The Business One Irwin Guide to Using The Wall Street Journal

Fourth Edition

Michael B. Lehmann

Business One Irwin
Homewood, Illinois 60430

Senior Editor: Amy Hollands
Project editor: Rita McMullen
Production manager: Bette K. Ittersagen
Compositor: Publication Services, Inc.
Typeface: 11/13 Times Roman
Printer: R.R. Donnelley & Sons Company

Library of Congress Cataloging-in-Publication Data
Lehmann, Michael B.
The Business One Irwin guide to using the Wall Street journal/
Michael B. Lehmann—4th ed.
p. cm.
Rev. ed. of: The Dow Jones-Irwin guide to using the Wall Street journal, 3rd ed. 1990.
Includes index
ISBN 1-55623-700-6 ISBN 1-55823-840-1 (CFP ed.)
1. Business cycles—United States. 2. Economic indicators—United States. I. Lehmann. Michael B. Dow Jones-Irwin guide to using the Wall Street journal. II. Business One Irwin. III. Wall Street journal. IV. Title.
HB3743.L44 1983
332.8—dc20 92–39045

Printed in the United States of America
1 2 3 4 5 6 7 8 9 0 DOC 9 8 7 6 5 4 3 2

To My Father
Dr. Frederick Lehmann

About the author . . .

MICHAEL B. LEHMANN is Professor of Economics at the University of San Francisco. He is a graduate of Grinnell College and received his Ph.D. from Cornell University.

Professor Lehmann lectures extensively on business and investment conditions and has developed a popular seminar based on this book, which he offers to investors, the business community, and corporations as an in-house training program.

PREFACE

When I first proposed this book to Business One Irwin, they asked me if its purpose was to show the reader "how to be your own economist." Not exactly, I said. The objective was to show the reader "how to use *The Wall Street Journal* to be your own economist."

After all, the *Journal* is the authoritative source for business news in America; it is published coast to coast; and it has the largest daily circulation of any newspaper in the country. By focusing on a handful of key statistical reports in the *Journal*, you can acquire a surprisingly quick and firm comprehension of the ups and downs of the American business economy. This book will facilitate that comprehension, clearly and accurately—but, I hope, in a pleasing and nontechnical manner.

The Business One Irwin Guide to Using the Wall Street Journal is designed to help you develop a sound overview of our economy so that your grasp of economic events as well as your business and investment decisions will be more informed and more confident. But it is not a get-rich-quick manual. You should always seek competent professional counsel before placing business or personal capital at risk.

Michael B. Lehmann

ACKNOWLEDGMENTS FOR THE FOURTH EDITION

I must begin by thanking Eric Scheide of the University of San Francisco's Office of Computer Services who desk-top published this edition. Eric can drive a Macintosh as easily as most folks drive a car. His skill and effort spared me the tedium of reading and rereading galley proofs and page proofs and then shipping them back and forth to BUSINESS ONE IRWIN. Thumb through the book and glance at the layout, the charts, the placement of *Wall Street Journal* articles, and the various type styles, and you will see for yourself that Eric did an outstanding job with an extraordinarily difficult task.

Patrick McGovern, president of Hilltop Software in San Francisco, and a former student of mine at the University of San Francisco, provided invaluable pinch-hit desk-top publishing assistance when impossible deadlines loomed. If you have a software problem, call Patrick. He's terrific.

Clint Powell, also with the University's Office of Computer Services, came to my assistance too.

Once again, as with the earlier editions, I owe a great debt to my wife, Millianne, and to Alan Heineman, my colleague at the University of San Francisco and my principal editor. Both criticized, amended, rewrote, and suggested deletions from and additions to the early drafts. Their editorial efforts spurred me to labor over revisions that otherwise would not have been undertaken, forcing me to clarify my ideas and manner of expression.

Bob Meier of DeKalb, Illinois reviewed the third edition and overhauled the entire second part, recommending important changes in the chapters on stocks and commodities, bonds, and money-market instruments. If you're interested in market techniques and technical analysis, he's the person to ask. I could not have upgraded these chapters without his assistance. Although I did my best to weave in his suggestions, any errors that remain are my responsibility. Bob also revised the list of suggested further reading that he kindly contributed to the third edition.

Dan Hinson in *The Wall Street Journal's* New York office once again assisted in my understanding of the statistical format and presentation in the *Journal's* money and investing section. Lottie Linberg of the New York office provided commodity prices and Gilbert Sherman of the Chicopee, Massachusetts office furnished data for the Dow Jones Industrial Average.

Barry Beckman of the Bureau of Economic Analysis at the Department of Commerce was kind enough to dig out many hard-to-find statistical series that are not available in *Business Cycle Indicators*. Jason Bram of the Conference Board in New York provided me with the Board's Index of Consumer Confidence. Janice Smith of the Office of Thrift Supervision clarified the intricacies of federal bank and thrift insurance for me.

Bob Ferraro reminded me not to delete what little I had said in earlier editions concerning social justice and those who really suffer because of the vagaries of the business cycyle.

My thanks also to Stanley Nel, Dean of the University of San Francisco's College of Arts & Sciences, and to Jack Clark, S.J. the University's Vice President for Academic Affairs, for their past and continuing support of my writingand research efforts.

And finally, last but not least, my thanks to Jessica Fisherman, Economics Department secretary at the University of San Francisco, who is always there when you need her.

CONTENTS

PART I

THE BIG PICTURE: THE ECONOMIC CLIMATE AND THE INVESTMENT OUTLOOK

CHAPTER 1

INTRODUCTION

GOLD VS. STOCKS

Some say that we learn best by doing . . . that we should plunge right in.

Give it a try. Examine Chart 1-1 on page 4 with an investor's eye. The vertical axis provides values for the Dow Jones Industrial Average and the price of gold. Years are on the horizontal axis. Where would you have placed your assets—into gold or stocks—at two critical junctures or turning points: 1970 and 1980? And where will you keep them in the 1990s?

Before you answer, you should be aware that the U.S. Treasury had set the price of gold at $35 an ounce from 1934 to 1971. Since the Treasury stood ready to buy or sell gold at $35 an ounce, and since the United States had most of the world's gold, there was no reason for any seller of gold to take one penny less than $35 or any buyer to pay one penny more than $35. So the price just sat at $35, year after year.

Just in case the stagnant price was not disincentive enough, Americans were prohibited by law from owning gold as an investment. Gold was to be used exclusively by the Treasury to settle international accounts. All that changed dramatically in the early 1970s, when the United States stopped selling gold for international settlement purposes and Americans were granted permission to own gold as an investment.

Although Americans were not permitted to own gold until December 31, 1974, place yourself in the hypothetical position of an investor who could have chosen between gold and stocks in 1970. With the wisdom of hindsight, can there be any doubt about your choice?

Look at Chart 1-1 again. You already know that gold was $35 in 1970. The Dow Jones Industrial Average, which most people view as a proxy for the stock market, began and ended the 1970s at about 800. It

CHART 1-1
Gold vs. Stocks: Gold-Engelhard High Price through 1987, Average Thereafter; Dow Jones Industrial Average

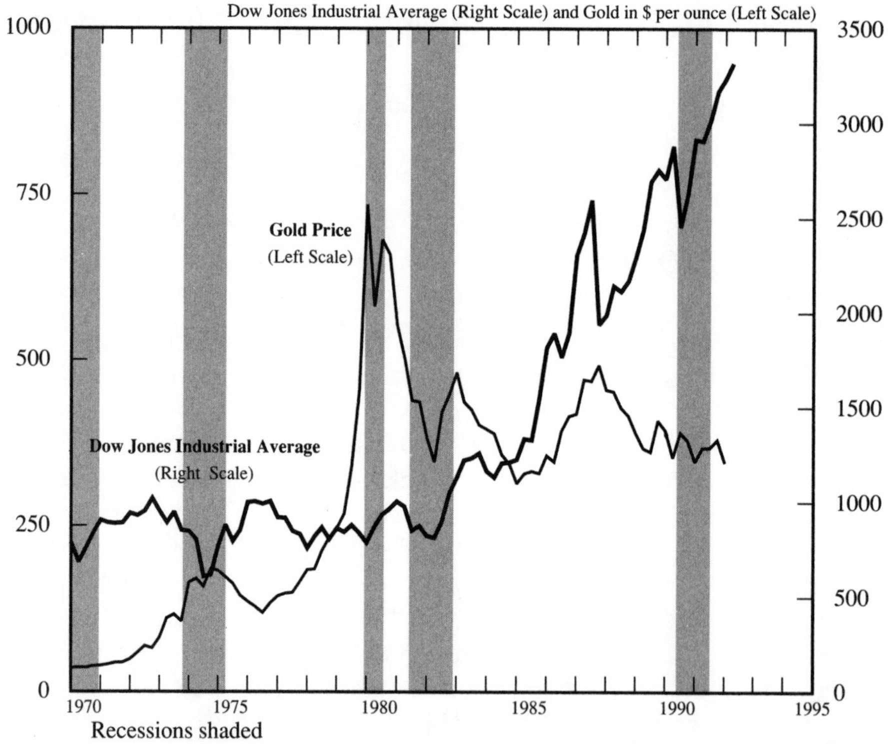

Source: U.S. Bureau of Mines, *Minerals Yearbook;* Standard & Poor's Statistical Service; Phyliis S. Pierce, ed., *The Dow Jones Investor's Handbook* (Homewood, IL: Dow Jones-Irwin, 1992); *Barron's*

fluctuated in a limited range for these 10 years, going nowhere. Had you bought stock in 1970, you would have enjoyed no investment appreciation. Gold, on the other hand, exploded in value, climbing to over $800 by early 1980. The smart money was in gold, not stocks.

Your choice was equally clear in 1980. Gold stood at over $800 an ounce; the Dow was under 1000. Then gold began to plunge. By mid-decade it had fallen to around $300. The price rose briefly to $500 in late 87 but by the end of the decade was down around the $400 mark. Stock prices, on the other hand, broke free in 1982, climbing intermittently, until in a burst of activity the Dow topped 2700 in August of 1987. Then came the crash and the recovery that followed, so that the Dow had made up its loss and reached 3000 by the end of the decade.

Looking back over the 1980s, there's no doubt that you should have taken all your money out of gold and put it all in stocks at the beginning of the decade. Stocks more than tripled (from under 1000 to over 3000), while gold was cut in half (from over $800 to under $400). You would have done very well in stocks, *despite the crash.* And even though the gain was not as great as the spectacular appreciation of gold during the 1970s, remember you could not have bought gold until December 31, 1974, when the price was $186.

But what do you do now? Are you trying to decide between stocks and gold once more? You can see from the chart that there is little evidence that stocks and gold move in the same direction for long. As a matter of fact, the chart indicates they are more likely to move in opposite directions over the long run. What should your investments be for the 1990s—gold or stocks?

Your response at this point might well be, "Now wait a minute, there are other investment avenues. I don't have to restrict my choice to gold or stocks." True, not every investment need be in the stock market or in gold, but most investments will be either "goldlike" or "stocklike" in their behavior. Conditions favorable to the stock market will also favor other paper investments such as bonds, while tangible investments such as commodities, collectibles (art, stamps), and real estate will move with gold. So, to simplify the discussion at this point, continue as if stocks and gold were the only investment opportunities. (Short-term money market investments will also be discussed later.) The principles illustrated will be easy to apply later to the full spectrum of investment possibilities.

In the meantime, diversification is one time-honored method for protecting investment income from the vagaries of the economic climate. Yet, putting half your money in stocks and half in gold in 1970 would have gained you much less over these decades. Diversification by itself is not an optimal strategy. Your store of investments must be minded. Investments must be shifted from gold (i.e., tangibles) to stocks (i.e., paper investments) and back again as conditions change. Investment timing is the key.

In order to call these moves, you will have to know why gold and stocks behaved as they did. What force propelled gold upward in the 1970s and held stocks back? And was it the same force or a different one that boosted stocks and depressed gold in the 1980s? Could the same force have generated such remarkably different turns of events?

Yes. Could and did. In a word, *inflation* was responsible for both sets of events. But you need to modify that word in order to describe the 70s and 80s accurately. *High* inflation drove gold upward and held stocks down in the 70s, and *low* inflation had the opposite effect in the 1980s—raising stocks and depressing gold.

That means you will need to forecast the investment climate of the 1990s from the perspective of inflation. In order to do that, you will not only have to make an educated guess with respect to inflation, you will also need to know how to forecast inflation based on the readily available economic data. And that forecast must be completed reasonably far in advance, so that your actions can anticipate investment trends (long-run movements in gold and stocks) before they occur. You don't want to react to events after the profitable opportunities have passed. You want to beat the market to the punch . . . and that's not easy.

Investor's Tip

- Diversification by itself is not an optimal strategy.
- Timing is the key
- Buy gold, commodities, and other tangibles when high (more than 8 percent) inflation threatens; sell if you expect low (less than 7 percent) inflation.
- Buy stocks, bonds, and other paper investments if you anticipate low inflation; get out when high inflation looms.

ON YOUR OWN

This means you will have to use the investment data on your own, without an interpreter. You will have to decipher the Dow Jones Industrial Average, GDP, capacity utilization, price/earnings ratio, housing starts, advance/decline line, auto sales, and other statistical series and reports. You must use them to gain an understanding of developing business and investment trends so that your judgments and opinions are not merely based on (and therefore biased by) popular analyses and secondary sources.

It's worth some time and effort to learn how to deal with the data on your own, because until you come to grips with the data you can't honestly say that you have formed your own opinion about current economic and business events, let alone about what the future holds. The news media now serve as intermediaries between you and the data. Furthermore, no matter how many experts are quoted, you still aren't dealing with the facts, only with someone else's interpretation of them. And these interpretations are often contradictory—and therefore confusing. At some point you have to wonder, do the "experts" know what they're talking about? And while you are waiting for them to sort things out, your investment opportunities may have passed.

On the other hand, your desire to master the data may also stem from your own business needs. Will demand for your product be weak or strong two quarters from now or two years from now? Is this the time to lay in additional inventory, hire key personnel, and build more plant? Or, despite the current level of orders, would it be more prudent to cancel those plans? Can you beat the competition to the punch, one way or another? Are interest rates likely to rise or to fall? Is disinflation (as deflation is sometimes called) merely a buzzword, or has inflation really been licked? That's just a hint of the issues you can begin to analyze on your own; all it takes is learning to come to grips with a small number of regularly released statistical reports.

You may also wish to conduct your own analysis of current economic events because they form the foundation for so many other social and political developments. Were President Reagan's tax cut and supply-side economics responsible for the early 1980s decline in inflation, or should the Federal Reserve System take the credit? And how serious are the problems of the federal government's budget deficit and the balance-of-trade deficit? Do your answers to these questions reflect your analysis of the data, your political point of view, or the opinions of your favorite commentator? Maybe they should reflect all three, but they can reflect only the last two until you learn to deal with the numbers on your own. Once you do that, your own judgment will be of greater importance to you and others.

Don't misunderstand: dispensing with expert advice is not the objective. Even the world's leading authority on a subject must consult other experts as a continual check on his or her understanding. This challenges the authority and helps prevent sloppy thinking. The point is: become the expert by handling the data on your own, and you will know whether or not the other experts make sense. Otherwise, you'll never be certain whether you're receiving sound or flimsy advice.

If you want to be your own economist and investment advisor, if you wish to master the daily data, you need two things: (l) a readily available, reliable, and comprehensive statistical source and (2) a guide to organizing and interpreting the information you receive.

As to the first requirement, *The Wall Street Journal* is your best source of investment, business, and economic information; you really don't need anything else. It contains all the reports necessary to conduct your own analysis.

With respect to the second requirement, this book can be your guide. In it, the nature of the statistics will be explained so that what they measure and how they are computed will be clear. GDP, capacity utilization, the price/earnings ratio, and the Dow Jones Industrial Average cannot remain vague and indefinite terms if you are going to be in control of the information.

For example, when the *Journal* reports that the money supply has increased, it is important to know that this fact has virtually nothing to do with the availability of currency. The money supply is composed largely of checking accounts; currency is the petty cash of the economy.

Understanding the nature of the various statistical series is, of course, not enough. You must be able to place them in both historical and contemporary context. For instance, the price/earnings (P/E) ratio for the Dow stocks hit a 25-year high of 22 in August 1987, just as the Dow peaked immediately prior to the October crash. A year later the P/E ratio was only 12, and the outlook for stocks was bright. The savvy investor understood these developments and was prepared to act on them.

These essential skills will develop and gain strength with each chapter. Your historical perspective will deepen, providing the background or benchmark for evaluating contemporary events. When a *Journal* article states that the trade deficit or the budget deficit is the largest ever, or that the Dow Jones Industrial Average has hit a new high, the comparison can provide perspective only if you grasp the frame of reference: knowledge of the past aids evaluation of the present by providing a standard against which recent developments are measured. For instance, auto sales and housing starts may be slightly higher or lower than they were a year ago, but if you know that current levels of activity are substantially lower than those of the 1980s, your perspective provides evidence that in the early 90s the economy is far from boom conditions.

As you read on, you will become aware that none of the statistical reports stands alone. Understanding the relationships among them provides insight into the economy's operation and the investment scene, for each is a piece of the puzzle, and together they compose the picture. For instance, mortgage interest rates and home construction have been featured in the *Journal* lately, and there is a simple, vital link between them: as mortgage interest rates fall, home construction increases.

Consider another example. In 1985 we asked our major trading partners to intervene in the foreign exchange markets in order to depress the value of the dollar. The hope was that cheaper dollars—and hence cheaper prices for American goods in world markets—would boost our exports and reduce our balance-of-trade deficit. Thus, the statistical reports on the value of the dollar and on our ability to export are inextricably linked, as you will see in more detail in Chapter 16.

All of the statistics analyzed in this book can be interrelated in this fashion, so they need not be a series of isolated events, released piecemeal on a day-to-day basis. Instead, they will form an unfolding pattern that clearly reveals the direction of economic and business activity.

Finally, you need a framework, a device to give a coherent shape to these historical insights and contemporary interrelationships. The business cycle, that wavelike rise and fall of economic activity, provides that necessary framework. You are already familiar with the cycle in your own investing, business, or personal situation, and the news media have provided increased coverage of the ups and downs of the economy in recent years. Economic expansion and contraction, easy or tight credit conditions, inflation, and unemployment are recurring facts of life. Who escapes them?

The business cycle is the best vehicle for illuminating the *Journal's* regularly appearing statistical series. Its phases bring life and meaning to the statistical reports. They establish the perspective through which the illustrations and examples in the book are interwoven into a unified exposition.

Each chapter will introduce one or more statistical series, and each will be devoted to a theme (such as the money and credit markets) that is used to describe and explain the statistical series introduced in the chapter, beginning with the simplest and most basic elements of the business cycle and proceeding to additional topics that will complete your understanding. This step-by-step progression of topics will not, however, prevent you from breaking into any chapter, out of order, if you wish to examine a particular statistical series or group of series. Indeed, you may already have a firm grasp of some of these topics and need only to fill in the missing elements to round out your comprehension of the essential workings of American business. A complete listing of all the statistical series discussed in this guide can be found in the appendixes following Chapter 17.

Each chapter will describe its statistical series in the context of the business cycle and explain the relationship of the new series to the overall picture. Analysis will be based on charts drawn from official publications so that you can visualize the data and put the current information in perspective. Recent articles in *The Wall Street Journal* containing the statistical series will be reproduced and discussed so that you can interpret the data in light of the visual presentation made by the charts. Finally, you will be alerted to what future developments can be expected.

You will enjoy putting the puzzle together yourself. Anyone can do it, with a little help. The ebb and flow of the business cycle will channel the stream of data that now floods you in seemingly random fashion, and you will experience a genuine sense of accomplishment in creating order out of something that may previously have appeared chaotic.

A word of caution before you begin. This will not be an economics or business cycle course or text, nor will it be a precise forecasting device. There will be no formula or model. The business cycle is used strictly as a vehicle to make the statistical information usable in as easy a manner as possible. The objective is not to make a professional economist out of you but to enable you to conduct your own analysis of the data just as soon as you are able. You will dive into the data and "get your hands dirty" by taking apart the cycle, analyzing it, and reassembling it. When you have finished this book, you will feel confident that you can deal with the data on your own.

Returning to the chart and example at the beginning of this chapter, you will be able to forecast the outlook for inflation and decide whether stocks (paper investments) or gold (tangible investments) are best for you. But a full discussion of that choice must wait until Chapter 8.

Now, before exploring the business cycle in detail, take time for a leisurely overview.

CHAPTER 2

THE BUSINESS CYCLE

A BIT OF HISTORY

The business cycle is nothing new. It's been a characteristic of every capitalist economy in the modern era. Nations have endured boom followed by bust, prosperity and then depression—periods of growth and confidence trailing off into a decade of despair.

It is all so familiar to us that images of its human effects are scattered among our popular stereotypes. Men in top hats peer at ticker tape emerging from a little glass dome. They wheel and deal, corner wheat markets, play with railroads, and organize steel companies. Fortunes are quickly won and just as quickly lost. Former tycoons are seen selling apples on street corners. Factory gates shut and signs go up saying, "No help wanted." Soup kitchens appear, and desperate families flee the dust bowl in Model A pickup trucks.

These caricatures—based on real history, actual power, blows of ill fortune, human suffering—persist in our collective consciousness, permanently etched by the Great Depression. Although the stock market collapse of 1929 is the most notorious such event in our history, it is by no means unique. Cycles in the American economy can be traced and analyzed going back to the beginning of the 19th century.

The settlement of the West is an example. The frontier assumes such importance in our history and folklore that we tend to think of the westward migration as a smooth, if hazardous, inevitable flow, driven by the doctrine of Manifest Destiny. It didn't happen that way. The settlement of the West proceeded in a cyclical pattern.

Farmers and ranchers were (and are) business people. The sod house and subsistence farming of the 1800s were temporary inconveniences, converted as quickly as possible to growing cash crops and raising livestock for the market. The settlers wanted to know the bottom line, the difference between revenue and expense. They wanted the best price for their cotton, corn, cattle, wheat, and hogs. They wanted to maximize production and minimize cost by using modern cultivation techniques and the latest equipment. Railroads and banks concerned them because transportation and interest rates affected the cost of doing business and thus their profit margin. Finally, and most important, farmers wanted their capital to grow. They expected their net worth to increase as their farms appreciated in value and their mortgages were paid.

This experience was not confined to the United States; European settlers in Canada, Australia, and Argentina produced the same commodities under similar conditions. All were part of the growing world economy. Every farmer and rancher counted on industrialization and urbanization at home and in Europe to build demand for his or her commodities.

And worldwide demand for food and fiber did increase rapidly. Farmers responded by boosting production as best they could on existing holdings. Eventually, however, their output reached its limit, even though demand continued to grow. As a result, prices began to creep, and then race, upward. The venturesome dreamed of moving west and doubling or tripling their acreage. Record crop and livestock prices made the costs of moving and financing a new spread seem manageable, and existing farms could always be sold to the less intrepid. Thousands upon thousands of families streamed across the frontier, claiming millions of acres offered by generous government policies or buying from speculators who held raw land.

Nobody planned the westward migration; nobody coordinated it; nobody governed it. Each individual involved made his or her own calculation of the market. Farmers borrowed in order to purchase land and building materials and to buy livestock, seed, and equipment. Newly opened banks faced an insatiable demand for credit. Towns sprang up at railroad sidings where grain elevators and livestock yards were constructed. Merchants and Main Street followed. High prices brought a land boom, and the land boom brought settlement and opened the West.

It took a while for the newly converted prairie to produce a cash crop. But when it did, thousands of new farms began dumping their output on the market. The supply of agricultural commodities increased dramatically. Shortage changed to surplus, and prices dropped. Time after time during the 19th century, commodity prices fell to record lows after a period of inflation and the subsequent land rush.

Many farmers were wiped out. They could not pay their debts while commodity prices scraped bottom, and banks foreclosed on farm property. If a bank made too many loans that went bad, then it was dragged down too. Merchants saw their customers disappear and had to close up shop. Settlers abandoned their land, and boomtowns became ghost towns.

Prices inevitably remained low for years, and most farmers, living on returns far below expectations, barely made it. In every instance, it took a while before the steady growth in world demand absorbed the excess agricultural commodities.

But as time passed, the cycle would repeat itself. After the inflation that accompanied the Civil War, western settlement continued to occur in waves until the end of the century, despite 30 years of deflation. The process happened at least half a dozen times until the frontier closed in the last years of the 19th century.

By the turn of this century, progress had been spectacular. Many thousands of acres of prairie had been transformed into productive field and pasture. Commodities worth billions of dollars were produced annually for the domestic and world markets. Billions of dollars of wealth had been created in the form of improved farmland. But the discipline of the business cycle governed the advance. For every two steps forward, there had been one step backward, as those who borrowed or lent the least wisely, settled the poorest land, or had the worst luck went broke.

Things haven't changed. Agriculture's fortunes are still guided by the cycle. Remember the boom of the early 70s? Consumption of beef was up; President Nixon negotiated the wheat deal with Russia; the Peruvian anchovy harvest had failed, and soy beans were used to fill the gap (as a protein extender). Agricultural commodity prices doubled, even tripled, and therefore, of course, farm income shot up. As a result, farmers spent the rest of the decade investing heavily in land and equipment. Ultimately, supply outstripped demand, and farm prices deteriorated throughout the early 80s.

We've seen the result. It's nothing that hasn't happened before: foreclosures, bankruptcies, falling land values, broken families, and ruined lives. Eventually, of course, prices stabilized—until the next cycle comes along to start the process all over again.

Oil presents a similar picture. Billions were spent on exploration, recovery, and production projects in Texas, Louisiana, Oklahoma, Wyoming, Colorado, and Alaska when prices were high. Houston, Dallas, Denver, and Anchorage were boomtowns in the early 1980s. Then, when prices fell (and they always do), the money dried up. Soon you could get a condominium in Anchorage or Denver for $15,000 because whole city blocks of new housing developments were abandoned—left by their owners for bank foreclosure.

What was true for farming and oil was equally true for the nation's railroads: they developed in the same cyclical pattern. On the eve of World War I, America's railway system was complete, representing a total capital investment second only to that of agriculture. It was a remarkable feat of creative engineering and equally creative financing.

We marvel at the colorful exploits of the Goulds, Fisks, Drews, Vanderbilts, Stanfords, Hills, and others. History refers to some of them as "robber barons"; they seemed to skim off one dollar for every two invested, and it's a wonder that the railway system was ever completed or operated safely. Yet there it was, the largest in the world, a quarter of a million miles of track moving the nation's freight and passenger traffic with unparalleled efficiency.

Promoters speculatively pushed the railroads westward in anticipation of the freight and passenger traffic that settlement would bring. Federal, state, and local governments, vying for the routes that would generate progress and development, gave the railroad companies 10 percent of the nation's land. Improving rights-of-way, laying track, building trestles, stations, and marshaling yards, and purchasing locomotives and rolling stock required the railway company to raise more capital than had ever been mobilized for any other single business venture. The companies floated billions of dollars in stocks and bonds, and investors eagerly ventured their capital to take advantage of prospective success. Flush with funds, the railroads raced toward the Pacific Coast, hoping that revenue would grow quickly enough to justify their huge investment. Periodically, however, the generous rate of expansion exceeded the growth in traffic. Prospects for profits, which had seemed so bright, grew dim. Investors stopped providing funds, and railroad track construction came to a halt. Since operating revenues could not recover costs, many railroads were forced into receivership and were reorganized. Stock and bond prices plunged, wiping out investors long after the promoters had made off with their killings.

Eventually, traffic grew sufficiently to justify existing lines and raise hopes that construction could profitably resume. Investors were once again lured into advancing their funds, and a new cycle of railway expansion began. It, too, was followed by a bust, and then by another wave of construction, until the nation's railway system was complete.

The tracks spanned a continent, from New York, Philadelphia, and Baltimore to Chicago, and from there to New Orleans, Los Angeles, San Francisco, Portland, and Seattle. Profit had motivated the enterprise, and enormous tangible wealth had been created. Losses had periodically and temporarily halted the undertaking and impoverished those who had speculated unwisely or who had been duped. Construction had proceeded in waves. It was an unplanned and often disorganized adventure but, given the institutions of the time, no other method could have built the system as rapidly.

In this century, we have seen the business cycle not only in the heroic proportions of the Roaring Twenties and the Great Depression but also during every succeeding business expansion or recession. We're in the cycle now, and we will be tomorrow and next year.

Business activity always expands and then contracts. There are periods when production, employment, and profits surge ahead, each followed by a period when profits and output fall, and unemployment increases. Then the entire cycle repeats itself once again. During the expansion, demand and production, income and wealth grow. Homes and factories are constructed, and machinery and equipment are put in place. The value of these assets grows too, as home prices and common stock prices increase. But then comes the inevitable contraction, and all the forces that mark the expansion shift into reverse. Demand, production, and income fall. The level of construction and the production of machinery and equipment are drastically curtailed. Assets lose their value as home prices and common stock prices fall.

No doubt you already realize that business cycles occur and repeat themselves in this way. But why? No completely satisfactory theory has yet been created. No one can accurately predict the length and course of each cycle. Economics, unlike physics, cannot be reduced to experiments and repeated over and over again under ideal conditions. There is no economic equivalent to Galileo on the Tower of Pisa, proving that objects of unequal weight fall with equal speed, because the economic "tower" is never quite the same height; the "objects" keep changing in number, size, and even nature; and the "laws of gravity" apply unequally to each object.

Yet one thing is certain: the business cycle is generated by forces within the economic system, not by outside forces. These internal forces create the alternating periods of economic expansion and contraction. And you should recognize that certain crucial features of the cycle endure.

A THUMBNAIL SKETCH

First, the forces of supply and demand condition every cycle. Our ability to enjoy increasing income depends on our ability to supply or create increased production or output; we must produce more to earn more. But the level of demand, and the expenditures made in purchasing this output, must justify the level of production. That is, we must sell what we produce in order to earn. With sufficient demand, the level of production will be sustained and will grow, and income will increase; if demand is insufficient, the reverse will occur. During the expansionary phase of the cycle, demand and supply forces are in a relationship that permits the growth of production and income; during the contractionary phase, their relationship compels a decrease in production and income.

Second, neither consumers nor businesses are constrained to rely solely on the income they have generated in the process of production. They have recourse to the credit market; they can borrow money and spend more than they earn. Spending borrowed funds permits demand to take on a life of its own and bid up a constantly and rapidly growing level of production. This gives rise to the expansionary phase of the cycle. Eventually, the growth in production becomes dependent on the continued availability of credit, which sustains the growth in demand. But once buyers can no longer rely on borrowed funds (because of market saturation, the exhaustion of profitable investment opportunities, or tight credit), demand falls and, with it, the bloated level of production and income. The contractionary phase has begun.

Third, every expansion carries with it the inevitability of "overexpansion" and the subsequent contraction. Overexpansion may be impelled by businesses that invest too heavily in new plant and equipment in order to take advantage of a seemingly profitable opportunity, or by consumers who borrow too heavily in order to buy homes, autos, or other goods. But when businesses realize that the expected level of sales will not support additional plant and equipment, and when consumers realize that they will have difficulty paying for that new home or car, then businesses and consumers will curtail their borrowing and expenditure. Since production and income have spurted ahead to meet the growth in demand, they fall when the inevitable contraction in demand takes place.

Fourth, during contractions, production and income recede to a sustainable level, that is, to a level not reliant on a continuous growth in credit. The contraction returns the economy to a more efficient level of operation.

Fifth, every contraction sows the seeds of the subsequent recovery. Income earned in the productive process, rather than bloated levels of borrowing, maintains the level of demand. Consumers and businesses repay their debts. Eventually, lower debt burdens and interest rates encourage consumer and business borrowing and demand. The economy begins expanding once more.

And there is progress over the course of the cycle. Overall growth takes place because some, or even most, of the increase in output remains intact. Nor is all the created wealth subsequently destroyed. The abandoned steel mills of the "rust belt" will be scrapped, but the plant and equipment used to make personal computers will remain on-stream. Residential construction completed in 1986 turned a profit for its developers, while homes completed in 1990, at the peak of the cycle, were liquidated at a loss after standing empty for a year. And so on. The tree grows, but the rings in its trunk mark the cycles of seasons that were often lush but on occasion were beset by drought.

Yet the American economy grew steadily throughout the 1980s after the recession of 1981-82. Had the business cycle been repealed? Some seemed to think so, just as others had thought so before them, only to be disappointed by the next recession.

Why did the economy just keep growing in the 1980s? Why didn't it stop? Did President Reagan and his supply-side policies deserve the credit? Was the Federal Reserve responsible?

And why did the economy lurch into recession in 1990? The chapters that follow will not only discuss the cycle's dynamic, they will also describe the forces that "stretched out" the cycle in the 1980s and postponed recession's expected return. And they will also discuss the cycle's dynamic in the 1990s: what we can reasonably expect and its impact on investors.

But as you may already suspect, the business cycle does not operate in a vacuum. It is conditioned, shortened and stretched, and initiated and forestalled by the institutions of our economy. So before embarking on an investigation of the cycle, take a quick look at Chapter 3, which discusses the attempts to influence the economy since World War II.

CHAPTER 3

THE TRANSFORMATION OF THE POSTWAR ECONOMY

To this point we have discussed the business cycle as if it were independent and autonomous. But in fact, in modern history, the American business cycle has been influenced by a variety of attempts to guide and direct it. The economic events of the 15 years from 1965 to 1980 provide a vivid example of well-intentioned economic meddling gone awry.

During these years the federal government and the Federal Reserve System attempted to stimulate demand for goods and services with liberal spending, tax, and credit policies. Their objective was to boost the economy higher and faster, thereby generating increased employment opportunities. They thought that as supply rose to meet demand, increased production would accomplish their objectives. Unfortunately, as demand grew more rapidly than supply, prices spiraled upward. As inflation became more severe, the only solution appeared to be a periodic reversal of those policies of liberal spending, tax, and credit—which invariably helped plunge the economy into recession. These policy reversals exacerbated the cycle so that inflation *escalated* during boom and unemployment *rose* during bust.

The actions of the Federal Reserve and federal government had their origin in the 1930s, when economists were attempting to cope with the ravages of the Great Depression. At that time it was obvious that the economy was stagnating due to insufficient demand for the goods and services business could produce. The factories were there; the machines were there; the labor was there; only the customers were missing. The great question of the day was, "How can we generate effective demand for goods and services?"

Traditional economists had no solution to the problem. They viewed the Depression as a trough in a particularly severe cycle that would correct itself with time. Therefore, they prescribed laissez-faire (leave it alone) as the best possible course of action. Why not? It had always worked in the past.

A new generation of economists surveyed the scene and came up with a different diagnosis. They saw the Great Depression as inaugurating an era in which demand was (and might remain) chronically depressed. To deal with the problem they recommended a two-pronged solution.

First, stimulate demand directly. Clearly consumers were not going to spend more, for many were unemployed, and those who were working were afraid to spend because they might lose their jobs. Business was not going to buy new factories and machinery since existing facilities were underutilized. Only the government was in a position to spend more. Such government spending would involve deficit financing as the level of expenditures exceeded tax revenues, but the New Dealers were prepared to run the risk. If the government had to borrow now, it could pay back later. In this way the government would be the employer of last resort, hiring people to build dams, bridges, roads, and parks.

Second, the Federal Reserve System (the nation's central bank, known as the Fed) could push interest rates down and thereby depress the cost of borrowing money. This would motivate businesses (to the extent that they could be motivated) to borrow funds in order to buy equipment and machinery and to build additional factories and other establishments. Making credit easy was a way of stimulating economic activity.

These policies, applied in the late 30s, were interrupted by World War II, which generated boom conditions. But when the war came to an end, it was feared that the economy would again slip back into a chronic state of depression. That anxiety was unfounded, but was so strongly felt that the ideological revolution of the 1930s survived. The new school of economists believed it was the government's duty to stimulate demand until the economy reached its maximum potential of full employment. This attitude meshed with other liberal and progressive views regarding government's responsibility for the social welfare of all.

Conservatives, on the other hand, continued to believe that laissez-faire was the best policy. Thus, throughout the Eisenhower years, the conservative administration drew fire from progressive economists for not implementing the lessons that had been learned in the 30s. They wanted additional federal spending and easy money in order to spur the economy.

When John F. Kennedy ran for office in 1960, he charged that the Eisenhower administration's conservative policies had reduced the rate of economic growth, and he promised to get the economy moving again. After he took office in 1961, he made good on that pledge by inviting the new school of economists into his administration, urging them to apply the progressive policies that had been developed under Roosevelt.

They did prescribe those policies, but with a new wrinkle. Rather than stimulate demand directly with increased government spending, they proposed putting more purchasing power in the pockets of consumers by cutting taxes. The government would still have to borrow to meet the deficit, except that this time it would do so to pay for a shortfall of revenue rather than a growth in expenditure. One way or the other, demand would grow.

Increased consumer spending was just as good as government spending—and, as a rule, politically more advantageous. The extra spending would stimulate economic growth and create jobs as production expanded to meet the surge in consumer demand. At the same time, President Kennedy's economists urged the Federal Reserve to maintain an easy policy so that liberal credit would be available at low rates of interest for consumer and business needs.

These views remained in fashion for two decades. A generation of students was trained to believe that an inadequate level of demand was the paramount problem facing the economy and that they should study economics in order to determine how the federal government and the Federal Reserve could best stimulate the level of economic activity to provide full employment. They all recognized that excessive stimulation of demand could lead to inflation, but they felt that inflation would not be a severe problem until the economy attained full employment.

In each recession the Federal Reserve depressed interest rates, and the government stimulated spending directly with tax cuts for consumers and business. Demand roared ahead in short order, and when it exceeded supply at current prices, prices surged upward. At this point the federal government and the Federal Reserve reversed course and employed policies designed to dampen inflation. They slammed on the brakes, raising taxes and interest rates, depressing demand temporarily, and causing recession. But as soon as the inflation rate dropped, they reversed course and helped bring on the next round of expanding demand and inflation.

No one—not the economists, not the government, not the Federal Reserve—realized that World War II had profoundly changed the underlying circumstances and that policies appropriate for the 30s were not suited for the 60s and 70s. The Great Depression, which preceded the war, was a time of inadequate demand. But government borrowing from banks during the war, and the expenditures of those funds, had placed a wealth of liquid assets at the consumer's disposal. When the war ended, consumers were prepared to spend those funds, and were also increasingly prepared to borrow in order to supplement their expenditures. In the postwar world, demand, buttressed by borrowing, would chronically exceed supply, thus bidding prices upward. Excessive demand, not inadequate demand, would be the problem.

Thus began the first American peacetime period with significant and continuing inflation. In all other eras inflation had been the product of wartime government spending financed by borrowing, while peacetime had been a period of stable prices or even deflation. Consequently, government spending financed by borrowing, whether in time of war or peace, was viewed by almost everyone as the single source of inflation, and this mindset spilled over into the postwar world. No one comprehended that a new economic dynamic was at work in which inflation would be generated by private (consumer and business) borrowing and spending. Ever greater waves of borrowing by the private sector (not government) would drive the inflationary cycle.

The new generation of economists and their students, whose intellectual mold had been cast during the New Deal, were like generals who conduct a war by fighting the previous campaign. But the real issue facing the postwar world was how to keep demand under control, how to restrain it and prevent it from generating inflation. The Eisenhower years, when demand did seem to stall, confused economists, making them believe that the chronically depressed conditions of the 1930s were a real possibility in the postwar world.

This was a major miscalculation. In fact, the escalating inflation of the 70s showed us that the potential runaway horse of the economy was champing at the bit—and all the while economists and policy makers were wondering how to apply the spurs more vigorously.

By 1980, after two decades of inappropriate policies, the Federal Reserve determined to come to grips with the problem. New Deal economics had to be discarded. The spurs had to be removed, the reins taken in hand, the runaway horse restrained. So the Fed tightened up, interest rates reached the stratosphere, borrowing and spending dried up, and the economy came closer to collapsing in 1981-82 than at any time since the war. After the recession of 1981-82 contained demand and eliminated inflation, the Fed slowly began to ease up. But the Fed was determined not to return to the errors of the past; it would not let credit become easy, or demand grow too rapidly, or inflation get out of control again.

Thus, the Fed acted single-handedly to stretch out the business cycle and forestall recession. By squashing the cycle flat in the early 1980s, and then restraining inflation in the mid and late 80s, the Fed interrupted the cycle's regular and periodic oscillations. This created a period of steady expansion during which the economy did not overheat. Inflation had been brought under control, giving the edge to stocks and other paper assets over gold and similar tangible investments.

But the recession of 1990-91 brought an end to the Fed's run of good luck. Why? What had gone wrong, and was the Federal Reserve or the federal government to blame once again?

So before you consider *The Wall Street Journal's* reports on business cycle developments, read Chapters 4 and 5 to review the role of the Federal Reserve System and the federal government in today's business and investment scene.

CHAPTER 4

THE FEDERAL RESERVE SYSTEM: MONETARY POLICY AND INTEREST RATES

THE FED AND INFLATION

Chart 1-1 on page 4 provides graphic evidence that inflation and the business cycle had the greatest imaginable impact on economic conditions and investment values from 1970 to 1990. Because the Federal Reserve System (the Fed) is the only modern American institution that has been able to constructively control and shape these forces, you should begin by learning how to use *The Wall Street Journal* to decipher the Fed's operations.

The Fed is your first order of business because the power of the Fed squashed the business cycle flat in the early 1980s, bringing an end to excessive inflation for the foreseeable future. Before that, during the high-inflation 70s, business cycle fluctuations had grown more severe and inflation's pace had accelerated. *Thus, the Fed's stand against inflation in 1981-82 was the most important turning point in our post World War II economic history.* And, as you already know, the Fed's anti-inflation policies of the late 80s were crucial in postponing recession and stretching out the cycle.

The business cycle and inflation had spun out of control in the late 1960s and 70s because consumers and businesses had borrowed ever more heavily to finance ever larger expenditures on homes, cars, and other durable goods, as well as plant, equipment, and inventory. As oceans of borrowing supported tidal waves of spending (i.e., demand for goods and services), supply could not keep pace, and prices rose.

To understand this phenomenon, consider a hypothetical example in which people had just as much to spend at the end of a given year as at the beginning, but had increased their output of goods and services by 5 percent during that year. Prices would have to fall by 5 percent before the same amount of spending (demand) could absorb an additional 5 percent of goods and services (supply). And if folks continued each year to produce 5 percent more while their spending did not grow, then prices would fall by 5 percent year after year. We would have chronic deflation.

Similarly, if people's ability to spend (demand) grew by 20 percent while output (supply) grew by 5 percent, you can imagine prices being bid up by 15 percent in that year. And if their spending continued to grow by 20 percent a year while their output grew by only 5 percent, you can imagine chronic inflation of 15 percent. Now you understand how changing supply and demand generate deflation and inflation.

But you may ask, "How is it possible for spending (demand) to grow more rapidly than the output (supply) of society? You can spend only what you have, after all." No, not if people have access to credit provided by banks. For instance, suppose you earn $50,000 a year and your income is a measure of the value of the goods and services that you produce or supply for the market. Also suppose that your spending (demand) is limited by your income. Demand and supply ($50,000) are equal, so prices don't change. Now suppose that you have access to bank credit, so that you can borrow $200,000 to have a house built. Your demand (spending) rises to $200,000 even though your income (supply) remains at $50,000. Demand exceeds supply in this case, and if your situation is repeated often enough in others, prices rise. Whenever demand exceeds supply at current prices, made possible by borrowing (credit), inflation (rising prices) occurs.

The $200,000 provided by the banks was *not* produced and saved by someone else, thereby equating earlier supply with new demand. It was created out of thin air by the banking system, and that is why your bank financed spending is inflationary. It also serves to illustrate the point that you have to understand the banking and credit system to comprehend the reasons for the ever-escalating business cycle and inflation of 1965-80.

And finally, you should also be aware that the decline in borrowing in the early 1990s signaled the drop in demand that led to both the recession of 1990-91 and the reduced inflation that accompanied it.

Private borrowing by consumers and businesses has always been a feature of our economy, but it did not begin to reach heroic proportions and grow at an explosive pace until the late 1960s. From that point on, credit *doubled* every five years. There was no way production could keep pace with these surges in demand, so rising inflation filled the gap.

But borrowing and spending did not grow smoothly. They surged forward periodically, generating the wavelike action of the business cycle. The rise of borrowing and spending carried inflation with it, and interest rates, too, as spiraling borrowing drove up the cost of credit. Steep increases in prices and interest rates eventually choked off the boom, discouraging consumers and businesses from continued borrowing and spending. The wave crashed and the cycle completed itself as the economy contracted into recession.

The Fed exacerbated the worst aspects of the cycle in the late 60s and throughout the 70s by attempting to alleviate them. Reining in credit expansion at the peak of the cycle, in order to curb inflation, merely contributed to the severity of the inevitable downturn and made recession worse. Easing up during recession, in order to encourage borrowing and spending and thus pull the economy out of a slump, contributed to the excesses of the next boom. And with each wave of the cycle, inflation and interest rates ratcheted higher and higher.

The Fed reversed course in 1981-82 and brought an end to 15 years of escalating inflation and cyclical instability by applying a chokehold of high interest rates. The economy was brought to the brink of collapse. But when the Fed relaxed its grip and interest rates declined from exorbitant to merely high, the manic rounds of boom and bust had ceased. The economy set out on a healthy expansion without inflation that lasted through the late 80s until Iraq's invasion of Kuwait eroded consumer sentiment, casting a pall over borrowing and spending that led to the 1990-91 recession.

Borrowing and Inflation

- Bank lending finances spending; spending generates inflation.
- The Fed controls bank lending and can thereby control inflation.
- But a drop in borrowing and spending will reduce inflation, and if sufficiently sharp will lead to recession.

But what is the Fed? How does it work? What, exactly, did it (and does it) do? Start your investigation with a bit of background.

THE FED'S HISTORY

The United States was the last major industrial nation to establish a central bank. The modern German state commissioned a central bank in 1875; the Bank of France was founded in 1800; and the Bank of England had entered its third century of operation when the Federal Reserve System was created in 1913.

America's tardiness was due to our traditional suspicion of centralized financial power and authority. Historically, we have felt more comfortable with small banks serving a single community. In fact, some states limit branch banking to this day. Ironically, The First National Bank of Chicago is one of the nation's biggest, even though Illinois law severely constrains its branch facilities in downstate Illinois. Similarly, the big New York City banks (until after World War II) were hampered by legislation that confined them to the city and its suburbs and kept their branches out of upstate New York. On the other hand, California's liberal branch banking laws once helped Bank of America build its position as the nation's largest bank. To this day, a rational, nationwide scheme for organizing our banking institutions does not exist.

Recall how many banks failed in the 1980s and the disaster that struck the savings and loan industry. There were many causes, but surely the small size and limited resources of many of our banks and S&Ls were contributing factors. Japan and Germany have a fraction of the number of banks that we have. Massive financial institution failure is unthinkable in those countries.

Alexander Hamilton proposed a central bank shortly after the country's founding. The two early attempts to create one failed when confronted with the nation's suspicion of the Eastern financial community. Consequently, our economy grew until the eve of World War I without benefit of coordination or control of its banking activity. Banking, like the sale of alcohol following the repeal of Prohibition, was largely subject to local option.

Under these circumstances, the banks had to fend for themselves, and the business cycle created perils for them as well as opportunities for profit. During recessions, when business income was down (usually following periods of speculative excess), banks found it difficult to collect on loans.

At the same time, nervous business persons and investors made large withdrawals, sometimes demanding payment in gold or silver specie. These precious metal coins composed the ultimate reserve for deposits; however, no bank possessed enough of them to secure every depositor, and the banking system functioned on the assumption that only a minority of depositors would demand their funds on any one day. When panic set in and a queue formed out the door and around the block, a bank could be wiped out in a matter of hours. As rumor spread, one bank after another failed, until only the most substantial institutions, with the greatest specie reserve, were left standing. The chain reaction damaged many people, not the least of whom were innocent depositors who could not reach their funds in time.

Congress took up the issue after the panic of 1907. In that crisis—as the story goes—J.P. Morgan kept New York's most important bankers locked up in his home overnight until they agreed to contribute a pool of specie to be lent to the weakest banks until the run subsided. It worked—but the near-disaster had made it clear that the time had come to establish an American central bank that could lend to all banks in time of panic; the nation's financial system could no longer rely on the private arrangements of J.P. Morgan. Thus, Congress established the Federal Reserve System in 1913. All member banks were required to make deposits to the system, creating a pool of reserves from which financially strapped banks could borrow during a crisis.

The system was originally conceived as a lender of last resort. In times of severe economic stress, it would use the pooled reserves of the banking system to make loans to banks under stress. When conditions improved, the loans were to be repaid. As time went by, however, the Fed discovered two things: first, that the reserve requirement could be used to control banking activity; and second, that control over the banking system provided a means of influencing the business cycle.

The reasoning was straightforward. Bank lending is a key ingredient in the business cycle, driving the cyclic expansion of demand. It cannot, however, grow beyond the limits set by bank reserves; so when the Fed wants to give the economy a boost by encouraging banks to lend more, it increases reserves. On the other hand, by decreasing reserves and thereby shrinking available credit, the Fed exerts a restraining effect on the economy.

OPEN-MARKET OPERATIONS

The mechanism used by the Fed to manipulate the banking system's reserves is astonishingly simple: it buys or sells securities on the open market. Briefly put, when the Fed buys securities, the sellers deposit the proceeds of the sale in their banks, and the banking system's reserves grow. On the other hand, when the Fed sells securities, buyers withdraw funds from their banks in order to make the purchases, and bank reserves fall.

This illustration may help you understand the process. Imagine that the Fed, a government-securities dealer, and all banks (not an individual bank) are the only players in this example. Keep in mind that there are trillions of dollars of U.S. Treasury securities outstanding and that anyone (domestic and foreign corporations, individuals, state, local and foreign governments, private banks, and central banks) can buy them. Billions of dollars of securities are traded each day in New York City.

The Fed increases and reduces bank reserves by its actions in this market. It trades in U.S. Treasury securities rather than some other instrument because the government securities market is so broad and Federal Reserve activities have a relatively small impact on that market.

When the Fed purchases a security from one of the dealers, it pays the dealer by instructing the dealer's bank to credit the checking account of the dealer by the amount of the transaction. At the same time, the Fed pays the bank by crediting the bank's reserve account at the Fed.

Returning to the example, Treasury bills are denominated in amounts of $10,000. Thus, when the Fed buys a Treasury bill from a securities dealer, it instructs the dealer's bank to credit the dealer's account by $10,000 to pay for the Treasury bill. At the same time the Fed credits the dealer's bank's reserve account by $10,000. As a result of the transaction, the dealer has exchanged one asset (Treasury bills ↓ $10,000) for another (checking account ↑ $10,000), the bank's assets (reserves at the Fed ↑ $10,000) and liabilities (dealer's checking account ↑ $10,000) have both increased, and the Fed's assets (Treasury bills ↑ $10,000) and liabilities (bank reserves ↑ $10,000) have both increased.

You may ask, "What gives the Fed the authority to execute these transactions: to pay for a Treasury bill by instructing the dealer's bank to credit the dealer's checking account and then to compensate the bank by crediting its reserve account at the Fed? It's as if the Fed has the right to fund the purchase of an asset by creating its own liability." That's how it works. The Fed has the right under the authority vested in it by the Federal Reserve Act of 1913.

In other words, the Fed can increase the nation's bank reserves by purchasing U.S. Treasury securities from securities dealers, and all it need do to pay for those securities is inform the banks that it has provided them with more reserves. And that's not all: be aware that unless the Fed continues to buy those securities and pay for them by crediting the banks' reserve accounts, bank reserves won't grow. The Fed can halt the economy's expansion by no longer purchasing Treasury bills. Once the Fed stops buying, bank reserves stop growing and so must bank lending. If the Fed wishes to keep a growing economy supplied with bank reserves, it must increase its holdings of Treasury securities over the long haul.

But suppose the Fed wishes to slow the economy's growth temporarily by curtailing banks' ability to lend. Easy—it just stops *buying* securities and starts *selling* them. The securities dealer pays for the Treasury bill it acquires (dealer's assets ↑) when the Fed instructs the dealer's bank to debit the dealer's bank account (dealer's assets ↓). The Fed collects from the dealer's bank by debiting the bank's reserve account at the Fed (bank's assets ↓) and the bank is compensated when it debits the dealer's checking account (bank's liabilities ↓). Consequently, bank lending must cease because the banks are deprived of reserves. Meanwhile, the Fed has merely reduced its assets (Treasury securities ↓) as well as its liabilities (bank reserves ↓).

Consider a few additional points. Don't worry whether or not the securities dealer is willing to buy or sell Treasury securities. There are dozens of dealers competing for the Fed's (and everyone else's) business. There's as much likelihood of the Fed not being able to find a buyer or seller for its Treasury securities as there is of someone not being able to buy or sell a share of stock at the market price. If one stockbroker won't do it, another will.

Also, don't be confused because these open-market operations involve the buying and selling of Treasury securities. Remember that the Fed is not an agency of the U.S. government. The Fed could just as easily deal in common stock or automobiles, but it wouldn't do that because it doesn't want its actions to upset the stock market or the car market. Nonetheless, keep in mind that the Fed could pay for shares of stock or autos by instructing banks to credit stockbrokers' or auto dealers' accounts (and then credit those banks' reserve accounts) in the same fashion that it instructs banks to credit U.S. Treasury securities dealers' accounts. Then the Fed would credit the reserve accounts of the banks that held the stockbrokers' and car dealers' accounts. If the Fed sold common stock or used cars, it would drain away bank reserves just as surely as when it sold Treasury bills in the open market.

Finally, keep in mind that the discussion refers to all banks collectively, not to individual banks. This distinction is important. Banks can competitively drain one another of reserves to augment their ability to lend, but this activity does not increase the entire system's reserves even though it explains the fierce rivalry among banks for deposits. When deposits are moved from one bank to another, the reserves of the first bank fall and those of the second bank increase. The first bank must restrain its lending, while the second bank can lend more. This competitive reshuffling of reserves, however, has not altered the overall level of reserves, and so the lending ability of the banking system remains the same.

To resume the historical account, the Fed has exercised increasing power over the economy since 1913. Periodically, this has led to conflict with the president and Congress. On occasion, politicians took the Fed to task for being too restrictive, for not permitting the economy to grow rapidly enough. At other times, the Fed was criticized for being too lenient and permitting demand to grow so rapidly that inflation threatened.

Why the conflict? Shouldn't the Fed's policy reflect the wishes of Congress and the president? Maybe, but it need not, for—as many do not realize—the Fed is *not* an agency of the U.S. government, but a corporation owned by banks that have purchased shares of stock. Federally chartered banks are required to purchase this stock and be members of the Federal Reserve System; state-chartered banks may be members if they wish. All banks, however, are subject to the Fed's control.

True, the Fed does have a quasi-public character because its affairs are managed by a Board of Governors appointed by the president of the United States with the approval of Congress. Nonetheless, once appointed, the Board of Governors is independent of the federal government and is free to pursue policies of its own choosing. New laws could, of course, change its status. That's why the chairman of the board is so frequently called upon to defend the policies of the Fed before Congress, and why Congress often reminds the Fed that it is a creature of

Congress, which can enact legislation to reduce, alter, or eliminate the Fed's powers. Indeed, legislators and others do suggest from time to time that the Fed be made an agency of the U.S. government in order to remove its autonomy. So far, however, Congress has kept it independent, and it is likely to remain so, exercising its best judgment in guiding the nation's banking activity.

In some ways, the Fed's control over the banking system's reserves is the most important relationship between any two institutions in the American economy. The Fed can increase or reduce bank reserves at will, making it easier or more difficult for the banks to lend, and thus stimulating or restricting business and economic activity.

THE FED AND THE MONEY SUPPLY

But how is it that bank lending increases the supply of money? Where does the money come from? There is an astonishingly simple answer to these questions: the banks create it by crediting the checking account deposits of their borrowers. Thus, bank lending creates money (deposits).

And the only limits to the money supply are:

1. The Fed's willingness to provide the banks with reserves, so that they can lend, and,
2. The banks' ability to find borrowers.

It may sound strange that banks create money, but nonetheless it's true.

The reason so much controversy surrounds the money supply is that many people misunderstand its nature. Checking accounts (or demand deposits, as they are formally called) constitute three-quarters of the money supply, and currency and coins in circulation together make up the remaining quarter. The one-quarter of the money supply that exists as cash comes from a two-tiered source: the U.S. Treasury mints coins and prints paper money for the Fed, and the Fed distributes them.

These arrangements have an interesting and important history. Before the Civil War, with the exception of the two short-lived attempts at a central bank that were mentioned earlier, all paper money was issued by private banks and was called bank notes. These bank notes resembled modern paper currency and entered circulation when banks lent them to customers.

The banks' incentive to issue bank notes to borrowers, instead of gold and silver coins, came from the limited supply of gold and silver coins (specie). If banks wished to lend more than the specie on hand, they would have to issue bank notes. Each bank kept a specie reserve that was no more than a fraction of its outstanding bank notes. This reserve was used to satisfy those who demanded that a bank redeem its notes with specie; as long as the bank could do so, its notes were accepted at face value and were "good as gold." Bank notes and minted coins circulated together.

After the Civil War, checking accounts replaced bank notes. They were safer and more convenient because the customer (borrower) had to sign them and could write in their exact amount. In modern times, all customers, whether depositors or borrowers, began to make use of checking accounts. The private bank note passed into history.

The U.S. Treasury first issued paper money during the Civil War, and it continued to do so until some time after World War II. During the 20th century, however, most of our paper money has been issued by the Federal Reserve System, and today the Fed has that exclusive responsibility; if you examine a piece of currency, you will see that it is a "Federal Reserve Note." Thus, ironically, bank notes constitute all of our currency today, just as they did before the Civil War. But today the notes are issued by the central bank rather than by a host of private banks.

Since the Treasury prints currency at the Fed's request to meet the public's needs, the common notion that the federal government cranks out more paper money to finance its deficits has no factual basis. The amount of paper money in circulation has nothing to do with the deficits of the federal government. When the federal government runs a deficit (expenditures exceed revenue), the Treasury borrows by issuing bonds that are bought by investors: the government gets the money, and the investors get the bonds. If a bond is sold to a bank (and banks are major purchasers of U.S. Treasury securities), the bank pays for it by crediting the checking account of the U.S. Treasury, thus increasing the total volume of all checking accounts. This is called *monetizing the debt;* it enlarges the money supply but does not affect currency in circulation. (If the bond is purchased by the Fed, the transaction is also characterized as monetizing the debt, and the effect is similar to an expansionary monetary policy in which the Fed buys U.S. Treasury securities through open-market operations.)

By contrast, the Fed issues paper money in response not to the budget deficits of the *federal government* but to the *public's* requirements for cash. It supplies banks with currency, and the banks pay for it with a check written on their reserve account. Checks written to "cash" by bank customers then determine the amount of currency circulating outside banks. This demand for currency has no impact on the money supply because checking accounts decrease by the amount currency increases when the check is "cashed."

How then does the money supply grow? In the same fashion that bank notes outstanding grew in the 19th century. When banks lend, they create demand deposits (checking accounts) or credit an existing demand deposit. The more that banks lend, the more that the money supply (which is mostly demand deposits) increases. Today, as 100 years ago, bank reserves set the only limit on bank lending and, therefore, on the money supply. The difference is that instead of keeping specie as reserves, the banks must maintain reserves with the Fed.

Remember: bank loans create deposits (checking accounts), not the other way around. As long as the banking system has sufficient reserves, it can make loans in the form of demand deposits (money). You must abandon the notion that depositors' funds provide the wherewithal for bank lending. That may be true for the traditional mortgage-lending activity of a savings and loan association, but it is not true for commercial banks. After all, where would depositors get the funds if not by withdrawing them from another checking account? But this actually does not increase deposits for the entire system; it only reshuffles deposits among banks. The total is unchanged.

Thus, demand deposits (checking accounts), and with them the money supply, grow when banks lend, and it makes no difference who the borrower is. When a business borrows from its bank in order to stock goods for the Christmas season, the bank creates a deposit (money) on which the business writes checks to pay for merchandise. If you borrow from your bank to buy a car, the loan creates a demand deposit that increases the money supply. Therefore, as you can see, it is not just the federal government that "monetizes debt" when it borrows from the banking system; businesses and consumers "monetize" their debt too.

One last point must be made about the nature of bank reserves. A hundred years ago, they consisted of gold and silver specie; today, they are deposits that banks maintain with the Federal Reserve System. Of what do these reserves consist, if not specie? They are merely checking accounts that the banks have on deposit with the Fed, very much like the checking account you have at your own bank.

Recall that the banks' checking accounts (reserves) increase when the Fed buys securities from a government securities dealer. In other words, banks' reserves are nothing more than accounts the banks maintain at the Fed, accounts that grow at the Fed's discretion whenever it buys securities in the open market.

If it sounds like a house of cards, or like bookkeeping entries in a computer's memory, that's because it is. Nothing "backs up" the money supply except our faith in it, expressed every time we accept or write a check. And those checking accounts, and hence the money supply, built on borrowing, *must keep growing* if the economy is to grow over the business cycle. The forward surge of the cycle, when demand grows rapidly and pulls the economy's output with it, is founded on spenders' ability and willingness to borrow, to go into debt.

This, then, is the critical significance of the money supply: it measures the increase in demand made possible by bank lending. With that in mind, it is now time to discuss the price borrowers are willing to pay for those funds.

THE FED AND INTEREST RATES

Every commodity has a price; the *interest rate* is the price of money. As with any commodity, that price fluctuates according to the laws of supply and demand.

The demand for money increases and interest rates rise during economic expansion as consumers and businesses finance increased spending. They do so by drawing on three sources of funds: current savings, liquidation of financial assets, and borrowing from banks and other financial intermediaries. It's easy to see that an increase in the demand for funds will drive up interest rates.

During recessions, however, as the economy moves from trough to recovery, cash becomes plentiful again. Savings grow, financial assets accumulate, and debt is repaid. Interest rates fall as the supply of funds exceeds the demand for funds at current rates.

The cyclical rise and fall of interest rates would occur with or without the Federal Reserve System. Yet the Fed's influence on interest rates is so pervasive that it is now time to study the Fed's actions in detail.

Begin with a summary statement of the Fed's objectives and actions that refers to neither the money supply or interest rates, which will be developed later:

- *Expansionary policy:* If the Fed buys securities, thus increasing member bank reserves, the banks will be able to lend more, stimulating demand. Such an expansionary policy has traditionally been pursued during a period of recession when the economy is at the bottom of the business cycle.
- *Contractionary policy:* If the Fed sells securities, and bank reserves are reduced, the banks will not be able to lend as much, which will curtail the share of demand that depends on borrowing and, hence, will reduce the total level of demand. This policy has been followed at the peak of the cycle to restrain the growth of demand and inflationary increases in prices.

These relationships can be easily summarized in the following manner: (Read ↑ as "up," ↓ as "down," and → as "leads to.")

Expansionary policy: Fed buys securities → Bank reserves ↑ → Bank lending ↑ → Demand ↑ .
Contractionary policy: Fed sells securities → Bank reserves ↓ → Bank lending ↓ → Demand ↓ .

Now include money in the analysis.

The Fed was traditionally activist, alternately pursuing easy (supplying banks with reserves) or tight (depriving banks of reserves) money policies, depending on the state of the business cycle. During periods of recession and through the recovery stage and the early period of expansion, the Fed's easy money policy contributed to rapid growth in the money supply (demand deposits or checking accounts) as banks lent money (demand deposits or checking accounts) freely in response to plentiful reserves. As the expansionary phase of the cycle reached its peak, the Fed switched to a tight money policy, restricting the growth of bank reserves and, hence, the money supply.

The Fed's actions with respect to the *money supply* may be added to the earlier set of directed arrows and summarized as shown:

Expansionary policy: Fed buys securities → Bank reserves ↑ → Bank lending ↑ → Money supply ↑ → Demand ↑.
Contractionary policy: Fed sells securities → Bank reserves ↓ → Bank lending ↓ → Money supply ↓ → Demand ↓.

As you can imagine, the Fed's actions also have an impact on interest rates. The Fed traditionally pursued an "easy money" policy to hold interest rates down and promote relaxed credit conditions in order to boost demand during the recovery phase of the cycle. Eventually, when the expansion was fully under way, the peak of the cycle was not far off, and credit availability was constricting on its own, the Fed switched to a "tight money" policy, which reduced the supply of credit even further and drove up interest rates.

The Fed's actions with respect to *interest rates* may be included with the directed arrows and summarized as follows:

Easy money policy: Fed buys securities → Bank reserves ↑ → Interest Rates ↓ → Bank lending ↑ → Money supply ↑ → Demand ↑.

Tight money policy: Fed sells securities → Bank reserves ↓ → Interest Rates ↑ → Bank lending ↓ → Money supply ↓ → Demand ↓.

FEDERAL RESERVE POLICY AND THE POSTWAR BUSINESS CYCLE

With these principles in mind, you can examine the Fed's record of expansionary (low interest rates) and contractionary (high interest rates) monetary policies since World War II. (See Charts 4-1 and 4-2 on pages 39 and 40.) Remember that the Fed's objective had always been to counteract the natural swing of the cycle, stimulating demand at the trough with low interest rates, making it easy for the banks to lend, and curbing inflation at the peak with high interest, making it difficult for the banks to lend. The peaks and valleys of the cycle are reflected in these oscillations. Recessions are shaded in gray.

CHART 4-1
Short-Term Interest Rates: The Prime Rate, the Federal Funds Rate, and the Treasury Bill Rate

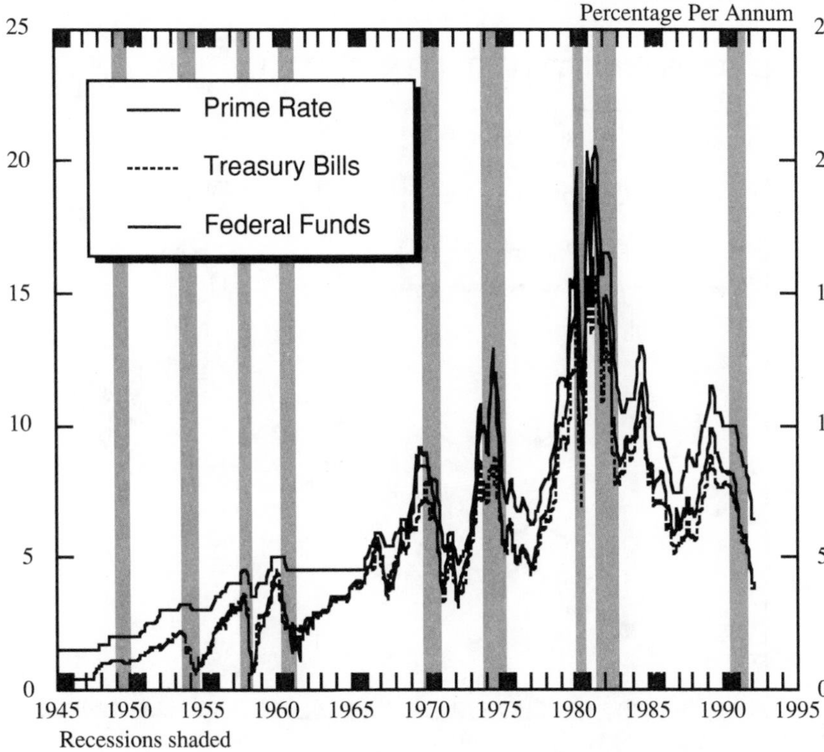

Source: U.S. Department of Commerce, *Business Cycle Indicators*, Series 109, 114, and 119.

The economic events that began in the early 70s clearly illustrate these ideas. Do you recall the feverish inflationary boom of 1973, when demand for autos and housing was so insistent that the United Auto Workers Union was complaining of compulsory overtime and there were shortages of lumber? The demand for borrowed funds was very strong and bank lending grew apace. Accordingly, the Fed instituted a tight money policy (see Charts 4-1 and 4-2 for years 1973 and 1974), forcing interest rates upward.

CHART 4-2
Long-Term Interest Rates: Secondary Market Yields on FHA Mortgages, Yield on New Issues of High-Grade Corporate Bonds, and Yield on Long-Term Treasury Bonds

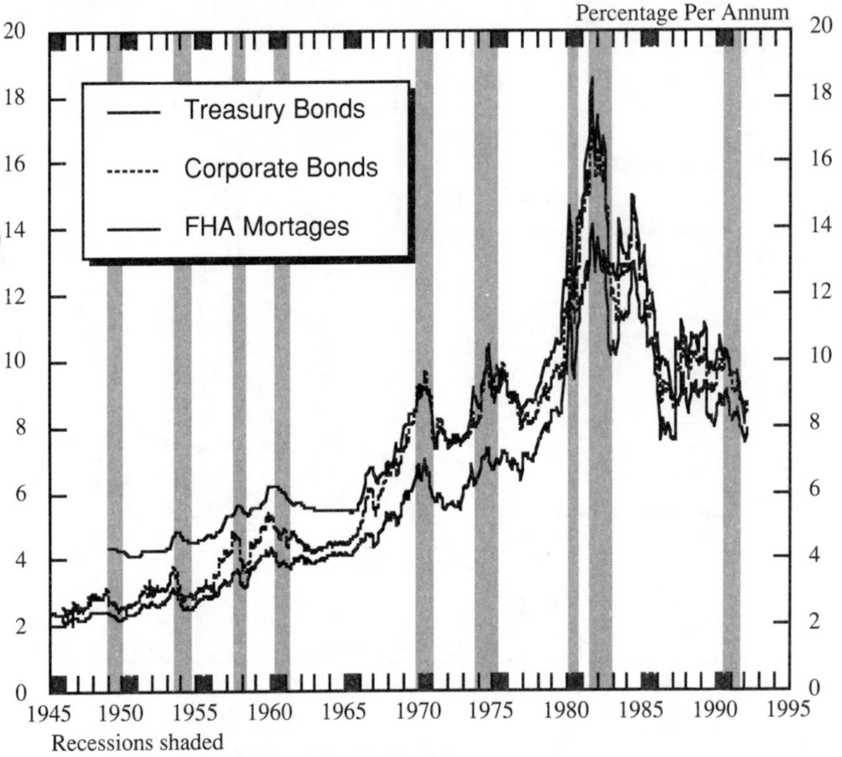

Source: U.S. Department of Commerce, *Business Cycle Indicators,* Series 115, 116, and 118.

As the Fed applied the brakes and raised interest rates, the boom came to a halt. More than 2 million people were thrown out of work when the full force of recession hit in late 1974 and early 1975. So the Fed switched to an easy money policy to stimulate the economy from 1975 through 1977 and interest rates fell. By 1977 the economy was expanding once more, and the Fed reversed itself again, adopting a tight money policy. It was 1974 all over again, except that inflation was even more severe. While the Fed pursued its traditional tight money policy, President Carter instituted voluntary wage and price controls.

President Carter reshuffled his cabinet in 1979, appointing Fed Chairman G. William Miller to the position of Secretary of the Treasury, and asking Paul Volcker, President of the Federal Reserve Bank of New York, to replace Mr. Miller. Paul Volcker accepted the appointment and immediately rallied the members of the Board to maintain the fight against inflation, obtaining a commitment from them to pursue the struggle beyond the cycle's present phase. Interest rates were at a postwar high, the cyclical peak had arrived, and a downturn was inevitable.

The 1980 downturn was so sharp that the Board of Governors set aside its inflation-fighting stance temporarily, providing banks with sufficient reserves and lowering interest rates to prevent undue hardship. Paul Volcker's battle plan, which will be described more fully in a moment, had been postponed by the exigencies of the moment.

In summary, then, the overall aim of the Fed since World War II had been to curb and ultimately reverse the extremes of the cycle: to dampen inflation and to stimulate a depressed economy.

THE MONETARIST CRITIQUE

However, another look at interest rates on pages 39 and 40 reveals that the Fed's policies contributed to the cycle's severity. Like an inexperienced driver with one foot on the gas and the other on the brake, attempting to achieve a steady speed but only able to surge forward after screeching to a halt, the Fed alternately stimulated and restrained the economy. Record interest rates at the cyclical peaks of the late 60s and the middle and late 70s provide evidence of the Fed's desperate attempts to bring inflationary expansion under control. Yet these sudden stops were partly the result of previous attempts, such as those made in 1972 and 1976, to stimulate rapid expansion by providing borrowers with low interest rates. As the economy accelerated and inflation began to go out of control, the Fed hit the brakes.

Meanwhile, the business cycle of the 1970s rose higher and higher, with inflation becoming more severe with each boom and unemployment becoming more severe with each bust. The Fed's policies had failed.

In the 70s, a growing group of economists began to criticize the Fed's policy, accusing the Fed of contributing to the severity of the business cycle instead of reducing cyclical fluctuations. In their view, the Fed's contractionary policy, applied at the peak of the cycle, only added to the severity of the impending recession, while its expansionary policy, during the early stages of recovery, only set the stage for the subsequent inflations .

These economists, known as the *monetarist* school, believe that the rate of increase in the money supply is the single most important determinant of business cycle conditions. If the money supply grows rapidly, the economy expands; if the money supply does not grow rapidly, or even contracts, economic activity also contracts. The monetarists also believe that because other forces intrinsic to the economy will lead to normal cyclical activity and fluctuation in the rate of growth in the money supply, the Fed's best course of action is to attempt to keep the money supply's growth on an even keel, preferably at a low rate, reflecting the economy's long-range ability to increase output. According to the monetarists' view, anything beyond that rate will lead to inflation, and attempts to reduce the swings of the cycle will instead only exacerbate them.

It's as if the monetarists were saying, "If you want a comfortable temperature, set the thermostat and leave it. Don't fiddle with it by alternately raising and lowering it every time you feel a little chilly or a bit too warm, because this will just cause wide swings in temperature, which only heighten discomfort rather than reduce it."

The Road to Hell Is Paved with Good Intentions

- The effect of the Fed's policies in the 70s was the opposite of its intentions.
- The Fed's policies increased the amplitude of the cycle's swings.
- The rate of inflation rose over the course of the cycle.

DEBT AND THE CYCLE

Now, although the Fed was unable to control the cycle or inflation in the 70s, it was not solely responsible for the course of events. You can see tidal waves of consumer and business borrowing (referred to earlier) in Chart 4-3 below, doubling every five years: $100 billion in 1969, $200 billion in 1974, and $400 billion in 1979. This borrowing drove demand forward during the expansionary phase of the cycle, creating the inflationary conditions that provoked the Fed's tight money policy and the subsequent crash into recession. The downturn would have occurred in the Fed's absence; the Fed's policies just made it more severe. Unfortunately, after recession took hold, the quick shift to an easy money policy fostered the next giant wave of borrowing, spending, and inflation, and this inevitably produced (once the wave's internal energy was spent and the Fed tightened up) a major collapse.

CHART 4-3
Total Private Borrowing

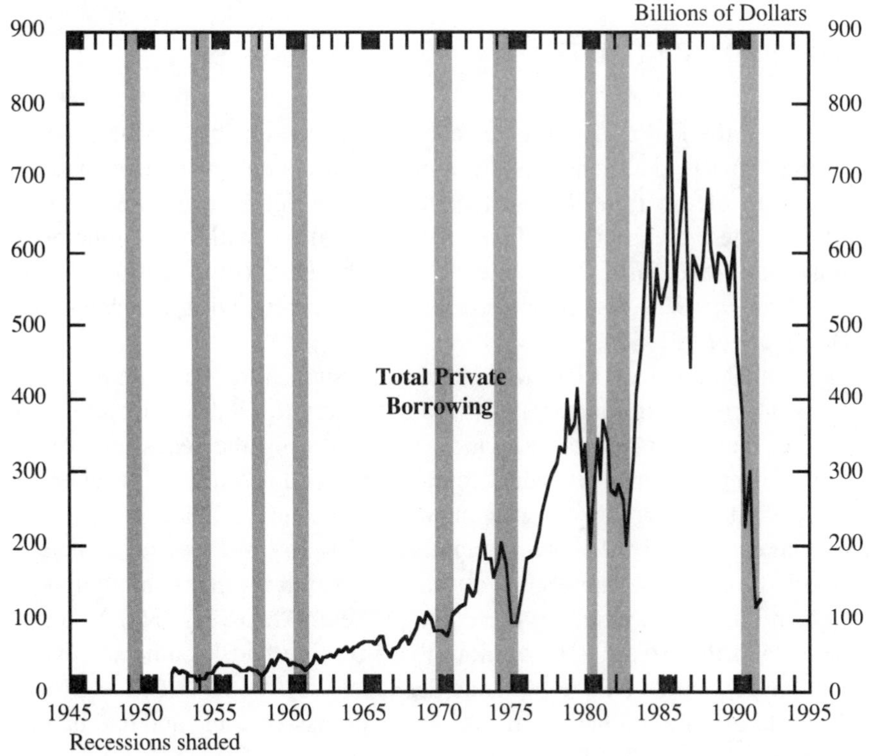

Source: U.S. Department of Commerce, *Business Cycle Indicators,* Series 110.

Be sure to notice as well that interest rates rose over time due to the ever-escalating demand for funds. You saw this in Charts 4-1 and 4-2 on pages 39 and 40, when consumer and business borrowing doubled every five years in the 1970s. Since the demand for funds continuously exceeded the supply of funds at current prices, interest rates (the price of borrowed money) climbed in the long run.

You can see that by the mid 80s interest rates had fallen from their record peaks although private borrowing reached an all-time high. More about this later.

Inflation's Engine: the 1970s

- Explosive borrowing → explosive spending → explosive inflation.

THE FED'S REVOLUTION

Although the Fed may not have been entirely responsible for the debacle of the late 70s, the monetarists' criticism of its "stop-go" policies had hit home. In October 1979, shortly after Paul Volcker began his term of office, the Fed announced an accommodation with the monetarist position. Henceforth, Mr. Volcker said, the Fed would set targets for monetary growth that it believed were consistent with an acceptable (low) rate of inflation.

In the summer of 1980, Mr. Volcker persuaded the Fed that it would have to renew immediately its commitment to halting inflation, a commitment that it had suspended briefly during the recession of the previous spring. After earlier recessions, the Fed had always reverted to an expansionary policy of a year or two's duration (see Charts 4-1 and 4-2 on pages 39 and 40). Following the 1980 slump, however, the Fed decided to prevent rapid recovery and expansion by maintaining a very tight money policy during the early phases of recovery. Mr. Volcker persuaded the Board of Governors that inflation had become so severe that the economy could not tolerate the usual easy-money-aided recovery. The rate of inflation had risen over each successive cycle and had barely declined during the 1980 recession. Rapid stimulation and recovery of demand would quickly bid prices up once again. This time, tight money was the only appropriate remedy, even if it stunted the recovery.

In consequence, the Fed's 1980, 1981, and 1982 tight money policies drove the prime rate to 21.5 percent and first mortgage rates to 18 percent, unleashing the worst recession since World War II. For the first time, the Fed had stopped a recovery in its tracks and watched the economy slide off into back-to-back recessions. The Fed had made up its mind that restraining demand in order to control inflation was worth the price of economic contraction.

But the Fed relaxed its grip in the summer of 1982, first, because inflation had been wrung out of the economy and unemployment had reached an intolerable level; and second, because there were strong signs that Congress was losing patience with the Fed's restrictive policies. The Fed had accomplished its objective, so there was no need to antagonize further those who had the power to terminate the Fed's independent status. Yet, despite the eventual relaxation, you should realize that the Fed's 1981 policies marked a major shift in strategy that had significant and far-reaching consequences for our economy. *If severe inflation has been eliminated for the foreseeable future, it is no exaggeration to say that the Fed beat it back single-handedly.*

The Fed Beats Back Inflation: Early 80s

- Restrictive policy → Bank reserves ↓ → Interest rates ↑ → Borrowing ↓ → Spending ↓ → Inflation ↓ .

Events in the 1980s nonetheless required the Fed's constant vigilance. When the Fed permitted easier conditions in late 1982, the economy roared ahead, as you can see from Chart 4-3 on page 43. Business and consumer borrowing grew rapidly in 1983, reaching $500 billion (a record high at the time) by early 1984. Was this to be a repeat of earlier inflationary cycles, where demand, financed by easy credit, would be permitted to leap upward, bidding the rate of inflation to a new record? Would the bitter and wrenching experience of 1981-82, which had brought inflation under control, have been suffered in vain?

Fortunately, there was so much slack in the economy due to the recession's severity, inflation did not immediately reappear. But, immediate action was required to avoid just such a painful reoccurrence.

So the Fed fine-tuned a mini-slowdown, restricting bank reserves and forcing up interest rates (Charts 4-1 and 4-2 on pages 39 and 40). That solved the problem: the growth in demand was stymied, and the economy cooled off.

The Fed's policies in the early 80s were a radical departure from those of the 60s and 70s. The 1981-82 recession and the mini slowdown of 1984 signaled a new era, a major turning point in postwar economic history. The Fed had abandoned its old game plan: spurring the economy onward during slack conditions only to apply a chokehold when boom and inflation got out of hand, and then dealing with a repeat performance in the next cycle but on a new, ratcheted, higher plateau. General restraint over the course of the cycle was the new master strategy.

Paul Volcker knew that easy conditions and a pro-growth attitude had contributed to the disaster of the 70s. He also knew that he was on a tightrope, and that the cautious attitude described above could not lapse into complacency. But by the mid-80s, new appointees to the Board of Governors who favored an easy-money policy had begun to undermine Mr. Volcker's go-slow approach. You will notice on pages 39 and 40 that interest rates fell, signaling dramatically easier conditions.

Why did these new appointees to the Board of Governors pursue a policy which appeared to be such a reckless reversal of the Fed's successful approach? And why were they appointed? Because President Reagan and his advisers, who called themselves "supply-side" economists, wanted supply-siders on the Board. And supply-siders favor easy credit and low interest rates. By 1987, at the end of Paul Volcker's second four-year term as the Board's chair, he was the only veteran of the tight money campaigns of the early 80s. As the supply-siders pushed easier and easier conditions, Mr. Volcker informed President Reagan that he did not wish to be appointed to another term as chair—a term in which the Board's policy of restraint could be undone by a new majority that favored easy money, and a term in which easy money could once again unleash the forces of inflation upon the economy.

So President Reagan appointed Alan Greenspan to succeed Paul Volcker. Many observers were pessimistic and did not believe that Mr. Greenspan would be any more successful in controlling the supply siders. But these fears were unfounded because under Mr. Greenspan the Board continued to be responsible, refusing to permit a rekindling of the inflation of the 1970s.

You can see in Chart 4-3 on page 43 that private borrowing did not increase in the late 1980s, fluctuating around $600 billion annually. Thus the Board maintained sufficient restraint to prevent the headlong expansion of private borrowing, and with it the explosion in demand that precedes a new round of inflation.

(The big jump in borrowing in the last quarter of 1985 was due to state and local government borrowing in anticipation of tax law changes that never came about. State and local borrowing is included with these private borrowing figures but is usually quite small.)

The Fed Controls Inflation: Late 80s

- Moderate restraint → Moderately high interest rates → Moderate borrowing → Moderate spending → Moderate inflation.

Instead, Mr. Greenspan's board had to confront a new problem at the turn of the 90s. Recession forced them to temporarily suspend the struggle against inflation. As private borrowing plunged to levels not seen since the 1970s (see Chart 4-3 on page 43), the Fed eased and short-term interest rates fell to 17-year lows, although long-term rates held steady (see Charts 4-1 and 4-2 on pages 39 and 40).

FINE-TUNING AND DEREGULATION

All of this raises the issue of economic "fine-tuning." How did the Fed manage to bring about an effective mini slowdown in 1984, when it seemed incapable of such sensitive fine-tuning in the 70s? And why should we be optimistic that the Fed can fine-tune in the future? The answer is partly that the Fed had a relatively small and easy task before it in 1984. But that's not all. In the 70s and earlier, interest rate regulations restricted the Fed to operating a switch that was either "off" or "on." But deregulation in the late 70s and early 80s permitted a metamorphosis; the switch became a valve, and the flow of credit could be more finely calibrated.

The history of this transition deserves some explanation. Until the end of the 70s, banks and savings and loan companies were not permitted to pay more than a statutory maximum of slightly over 5 percent on consumer savings accounts. During the rapid expansions of 1968-69 and 1973-74, Treasury bill interest rates climbed to well above 5 percent, providing an incentive for large depositors to withdraw their funds from these financial intermediaries and invest them in Treasury bills in order to earn the higher market return.

This process was called *disintermediation* (a coinage only an economist could love) because savers bypassed the financial intermediaries to invest their funds directly in Treasury bills; S&Ls suffered severely because of their dependence on consumer savings accounts.

The upshot was that as soon as boom conditions developed and the Fed began exercising a tight money policy, driving interest rates up, an ocean of deposits drained out of the banks and especially out of the S&Ls. The savings and loans literally ran out of money. They couldn't make mortgage loans, even if borrowers were willing to pay exorbitant rates of interest.

You can understand, then, why the Fed's tight money policies during these earlier periods did not cause credit to constrict gradually as interest rates climbed; instead, the availability of credit suddenly dried up for certain key areas of the economy (e.g., residential construction almost shut down).

Then, when the boom peaked and the economy slipped off into recession, the Fed switched to an easy money policy. As soon as Treasury bill interest rates fell below the statutory maximum that banks and S&Ls were able to pay, depositors sold their Treasury bills and redeposited the funds, propelling a tidal wave of deposits back into the financial intermediaries. As a result, S&Ls practically gave money away to finance home building.

These fund flows out of and then back into the banks and S&Ls exacerbated the business cycle. In 1969 and 1974, analysts didn't talk about tight conditions; they talked about the "credit crunch" and how it had stopped the economy in its tracks. Then, as deposits came flooding back into the system in 1970-72 and 1975-77, demand fueled by cheap credit took off like a rocket.

By 1980 deregulation had begun to remove interest rate ceilings from consumer savings accounts. The new, flexible-rate accounts were even called "T-bill accounts" for a while because they were pegged to the Treasury bill rate and were designed to prevent savers from defecting to the savings account's chief competitor, the Treasury bill, as interest rates rose.

When the Fed made its desperate stand against inflation in 1981-82, deregulation had been partially accomplished: the T-bill accounts prevented a run on the savings and loan companies' deposits. These accounts required a minimum deposit of $10,000, however, so many savers were attracted by recently created money market mutual funds that had much smaller minimum deposit requirements. The money market funds invested in commercial paper and other short-term instruments, thus providing yields slightly higher than those of Treasury bills. Consequently, banks and S&Ls still faced a partial drain on their deposits.

But deregulation had begun to work. The S&Ls did not run out of money in 1981-82, although they were obliged to raise mortgage rates to prohibitive levels as T-bill account interest rates went up with the yield on Treasury bills. Residential construction was at last constrained by the *price* borrowers had to pay for funds rather than by the *availability* of those funds.

After the Fed eased up in mid-1982, and as the economy rebounded strongly in 1983, banks and S&Ls received permission to offer "money market accounts," which competed directly with the money market funds. Although deregulation was not 100 percent complete, depositors now had little reason to keep their funds elsewhere, and so a large volume of funds returned to the banks and S&Ls from the money market mutual funds.

Now that the Fed had a finely honed scalpel, it could maintain interest rates at sufficiently low levels to encourage demand but could easily nudge them upward whenever inflationary conditions threatened. And it would not have to fear disintermediation, the destructive flows of funds out of banks and S&Ls.

Early 1984 provided the first test; to confirm the results, review the interest rate record in Charts 4-1 and 4-2 on pages 39 and 40 once again. Interest rates collapsed in late 1982, but the Fed didn't wait long before it began to tighten up again. Demand had roared ahead throughout 1983; and, by the end of the year, there were many alarming signs that inflation was about to be rekindled. Although the Fed had allowed interest rates to drift upward throughout 1983, by early 1984 more decisive, positive action was required.

Recall from Charts 4-1 and 4-2 that the Fed's tight money policy in the spring of 1984 had forced interest rates quickly upward, inducing the mini-slowdown of 1984. There was talk of recession, but the Fed had carefully tuned the slowdown and did not let it develop into recession. Once the danger was past, the Fed permitted interest rates to drop sharply, and demand began to grow once again.

Although deregulation became suspect in the late 80s because of the excesses and consequent failures associated with unregulated lending practices by the savings and loan industry, the deregulation of interest rates helped the Fed alter the course of America's economic history.

By the early 1990s, of course, the Fed faced a different problem. Private borrowing tumbled so steeply during the 1990-91 recession that the Fed redirected its efforts to stimulating demand with low interest rates. You can see on page 39 how steeply short-term rates plunged, although long-term rates hardly dipped (see page 40). The Fed insisted it was at a loss to explain this divergence.

THE NEW CREDIT RATIONING

Recall once again the credit craziness of the late 70s, when rampant recourse to borrowed funds pumped up the inflationary balloon. Many observers suggested credit rationing as a solution. That was the only way, they argued, to provide funds for productive business investment in new technology and capital goods, while curtailing unproductive consumer expenditures financed by installment plans, credit cards, and so forth. Otherwise, industry had to compete with consumers in the capital markets for scarce funds. Consumers, the argument continued, were notoriously insensitive to interest rates; all they cared about was the size of the monthly payment, and this could be held down by stretching out the length of payment.

Consequently, as consumers borrowed more and more for second homes, boats, the latest electronic gadget, or whatever, business was forced to pay ever higher interest rates as it competed for scarce funds. This not only limited industry's ability to modernize and improve our nation's capital stock, it also added *business* debt-financed demand on top of *consumer* debt-financed demand (see Chart 4-3 on page 43). Too many dollars chased too few goods (i.e., supply could not keep pace with demand at current prices) and therefore prices inevitably rose too quickly. So the advocates of credit rationing recommended their solution.

They suggested that legal minimums be set for auto and home loan down payments and legal maximums established for the term of the loan: for instance, 50 percent minimum down payments with a 10-year maximum loan term for housing and 2 years for autos. Yet, there was no way Congress would enact, or the President sign, such legislation. The auto and construction industries would not permit it.

And then, beginning in the early 80s, the Fed stepped in and throttled inflation with its tight money policy. Inflation collapsed; the Fed was the victor and remained vigilant ever-after.

The Fed has a unique opportunity in the 1990s to keep interest rates at just the right level to maintain an adequate, but not too rapid, growth in demand without inflation. But that means that interest rates in the 1990s cannot return to the low levels of yesteryear, especially when compared to the rate of inflation. *High interest rates (which is not to say chronically rising rates) are the new credit rationing, and they will be with us for many years.*

Investors should keep that in mind. And they should be aware that the Fed's anti-inflation posture will bode ill for gold and other tangibles but well for stocks and other paper investments. All of which Chapter 8 will discuss in greater detail.

SUMMARY

To summarize this experience, think of the economy as a frisky horse where the rider (the Fed) must continually pull back on the reins (tight money) in order to prevent a runaway, breakneck gallop (inflation). The rider has learned a lesson the hard way, by periodically letting the reins go slack and permitting the horse to break into a gallop, only to be thrown from the horse as it reared when the rider desperately yanked on the reins (pre-1981/82 stop-go policy).

The stop-go policy is over; the Fed has a firm grip on the reins. Its present governors know it must restrain borrowing with high interest rates into the foreseeable future in order to dampen both the business cycle and inflation.

CHAPTER 5

FEDERAL FISCAL POLICY

THE CONVENTIONAL WISDOM

The federal deficit needs no introduction. It's been an issue for debate in every presidential election campaign since 1980. The federal government borrowed $200 billion in some years of that decade and over a trillion dollars throughout the decade. By the early 1990s the annual deficit had risen to around $300 billion and the outstanding debt to more than $3 trillion. This chapter will deal principally with one aspect of that issue: the deficit's impact on the rate of inflation.

Chapter 4 asserted that the Fed had "single-handedly" overcome inflation in the 1980s by the exercise of monetary policy. This runs contrary to the conventional wisdom that it is federal deficits that generate inflation. How do we reconcile the conventional wisdom that deficits generate inflation with the earlier analysis of the Fed's role? Let's look at the evidence.

The facts portrayed in Chart 5-1 on page 54 show that the deficit grew dramatically in 1975 and 1981-82, and shrank to an insignificant number in 1979. If the conventional wisdom made sense, inflation should have jumped in 1975 and 1981-82 with the increase in the federal deficit and subsided in 1979 when the budget balanced.

But that didn't happen. As a matter of fact, the opposite occurred. Inflation narrowed in 1975 and 1981-82 and peaked in 1979. In other words, not only do the facts not support the conventional wisdom, they seem to indicate the opposite. Inflation fell with the increases in the federal deficit (1975 and 1981-82) and rose when the deficit declined (1979). Does this mean that balanced budgets *generate* inflation while deficits *reduce* inflation? Now that *would* be a scoop.

CHART 5-1
Federal Government Expenditures, Receipts, and Deficit

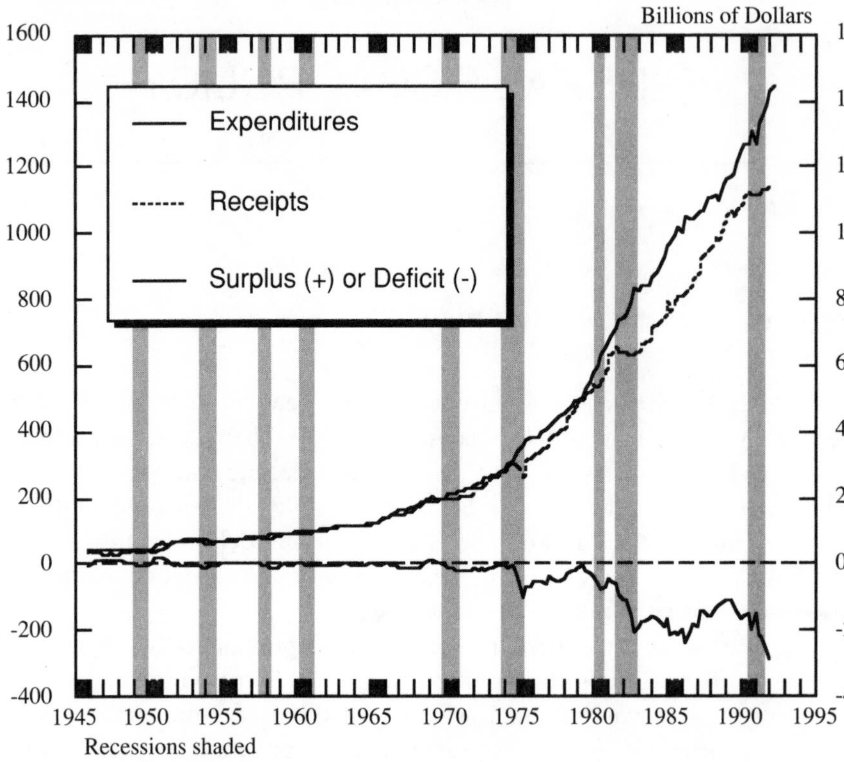

Source: U.S. Department of Commerce, *Business Cycle Indicators,* Series 500, 501, and 502.

To resolve the problem, you must put the federal deficit in perspective. Chart 4-3 on page 43, reproduced as Chart 5-2 on page 55, depicts private borrowing. Compare it with the federal deficit in Chart 5-1 on page 54. Recall that private borrowing includes mortgage borrowing to support residential construction, installment credit to finance the purchase of autos and other consumer durables, and business indebtedness to pay for expenditures on plant, equipment, and inventory. But it also includes (unfortunately, because it is confusing) borrowing by state and local governments, for reasons that need not be developed here.

CHART 5-2
Total Private Borrowing

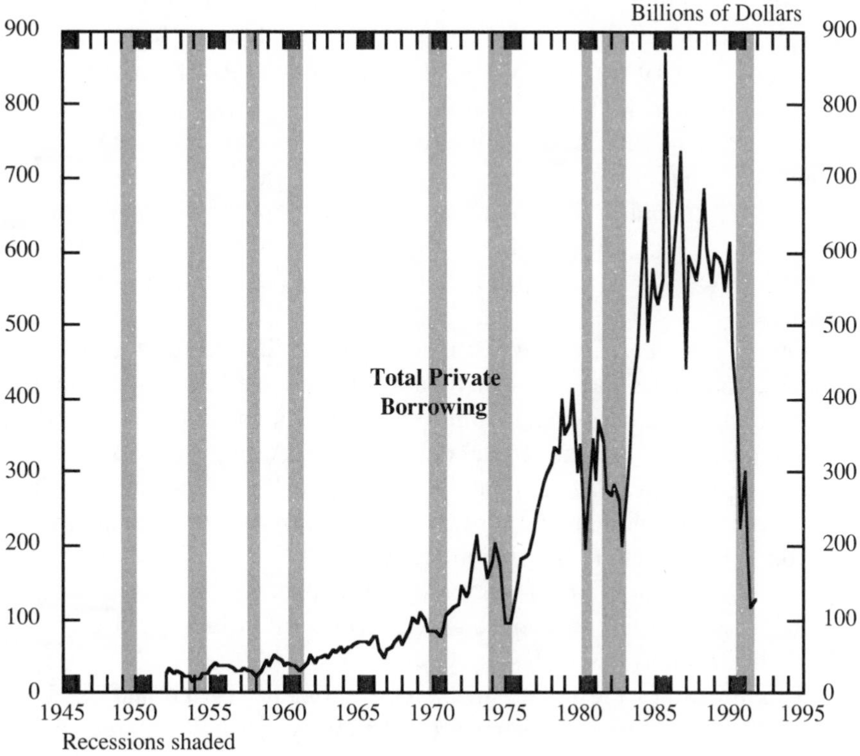

Source: U.S. Department of Commerce, *Business Cycle Indicators*, Series 110.

Keep in mind that both charts portray annual borrowing, not outstanding debt. By the early 1990s, outstanding federal debt was over $3 trillion and outstanding private debt was over $10 trillion. Each year's borrowing adds to the outstanding figure, so that an annual federal deficit of $300 billion would boost the outstanding federal figure from $3 trillion to $3.3 trillion and annual private borrowing of $200 billion might lift the private total to $10.2 trillion. (Don't confuse either of these with the balance of trade deficit, to be examined in Chapter 16.)

Now compare private borrowing with the federal deficit in 1975, and note that both were approximately $100 billion. Then they move in opposite directions: the federal deficit shrinks to nothing in 1979 and private borrowing balloons to $400 billion. So total borrowing grew from $200 billion in 1975 ($100 billion of private plus $100 billion of federal) to $400 billion in 1979 (all private).

This explains the burst of inflation in the late 70s. Total borrowing doubled, financing the huge increase in demand (greater than the economy's increase in production at current prices) that drove up inflation. Thus, the growth in private borrowing in the late 70s overwhelmed the decline in federal borrowing, generating rapid price increases.

On the other hand, if you continue to look at the record in Charts 5-1 and 5-2 on pages 54 and 55, you'll notice that private borrowing slumped in 1981 and 1982, dropping to almost $200 billion annually from its $400 billion peak in 1979. The federal deficit, however, popped back up from next to nothing in 1979 to about $200 billion in 1982. Once again, when you add private and federal borrowing, you see an offset: the total is $400 billion in both years ($400 billion private in 1979 with no federal deficit and $200 billion for each in 1982). When total borrowing stopped growing from 1979 through 1982, the rate of inflation subsided as demand came into line with supply.

This illustrates the fallacy in the conventional wisdom and explains why inflation seemed to behave so perversely when compared to the federal deficit. You can't ignore private borrowing when analyzing inflation. As a matter of fact, the explosion of private borrowing from 1970 to 1973 ($100 billion to $200 billion) and from 1975 to 1979 ($100 billion to $400 billion) explains that decade's two great rounds of inflation. Inflation did not grow in the 1980s because private borrowing fluctuated in a narrow range (except for 1985) and demonstrated no upward trend after 1984. By the end of the decade, private borrowing was still fluctuating around $600 billion annually, the level it had reached more than five years earlier. Then it plunged to $200 billion in the early 90s and inflation withered. Federal borrowing's growth to $400 billion was not large enough to offset private borrowing's decline.

Another development also requires clarification: the burst of private borrowing in late 1985. It was due to state and local governments' trying to beat an anticipated change in tax laws that never came to pass. Some Congressmen had suggested that interest paid on state and local bonds no longer be tax-exempt. Enactment of this legislation would have increased state and local interest payments because their bonds had paid below-market rates for years due to the tax-exempt benefit to investors (i.e., bond holders were willing to receive below market yields, provided they were tax-exempt). State and local governments moved up their borrowing in anticipation of the 1986 change that never came to pass.

But the main point to bear in mind is that the large federal deficits of the 1980s and early 90s have not generated inflation despite the attention paid them. The recessionary drop in private borrowing overshadowed them.

Investor's Tip

- Forget about the federal deficit; it won't influence our rate of inflation for the foreseeable future and therefore *won't* influence the value of your investments.

ALONG CAME KEYNES

Nonetheless, you ought to consider the federal government's deficits in some detail for no other reason than that they have drawn so much attention. In order to sort out the continuing debate surrounding the federal government's taxing and spending programs and their impact on the economy, you must go back to the 19th and early 20th centuries. Economics then was governed by an axiom known as *Say's Law:* "Supply creates its own demand." This meant that economic recession and depression and their accompanying unemployment were temporary and self-correcting phenomena. After all, capitalists produce goods for market, and workers offer their labor for hire *so that they in turn can demand goods in the marketplace*. If the goods cannot be sold or the labor is not hired, then a lower price or wage will be asked, until price and wage cutting permit all of the goods or labor to be sold. No goods will remain chronically unsold and no labor will remain chronically unemployed as long as prices and wages remain flexible.

Using this line of reasoning, 19th-century economists argued that recession and its concomitant unemployment were transitory phenomena and should generate neither a great deal of concern nor any corrective policy prescription by the government. Society and government ought to let well enough alone (i.e., follow the policy of laissez-faire) and let market forces prevail. The operation of the market would eventually restore full employment.

With Say's Law as their guide, no wonder economists could not understand the Great Depression, which began in 1929 and hit bottom in 1933. Nor could they understand why the economy's performance remained anemic for so long after 1933. After all, they reasoned, the economy should naturally return to conditions of full production and full employment as business cut prices in order to sell its products and workers took wage cuts in order to find employment. If the economy continued in a slump, that was the fault, not of the economists and their theories, but of employers and employees who refused to cut prices and wages.

The economists' logic did not help the businesses that were failing or the workers who were out of jobs. Prices and wages had fallen, yet conditions remained dismal; something was dreadfully wrong, and somebody had to do something about it.

In America, President Roosevelt was elected. He responded with massive public-works programs, which, by the way, were funded by federal deficits. The economics community was horrified and they insisted that the federal government's efforts would merely deny resources to the private sector, and thus provide no net benefit. F.D.R. ignored economic theory. He was a practical man with a practical solution: if people were out of work, then the government would be the employer of last resort and put them to work building roads, parks, bridges, dams, and other public projects.

In 1936 an Englishman named John Maynard Keynes (rhymes with *brains)* gave intellectual credentials to F.D.R.'s practical policies by proposing that the problem was the economists' theories, not the economy. Keynes tackled Say's Law (and the economics establishment) at the knees by declaring that demand *could* be chronically insufficient and the economy *could* be chronically plagued with substantial excess capacity and unemployment. Keynes scolded his fellow economists for arguing that their theories were right and that the problem lay with the practical world of business and work that was not living up to theoretical expectations. Science—even "the dismal science" of economics—dictates that a theory that does not conform to the facts must be discarded.

Keynes declared that it was ridiculous to expect price and wage cuts to solve the economy's problem. A totally new approach had to be devised. He believed the only answer was to boost demand by the use of some exogenous (outside) force. Workers could not be expected to buy more under conditions of actual and threatened unemployment nor business to spend more on plant and equipment when excess capacity and weak profits were the rule. But if consumers and business would not spend, how could the economy pull out of its slump? Through government spending, Keynes argued, even if the government had to borrow funds. Once government began to spend on public works, the people who were employed on these projects would spend their earnings on privately produced goods and services. In a multiplier effect, the total level of demand would be lifted and full employment restored. When the pump-priming operation was over and the private economy was back on its feet, the government could gradually withdraw from the economic scene. Pump-priming by government intervention became known as *Keynesian* economics.

Keynesian (rhymes with "brainsian") theory came to dominate economics, rendering Say's Law archaic. The next generation of economists pushed Keynesian theory a bit further, reasoning that a tax cut could be as effective in priming the pump as an increase in government expenditures. Reducing taxes would increase consumers' disposable income and their consumption expenditures. The new generation believed this would be as effective as an increase in government expenditures for restoring demand to a level sufficient to ensure full employment.

Economists now argued that it didn't matter how the pump was primed, whether through expenditure increases or tax cuts. Putting more into the expenditure stream than was removed from the income stream (in the form of taxes) would always create a net boost in total demand. If government expenditures increased while tax revenues remained the same, the increase in public expenditures would boost demand. If government expenditures remained the same while taxes were cut, the increase in private consumption expenditures would boost demand. In either case, or in both together, the increased government deficit and the borrowing needed to fund that deficit made possible a net addition to total demand.

The increase in the deficit measures the increase in demand, and the government finances that deficit by borrowing from the public through the sale of U.S. Treasury securities. Now, it might seem that borrowing from the public would have the same effect as taxing the public since it removes funds from the private sector and would thus neutralize the spending increase. After all, if the public refrains from spending to buy government bonds, isn't the public's expenditure reduced? The answer is yes, if the bonds are purchased by private citizens; however, this is generally not the case. The largest share of bonds is sold to the banking system, which purchases them by creating a demand deposit (checking account) for the government. This is known as "monetizing" the debt, as described in Chapter 4. The fact that the government borrows from the banks permits an increase in government spending without a decrease in private spending.

The federal government's attempts to influence economic activity through its power to tax and spend is known as *fiscal policy*. Although this chapter discusses fiscal policy in the context of the need to stimulate demand in order to deal with recession, it should be clear that fiscal policy could also be employed to deal with inflation. For example, increasing taxes or reducing government expenditures, which would create a surplus, drains spending from the economy, reducing total demand and, consequently, cooling inflation.

As the discussion of fiscal policy continues, remember that it is not the same thing as *monetary policy,* which was discussed in Chapter 4.

Monetary policy refers to the actions of the Federal Reserve System; *fiscal policy* refers to the actions of the federal government. Monetary policy works through its influence on the banking system, the money supply, bank lending, and interest rates, whereas fiscal policy works through its direct impact on aggregate demand.

Also keep in mind that fiscal policy is the province solely of the federal government, not of state or local government. Only the federal government has the flexibility to run the necessary budget deficits or surpluses large enough to influence total demand. Most state and local governments are limited, either de facto or de jure, to operating with a balanced budget.

THE KENNEDY TAX CUT

Keynesian economics, with its emphasis on fiscal policy, had won the hearts and minds of academic economists by the early 1960s. Not everyone, however, was convinced. When President Kennedy assumed office in 1961 and proposed a tax cut to stimulate the level of economic activity, Republicans and conservative Democrats in Congress attacked it as fiscally irresponsible. They demanded a balanced budget and argued that tax cuts would generate unacceptable deficits. President Kennedy's Keynesian reply was that the deficits would disappear as soon as the tax cut stimulated the level of demand, output, and income, providing even greater tax revenues despite the decline in the tax rate. These arguments did not immediately persuade Congress, and the tax cut did not pass until the spring of 1964, following President Kennedy's assassination.

The nation enjoyed full employment and a balanced budget in 1965, and Keynesian fiscal policy became an accepted method of "fine-tuning" the economy. Indeed, this technique became so legitimate that it was employed by the next two Republican presidents. President Nixon cut taxes to deal with the 1970 recession, and President Ford cut taxes to deal with the 1974-75 recession. In each case, the Federal Reserve also pursued an easy money policy in order to stimulate demand. Conservatives joined liberals and Republicans agreed with Democrats that tax cuts were necessary to get the economy moving.

By the late 1970s, however, severe inflation prompted a new and growing group of economists to conclude that attempts to stimulate demand with easy money and easy fiscal policies had gone awry. Escalating inflation, which reduced real income, had drawn more and more people into the labor force. The new entrants to the labor force, usually the secondary or tertiary wage earners in the family, had fewer skills and thus were more difficult to employ. Unemployment grew as inflation escalated. The economy had the worst of both worlds. Thus, this new group of economists and politicians argued that what was known as "full-employment policy," actually the Keynesian prescription of stimulating demand through easy monetary and easy fiscal policies, had been a failure.

Moreover, they continued, increased inflation had discouraged savings and investment. Rising prices penalized savers for their thrift, because the value of real savings fell. This encouraged personal indebtedness rather than saving, and inasmuch as saving is the ultimate source of all funds for investment, the level of investment was bound to shrink over time. These critics charged that the lack of savings and the resulting lack of investment were reflected by the low levels of business investment in new machinery and technology and by the resulting decline in productivity.

Finally, they attacked the progressive income tax, which propelled people into higher tax brackets despite a drop in real income. Higher marginal tax rates, they said, removed the incentive to work more and to work harder. Why should businesses invest in new ideas, new products, and more efficient ways of doing things if higher taxes confiscated the profits? Why should workers put in more hours on the job if higher taxes reduced the additional pay to a meaningless figure?

SUPPLY-SIDE ECONOMICS

The views of these economists and politicians came to be called *supply-side* economics, which they developed in contrast to *demand-side,* or Keynesian, economics. The supply-siders argued that it was more important to support policies that bolstered the economy's ability to supply or produce more goods than to enhance demand. Therefore, the supply-side economists advocated drastic federal income tax reductions over a three-year period, with deficits to be avoided by a parallel reduction in federal spending. Federal expenditure programs, in their view, tended to over-regulate private activity and to waste tax dollars in a variety of boondoggles and unnecessary transfer payments.

Supply-side theory claimed that a massive, across-the-board tax cut would accomplish two major objectives. First, it would provide incentives for increased work, thus boosting output. A greater supply, or output, of goods and services would dampen inflation. Second, increased disposable income would lead to increased savings, providing a pool of funds to finance investment. Once again, the supply of goods and services would be stimulated, and increased output would reduce inflation.

Supply-side economics was a total contradiction of Keynesian fiscal policy, which had prevailed for almost half a century. It was widely and correctly viewed as a device to restrict and contract the federal government and so was admired and promoted by conservatives and viewed with suspicion by liberals. The supply-siders began to make their voices heard during President Carter's administration, placing him in a potential quandary. He had pledged to balance the federal budget by the end of his first term in office. Rapid economic expansion and inflation had pushed revenues upward more rapidly than expenditures; consequently, his goal was in sight by late 1979. The tax cut proposed by the supply-siders would have postponed that goal, unless, of course, it was accompanied by large reductions in federal expenditures, which, as a Democrat, President Carter could not endorse.

The 1980 recession created an even sharper dilemma for him. He might have advocated a tax cut (the traditional Keynesian prescription for recession), but this would have played into the hands of the supply-siders, who would have demanded compensating spending cuts. By now the supply-siders had a presidential candidate, Ronald Reagan, as their principal spokesman. The situation was further complicated for President Carter by the fact that the supply-side tax cut favored upper-income groups, rather than the lower-income groups traditionally targeted for tax cuts by the Democrats. Thus, political circumstances precluded President Carter from trying to deal with the 1980 recession by means of tax reductions.

After his inauguration in 1981, as the economy slid into the 1981-82 recession, President Reagan pushed for and obtained the supply-side tax cuts. What a strange historical reversal: 20 years after President Kennedy battled Republicans and conservatives for his tax cut, President Reagan now had to battle Democrats and liberals for his. Whereas Democrats had once advocated tax cuts to stimulate the economy and the Republicans had opposed those cuts, it was now the Republicans who were advocating tax cuts over the opposition of the Democrats. The parties had done a complete about-face.

The shift of the mantle of fiscal conservatism from Republicans to Democrats is one of the most important political changes since World War II. President Reagan's supply-side tax cut of 1981-83 accompanied the recession of 1981-82. It generated a chaotic reduction in federal revenue, because a smaller proportion of a declining level of income was collected in taxes. Meanwhile, total expenditures continued to grow despite reductions in the budget left by President Carter. Democrats criticized the resulting deficit and demanded that the tax cuts be rescinded. Republicans insisted that there be no tax increase, despite the deficits.

The debate occurred in the midst of recession and recovery. The Republicans contended that any tax increase would jeopardize the supply-side expansion. The Democrats countered that continued deficits and the accompanying government borrowing drove up interest rates and jeopardized the expansion. Beneath the economic details of the debate, both sides had ideological positions to defend. The Democrats realized that continued deficits put relentless pressures on domestic expenditures. Only a tax increase could generate the revenue that made these expenditure programs affordable. The Republicans too were aware that the only way to deliver a knockout punch to the domestic programs, while increasing military expenditures, was to hold taxes down and let the clamor to end the deficits force legislators to curtail domestic spending. So the real battle was over domestic programs, not taxes, the deficit, or even supply-side economics. Indeed, there are some political analysts who believe that the whole supply-side argument was only a cynical "Trojan Horse" whose sole purpose was to decimate federal assistance programs and repeal the New Deal.

In the end, no compromise of these issues was attained. The Democrats held on to the social programs, the Republicans held on to the military programs, and President Reagan made it clear that he would veto any tax increase. The deficit remained. Finally, in a desperate attempt to at least seem to be doing something about the problem, Congress passed the Gramm-Rudman Balanced Budget Act in late 1985, mandating gradual elimination of deficits over a five-year period. The political fight was pushed into the future. The Democrats hoped that military expenditures would be cut and taxes raised, the Republicans and the president hoped that domestic expenditures would be cut, and they all hoped that this procrustean bed would dismember someone else.

CROWDING OUT

Meanwhile, the argument over supply-side economics (never the real issue) was lost in the shuffle as the political wrangling over the impact of the deficit continued. The Democrats insisted that the increased federal borrowing due to the tax cut would crowd-out private borrowing (and hence capital expenditures). Ironically, Republicans had criticized President Carter's (shrinking) deficits in the late 1970s on precisely the same grounds. Yet you have seen that private borrowing exploded in those years. The inconsistencies in the political debate provide further evidence that the real issues were not (and are not) economic.

Indeed, any fear about "crowding out" was misplaced, for it was the actions of the Federal Reserve that largely determined whether private borrowing at reasonable rates was possible. Whenever the Fed pursues a tight money policy, private borrowers must compete with the government for funds; whenever the Fed pursues a sufficiently easy policy, there is room for both private and public borrowing. The point is that difficulty or ease of credit conditions is determined largely by the Fed and not by any crowding-out dynamic.

Keep in mind that the Fed's objective throughout the 80s was to restrain the expansion rather than stimulate it, so perhaps a little crowding out, if it helped prevent credit conditions from becoming too easy, was not so unhealthy. Tight money restricted consumer borrowing more than business borrowing, allocating funds (and resources) away from consumption expenditures toward investment expenditures in new plant and equipment. And as the economy and tax revenues grew in the late 80s, private borrowing held its own while federal borrowing shrank (see Chart 5-1 on page 54 and Chart 5-2 on page 55). Then the recession of 1990-91 and the full impact of the S & L crisis hit, multiplying the deficit but without crowding-out private borrowing.

Forget about Crowding Out

- The Fed's influence on interest rates is far more important than the federal government's borrowing.

In order to relate this discussion of fiscal policy to the business cycle, you need to know how *not* to relate it. Please realize that the huge federal deficits were responsible for neither the 1981-82 recession nor the subsequent recovery and expansion. The Federal Reserve's tight money policy generated the recession; the recession choked off inflation; and the stifling of inflation, along with the release of the Fed's grip, is what produced recovery and expansion in the mid and late 80s.

Thus, President Reagan's administration should be neither blamed for the recession nor lauded for the recovery and expansion or inflation's demise. Those phenomena were created by monetary policy, not fiscal policy.

BALANCING THE BUDGET

You can see from Chart 5-1 on page 54 that the federal deficit has grown enormously with each recession—for two chief reasons. First, recession reduced receipts because of lower personal income tax revenues, unemployment (the unemployed paid no income tax), and lower profits-tax revenues. Second, tax cuts accompanied the recessions of 1970, 1974-75, and 1981-82. In addition, note that federal expenditures continued to grow during each recession despite revenue's setback, generating the budget gap. Since the deficit grew with each successive recession, closing this deficit gap became more difficult and took longer every time.

In order to close the continuing deficit gap following the 1990-91 recession without a tax increase, receipts must grow more rapidly than expenditures. It took four years after the 1970 recession and five years after the 1974-75 recession to balance the federal budget. How long will it take this time? That's hard to say. The gap began to shrink in the late 80s until the S & L crisis and the 1990-91 recession hit, and it will shrink once again as long as a growing economy generates additional tax revenues. Another recession, however, will bring about renewed deficits by reducing tax revenues. If future deficits are to be avoided, a substantial budgetary surplus must be built to provide a cushion for the inevitable decline in revenue that accompanies recession.

In other words, it's not reasonable to assume that the massive budget deficits of the early 1990s can be eliminated and changed to surpluses before the next recession unless a tax increase is enacted. We waited ten years in vain for a growing economy to eliminate the deficit following the 1981-82 recession, and that gap was a mere $200 billion. How long will it take, starting from a $300 billion shortfall? It can't be done without a tax increase.

But wait a minute. Perhaps we should stop worrying about the deficit altogether since its impact on the business cycle and on crowding out is so negligible. Not quite. There are still two good reasons for concern. First, as the federal government's debt mounts, interest payments become an increasing share of federal expenditures. There are historical examples of nations borrowing to the point that debt service composed the majority of their budget, compelling increased borrowing to meet the interest payments on old debt and thereby severely restricting the nation's ability to cope with any social or military issue. Second, if the financial markets begin to question whether the federal government can meet its debts, it could become increasingly difficult for the government to obtain credit, subjecting its day-to-day operations to cash-flow irregularities.

Therefore, the soundness of both government finance and the economy would be strengthened by deficit reduction and a balanced budget. But, to repeat, that does not mean that continued federal deficits should be your primary concern with respect to inflation's outlook. Your attention should focus on the private sector and whether or not the Fed will continue to rein in private borrowing and spending.

CHAPTER 6

THE POSTWAR BUSINESS CYCLE: THE ROLE OF CONSUMER DEMAND

CONSUMER DEMAND AND INFLATION

Chapter 4 developed three concepts:

1. The Fed's policies aided and abetted inflation through the end of the 1970s and exacerbated the business cycle.
2. The Fed's 1981-82 tight money policy was the major turning point in our post-World War II economic history, ending inflation's upward spiral.
3. Fighting inflation continues to be the Fed's primary concern, and therefore interest rates will remain relatively high (when compared with the rate of inflation) despite weak economic conditions.

This chapter will build on these concepts by analyzing the role of the consumer in the post-World War II business cycle, showing how consumer demand led the business cycle by generating ever higher waves of inflation, until that inflation broke on the rocks of the Fed's 1981-82 tight money policy. It will also illustrate how the Fed's fine-tuning smoothed out consumer demand after the 1981-82 crackdown, thereby limiting inflation and postponing recession until the start of the Persian Gulf War.

To begin the analysis of inflation, start with a definition and consider that definition in its historical context. *Inflation* is an increase in prices due to excessive spending financed by borrowing from banks. "Too many dollars chasing too few goods" is a standard way of putting it. Economists are more formal: "Inflation occurs when demand exceeds supply at current prices, and prices are bid up."

Both explanations conjure up the image of a gigantic auction at which customers bid for both goods and services. The more money the customers have to spend, the higher prices go. Where do they get the money? From banks that create it.

Now look at inflation's record in Chart 6-1.

Although we wait and hope for it to subside, we tend to assume that inflation, like death and taxes, is inevitable. In fact, however, chronic inflation is a recent problem. Before the late 1940s, severe inflation was a temporary phenomenon, usually associated with war. When the federal

CHART 6-1
Wholesale Prices

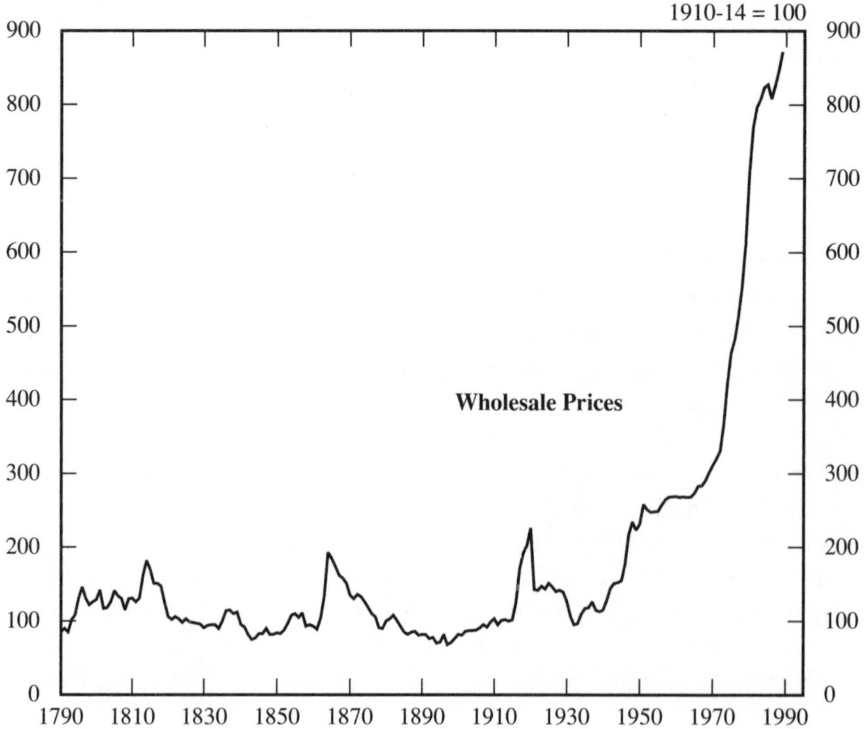

Source: U.S. Bureau of the Census, *Historical Statistics of the U.S.* (Washington, D.C., 1975), series E52 and 23; U.S. Department of commerce, *Business Cycle Indicators,* series 334.

government's wartime expenditures overshot tax revenues and the government covered the difference by selling bonds to the banking system or by printing paper money (which the federal government has not done recently), prices increased swiftly. That's how the conventional wisdom arose that government deficits cause inflation.

From 1789 until after World War II, except for war-related inflations, prices in America fell more often than they rose. As a matter of fact, prices were actually lower in 1914, on the eve of World War I, than they were in 1815, at the end of the Napoleonic Wars and the War of 1812!

Prices dropped during the 19th century because supply grew more rapidly than demand. Railroads and steamships opened new continents and made their agricultural products available throughout the world. Business mobilized the technological advances of the Industrial Revolution to produce standard items of consumption in large quantities at considerably lower cost. Occasionally, prices rose during the upswing of the business cycle, because investment expenditures were financed by bank borrowing or because there were temporary shortages of agricultural commodities. But these increases were more than offset in recession years when prices tumbled as huge additions to supply were brought to market.

The institutions that, in our day, enabled and encouraged headlong private borrowing and spending had not yet evolved. A hundred years ago it wasn't easy to obtain a home mortgage. Typically, the purchase of a new home required a 50-percent down payment with interest-only mortgage payments on a seven-year loan, followed by a balloon payment of the entire principal. If you go back far enough, most of the major consumer durables that we now buy on credit were available exclusively to a small portion of the population on a cash-only basis, if they existed at all.

It was not until after World War II that vast amounts of consumer borrowing came into common use, financing residential construction, autos, and other goods. At the same time, new institutions evolved to facilitate business borrowing.

Only the Civil War and World Wars I and II had provided great inflationary experiences; even the period between World War I and World War II was a time of deflation (falling prices). War brought inflation, and peace brought deflation, because government borrowed and spent more massively in wartime than business borrowed and spent in peacetime. The difference was more a matter of degree than a matter of kind; peacetime investment expenditures and borrowing by farmers, railroads, and manufacturers, though substantial, were usually not large enough to boost the growth in demand beyond the increase in supply. Thus prices fell in most years because supply exceeded demand at current prices.

To summarize, prices fell unless there was a rapid increase in demand (spending) financed by bank borrowing or the printing press (greenbacks during the Civil War). Only when outside financing provided a boost did demand take on a life of its own and grow more rapidly than supply. It made little difference whether it was government spending for war or business spending for investment, as long as banks printed bank notes or created demand deposits, or the government printed paper money. Once demand grew more rapidly than supply, and too many dollars chased too few goods, prices rose.

History does not note or dwell upon the pre-World War II examples of private borrowing and spending that generated inflation because there were so few of them; they were insignificant when compared to wartime episodes.

But what was responsible for the post-World War II inflationary experience? Why did prices rise so steadily? The answer lies in consumer spending. This period marked the first time that consumers borrowed continually and prodigiously to finance purchases of luxury goods. The level of activity grew decade after decade, and with each cycle, so that in the 1970s tidal waves of credit roared through the system, rapidly swelling demand to record levels.

It started in the 1920s, a kind of brief test run for the full-scale activity that followed World War II. Credit-backed demand included kitchen and laundry appliances, furniture and furnishings, and electronic equipment such as television sets, VCRs, stereos, and personal computers, as well as residential construction and automobiles. All were financed by credit, and the terms became more liberal over time, even as interest rates rose. The American consumer was encouraged—indeed, came to feel obligated—to mortgage the future so that present expenditures could exceed present income, with borrowing covering the difference.

The economy's health thus developed a dependence on the chronic fix of greater consumer expenditures, financed by borrowing. These circumstances were entirely different from the circumstances of the 19th century; during that era, consumers were largely confined to standard items of consumption purchased with current income (not debt), and economic growth was propelled by increased supply, which pushed prices downward. Now the situation became quite different. Full production and employment became the hostages of ever larger waves of consumer expenditure on discretionary purchases financed by borrowing.

CONSUMER DEMAND AND THE BUSINESS CYCLE

Unfortunately, these surges in consumer demand always led to their own demise, because expansion brought inflation, which depleted real incomes and generated the downturn of the cycle. Only then did inflation abate, real income recover, and expansion begin anew. Thus every boom inevitably went bust and each recession was also self-correcting and carried with it the seeds of economic recovery.

But why did the business cycle always rebound from recession, never falling into permanent depression, and why wasn't expansion continuous?

Well, to begin with, every expansion ended inevitably in recession because every expansion was fueled by credit. Consumers and businesses borrowed to buy new homes, cars, factories, and machinery. The more they borrowed and spent, the faster demand grew, pushing production into high gear in order to keep pace with demand. But sooner or later, the upward spiral of borrowing and spending came to an end. The strain on productive facilities forced costs higher, pushing prices up, too. Inflation depressed consumer sentiment and consumers responded by curtailing their expenditures. Consumers also found that their incomes could not support the burden of additional debt repayment. Businesses, having accomplished their targeted growth in plant and equipment, cut back or ceased their expenditures in this area. Once business and consumer borrowing and spending started to decline, the slump began and production and income fell. Inflation subsided with the drop in demand.

The recessions hit bottom just before consumers recovered their confidence, due to inflation's decline, and began spending again. Components of demand that were financed by credit stopped shrinking. Remember that these components were a limited, though highly volatile, share of total demand. (The demand for many items that were not financed by credit, such as food and medical care, hardly declined at all during recession.) As consumers and businesses ceased borrowing and turned their attention to liquidating their expansion-generated debts, the price of credit, namely interest rates, fell until finally the debt burden and interest rates were low enough that consumers and businesses could borrow and spend again. At this juncture, auto production, home construction, and business investment in new plant and equipment stopped falling, the slide ended, and economic recovery was in sight.

Generally speaking, expansion ceased when consumers were no longer willing to borrow and spend; contraction ended when their confidence returned. In the 1970s, these cyclical changes in consumer confidence were closely tied to the rate of inflation. Rapid economic expansion brought swiftly rising prices with an attendant and sobering drop in real income and consumer confidence. Recession cooled the pace of inflation, encouraging a resurgence of confidence.

In the 1980s, the Fed interrupted the normal course of the cycle by implementing its tight money policy of 1981-82, and then strongly influenced the cycle through its new posture toward inflation. The Fed squashed the cycle flat and squeezed high inflation out of the system, permitting the economy to expand gradually and steadily in the mid and late 80s.

Yet the Fed could not repeal the business cycle. When Iraq invaded Kuwait, and it appeared that we would be drawn into the conflict, consumer sentiment plunged and dragged the economy down with it.

Chapter 4, which examined the Federal Reserve System and the money and credit markets, described the 70s cycle, and the new climate of the 80s and 90s, in financial terms. Look at the cycle now from a different perspective, weaving in the elements of production, income, and consumer demand.

Consumers borrowed heavily in 1972 and 1973 to make record purchases of new homes and automobiles. Business responded by adding plant and equipment to meet the demand and by stockpiling inventory to satisfy customer orders. The sharp growth in consumer and business demand boosted prices rapidly, and the rate of inflation increased from 4 percent in 1972 to 12 percent in 1974. Interest rates moved in parallel fashion. Soon consumers became discouraged because their incomes failed to keep pace, so their expenditures on homes, autos, and other goods plunged.

This led to a general decline in production, and by early 1975 unemployment was at a postwar record high. The cycle was complete. The drop in demand reduced both inflation and interest rates, thereby restoring consumer confidence and spending. Recovery and expansion brought boom conditions. Rising inflation and interest rates returned in

1978, eroding consumer confidence once again. Consumer demand fell, and the 1980 recession began; another cycle had come full circle.

Recovery from the 1980 recession had barely begun when the Fed strangled the credit markets in 1981-82. The ensuing recession, designed to curb inflation, had the typical impact on consumer confidence (dramatic improvement due to reduced inflation), and as soon as the Fed relaxed its grip, consumer expenditures surged forward in 1983.

But why didn't the 80s repeat the experience of the 70s? Why didn't burgeoning consumer demand, backed by exploding credit, drive inflation upward once again? Because the Fed fine-tuned demand by maintaining interest rates at relatively high levels, high enough to sustain moderate expansion but not so high as to rekindle inflation. And even though Saddam Hussein had to spoil it all by invading Kuwait and plunging us into recession, the Fed will continue to maintain its vigilant stance against inflation despite 1990-91's temporary interest rate dip. Thus, you should now learn which signposts to observe in order to follow the dynamic of inflation and consumer demand.

So far, the business cycle has been painted with fairly broad strokes. The time has come to take up a finer brush so that essential details and connections can be clearly drawn. This chapter shows you how to use *The Wall Street Journal* to understand each step in the growth of consumer demand.

The first statistical series to be examined in this chapter is the *consumer price index* (CPI), whose fluctuations chart the course of inflation. Lower inflation leads to improved consumer sentiment and demand, which drives economic expansion forward. You can gauge the latter through data on auto sales, consumer credit, and housing starts, which will serve as the leading indicators of consumer demand.

CONSUMER PRICE INDEX (CPI)

The Bureau of Labor Statistics' CPI release usually appears mid-month in *The Wall Street Journal*. In the Thursday, May 14, 1992 article, the headline and first paragraph inform you of the CPI's monthly increase. Multiply by 12 to approximate the annual rate. (See pages 76 and 77.)

The CPI compares relative price changes over time. An index must be constructed because consumers purchase such a wide variety of goods and services that no single item could accurately reflect the situation. (See Chart 6-2 on page 78.)

Consumer Prices Rose a Modest 0.2% in April

Data Ease Inflation Fears; Broad Retail Sales Gain Was 0.9% for the Month

By LUCINDA HARPER
Staff Reporter of THE WALL STREET JOURNAL

CPI

WASHINGTON—The prices Americans paid for goods and services rose a modest 0.2% in April, the Labor Department said, reversing a string of larger increases that brought worries of renewed inflation.

Prices were restrained mainly by declines in the cost of food and clothing and a slowdown in increases for housing, transportation and energy. Excluding the volatile food and energy sectors, the so-called core rate of inflation rose 0.3% in April following a 0.5% increase in March.

The slowing in consumer prices follows increases of 0.5% in March and 0.3% in February, raising concerns that increasing demand was causing a run-up in prices. But analysts say economic activity hasn't picked up enough to do that.

Demand Is Still Weak

"There is still not enough demand in the system to bring prices up swiftly," said David Ramsour, chief economist at the Bank of Hawaii in Honolulu.

The financial markets yesterday were rife with speculation that the Federal Reserve would cut interest rates following the inflation report. A move yesterday by the Fed to add reserves to the banking system led some to conclude that an easing was already under way. But Fed officials indicated the move was merely a technical one, and no policy change had occurred.

Consumer Prices

Year-to-year percent change

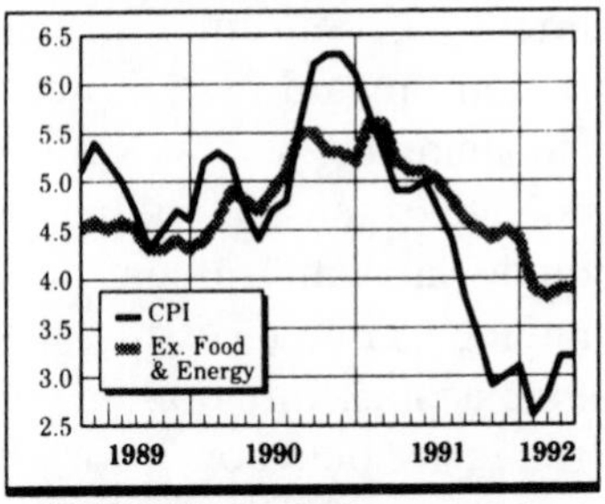

CONSUMER PRICES rose 3.2% in the 12 months ending in April 1992. Excluding the food and energy sectors, the increase was 3.9%. (See story on page A2.)

CONSUMER PRICES

Here are the seasonally adjusted changes in the components of the Labor Department's consumer price index for April.

	% change from March 1992	% change from April 1991
All items	0.2	3.2
Minus food & energy	0.3	3.9
Food and beverage	0.0	1.2
Housing	0.1	3.0
Apparel	−0.7	2.5
Transportation	0.5	2.5
Medical care	0.5	7.9
Entertainment	0.6	3.1
Other	0.7	6.8

April consumer price indexes (1982-1984 equals 100), unadjusted for seasonal variation, together with the percentage increases from April 1991 were:

All urban consumers	139.5	3.2%
Urban wage earners & clerical	137.3	3.0
Chicago	139.8	2.7
Detroit	135.3	2.7
Los Angeles	145.8	3.6
New York	149.2	3.8
Philadelphia	145.4	3.3
San Francisco	141.6	4.3
Dallas-Fort Worth	132.5	2.3
Houston	128.7	4.2
Pittsburgh	135.1	2.7

Source: *The Wall Street Journal,* May 14, 1992

CPI–First Paragraph

By LUCINDA HARPER
Staff Reporter of THE WALL STREET JOURNAL

WASHINGTON—The prices Americans paid for goods and services rose a modest 0.2% in April, the Labor Department said, reversing a string of larger increases that brought worries of renewed inflation.

Source: *The Wall Street Journal,* May 14, 1992

After a base period (1982-84) is selected and assigned an index number of 100.0, prices for other periods are then reported as percentage changes from this base. For instance, if prices rose 5 percent, the index would be 105.0. If prices fell by 10 percent, the index would be 90.0.

The Bureau of Labor Statistics (BLS) calculates the CPI by compiling a list of the goods and services purchased by the typical consumer, including such items as food, clothing, shelter, public utilities, and medical care. These make up the "market basket." The base-period price of each item is recorded and assigned a weight according to its relative importance in the basket. Changes in the price of each item are noted, and the percentage change in the total price is reflected in the change of the index number.

The ways consumers spend are continuously shifting because tastes change, as do incomes and the relative prices of goods. New goods and services are frequently introduced. It would be impossible, however, to generate a consistent index of consumer prices if the components of the market basket were constantly changed; a balance must be struck between the need for consistency and the need for an accurate reflection of consumer buying patterns. Therefore, the BLS revises the contents of the market basket only occasionally, after conducting a survey of consumer expenditure patterns.

Contrary to the popular image, the CPI is not really a "cost-of-living" index. The BLS's market basket is fixed; the individual consumer's is not. Substitutions are made with changes in prices and with changes in income. Your cost of living can vary (or can be made to vary) independently of any change in the CPI.

CHART 6-2
Consumer Price Index (CPI) (1982-84 = 100); **Change in Index at Annual Rates** (smoothed)

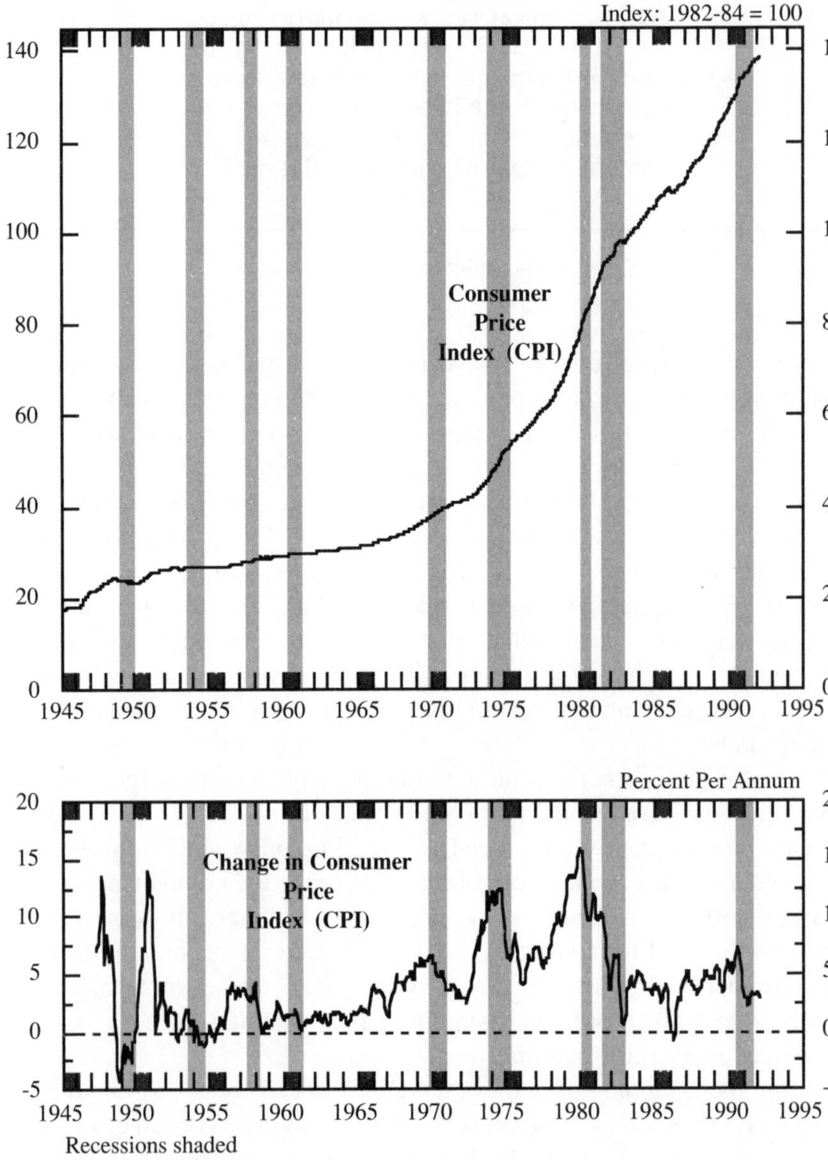

Source: U.S. Department of Commerce, *Business Cycle Indicators,* series 320 and 320c.

A final point should be made. In the early 80s, the BLS replaced the cost of home ownership with an imputation (or estimate) of the rental value of owner-occupied homes. The cost of home ownership, which includes mortgage interest rates and home purchase prices, had swiftly escalated in the late 1970s, so that this component of the CPI pulled the entire index upward. Many found this an unjustified upward bias. Accordingly, the BLS adjusted the shelter component to estimate the increase in rental value of an owner-occupied home, which more closely approximates its usage value than does actual appreciation in price. Ironically, interest rates and home prices fell soon afterward, so that the old index, had it remained in use, would have displayed a downward bias and risen less rapidly than the new index.

Make a mental note that the *Journal's* May 14, 1992 report updates Chart 6-2 on page 78 and confirms inflation's continued abatement since the late 70s peak; the CPI increased by about 5 percent annually in the mid and late 80s and then fell to half that level with the 1990-91 recession. As always, weak demand had done the trick.

Investor's Tip

- If the CPI increases by 8 percent or more (at an annual rate) for three months running, watch out!
- If that performance is repeated over the next three months, the Fed has failed.
- Bail out of paper investments like stocks and bonds; get into gold and other tangible assets.

CONSUMER SENTIMENT

The Fed's tight money policies and the ensuing recession forced the rate of inflation down to a moderate level in 1982, and the recession of 1990-91 reduced it even further. Let's now consider the impact of that on economic recovery in general and on the consumer's leading role in particular.

The Survey Research Center at the University of Michigan compiles the *Index of Consumer Expectations*. Consumers are asked a variety of

Economy Rose in Quarter, Led by Consumer Spending

Advance Estimates Put Gain At an Annual Rate of 2%; Confidence Index Jumps

By LUCINDA HARPER
Staff Reporter of THE WALL STREET JOURNAL

WASHINGTON – Economic activity picked up in the first quarter, rising at an annual rate of 2%, according to advance estimates from the Commerce Department.

The growth in gross domestic product, following a fourth quarter that was nearly stagnant, was driven mainly by consumers, who boosted their spending by a hefty 5.3% annual rate between January and March after nearly flat outlays in the quarter before.

Consumer Confidence

The renewed spirit of the consumer was also reflected in the Conference Board's measure of consumer confidence, which jumped eight points in April to 64.8 on a scale of 100 – its highest point in seven months. The index has gained 17 points in the past two months but, "while consumers are increasingly hopeful about the future, they remain uneasy with the present situation," said Fabian Linden, executive director of the Conference Board's Consumer Research Center.

Consumer Confidence

Index (1985=100)

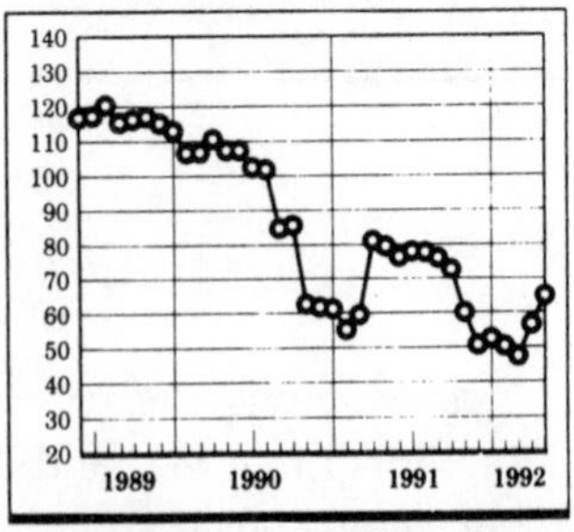

CONSUMER CONFIDENCE index rose to 64.8 in April from a revised 56.5 in March, the Conference Board reports. (See story on page A2.)

Source: *The Wall Street Journal,* April 29, 1992

Consumer Confidence–Third Paragraph

The renewed spirit of the consumer was also reflected in the Conference Board's measure of consumer confidence, which jumped eight points in April to 64.8 on a scale of 100 – its highest point in seven months. The index has gained 17 points in the past two months but, "while consumers are increasingly hopeful about the future, they remain uneasy with the present situation," said Fabian Linden, executive director of the Conference Board's Consumer Research Center.

Source: *The Wall Street Journal,* April 29, 1992

questions regarding their personal financial circumstances and their outlook for the future. Responses are tabulated according to whether conditions are perceived as better or worse than a year earlier, and an index is constructed comparing the outcome to that for a base year (1966). *The Wall Street Journal* occasionally reports this index, but more often publishes the Conference Board's index of consumer confidence. (See the Wednesday, April 29, 1992 article on page 80.) A glance at Chart 6-3 on page 82 shows you that the Michigan and Conference Board indexes have similar records, although the Conference Board index is more volatile.

Compare the CPI with the Michigan index (see Chart 6-4 on page 82), and you will find that inflation and consumer sentiment moved in opposite directions during the 1970s as consumers responded to the rate of inflation.

Begin by comparing the 1955-65 period with 1965-80. The principal difference between these periods is the moderate rate of inflation in the first decade and the cyclical increase of inflation after that. With each boom (1969, 1974, 1979), the rate of inflation hit a new high and consumer sentiment reached a new low. Although the mid-70s recession was worse than the 1970 recession, the rate of inflation did not drop to as low a number. No wonder consumer sentiment deteriorated for 15 years: inflation and the attendant swings of the business cycle were becoming more severe. Once inflation's grip was broken in the early 80s, however, consumers began feeling positively upbeat again for the first time in 20

CHART 6-3
Consumer Expectations: Michigan and Conference Board Surveys

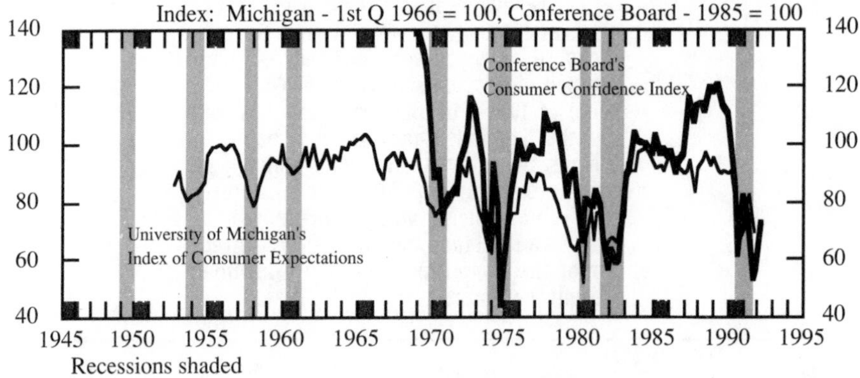

Source: U.S. Department of Commerce, *Business Cycle Indicators,* Series 83; The Conference Board.

CHART 6-4
Index of Consumer Expectations and Change in CPI at Annual Rate

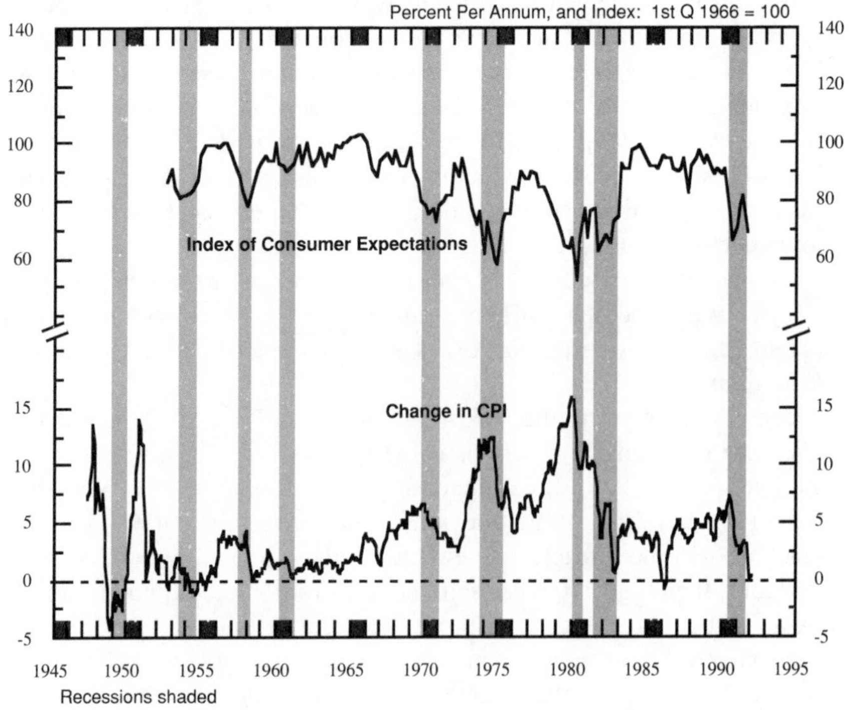

Source: U.S. Department of Commerce, *Business Cycle Indicators,* Series 83 and 320c.

years. The key had been the interruption of the inflationary boom/bust cycle.

Note the dramatic improvement in consumer sentiment after 1980 as inflation slackened due to the recession forced on the economy by the Fed's 1981-82 tight money policy. Then, when the Fed relaxed its grip and the economy began to recover, consumer sentiment exploded in the most dramatic gain since the construction of the index. Consumer sentiment remained robust for the rest of the 1980s, a dramatic testimony to consumers' relief that ever-increasing inflation was behind them.

But consumers are influenced by more than inflation. Employment opportunities, interest rates, and current events (like the Persian Gulf war) all play a role. Consumer psychology is complicated. Yet you can see the singular impact of inflation before the Fed came to grips with it in the early 1980s; inflation and consumer sentiment demonstrated a clear and predictable inverse relationship.

Iraq's invasion of Kuwait on August 2, 1990 broke that relationship and depressed consumer sentiment for two reasons. First, consumers expected that gasoline prices would rise quickly. Second, and even more important, no one knew whether we would be drawn into the conflict and what the consequences would be. How many lives would be lost? How long would the fighting last? As a result, consumer sentiment plunged dramatically and drastically without a severe and protracted surge of inflation.

Consumer sentiment remained in the doldrums until the fighting stopped, and then snapped back, only to fade as the recession lingered. For the first time in two decades, consumer sentiment seemed to follow the cycle rather than lead it.

Nonetheless, here's the nub of this discussion: *consumer sentiment drives consumer borrowing and spending*. Strong consumer sentiment propels consumer demand forward, while low consumer sentiment depresses consumer demand. That's why inflation traditionally brought on recession (it depressed consumer sentiment) and why low inflation generated recovery and expansion (it boosted consumer sentiment). Low inflation in the 1980s maintained consumer sentiment and postponed the cycle's peak and the next recession. Credit the Fed's fine-tuning for that. Events in the Persian Gulf depressed consumer sentiment and led to the 1990-91 recession. Credit Saddam Hussein for that.

Feelings Are Facts

- When consumer sentiment falters, watch out for recession.

CONSUMER DEMAND

The Wall Street Journal regularly publishes articles on three indicators of consumer demand that merit your close attention: auto sales, consumer credit, and housing starts. Let's examine each in turn.

Auto Sales

Around the 5th, 15th, and 25th of the month, *The Journal* reports automobile sales data compiled by the manufacturers. Look at the Wednesday, May 6, 1992 report on page 85.

The first paragraph includes truck and van sales while the third paragraph does not. But you need the *seasonally adjusted data at an annual rate* for cars only, as reported in the third paragraph, to make a comparison with the data included in the chart accompanying the article. Thus, the third paragraph and the accompanying chart report the April 21-30 rate of 6.0 million domestically-produced automobiles as slightly better than the pace over the previous 30 days, and much better than the same period a year ago. (See Chart 6-5 on page 86 for a historical comparison.)

The well-equipped auto has symbolized the American consumer economy since the 1920s. The automobile industry pioneered such now familiar techniques as planned obsolescence, mass production, and mass marketing and advertising campaigns in the 1920s and 30s. Henry Ford's Model T was the first mass-produced automobile. His assembly line production methods were state-of-the-art; his marketing concept, however, was vintage 19th century. He emphasized the cheapest possible serviceable car at the lowest price. Henry Ford reduced the price of a Model T to $300 in the early 1920s, and provided customers with any color they wanted, as long as it was black. Ford dominated the market until the late 1920s, when General Motors saw the profit potential in continually inflating the product by offering colors, options, and model changes and increased size, weight, and speed. This strategy enabled GM to take the sales lead from Ford; and, from then on, competition in autos meant more (and different) car for more money, not the same car for a

U.S. Car Sales Stayed Sluggish In Late April

Continued Surge in Demand For Light Trucks Spurs Hopes for Industry Rally

By GREGORY A. PATTERSON
Staff Reporter of THE WALL STREET JOURNAL

DETROIT – Sales of domestically built cars remained in low gear in late April, but a continuing surge in light-truck demand sustained flickering hopes for an industry rebound.

April's mixed sales results buoyed the outlook of some automotive analysts. But most said it's far too early to declare a recovery is at hand.

Auto Sales

Overall, domestically produced cars sold at a seasonally adjusted annual rate of six million vehicles. That's better than the 5.8 million-car pace in the prior 30 days and much better than the tepid 5.3 million rate of the year-earlier period.

For the entire month, sales of U.S.-made cars improved 7% from a year earlier, while sales of domestic trucks leaped 21.6%.

Industry analysts said truck sales have jumped with the arrival of new models to the market, such as **Chrysler** Corp's. Jeep

U.S. Auto Sales

Seasonally adjusted annual rate of domestic cars sold, in 10-day selling periods, in millions

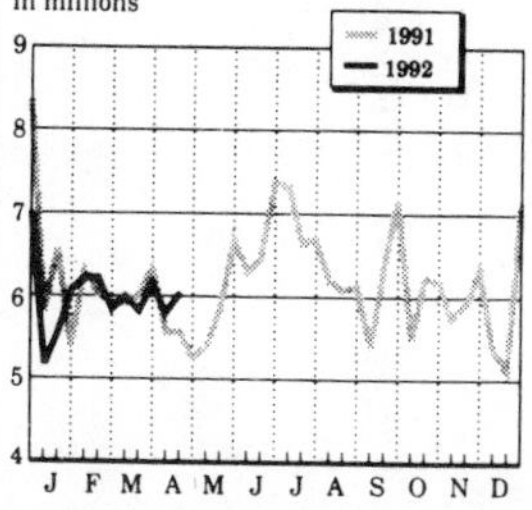

Source: Commerce Department

Grand Cherokee and restyled versions of Ford's full-sized F-Series pickup trucks. Chrysler said it exceeded early sales expectations for its newest Jeep by selling 4,877 of the vehicle in April.

Source: *The Wall Street Journal,* May 6, 1992

Seasonally Adjusted Annual Data–Third Paragraph

Overall, domestically produced cars sold at a seasonally adjusted annual rate of six million vehicles. That's better than the 5.8 million-car pace in the prior 30 days and much better than the tepid 5.3 million rate of the year-earlier period.

Source: *The Wall Street Journal,* May 6, 1992

CHART 6-5
New Auto Sales, Domestic Type (excluding imports)

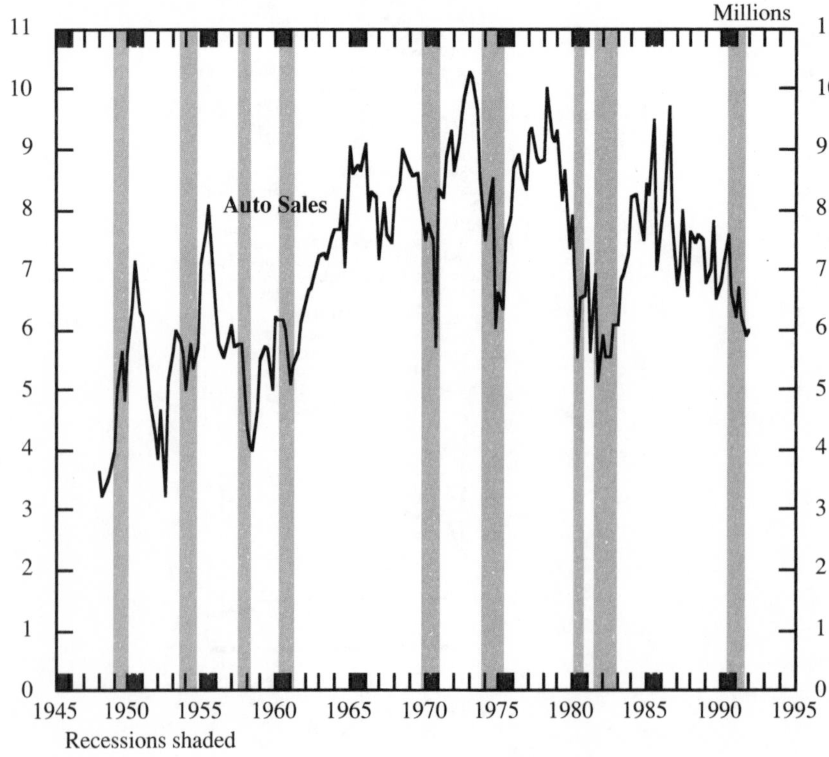

Source: U.S. Department of Commerce, *Survey of Current Business.*

lower price. The option of less car for less money was eliminated until the German and Japanese imports arrived.

Ford had grafted 20th-century technology onto 19th-century marketing techniques, driven the price down as far as it could go, and seen sales go flat in the mid-1920s as the market was saturated. GM pioneered the 20th-century marketing technique of product inflation on a mass scale and gambled that the consumer would borrow ever more in order to buy next year's model.

Product inflation boosts sales by cajoling the consumer into buying something new at a higher price. The customer isn't swindled, just convinced by marketing and advertising techniques that he or she needs an improved product for more money. Planned obsolescence is a corollary, because style and model changes, as well as product improvement, aid in persuading the consumer that the present (and still serviceable) model should be replaced with a better, more expensive model, not a lower cost repeat of the old model.

That set the pattern for American marketing of consumer goods. You can see it in your kitchen, laundry room, and living room, not just your driveway. TV replaced radio, color TV replaced black-and-white TV, and VCRs are now perceived as near-compulsory accessories. With each innovation, the price goes up and so does debt.

The 1970s and 80s, however, brought a rude shock to the domestic automobile manufacturers. The American public was no longer willing to buy whatever the manufacturers wished to sell. Consumers balked at continued product inflation, especially if it meant buying features, such as increased size and weight, that were no longer attractive. In addition, consumers were willing to accept less car for less money, especially if it meant a better made and more fuel efficient vehicle. So the domestic manufacturers lost market share to the imports, and are still struggling to stem the tide.

Yet domestic auto sales remained a leading indicator of economic activity because foreign makes manufactured here count as domestically produced models while domestic makes manufactured overseas do not. We measure activity that affects our own economy, not somebody else's. You can see that sales turned down as soon as escalating inflation eroded consumer sentiment (see Charts 6-4 and 6-5 on pages 82 and 86) and recovered quickly when inflation subsided and consumer sentiment improved. Domestic auto sales have led the cycle into both expansion and contraction.

This will help you understand domestic auto sales' role in the economy and why you should regularly track them. It's not just that the auto industry, along with the cluster of industries that depends upon it (e.g., rubber tire, steel, glass, upholstery, fuzzy dice), represents a significant share of total economic activity. It's also that the fortunes of the auto industry lead the cycle, foretelling recession and prosperity. What's good for GM may not necessarily be good for America, but GM's sales are a reliable leading indicator of overall economic activity.

The Fed's high interest rate policies in the 80s helped restrain auto sales, keeping them in the 7 to 8 million annual range (see Chart 6-5) and thus holding down costs and inflation. Will auto sales break out of their early 1990s slump and soon reach the l0-million-a-year sales volume they occasionally enjoyed in the 70s? Not unless the Fed dramatically reverses course and deliberately depresses interest rates.

Investor's Tip

- Auto sales above 8 million threaten inflation; 10 million assure inflation.

Consumer Credit

The Wall Street Journal publishes the Commerce Department's release on *consumer installment debt* in the second week of the month. Changes in consumer credit have been an important barometer of consumer activity because they have borrowed heavily to finance purchases of autos and other expensive and postponable items. But the Friday, May 8, 1992 article reproduced on page 90 informs you that the 1990-91 recession brought an end to consumer installment borrowing.

Did this mark the trend's reversal? Chart 6-6 on page 91 illustrates the dramatic turnaround. Consumer credit rose gradually and cyclically until the 1970s. Then it exploded. You can see the cyclical maximum of $10 billion in the late 60s, $20 billion in the early 70s, $50 billion in the late 70s, and $80 billion by the mid 1980s. No wonder the Fed maintained its guard throughout the 80s; indeed, it's amazing that inflation was not more severe in the face of this stimulus to demand.

Investor's Tip

- Consumer credit growth of $80 billion threatens inflation; $100 billion assures inflation.
- There's no threat of inflation when consumer credit fails to grow.

Both consumer sentiment and consumer credit fell steeply in the 1990-91 recession, and you can see their historical relationship when you compare Chart 6-6 on page 91 with Chart 6-4 on page 82. Increases in consumer credit trailed off with the surge of inflation and the drop in consumer sentiment in the late 60s, 1973-74, and 1979. Then, with each recession and the return of consumer confidence, consumer credit rebounded.

In 1991 consumers actually reduced their installment debt for the first time since World War II. It may be quite a while before consumer credit returns to the heydays of yesteryear. Since these figures do not include home equity loans, by the early 90s it was not yet clear whether consumers had switched to alternative sources of funds or fundamentally changed the way they financed their expenditures on durable goods. Or, worse yet for the health of aggregate demand, although better for the inflation outlook, had consumers decided to curtail their expenditures on big-ticket items?

Housing Starts

The Commerce Department's monthly release on *housing starts* is usually published in *The Wall Street Journal* between the 17th and the 20th of the month. Always direct your attention to the seasonally adjusted monthly figure, presented at an annual rate. The fourth paragraph and the chart accompanying the Wednesday, May 20, 1992 story on page 93 tell you that there were 1.1 million home and apartment unit construction starts in April of 1992.

Consumer Borrowing Declined in March, Auto Loans Shrank

By a WALL STREET JOURNAL *Staff Reporter*

WASHINGTON – Consumer borrowing dropped again in March, as auto loans fell for the 14th time in 15 months, the Federal Reserve Board said.

Consumer Credit

The Fed said consumer-installment credit outstanding fell $1.61 billion in March to $727.40 billion, after declining a revised $500 million in February. The March decrease was at a 2.7% annual rate.

The biggest decline came in a catchall category that includes loans for education, boats, vacations, recreational vehicles, motorcycles, tax payments and home improvements as well as loans that aren't backed by anything more than a person's signature. That category tumbled $1.45 billion, or at an 8.4% annual rate, after dropping $721 million the month before.

Outstanding automobile credit shrank $263 million in March, or at a 1.2% annual rate, after falling $489 million in February.

Revolving credit, which includes bank cards and store cards, was fairly flat, rising $55 million in March after a $1.14 billion climb the month before.

Meanwhile, mobile home credit bounced back after steep declines in January and February, at a 3.5% annual rate by $53 million.

The figures were adjusted for seasonal fluctuations and don't include home-equity lines.

CONSUMER CREDIT

Here are the seasonally adjusted totals of consumer installment credit outstanding for March:

Total	**$727.40**	**-2.7%**
Automobile	267.50	-1.2
Revolving	236.01	0.3
Mobile home	18.31	3.5
Other	205.58	-8.4

Source: *The Wall Street Journal,* May 8, 1992

Consumer Credit–Second Paragraph

The Fed said consumer-installment credit outstanding fell $1.61 billion in March to $727.40 billion, after declining a revised $500 million in February. The March decrease was at a 2.7% annual rate.

Source: *The Wall Street Journal,* May 8, 1992

CHART 6-6
Change in Consumer Installment Credit

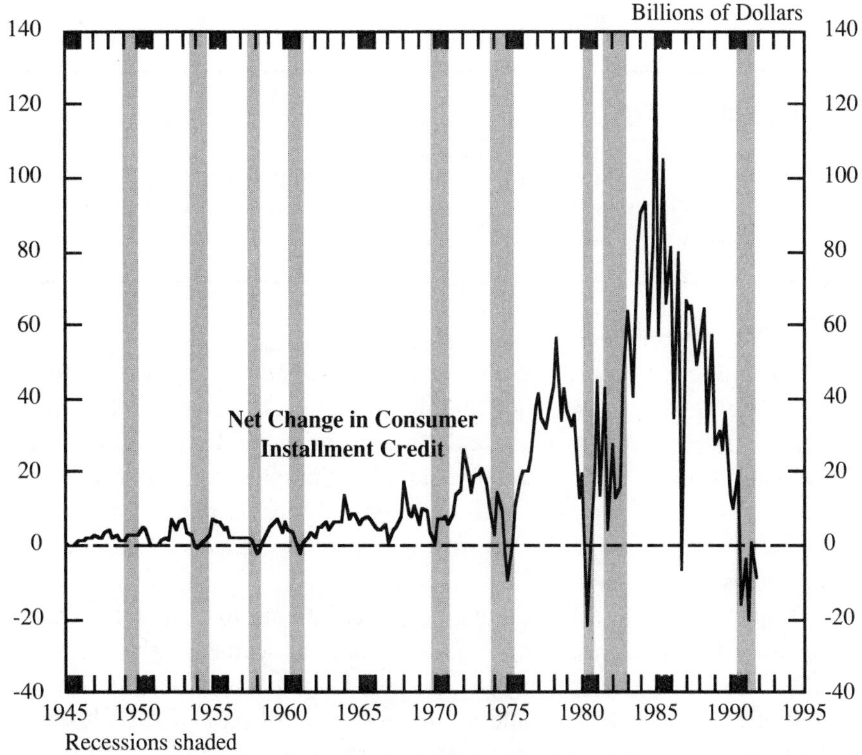

Source: U.S. Department of Commerce, *Business Cycle Indicators,* series 113.

The cyclical sensitivity of housing starts to consumer sentiment and the availability of mortgage credit is striking. (See Chart 6-7 on page 94.) Housing starts turned down well before the onset of recession, as soon as rising inflation reduced consumer confidence and the Fed slammed on the brakes, drying up mortgage credit. But you can see that they turned back up even before the recession ended as consumer confidence returned with the decline of inflation and the Fed's switch to an easy money policy.

You have already reviewed the dramatic impact of the Fed's 1981-82 tight money policy on residential construction. The Fed's policy put a new home beyond the reach of most consumers, and mortgage borrowing and housing starts plunged. Although housing starts and mortgage borrowing recovered in the mid-1980s, housing starts did not surpass the record levels of the early 70s (2.5 million at an annual rate in 1972). That fit well with the Fed's plan of restraint.

Investor's Tip

- As housing starts approach 2 million, inflation looms.
- It will be a long time before housing starts recover their past glory and threaten inflation.

Although residential construction withered during the 1990-91 recession, there's no evidence that the Fed plans to depress interest rates to a level that would provide real stimulus to this industry. Land prices and interest costs have risen more rapidly than other consumer prices, so that a new home is now relatively more expensive than it was before 1980. That's enough to keep housing starts in check and prevent inflation's resurgence.

What was said earlier about industries related to auto sales can be repeated for residential construction. Lumber, cement, glass, roofing materials, heating, plumbing and electrical supplies, kitchen and laundry appliances, and furniture and furnishings are all part of the cluster of industries that fluctuate with housing starts. The Fed's policy of restraint holds all of these activities in check and thereby maintains moderate levels of inflation in those industries as well.

Housing Starts Dropped by 17% During April

All Regions Posted Declines; Plunge Follows Surges Three Months in a Row

By CHRYSTAL CARUTHERS
Staff Reporter of THE WALL STREET JOURNAL

WASHINGTON – Housing starts tumbled 17% in April, the Commerce Department said, with all areas of the country posting declines.

The plunge follows three months of impressive gains. As a result, despite the April decline, housing starts for the first four months of this year are a strong 14% above levels of a year earlier, when the industry was in the doldrums.

Norman Robertson, chief economist for Mellon Bank in Pittsburgh, said the numbers simply indicate continued slow growth. "The road to economic recovery will be slow and shaky," he said. "However, the magnitude of the drop exaggerates the degree of weakness in the housing market. We cannot view one month's figures as a signal that we're heading into a housing recession."

Setting Up House

A New Jersey judicial panel rules that lawyers are indispensable in housing transactions. Separately, Merrill Lynch Credit will provide 100% financing if a family member puts up enough collateral. Stories on pages B12 and C1.

Housing-starts figures often vary widely from month to month and are sometimes substantially revised. According to the latest report, construction was begun on privately owned housing last month at an annual rate of 1,115,000 units, down from the March rate of 1,344,000. Spurred by lower interest rates, housing starts grew 5.5% in January, 6.5% in February and 6.9% in March. The figures are adjusted for seasonal changes.

White House spokesman Marlin Fitzwater said that as a result of such strong and surprising gains, the switch to a "more sustainable" rate of expansion as the year progressed was expected.

Analysts said the real shock in the April figures was the low number of single-family starts. They tumbled 11% during the month to a 963,000 annual rate. That caused concern because single-family homes are a big part of the economy.

Another worrisome sign: There was a 3.3% decline in applications for building permits in April following a 4.5% drop in March. Building permits often are a measure of future activity.

David Seiders, chief economist for the National Association of Homebuilders, said he believes that the April figures are a sign suggesting the economy could peter out once again.

"Hopefully, these numbers will encourage the federal government to decrease interest rates," he said.

But so far there has been no sign that the Federal Reserve would ease interest rates further, though prices of U.S. government securities went higher yesterday on speculation that poor housing numbers would push the Fed to cut rates. The Fed's policy committee met yesterday to set interest-rate policy for the coming weeks.

Wayne Barnette, president of **Woodcrest Development** Co., a San Diego, Calif., developer, said slower loan approvals have been a problem. He acknowledged that traffic has slowed sharply from two years ago, but he added: "We're waiting for lenders to finish their analysis so we can go forward – we have the permit in place, land available, but the lender is causing the delay."

Housing Starts

Annual rate, in millions of dwelling units.

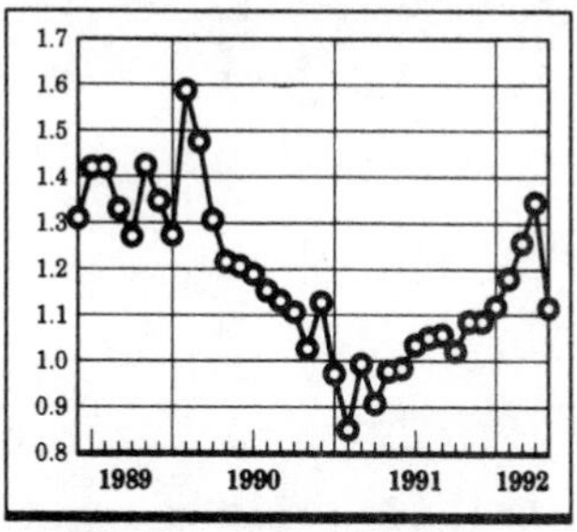

HOUSING STARTS in April fell to a seasonally adjusted rate of 1,115,000 units from a revised 1,344,000 units in March, the Commerce Department reports. (See story on page A2.)

Source: *The Wall Street Journal,* May 20, 1992

Housing Starts–Fourth Paragraph

Housing-starts figures often vary widely from month to month and are sometimes substantially revised. According to the latest report, construction was begun on privately owned housing last month at an annual rate of 1,115,000 units, down from the March rate of 1,344,000. Spurred by lower interest rates, housing starts grew 5.5% in January, 6.5% in February and 6.9% in March. The figures are adjusted for seasonal changes.

Source: *The Wall Street Journal,* May 20, 1992

CHART 6-7
Housing Starts

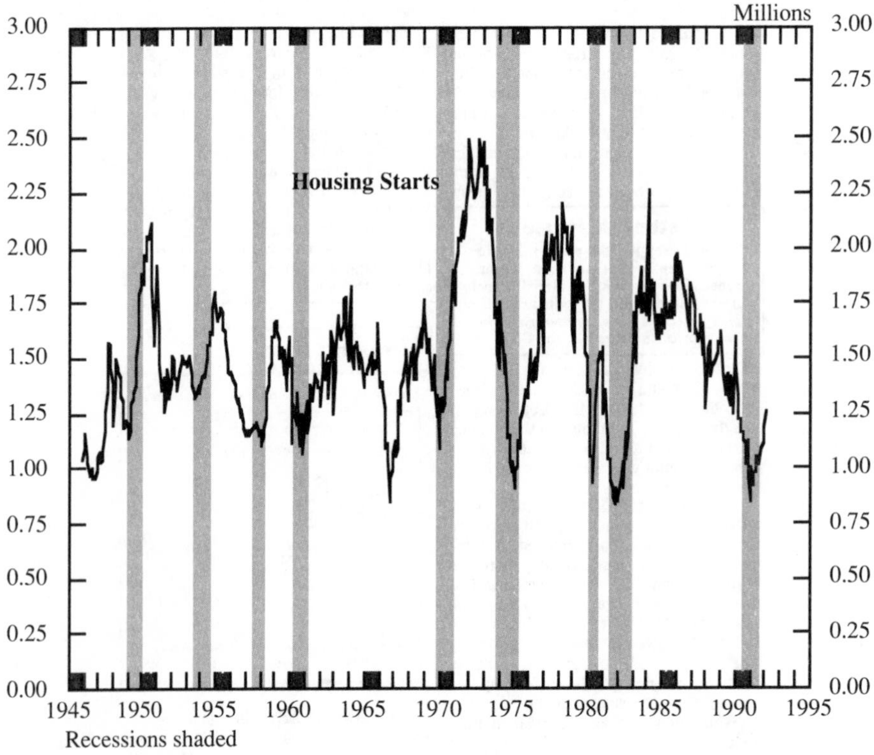

Source: U.S. Department of Commerce, *Business Cycle Indicators,* series 28.

SUMMING UP: THE CYCLE AND ITS CONSEQUENCES

So now you can see how much the modern American economy has come to depend on product inflation and ever larger volumes of debt. These sustain the growth in demand required to maintain production and income at adequate levels. Moreover, consumer debt and consumer demand have been the leading edge of the post-World War II business cycle. Paradoxically, their strong growth led to cyclical problems with inflation, which periodically tended to choke off credit, demand, and economic expansion, generating recession.

In summary, as the cycle moved from *peak to contraction,* rapidly rising inflation depressed consumer real income and consumer sentiment, bringing on a collapse in consumer demand and inevitable recession.

CPI ↑ → Consumer sentiment ↓ → Consumer demand ↓ (Auto sales ↓ + Consumer credit ↓ + Housing starts ↓).

Recession let the steam out of the economy and that cooled inflation. The temporary reduction in the rate of inflation permitted the business cycle to resume its course after each recession. Reduced inflation encouraged consumers to indulge in a new wave of borrowing and spending, moving the cycle from *recovery to expansion* and launching another round of inflation.

CPI ↓ → Consumer sentiment ↑ → Consumer demand ↑ (Auto sales ↑ + Consumer credit ↑ + Housing starts ↑).

There was no human villain in this drama. Blame the inanimate forces of credit and inflation, which periodically swept over the economy to leave recession's wreckage behind. The Fed finally came to grips with the problem in 1981 when, in its attempt to bring inflation under control, it tightened credit sufficiently to turn recovery into recession.

There are no villains, but there are victims. There is no doubt who bore the burden of recession: the unemployed. Their loss of income is not shared by the rest of us as the economy contracts. Moreover, unemployment hits hardest those industries that depend heavily on big-ticket consumer expenditures financed by borrowing. It is worst in construction, autos, and other durable goods industries and in the steel and nonferrous metal industries. Workers in communications, services, finance, and government are largely spared.

Through no fault of their own, therefore, workers (and their families) in a narrow band of industries must bear most of the cycle's burden. They are not responsible for the economy's fluctuations, but they are the chief victims in every downturn. Someone must build the homes and cars and mill the lumber and steel. Yet, as if caught in a perverse game of musical chairs, those who do are always left without a seat when the music stops.

WHAT NEXT?

Is the next recession inevitable? Yes, because all economic expansions end in recession. The 1990-91 recession departed from the cyclical pattern described above when the Persian Gulf crisis depressed consumer sentiment even though there was no surge of inflation. That recession created so much slack that it did not appear that the old cyclical pattern of inflation and recession would reappear. Severe inflation was no longer a concern.

But what have we learned from the past? A strong and rapid expansion, driven by large increases in consumer and business borrowing and ending in virulent inflation, will produce a sharp and severe recession. A mild and gradual expansion, lacking excessive borrowing and ending with only slight inflation, will produce a mild recession.

Data on auto sales, consumer credit, and housing starts in the late 80s provided evidence that the excesses of the 70s can be avoided if the Fed has the resolve to keep interest rates at restrictive levels. It is better to avoid the rapid growth of demand and the resurrection of inflation, the lethal twins that have killed all previous booms. If demand grows slowly because credit is restrained, expansion will last longer and not be set back so severely by the next recession.

Investor's Tip

- If housing starts exceed 1.8 million, consumer credit $80 billion, and auto sales 8 million, inflation is around the corner.

CHAPTER 7

THE POSTWAR BUSINESS CYCLE: THE ROLE OF COSTS AND INFLATION

INTRODUCTION

The Fed's tight money policy postponed recession in the 1980s by restraining aggregate demand and curbing inflation. But the Iraqi invasion of Kuwait on August 2, 1990 chilled consumer sentiment, and the economy faded into recession without inflation's preliminary phase.

This chapter will develop the relationship between production, costs, and prices, so that you will be able to understand the dynamic whereby rapid growth is transformed into severe inflation. By fathoming this dynamic you will see why there is little likelihood of inflation's resurgence in the 1990s.

You can find inflation's bellwether in the statistical series that chart output and efficiency. Gross national product, industrial production, and capacity utilization measure the economy's output; productivity measures its efficiency. As output increases, efficiency decreases, and inflation (as reported by the producer price index) inevitably becomes a problem.

At the peak of the cycle, when output is at its maximum, production facilities are strained to the point where production costs rise sharply. Overburdened equipment fails, accelerating the expense of maintenance and repair. The quantities of labor added to the production process are relatively greater than the increase in output. Inevitable inefficiencies force up costs and consequently prices, even though the product itself has not changed. As the obvious result, inflation increases rapidly.

With the recession's drop in production, the strain on facilities and labor eases. Costs fall, inflation declines, and the stage is set for a new round of expansion and growth.

The connections between output, efficiency, and inflation form this chapter's central theme. Turn now to an examination of the statistical releases that will be of particular importance in charting the course of production and the interaction of efficiency and inflation as the economy moves from trough to recovery.

GROSS DOMESTIC PRODUCT (GDP)

GDP is a good place to start. As the broadest available measure of economic activity, it provides the official scale with which fluctuations in the economy are measured.

The Wall Street Journal publishes data from the U.S. Department of Commerce's quarterly release on the GDP about three weeks after the close of each quarter. Then, around the 25th of the two subsequent months of the next quarter, it reports revisions of the data. The first quarter of 1992 figures appeared in the Wednesday, April 29, 1992 *Journal.*

Look for the following features: *constant-dollar (real) GDP, current dollar (nominal) GDP,* the *rate of inflation,* and the *statistical summary.*

Constant-Dollar (Real) GDP

The first paragraph and accompanying chart tell you, "Economic activity picked up in the first quarter, rising at an annual rate of 2%..." What does this mean?

Constant-dollar (real) GDP measures the final output of goods and services produced in the U.S. in one year, without including the impact of changed prices on the value of those goods. Thus, this year's output (as well as last year's output, next year's, or any year we wish to measure) is calculated in the prices of the base year (1987).

This kind of aggregate measure was once referred to as the Gross National Product (GNP) and there is a slight difference between the two. Put simply, GNP measures the output and earnings of Americans, no matter where they live and work, whereas GDP measures output and earnings in the U.S. regardless of the earner's nationality. Thus, for

Economy Rose in Quarter, Led by Consumer Spending

Advance Estimates Put Gain At an Annual Rate of 2%; Confidence Index Jumps

By LUCINDA HARPER
Staff Reporter of THE WALL STREET JOURNAL

GDP

WASHINGTON – Economic activity picked up in the first quarter, rising at an annual rate of 2%, according to advance estimates from the Commerce Department.

The growth in gross domestic product, following a fourth quarter that was nearly stagnant, was driven mainly by consumers, who boosted their spending by a hefty 5.3% annual rate between January and March after nearly flat outlays in the quarter before.

"An increasing number of positive factors appear in the current picture and on the horizon, so we are more confident now that the economic recovery will carry forward," said J. Antonio Villamil, the Commerce Department's chief economist. Aside from consumer spending, foreign trade, residential investment and increased government purchases also helped the economy grow.

Business inventories fell $26.1 billion, which detracted from first-quarter GDP–goods and service produced in the U.S. But economists said the drop was a positive sign for future growth, as demand picks up and businesses must increase production to restock their shelves.

Analysts cautioned, however, that the upsurge in consumer expenditures seen in the government's figures probably won't be sustained at its present pace.

"Large increases in government transfer payments and tax refunds along with mild winter weather gave spending a boost" in the first quarter, said Mellon Bank chief economist Norman Robertson. Rising transfer payments included Social Security and unemployment compensation.

However, the high unemployment rate – 7.3% of the work force in March – is likely to restrain future spending, Mr. Robertson said.

Indeed, while Michael Boskin, the chief economic adviser at the White House, said the Bush administration was encouraged by the "pattern of growth," it is looking for even stronger growth "so that we get enough new jobs so that unemployment comes down and comes down substantially."

President Bush said "there are some areas that are still hurting, but clearly, this is a good sign and there are a lot of other good signs and I think most people that I talk to . . . do feel that things are getting better."

Real GDP

Percentage change at annual rate.

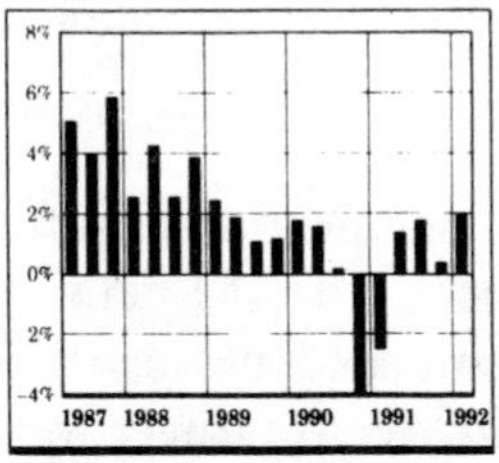

The GDP figures will be revised twice in the coming months, but analysts said the overall picture isn't likely to change.

In other economic news:

Inflation

–The fixed-weight price index for gross domestic purchases–everything bought in the U.S., including imports–rose at a moderate annual rate of 2.7% in the first quarter, compared with 2.2% in the last quarter of 1991, the Commerce Department said. Most of the step-up was due to a federal pay raise, which represents an increase in prices paid by the government for employee services.

–In another indication that inflation is under control, the Labor Department said workers' wages, salaries and benefits rose 0.9% in the first quarter–the same as in the final quarter of 1991. Benefits costs rose 1.3%, following a 1.2% increase in the fourth quarter, their slowest quarterly rise since 1987.

–And in a revision of a previous report, the Commerce Department said after-tax corporate profits sagged 4.6% to $306.8 billion last year, the third consecutive annual decline. For the fourth quarter, profits ran at an annual rate of $315.6 billion.

All figures have been adjusted for normal seasonal variations.

Statistical Summary

GROSS DOMESTIC PRODUCT

Here are some of the major components of the gross domestic product expressed in seasonally adjusted annual rates in billions of constant (1987) dollars:

	1st Qtr. 1992	4th Qtr. 1991
GDP	4,891.9	4,868.0
less: Inventory chng	–26.1	7.6
equals: final sales	4,918.0	4,860.3
Components of Final Sales		
Personal Consumption	3,313.8	3,271.1
Nonresidential Invest.	503.7	505.6
Residential Invest.	188.5	181.7
Net Exports	–17.8	–21.3
Gov't Purchases	929.8	923.3

Source: *The Wall Street Journal*, April 29 1992

GDP–First Paragraph

WASHINGTON – Economic activity picked up in the first quarter, rising at an annual rate of 2%, according to advance estimates from the Commerce Department.

Source: *The Wall Street Journal,* April 29, 1992

instance, GNP includes the profits of American corporations overseas and excludes the profits of foreign corporations in America, while GDP excludes the former and includes the latter.

GDP includes only final goods and services. This eliminates measuring the same thing more than once at various stages of its production. For instance, bread purchased by the consumer appears in GDP, but both the flour from which the bread is baked and the wheat from which the flour is milled are omitted because the value of the bread comprises the value of all its ingredients. Thus, the economy's output of *all* goods and services is far greater than its output of *final* (GDP) goods and services. We use very little steel, chemicals, or advertising agency services directly. Their value is subsumed in our purchases of well-promoted Chevrolets and Saran Wrap.

The first paragraph refers to a two percent increase in final output. This measurement was made at a *seasonally adjusted annual rate* in the fourth quarter. Adjusting for seasonal factors merely means correcting the distortion in the data arising from the measurement being taken during this rather than any other quarter. Obviously, no seasonal adjustment is required when a whole year's data is measured, but when the year is divided up and data extracted for a run of months, the risk of distortion attributable to the season is great. For instance, retail trade is particularly heavy around Christmas and particularly light immediately after the first of the year; you could not make a useful comparison of the first quarter's retail sales with the last quarter's without first making a seasonal adjustment.

The reference to "annual rate" shows that the data for the first quarter, which of course covers only three months' activity, has been multiplied by four to increase it to a level comparable to annual data.

The constant-dollar or real GDP calculation is made in order to compare the level of output in one time period with that in another without inflation's distorting impact. If the inflation factor were not removed, you would not know whether differences in dollar value were due to output changes or price changes. Real GDP gives you a dollar value that measures output changes only.

One last point should be made before moving on. The first paragraph said that economic activty picked up in the first quarter, but a glance at the accompanying chart shows that it remained anemic. You can also see the two consecutive quarterly declines in real GDP that traditionally define recession. The 1990-91 slump was the first in almost a decade.

But once the economy had begun to recover, what pace could be viewed as adequate? Three percent or better is good, and more than 5 percent is unusual and unsustainable for any length of time. The economy just can't supply (turn out) more than that without an increase in prices because of the limits on our productive capacity at any moment. On the other hand, three percent is well above the rate of population growth and therefore provides a substantial per capita gain.

Current-Dollar (Nominal) GDP

Nominal (current-dollar) GDP includes inflation and is therefore higher than real (constant-dollar) GDP, which does not. Most *Journal* GDP reports include a brief mention of nominal GDP, although this one does not.

Before adjustment for inflation (i.e., including current, inflated prices) GDP was slightly more than $5 trillion at the time, slightly more than the real figure (at 1987 prices) of $4.891 trillion, reported in the statistical summary at the end of the article. You can see how rising prices inflate the nominal value of GDP. Both measurements calibrate the same level of output, but the greatly increased value of the current-dollar GDP figure is a direct consequence of the higher level of prices prevailing now.

Rate of Inflation

The fourth paragraph from the end of the article reports that the *price index* "...rose at a moderate annual rate of 2.7% in the first quarter..." This index yields the broadest measure of inflation, since GDP is the most broadly based yardstick of economic activity. The more familiar consumer price index includes consumption expenditures only, while this index includes production for business and government use as well. The producer price index, which is explained later in this chapter, covers wholesale prices of goods but not services.

Inflation–Fourth Paragraph From End of Article

—The fixed-weight price index for gross domestic purchases—everything bought in the U.S., including imports—rose at a moderate annual rate of 2.7% in the first quarter, compared with 2.2% in the last quarter of 1991, the Commerce Department said. Most of the step-up was due to a federal pay raise, which represents an increase in prices paid by the government for employee services.

Source: *The Wall Street Journal*, April 29, 1992

Statistical Summary

The statistical summary at the end of the article provides a convenient breakdown of the major GDP components.

Now you are ready to put GDP's current performance in historical perspective. Compare it with Chart 7-1.

Statistical Summary–End of Article

GROSS DOMESTIC PRODUCT

Here are some of the major components of the gross domestic product expressed in seasonally adjusted annual rates in billions of constant (1987) dollars:

	1st Qtr. 1992	4th Qtr. 1991
GDP	4,891.9	4,868.0
less: Inventory chng	−26.1	7.6
equals: final sales	4,918.0	4,860.3
Components of Final Sales		
Personal Consumption	3,313.8	3,271.1
Nonresidential Invest.	503.7	505.6
Residential Invest.	188.5	181.7
Net Exports	−17.8	−21.3
Gov't Purchases	929.8	923.3

Source: *The Wall Street Journal*, April 29, 1992

CHART 7-1
Gross Domestic Product (GDP) in Constant (1987) Dollars; Quarterly Change in GDP at Annual Rates

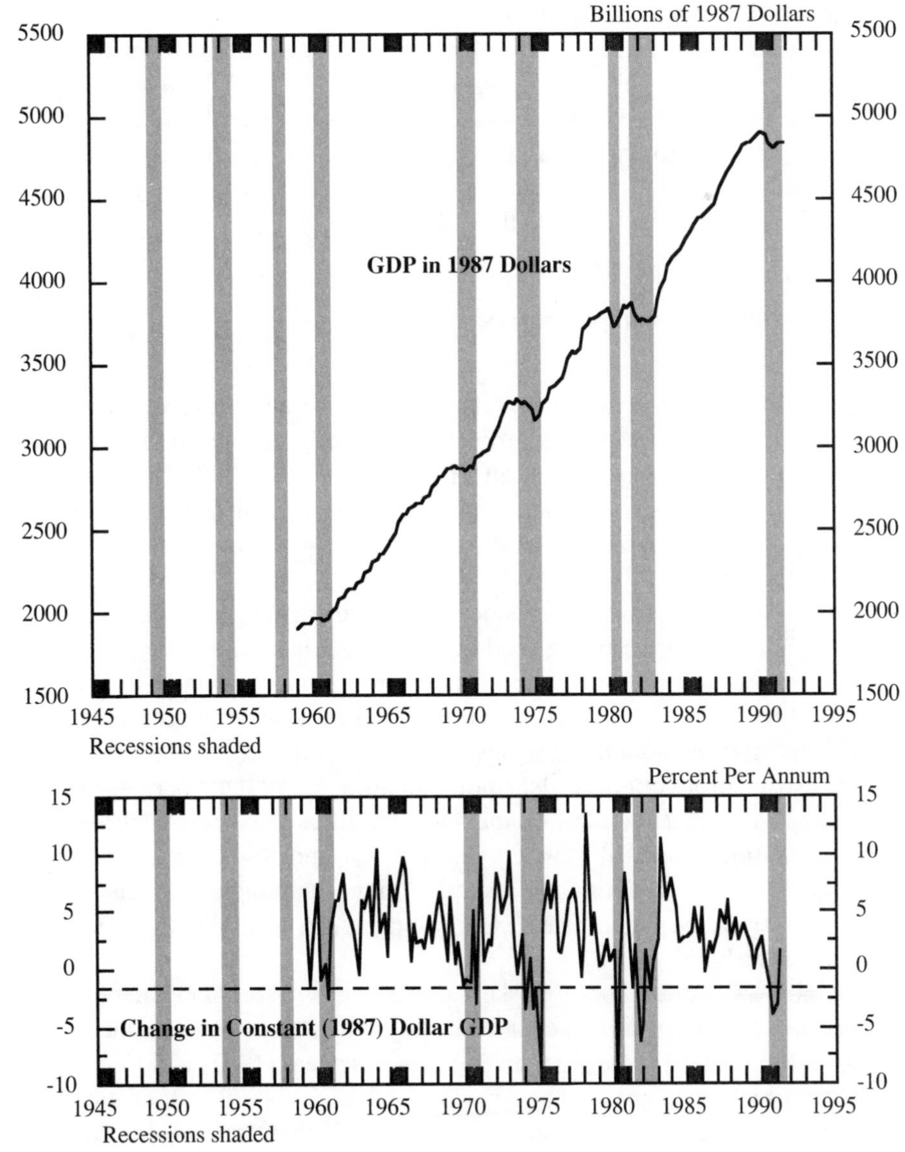

Source: U.S. Department of Commerce, *Business Cycle Indicators,* series 50 and 50c.

The top graph portrays the actual level of GDP, while the bottom graph depicts quarterly percentage changes at annual rates. When the bottom series is above the zero line, GDP has increased; a drop in GDP is indicated by points below the zero line.

As you look at these graphs, pay special attention to the setback to GDP growth during the recession of 1990-91. "Two consecutive quarters of declining GDP" is the traditional definition of recession.

Industrial production and capacity utilization will mirror GDP's performance and also provide important additional detail, so you should now become acquainted with these series.

INDUSTRIAL PRODUCTION

The Wall Street Journal reports data from the Federal Reserve's report on *industrial production* in an article that usually appears mid-month. A typical report was published on Monday, May 18, 1992. The headline, accompanying chart, second paragraph, and statistical table at the end of the story summarize matters, while the article provides detail and commentary.

The index of industrial production measures changes in the output of the mining, manufacturing, and gas and electric utilities sectors of our economy. Industrial production is a narrower concept than GDP because it omits agriculture, construction, wholesale and retail trade, transportation, communications, services, finance, and government. Industrial production is also more volatile than GDP, because GDP, unlike industrial production, includes activities that are largely spared cyclical fluctuation, such as services, finance, and government. The brunt of cyclical fluctuations falls on the mining, manufacturing, and public utilities sectors. Nonetheless, GDP and industrial production move in parallel fashion.

Industrial production is measured by an *index,* a technique that focuses on the relative size and fluctuation of physical output without concern for its dollar value. To construct the index, a base year (1987) was selected to serve as a benchmark and assigned a value of 100.0. (Think of it as 100 percent.) Data for all other months and years is then expressed in relative proportion (numerical ratio) to the data for the base year. For example, according to the statistical summary at the end of the article, industrial production had an index value of 108.2 percent in April of 1992. This

Manufacturing Output Grew By 0.5% in April

By LUCINDA HARPER
Staff Reporter of THE WALL STREET JOURNAL

Industrial Production

WASHINGTON – U.S. industrial production rose in April for the third consecutive month, suggesting the manufacturing sector is becoming more robust.

Output moved up 0.5% last month, according to the Federal Reserve Board. Illustrating further strength, the March gain was revised upward to 0.4% from the 0.2% originally reported.

The Fed said the increase in industrial production in the past three months "has retraced much of the decline between October and January," when the manufacturing sector faltered after an encouraging summer of improving health.

Industrial Production

In percent (1987=100), seasonally adjusted.

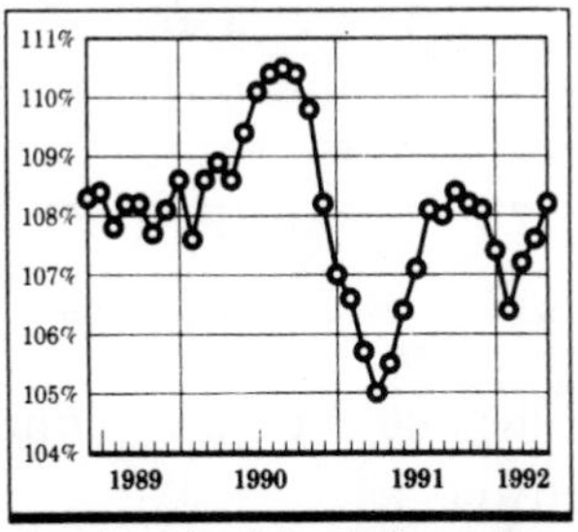

Most of the output gains in April came from a sharp rise in auto production. But even aside from motor vehicles and parts, overall production was up 0.3% in April and fairly broad-based.

Production of consumer goods and business equipment increased in April, as did that of furniture, paper products and coal.

The pick up in growth was especially encouraging because an earlier survey of purchasing managers indicated that manufacturing expanded in April at a slower pace than in March. Also, the most recent employment report showed only a small increase in manufacturing jobs last month.

In a companion report, the Fed said that factory operations ran at 77.7% of capacity in April, up from 77.5% the month before and continuing a string of small increases since the start of the year. Total industrial output was at 78.7% of capacity, up from 78.4% in March.

Capacity Utilization

The "underlying strength in industrial activity suggests that the recovery is sustainable, although the pace should be moderate," said Gordon Richards, economist for the National Association of Manufacturers here.

All figures have been adjusted for normal seasonal variations.

INDUSTRIAL PRODUCTION

Here is a summary of the Federal Reserve Board's report on industrial production in April. The figures are seasonally adjusted.

	% change from March 1992	% change from April 1991
Total	**0.5**	**2.5**
Consumer goods	0.4	4.2
Business equipment	0.8	1.2
Defense and space	−1.6	−7.0
Manufacturing only	**0.5**	**2.9**
Durable goods	0.8	1.9
Nondurable goods	0.3	4.2
Mining	**0.8**	**−2.4**
Utilities	**−0.2**	**2.6**

The industrial production index for April stood at 108.2% of the 1987 average.

Statistical Summary

Source: *The Wall Street Journal,* May 18, 1992

means that industrial production was 8.2 percent higher than the average rate of production in 1987.

As with GDP, two graphs are used to illustrate industrial production (see Chart 7-2 on page 107). The top graph displays actual index values, and the bottom graph illustrates monthly changes.

Statistical Summary–End of Article

INDUSTRIAL PRODUCTION

Here is a summary of the Federal Reserve Board's report on industrial production in April. The figures are seasonally adjusted.

	% change from March 1992	April 1991
Total	**0.5**	**2.5**
Consumer goods	0.4	4.2
Business equipment	0.8	1.2
Defense and space	−1.6	−7.0
Manufacturing only	**0.5**	**2.9**
Durable goods	0.8	1.9
Nondurable goods	0.3	4.2
Mining	**0.8**	**−2.4**
Utilities	**−0.2**	**2.6**

The industrial production index for April stood at 108.2% of the 1987 average.

Source: *The Wall Street Journal*, May 18, 1992

These developments are reflected in the rate of capacity utilization and in the efficiency with which the economy operates.

Industrial Production–Second Paragraph

Output moved up 0.5% last month, according to the Federal Reserve Board. Illustrating further strength, the March gain was revised upward to 0.4% from the 0.2% originally reported.

Source: *The Wall Street Journal*, May 18, 1992

CHART 7-2

Industrial Production Index (1987 = 100);
Quarterly Change in Index at Annual Rates

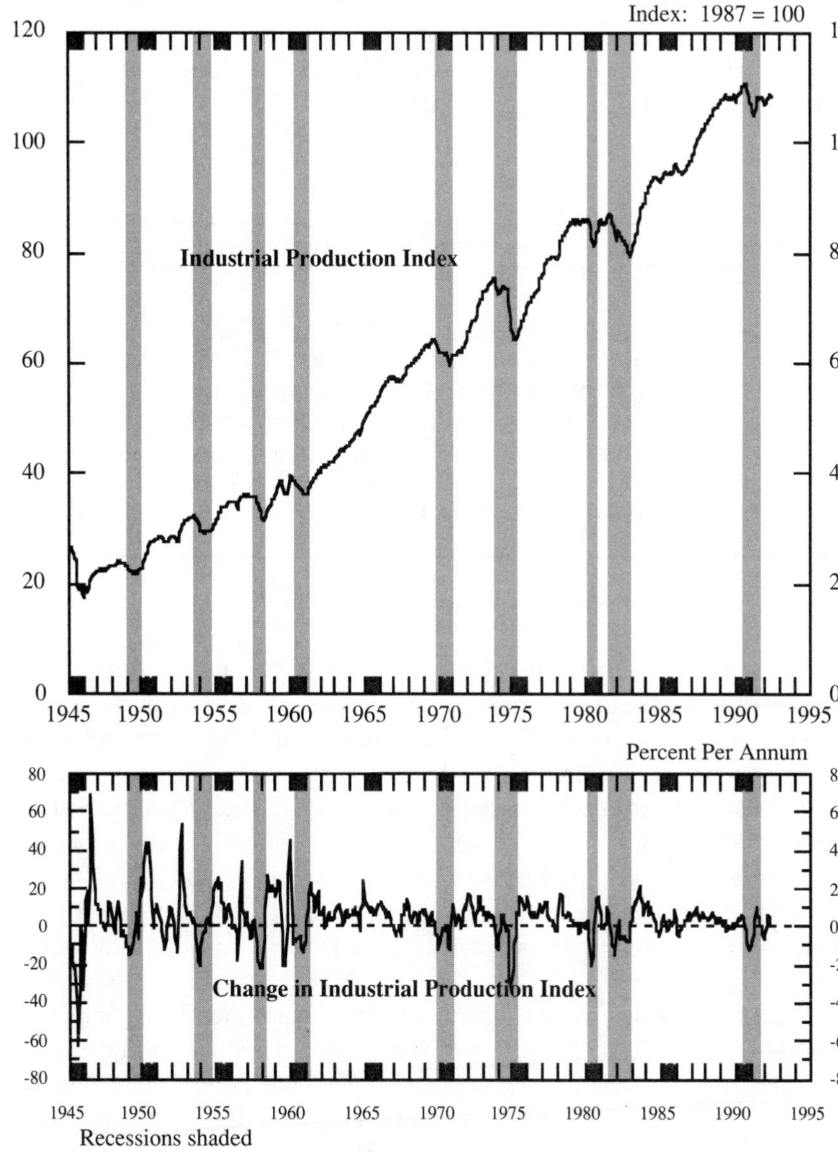

Source: U.S. Department of Commerce, *Business Cycle Indicators,* series 47 and 47c.

CAPACITY UTILIZATION

The Wall Street Journal publishes information from the Federal Reserve's monthly statistical release on *capacity utilization,* or, as it is often called, *the factory operating rate,* along with the industrial production figures. The third paragraph from the end of the May 18, 1992 article on page 105 informs you of April's 77.7 percent rate.

Capacity Utilization–Third Paragraph from the end of Article

In a companion report, the Fed said that factory operations ran at 77.7% of capacity in April, up from 77.5% the month before and continuing a string of small increases since the start of the year. Total industrial output was at 78.7% of capacity, up from 78.4% in March.

Source: *The Wall Street Journal,* May 18, 1992

Capacity utilization is the rate at which mining, manufacturing, and public utilities industries operate, expressed as a percentage of the maximum rate at which they could operate under existing conditions. Putting the matter differently, think of capacity utilization as measuring what these industries are currently producing compared (in percentage terms) to the most they could produce using all of their present resources. Thus, if an industry produces 80 tons of product in a year, while having plant and equipment at its disposal capable of producing 100 tons a year, that industry is operating at 80 percent of capacity; its capacity utilization is 80 percent.

Capacity utilization is a short-run concept determined by a company's current physical limits; at any moment in which capacity utilization is reported, it is assumed that the company's plant and equipment cannot be increased, although labor and other inputs can. This defines the short run. Although manufacturing industry continually adds new plant and equipment, it is useful to snap a photograph at a particular moment to enable measurement and comparison.

What bearing does capacity utilization have on the efficiency or productivity of industry? Consider a hypothetical analogy. Your car operates more efficiently at 50 miles per hour than at 70 miles per hour if its maximum speed is 80, for you will obtain better gas mileage at the lower speed. Efficiency is expressed as a relationship between inputs (gas gallons) and outputs (miles driven). Your car's engine operates more efficiently at lower speeds, or at lower levels of capacity utilization.

You are therefore confronted with the problem of diminishing returns: as your speed increases, you obtain fewer miles for each additional gallon of gas. At 50 miles per hour, you can go 30 miles on an additional gallon of gas; at 52 miles per hour, 29 miles on an additional gallon; at 54 miles per hour, 28 miles; and so on. Your output (miles) per unit of input (gallon) falls as you push toward full capacity utilization (maximum speed).

Likewise, as capacity utilization increases, an industry also passes the point of diminishing returns. This may be at 70 percent, 80 percent, or 90 percent of capacity utilization, depending on the industry, but the point will ultimately be reached where the percentage increases in output will become smaller than the percentage increases in input. For instance, a 15 percent increase in labor input, once we have passed the point of diminishing returns, may provide only a 10 percent increase in output. This phenomenon does not occur because of some mystical mathematical relationship nor because people are just like automobile engines. There are common-sense reasons for it, and you probably know many of them already.

First, at low levels of capacity utilization, there is ample time to inspect, maintain, and repair equipment; accidental damage can be held to a minimum; and production increases can be achieved easily in a smoothly efficient plant. Above a certain level of capacity utilization, however, management finds it more difficult to inspect, maintain, and repair equipment because of the plant's heavier operating schedule. Perhaps a second shift of workers has been added or additional overtime scheduled. There is less time for equipment maintenance, and accidental damage becomes inevitable. The labor force is in place and on the payroll, and production does increase, but not as rapidly as does labor input, because equipment frequently breaks down.

Second, as production increases and more labor is hired, the last people hired are less experienced and usually less efficient than the older workers; furthermore, crowding and fatigue can become a problem if more overtime is scheduled. Poor work quality and accidental damage result. All of this ensures that output will not increase as rapidly as labor input.

Third, low levels of capacity utilization occur at the trough of a recession. Business firms typically suffer a sharp drop in profit, if not actual losses, and under these circumstances, the employer reduces the work force as much as possible. In fact, he or she usually reduces it more than the drop in output, once the decision to cut back has been made. Why more than the drop in output? Because by the trough of recession, the seriousness of the situation is recognized, and industry has embarked on a thorough restructuring. The alarm has sounded and costs (work force) are slashed. That's why recession often generates the sharpest increases in efficiency.

Even after output has begun to recover, an extended period of labor reduction may continue as part of a general cost-cutting program. As recovery boosts capacity utilization, however, hiring additional workers becomes inevitable. When a factory reaches full capacity utilization near the peak of a boom, the cost-cutting program will be long forgotten as management scrambles for additional labor in order to meet the barrage of orders. At this point, additions to labor are greater than increments in output, even though (to repeat) output will be rising somewhat.

You can summarize business's decisions regarding labor as follows. During rapid expansion and into economic boom, when orders are heavy and capacity utilization is strained, business will sacrifice efficiency and short-run profits to maintain customer loyalty. Management adds labor more rapidly than output increases in order to get the job done. But when the recession hits in earnest, and it becomes apparent that orders will not recover for some time, management cuts labor costs to the bone with layoffs and a freeze on hiring. This is especially true during a prolonged recession, such as that of 1981-82, which followed on the heels of an earlier recession (in 1980) and an incomplete recovery. Even after recovery and expansion begin, however, business will still attempt to operate with a reduced labor force in order to reap the benefits of cost cutting in the form of higher profits. Operating efficiency (productivity) improves rapidly, and it will not be threatened until the expansion heats up and boom conditions develop.

Remember the motor in your car? Efficiency is expressed as the relationship between inputs (fuel) and outputs (distance traveled). It is useful to think of the economy as if it were a machine, like the engine.

Since your engine is fixed in size (at any moment in time), you can only push a finite amount of fuel through it. Depressing the accelerator rapidly increases your speed and the distance traveled, but the increment in fuel used is greater than the increment in speed and distance. Hence the efficiency of your engine falls despite your greater speed and distance. You are getting fewer miles per gallon and it's taking more fuel to go a mile because you are driving faster.

Just as a bigger engine would help you accelerate more quickly, more industrial capacity would permit the economy to operate more efficiently. But for the moment the economy is limited to the amount of capacity at hand, making it useful to speak about the rate of capacity utilization now. And it is important to realize that, like your car engine, the economy becomes less efficient if it is pushed too hard.

Now compare capacity utilization's historical record with that of GDP and industrial production, noting once again the figure reported in the May 18, 1992 *Journal* article (see Chart 7-3 on page 112). Each of the series examined thus far (GDP, industrial production, capacity utilization) tells the same story. The economy has moved well past the trough of the cycle in 1990-91, although the impact of the recession is clear in all three series.

The mid-80s capacity utilization plateau (hovering around 80 percent for almost five years) and the 1990-91 recession explain the low inflation rates we have had since 1982. The economy has not been pushed to a sufficiently high level of capacity utilization to produce the inefficiencies that generate rapidly rising costs and prices.

When you examine the 1970s, on the other hand, you can see that the rate of capacity utilization periodically rose to the 90 percent level, generating the inefficiency that brings on inflation. That's why the severe cyclical fluctuations of the 70s were bad for the economy and the slow, steady growth of the 80s was good.

Capacity Utilization and Inflation

- Robust consumer demand for housing and autos and other durables leads to surging capacity utilization and inflation.
- Capacity utilization over 85% generates inflation.

CHART 7-3
GDP, Industrial Production, and Capacity Utilization

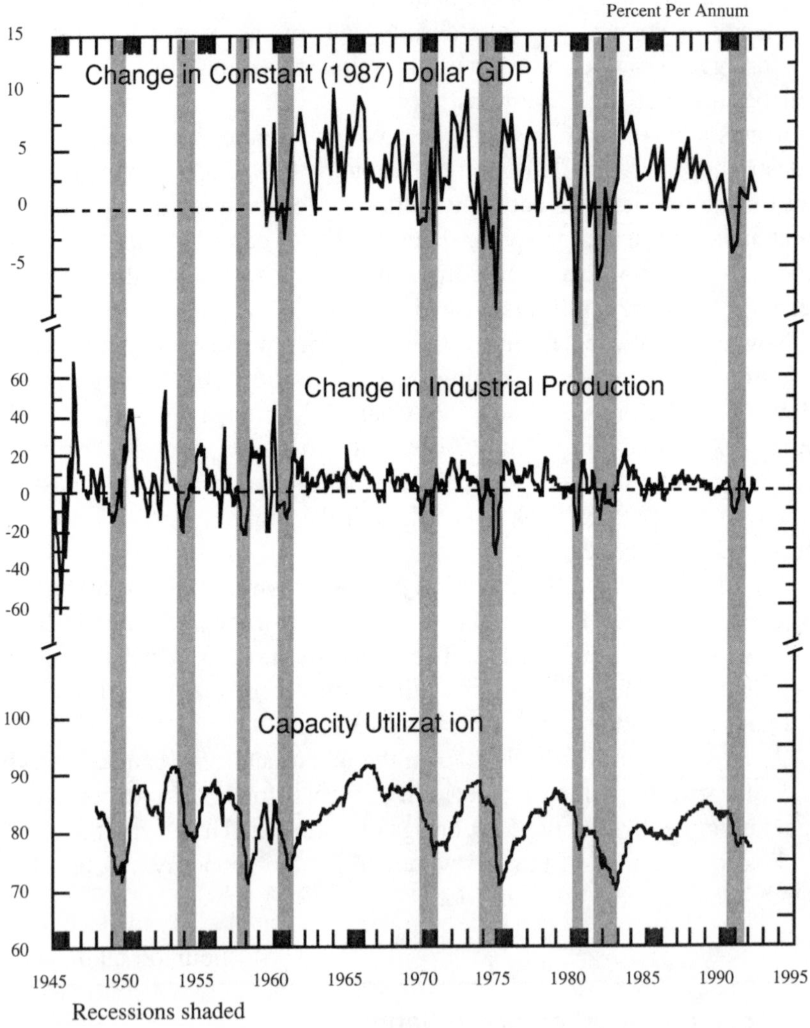

Source: U.S. Department of Commerce, *Business Cycle Indicators,* series 47c, 50c, and 82.

The next series in this chapter, labor productivity and unit labor costs, will provide the statistical measurements needed to calibrate these fluctuations in efficiency.

LABOR PRODUCTIVITY AND UNIT LABOR COSTS

The Wall Street Journal reports figures from the U.S. Department of Labor's preliminary release on *labor productivity* about a month after the end of the quarter, and publishes a revision about a month later. The Thursday, February 6, 1992 article presents 1991 data. (See page 114.)

The first and sixth paragraphs inform you that no change in fourth quarter output, combined with a 0.9 percent decrease in labor input, drove up output per worker by 1.1 percent for all *nonfarm business* in 1991's last quarter. It's simple subtraction: 0.0 minus -0.9 equals (roughly) 1.1.

Chart 7-4 on page 116 presents the record for all business (including farms). The series are similar.

Labor productivity measures output or production per unit of labor input (e.g., output per hour) and is *the most important gauge* of our nation's efficiency. Its significance cannot be overemphasized, for *per capita real income cannot improve*—and thus the country's standard of living cannot rise—*without an increase in per capita production.*

Unit labor cost measures the cost of labor per unit of output. Thus, unit labor cost is the *inverse* of labor productivity, since unit labor costs fall as labor productivity rises, and vice versa. Unit labor cost tells you how much added labor is required to produce an additional unit of output. Because labor is hired for a wage, requiring more labor time to produce each unit of output will raise labor costs per unit of output, and vice versa.

Consider, for instance, a factory that assembles hand-held calculators. If the production of a calculator has required an hour of labor and a technological innovation permits the production of two calculators per hour, labor productivity has doubled, from one to two calculators per hour. The output per hour of work is twice what it was.

If the wage rate is $10 per hour, and before the innovation an hour of work was required to produce a calculator, the labor cost per unit of output was then $10. After the innovation, however, two calculators can be produced in an hour, or one calculator in half an hour, so unit labor cost has fallen to $5. Note that as labor productivity doubled, from one to

Productivity Increased at Rate of 1.1% In Fourth Quarter and 0.2% in the Year

By RICK WARTZMAN
Staff Reporter of THE WALL STREET JOURNAL

Productivity

WASHINGTON – Non-farm business productivity rose at an annual rate of 1.1% in the fourth quarter, but edged up only 0.2% for all of 1991, the Labor Department said.

Although the numbers were anemic, economists said it was surprising that there was any increase at all given the sluggish state of the economy. By comparison, non-farm productivity in 1990 tumbled at a 0.3% rate in the fourth quarter and fell 0.1% for the full year.

"Just to be in the positive column is remarkable," said Adrian Dillon, chief economist at Eaton Corp., a Cleveland manufacturer of transportation and capital-equipment components. Productivity is defined as output per hour of work.

The biggest gains were lodged by the manufacturing sector, where productivity rose at a 1.5% annual rate in the fourth quarter and 1.4% for the year.

Economists said the overall increase by non-farm businesses reflected aggressive moves by both heavy industry and service-oriented concerns to cut employment levels. "What this suggests is that we're adapting very nimbly to changing economic circumstances," Mr. Dillon said.

Output and Employment

Indeed, while output was unchanged in the fourth quarter, employment fell 0.9% and the average work week was shortened 0.2%.

In the near term, "people pay a personal price" because of these adjustments, noted Robert Dederick, chief economist at Northern Trust Co. in Chicago. But over the long haul, he added, they are "beneficial" because companies will be more competitive when the economy picks up.

Reductions in hours worked also help keep inflation down, economists said. During the fourth quarter, in fact, the government's measure of changes in labor costs and other payments rose a scant 1%, the smallest jump since 1970.

Economists generally agree that advancements in productivity are crucial for a healthy economy. Just yesterday, the White House asserted in the president's annual economic report that "the major long-run challenge confronting the American economy is to increase the nation's rate of productivity growth." Without such improvement, the report warned, "America's standard of living will neither keep pace with the expectations of our citizens nor remain the highest in the world."

Productivity for all businesses, including agriculture, grew at a 1.6% annual rate in the fourth quarter and 0.2% for the year.

All of the quarterly figures are adjusted for seasonal changes. They are often revised later by the government.

Source: *The Wall Street Journal*, February 6, 1992

Labor Productivity–First Paragraph

Indeed, while output was unchanged in the fourth quarter, employment fell 0.9% and the average work week was shortened 0.2%.

Source: *The Wall Street Journal*, February 6, 1992

Output and Hours–Fifth Paragraph

WASHINGTON – Non-farm business productivity rose at an annual rate of 1.1% in the fourth quarter, but edged up only 0.2% for all of 1991, the Labor Department said.

Source: *The Wall Street Journal*, February 6, 1992

two calculators per hour, unit labor costs were halved, from $10 to $5 per unit of output. The gain in labor productivity drove down unit labor costs without any change in the wage rate.

Now compare the record of labor productivity and unit labor costs with the other indicators examined so far (see Chart 7-5 on page 117).

GDP, industrial production, and capacity utilization together define the business cycle in the 1970s. Since 1970 their fluctuations have indicated prosperity and recession. You can also see that labor product-

CHART 7-4

Productivity: Output per Hour, All Persons, Private Business Sector (1982 = 100); **Change in Output per Hour** (smoothed)

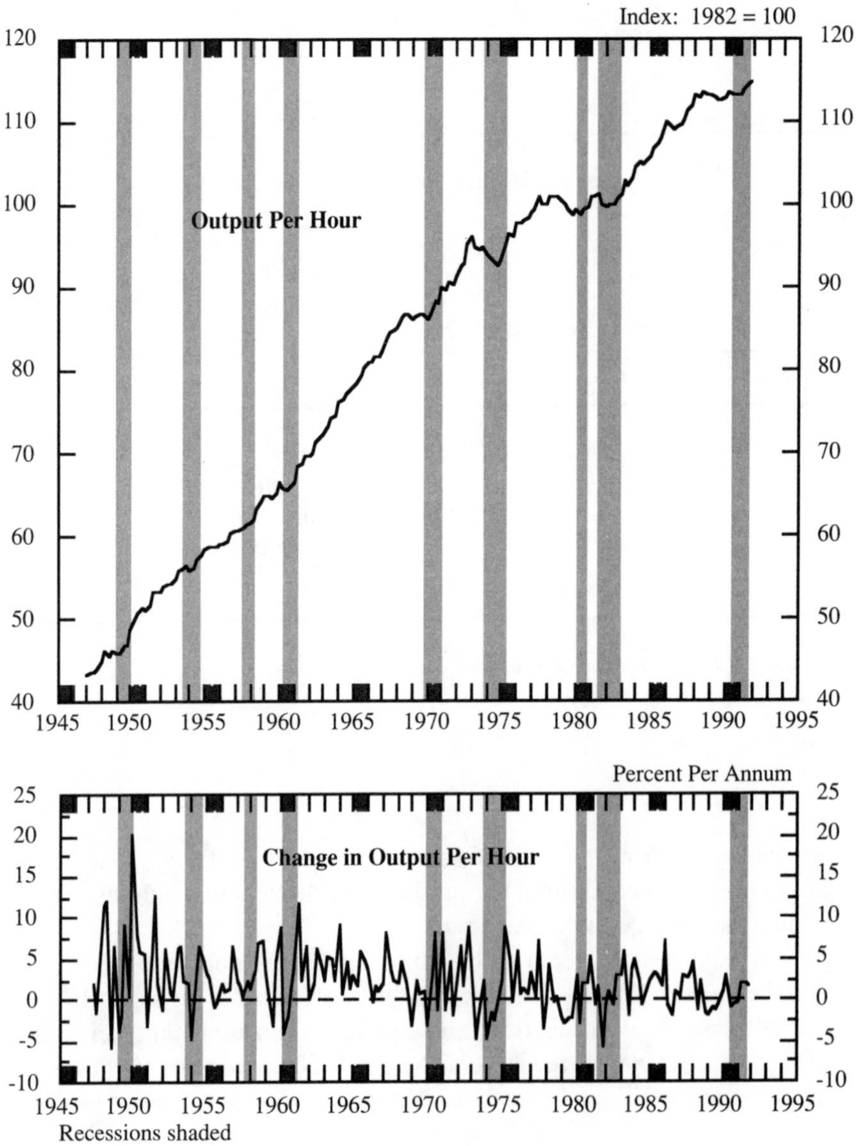

Source: U.S. Department of Commerce, *Business Cycle Indicators,* series 370 and 370c.

CHART 7-5

GDP, Industrial Production, Capacity Utilization, Labor Productivity, and Unit Labor Cost

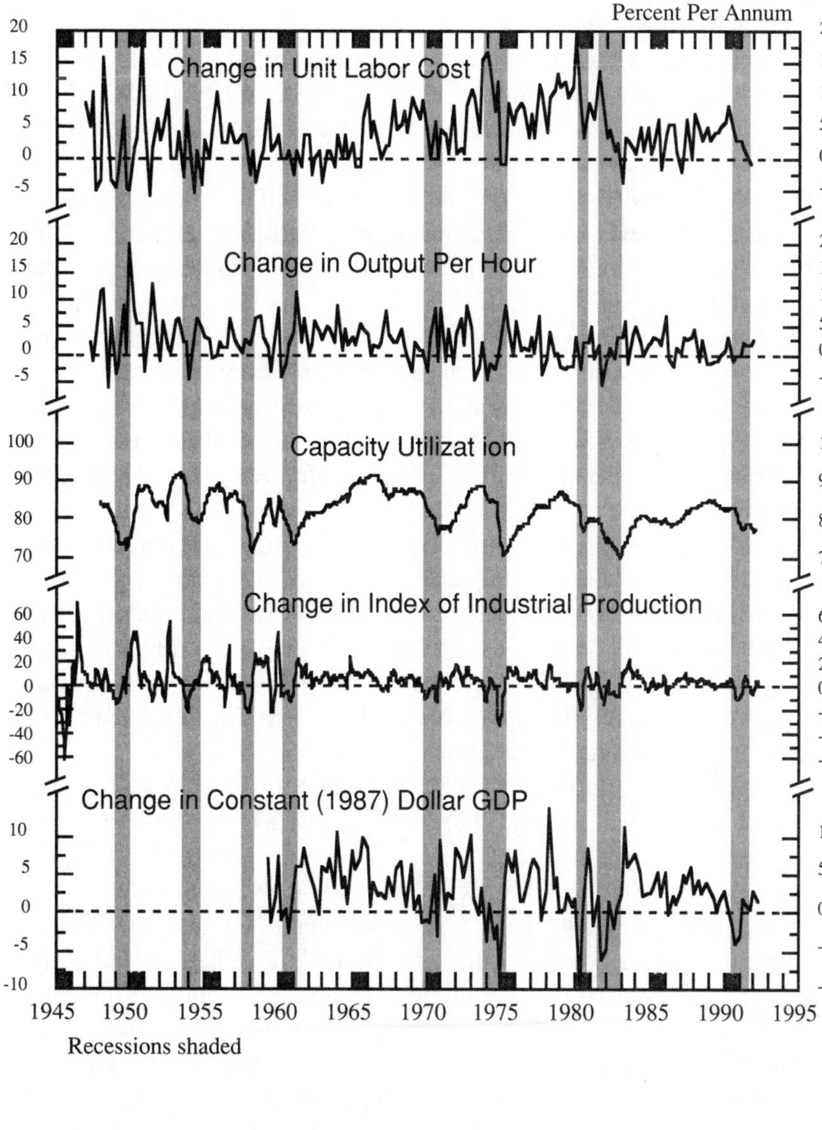

Source: U.S. Department of Commerce, *Business Cycle Indicators,* series 47c, 50c, 62, 82 and 370c

ivity plunged and unit labor costs soared with the peak of each cycle in the 1970s. Then labor productivity improved and unit labor costs declined with each recession and into the next recovery. But as soon as expansion got under way, labor productivity's growth began to weaken and unit labor costs began to rise, until productivity slumped and costs peaked at the end of the boom.

And this brings you full circle to the discussion of efficiency included in the earlier investigation of capacity utilization: the economy's efficiency deteriorated in the 70s with each boom and improved in each recession and into recovery. All that this section has done is to provide the labels and devices (labor productivity and unit labor costs) necessary to measure that efficiency. During boom conditions, efficiency (labor productivity) declines and expenses (unit labor costs) mount. During recession the opposite is true.

At first you might ask yourself, "Why would management ever place itself in the position of risking a drop in the efficiency of its operations in order to push output and capacity utilization too far? Why not limit production to an efficient level of operations, at say 80 percent capacity utilization, rather than risk declining productivity at 90 percent of capacity utilization?"

The answer is easy, if you put yourself in management's shoes. Suppose you're the boss at Bethlehem Steel, and Ford Motor Co. is your best customer. Suppose also that you're running two production shifts at your mill, sixteen hours a day, and a small maintenance crew is employed during the remaining eight-hour shift. The maintenance crew inspects, maintains, and repairs the equipment so that everything is up and running during the daily sixteen hours of production.

Now Ford calls and says their Taurus model has been a big success and they need more steel in a hurry. Do you tell Ford that you're sorry, that you're running flat out, that you have no idle capacity, and that they should come back during the next recession when you have plenty of idle capacity and would be happy to take their order? Only if you want to lose your best customer. No, you tell them you will move heaven and earth to fill their order, and you cancel the maintenance shift and put on another production shift.

Putting on another shift of workers increases the size of your production crew (and labor costs) by 50 percent (from sixteen to twenty-four hours a day). Yet your output increases by only 30 percent because of periodic breakdowns in equipment that cannot be properly maintained.

But if you only require a 30 percent increase in output in order to fill the order, you may very well be willing to put up with a 50 percent increase in labor hours and costs. Sure, output per worker (productivity) falls on this order and maybe you won't turn a profit either. That's okay as long as you keep your best customer. You're interested in maximizing your profit in the long run, not the short run.

As a result, you've met your deadline by pushing your mill's output to the maximum. Productivity has declined and costs have increased. But that's acceptable, especially if you can pass those higher costs on in the form of higher prices (the subject of the next section of this chapter).

The charts inform you that productivity growth was moderate during the 80s as output grew more rapidly than labor input. The economy was far better off than in the 70s, when periodic declines in productivity were associated with excessive rates of capacity utilization.

Notice as well that productivity improved nicely coming out of the 1990-91 recession. That illustrates, once again, that efficiency rebounds in the trough of the cycle and during recovery.

Productivity and the Cycle

- The economy is like your car's engine—far more efficient at a steady, moderate pace than in stop-and-go traffic.
- If you push the accelerator to the floor and rev the engine (high capacity utilization), efficiency (productivity) drops.

Perhaps by now you are wondering about the long-run influences on productivity. Our economy's efficiency depends on more than cyclical developments. What about industry's efforts to improve efficiency? Where do these fit in?

An economy's productivity improves when enterprise mobilizes improved technology and additional capital goods to raise output per worker and an increasing share of the economy's work shifts to those enterprises that have upgraded their technology and capital goods. These changes occur year-in and year-out, regardless of short-run developments and the cycle's phase. But pushing production to the limit can set these efforts back in the short run.

Turn now to the object of all the effort to contain costs: producer prices.

PRODUCER PRICES

The *producer price index,* until recently referred to as the wholesale price index, is compiled by the U.S. Department of Labor and shows the changes in prices charged by producers of finished goods—changes that are, of course, reflected in the prices consumers must pay. Data from the Labor Department's news release on producer prices is usually published by *The Wall Street Journal* in mid-month.

The Wednesday, May 13, 1992 article is an example, and the headline, accompanying chart and first paragraph tell you that the producer price index rose 0.2 percent in April of 1992.

Chart 7-6 (see page 122) confirms that in the early 90s, inflation as measured by the producer price index, was still well below the double-digit levels of the 1970s. The drop since the 1979-80 peak has been dramatic.

You can also see from Chart 7-7 on page 123 that in the 70s the cyclical trends in producer prices mirrored those of unit labor costs. With each boom in output and capacity utilization, productivity dropped and unit labor costs rose, driving producer prices up. Then, when recession hit and output and capacity utilization fell, improved labor productivity and lower unit labor costs were reflected in reduced inflation. The 1981-82 recession illustrates the principle: inflation's trend followed unit labor costs downward. As the economy's efficiency improved, stable prices followed on the heels of stable costs. Inflation remained low throughout the 1980s and early 90s because unit labor costs increased at a moderate pace.

"But isn't it true," you may ask "that moderate wage increases have restrained unit labor costs recently? Perhaps the emphasis on productivity is misplaced and we should instead focus attention on wages as the driving force propelling prices upward."

True, wage increases subsided in the low-inflation 80s and have remained low ever since, contributing to the meager growth in unit labor costs. But generally speaking, *wage rates follow the cycle, they do not lead it.* Wages lagged behind prices during inflation's surge in the late 70s and fell less rapidly than prices in the early 80s. If boom conditions

Producer Prices Rose Just 0.2% Last Month

ECONOMY

By Lucinda Harper
Staff Reporter of The Wall Street Journal

WASHINGTON – Producer prices rose a modest 0.2% in April, the Labor Department said, indicating that inflation still isn't much of a problem despite the recent, modest increase in economic activity.

The small rise in producer prices matches the gains in March and February. Energy prices last month rose 0.5%, while food prices fell 0.3%. Excluding those volatile sectors, producer prices for finished goods still rose just 0.2% in April, the same as in March.

"There has been no pickup in inflation," said Samuel Kahan, chief economist for Fuji Securities Inc. in Chicago. "As the pace of economic activity has been firming, that's what people have been really worried about."

But Mr. Kahan said the true test of inflationary pressures will come today, with the release of the Consumer Price Index. It rose just 0.1% in January, but then jumped 0.3% in February and accelerated to a 0.5% rise in March.

"We don't want to see any more pickup on the consumer level," Mr. Kahan said. "The producer price numbers seem to point to good news at the consumer level."

If consumer prices prove to have been in check in April, the door may well be opened even wider for the Federal Reserve to consider cutting interest rates again to spur the economy.

Prices for crude materials, other than food and energy, increased only 0.2% last month after jumping 2.2% in March and 1.4% in February. But most of the April slowdown came from a 17% drop in leaf tobacco prices; otherwise, nonenergy and nonfood crude-goods prices would have risen 0.4%.

Analysts considered the pickup in crude-material prices good news, because it showed that industrial activity is gaining steam. Moreover, such increases normally don't translate into higher consumer prices.

"When you have an economy that's this flat, and you start to see aggressiveness in crude prices, it means that there is some activity out there – finally. It's not bad news," said Ron Schreibman, vice president of the National Association of Wholesaler-Distributors here.

Norman Robinson, chief economist for Mellon Bank in Pittsburgh, agreed that the latest producer-price report indicates that the economy is in the midst of a weak recovery where demand for goods is still too mild to make prices go up significantly. "There is very little inflation in the system right now," he said. "These numbers represent a weak recovery is taking place."

The largest price increases in April for finished consumer goods came in toys, tobacco and tires. Prices for household items fell. In foods, there was a huge drop in vegetable prices, while the cost of fish rose substantially.

All figures have been adjusted for normal seasonal variations.

PRODUCER PRICES

Here are the Labor Department's producer price indexes (1982=100) for April, before seasonal adjustment, and the percentage changes from April 1991.

Finished goods	122.2+	0.9%
Minus food & energy	133.6+	2.4%
Intermediate goods	113.8–	0.1%
Crude goods	98.9–	1.9%

Producer Prices

Percentage change from previous month, seasonally adjusted

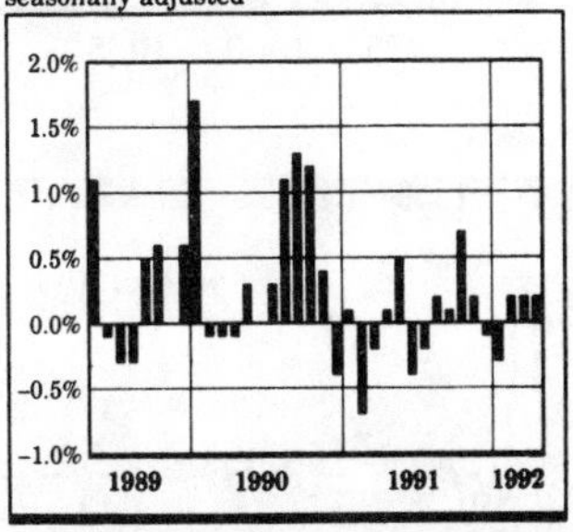

PRODUCER PRICES of finished goods rose a seasonally adjusted 0.2% in April compared with a 0.2% increase in March, the Labor Department reports. (See story on page A2.)

Source: *The Wall Street Journal,* May 13, 1992

CHART 7-6

Producer Price Index (1982 = 100);
Quarterly Change in Index at Annual Rates (Smoothed)

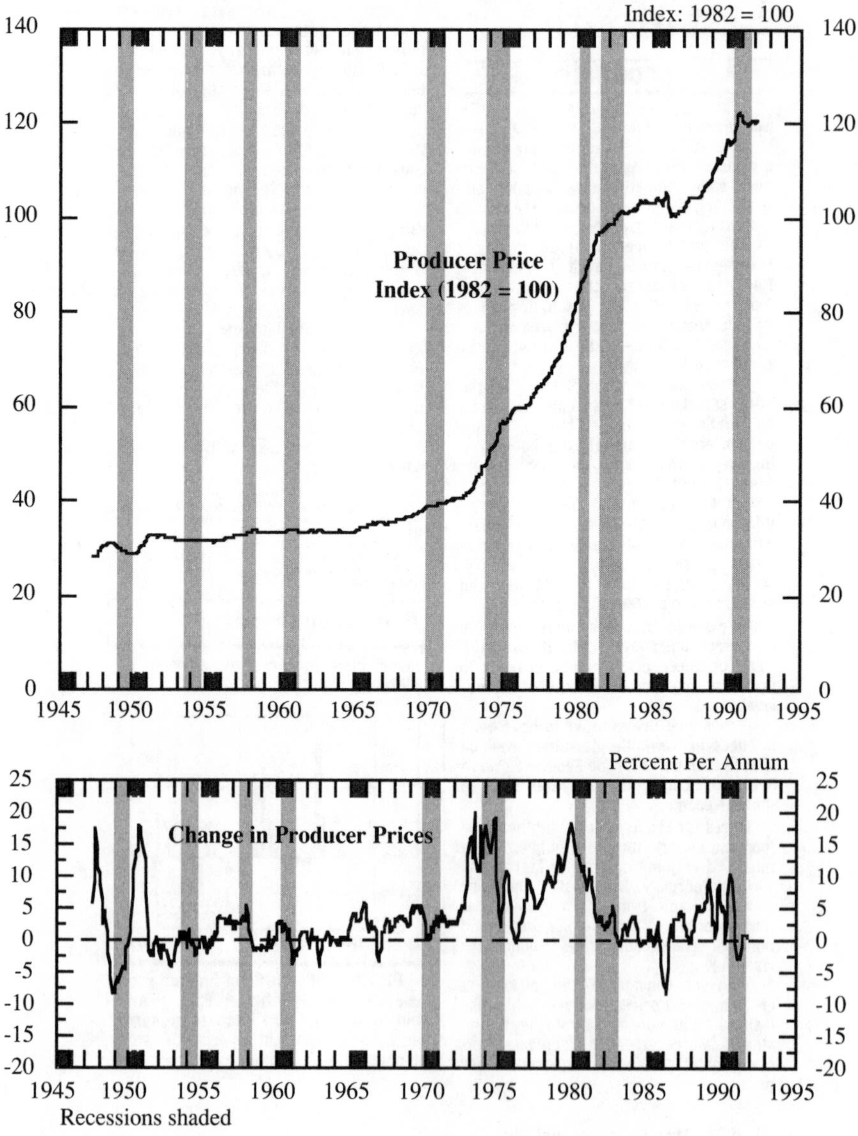

Source: U.S. Department of Commerce, *Business Cycle Indicators,* series 334 and 334c.

CHART 7-7
Changes in Unit Labor Cost and Producer Prices

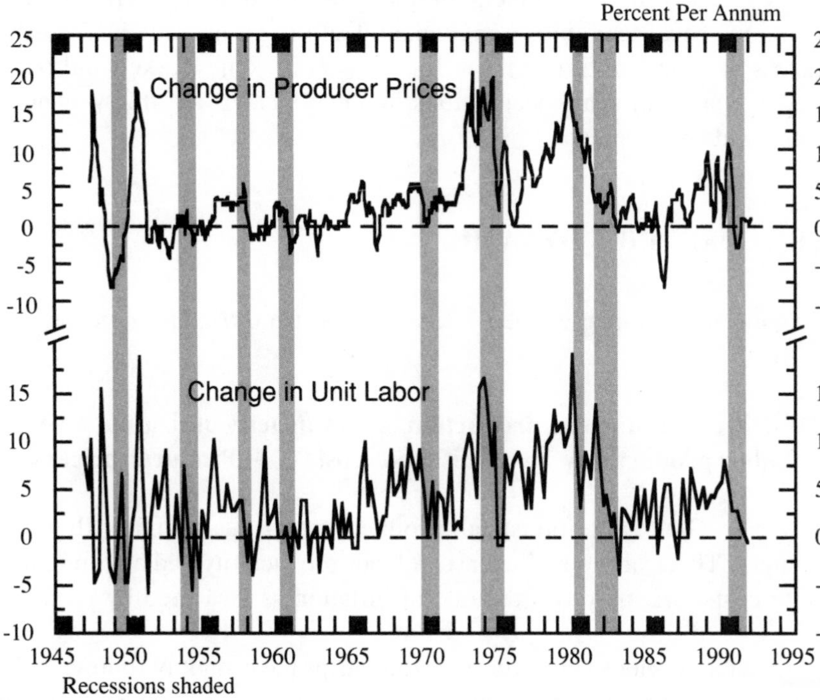

Source: U.S. Department of Commerce, *Business Cycle Indicators,* series 62 and 334c.

Producer Prices- First Paragraph

WASHINGTON – Producer prices rose a modest 0.2% in April, the Labor Department said, indicating that inflation still isn't much of a problem despite the recent, modest increase in economic activity.

Source: *The Wall Street Journal,* May 13, 1992

return and sharp cost increases due to declining productivity are the result, expect wage increases to lag behind inflation once again.

Even the full employment of the late 80s didn't generate "wage inflation" because employers remained loath to grant wage increases in excess of inflation. Competition for workers in some markets did boost wages rapidly in some occupations in some locales, but this was not a nationwide phenomenon.

THE COST/PRICE DYNAMIC

To conclude, summarize the cycle's progress from *trough to recovery* as follows:

GDP $\downarrow$ $\rightarrow$ Industrial production $\downarrow$ $\rightarrow$ Capacity utilization $\downarrow$ $\rightarrow$ Labor productivity $\uparrow$ $\rightarrow$ Unit labor costs $\downarrow$ $\rightarrow$ Producer prices $\downarrow$.

When GDP and industrial production fall, capacity utilization declines. This leads to an increase in labor productivity and a drop in unit labor costs, driving down the rate of inflation as measured by producer prices.

Like the reveler's hangover, recession grips the economy following the bender of boom and inflation. Rest is the only cure, and recovery is marked not by a renewed round of expansion and growth but by a slack period in which steadiness is restored.

But it would surely be naive to assume that low inflation will be forever with us. What forces can propel it upward once again? Why may we have a renewed round of price increases?

If you ask a business person why prices rise, he or she will answer, "Rising costs," probably referring to personal experience. When you ask an economist the same question, the response will be, "Demand exceeds supply at current prices, and therefore prices rise," probably referring to the textbook case. These points of view seem to have nothing in common. Yet an analysis of economic expansion shows that they meld into a single explanation. Consider an idealized (and hypothetical) situation.

Suppose all the indicators of economic expansion (demand)—auto sales, consumer credit, housing starts—are strong. This will initiate broad-based growth as incomes increase in the construction, auto, and other durable goods industries, spilling over and boosting demand for other consumer goods. Boom conditions will intensify as business invests in additional factories and machinery to meet the rush in orders.

As the expansion unfolds, capacity utilization increases with the growth in demand and production. Soon factories move from, say, 70 percent to 90 percent of their rated maximum. Productive facilities strain to meet the demands and retain the loyalty of customers.

Next, high levels of capacity utilization drive labor productivity down and unit labor costs up; efficiency is sacrificed for increased output. Machinery that is always in use cannot be adequately maintained, and so it breaks down. Inexperienced workers often do not make the same contribution as old hands. The amount of labor employed increases more rapidly than output, and as output per worker falls, the labor cost per unit of output rises. This generates a surge in production costs.

Finally, rapidly increasing costs are translated into rapidly increasing prices, and a renewed round of inflation begins.

All the forces that led to a reduction in the rate of inflation are now reversed as the cycle moves from *expansion to peak.*

**GDP ↑ → Industrial production ↑ →Capacity utilization ↑ →
Labor productivity ↓ → Unit labor costs ↑ → Producer prices ↑.**

So the practical (business person's) and the theoretical (economist's) explanations of inflation are not at odds. During expansion, demand bids production to a level that is inefficient and costly. The business person experiences the increased cost and attributes inflation directly to that experience. The economist sees increased demand as the ultimate cause of the production gain that drives costs up. Each explanation covers different aspects of the single phenomenon, economic expansion.

THE 1970s AS AN ILLUSTRATION

The late 1970s illuminate the process graphically. You will need the same statistical series employed earlier to illustrate expansion's impact on inflation: *GDP, industrial production, capacity utilization, labor productivity* and *unit labor costs,* and the *producer price index.* Each of these statistical series has already been introduced, so excerpts from *The Wall Street Journal* will not be presented again.

Although subsequently eclipsed by the 1981-82 recession, the 1974 recession established a postwar record at the time. GNP declined for four quarters, and industrial production tumbled 15 percent. By the spring of 1975, the unemployment rate was over 9 percent.

Like all recessions, however, this one prepared the way for the subsequent recovery. Capacity utilization fell to a postwar low, and labor productivity began to rise immediately. The resulting decline in unit labor costs cut the rate of inflation.

At the same time, the Federal Reserve System switched from a tight to an easy money policy, reducing interest rates and providing ample credit. A sharp recovery and strong expansion began as the decline in the rate of inflation dramatically improved consumer real income and boosted consumer sentiment. At long last, consumers were pulling ahead of inflation; their pleasure was reflected in demand's rapid increase.

By 1977-78, new housing starts were 2 million annually and domestic automobile sales peaked at approximately 10 million, while consumer installment borrowing hit annual rates of $50 billion.

The evidence of a robust economic expansion was all around as GNP and industrial production surged ahead. Rapid growth in demand, production, and capacity utilization had its inevitable result: the nation's factories and other productive facilities were strained, and increases in the labor force no longer made a proportional contribution to output (see Chart 7-5 on page 117).

In 1979 labor productivity stopped improving and began to fall. As a result, unit labor costs increased steadily, and by early 1980 the rate of inflation, as measured by the producer price index, had reached 15 percent (see Chart 7-7 on page 123).

Declining labor productivity is the focal point of this analysis. Once output is pushed past the point of diminishing returns, unit labor costs become an inevitable problem. Most people believe that rising wages are chiefly responsible for this condition; wages do play a minor role, naturally, but unit labor costs will increase swiftly even if wage gains run well below the rate of inflation (i.e., even if real wages are falling).

Falling real wages, coupled with the forward surge in labor costs, creates one of the cruelest features of inflation. Because labor productivity has declined, there is less per capita output and therefore less real income per person. Declining real income pits one segment of American society against another, fighting over a shrinking pie. Labor management relations become especially bitter in these periods of boom without prosperity. Employers blame workers' wages for rising labor costs and shrinking profits, while workers blame employers' profits for shrinking real wages; in reality, neither one is responsible for the other's misfortune.

In such times, the public's support for wage and price controls becomes insistent (although, of course, management has a greater interest in controlling wages and labor has a greater interest in controlling prices). Yet you can see from this chapter's analysis that rising costs due to reduced efficiency (falling labor productivity) are responsible for the increase in prices that captures everyone's attention. No one's greed is to blame. And therefore controls designed to limit greed are bound to be ineffective.

There have been two recent attempts at wage and price controls: the first under President Nixon in 1971-72 and the second under President Carter in 1979-80. President Nixon's controls were certain to "succeed" because they were implemented during the transition from recovery to expansion, while capacity utilization was low and labor productivity was high. As a result, the rate of inflation was still falling from its 1970 cyclical peak. It would have continued to decline in any event and remain low until the expansion gained strength. The controls did slightly dampen inflation, but their impact was marginal.

President Carter's controls were destined to "fail," just as President Nixon's were destined to succeed, because President Carter's were implemented during the virulent expansion of 1977-79. As labor productivity fell and unit costs climbed, business merely passed its increased costs on to the consumer. Rising prices reflected rising costs, not greed, and business did not earn excessive profits.

Keep in mind also that more stringent wage controls could not have restrained business costs. Some of the increase in unit labor costs was due to the increase in wage rates, but most of it was due to declining productivity caused by high capacity utilization. Workers were no more culpable than their employers.

This is an important point. We really can't blame the declines in labor productivity in the 1970s on the American worker, as some are prone to do. Productivity lapses in that decade occurred cyclically, when the economy overheated, and thus they really reflected the limitations of plant and equipment under extreme conditions rather than failures of diligence in the labor force.

And harking back to World War II for an example of successful wage and price controls is not the answer, either. Wage and price (and profit) controls worked then because the economy was on a war footing. About half of the economy's output was devoted to the war effort, much of it under a system of planning and direct resource allocation that operated outside ordinary market relationships. You couldn't bid up the price of a car (none were produced because the auto plants were converted to war production) or buy all the gasoline and steak you wanted (these were rationed). And despite the patriotism aroused by the war effort, black markets arose to subvert the controls. Therefore, it's doubtful whether such a system could work to contain peacetime inflation, for which, unlike war-induced inflation, there is no end in sight.

Imposing wage and price controls during the expansionary phase of the business cycle (as was attempted in the late 70s) is a little like trying to stop the rattle of a boiling kettle by taping down the lid. Demand heats the expansion, and inflation is the natural result. Turning down the heat is the only practical solution.

Investor's Tip

- Moderate levels of consumer demand (auto, housing, consumer credit) → Moderate capacity utilization → Moderate inflation.
- Booming auto sales (8 million +) + Housing starts (1.8 million +) + Consumer credit ($80 billion +) → High capacity utilization (85 + percent) → rapid (8 + percent) producer price inflation.
- A booming economy is your first hint that you should anticipate inflation by disposing of paper investments and buying tangible investments.

Finally, there's the question of "supply-side shocks." These are sudden increases in the price of important commodities (imposed by the sellers) or reductions in supply due to forces beyond our control. Some believe that the late 70s' inflation was due to these sorts of shocks, but this argument should be taken with a grain of salt. First, any explanation that places the blame on others should be suspect; if you wish to find fault, it is always best to look in the mirror. Second, neither OPEC nor the Russian wheat deal nor the failure of the Peruvian anchovy harvest can explain the price explosions of the 70s. They may have contributed to the inflation, but they did not cause it. If demand had been weak, prices would have remained stable. After all, prices stopped climbing as soon as recession hit in 1981-82, well before the oil price collapse of early 1986.

And whether you are dealing with free-market farm prices or OPEC, repealing the laws of supply and demand is not easy. Farm prices eased down in the commodity deflation of the 80s, while oil prices collapsed in a matter of months in early 1986. In both cases, high prices and profits in the 70s had attracted investment in new productive facilities and therefore created excess capacity (supply). Once supply exceeded demand at current prices, the price collapse was inevitable.

CONCLUSION

The expansion of the late 80s did not generate inflation as virulent as that of 1977-79 because the Fed restrained the growth in demand by restraining the growth in credit. The 1980s confirm the Fed's resolve to keep demand under control by restraining credit and keeping interest rates high.

The Fed's posture had not changed by the early 90s, and continued languid GDP growth restrained capacity utilization, costs and prices.

CHAPTER 8

STOCKS VS. GOLD

If you return to the comparison of stocks' and gold's performance (see Chart 8-1 on page 132) first mentioned in Chapter 1, you will note, to repeat, that stocks did poorly in the high-inflation 70s and well in the low-inflation 80s and early 90s, and that gold performed in the opposite fashion. Recall the promise in Chapter 1 that you would be able to forecast stocks' and gold's future performance once you had mastered (I) an understanding of the forces that shaped inflation, and (2) an ability to use *The Wall Street Journal* to analyze those forces. Now is the time to put your knowledge to work.

GOLD

Compare gold's performance to an index of a dozen commodity prices (including gold) presented on page 133 in Chart 8-2, and recall the suggestion in Chapter 1 that you view gold as a proxy for all tangible investments. When you mention commodities as an investment, most people think of gold.

The similarity in movement between gold prices and the commodity index is easily explained. All commodity prices (and gold is a commodity) measure inflation, which is after all nothing more than rising prices. Copper, cattle, hogs, lumber, wheat, and gold will move along the same path in the long run because the price of each is subject to the same supply and demand forces. When demand exceeds supply at current prices because spenders have access to credit, all prices rise. Sure, there are occasions when a commodity will defy the price trend for a while because of circumstances peculiar to its production and market. But these are exceptional cases.

CHART 8-1

Gold vs. Stocks: Gold–Engelhard High Price through 1987, Average Thereafter; Dow Jones Industrial Average

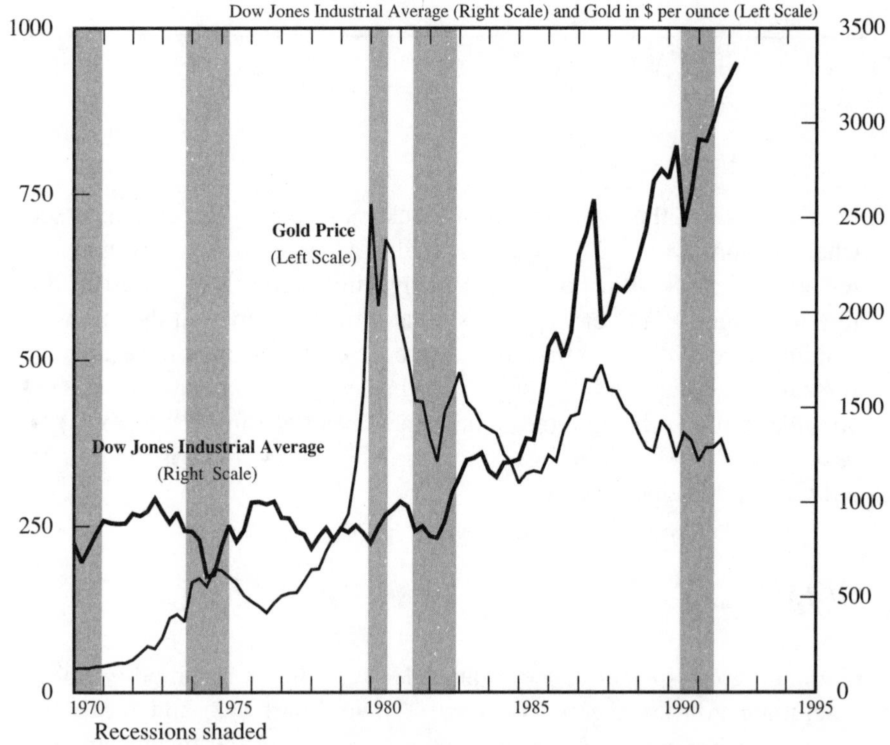

Source: U.S. Bureau of Mines, *Minerals Yearbook;* Standard & Poor's Statistical Service; Phyllis S. Pierce, ed., *The Dow Jones Investor's Handbook* (Homewood, IL: Dow Jones-Irwin, 1992); *Barron's*

Gold is a good investment (as are most tangibles) in times of high and rising inflation because its price climbs more rapidly than standard measures of inflation such as the CPI. In times of low inflation, gold prices will be weak or actually fall. Why does gold beat the averages during a period of severe inflation and then fall when inflation subsides (although prices generally are still rising)?

CHART 8-2
Gold and Dow Jones Commodity Futures Index

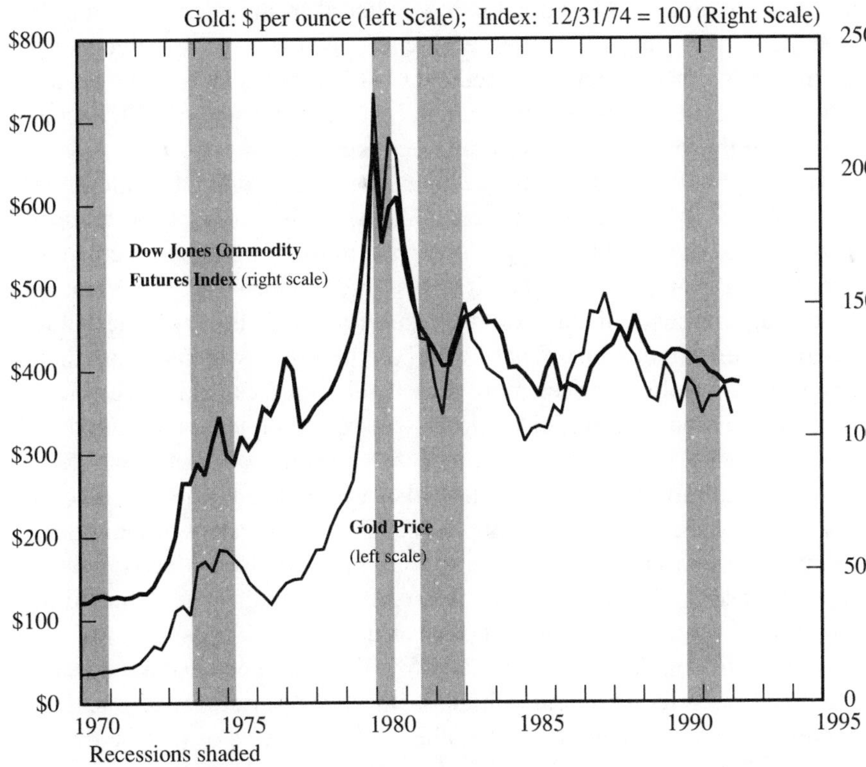

Source: U.S. Bureau of Mines, *Minerals Yearbook;* Standard & Poor's Statistical Service; Phyllis S. Pierce, ed., *The Dow Jones Investor's Handbook* (Homewood, IL: Dow Jones-Irwin, 1992); *Barron's*

What is true for gold is true for commodities generally. All occupy a position early in the production chain, before a great deal of value has been added in the productive process. Value added, which is the labor and technology applied to raw materials that turn them into useful products, acts as a cushion between the prices we pay for the finished product and the volatile prices paid for the commodities from which the product was fashioned.

Consider an example. If air travel increases, airlines order more planes from the aircraft manufacturers. Aircraft prices may rise 10 percent with the costs of designing, developing, manufacturing, and assembling. Most of these costs are payments to people. Yet the price of aluminum, the aircraft's principal ingredient, may rise 50 percent in the face of rapidly growing demand. And bauxite, the raw material from which aluminum is produced, may jump 100 percent, even as the cost of electricity (aluminum's other principal ingredient) hardly grows at all. Thus, a 10 percent increase in airplane prices may be consistent with a 100 percent increase in the price of bauxite, a mineral taken from the ground.

The point is that prices of the raw material out of which the aircraft is manufactured will surge far more rapidly than the price of the aircraft because the value added costs (design, engineering, manufacturing, assembly, etc.) required for the aircraft's production will not increase as rapidly as the costs of the raw materials (which had very little value added in their production). That's why bauxite prices will rise more than aircraft prices, tomato prices more than ketchup prices, and cattle prices more than hamburgers at McDonald's—in a period of general inflation.

Conversely, a drop in the demand for aircraft will not generate a decline in aircraft prices as labor and other value added costs continue to grow. Yet bauxite prices may fall. Wheat was six dollars a bushel in the summer of 1973 and not much more than half that by the early 1990s. Thus, the prices of finished goods will continue to climb in a climate of low inflation even as raw material prices slump.

It's as if fluctuations in the demand for finished goods had a whipsaw effect on the price of commodities, with slight variations at one end magnified in the fluctuations at the other end. It's a kind of reverse ripple effect, with the waves escalating in size and intensity as you move away from the splash.

That's why investors want to position themselves in the raw commodity during high inflation and not in finished goods. And gold is the raw commodity investment vehicle—par excellence. This explains why gold surges whenever there's a whiff of inflation. But look out when deflation hits. Gold will fade along with all other commodities.

Chart 8-3 on page 136 provides an illustration by presenting a number of price indexes, from raw commodity prices to semifinished goods to the CPI.

The sharp break presented by the early 1980s is never lost, but is clearly muted as you go up the productive process from raw to finished goods. Commodity prices rise most steeply among all the indexes and actually fall in the 80s. The CPI rises least rapidly of all the indexes in the 1970s, yet continues to rise most rapidly in the 1980s, a period in which many commodity prices fell.

As a general rule, commodity prices rise more rapidly than consumer prices in high inflation, but rise less rapidly than consumer prices when inflation is low (and can actually fall).

Once again, the farther back you go in the chain of production, the more volatile the price index. Gold is no exception to this rule. Glance back to Chart 8-2 on page 133 and you can see gold's explosion in the 70s and its weak performance in the 80s and early 90s. It will stay weak in the 90s if inflation remains in check. It will climb to its 1980 high of about $900 an ounce only if inflation is rekindled.

Investor's Tip

- Stay away from gold, commodities, and other tangibles unless inflation exceeds 8 percent at a seasonally adjusted annual rate for at least a quarter year.

PROFITS AND STOCKS

Stocks are more complex than commodities because you must analyze profits first. You can't measure a company's value until you know how much it can earn. *The Wall Street Journal* survey of corporate profits for over 500 corporations (see page 140) appears about two months after the close of the quarter, while the Commerce Department estimate is included with the last revision of GDP data (see page 138). The fifth paragraph of the June 26, 1992 report (see page 138) for the first quarter of 1992 states that profits rose 11.3 percent over the previous quarter, and the first paragraph of the May 4, 1992 report on page 140 reports a 34 percent gain over the year-earlier quarter. You should note the different bases of comparison.

Profits measure efficiency by comparing revenues to costs. Recall that the economy's efficiency improves during the early phases of the cycle and deteriorates during the latter phases. Thus, profits grow during recovery and expansion and deteriorate during peak and contraction.

CHART 8-3
Price Index Comparisons: Dow Jones Commodity Futures Index, Raw Industrial Materials (spot), Producer Price Index, Consumer Price Index

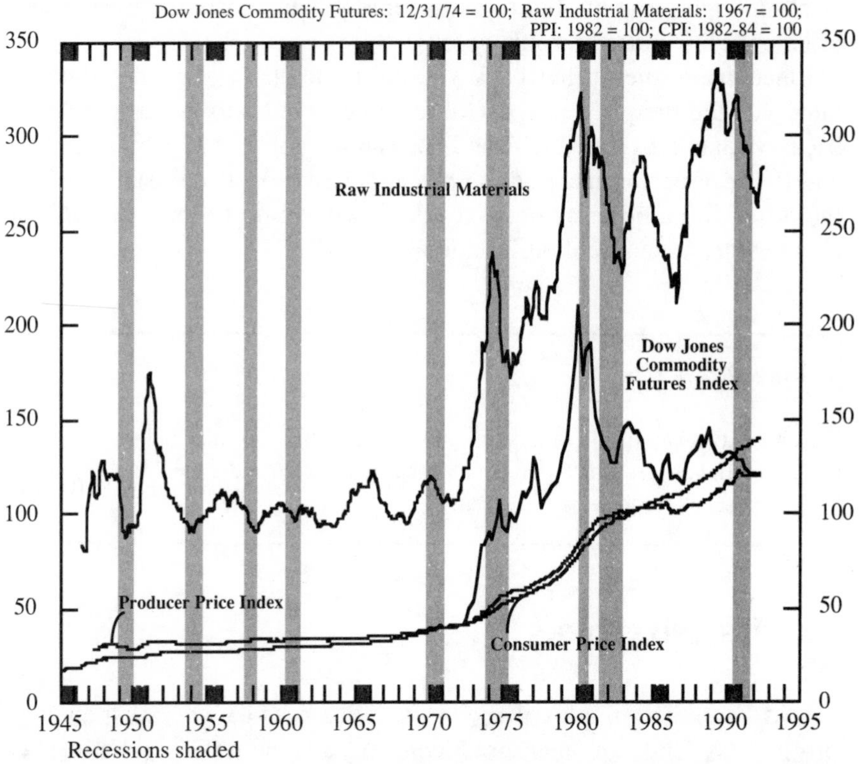

Source: U.S. Department of Commerce, *Business Cycle Indicators,* series 320 and 320c. Phyllis S. Pierce, ed., *The Dow Jones Investor's Handbook* (Homewood, IL: Dow Jones-Irwin, 1992); Knight-Ridder, Commodity Research Bureau

A bit of logic reveals the relationship between general changes in economic efficiency over the cycle and the specific measurement of profit. Efficiency rises early in the cycle because factories operate with excess capacity and produce less than maximum output. The general reduction in costs due to enhanced productivity increases the spread between prices and costs, known as the profit rate or profit per unit of output. As sales increase, total profit grows because of both higher output and higher profits per unit of output.

Efficiency deteriorates late in the cycle as factories strain to produce maximum output. Costs rise as productivity falls, and industry is forced into a "profit squeeze," meaning that costs push up against prices. Total profits fall as sales volume stops growing, or actually contracts with the onset of recession, and profit per unit of output (the profit rate) falls.

It may help to think of it in these terms: costs rise as output increases and industry reaches full capacity utilization. As costs come up from below, they bump prices upward. But competition prevents management from raising prices as rapidly as it would like. If costs rise more rapidly than prices, the margin between price and cost is squeezed. Profit margins decline.

On the other hand, management has the opportunity to rebuild its profit margins in the slack period following recession. Costs are no longer rising as rapidly because capacity utilization is low. This provides management with the opportunity to recover profit margins by raising prices more rapidly than costs.

Thus, paradoxically, profit margins shrink when prices rise most rapidly, typically before the peak of the cycle, and grow when inflation abates in the slack period immediately after recession and when recovery begins.

That's why both productivity and profitability recovered nicely as the economy emerged from the 1990-91 recession. There's a strong correlation between productivity and profit margins. As the economy's efficiency improves, so does the spread between price and cost. Business earns more per unit of output. But in the superheated economy at the business cycle's peak, such as during the highly volatile 1970s, efficiency and profitability deteriorated. Profit margins shrank.

Chart 8-4 on page 139 depicts the ratio of price to unit labor cost (i.e., the relative strength of prices and unit labor cost) and is therefore a proxy for profit margins. This informs you of the extent of labor cost's encroachment on prices and of business's ability to hold down labor costs in relation to the prices received. Keep in mind that the ratio of price to unit labor cost is a fraction in which price is the numerator (top half) and cost the denominator (bottom half). In boom conditions, when costs are rising rapidly and pushing prices upward, profit margins are squeezed because competition prevents management from raising prices as rapidly as costs increase. Thus, the value of the fraction (ratio of price to unit labor cost) falls as the denominator (cost) rises more rapidly than the numerator (price).

Economy Grew At Rate of 2.7% In First Quarter

ECONOMY

By DAVID WESSEL
Staff Reporter of THE WALL STREET JOURNAL

WASHINGTON – The U.S. economy grew at a slightly faster pace in the first quarter than previously estimated, the Commerce Department said. But the revision didn't dispel new worries about the strength of the recovery.

The Commerce Department said the gross domestic product, the value of all goods and services produced in the country, rose at an annual rate of 2.7% in the first quarter, the biggest increase since the fourth quarter of 1988. Previously, the department put the rise at 2.4%.

"It tells us that the economy really did have a pretty good first quarter, particularly in domestic demand," said Richard Rippe, economist at Prudential Securities Inc. "The real question about where we are headed isn't resolved. Certainly, the recent signs have been slower."

Indeed, the Labor Department reported yesterday that initial claims for state unemployment benefits rose by 16,000 to 422,000 in the week ended June 13. Although the increase could be an aberration, it added to worries that weak consumer spending threatens to damp hiring. The four-week average, tracked by some analysts because it isn't as volatile, rose to 411,000 from 406,000.

Corporate Profits

The Commerce Department also said yesterday that corporate profits rose even more sharply in the first quarter than previously reported. After-tax profits were up 11.3% to an annual rate of $211.2 billion; previously the increase was estimated at 8%. Pretax profits adjusted for inventory-valuation changes, the department's preferred measure of profits, increased in every major industry except trade.

Source: *The Wall Street Journal*, June 26, 1992

Corporate Profits–Fifth Paragraph

The Commerce Department also said yesterday that corporate profits rose even more sharply in the first quarter than previously reported. After-tax profits were up 11.3% to an annual rate of $211.2 billion; previously the increase was estimated at 8%. Pretax profits adjusted for inventory-valuation changes, the department's preferred measure of profits, increased in every major industry except trade.

Source: *The Wall Street Journal*, June 26, 1992

CHART 8-4
Ratio, Price to Unit Labor Cost, Manufacturing

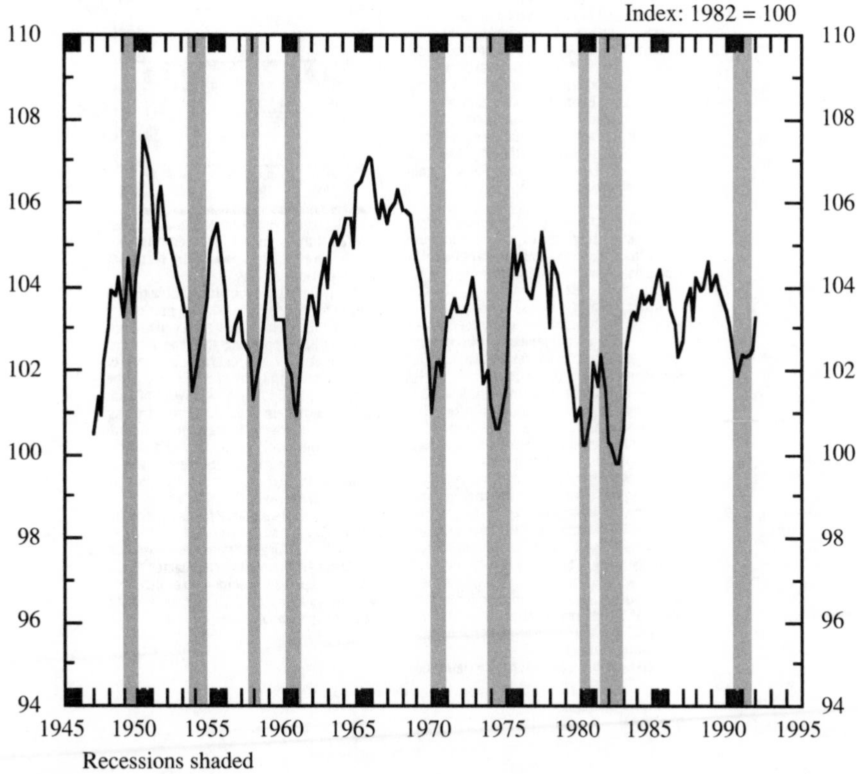

Source: U.S. Department of Commerce, *Business Cycle Indicators*, series 62

Corporate Profits

Companies' Net Income Rose 34% As Economy Begins to Perk Up

A WALL STREET JOURNAL *News Roundup*

Corporate profits, like the economy, are beginning to show signs of life. For the first quarter of this year, net income of 616 major corporations rose 34%, the first year-to-year increase since the third quarter of 1990.

But there were far fewer write-offs in this year's first quarter than there were in the 1991 period, and after-tax earnings from continuing operations rose only 9%.

The results in the quarter generally were better than expected. Melissa R. Brown of Prudential Securities thinks the pleasant surprise stems less from a strong economy than from the fact that analysts, after several quarters of disappointments, had begun to hold down their predictions.

Now that an upturn has occurred, the forecasters think earnings will continue to gather strength. "No matter how you keep score, profits growth will be strong both this year and next, even though the pace of business activity will accelerate only moderately," says Daniel E. Laufenberg, senior economist of IDS Financial Services.

The 50 economists interviewed monthly by Blue Chip Economic Indicators, a newsletter published in Sedona, Ariz., on the average now look for pretax profits to rise by 10.9% this year and then by 13.4% in 1993. They expect the inflation-adjusted gross domestic product to rise by 3.1% in 1993.

Several analysts point out that corporate cost-cutting has expanded company profit margins so that earnings are likely to rise briskly even though economic growth remains moderate.

Among major groups, earnings recovered for auto makers while securities firms, banking companies and aerospace concerns posted strong results. Oil companies were hit hard in the quarter.

The Big Three auto makers staged a comeback in the first quarter after five collective quarters of record red ink.

Ford Motor and General Motors turned profits because they sold more vehicles, and a more profitable mix of vehicles, including more trucks and fewer fleet cars. Chrysler, however, remained in the red because of launch costs for new vehicles and because its share of the car market has been declining. Chrysler's results included one-time gains of $218 million for new accounting rules and $88 million for selling some of its shares in Mitsubishi Motors, and a $63 million loss for investments in a real estate company.

Although the car market remains depressed, analysts expect the industry to do somewhat better in the second quarter. That's partly because all three companies have aggressively cut costs and because they're using relatively strong truck sales to offset weak car sales.

Earnings at Wall Street securities firms continued to soar because of lower interest rates. The securities industry posted one of its best quarters, buoyed by active trading and a record issuance of new stocks and bonds.

All the major firms posted record profits, with rises of at least 50%, compared with a strong year-earlier quarter. Most showed jumps in trading commissions, which were offset somewhat by increases in compensation costs.

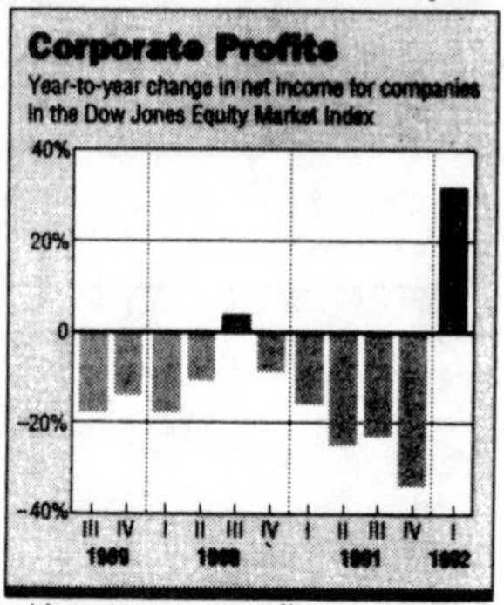

Analysts expect the blockbuster profits to ease for the rest of 1992. The market for initial public stock offerings has cooled off. "Signals are appearing that the forward momentum in the brokerage business of the past year may be starting to cut the other way," said Guy Moszkowski of Sanford C. Bernstein & Co. "Market trading volumes have begun to weaken considerably from the levels of January and February." Still, even if profits slow down, it should be an "excellent year" for brokers, if not for brokerage stocks, he added.

Results for two major firms – Morgan Stanley Group and Salomon – haven't been released yet. Morgan Stanley has switched to a fiscal year, and its first quarter didn't end until April 30. Salomon's results have been delayed so they can coincide with Wednesday's annual meeting.

Source: *The Wall Street Journal*, May 4, 1992

In recession and recovery from recession, management can rebuild profit margins because costs are no longer rising rapidly. Management raises prices somewhat more quickly than costs increase, and profit margins are rebuilt. As a result, the ratio of price to unit labor cost rises as the numerator of the fraction now gains more rapidly than the denominator.

Each of the cycles in the 1970s demonstrates the same sequence of events. Start with a typical recovery and expansion, such as the recovery and expansion of 1971-72 or 1975-77. Unit labor cost was kept down by good gains in labor productivity due to modest levels of capacity utilization. As a result, the ratio of price to unit labor cost (our proxy for the term profit margins) improved and held up well. Since sales volume and output were growing, total real profits grew sharply.

Then, in 1973 and 1978-79, as production and capacity utilization peaked, labor productivity declined and unit labor cost increased. As a result, the ratio of price to unit labor cost fell, pinching profit margins. Since, at the peak of the cycle, sales and output had also stalled, real profits tumbled and continued to fall throughout the ensuing recessions of 1974-75 and 1980.

Chapter 7 discussed wage and price controls, and Chart 8-4 on page 139 illustrates the foolishness of this adventure. The rate of inflation declined in 1971-72, during President Nixon's controls, despite rising profit margins (ratio of price to unit labor cost). Since profit margins rose, why didn't inflation climb with them? Because the rate of cost increase subsided due to improved productivity brought about by the recovery phase of the business cycle. In other words, the drop in costs exceeded any increase in margins.

The rate of inflation rose in 1979-80, during President Carter's controls, despite falling profit margins (ratio of price to unit labor cost). Since profit margins fell, why weren't controls effective in limiting inflation? Because the inflation was not due to excessive profit margins, it was due to the increasingly rapid rise in costs brought on by cyclical expansion's negative impact on productivity. Controls could not stem the rising spiral of prices.

To summarize, profits, when calculated for the entire economy, measure efficiency, not greed. Prices simply can't be controlled by limiting profits.

You can see in Chart 8-4 on page 139 that profit margins recovered in the mid-80s, as low rates of capacity utilization boosted labor

CHART 8-5
Dow Jones Industrial Average (Price), Earnings per Share, and Price/Earnings Ratio

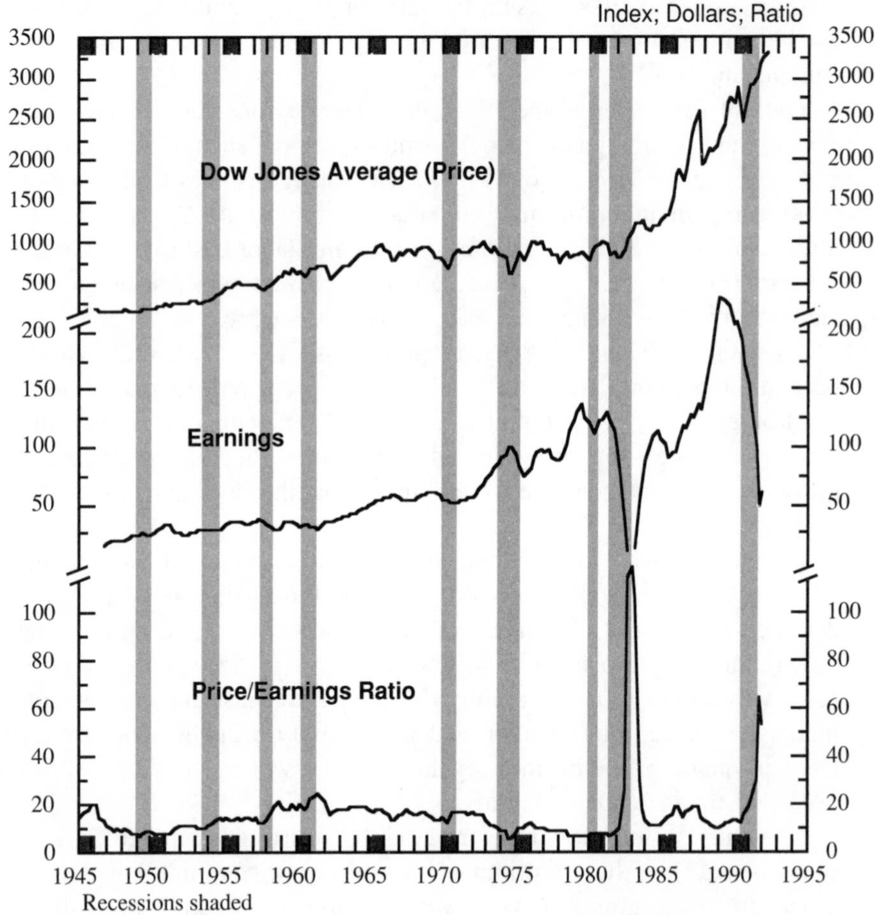

Source: Phyllis S. Pierce, ed., *The Dow Jones Investor's Handbook* (Homewood, IL: Dow Jones-Irwin, 1992); *Barron's*

productivity and held down unit labor costs, providing an increased spread between prices and costs (improved profit margins).

Profit margins stumbled in the late 80s because the economy grew too languidly and slid even further with the start of the 1990-91 recession, an anomaly caused by the Persian Gulf war. Keep in mind, however, that margins did not fall as severely as they had in the 70s during the cyclical course of boom conditions.

The important point (see Chart 8-5 on page 142) is that inflation's cyclical squeeze on profit margins and real earnings in the 1970s regularly depressed the stock market so that it could not advance out of the trading range in which it was trapped. Inflation is murder on profit margins and therefore is the death of the stock market. On the other hand, once inflation subsided, continued strong margins provided a boost to the stock market in the 1980s and early 1990s.

Investor's Tip

- Stay away from stocks if the annual inflation rate exceeds 8 percent for a quarter.

STOCKS AND THE PRICE/EARNINGS RATIO

Let's return to the Dow Jones Industrial Average. You know that the price of a share of stock reflects the ability of the corporation to earn profits. This relationship is expressed as the price/earnings (P/E, or price divided by per share earnings) ratio between the price of the stock and the profits per share of stock earned by the corporation (profits divided by number of shares outstanding). The price/earnings ratio answers this question: "What is the price an investor must pay to capture a dollar of earnings?" For instance, a P/E ratio of 10 might mean that a company earned $10 per share per annum and that a share sold for $100, or it might mean that a company earned $7 per share per annum and that a share sold for $70, and so on.

The investor, of course, seeks the highest yield consistent with safety. The earnings yield is annual profit expressed as a percentage of market price. If you earn $100 a year on an investment of $1,000, the yield is 10 percent. A P/E ratio of 10 (10/1) represents a 10 percent yield because earnings are 1/10 (10 percent) of the price per share. Similarly, a P/E ratio of 5 (5/1) is the equivalent of a 20 percent yield because earnings per share are one fifth (20 percent) of invested capital. A P/E ratio of 20 (20/1) represents a 5 percent earnings yield. And so on.

Chart 8-5 on page 142 shows that the Dow's P/E ratio fell from the end of World War II until the beginning of the Korean War, because earnings grew while share prices languished. Following the uncertainties of the 1930s and World War II, investors were still tentative about the market.

Then the great bull market (stock prices fall in a bear market) of the 1950s began, and the P/E ratio rose as investors bid up share prices more rapidly than earnings increased. Investors were at last convinced of a "return to normalcy" and were willing to stake their future in shares of stock. The market was clearly "undervalued" (a P/E ratio of seven was roughly a 15 percent earnings yield), so it is not surprising that stock prices climbed rapidly. Stocks were a good buy because their price was very low compared to their earnings per share and their potential for even higher earnings. As investors rushed into the market, stock prices soared. Enthusiasm was so great and share prices advanced so rapidly that the P/E ratio rose despite stronger earnings per share.

The P/E ratio had climbed to more than 20 (a 5 percent yield) by the early 60s, so the market was no longer undervalued. The ratio plateaued or fell slightly to the end of the 60s because share prices were no longer increasing faster than corporate earnings. The great bull market had ended.

During the 70s, investors became frightened of the impact of inflation and severe cyclical fluctuation on profit margins, since margins fell sharply with each burst of inflation. At the first hint of declining margins, investors unloaded their shares and stock prices plunged. As a result, the Dow remained mired within a range for a decade, fluctuating between the high 500s and just over 1,000. Investors had been so badly burned by the market's decline in 1969 and 1974 that they refused to be swayed by the strong recovery of profits after each recession.

Yet nominal (not adjusted for inflation) profits rose over the decade, and thus the P/E ratio fell, so that by the early 1980s it was almost as low as it had been at the outset of the Korean War. The market had not kept pace with nominal earnings, and stocks were undervalued once again.

To some, this indicated that we were on the verge of another bull market. The situation seemed similar to that of the late 1940s, with investors hesitant after years of bad news, yet willing to take the plunge when it became clear that the fundamentals had changed. One indication of this sentiment was that stock prices fell little in the recessions of 1980 and 1981-82 when compared with those of 1970 and 1974. It was as if investors were positioning themselves for the bull market that was just around the corner.

There were two very auspicious signs. First, the breaking of the boom-and-bust inflationary spiral with the back-to-back recessions of 1980 and 1981-82 was a key signal that henceforth corporations could enjoy high profit margins. Second, the low P/E ratio meant that stocks were undervalued. Growing earnings would generate rising share prices, and when sufficient numbers of investors realized that the earnings improvement was permanent, the P/E ratio would rise to higher levels as buying pressure drove stock prices up.

The bull market of the 80s began in the summer of 1982, when it became clear that the Fed had loosened its monetary vise. The decline in interest rates mattered to investors because interest-earning assets are an alternative to stocks. As interest rates fell, investors moved out of interest-earning instruments and into stocks.

But Chart 8-5 on page 142 demonstrates that investors responded too enthusiastically to the improved profit potential. Speculation bid share prices up much faster than either real or nominal earnings. By August 1987 the Dow had doubled its 1985 level and stood at more than 2700, while earnings per share at $125 were not much greater than they had been four years earlier. The P/E ratio climbed to 22, higher than it had been since the early 60s.

Clearly the market was overvalued, ripe for a correction. It began to fold after its peak of 2722.42 on August 25, 1987, and declined 500 points by October 16. Then on October 19 it crashed another 500 points.

P/E RATIOS & YIELDS ON INDEXES

	--P/E Ratios--		Dividend Yields	
	07/10/92	Yr. Ago	07/10/92	Yr. Ago
DJ Industrials	68.5	19.9	3.13%	3.08%
DJ Tranportations ..	....	....	1.52%	1.55%
DJ Utilities	14.6	15.1	6.33%	7.06%
S&P 500	25.61	18.16	3.00%	3.20%

Price earnings ratios for the Dow Jones Averages are based on per share earnings for the most recent four quarters of $48.61 for the 30 Industrials; ($30.21) for the 20 transportation issues; $14.95 for the 15 utilities.

Source: *The Wall Street Journal*, July 13, 1992

Yet earnings per share continued to grow in a climate of low inflation. They exceeded $200 by early 1989, sending the P/E back down to 12. Now the Dow was undervalued once again and investors began to recover from their post crash jitters. By early 1990 investors had propelled the Dow passed its 1987 high; in the summer of 1990 it reached 3000.

What was the source of their bullish attitude? Strong margins, low inflation, and a low P/E. What did investors have to fear? Either inflation's return or speculation; the first because of its depressing impact on profit margins, the second because excessive stock market appreciation would create overvaluation (a high P/E) of the kind that existed before the 1987 crash.

Then Iraq invaded Kuwait. As consumer sentiment collapsed and recession unfolded, the Dow fell to 2400. But consumer sentiment rebounded with the success of Desert Storm and the stock market anticipated economic recovery. The Dow quickly regained the 3000 range and remained there for some time.

Unfortunately, the economic recovery took longer than forecast and earnings continued to decline. The 1990-91 recession repeated the experience of 1981-82 by sharply depressing earnings. Moreover, as you can see in Chart 8-5 on page 142, the drop in earnings drove the P/E ratio to absurdly high figures. Was that a sign of speculation and a signal for investors to sell?

Clearly not. Abysmal earnings for the Dow stocks, not speculation, had generated the extraordinary P/E ratios. Circumstances at the close of the 1990-91 recession were quite different from those before the crash of 1987. Depressed earnings, not speculation, were responsible for the extraordinarily high P/E ratio.

Yet the Dow was overvalued in some sense, even if a crash was not imminent. Earnings would have to recover before the Dow could resume its upward march.

Investor's Tip

- If the P/E exceeds 15, be cautious: stocks may be overvalued; if the P/E reaches 20, get out unless you have firm evidence that speculation is absent.

Follow the earnings and P/E for the Dow stocks each Monday on the third page (C3) of the *Journal*'s third section, called Money and Investing. An example from the July 13, 1992 *Journal* appears on page 145.

STOCKS VS. GOLD

Smart investors picked stocks and stayed away from gold in the 1980s and 1990s. The Fed had inflation under control, which was a good omen for stocks (and bonds and other paper investments) and a bad omen for gold (and commodities and other tangible investments).

As for the crash of 1987, that proved to be a correction for excessive speculation in stocks, for which a lofty P/E ratio was an omen. The smart money left the market when it became overvalued (P/E exceeded 20), and returned immediately after the crash.

WHAT ABOUT REAL ESTATE?

In general, invest in tangible assets when inflation is high and invest in paper assets when inflation is low.

Then what happened to real estate in the 1980s? Why did this tangible asset soar in many locales despite low rates of inflation?

Don't confuse the real estate markets of the 1970s and 80s. The rising tide of inflation lifted all the boats in the inflationary 70s. Whether you owned urban, suburban, or rural real estate, all values rose. Like Rip Van Winkle, you could have gone to sleep in 1970 and awakened in 1980 to find an increase in the value of your assets no matter where their location. But most real estate markets languished in the 1980s because most of America is rural and farmland values collapsed with agricultural commodity prices in the early 80s. There were important exceptions, such as California and the Northeast, whose values soared with local job conditions, but those situations were local, not general. The oil boomlets are another illustration of this phenomenon.

These special situations collapsed too, of course, so that the 1990s began with all real estate markets in slack condition. And since low inflation should continue from the 1980s right through the 90s, real estate should not be a good investment in the 90s. Sure, special situations and local booms will continue to occur, but that will be against a backdrop of generally weak conditions. Remember, too, that falling interest rates drove much of the mid-80s boom (where it did occur), and that interest rates are not likely to decline so dramatically in the 90s.

PART II

YOUR CHOICE OF INVESTMENTS

CHAPTER 9

THE STOCK MARKET

A FIRST GLANCE: MARKETS DIARY

Chapter 8 compared the fortunes of stocks and gold in condition of high and low inflation. Now it's time to study these competing investments in depth.

Start with stocks, not only because they are a more common investment, but also because you have seen that our economy's health and the stock market's health are inextricably intertwined.

You probably want to plunge right in and find out how you can make money in the market and use *The Wall Street Journal* to see how much you've made, but slow down a little instead and take the time for a step-by-step approach.

The stock market is a good barometer of economic activity because it reflects the value of owning the businesses responsible for most of our economy's output. *The Dow Jones Industrial Average* is the most popular indicator of stock market performance, and that's why Chapters 1 and 8 employed it to portray the entire market.

The Dow represents share prices of 30 blue-chip industrial corporations, chosen because their operations cover the broad spectrum of industrial America, although you can see from the list presented below that not all of these firms are literally "industrials" (e.g., American Express, AT&T, McDonald's, and Woolworth are in financial services, communications, and retailing). (Dow Jones publishes separate indexes for public utilities and transportation companies.)

There are broader stock market barometers that include more corporations, but the Dow Industrials remains the most closely watched average because it was first and, more significant, because its handful of

MARKETS DIARY 9/30/92

STOCKS Dow Jones Industrial Average

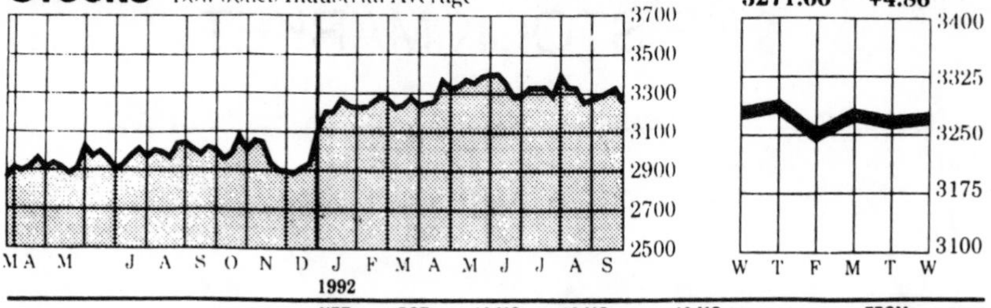

INDEX	CLOSE	NET CHNG	PCT CHNG	12-MO HIGH	12-MO LOW	12-MO CHNG	PCT	FROM 12/31	PCT
DJIA	3271.66	+ 4.86	+ 0.15	3413.21	2863.82	+ 259.14	+ 8.60	+ 102.83	+ 3.25
DJ Equity	394.01	+ 1.22	+ 0.31	400.79	352.36	+ 30.36	+ 8.35	+ 2.11	+ 0.54
S&P 500	417.80	+ 1.00	+ 0.24	425.27	375.22	+ 29.54	+ 7.61	+ 0.71	+ 0.17
Nasdaq Comp.	583.27	+ 5.64	+ 0.98	644.92	513.81	+ 56.94	+ 10.82	− 3.07	− 0.52
London (FT 100)	2553.0	− 12.5	− 0.49	2737.8	2281.0	− 91.2	− 3.45	+ 59.9	+ 2.40
Tokyo (Nikkei)	17399.08	− 349.01	− 1.97	25222.28	14309.41	− 6976.03	− 28.62	− 5584.69	− 24.30

Source: *The Wall Street Journal,* October 1, 1992

blue-chip companies do reflect stock market activity with surprisingprecision. Other measures of the stock market's performance will be mentioned shortly.

You probably already know a fair bit of the information in the next several pages, but it will provide a good basis for some more complex ideas presented later in this chapter.

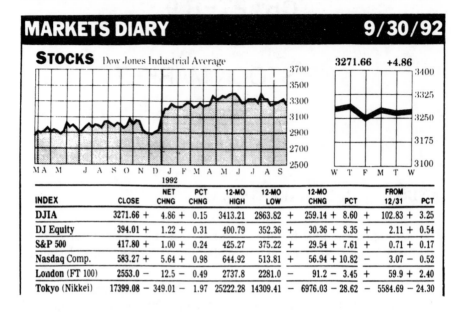

Every day, on the first page (Cl) of the third section, *The Wall Street Journal* publishes a summary account of the activity of the stock market as measured by several major indexes. It is always the lead item under the heading **Markets Diary** (see the excerpt from the Thursday, October 1, 1992 *Journal* above). The Dow Jones Industrial Average is featured in the two charts under the **Stocks** caption. The chart on the left pictures the fluctuations in the Dow over the past year-and-a-half, while the one on the right shows the Dow's weekly movement. The table just below the charts features four major domestic indexes and two international indexes that will be discussed more fully below.

You should use this chart and table for your first quick assessment of the previous day's stock market activity. Notice that while all American indexes improved by about the same (percentage) amount over the past twelve months, the London and Tokyo markets fell.

But take a moment to consider the Dow Industrials in more detail.

CALCULATING THE DOW

Each day, on the third page (C3) of the last section, the *Journal* publishes in chart form a detailed summary of the **Dow Jones Averages** over the past six months (see pages 155 and 156). It records the progress of the 30 industrials, the 20 stocks in the transportation average, and the 15 stocks in the utility average, as well as trading volume.

After glancing at the top chart of the Dow Jones Averages, your first question—once you know what this index signifies—probably is, "How can an average of stock market prices be over $3,000? I don't know of *one* stock that trades that high, much less 30 of them."

The answer involves the manner in which the Dow deals with "stock splits." Companies split their stock (say, two for one) to prevent the stock from becoming too expensive. Shareholders receive two shares for each share they own and the stock's price is halved; thus, the total value of the shares remains the same.

This usually occurs when the price of a "round-lot" transaction (100 shares) climbs too high. Round-lot transactions are popular with large investors because of the lower commission per share, and it's much easier

The 30 Stocks in the Dow Jones Industrial Average (April 15, 1992)

Alcoa	Goodyear
Allied-Signal	IBM
American Express	International Paper
AT&T	McDonald's
Bethlehem Steel	Merck
Boeing	Minnesota Mining & Manufacturing
Caterpillar	JP Morgan
Chevron	Phillip Morris
Coca-Cola	Procter & Gamble
Disney	Sears
DuPont	Texaco
Eastman Kodak	Union Carbide
Exxon	United Technologies
General Electric	Westinghouse
General Motors	Woolworth

to buy a round lot at $50 than $100 a share. So most companies would rather split their stock than see it become too expensive and discourage investors' purchases.

Here's how this applies to the Dow Jones Industrial Average. Suppose you are calculating the average of a group of 30 stocks (such as the Dow) by adding the share prices of all of them and dividing by 30. If (to make the arithmetic simple and the point clear) each of the 30 were selling at $100, obviously the average would be $100 ($3,000/30). However, if each of the 30 happened to split two for one, then each would be worth $50, per share; that is, the average price per share of these 30 stocks would suddenly be $50 not $100. Clearly it makes no sense to reduce the average because of such splits, since someone who owns the stock has exactly as much equity (percentage ownership) value after a split as before it.

Lowering the divisor from 30 to 15 is one solution: 30 shares at $50 each ($1,500) divided by 15 (not 30) keeps the average at 100. Future stock splits can be handled in a similar fashion with an appropriate adjustment in the divisor.

Another, though less important, reason for changing the divisor is that occasionally Dow Jones replaces one of the 30 industrial stocks with another. Here, too, it wouldn't make sense to change the average; just because one stock is substituted for another doesn't mean the market, itself, has changed. Therefore, the divisor is adjusted at the same time, to keep the average constant.

Now consider a real-life example (see page 157) using the Dow on June 11, 1992. Add the share prices of all 30 companies in the Dow. The total comes to $1,616.125, and, when you divide that by the divisor of 0.48220767, you get $3,351.51—the Dow average for June 11, 1992.

The figures used on page 157 to compute the Dow are the closing June 11, 1992 prices for the New York Stock Exchange (NYSE). NYSE *Composite Transactions* prices (to be discussed below) vary slightly from the prices used here. Why the discrepancy? Because the composite includes the closing prices of NYSE stocks listed on other exchanges such as the Pacific Stock Exchange, which continues its operations for half an hour after the New York Exchange closes.

So much for the Dow; you are now ready to move on to a more detailed analysis of the other stock market indicator and stock market performance.

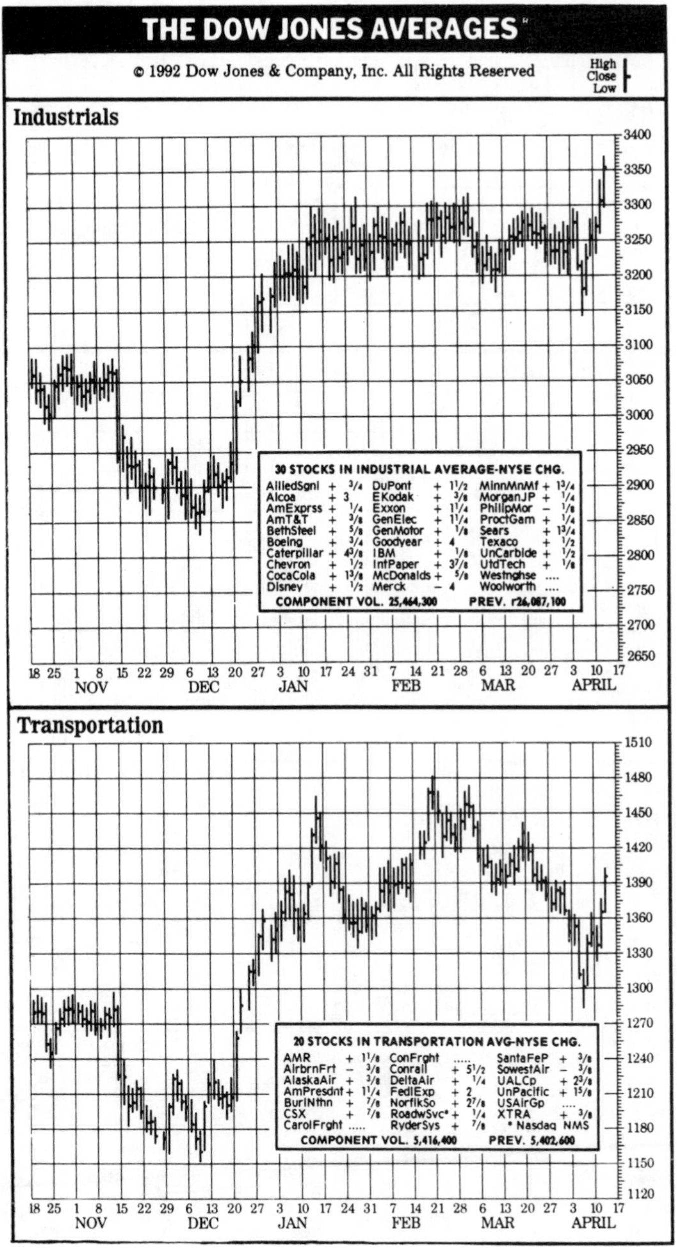

Source: *The Wall Street Journal*, April 16, 1992

Utilities

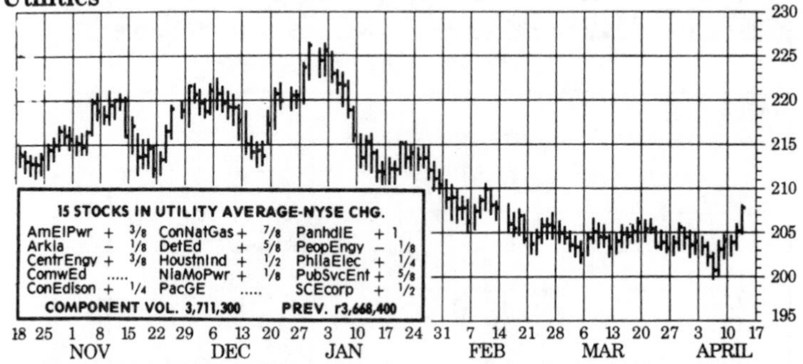

NYSE Volume (9:30 a.m. to 4 p.m. EDT)

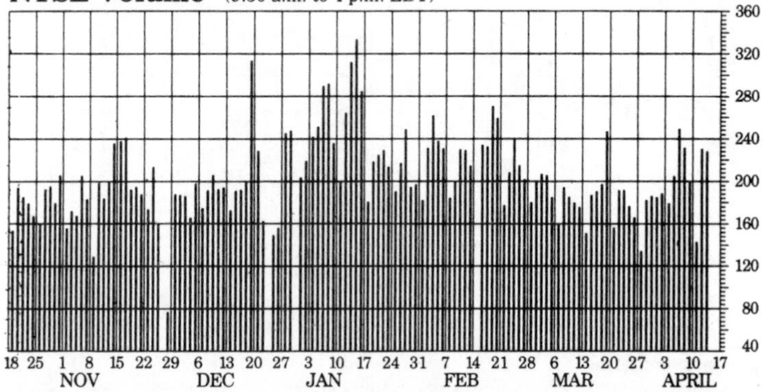

Following are the Dow Jones averages of INDUSTRIAL, TRANSPORTATION and UTILITY stocks with the total sales of each group for the period included in the chart.

DATE	OPEN	10 AM	11 AM	12 NOON	1 PM	2 PM	3 PM	CLOSE	CH	%	HIGH*	LOW*	HIGH[a]	LOW[a]
30 INDUSTRIALS											(THEORETICAL)		(ACTUAL)	
Apr 15	3328.26	3317.75	3328.26	3334.30	3338.55	3331.62	3334.08	3353.76	+ 47.63	+ 1.44	3370.08	3296.51	3354.20	3307.02
Apr 14	3283.54	3279.07	3278.85	3292.93	3302.77	3308.59	3308.36	3306.13	+ 36.23	+ 1.11	3336.54	3259.39	3322.23	3269.45
Apr 13	3254.70	3248.66	3262.08	3259.17	3261.18	3260.51	3262.75	3269.90	+ 14.53	+ 0.45	3283.54	3230.77	3270.57	3248.43
Apr 10	3255.59	3252.01	3258.50	3254.70	3251.12	3256.04	3253.13	3255.37	+ 30.41	+ 0.94	3280.86	3227.64	3262.97	3225.63
Apr 9	3193.43	3184.70	3197.23	3207.74	3214.00	3226.97	3212.21	3224.96	+ 43.61	+ 1.37	3245.08	3171.06	3231.66	3181.80
20 TRANSPORTATION COS.											(THEORETICAL)		(ACTUAL)	
Apr 15	1375.93	1375.56	1379.11	1380.04	1389.76	1386.40	1390.32	1395.74	+ 30.27	+ 2.22	1403.03	1364.72	1395.74	1365.28
Apr 14	1340.81	1346.41	1344.92	1351.27	1358.00	1365.47	1369.96	1365.47	+ 28.21	+ 2.11	1377.06	1334.45	1372.38	1337.07
Apr 13	1346.23	1343.61	1338.19	1334.64	1334.64	1332.03	1336.88	1337.26	– 10.09	– 0.75	1354.07	1323.24	1347.35	1331.65
Apr 10	1349.59	1348.65	1350.52	1348.84	1347.53	1350.15	1351.08	1347.35	+ 8.79	+ 0.66	1365.28	1335.76	1354.07	1338.75
Apr 9	1306.24	1306.61	1317.83	1326.42	1331.28	1337.44	1334.64	1338.56	+ 36.99	+ 2.84	1346.04	1302.50	1340.81	1301.57
15 UTILITIES											(THEORETICAL)		(ACTUAL)	
Apr 15	205.75	206.00	205.81	206.18	206.50	206.87	206.94	207.81	+ 2.63	+ 1.28	208.19	204.81	207.81	205.18
Apr 14	203.87	203.81	204.06	204.37	204.74	205.18	205.50	205.18	+ 1.25	+ 0.61	206.06	202.99	205.75	203.62
Apr 13	203.93	203.87	203.56	203.43	203.24	203.43	203.30	203.93	– 0.19	– 0.09	204.74	202.30	204.18	203.05
Apr 10	203.56	203.37	203.18	203.05	203.24	203.81	203.87	204.12	+ 1.00	+ 0.49	204.81	201.99	204.18	202.93
Apr 9	200.99	200.68	201.30	202.62	202.80	203.05	203.05	203.12	+ 2.38	+ 1.19	204.18	200.05	203.43	200.49
65 STOCKS COMPOSITE AVERAGE											(THEORETICAL)		(ACTUAL)	
Apr 15	1179.12	1177.04	1179.95	1181.70	1185.21	1183.23	1184.75	1190.80	+ 19.25	+ 1.64	1196.25	1169.10	1190.80	1171.55
Apr 14	1159.82	1160.23	1160.00	1164.71	1168.68	1172.05	1173.35	1171.55	+ 15.38	+ 1.33	1181.34	1152.61	1176.72	1156.03
Apr 13	1155.25	1153.31	1154.51	1152.94	1153.21	1152.57	1154.14	1156.17	+ 0.37	+ 0.03	1163.74	1143.42	1156.17	1152.29
Apr 10	1155.98	1154.88	1156.54	1155.25	1154.32	1156.40	1156.08	1155.80	+ 9.19	+ 0.80	1166.00	1146.64	1157.79	1146.66
Apr 9	1130.54	1128.60	1134.42	1139.68	1142.32	1146.70	1142.96	1146.61	+ 19.90	+ 1.77	1153.40	1124.31	1148.13	1126.80

Source: *The Wall Street Journal*, April 16, 1992

Calculating the Dow

Company	*June 11, 1992 NYSE Price*
AT&T	43
Allied Signal	57.875
Alcoa	75.75
American Express	23.875
Bethlehem Steel	16.375
Boeing	44.25
Caterpillar	56.75
Chevron	73.375
Coca Cola	42.75
Disney	36.75
DuPont	52
Eastman Kodak	39.875
E**XX**on	63.25
General Electric	76.625
General Motors	43
Goodyear	66.375
IBM	92
International Paper	66.375
McDonald's	44.5
Merck	49.25
Minnesota Mining & Manufacturing	95.25
JP Morgan	55.25
Philip Morris	72.375
Procter & Gamble	99.375
Sears	41.375
Texaco	66
Union Carbide	27.5
United Technologies	50.625
Westinghouse	18.25
Woolworth	26.125
Total	1616.125

$$\frac{1616.125}{0.48220767} = 3351.51 \text{ (The Dow average on June 11, 1992)}$$

$$\frac{\text{Sum of stock prices}}{\text{Divisor}} = \text{The Dow Jones Industrial Average}$$

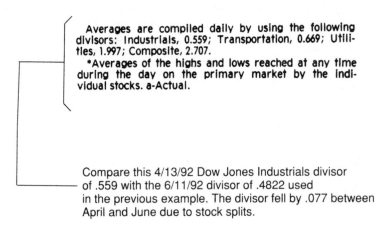

Averages are compiled daily by using the following divisors: Industrials, 0.559; Transportation, 0.669; Utilities, 1.997; Composite, 2.707.
*Averages of the highs and lows reached at any time during the day on the primary market by the individual stocks. a-Actual.

Compare this 4/13/92 Dow Jones Industrials divisor of .559 with the 6/11/92 divisor of .4822 used in the previous example. The divisor fell by .077 between April and June due to stock splits.

Source: *The Wall Street Journal*, April 16, 1992

STOCK MARKET DATA BANK

The Stock Market Data Bank appears daily on the second page (C2) of the third section. See pages 159 through 166 for an example from the Thursday, April 16, 1992 *Wall Street Journal*. It presents a comprehensive summary of stock market activity in seven sections: **Major Indexes, Most Active Issues, Diaries, Price Percentage Gainers and Losers, Volume Percentage Gainers and Losers, Volume Percentage Leaders, and Breakdown of Trading in NYSE Stocks**. Look at it after you have examined the **Markets Diary** in order to get a more detailed view of the previous day's trading activity.

Major Indexes on page 161 lists the Dow averages as well as a variety of other indexes in greater detail than provided in the **Markets Diary** on the first page (Cl) of the third section. These statistics permit you to compare the performance of your own investments with the broadest gauges of stock market activity.

The **Dow Jones Equity Market Index** is a very broad-based index (June 30, 1982=100) of about 700 stocks (see pages 161 and 204).

The **New York Stock Exchange Composite** tracks the movements of all stocks listed on that exchange. Notice that this composite, like most others, is broken out into a number of components.

STOCK MARKET DATA BANK 4/15/92

MAJOR INDEXES

HIGH	LOW (†365 DAY)		CLOSE	NET CHG	% CHG	†365 DAY CHG	% CHG	FROM 12/31	% CHG
DOW JONES AVERAGES									
3353.76	2863.82	30 Industrials	3353.76	+ 47.63	+ 1.44	+ 349.30	+ 11.63	+ 184.93	+ 5.84
1467.68	1129.06	20 Transportation	1395.74	+ 30.27	+ 2.22	+ 229.48	+ 19.68	+ 37.74	+ 2.78
226.15	195.17	15 Utilities	207.81	+ 2.63	+ 1.28	− 11.95	− 5.44	− 18.34	− 8.11
1192.83	1028.33	65 Composite	1190.80	+ 19.25	+ 1.64	+ 120.77	+ 11.29	+ 33.98	+ 2.94
396.64	343.91	Equity Mkt. Index	391.57	+ 3.69	+ 0.95	+ 26.84	+ 7.36	− 0.33	− 0.08
NEW YORK STOCK EXCHANGE									
231.84	202.10	Composite	229.15	+ 1.84	+ 0.81	+ 15.94	+ 7.48	− 0.29	− 0.13
290.02	253.72	Industrials	288.35	+ 2.36	+ 0.83	+ 21.10	+ 7.90	+ 2.53	+ 0.89
102.27	87.76	Utilities	95.72	+ 1.06	+ 1.12	+ 1.45	+ 1.54	− 6.41	− 6.28
212.02	166.15	Transportation	206.70	+ 4.55	+ 2.25	+ 37.27	+ 22.00	+ 4.83	+ 2.39
177.72	147.12	Finance	173.06	+ 0.35	+ 0.20	+ 14.87	+ 9.40	+ 0.38	+ 0.22
STANDARD & POOR'S INDEXES									
420.77	368.57	500 Index	416.28	+ 3.89	+ 0.94	+ 25.83	+ 6.62	− 0.81	− 0.19
499.27	438.51	Industrials	496.40	+ 4.67	+ 0.95	+ 33.28	+ 7.19	+ 3.68	+ 0.75
362.50	277.02	Transportation	355.03	+ 9.70	+ 2.81	+ 75.05	+ 26.81	+ 13.57	+ 3.97
155.70	133.52	Utilities	142.58	+ 1.69	+ 1.20	− 2.52	− 1.74	− 12.58	− 8.11
35.14	28.77	Financials	34.42	+ 0.06	+ 0.17	+ 2.73	+ 8.61	+ 0.32	+ 0.94
154.74	119.18	400 MidCap	145.83	+ 0.27	+ 0.19	+ 17.82	+ 13.92	− 0.76	− 0.52
NASDAQ									
644.92	473.08	Composite	600.03	+ 5.22	+ 0.88	+ 88.72	+ 17.35	+ 13.69	+ 2.33
741.92	523.54	Industrials	666.10	+ 5.61	+ 0.85	+ 90.43	+ 15.71	− 2.85	− 0.43
632.09	522.07	Insurance	603.30	+ 2.92	+ 0.49	+ 18.22	+ 3.11	+ 2.21	+ 0.37
402.20	317.36	Banks	402.20	+ 5.11	+ 1.29	+ 69.34	+ 20.83	+ 51.64	+ 14.73
285.08	208.31	Nat. Mkt. Comp.	265.34	+ 2.37	+ 0.90	+ 39.42	+ 17.45	+ 5.60	+ 2.16
296.32	207.84	Nat. Mkt. Indus.	266.22	+ 2.30	+ 0.87	+ 36.29	+ 15.78	− 1.57	− 0.59
OTHERS									
418.99	356.79	Amex	394.16	+ 2.02	+ 0.52	+ 21.70	+ 5.83	− 0.89	− 0.23
266.85	228.21	Value-Line (geom.)	257.06	+ 1.45	+ 0.57	+ 10.17	+ 4.12	+ 7.72	+ 3.10
212.61	167.00	Russell 2000	199.68	+ 0.77	+ 0.39	+ 20.98	+ 11.74	+ 9.75	+ 5.13
4121.28	3529.97	Wilshire 5000	4044.24	+ 33.66	+ 0.84	+ 312.76	+ 8.38	+ 3.14	+ 0.08

†-Based on comparable trading day in preceding year.

MOST ACTIVE ISSUES

NYSE	VOLUME	CLOSE	CHANGE
Archer-Daniel	2,972,100	24⅜	− 1⅛
Ford Motor Co	2,737,600	40⅞	− ⅛
Gen Motors	2,473,300	39⅞	.....
Sprint	2,255,400	23¾	+ 2¼
IBM	2,215,600	88½	+ ¼
AT&T	2,205,900	42⅞	+ ¼
Glaxo Hldgs	2,148,600	28⅝	− ⅛
Chrysler Corp	1,986,900	18½	+ ⅝
Grace (W R)	1,872,400	35¾	− ⅛
Banc One Corp	1,856,000	44⅜	− 1¼
PepsiCo	1,732,400	35⅜	− ⅛
Conner Prphls	1,692,800	20⅝	+ ½
Merrill Lynch	1,675,800	49¼	− ⅞
RJR Nab Hldg	1,644,400	9¾	+ ⅛
1st Data Cp	1,620,600	23⅝	+ ⅜
NASDAQ			
Centocor	17,076,000	18½	− 12¾
Microsoft Corp	4,657,000	128⅞	+ 11⅞
Xoma Corp	4,426,200	14½	− 4
Intel Corp	2,594,100	53½	+ 1¼
Tele-Comm A	2,447,300	17⅞	+ ⅜
Greenw Pharm	2,043,600	8⅝	− 2⅛
Valley Natl Cp	2,041,800	47⅞	− 1⅞
M C I Comm	2,022,800	33⅜	+ 1¼
Apple Cmptr	1,940,700	60½	+ 1¾
Mens Wearhous	1,835,900	13	.....
Oracle Sys	1,743,600	14⅛	+ ¼
Lotus Dvlp	1,637,900	33¼	− 1⅛
Sun Microsys	1,555,100	28¾	+ 1⅛
AMEX			
Chambrs Dvl A	783,100	7⅞	.....
Parker Parsley	604,900	11½	− ⅜
Fruit Loom Inc	476,400	38⅜	+ ⅝
Echo Bay Mns	441,500	5⅝	− ⅜
Wang Labs B	438,300	5⅛	.....

DIARIES

NYSE	WED	TUE	WK AGO
Issues traded	2,248	2,243	2,234
Advances	1,111	1,220	435
Declines	651	512	1,388
Unchanged	486	511	411
New highs	94	59	9
New lows	20	11	84
zAdv vol (000)	141,646	167,597	52,667
zDecl vol (000)	66,007	42,218	175,597
zTotal vol (000)	228,360	230,620	249,210
Closing tick[1]	+388	+223	+75
Closing Arms[2] (trin)	.80	.60	1.04
zBlock trades	5,161	5,290	5,792
NASDAQ NMS			
Issues traded	4,241	4,238	4,228
Advances	1,214	1,283	600
Declines	971	905	1,819
Unchanged	2,056	2,050	1,809
New highs	140	109	30
New lows	80	86	468
Adv vol (000)	101,581	111,836	61,768
Decl vol (000)	83,610	51,229	152,377
Total vol (000)	218,575	195,596	243,470
Block trades	4,349	3,684	4,551
AMEX			
Issues traded	809	796	818
Advances	300	338	163
Declines	251	230	446
Unchanged	258	228	209
New highs	21	19	11
New lows	9	8	26
zAdv vol (000)	5,519	12,564	3,977
zDecl vol (000)	4,710	3,220	9,581
zTotal vol (000)	13,008	18,935	16,035
Comp vol (000)	16,611	22,310	20,628
zBlock trades	n.a.	285	214

Source: *The Wall Street Journal*, April 16, 1992

PRICE PERCENTAGE GAINERS . . .

NYSE	CLOSE	CHANGE	% CHG
Sahara Casino	3⅞	+ ⅞	+ 29.2
CarriageIndus	6⅞	+ ⅞	+ 14.6
CurraghResou	3⅜	+ ⅜	+ 12.5
Sprint	23¾	+ 2¼	+ 10.5
Schwitzer	9⅜	+ ⅞	+ 10.3
JennyCraig	23⅛	+ 2⅛	+ 10.1
Rohm&Haas	53⅝	+ 4⅞	+ 10.0
Enron.pfJ	260	+ 22½	+ 9.5
SuperiorIndus	54⅛	+ 4⅝	+ 9.3
TCFFncl	20½	+ 1¾	+ 9.3
MaytagCorp	19⅞	+ 1⅝	+ 8.9
CaterpillarInc	53⅞	+ 4⅜	+ 8.8
TalleyIndus	3⅛	+ ¼	+ 8.7
Safeway.wt	3¼	+ ¼	+ 8.3
SizzlerIntl	13¼	+ 1	+ 8.2
Merry-Go-Rnd	11¾	+ ⅞	+ 8.0
BirminghmStl	27	+ 2	+ 8.0
MotorolaInc	82	+ 6	+ 7.9
ChemWaste	18¾	+ 1⅜	+ 7.9
CarlislePlsA	10¼	+ ¾	+ 7.9
NASDAQ NMS			
WashBncp-NJ	5	+ 1	+ 25.0
GeneLabs	7¾	+ 1⅜	+ 21.6
CareGrp.wt	3⅝	+ ⅝	+ 20.8
InfodataSys	3⅞	+ ⅝	+ 19.2
FNBRochstr	6¼	+ 1	+ 19.0
BrynMawrBk	18	+ 2⅞	+ 19.0
TCIIntl	4	+ ⅝	+ 18.5
BankAtlantic	4	+ ⅝	+ 18.5
Baker (J.) Inc	15	+ 2⅛	+ 16.5
FLSHldg.pfA	14½	+ 2	+ 16.0
AndoverBncp	5¾	+ ¾	+ 15.0
MerrillCorp	11¾	+ 1½	+ 14.6
NewImageIndus	5	+ ⅝	+ 14.3
RotechMed	15½	+ 1⅞	+ 13.8
AMEX			
LarizzaIndus	2⅝	+ ⅜	+ 16.7
CavalierHomes	6⅛	+ ¾	+ 14.0
TeneraL.P	2⅜	+ ¼	+ 11.8
PrefHlthCare	12¼	+ 1	+ 8.9
GeneralMicwv	9⅜	+ ¾	+ 8.7

AND LOSERS

NYSE	CLOSE	CHANGE	% CHG
LiveEntmt	2¼	– ¾	– 25.0
LiveEntmt.pf	7	– 2⅛	– 23.3
RobertsnCeco	1¾	– ¼	– 12.5
PHMCorp	23⅛	– 2⅝	– 10.2
CalifREIT	2¼	– ¼	– 10.0
PrideCos.pf	15⅛	– 1⅝	– 9.7
BattleMtGold	6⅛	– ⅝	– 9.3
GlobalNatRes	8⅝	– ⅞	– 9.2
Equimark	4	– ⅜	– 8.6
TeradyneInc	13¾	– 1¼	– 8.3
PharmResou	5¾	– ½	– 8.0
Grainger (W.)	55¼	– 4⅝	– 7.7
Amphenol	7½	– ⅝	– 7.7
EmplyeBenefit	13⅞	– 1⅛	– 7.5
ParkerDrilling	4⅝	– ⅜	– 7.5
NoForkBncp	5¼	– ⅜	– 6.7
OrionPictures	1⅞	– ⅛	– 6.3
AtlasCorp	5⅝	– ⅜	– 6.3
AT&TCap.wt	3¾	– ¼	– 6.3
PaineWebber	19½	– 1¼	– 6.0
NASDAQ NMS			
Centocor.wt	18½	– 24	– 56.5
Centocor	18½	– 12¾	– 40.8
Cherokee	2⅜	– ⅞	– 26.9
XomaCorp	14½	– 4	– 21.6
GreenwPharm	8⅝	– 2⅛	– 19.8
GrantTensor	7	– 1½	– 17.6
FairIsaac	12½	– 2½	– 16.7
CheckTech	2	– ⅜	– 15.8
AmVangrd	8⅞	– 1⅝	– 15.5
InterspecInc	4⅛	– ¾	– 15.4
Geriatrc&Med	4¾	– 13/16	– 14.6
SciCloPharm.wt	3	– ½	– 14.3
ImmuneResp	21	– 3	– 12.5
LaserPac	2⅝	– ⅜	– 12.5
AMEX			
LifetimeProd	1⅞	– ½	– 21.1
AllouHlth.wt	2⅞	– ½	– 14.8
Allou.wtB	1¾	– ¼	– 12.5
CXRCorp	2⅛	– ¼	– 10.5
LittlefieldAdm	11⅞	– 1⅜	– 10.4

VOLUME PERCENTAGE LEADERS

NYSE	VOL	%DIF*	CLOSE	CHANGE
PrptyTrAm	1,012,400	10000.0	10⅜	...
WarnerIns	249,500	2910.4	7½	– ⅜
AthloneIndus	134,200	1787.0	13½	+ ½
ThomasBetts	538,800	1705.5	57⅝	– 1⅛
Rohm&Haas	934,400	1087.6	53⅝	+ 4⅞
Grainger (W.)	497,200	616.5	55¼	– 4⅝
Bass.adr	33,300	527.4	21⅜	+ ⅜
TrinityIndus	358,000	526.3	27	– ½
1stFidelity	695,600	489.6	35¼	+ ½
NatnwdHlth	166,200	458.3	26¾	– ¼
MarshallInd	86,100	457.7	33⅝	+ 1⅛
BancOneCorp	1,856,000	446.8	44⅜	– 1¼
VanKampenIns	42,600	a442.8	14⅜	...
GenPhysics	95,400	424.3	11½	+ ¼
IMOIndus	158,100	393.6	11⅛	– ⅛
CyclopsIndus	76,500	382.4	22⅛	+ ⅛
FranklinTrsbl	167,600	381.2	8¼	+ ⅛
Grace (WR)	1,872,400	362.3	35¾	– ⅛
BritishTelepp	529,200	358.5	22⅜	+ ⅝
Austria1996	61,900	355.2	10⅞	...

*Common stocks of $5 a share or more with average volume over 65 trading days of at least 5,000 shares.
a–has traded fewer than 65 days on any exchange.

NASDAQ NMS	VOL	%DIF*	CLOSE	CHANGE
HomeFncl	157,700	1490.5	32¾	+ ¼
F&CBncshr	85,300	1386.8	12⅝	+ ⅜
DynatechCorp	349,900	1293.6	18	– ¼
Centocor	17,076,000	1171.1	18½	– 12¾
HarmonIndus	151,500	964.5	7	+ ⅛
PsicorInc	101,800	886.2	13½	+ 1
SeibelsBruce	243,100	845.7	5⅝	+ ¼
UnilabCorp	1,145,100	786.3	8⅛	+ ¼
WolfFnclGrp	562,000	754.8	7½	...
XomaCorp	4,426,200	752.7	14½	– 4
CanonInc	49,200	740.9	51	+ 1
Inforum	207,400	723.5	11¼	+ ¼
USTrustCorp	81,400	663.0	44¼	+ ¾
Hologic	328,800	659.3	9⅜	– ⅜
FlexsteelInd	67,700	651.7	13½	...
AmPacific	578,800	641.6	31½	– ⅝
AMEX				
ParkerParsley	604,900	1516.5	11½	– ⅜
CavalierHomes	56,700	785.5	6⅛	+ ¾
WestamBncp	42,500	550.1	20⅝	+ ⅛
Fibreboard	185,300	488.9	7⅜	– ⅝
Baker (Michl)	37,600	440.5	23⅞	– 1

BREAKDOWN OF TRADING IN NYSE STOCKS (9:30 a.m. to 4 p.m. EST)

BY MARKET	Wed	Tues	WK AGO
New York	228,360,000	230,620,000	249,210,000
Midwest	12,520,400	11,779,100	13,236,000
Pacific	8,148,200	7,913,100	8,847,300
NASD	14,684,990	16,944,020	16,299,270
Phila	4,235,100	3,654,600	4,714,600
Boston	3,975,500	3,482,400	4,680,300
Cincinnati	2,585,700	2,523,300	2,676,900
Instinet	256,300	300,200	496,100
Composite	274,766,190	277,216,720	300,160,470

[1]The net difference of the number of stocks closing higher than their previous trade from those closing lower. NYSE trading only.
[2]A comparison of the number of advancing and declining issues with the volume of shares rising and falling. Generally, an Arms of less than 1.00 indicates buying demand, above 1.00 indicates selling pressure.
z NYSE or Amex only

½-HOURLY	Wed	Tues	WK AGO
9:30-10	32,570,000	31,390,000	33,240,000
10-10:30	19,730,000	22,120,000	23,640,000
10:30-11	19,090,000	14,980,000	28,040,000
11-11:30	17,030,000	14,440,000	26,150,000
11:30-12	15,360,000	18,270,000	18,970,000
12-12:30	16,760,000	15,540,000	16,150,000
12:30-1	13,610,000	15,100,000	10,640,000
1-1:30	12,450,000	17,490,000	10,700,000
1:30-2	13,190,000	17,600,000	12,620,000
2-2:30	14,050,000	16,970,000	13,570,000
2:30-3	13,730,000	14,370,000	16,930,000
3-3:30	17,170,000	14,730,000	17,830,000
3:30-4	23,620,900	17,620,000	20,730,000

Source: *The Wall Street Journal*, April 16, 1992

STOCK MARKET DATA BANK 4/15/92

MAJOR INDEXES

HIGH	LOW (†365 DAY)		CLOSE	NET CHG	% CHG	†365 DAY CHG	% CHG	FROM 12/31	% CHG
DOW JONES AVERAGES									
3353.76	2863.82	30 Industrials	3353.76	+ 47.63	+ 1.44	+ 349.30	+ 11.63	+ 184.93	+ 5.84
1467.68	1129.06	20 Transportation	1395.74	+ 30.27	+ 2.22	+ 229.48	+ 19.68	+ 37.74	+ 2.78
226.15	195.17	15 Utilities	207.81	+ 2.63	+ 1.28	− 11.95	− 5.44	− 18.34	− 8.11
1192.83	1028.33	65 Composite	1190.80	+ 19.25	+ 1.64	+ 120.77	+ 11.29	+ 33.98	+ 2.94
396.64	343.91	Equity Mkt. Index	391.57	+ 3.69	+ 0.95	+ 26.84	+ 7.36	− 0.33	− 0.08
NEW YORK STOCK EXCHANGE									
231.84	202.10	Composite	229.15	+ 1.84	+ 0.81	+ 15.94	+ 7.48	− 0.29	− 0.13
290.02	253.72	Industrials	288.35	+ 2.36	+ 0.83	+ 21.10	+ 7.90	+ 2.53	+ 0.89
102.27	87.76	Utilities	95.72	+ 1.06	+ 1.12	+ 1.45	+ 1.54	− 6.41	− 6.28
212.02	166.15	Transportation	206.70	+ 4.55	+ 2.25	+ 37.27	+ 22.00	+ 4.83	+ 2.39
177.72	147.12	Finance	173.06	+ 0.35	+ 0.20	+ 14.87	+ 9.40	+ 0.38	+ 0.22
STANDARD & POOR'S INDEXES									
420.77	368.57	500 Index	416.28	+ 3.89	+ 0.94	+ 25.83	+ 6.62	− 0.81	− 0.19
499.27	438.51	Industrials	496.40	+ 4.67	+ 0.95	+ 33.28	+ 7.19	+ 3.68	+ 0.75
362.50	277.02	Transportation	355.03	+ 9.70	+ 2.81	+ 75.05	+ 26.81	+ 13.57	+ 3.97
155.70	133.52	Utilities	142.58	+ 1.69	+ 1.20	− 2.52	− 1.74	− 12.58	− 8.11
35.14	28.77	Financials	34.42	+ 0.06	+ 0.17	+ 2.73	+ 8.61	+ 0.32	+ 0.94
154.74	119.18	400 MidCap	145.83	+ 0.27	+ 0.19	+ 17.82	+ 13.92	− 0.76	− 0.52
NASDAQ									
644.92	473.08	Composite	600.03	+ 5.22	+ 0.88	+ 88.72	+ 17.35	+ 13.69	+ 2.33
741.92	523.54	Industrials	666.10	+ 5.61	+ 0.85	+ 90.43	+ 15.71	− 2.85	− 0.43
632.09	522.07	Insurance	603.30	+ 2.92	+ 0.49	+ 18.22	+ 3.11	+ 2.21	+ 0.37
402.20	317.36	Banks	402.20	+ 5.11	+ 1.29	+ 69.34	+ 20.83	+ 51.64	+ 14.73
285.08	208.31	Nat. Mkt. Comp.	265.34	+ 2.37	+ 0.90	+ 39.42	+ 17.45	+ 5.60	+ 2.16
296.32	207.84	Nat. Mkt. Indus.	266.22	+ 2.30	+ 0.87	+ 36.29	+ 15.78	− 1.57	− 0.59
OTHERS									
418.99	356.79	Amex	394.16	+ 2.02	+ 0.52	+ 21.70	+ 5.83	− 0.89	− 0.23
266.85	228.21	Value-Line (geom.)	257.06	+ 1.45	+ 0.57	+ 10.17	+ 4.12	+ 7.72	+ 3.10
212.61	167.00	Russell 2000	199.68	+ 0.77	+ 0.39	+ 20.98	+ 11.74	+ 9.75	+ 5.13
4121.28	3529.97	Wilshire 5000	4044.24	+ 33.66	+ 0.84	+ 312.76	+ 8.38	+ 3.14	+ 0.08

†-Based on comparable trading day in preceding year.

Source: *The Wall Street Journal*, April 16, 1992

MOST ACTIVE ISSUES

NASDAQ			
Centocor	17,076,000	18½	− 12¾
Microsoft Corp	4,657,000	128⅞	+ 11⅞
Xoma Corp	4,426,200	14½	− 4
Intel Corp	2,594,100	53½	+ 1¼
Tele-Comm A	2,447,300	17⅞	+ ⅜
Greenw Pharm	2,043,600	8⅝	− 2⅛
Valley Natl Cp	2,041,800	47⅞	− 1⅞
M C I Comm	2,022,800	33⅜	+ 1¼
Apple Cmptr	1,940,700	60½	+ 1¾
Mens Wearhous	1,835,900	13	.....
Oracle Sys	1,743,600	14⅛	+ ¼
Lotus Dvlp	1,637,900	33¼	− 1⅛

← 17 million shares of Centocor change hands under heavy selling pressure.

Source: *The Wall Street Journal*, April 16, 1992

Since this index includes all stocks listed (almost 2,000), rather than a sample like the Dow, you may wonder why it isn't preferred to the Dow. Because most investors aren't interested in all the stocks listed, just the most important ones. For that reason, the next measure of the market strikes a compromise.

The Standard and Poor's 500 includes some stocks not listed on the New York exchange and is a composite. Since it weights (measures the importance of) its constituent companies by their market value (share price multiplied by the number of share outstanding), unlike the Dow which weights by price alone, and since it includes far more companies then the Dow, most observers prefer this index to the Dow.

NASDAQ (National Association of Securities Dealers Automated Quotations) Stocks are traded over-the-counter (electronically), not on an organized exchange, and usually represent ownership of smaller and less widely-held companies.

The **AMEX** index measures all the stocks (almost 1,000) traded on the American Stock Exchange. Most of these companies were traditionally between the New York and over-the-counter companies in size, but this distinction has evaporated with the rapid growth of many of the over-the-counter companies. This exchange was once known as the Curb Exchange when its business was conducted in the street and it had no premises.

The **Value-Line** composite is prepared by the investment service of the same name. It contains about 1,700 stocks traded on the two major exchanges as well as over-the-counter.

The **Russell 2000** tracks stocks issued by smaller companies.

The **Wilshire 5000** measures all the 5,000 or so stocks that are actively traded on the two major exchanges as well as over-the-counter. This excludes the one or two thousand stocks that are not actively traded.

Now, return to **Most Active Issues** (C2) on page 161, which lists the day's most heavily traded stocks on the three major markets: New York Stock Exchange (NYSE), the National Association of Security Dealers Automated Quotation (NASDAQ) system in the over-the-counter (OTC) market, and the American Stock Exchange (AMEX). For instance, under NASDAQ you can see that over 17 million shares of Centocor changed hands on Wednesday, April 15, 1992 under heavy selling pressure.

The **Diaries** provide another important measure of the day's trading activity: *advances versus declines, new highs versus new lows,* and the *volume of the stocks advancing and declining.* On Wednesday, April 15, 1992, 1,111 issues advanced and 651 declined on the New York

DIARIES

NYSE	WED	TUE	WK AGO
Issues traded	2,248	2,243	2,234
Advances	1,111	1,220	435
Declines	651	512	1,388
Unchanged	486	511	411
New highs	94	59	9
New lows	20	11	84
zAdv vol (000)	141,646	167,597	52,667
zDecl vol (000)	66,007	42,218	175,597
zTotal vol (000)	228,360	230,620	249,210
Closing tick[1]	+388	+223	+75
Closing Arms[2] (trin)	.80	.60	1.04
zBlock trades	5,161	5,290	5,792

Advancing Issues led Declining Issues

New Highs exceeded New Lows

Positive (+) tick indicates more stocks advanced than declined in last trade

Arms Index of less than one (1) indicates buying pressure

Source: *The Wall Street Journal*, April 16, 1992

exchange. The advancers were far more actively traded: 141,646,000 to 66,007,000. These figures confirm the Dow's big gain that day (47.63 points), and so does the margin of stocks that hit new highs (94) over those that hit new lows (20).

Closing tick and *closing Arms (trin)* are even finer measures of stock market strength or weakness.

A tick is a measure of movement in closing stock prices: a positive (+) tick means prices were rising at the end of the day, and the negative (-) tick indicates falling prices. The closing tick nets all stocks whose last trade was higher than the previous trade (+) on the NYSE against all stocks whose last trade was lower (-); a " + " closing tick means that more stocks were rising than falling and a " - " closing tick means that more stocks were falling than rising. On April 15, 1992, 388 more stocks were rising than falling at their last trade, and so the closing tick for the day was +388.

The Arms index (trin), named for Richard W. Arms, Jr., its creator, measures market strength. A trin less than one (0.80 on April 15, 1992) indicates money flowing into stocks (bullish sign), while a trin greater than one indicates money flowing out of stocks (bearish sign). The Arms index is computed by dividing two ratios:

$$\frac{\dfrac{\text{Advances}}{\text{Declines}}}{\dfrac{\text{Advance Volume}}{\text{Decline Volume}}} = \frac{\dfrac{1{,}111}{651}}{\dfrac{141{,}646}{66{,}007}} = 0.80 = \text{Arms index}$$

In this example, a trin of less than one indicates that the (denominator) ratio of the *volume* of advancing stocks to declining stocks (141,646/66007) exceeded the (numerator) ratio of advancing stocks to declining stocks (1,111/651) *and therefore a disproportionate share of the trading volume was in advancing stocks (a bullish sign).* A trin of more than one would indicate the opposite.

This example, drawn from the April 16, 1992 *Journal*, is confusing because it employs actual trading data for April 15, 1992. Consider, instead, the simple hypothetical examples on the next page. The first illustrates a bull (rising) market, the second a bear (falling) market.

AND LOSERS

NASDAQ NMS					
Centocor.wt	18½	–	24	–	56.5
Centocor	18½	–	12¾	–	40.8
Cherokee	2⅜	–	⅞	–	26.9
XomaCorp	14½	–	4	–	21.6
GreenwPharm	8⅝	–	2⅛	–	19.8
GrantTensor	7	–	1½	–	17.6
FairIsaac	12½	–	2½	–	16.7
CheckTech	2	–	⅜	–	15.8
AmVangrd	8⅞	–	1⅝	–	15.5
Intersp ecInc	4⅛	–	¾	–	15.4
Geriatrc&Med	4¾	–	13/16	–	14.6
SciCloPharm.wt	3	–	½	–	14.3
ImmuneResp	21	–	3	–	12.5
LaserPac	2⅝	–	⅜	–	12.5

Centocor loses almost half its value in one day → Centocor

Source: *The Wall Street Journal,* April 16, 1992

Use hypothetical numbers of your own to create additional examples. This will establish your understanding of the Arms index.

Bull Market

$$\frac{\frac{\text{Advances}}{\text{Declines}}}{\frac{\text{Advance volume}}{\text{Decline volume}}} \quad \frac{\frac{1}{1}}{\frac{2}{1}} = \frac{1}{2}$$

Although advances and declines were equal, advance volume was twice decline volume and therefore a trin of 1/2 is a bullish sign.

$$\frac{\frac{\text{Advances}}{\text{Declines}}}{\frac{\text{Advance volume}}{\text{Decline volume}}} \quad \frac{\frac{1}{2}}{\frac{1}{1}} = \frac{1}{2}$$

Although declines exceeded advances, advance volume equaled decline volume and a trin of 1/2 remained a bullish sign.

Bear Market

$$\frac{\frac{\text{Advances}}{\text{Declines}}}{\frac{\text{Advance volume}}{\text{Decline volume}}} \quad \frac{\frac{1}{1}}{\frac{1}{2}} = 2$$

Although advances and declines were equal, decline volume was twice advance volume and therefore a trin of 2 is a bearish sign.

$$\frac{\frac{\text{Advances}}{\text{Declines}}}{\frac{\text{Advance volume}}{\text{Decline volume}}} \quad \frac{\frac{2}{1}}{\frac{1}{1}} = 2$$

Although advances exceeded declines, decline volume equaled advance volume and a trin of 2 remained a bearish sign.

As an investor, you want to know the percentage performance of your stocks. A $1 rise in the price of a stock that you purchased at $100 a share is an event to note, but if you had paid $2 a share for the stock, the same $1 rise is a cause for celebration. In the first case your investment increased by 1 percent, in the second by 50 percent. In **Price Percentage Gainers and Losers** (opposite page) you can track this daily. On April 15, 1992 Centocor (NASDAQ), the most heavily traded issue that day, lost about 40% of its value (ouch!). You may notice it was a bad day for other biotech stocks, too.

Volume Percentage Leaders represent the stocks that traded the largest volume of shares on April 15. The percentage gain refers to the increase in volume over the average for the previous 65 trading days.

The **Breakdown of Trading in NYSE Stocks** on page 166 provides trading volume on all stock exchanges of securities listed on the New

York Stock Exchange, as well as trading volume by half-hours. As mentioned earlier in the discussion on how to compile the Dow, shares listed on the NYSE trade on a variety of exchanges as well as electronically, and therefore the composite of all trades will be greater than the New York volume. Trading of all NYSE stocks on all exchanges was a composite volume of 274,766,190 shares on April 15, 1992.

Finally, the **Diaries** component of the **Stock Market Data Bank** on page 163 listed the number of stocks that hit new highs and lows (i.e., the number that closed higher or lower than at any time in the past 52 weeks). You saw that on April 15, 1992, 94 reached new highs and 20 reached new lows. **NYSE Highs/Lows** (in the front-page indexes of the first and last sections) lists these stocks. Consider the example on the next page from the Thursday, April 16, 1992 *Journal.*

THE ODD-LOT TRADER

So far this discussion has proceeded without regard to the magnitude of individual investments, except for the observation that companies split

BREAKDOWN OF TRADING IN NYSE STOCKS (9:30 a.m. to 4 p.m. EST)

BY MARKET	Wed	Tues	WK AGO
New York	228,360,000	230,620,000	249,210,000
Midwest	12,520,400	11,779,100	13,236,000
Pacific	8,148,200	7,913,100	8,847,300
NASD	14,684,990	16,944,020	16,299,270
Phila	4,235,100	3,654,600	4,714,600
Boston	3,975,500	3,482,400	4,680,300
Cincinnati	2,585,700	2,523,300	2,676,900
Instinet	256,300	300,200	496,100
Composite	274,766,190	277,216,720	300,160,470

[1]The net difference of the number of stocks closing higher than their previous trade from those closing lower; NYSE trading only.
[2]A comparison of the number of advancing and declining issues with the volume of shares rising and falling. Generally, an Arms of less than 1.00 indicates buying demand, above 1.00 indicates selling pressure.
z-NYSE or Amex only.

½-HOURLY	Wed	Tues	WK AGO
9:30-10	32,570,000	31,390,000	33,240,000
10-10:30	19,730,000	22,120,000	23,640,000
10:30-11	19,090,000	14,980,000	28,040,000
11-11:30	17,030,000	14,440,000	26,150,000
11:30-12	15,360,000	18,270,000	18,970,000
12-12:30	16,760,000	15,540,000	16,150,000
12:30-1	13,610,000	15,100,000	10,640,000
1-1:30	12,450,000	17,490,000	10,700,000
1:30-2	13,190,000	17,600,000	12,620,000
2-2:30	14,050,000	16,970,000	13,570,000
2:30-3	13,730,000	14,370,000	16,930,000
3-3:30	17,170,000	14,730,000	17,830,000
3:30-4	23,620,000	17,620,000	20,730,000

Source: *The Wall Street Journal,* April 16, 1992

their stock chiefly in order to keep its price within the small investor's reach. Remember that round lots are trades of 100 shares whose commission per share is lower than that on *odd-lot* (less than 100 shares) transactions. Yet many small investors still trade in odd lots because they cannot afford to deal in round lots. For instance, Merck closed at $151.25 on Wednesday April 15, 1992, putting the cost of a round-lot purchase at $15,125 ($151.25 multiplied by 100) and out of the reach of many small investors.

NYSE HIGHS/LOWS

Wednesday, April 15, 1992

NEW HIGHS – 94

AirProd s	CrownCork	KemprHiIn	RohmHaas
AlaP pfA	Dexter	KnightRid	RussBerr
Alcoa	EatonCp	Lawtin s	Ryder
ABusP s	Empresica n	LbtyTerm n	Schwitzr
AmCapInco	Enron s	La Pacif	SearsRoeb
Amer T&T	FstAm	MBIA	Sears pfP
AmSth s	FstData n	MagmaCpr wt	SherwinW
AtlEnergy	FstUnionCp	MagmaCppr	SIGNET
BancFlorida	FishrSci n	MarshInd	Singer n
BassPubl n	FleetNrstr	Mattel s	SourceCap pf
Bemis s	GnDynam	Maytag	SpringsInd
BenetonGp	GenSignal	MetEd pfG	Standex
BrazilEqF n	Goodrich	NatlCity	SuperInds
BritAir	Gdrich pfD	NII pf	Sysco
CBS	Goodyear	NewsCorp	TRW Inc
CabotCp	GtLkCh s	Norwest	TRW 4.40pf
CarriageInd	Guilfrd s	OxfordInd	TimeWrn pfD
Caterpllr	HerculesInc	ParamtCom	TycoToys
ChileFd	HiltonHtl	Phelps Dod	Unifi s
ChileTel	IP Timber	PhEl 9.87pf	UnCarbde
Chrysler	ImperChem	Potlatch	VF Corp
Circus s	IpalcoEnt	PutnamHiInc	Whirlpool
Coltec n	KansPL wi	RTZ	Whitakr n
Conrail		Raytheon s	

NEW LOWS – 20

ASA	CyprSemi	Homestake	NuvQIInc n
Ameron	EmplBenft	Horsham g	PS Group
BattleMt	GATX Cp pf	LiveEnt	PennCtrl
ChockFON	HancFb s	MaunaLoa	PrideCos
ConsFrt pf	HiShear	Nerco	Sprint pf

s-Split or stock dividend of 25 per cent or more in the past 52 weeks. High-low range is adjusted from old stock. n-New issue in past 52 weeks and does not cover the entire 52 week period.

ODD-LOT TRADING

NEW YORK – The New York Stock Exchange specialists reported the following odd-lot transactions (in shares):

	Customer Purchases	Short Sales	Other Sales	Total Sales
April 14, 1992	1,442,971	3,328	778,603	781,931

Odd-lot purchases exceeded odd-lot sales on April 15,1992.

Source: *The Wall Street Journal*, April 16, 1992

Many market analysts used to believe that odd-lot transactions were a contrary (negative) indicator, because they saw the small investor as a market follower who buys more as the market peaks and sells more as it bottoms out (the opposite of the savvy, big time trader who gets in at the bottom and out at the top). Therefore, according to this wisdom, a high ratio of odd-lot buying to selling is a sign of a market peak (time to sell), while the opposite indicates a market trough (time to buy). However, since a great many small investors in recent years have abandoned odd-lots in favor of mutual funds, this omen has become less significant to analysts.

The *Journal* provides a daily record of **Odd-Lot Trading** for the day preceding the previous trading day. You'll find it beneath NYSE Highs/Lows. See the example on page 167 from the Thursday, April 16, 1992 issue that indicated sales of 781,931 and purchases of 1,442,971 on April 14, 1992. The market had rallied to new highs in mid-April of 92, and now the small investors were pouring in. Was it time for the smart money to leave the market?

A more detailed report appears on Mondays (also beneath NYSE Highs/Lows). See for yourself when examining the **Odd-Lot Trading** report from the Monday, April 13, 1992 *Wall Street Journal.* Odd-lot purchases (1,307,501 shares) exceeded odd-lot sales (719,289) on Thursday, April 9, 1992 in NYSE trading by odd-lot specialists and shares purchased (4,435,320) exceeded shares sold (4,213,568) by all NYSE member firms for the week ended Friday, March 27, 1992.

FOLLOW YOUR STOCK

Suppose now that you have studied the various stock market indicators and indexes, decided that the time was right to get into the market, and did so. You will want to follow the progress of your investment. Here's how you do it.

If you own shares of Anheuser-Busch, you can follow their daily performance in *The Wall Street Journal* by turning to **New York Stock Exchange Composite Transactions**. Recall that this composite report includes a small amount of trading activity on regional exchanges. You'll find a reference to all exchanges in the index on the front pages of the first (Al) and third (Cl) sections.

In the accompanying Thursday, April 16, 1992 excerpts (page 170 and 171), the first and second columns tell you the highest and lowest value

ODD-LOT TRADING

NEW YORK—The New York Stock Exchange specialists reported the following odd-lot transactions (in shares):

	Customer Purchases	Short Sales	Other Sales	Total Sales
April 9, 1992	1,307,501	40,496	678,793	719,289

New York Stock Exchange odd-lot trading for all member firms dealing in odd-lots, for the week ended March 27, 1992:

	Shares	Values
Customers' Orders to Buy ..	4,435,320	$232,706,756
Customers' Orders to Sell ..	4,213,568	$174,723,830
Customers' Short Sales	399,894	$18,014,834

Odd-lot purchases exceeded odd-lot sales on April 9, 1992

Round-Lot transactions (in shares) for the week ended March 27, 1992:

	Purchases	Sales (incl. Short Sales)	Short Sales
Total	884,145,680	884,145,680	63,391,700
For Member Accounts:			
As Specialists-a,b	86,797,600	82,089,740	25,683,240
As Floor Traders	17,300	19,500	....
Others-a	112,753,609	124,984,315	19,282,380

a-Including offsetting round-lot transactions arising from odd-lot dealer activity by specialists and other members.

b-Includes transactions effected by members acting as Registered Competitive Market Makers.

American Stock Exchange round-lot and odd-lot trading statistics for the week ended March 27, 1992:

	Purchases	Sales (incl. Short Sales)	Short Sales
Total	70,810,575	70,810,575	1,457,873
For Member Accounts:			
As Specialists	7,616,970	7,560,985	7,200
As Floor Traders	187,100	181,600	47,500
Others	4,581,077	6,070,375	407,400
Customer odd-lots	70,215	94,995	....

Source: *The Wall Street Journal*, April 13, 1992

of one share of the stock in the past 52 weeks, expressed in dollars and fractions of a dollar. Thus, **Anheuser-Busch** stock was as low as $47.375 (47-3/8) and as high as $62 (62) in the year preceding April 15, 1992.

Footnotes and symbols, including arrows and underlining, are fully explained in the box on the lower left of the first page of the Composite listings.

The third and fourth columns give the company name and stock ticker symbol **(BUD)**.

The fifth column of data reports the latest annual cash dividend of $1.12 per share. The dividend is expressed as a percentage of the closing price in the next column ($1.12/$56.875 = 1.97 percent, rounded to 2.0 percent).

NEW YORK STOCK EXCHANGE COMPOSITE TRANSACTIONS

Quotations as of 5 p.m. Eastern Time
Wednesday, April 15, 1992

Anheuser Busch → (points to the AnheuserB row)

	52 Weeks Hi	52 Weeks Lo	Stock	Sym	Div	Yld %	PE	Vol 100s	Hi	Lo	Close	Net Chg
	29⅝	**18⅜**	**AmBarrick**	**ABX**	**.10a**	**.4**	**34**	**4586**	**24⅞**	**23¼**	**23⅜**	**−1½**
	47¾	38⅛	AmBrand	AMB	1.75	3.7	12	3079	47¾	46⅝	46¾	−1
	33½	31	AmBrand pf		2.75	8.5	...	3	32⅜	32⅜	32⅜	− ⅛
	40⅝	28½	AmBldgMaint	ABM	.96	2.7	13	144	36	35⅞	36	− ⅛
s▲	30	16⅜	AmBusnPdts	ABP	.70	2.3	20	204	31⅛	29¾	30½	+ ½
	20⅛	17⅝	AmCapBdFd	ACB	1.68	8.5	...	137	19⅞	19⅝	19⅞	+ ⅛
	20¼	17	AmCapCvSec	ACS	1.35e	7.0	...	15	19⅜	19⅛	19⅜	+ ¼
▲	8	6⅝	AmCapIncTr	ACD	.84a	10.3	...	468	8⅛	8	8⅛	+ ¼
	69	53⅜	AmCyanmd	ACY	1.50	2.3	17	1291	64¾	63¾	64½	+ ⅛
	34¼	27⅞	AmElecPwr	AEP	2.40	7.5	12	2196	32	31½	32	+ ⅜
	30⅝	18	AmExpress	AXP	1.00	4.4	14	13007	22⅞	22½	22⅞	+ ¼
	45⅝	36⅜	AmGenerl	AGC	2.08	4.9	10	1102	42⅜	42	42⅜	+ ¼
	8⅝	7½	AmGvIncFd	AGF	.77a	9.3	...	309	8⅜	8⅛	8¼	...
	11	9	AmGvIncoP	AAF	.96a	8.9	...	481	10¾	10½	10¾	+ ¼
	11	10	AmGvTermTr	AGT	.94	9.0	...	88	10⅝	10½	10½	...
	37	25¼	AmHlthProp	AHE	2.69	9.5	14	612	28⅞	28¼	28¼	− ¼
s	30	17⅜	AmHeritgLf	AHL	.84	3.3	13	140	25½	25⅛	25½	+ ⅜
	86¼	57¾	AmHomePdts	AHP	2.60	3.3	18	4439	81⅞	79¾	80	−1⅝
n	19	16½	AmIncHldg	AIH		...	...	93	18	17¾	18	+ ⅜
	101⅞	78⅝	AmIntGroup	AIG	.50	.6	12	3547	87½	86¼	87⅜	+ ½
n	10⅜	9½	AmMunTermTr2	BXT	.62	6.3	...	8	9⅞	9⅞	9⅞	− ⅛
	10⅝	9⅝	AmMunTermTr	AXT	.65e	6.4	...	25	10⅛	10	10⅛	+ ⅛
	11¾	9⅜	AmOpIncoFd	OIF	1.00a	9.1	...	275	11⅛	10⅞	11	...
	8⅝	6¼	AmPrecInd	APR	.20	2.6	16	76	7¾	7⅝	7¾	...
	43⅞	24¼	AmPresidnt	APS	.60	1.8	9	938	34½	33½	34¼	+1¼
	11½	7⅛	AmRE Ptnrs	ACP	1.00	12.7	6	98	8⅛	7⅞	7⅞	− ⅛
	8¼	5	AmRltyTr	ARB		...	...	2	6⅛	6⅛	6⅛	...
	3½	1½	AmShipBldg	ABG		...	...	130	2⅞	2½	2⅞	+ ⅛
s	46⅛	26	AmStores	ASC	.70	2.0	10	1494	34⅜	33¾	34⅜	+1
n	15⅞	14¾	AmStratInco	ASP	1.35	9.2	...	40	14⅞	14¾	14¾	...
▲	42¾	35⅛	AmT&T	T	1.32	3.1	107	22059	43⅛	42⅝	42⅞	+ ¼
	11½	3⅜	AmWasteSvc	AW		...	14	608	4	3⅝	3⅞	+ ⅛
	28½	19⅜	AmWaterWks	AWK	.92	4.3	10	223	21⅞	21½	21⅝	...
	19	14⅝	AmWaterWks pf		1.25	7.2	...	z100	17⅜	17⅜	17⅜	− ½
	14¾	7½	Ameriscribe	ACR		...	17	202	11¼	10⅝	11⅛	− ¼
	66	55¾	Ameritech	AIT	3.52	5.9	13	2557	59⅝	59¼	59⅝	+ ⅛
▼	43¼	30	Ameron	AMN	1.28	4.2	19	60	30½	29¾	30½	...
	2½	¼	vjAmesDeptStr	ADD		...	...	561	7/16	⅜	7/16	...
	17⅜	11½	Ametek	AME	.68	4.3	18	916	16¼	15⅞	16	+ ⅛
	55	41¾	Amoco	AN	2.20	4.9	19	5616	45¼	44¼	45¼	+ ¾
	68¾	47	AMP	AMP	1.52	2.5	25	1858	60¾	59⅞	60⅝	+ ⅞
	9	**5⅞**	**AmpcoPgh**	**AP**	**.30**	**4.1**	**...**	**126**	**7¼**	**6⅞**	**7¼**	**+ ⅜**
n	**10⅝**	**7**	**Amphenol**	**APH**		**...**	**...**	**409**	**8⅛**	**7⅜**	**7½**	**− ⅝**
	12⅛	4⅝	AMRE	AMM	.12	1.5	35	198	8	7⅜	7¾	− ⅜
	6¼	3½	AMREP	AXR		...	...	41	6¼	6¼	6¼	...
	25⅝	15¼	AmscoInt	ASZ		...	22	1368	22	21	21¼	...
s▲	27⅜	17½	AmSouthBcp	ASO	1.04	3.8	12	568	27½	27	27⅜	+ ¼
	5⅜	2⅞	Anacomp	AAC		...	12	918	4⅝	4½	4⅝	...
	33⅛	18½	AnadrkPete	APC	.30	1.4	38	898	22⅜	22⅛	22⅛	− ⅛
	12½	7	AnalogDevcs	ADI		...	145	1087	10⅛	10	10⅛	+ ⅛
	40¼	32	Angelica	AGL	.92	2.7	14	32	34⅜	34	34	− ½
	62	47⅜	AnheuserB	BUD	1.12	2.0	17	5407	57¼	56⅜	56⅞	+ ⅜
n	36½	12	AnnTaylor	ANN		...	58	313	18	17⅝	17⅞	+ ½
	47¾	24	AnthemElec	ATM		...	22	257	46¼	45¾	46	+ ⅛
	14¾	7½	AnthonyInd	ANT	.44a	3.8	18	9	11¾	11⅝	11⅝	...
	45¼	34¾	AonCp	AOC	1.68	3.9	12	678	43	42⅝	42¾	− ⅛
	42½	36⅜	AonCp pf		3.04	7.4	...	26	41¼	41	41¼	+ ¼
	20¾	12	ApacheCp	APA	.28	1.9	20	1322	15¼	14¾	15	+ ⅛
	12	11⅛	ApexMunFd	APX	.88	7.7	3	953	11⅝	11⅜	11⅜	− ⅛
	102	88	AppalchPwr pf		8.12	8.4	...	z40	97	97	97	− ⅝
	92½	80½	AppalchPwr pf		7.40	8.2	...	z16300	89⅞	89⅞	89⅞	+ ⅛
	29¾	26⅝	AppalchPwr pf		2.65	9.5	...	4	28	27¾	28	+ ⅝
	12	4⅜	AppliedMagn	APM		...	...	404	7½	7⅛	7⅜	+ ⅛
	27¼	20⅛	Aquarion	WTR	1.62	7.9	15	70	21	20⅝	20⅝	− ⅜
	33¼	21⅞	ArcherDan	ADM	.10b	.4	15	29721	25⅞	24	24⅜	−1⅛
	10⅜	5½	ArcticAlsk	ICE		...	8	232	8¼	7⅞	8⅛	...
n	16¼	12	ArgntnaFd	AF	.06e	.4	...	316	15½	15⅛	15¼	...
	28⅞	24½	ArkPower pf		2.40	8.7	...	23	27¾	27½	27½	...
	19⅜	7¾	Arkla	ALG	1.08	13.7	88	4598	8	7¾	7⅞	− ⅛
	39⅜	29½	Arkla pf		3.00	9.3	...	65	32⅝	32⅛	32⅛	− ½
	6⅜	4	Armco	AS		...	...	2092	5⅞	5¾	5⅞	+ ¼
	39¼	30½	Armco pf		4.50	11.9	...	10	37¾	37⅝	37¾	+ ⅝
	34½	23¼	ArmstrngWld	ACK	1.20	3.7	30	1407	33	32½	32¾	+ ¾

NYSE EXTENDED TRADING

April 15, 1992

	Total Volume	Market Value
First crossing session	44,600	b-$2,829,525
Second session (baskets)	1,281,150	$52,147,500

MOST ACTIVE ISSUES

(First session)

Issue	Sym.	a-Volume 100s	NYSE Close	Comp. Close
Royal Dutch	RD	74	80⅞	80⅞
Merck & Co	MRK	73	151¼	151¼
Advest Group	ADV	50	7⅛	7⅛
Schering-Plou	SGP	40	56	56¼
Bausch & Lomb	BOL	30	49¼	49¼
Digital Equip	DEC	21	44½	44½
Lilly (Eli)	LLY	15	72⅜	72⅜
Glaxo Hldgs	GLX	15	28⅝	28⅝
Crompton Knl	CNK	11	40⅞	40⅞
Texas Utilities	TXU	11	37⅞	37⅞

a-From 4:15 p.m. to 5:00 p.m. Eastern time, NYSE only. b-WSJ calculation, estimate.

	52 Weeks Hi	52 Weeks Lo	Stock	Sym	Div	Yld %	PE	Vol 100s	Hi	Lo	Close	Net Chg
	31⅞	26⅝	BRE Prop	BRE	2.40	8.0	15	40	30	29¾	29⅞	+ ⅛
	4¼	**1¾**	**BRT RltyTr**	**BRT**		**...**	**...**	**30**	**2¼**	**2⅛**	**2¼**	**+ ⅛**
	9	4⅞	Bairnco	BZ	.20	3.0	16	181	6⅞	6¾	6¾	− ⅛
	19	15⅞	BakrFentrs	BKF	1.73e	9.2	...	78	18⅞	18⅝	18⅞	+ ¼
	30¼	15⅞	BakrHughs	BHI	.46	2.5	16	9243	19⅛	18⅝	18¾	− ¼
	25	19⅞	BaldorElec	BEZ	.48	2.0	20	39	24⅛	24	24⅛	...
	39½	25¾	Ball Cp	BLL	1.20	3.3	15	424	36¼	35½	36⅛	+ ⅜
	8¼	2⅞	BallyMfg	BLY		...	...	767	6¼	6	6	− ¼
	11⅜	4⅛	BaltimrBcp	BBB		...	...	422	5⅞	5½	5¾	...
	34⅝	28½	BaltimrGE	BGE	2.10	6.6	14	2411	31¾	31⅛	31⅝	+ ⅜
	65	52½	BaltimrGE pfB		4.50	7.1	...	z100	63	63	63	...
▲	7¾	2⅜	BancFla	BFL		...	...	605	8⅜	7¾	8	+ ¼
	50	32	BancOne	ONE	1.16b	2.6	14	18560	45⅝	44¼	44⅜	−1¼
	3¾	**5/16**	**BancTexas**	**BTX**		**...**	**...**	**442**	**2⅜**	**2¼**	**2⅜**	**+ ⅛**
	27⅛	24⅜	BancoBilV pf			...	...	874	25⅜	25¼	25⅜	...
	32¾	23¾	BancoBilV	BBV	1.73e	6.3	6	2	27⅜	27⅛	27⅜	...
	55	38¾	BancoSantdr	STD	2.17e	4.8	8	257	45¼	44¾	45¼	+1¼
s	52	37½	BcpHawii	BOH	1.20	2.6	11	1750	45½	44¼	45½	+1¼
	134½	93	Bandag	BDG	1.20b	.9	22	240	131	129½	131	...
	18⅛	14¼	BangorHyd	BGR	1.32	7.5	13	9	17½	17½	17½	...
	20½	6½	BankBost	BKB		...	...	5678	18⅜	17⅞	18¼	− ⅛
	38¾	23⅞	BankBost pfA		3.30e	8.7	...	2	38¼	38	38	...
	36⅞	22	BankBost pfB		3.18e	8.8	...	5	36	36	36	+ ¼
	64¼	38¾	BankBost pfC		5.83e	9.2	...	z6500	63⅜	63	63⅜	+ ⅛
	41⅝	24¾	BankNY	BK	1.52	3.7	32	5908	41½	40⅝	40¾	+ ½
	42½	33⅞	BankNY adj pfA		3.29e	7.9	...	25	41¾	41½	41½	− ¼
	46¼	30⅝	BankAmer	BAC	1.30	3.0	9	9329	43⅜	42½	42⅝	− ⅜
	46¾	38	BankAmer pfA		3.25e	7.5	...	59	43⅜	43⅜	43⅜	...
	79½	64⅝	BankAmer pfB		6.00	8.0	...	4	75⅜	75⅛	75¼	− ⅛
	29	25	BankAmer pfF		2.41	8.9	...	75	27¼	27	27⅛	+ ⅛
	58	45½	BankAmer pfG		3.25	5.8	...	34	56	55½	55¾	− ¼
	27¼	25¼	BankAmer pfH		2.25	8.7	...	103	26	25¾	25¾	− ¼
	26⅜	24½	BankAmer pfK		2.09	8.4	...	141	25	24¾	25	...
	68	45⅝	BankTrst	BT	2.80	5.3	7	1797	53⅝	52⅝	52⅞	− ⅜
	24¾	24	BkTr pur un			...	...	148	24⅝	24½	24⅝	+ ⅛
	10¾	6¾	BannerAero	BAR		...	13	101	8½	8⅜	8½	+ ¼
	1⅛	5/16	BanyanMtgInv	VMG		...	...	199	11/16	⅝	11/16	...
	27⅝	24⅜	Barclays pr		2.78	10.4	...	92	27	26¾	26¾	− ¼
	28	24	Barclays prB		2.72	10.2	...	92	26⅝	26⅜	26⅝	+ ⅛
	28½	24⅜	Barclays pfC		2.81	10.1	...	143	27¾	27⅜	27¾	+ ⅛
	28¾	24¾	Barclays pfD		2.87	10.3	...	135	28⅛	27⅞	28	− ⅛
	33	20⅝	Barclays	BCS	1.92e	8.0	18	38	24	23¾	24	+ ½
	34	22	Bard CR	BCR	.48	1.7	26	1802	28⅝	28⅛	28¼	− ¼
	38	29⅞	BarnesGp	B	1.40	4.3	12	177	32⅜	31½	32⅜	+1⅛
	37½	24½	BarnettBks	BBI	1.32	3.7	18	3211	35½	34⅝	35⅜	+ ⅝
	75¾	55¼	BarnettBks pf		4.50	6.1	...	45	74	73½	74	+2
	57½	45½	BarnettBks C			...	...	50	56¾	54¾	56¾	+2⅜
	7½	4½	BaroidCp	BRC	.20	3.7	16	783	5⅜	5⅜	5⅜	− ¼
n▲	21	14½	Bass	BAS	.83e	3.9	12	333	21⅜	21	21⅜	+ ⅜

Source: *The Wall Street Journal*, April 16, 1992

	n	10⅝	7	**Amphenol**	**APH**	...	...		**409**	**8⅛**	**7⅜**	**7½**	**– ⅝**
		12⅛	4⅝	AMRE	AMM	.12	1.5	35	198	8	7⅜	7¾	– ⅜
		6¼	3½	AMREP	AXR	...	...		41	6¼	6¼	6¼	...
		25⅝	15¼	AmscoInt	ASZ		...	22	1368	22	21	21¼	...
	s▲	27⅜	17½	AmSouthBcp	ASO	1.04	3.8	12	568	27½	27	27⅜	+ ¼
		5⅜	2⅞	Anacomp	AAC		...	12	918	4⅝	4½	4⅝	...
		33⅛	18½	AnadrkPete	APC	.30	1.4	38	898	22⅜	22⅛	22⅛	– ⅛
		12½	7	AnalogDevcs	ADI		...	145	1087	10⅛	10	10⅛	+ ⅛
		40¼	32	Angelica	AGL	.92	2.7	14	32	34⅝	34	34	– ½
Anheuser Busch ⟶		62	47⅜	AnheuserB	BUD	1.12	2.0	17	5407	57¼	56⅜	56⅞	+ ⅜
	n	36½	12	AnnTaylor	ANN		...	58	313	18	17⅝	17⅞	+ ½
		47¾	24	AnthemElec	ATM		...	22	257	46¼	45¾	46	+ ⅛
		14¾	7½	AnthonyInd	ANT	44a	3.8	18	9	11¾	11⅝	11⅝	...
		45¼	34¾	AonCp	AOC	1.68	3.9	12	678	43	42⅝	42¾	– ⅛

Source: *The Wall Street Journal*, April 16, 1992

The seventh column shows the price-earnings (P/E) ratio, which is obtained by dividing the price of the stock by its earnings per share. (This important statistic is discussed in detail in Chapter 8.) On April 15, Anheuser-Busch's stock was worth 17 times the profits per share of stock.

The eighth column informs you of the number of shares traded that day, expressed in hundreds of shares. Thus, 540,700 shares of Anheuser-Busch traded on April 15,1992. If a z appears before the number in this column, the figure represents the actual number (not hundreds) of shares traded.

The ninth, tenth, and eleventh columns reveal the stock's highest, lowest, and closing (last) price for the trading day. Thus, on Wednesday, April 15, 1992, Anheuser-Busch stock traded as high as 57-1/4 and as low as 56-3/8 before closing at 56-7/8.

The last column provides the change in the closing price of the stock from the price at the close of the previous day. You can see that this stock closed at a price 37.5 cents (3/8 of a dollar) higher than the previous closing price.

You may wonder why share prices are quoted with figures such as 3/8 which must be converted into fractions of a cent. Because trading is usually conducted in round lots of 100 shares, and payment for a round lot eliminates the problem. For instance, 56-3/8 X 100 = $5,637.50.

Shares of other companies, usually smaller than those listed on the NYSE, trade on the American Stock Exchange (AMEX). *The Wall Street Journal's* AMEX report, called **American Stock Exchange Composite Transactions**, is identical in form to **NYSE Composite Transactions.**

Over-the-counter (OTC) stocks are not traded on an exchange. Instead, dealers have established a market for them using a computer network referred to as *NASDAQ* (National Association of Securities Dealers Automated Quotations). You can follow this market in **NASDAQ National Market Issues**, which is similar to the New York and American Exchange listings. Take a look at the reprint from the Thursday, April 16, 1992 *Journal* (on the next page, using **Microsoft (MSFT)** as an example.

The first two columns give the high and low prices for the past year. The column after the price-earnings ratio lists sales in hundreds, informing you that 4,657,000 shares of Microsoft traded on Wednesday, April 15,1992.

The next three columns provide the high (129-1/4), low (126-1/2) and closing (128-7/8) prices of the day, and the final column tells you that Microsoft's stock closed at a price $11.875 higher than its price at the previous close.

OTC stocks traded less actively than the National Market Issues are quoted currently with bid (what buyers are willing to pay) and ask (what sellers are willing to offer) prices, although all OTC stocks will eventually be quoted with closing prices.

With this information, you can track the performance of any share of stock traded on the New York or American exchanges or the OTC market.

MUTUAL FUNDS

But at this point you may feel that the discussion has strayed from the goals established in Chapters 1 and 8. If you've decided to pick stocks instead of gold, can the wisdom of that decision be offset by the selection of the wrong stock? If so, is there a way to get into the stock market without purchasing a particular stock?

Yes, and yes. Mutual funds provide a way to invest in the stock market indirectly. Investment companies establish mutual funds to pool the resources of many investors and thus create a large, shared portfolio of investments. Individuals invest in mutual funds by purchasing shares in the fund from the investment company. These mutual funds are open-ended, which means the investment companies are always willing to sell more shares to the public and to redeem outstanding shares. Therefore, the pool of capital, the number of investors, and the number of shares outstanding can expand or contract.

NASDAQ NATIONAL MARKET ISSUES

	52 Weeks Hi	Lo	Stock	Sym	Div	Yld %	PE	Vol 100s	Hi	Lo	Close	Net Chg
▼	7⅛	2¼	**MachTech**	**MTEC**		...	**5**	**524**	**2⅜**	**2⅛**	**2⅛**	**−⅛**
s▲	31⅜	24	MadsnGas	MDSN	1.76	5.6	14	51	31¾	30¾	31⅜	...
	14¾	6¼	MagainPharm	MAGN		...	...	110	7	6½	6½	...
	11	5⅞	MagicSftwr	MGICF		...	...	110	9⅛	8⅞	9⅛	+⅜
	32	19¼	MagmaPwr	MGMA		...	15	667	22	21	21¾	+¼
▲	14⅛	10⅜	MagnaGp	MAGI	.68	4.8	51	2826	14¾	13⅞	14¼	+⅛
	26⅝	6¾	MagnaInt g	MAGAF	.10e	...	...	5828	25¼	24½	25	+⅜
s	21	8⅞	MailBoxEtc	MAIL		...	48	1497	18¾	18¼	18¾	+¼
s	17	12¼	MakitaCp	MKTAY	.14e	1.0	25	18	14⅜	14¼	14¼	+⅛
	7¼	1½	**MellonRes**	**MLRC**		...	...	**223**	**6½**	**6**	**6¼**	**−½**
	4¼	1⅞	Manatrn	MANA		...	21	39	4	3 15/16	3 15/16	−1/16
	24½	17¼	Manitowc	MANT	1.00	4.6	18	613	22¼	20¾	21¾	−½
s	48	28⅞	MfrsNtl	MNTL	1.32	2.8	13	739	48	46½	47¾	+1
	5¼	1¾	**MarblFnl**	**MRBL**		...	...	14	5¼	4½	4½	−¾
	29¾	15	Marcam	MCAM		...	33	319	23	22	22¾	+1
	18	**15**	**MarcusCp**	**MRCS**	**.33**	**1.8**	**12**	**83**	**18**	**17**	**18**	**+1**
	8½	**3½**	**MariettaCp**	**MRTA**		...	...	**939**	4½	**4**	4½	+½
	1⅞	1/32	**MarineDrill**	**MDCO**		...	...	**29**	3/16	3/16	3/16	+1/32
	9½	5¾	MarkCtrl	MRCC		...	14	73	9¼	8¾	9⅛	...
▲	25¾	17	MkTwainB	MTWN	1.04	4.0	11	52	26	25	25¾	...
	28¼	14	MarkelCp	MAKL		...	10	80	26¾	26⅝	26⅝	+⅜
	7	3½	MktFacts	MFAC	.20	4.0	10	11	5	5	5	...
	14¼	6½	MarqstMed	MMPI		...	...	293	8⅜	8⅛	8⅜	+¼
	23½	16	MarquetEl	MARQA		...	...	32	17	16¼	17	...
s	16¾	7¾	MarsmPharm	MSAM		...	136	259	9¾	9¼	9½	−¼
	22	13	MarshSupr B	MARSB	.44	2.7	13	92	17	16¼	16¼	−¼
s	23½	13½	MarshSupr A	MARSA	.44	2.6	14	109	17¼	16½	17¼	...
	56	35½	MarshIlsly	MRIS	1.32	2.5	12	92	54	53¼	53¼	−½
	16¼	9½	MaryldBcp	MFSL	.24	1.6	9	3	15¾	15¼	15¼	−½
	11	4¾	MascoInd	MASX		...	...	486	9⅞	9⅝	9⅝	−¼
	2 1/16	13/32	MassMicrsys	MMIC		...	...	715	1 7/32	1 1/16	1⅛	+1/32
	27½	16	Massbk	MASB	.50	1.8	23	117	27½	27	27¼	+¼
	1 3/16	5/16	**MasstrSys**	**MSCO**		...	...	**1098**	¾	21/32	¾	+⅛
	18¼	8½	MatrixPharm	MATX		...	...	105	10¼	9½	10¼	+¼
	30¼	17	MatrixSvc	MTRX		...	23	42	18¾	18½	18½	+¾
	6⅜	2¾	MattStudio	MATT		...	...	268	4⅝	4⅜	4½	+⅛
	6	3¼	MaxErmRestr	MAXE	t	...	26	15	5½	5½	5½	+¼
	4⅜	1⅝	Maxco	MAXC		...	9	245	4¼	3¾	3⅞	+⅛
	11½	6⅜	MaxicareHlth	MAXI		...	71	54	10¼	9¾	10	+¼
	29¾	14¼	MaximInPdt	MXIM		...	28	2476	23¾	23¼	23¾	+⅜
	12¼	1⅝	Maxtor	MXTR		...	...	4133	12	11½	11¾	...
	17	11¼	MaxwlLab	MXWL	.40e	3.2	9	41	12⅜	11½	12⅜	−⅛
	7⅞	4⅞	MaynrdOil	MOIL		...	...	24	5⅝	5⅜	5⅜	...
	11¾	6	MetropS&L	MSEA		...	9	21	11¼	10⅞	10⅞	−⅜
	29¼	16	MeyerFred	MEYR		...	14	1891	26	25¼	25¾	+½
	6¼	2½	MiamiSubs	SUBS		...	...	875	5⅛	5	5⅛	+1/16
s	23⅝	12½	MichlFood	MIKL	.20	1.3	14	1107	15¾	14⅞	14⅞	−⅝
	26	**6**	**MichaelStr**	**MIKE**		...	**42**	**4582**	**23⅝**	**21⅝**	**23¼**	**+2⅛**
	52	21	MichNtl	MNCO	2.00	4.0	15	966	50½	49½	50	+¼
	25¼	**10¾**	**MicroHlth**	**MCHS**		...	**24**	**336**	**15½**	**14½**	**14½**	−1
	15¾	5¾	MicroAge	MICA		...	19	986	13	12½	12½	...
	14½	5	Microcom	MNPI		...	...	308	11¼	11	11	...
	13¾	7⅞	Microdyne	MCDY		...	16	603	12½	12	12¼	−¼
	30¼	9¾	Micrografx	MGXI		...	32	256	27¼	26¼	27¼	+½
	3⅛	**¾**	**Microlog**	**MLOG**		...	...	**100**	1½	1¼	1⅜	−⅛
	9¾	5⅜	Micronics	MCRN		...	6	583	6⅜	6	6⅛	+⅛
	17¾	5½	Micropolis	MLIS		...	164	1976	11½	11	11½	...
	17	9¾	Microprose	MPRS		...	...	413	16¼	14⅞	15	−½
	7½	4⅛	MicrosSys	MCRS		...	15	55	7½	7¼	7¼	−¼
	3⅜	**1**	**Microsemi**	**MSCC**		...	**10**	**120**	**2**	**1⅞**	**2**	**+⅛**
s	**133¼**	**68½**	**Microsoft**	**MSFT**		...	**43**	**40570**	**129¼**	**126½**	**128⅞**	**+11⅞**
	23	15¾	MidAmInc	MIAM	.96	4.3	23	185	22½	22	22⅛	−⅛
	18⅞	6½	MidAtlMed	MAMS		...	15	726	10¾	10⅛	10½	+¼
	9¾	4	MidConnBk	MIDC	.20	2.8	12	2	7¾	7¼	7¼	+¼
	11	6½	MidSouthIns	MIDS	.24	2.4	6	25	10½	10⅛	10⅛	−⅛
	14	7½	MidStS&L	MSSB		...	13	2	12	12	12	...
	11½	6¾	MidSouth	MSRR		...	14	111	10¾	10⅝	10⅝	...
▲	30	24	MidsexWtr	MSEX	1.92	6.5	13	15	30¼	29¾	29¾	+1¼
	9⅜	3½	Midlantc	MIDL		...	...	2403	7⅞	7½	7¾	...
	7¾	**3⅝**	**Midwesco**	**MFRI**		...	**24**	**24**	**6**	**6**	**6**	−½
	36	24¾	MdwGmProd	MWGP	.70	2.2	16	39	32½	31½	32	−½
	4¾	2½	MillerBldg	MTIK	.10	2.8	13	35	3⅞	3⅝	3⅝	...
	22½	15	MillerHrm	MLHR	.52	2.6	25	156	19⅞	19⅝	19⅝	...
	13⅛	2¾	Millfeld	SHOE		...	...	15	2¾	2¾	2¾	−⅛
	10¼	4¼	Millicom	MILL		...	...	134	7	6⅝	7	...
	59	42	MineSftyAp	MNES	.88	1.9	15	7	45¼	44¼	45¼	+⅜
s	18¼	10	Minntch	MNTX		...	32	135	15½	14¾	15¼	+½
	20⅝	7⅞	MipsCptr	MIPS		...	...	871	11⅜	11	11⅜	+⅜
	12⅛	7	Missimer	MSMR		...	...	1056	8½	7⅞	8⅛	+¼
	45¼	22	MitekSurg	MYTK		...	48	120	25½	23	25½	...
	134	80¾	Mitsui&Co	MITSY	1.05e	1.2	...	6	88½	88¼	88½	+1¾
	18½	13	MoblGsSv	MBLE	.88	5.3	11	5	17¾	16¾	16¾	−¼
	13¾	6¾	MoblTelcm	MTEL		...	...	648	9⅞	9⅝	9⅝	...
	13½	7½	MobleyEnvr	MBLYA		...	28	12	8½	8⅜	8½	−¼
s	21¼	10¾	ModnCtrls	MOCO	.16	1.2	22	40	13½	12½	13¼	+¼
	36¼	**19¼**	**ModineMfg**	**MODI**	**.76**	**2.3**	**22**	**1854**	**33¼**	**30**	**32⅝**	**+2⅛**

Source: *The Wall Street Journal*, April 13, 1992

	9¾	5⅜	Micronics	MCRN		...	6	583	6⅜	6	6⅛	+⅛	
	17¾	5½	Micropolis	MLIS		...	164	1976	11½	11	11½	...	
	17	9¾	Microprose	MPRS		...	...	413	16¼	14⅞	15	−½	
	7½	4⅛	MicrosSys	MCRS		...	15	55	7½	7¼	7¼	−¼	
	3⅜	**1**	**Microsemi**	**MSCC**		...	**10**	**120**	**2**	**1⅞**	**2**	**+⅛**	
s	**133¼**	**68½**	**Microsoft**	**MSFT**		...	**43**	**40570**	**129¼**	**126½**	**128⅞**	**+11⅞**	← Microsoft
	23	15¾	MidAmInc	MIAM	.96	4.3	23	185	22½	22	22⅛	−⅛	
	18⅞	6½	MidAtlMed	MAMS		...	15	726	10¾	10⅛	10½	+¼	
	9¾	4	MidConnBk	MIDC	.20	2.8	12	2	7¾	7¼	7¼	+¼	
	11	6½	MidSouthIns	MIDS	.24	2.4	6	25	10½	10⅛	10⅛	−⅛	
	14	7½	MidStS&L	MSSB		...	13	2	12	12	12	...	
	11½	6¾	MidSouth	MSRR		...	14	111	10¾	10⅝	10⅝	...	

Source: *The Wall Street Journal*, April 13, 1992

The value of the fund's assets divided by the number of shares outstanding determines the value of each share. Any gain in the fund's portfolio is passed through to the individual investors. Purchases of additional shares by new investors do not reduce the value of existing shares because the purchaser makes a cash contribution equal to the value of the share.

Which raises an important point: mutual fund shares are not traded on the open market. They are purchased from and sold back to the investment company.

Mutual funds are popular with individual investors because they permit diversification in a wide variety of securities with very small capital outlay. In addition, a mutual fund lets you take advantage of the professional management skills of the investment company.

When you purchase a mutual fund share, you own a fraction of the total assets in the portfolio. The price of that share is equal to its *net asset value* (net value of assets held by the fund divided by the number of mutual fund shares outstanding plus any sales commission.). As with any pooled investment in common stock, price appreciation and dividends earned will determine the gain in net asset value.

Mutual funds are classified according to whether or not they charge a sales commission called a *load*. Every day, **Mutual Fund Quotations lists** the major funds available to investors, and it can be found using the indexes on the front pages of the first (Al) and third (Cl) sections. Pages 175 and 176 provide excerpts from the Thursday, April 16, 1992 edition of the *Journal*.

No-Load (NL) Funds don't require a commission to purchase or sell the shares of the fund. There is, however, a "management fee" on these funds' and all other funds' assets that is generally less than 1 percent of the investment. Net asset values are calculated after management takes its fee.

You can tell if a fund has no load by the symbol *NL* under the offer price. Even if the fund's offer price is the same as its net asset value, absence of the "NL" symbol indicates a sales commission (load). This is explained below.

Front-End Loaded Funds charge a one-time admission or sales fee to purchasers of their shares as well as the management fee levied by all funds. This "sales" or commission fee can be as high as 8 percent, which will effectively reduce your overall rate of return depending on how long you hold the fund. A *p* after the fund's name indicates there is a distribution charge, or front-load, on the fund.

MUTUAL FUND QUOTATIONS

	NAV	Offer Price	NAV Chg
ST GIA	9.66	9.96	...
ST GIB	9.66	9.66	...
TxFH p	15.39	16.18	...
USGv p	15.71	16.52	−.01
Vance Exchange:			
CapE	156.98	NL	+1.01
DBst	84.15	NL	+.64
Divrs	162.17	NL	+.82
EBos	195.08	NL	+.90
ExFd	233.29	NL	+1.42
FdEx	142.16	NL	+.53
ScFld	119.78	NL	+.77
Vanguard Group:			
AssetA	13.28	NL	+.05
BdMkt	9.77	NL	−.01
Convrt	10.85	NL	+.05
EqInc	12.45	NL	+.13
Explr	39.86	NL	+.22
Morg	12.22	NL	+.10
Prmcp	15.22	NL	+.14
V Pref	9.15	NL	+.01
Quant	16.29	NL	+.09
STAR	12.52	NL	+.06
TC Int	26.21	NL	+.24
TCUsa	27.84	NL	+.20
GNMA	10.30	NL	...
HYCorp	7.33	NL	...
IGCorp	8.65	NL	...
STCorp	10.81	NL	−.01
STFed	10.20	NL	−.01
ST Tr	10.12	NL	−.01
IT Tr	10.16	NL	−.02
LT Tr	9.97	NL	−.01
Idx 500	39.30	NL	+.37
IdxExt	15.98	NL	+.07
IdxEur	10.10	NL	+.10
IdxPac	7.24	NL	+.16
IdxInst	39.91	NL	+.38
SmCap	13.00	NL	+.04
MuHY	10.47	NL	+.01
MuInt	12.55	NL	+.01
MunLd	10.50	NL	+.01
MuLg	10.65	NL	+.01
MInLg	11.96	NL	...
MuShf	15.56	NL	...
Cal Ins	10.62	NL	+.01
NJIns	10.88	NL	+.01
NYIns	10.20	NL	...
OhioIn	10.77	NL	+.02
PennIn	10.61	NL	...
VSPE r	12.70	NL	+.07
VSPG r	8.63	NL	−.09
VSPH r	34.12	NL	−.17
VSPS r	19.48	NL	+.21
VSPT r	16.17	NL	+.05
WellsI	17.50	NL	+.07
Welltn	18.78	NL	+.12
Wndsr	12.36	NL	+.08
Wnds II	15.24	NL	+.12
WldInt	9.81	NL	+.11
WldUS	14.89	NL	+.06
Venture Advisers:			
IncPl	4.90	5.14	...
Muni t	9.43	9.43	+.01
NY Ven	9.99	10.49	+.04
RPFB t	6.69	6.69	−.01
RPFE t	24.93	24.93	−.05
Vista Funds:			
CapGr	24.77	25.94	+.05
GvInc	11.47	12.01	−.01
GrInc	26.72	27.98	+.18
NY TF	11.02	11.54	+.02
TF Inc	11.25	11.78	+.04
Volumet	15.37	NL	+.08
Voyageur Fds:			
AZIns	10.33	10.85	+.02
CO TF	10.26	10.68	...
GrSt fp	24.18	25.66	+.19
MNIns f	9.98	10.48	...
MNInt f	10.62	10.92	...
MNTF f	11.97	12.57	...
US Gv f	10.33	10.85	−.01
WallSt	7.20	7.50	+.01
Warburg Pincus:			
CapAp	12.91	NL	+.07
EGth	17.83	NL	+.02
FixInc	9.69	NL	−.01
GblFxd	10.44	NL	−.06
IntEqu	13.11	NL	+.14
IntGvt	10.87	NL	−.02
NYMu	9.97	NL	+.02
Weiss Peck Greer:			
Tudor	25.10	NL	+.18
Govt	10.36	NL	+.01
Gwth	130.06	NL	+.49
GrInc	24.99	NL	+.16
Westcore:			
BalInv	17.98	18.83	+.12
BasVl	21.92	22.95	+.25
BdPlu	15.67	16.41	−.01
IntBd	10.14	10.62	...
LT Bd	10.59	11.09	...
Midco	15.16	15.87	+.11
ModVl	13.44	14.07	+.12
ST Bd	....	....	...
Westwood Funds:			
Balan	10.67	11.11	+.07
Equity	14.80	15.42	+.19
IntBd	10.20	10.63	...
WmBlGr	9.25	NL	+.05
WmBlIn	10.61	NL	...
William Penn:			
PennS p	10.60	11.13	+.12
PATF	10.63	11.16	...
US Gov	10.32	10.83	+.01
Wood Struthers:			
Neuw	14.39	NL	+.13
Pine	12.08	NL	+.07
WinFI	10.15	10.15	...
WinG t	11.09	11.09	+.14
Woodward Fds:			
Bond	10.37	10.85	...
GrVal	10.22	10.70	+.10
IntBd	10.41	10.90	...
Intrns	10.65	11.18	+.04
Opport	10.97	11.48	+.07
World Funds:			
NwpTlg	12.46	13.12	+.13
VontEP	12.67	13.34	+.07
VontblV	11.82	12.44	+.03
Wright Funds:			
CurIn	10.57	NL	...
GvOb	12.63	NL	−.02
InBlCh	11.03	NL	+.09
JrBlCh	14.66	NL	+.15
NearB	10.55	NL	−.01
QulCor	14.71	NL	+.11
SIBlCh	16.40	NL	+.03
TotRet	12.24	NL	−.01
YamGlb	7.51	7.88	+.06
Zweig Funds:			
StratA	12.80	13.54	+.07
ZS AppA	12.22	12.93	+.04
ZS GvA p	9.81	10.30	...
ZS P A p	12.57	13.30	+.07
StratB	12.81	12.81	+.07
ZS AppB	12.21	12.21	+.04
ZS GvB	9.80	9.80	...
ZS P B	12.56	12.56	+.07

e-Ex-distribution. f-Previous day's quotation. s-Stock split or dividend. x-Ex-dividend. NL-No load. p-Distribution costs apply, 12b-1 plan. r-Redemption charge may apply. t-Both p and r footnotes apply.

Source: *The Wall Street Journal*, April 16, 1992

Back-End Loaded Funds levy a fee of up to 8 percent when the shares are sold back to the investment company. An *r* indicates this *redemption* charge. Some back-loaded funds vary their fees according to the length of time the shares are held. If you sell your shares after one year, the fee may be as high as 8 percent. But if you hold the shares for a long time (say, 30 years), no fee may be charged. (Remember that *all* funds have built-in management fees in addition to any loads.)

Therefore, the net asset value and offer price of a back-loaded fund may be identical, yet the fund may still charge you a sales commission when it redeems your shares.

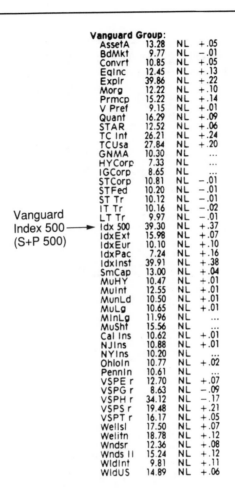

Vanguard Group:			
AssetA	13.28	NL	+.05
BdMkt	9.77	NL	−.01
Convrt	10.85	NL	+.05
EqInc	12.45	NL	+.13
Explr	39.86	NL	+.22
Morg	12.22	NL	+.10
Prmcp	15.22	NL	+.14
V Pref	9.15	NL	+.01
Quant	16.29	NL	+.09
STAR	12.52	NL	+.06
TC Int	26.21	NL	+.24
TCUsa	27.84	NL	+.20
GNMA	10.30	NL	...
HYCorp	7.33	NL	...
IGCorp	8.65	NL	...
STCorp	10.81	NL	−.01
STFed	10.20	NL	−.01
ST Tr	10.12	NL	−.01
IT Tr	10.16	NL	−.02
LT Tr	9.97	NL	−.01
Idx 500	39.30	NL	+.37
IdxExt	15.98	NL	+.07
IdxEur	10.10	NL	+.10
IdxPac	7.24	NL	+.16
IdxInst	39.91	NL	+.38
SmCap	13.00	NL	+.04
MuHY	10.47	NL	+.01
MuInt	12.55	NL	+.01
MunLd	10.50	NL	+.01
MuLg	10.65	NL	+.01
MInLg	11.96	NL	...
MuSht	15.56	NL	...
Cal Ins	10.62	NL	+.01
NJIns	10.88	NL	+.01
NYIns	10.20	NL	...
OhioIn	10.77	NL	+.02
PennIn	10.61	NL	...
VSPE r	12.70	NL	+.07
VSPG r	8.63	NL	−.09
VSPH r	34.12	NL	−.17
VSPS r	19.48	NL	+.21
VSPT r	16.17	NL	+.05
WellsI	17.50	NL	+.07
Welltn	18.78	NL	+.12
Wndsr	12.36	NL	+.08
Wnds II	15.24	NL	+.12
WldInt	9.81	NL	+.11
WldUS	14.89	NL	+.06

Vanguard Index 500 (S+P 500) → Idx 500

Source: *The Wall Street Journal,* April 16, 1992

When both redemption and distribution fees are charged, the fund is identified by a *t* after the fund's name.

If there is no letter following the fund name and the offer price exceeds the net asset value, it is impossible to tell from the listing how the fund is loaded; the mutual fund company can provide that information to you.

Loaded funds are sold through brokers, which explains the commission fee. The investment company contracts with the broker to act as the fund's marketer.

Since no-load funds are directly marketed and have no outside sales force, there is no commission fee. In order to invest in a no-load fund, you must select the fund (e.g., in response to a newspaper ad or direct mail solicitation) and contact the investment company directly. A broker customarily will not act for you in the purchase of no-load funds because he or she will not receive a commission fee of any kind.

Some companies offer many funds, each with its own special objective. Take the *Vanguard Group* (opposite page), for example. In the first column, NAV stands for net asset value (per share). As you recall, this is calculated by totaling the market value of all securities owned by the fund, subtracting the liabilities (if any), and then dividing by the number of fund shares outstanding. In short, NAV equals the dollar value of the pool per mutual fund share. For instance, at the close of business on April 15, 1992, Vanguard Groups Index 500 fund, which invests only in the S & P 500, had a net asset value of $39.30. The last column informs you that this was a 37 cent gain from the previous day.

Notice that the offer price of $39.30 is the only figure given because the Index 500 Fund is a no-load fund. Also note that for $39.30 you could have bought a "share" in the S & P 500. Imagine the cost of buying a share in each of these 500 companies.

The *Journal* publishes a report daily on the third-to-last page of the third (C) section called **Mutual Fund Scorecard**. (See the example from the Thursday, April 16, 1992 *Wall Street Journal* on page 178). It lists the top and bottom performers of a wide variety of mutual funds. Here is a list of some of the different kinds of funds that are covered in the *Journal's* **Mutual Fund Scorecard**:

- A-Rated Bond
- Balanced
- BBB-Rated Bond
- Capital Appreciation
- Closed End Bond
- Closed End Equity
- Convertible Securities
- Equity Income
- General Municipal Bond
- Ginnie Mae
- Global
- Growth
- Growth and Income
- High Current Yield
- International
- Money Market
- Natural Resources and Gold
- Short-Term Municipal Bond
- Small Company Growth
- Specialty and Miscellaneous
- U. S . Government Bond
- Variable Annuity Bond
- Variable Annuity Equity
- World Income

Mutual Fund Scorecard/Money Market

INVESTMENT OBJECTIVE: Holds financial instruments with average maturity of 90 days or less; intends to keep constant net asset value

(Ranked by 12-month return)	NET ASSET VALUE[1] MAR. 31	TOTAL RETURN[2] IN PERIOD ENDING MAR. 31				ASSETS DEC. 31 (In millions)
		1 MONTH	SINCE 12/31	12 MONTHS	5 YEARS	
TOP 15 PERFORMERS						
Sessions:Riverside MM[3]	$1.00	0.36%	1.10%	6.20%	**%	$171.0
Elfun Money Mkt[3,5,6]	1.00	0.36	1.13	5.84	**	47.6
Infinity:Pegasus Prime[3,6]	1.00	0.39	1.20	5.83	**	205.3
Alger:Money Market[3,6]	1.00	0.34	1.10	5.76	44.37	151.8
Dreyfus Worldwide Dlr[3]	1.00	0.37	1.13	5.74	**	8119.3
Olde Premium MM[3,7]	1.00	0.33	1.01	5.71	**	274.1
Emerald:Prime Shares[3]	1.00	0.37	1.12	5.64	**	571.2
GW Sierra:Global Inc MM[3]	1.00	0.34	1.08	5.62	**	80.3
Evergreen MM Trust[3]	1.00	0.36	1.13	5.60	**	397.1
Fidelity Spartan MM[3]	1.00	0.37	1.16	5.59	**	5334.8
Nth Am Sec Tr:MM[3]	1.00	0.32	1.03	5.54	**	3.0
AARP Hi Ql Mon[3,5,6]	1.00	0.30	1.27	5.53	38.58	361.1
Boston Co:Cash Mgt[3,7]	1.00	0.32	1.00	5.51	40.89	242.4
Pac Hzn:Prime Pac Hzn[3]	1.00	0.35	1.06	5.50	42.25	1113.5
RBB:Sansom St MM[3]	1.00	0.35	1.08	5.49	**	152.4
AVG. FOR CATEGORY		0.31%	0.95%	4.98%	40.33%	
NUMBER OF FUNDS		256	257	243	156	
BOTTOM 10 PERFORMERS						
Declaration Fund:Cash[3]	$1.00	0.20%	0.60%	3.61%	33.46%	$48.4
PaineWbr Money Mkt B[3]	1.00	0.21	0.60	3.63	35.43	31.8
Providentmut Money[3]	1.00	0.23	0.68	4.14	37.67	33.1
Country Capital MM[3,6]	1.00	0.22	0.69	4.14	36.39	15.0
Thomson:Money Mkt B[3]	1.00	0.28	0.84	4.27	34.77	52.9
SunAmer Cash Fund[3]	1.00	0.26	0.79	4.34	**	22.9
MacKenzie Cash Mgt Fd[3]	1.00	0.26	0.73	4.35	37.03	4.8
Finl Hrzns:Cash Rsv[3]	1.00	0.27	0.82	4.38	**	2.5
Thomson:Money Market A	1.00	0.23	0.80	4.42	**	0.5
State Bond Cash Mgt[3]	1.00	0.28	0.82	4.42	38.00	6.6

[1]Some funds don't qualify for newspaper share price quotation
[2]Change in net asset value with reinvested dividends and capital gains
[3]No initial load
[4]Low initial load of 4.5% or less
[5]Fund may not be open to all investors
[6]Reflects non-standard dividend period
[7]Capital gain in period

**Fund didn't exist in period
N.A.=Not available

Source: Lipper Analytical Services Inc.

Source: *The Wall Street Journal,* April 16, 1992

At this point you may very well feel that the objective outlined in Chapters 1 and 8 has been lost. Mutual funds seem to have no advantage over individual stocks because the choice among funds, even among different kinds of funds, has become tremendously difficult due to the proliferation of funds. What happened to gold vs. stocks?

Don't despair. You can still invest in the overall stock market by selecting an *index fund* that places your capital in one of the better known stock market barometers. For instance, return to page 176 and the *Journal's* April 16, 1992 quote of the Vanguard Group's Index 500 fund: all of its resources are invested in the S & P 500.

CLOSED-END FUNDS

The mutual funds described above are open-ended because they continually issue new shares in order to expand their pool of capital. They sell their shares to investors and buy them back. But after their initial offering, *closed-end funds* do not issue additional shares and do not buy them back. The shares of the closed-end fund trade on an organized exchange or over-the-counter and appreciate or depreciate with investor demand like any other share of stock. Meanwhile, the investment company has its initial (fixed) pool of capital with which to make investments.

The success of the fund's investments determines the net asset value of the fund's shares (a fluctuating numerator to be divided by a fixed denominator), which can differ from their market value (stock price) as determined by supply and demand. The stock price may be above net asset value, trading at a premium, or below, trading at a discount. Either way, the fund's management takes its fee for administering the fund.

Why would fund managers choose to be confined by a closed-end fund rather than grow with a conventional open-end mutual fund? Because their pool of capital is not subject to the volatile swings generated by purchases and redemptions. Why would investors buy this kind of fund? Because they can purchase a closed-end fund at a discount, at less than net asset value, and enjoy a substantial potential gain if the stock price climbs back up to net asset value.

The Wall Street Journal publishes a report on closed-end funds each Monday under the heading **Publicly Traded Funds.** You can find it in the index on page C1. Page 181 has an example from the April 13, 1992 issue. Notice the broad array of investments and investment objectives.

Notice also that you may be able to purchase shares in a fund at a substantial discount from its net asset value. This may signal an unusual and temporary investment opportunity.

RISKY BUSINESS

Margin and Option Trading

If you are confident a stock will rise, you may purchase it and realize your gain if your prediction proves true. But there are a number of ways you can *leverage* your purchase in order to increase your gain (i.e., you can capture the increase on a larger number of shares of stock than you can currently afford to purchase). Your *leverage* is the ratio between the value of the shares you control (and from which you will reap a profit) and the amount of capital (money) you have invested. The smaller your investment and the larger the value of the shares you control, the greater your leverage.

For instance, under current regulations set by the Fed, you may borrow from your broker up to half the initial value of the shares of stock you purchase, which provides leverage of two to one. It's called *buying on margin*. If you buy $200 worth of stock from your broker, with a margin (your capital) of $100 (50 percent margin) and a $100 loan from the broker, and the stock doubles in value (from $200 to $400), you have made $200 on a $100 investment (less interest and brokerage costs) instead of $100 on a $100 investment that was not margined. That's leverage.

Options provide another opportunity to leverage your investment. They give you the right (option) to buy or sell stock at a stated price for future delivery at a premium (cost to buy the option). People do this for the same reason they buy or sell any stock: they think it's going up or down in value. Only in this case, they believe the market price of the stock will be higher or lower than the price at which they agreed to buy or sell it. Investors stand to gain if they can buy a stock below its market price (and can then sell it at the market price), or can sell it above market price (after having purchased it below market price).

For instance, suppose you had the option to buy a share of stock for $25 in a few months' time that currently trades at 23-1/2, and you were convinced the stock would be trading at 28 by then. Wouldn't you pay a premium for the right to buy a $28 stock for $25? That's a good deal, as

PUBLICLY TRADED FUNDS

Friday, April 10, 1992

Following is a weekly listing of unaudited net asset values of publicly traded investment fund shares, reported by the companies as of Friday's close. Also shown is the closing listed market price or a dealer-to-dealer asked price of each fund's shares, with the percentage of difference.

Fund Name	Stock Exch.	N.A. Value	Stock Price	% Diff.
Diversified Common Stock Funds				
Adams Express	NYSE	19.56	18 1/4	– 6.70
Allmon Trust	NYSE	10.39	9 3/4	– 6.16
Baker Fentress	NYSE	21.62	18 5/8	– 13.85
Blue Chip Value	NYSE	7.73	7 5/8	– 1.36
Clemente Global Gro	NYSE	b10.13	8 5/8	– 14.86
Gemini II Capital	NYSE	16.63	12 3/4	– 23.33
Gemini II Income	NYSE	9.52	13 5/8	+ 43.12
General Amer Invest	NYSE	27.11	27 7/8	+ 2.82
Jundt Growth Fd	NYSE	14.52	13 3/4	– 5.30
Liberty All-Star Eqty	NYSE	10.52	10 3/8	– 1.38
Niagara Share Corp.	NYSE	15.08	14 1/2	– 3.85
Quest For Value Cap	NYSE	24.07	19 1/8	– 20.54
Quest For Value Inco	NYSE	11.57	13 1/4	+ 14.52
Royce Value Trust	NYSE	11.97	11 1/4	– 6.02
Salomon Fd	NYSE	15.01	13 5/8	– 9.23
Source Capital	NYSE	41.43	44 5/8	+ 7.71
Tri-Continental Corp.	NYSE	27.70	26 7/8	– 2.98
Worldwide Value	NYSE	15.86	13 1/8	– 17.24
Zweig Fund	NYSE	a11.16	13	+ 16.49
Closed End Bond Funds				
CIM High Yield Secs	AMEX	7.66	7 3/8	– 3.72
Flexible Portfolio Funds				
America's All Seasn	OTC	5.56	4 7/8	– 12.32
European Warrant Fd	NYSE	7.57	6 1/8	– 19.09
Zweig Total Return Fd	NYSE	9.14	10 1/2	+ 14.88
Loan Participation Funds				
Pilgrim Prime Rate	NYSE	9.96	9 1/4	– 7.13
Specialized Equity and Convertible Funds				
Alliance Global Env Fd	NYSE	12.02	10 3/8	– 13.69
American Capital Conv	NYSE	21.85	19	– 13.04
Argentina Fd	NYSE	12.00	14 7/8	+ 23.96
ASA Ltd	NYSE	bc38.16	44	+ 15.30
Asia Pacific	NYSE	12.91	15 1/8	+ 17.16
Austria Fund	NYSE	9.42	8 1/8	– 5.79
Bancroft Convertible	AMEX	21.82	18 7/8	– 13.50
Bergstrom Capital	AMEX	94.31	106 1/2	+ 12.93
BGR Precious Metals	TOR	be7.59	5 3/4	– 24.24
Brazil	NYSE	b21.76	21	– 3.49
Brazilian Equity Fd	NYSE	13.77	16	+ 16.19
CNV Holdings Capital	NYSE	11.38	7 1/2	– 34.09
CNV Holdings Income	NYSE	9.70	12 3/8	+ 27.58
Castle Convertible	AMEX	23.83	20 5/8	– 13.45
Central Fund Canada	AMEX	b4.23	3 3/4	– 11.35
Central Securities	AMEX	11.93	10	– 16.18
Chile Fund	NYSE	39.04	34 1/8	– 12.59
Couns Tandem Secs	NYSE	15.20	13	– 14.47
Duff&Phelps Utils Inc.	NYSE	8.96	9 5/8	+ 7.42
Ellsw Conv Gr&Inc	AMEX	8.93	7 5/8	– 14.61
Emerging Ger Fd	NYSE	9.12	7 7/8	– 13.65
Emerging Mexico Fd	NYSE	b22.29	21 1/8	– 5.23
Engex	AMEX	11.37	9 3/8	– 17.55
Europe Fund	NYSE	12.61	11 3/8	– 9.79
1stAustralia	AMEX	10.43	8 7/8	– 14.91
First Financial Fund	NYSE	10.38	9 1/2	– 8.48
First Iberian	AMEX	9.13	7 3/4	– 15.12
First Philippine Fund	NYSE	11.88	9	– 24.24
France Growth Fund	NYSE	11.33	9 1/4	– 18.36
Future Germany Fund	NYSE	15.02	12 5/8	– 15.95
Gabelli Equity Trust	NYSE	10.68	10 7/8	+ 1.83
Germany Fund	NYSE	11.34	11 3/8	+ 0.31
Global Health Sciences Fd	NYSE	13.18	12 1/2	– 5.16
Growth Fund Spain	NYSE	11.50	9 5/8	– 16.30
GT Greater Europe Fd	NYSE	11.15	9 1/2	– 14.80
H&Q Healthcare Inv	NYSE	19.43	21 7/8	+ 12.58
India Growth Fund	NYSE	f27.20	23 5/8	– 13.14
Indonesia Fund	NYSE	8.55	9 1/8	+ 6.73
Inefficient Market Fund	AMEX	11.39	10 3/8	– 8.91
Irish Investment Fd	NYSE	9.51	7 5/8	– 19.82
Italy Fund	NYSE	10.17	8 7/8	– 12.73
Jakarta Growth Fd	NYSE	6.44	6 5/8	+ 2.87
Japan OTC Equity Fund	NYSE	8.06	9 7/8	+ 22.52
Korea Fund	NYSE	11.52	12 1/2	+ 8.51
Korean Investment Fd	NYSE	11.02	9 7/8	– 10.39
Latin America Equity Fd	NYSE	19.25	17 3/4	– 7.79
Latin America Inv Fd	NYSE	32.74	31 1/4	– 4.55
Malaysia Fund	NYSE	14.55	13 1/8	– 9.79
Mexico Equity Inc Fd	NYSE	b17.27	16 7/8	– 2.29
Mexico Fund	NYSE	b31.47	25	– 20.56
Morgan Grenf SmCap	NYSE	12.00	11 3/4	– 2.08
Morgan Stan Em Mks Fd	NYSE	16.91	18 1/8	+ 7.19
New Germany Fund	NYSE	13.21	10 7/8	– 17.68
Pacific Eur Growth Fd	NYSE	b9.76	9 1/2	– 2.66
Patriot Prem Div Fd	NYSE	9.56	9 3/8	– 1.94
Patriot Prem Div Fd II	NYSE	11.39	10 7/8	– 4.52
Patriot Select Div Trust	NYSE	15.28	16 5/8	+ 8.80
Petrol & Resources	NYSE	26.47	25 3/8	– 4.14
Pilgrim Regional	NYSE	10.86	10 3/8	– 4.47
Portugal Fund	NYSE	10.96	12 7/8	+ 17.47
Preferred Income Fd	NYSE	17.58	18 1/4	+ 3.81
Preferred Inc Opport Fd	NYSE	11.91	12 3/4	+ 7.05
Putnam Dividend Inco	NYSE	11.11	12	+ 8.01
Rl Estate Sec Inco Fd	AMEX	7.29	7 1/4	– 0.55
ROC Taiwan Fund	NYSE	9.62	10	+ 3.95
Scudder New Asia	NYSE	15.06	16 1/8	+ 7.07
Scudder New Europe	NYSE	9.86	8 5/8	– 12.53
SE Thrift & Bank Fd	OTC	b10.17	8 3/4	– 13.96
Singapore Fd	NYSE	b10.66	11	+ 3.19
Spain Fund	NYSE	11.74	11 1/8	– 5.24
Swiss Helvetia Fd	NYSE	13.51	13 1/2	– 0.07
Taiwan Fund	NYSE	b21.76	25 7/8	+ 18.91
TCW Convertible Secs	NYSE	7.98	8 1/2	+ 6.52
Templeton Em Mkts	NYSE	b19.16	21 1/2	+ 12.21
Templeton Global Util	AMEX	12.50	12 1/4	– 2.00
Thai Capital Fund	NYSE	10.23	8 5/8	– 15.69
Thai Fund	NYSE	17.19	15 1/8	– 12.01
Turkish Inv Fund	NYSE	5.80	6 1/2	+ 12.07
United Kingdom Fund	NYSE	10.59	9 1/2	– 10.29
Z-Seven	OTC	16.89	19 3/4	+ 16.93

a-Ex-dividend. b-As of Thursday's close. c-Translated at Commercial Rand exchange rate. e-In Canadian Dollars. f-As of Wednesday's close, using the Free–Market Spot Rate.

Source: *The Wall Street Journal*, April 13, 1992

LISTED OPTIONS QUOTATIONS

Friday, November 22, 1991

Options closing prices. Sales unit usually is 100 shares.
Stock close is New York or American exchange final price.

CHICAGO BOARD

Option & NY Close	Strike Price	Calls-Last			Puts-Last		
		Dec	Jan	Feb	Dec	Jan	Feb
AirbFr	20	11/16	1¼	r	1 1/16	r	r
AllanP	22½	r	r	r	r	r	2⅝
23½	25	r	2 3/16	r	r	r	r
23½	30	r	1⅛	r	r	r	r
Amdahl	12½	r	⅞	1	⅞	r	1½
12⅛	15	¼	r	½	2¾	r	r
A E P	30	r	r	1	r	r	11/16
AInGrp	80	r	r	r	¾	r	2
83¾	85	1¾	r	3⅝	r	r	r
83¾	90	⅜	r	r	r	r	7⅛
Amoco	45	3⅝	r	r	r	⅜	½
48¼	50	r	15/16	r	1⅜	r	2 13/16
48¼	55	r	⅛	5/16	6⅜	r	r
A M P	45	r	s	r	r	s	¾
51⅛	50	r	2½	r	⅞	r	r
30⅜	30	r	r	r	1 3/16	r	r
TelMex	35	8½	s	9½	r	s	
43⅛	40	4	4⅞	r	11/16	[illegible]	
43⅛	45	1	1 15/16	2 13/16	2⅝		
43⅛	50	⅛	¾	1⅜			
Tribune	35	r	r				
TritEn	35	r					
42⅛	40	[illegible]					
42⅛	45						
42⅛							
[illegible]							
					s	s	2¾
				s	2⅜	r	s
			r	s	4¼	r	s
		1⅜	3⅛	5	6⅞	8½	r
		11/16	r	3¼	r	r	r
	140	¼	r	r	r	r	
[illegible]	145	r	s	1⅜	r		
124	150	s	s	¾	s		
124	155	s	s	r			
UST	50	r	r				
52⅞	55	[illegible]					
U Tech	45						
46⅝							
Willm[illegible]							

Option & NY Close	Strike Price	Dec	Jan	Mar	Dec	Jan	Mar
[illegible]	5	1¼	1⅜	1½	r	⅛	r
	7½	r	5/16	7/16	1⅜	r	1¾
[illegible]	10	r	r	1/16	r	r	r
APwrCv	35	5⅜	r	r	r	1 9/16	r
40	40	2⅝	3⅝	5⅜	3	r	r
40	45	1⅜	r	r	r	r	r
40	50	¼	r	r	r	r	r
BergBr	22½	r	r	7/16	r	r	r
Blkbst	7½	r	s	r	r	s	¼
11⅛	10	1 7/16	r	2 5/16	¼	r	r
11⅛	12½	3/16	½	⅞	r	r	r
11⅛	15	1/16	s	⅜	r	s	r
BrMSq	70	10¾	s	s	⅛	s	s
80¼	75	6⅛	6	7¾	½	1⅛	1⅞
80¼	80	2⅜	3⅛	4⅝	2	3	3¾
80¼	85	⅝	1⅛	2⅝	5	r	6¾
80¼	90	⅛	r	1⅛	10	10½	r
Bruns	10	r	r	2 3/16	r	5/16	r
11¾	12½	¼	r	⅞	1	r	1½
11¾	15	1/16	r	r	r	r	r
Chamln	22½	1 7/16	r	r	r	r	r
23½	25	⅜	r	1 3/16	1½	r	r
Cirrus	17½	r	1⅛	r	r	r	r
Coastl	30	r	r	r	r	3⅛	r
CompSc	65	r	r	r	1 11/16	r	r
65⅜	75	r	s	r	9⅝	s	r
ContBk	7½	r	r	r	⅛	r	¾
9	10	¼	r	¾	r	1⅜	r
9	12½	1/16	r	r	3⅜	r	r
CypSem	15	1¼	r	r	1	r	r
15⅜	17½	½	r	1⅜	2½	r	r
15⅜	20	r	⅜	⅞	r	r	5⅜
Dow Ch	45	5	5⅛	r	⅛	⅝	1
49¾	50	1⅝	2	2½	1½	r	2¾
49¾	55	⅛	r	1	5¼	r	5⅞
49¾	60	1/16	s	⅜	r	s	r
Duracl	22½	3¾	r	r	r	r	r
25⅞	30	r	¼	r	r	r	r
EleArt	35	1 13/16	3⅛	r	r	r	r
34½	40	¾	r	r	r	r	r
Ford	22½	2¼	r	r	3/16	7/16	⅞
24⅝	25	11/16	1⅛	1⅝	⅞	1 3/16	1⅞
24⅝	30	r	⅛	7/16	5⅜	r	5¾
24⅝	35	r	s	3/16	10⅜	s	r
FundAm	60	7	s	r	r	s	r
67	65	r	r	r	r	1 3/16	1 13/16
Fuqua	15	5/16	r	⅞	r	r	r
Gap	35	15⅝	s	r	⅛	s	r
50⅞	40	r	s	r	¼	s	⅞
50⅞	45	5½	6⅞	r	½	1 3/16	1 13/16
50⅞	50	2⅜	3⅞	5¼	1½	r	r

Option & NY Close	Strike Price	Calls-Last			Puts-Last		
		Dec	Jan	Mar	Dec	Jan	Mar
K mart	35	4⅞	r	r	r	r	r
39½	40	1¼	2	2⅞	1¼	r	2⅝
39½	45	⅛	⅜	1	5½	r	r
39½	50	r	s	⅜	10	s	r
LandsE	25	r	r	r	r	r	2
Litton	80	r	r	r	7/16	r	r
86⅛	85	r	4	r	1 9/16	r	r
86⅛	90	⅞	r	r	r	r	
Loews	95	10½	s	r	r		
105¼	100	r	r	r	[illegible]		
105¼	105	r	r	[illegible]			
105¼	110	1⅜	[illegible]				
LongvF	15	r					
MBNA	25						
29⅞	30						
29⅞							
Mar[illegible]							
					r	r	13/16
				[illegible]	⅞	r	r
				¾	r	r	r
			r	3/16	s	r	r
		r	r	r	r	¼	½
	12½	¼	½	1	r	1¼	1⅜
	15	r	1/16	⅜	3⅜	3⅜	r
11¾	17½	r	1/16	r	r	r	
Biogen	25	s	r	r	s		
37	30	s	8⅜	r			
37	35	3¾	5				
37	40	1 11/16					
37	45						
37	[illegible]						
Biome[illegible]							
						1½	r
					[illegible]	r	r
					r	r	r
				s	s	⅛	s
			r	r	r	r	r
		r	r	r	⅛	r	1
	55	r	18⅛	r	r	r	r
	60	r	15	r	⅜	¾	2½
74½	65	9½	12⅝	r	⅞	2	4⅜
74½	70	6	8½	11¼	2	3½	5⅞
74½	75	3¼	5¾	9⅞	4¾	5¾	r
74½	80	1 11/16	3⅛	6⅝	8½	8½	r
BurlN	30	s	r	r	s	r	5/16
36	35	2⅜	3⅛	r	r	r	r
36	40	r	⅝	r	r	r	r
CIGNA	45	r	r	7¾	r	¾	1 13/16
51¼	50	2½	3	r	1½	2 3/16	r
CarnCr	22½	1¼	1⅞	r	11/16	1	1 15/16
23	25	¼	¾	1¾	2½	r	r
Cntocr	27½	s	21⅝	s	s	r	s
49	35	s	14⅞	r	s	r	r
49	40	9½	10	13	⅝	1¼	3⅛
49	45	6⅛	6¾	9⅜	1⅜	2¾	r
49	50	2⅜	4⅛	7½	3½	4¼	7⅛
49	55	1	2¼	5¼	r	r	r
49	60	½	1⅜	3⅞	11¼	r	r
Chiron	60	3⅞	r	r	r	r	r
61¼	65	1⅞	3⅜	r	r	r	r
61¼	70	r	r	r	9½	r	r
61¼	80	r	r	2	r	r	r
Chryslr	7½	r	r	r	r	1/16	r	← Chrysler
11¾	10	1⅝	1⅞	2⅜	⅛	3/16	r
11¾	12½	¼	9/16	1	r	1⅜	1½
11¾	15	r	1/16	½	r	3¼	r
CinBel	22½	r	r	13/16	r	r	r
Cisco	45	5¼	r	r	1	1 7/16	r
49¼	50	2 3/16	3¼	5¼	2¾	4	r
49¼	55	½	1½	r	r	r	r
Citicp	10	1	1¼	1 15/16	¼	⅜	13/16
10¾	12½	⅛	¼	11/16	r	2	r
10¾	15	s	1/16	⅜	s	r	r
CmprsL	20	3	r	4¾	11/16	1 7/16	r
22¼	22½	1½	2⅛	r	r	r	r
22¼	25	¾	1⅜	2 13/16	3½	4½	r
CmpAsc	7½	r	2	r	r	r	r
9⅜	10	⅛	7/16	r	r	r	r
CyprMn	17½	s	4⅛	r	s	r	r
21⅛	20	r	1 13/16	2 11/16	r	r	r
21⅛	25	r	r	11/16	r	r	r
Delta	55	3⅛	4⅛	5⅞	1	1⅝	2⅞
57¼	60	13/16	1 11/16	3½	3¼	4⅛	5
57¼	65	⅛	⅝	2	7	7⅞	r
57¼	70	r	r	⅞	13	r	r
57¼	75	r	r	r	r	17½	r
DiaSrk	22½	r	r	1 1/16	r	r	r
Dryfus	40	1⅞	r	r	1	r	r
EKodak	35	s	r	s	s	⅛	s	← Eastman Kodak
46⅜	40	r	6⅞	r	r	7/16	¾
46⅜	45	2⅛	2⅝	3⅞	⅞	1¼	2¼
46⅜	50	¼	9/16	1 9/16	r	r	r
46⅜	55	r	⅛	r	r	r	r
Eaton	55	r	r	r	13/16	r	r
56¾	60	r	r	r	3½	r	r
Elan	40	r	r	r	½	r	r
43½	45	r	2⅛	r	r	r	r
Enron	70	r	3¼	r	1	r	r
72	75	r	r	r	r	4¾	r
Epitpe	17½	r	r	6½	r	r	r

Source: *The Wall Street Journal*, November 25, 1992

Chryslr	7½	r	r	r	r	1/16	r	
11¾	10	1⅝	1⅞	2⅜	⅛	3/16	r	
11¾	12½	¼	9/16	1	r	1⅜	1½	
11¾	15	r	1/16	½	r	3¼	r	←Chrysler

Source: *The Wall Street Journal*, November 25, 1991

long as the premium is smaller than the spread between $25 and the $28 price at which you think the stock will trade. Conversely, if you were convinced that a stock, currently trading at 23-1/2, would fall to 18, wouldn't you pay a fee (premium) for the right to sell it at $20, knowing you could obtain it at $18?

The excerpt from the Monday, November 25, 1991 *Journal* presents a summary of options trading on Friday, November 22, 1991. This report, called **Listed Options Quotations,** appears daily and you can find it listed in the front-page indexes of the first (Al) and last (Cl) sections. This excerpt takes Chrysler as an example (first column).

The first column informs you that Chrysler closed at 11-3/4 on Friday, November 22, 1991.

The second column lists the *strike prices* (7-1/2, 10, 12-1/2, 15) at which you have the option of buying or selling (striking a deal for) the stock in the future. Note that some prices are higher and some are lower than the current price (11-3/4). Think of the strike price as the price at which you strike a deal.

The third through the fifth columns list the premium you must pay per share to purchase the option to *call* (buy) Chrysler stock at the applicable strike price by the third Friday of the months listed (December, January, April). Take April as an example. On November 22, 1991 you had to pay a premium of 50 cents (1/2 of a dollar) for the right (option) to buy a share of Chrysler stock at $15.00 (15) by the close of trading on April 17, 1992 (third Friday of April). Once the deal was struck, the seller (writer) of the option would be bound to deliver the stock to you at that price at any time before the close of business on April 17, 1992, *at your option.* That is, the decision would be up to you.

Why would you buy such a contract? Because you were convinced that Chrysler would trade at more than $15.50 (strike price of $15.00 plus premium of $0.50) at any time before the third Friday in April. Then you would have the option to buy it at $15.00 (the strike price) from the option writer and sell it at the higher market price. When the call price rises above the strike price, an option is said to be *in the money*.

Trading is done in round lots of 100 shares. Thus, on November 22, 1991, when Chrysler was $11.75, you could have purchased an option for $50 (100 X $0.50) to buy 100 shares at $15.00 by April 17, 1992. How would you have done?

Not bad. As you can see below in the excerpt from the Thursday, April 16, 1992 *Journal,* Chrysler traded at $18.50 on April 15, two days before the option expired. Back in November you paid a $50 premium (100 x $0.50) for the option to call 100 shares at $15.00 share, and now exercise your option for $1,500 (100 X $15.00). Those shares are worth $1,850 (100 x $18.50) on the market. Thus, you've obtained $1,850 of securities for $1,500, less your premium of $50, for a gain of $300 ($1,850 - $1,500 - $50 = $300) on your $50 investment. That's leverage.

Notice that purchasing the option provided you a much higher return than buying Chrysler stock at $11.75 on November 22, 1991. By April 15, 1992 that investment had appreciated by 57%, considerably less than the 600% gain on the option. But notice that the option carried considerably greater risk. When a stock does not appreciate, you at least preserve your capital. When an option expires, your money's gone.

Option & NY Close	Strike Price	Calls-Last Apr	May	Jul	Puts-Last Apr	May	Jul	
G M	25	s	s	14 5/8	s	s	r	
40	30	s	s	10	s	s	1/8	
40	35	4 7/8	5	5 1/4	r	3/16	7/16	
40	40	1/4	1 1/8	1 11/16	5/16	1 1/2	2 1/16	
40	45	r	1/8	5/16	r	r	5 5/8	
Gensia	30	r	r	r	r	9/16	r	
36	33 3/8	r	s	r	r	s	2 1/16	
36	35	4	r	r	7/16	r	2 7/8	
36	40	r	r	2 1/2	r	r	r	
36	45	1/16	r	r	r	r	r	
36	46 5/8	s	s	1	s	s	r	
GtLCh	50	r	s	14 1/2	r	s	r	
63 5/8	55	r	9 1/8	10 1/8	r	r	5/8	
63 5/8	60	3 1/4	r	5 1/2	r	r	r	
63 5/8	65	1/4	2	2 5/8	r	r	r	
ChamDv	7 1/2	3/8	r	1 1/16	r	9/16	13/16	
7 7/8	10	r	r	1/2	2 3/8	r	r	
7 7/8	12 1/2	r	r	5/16	r	r	r	
Chiron	40	1/2	2 3/16	4 5/8	1	2 9/16	4	
39 1/2	45	r	3/4	r	2 7/8	r	r	
39 1/2	50	r	1/4	1 5/16	r	r	r	
Chrs o	29 3/8	r	s	r	3 3/8	s	r	
Chryslr	10	8	s	8	r	s	r	
18 1/2	12 1/2	6	s	6	r	s	1/8	
18 1/2	15	3 1/2	3 3/8	4	r	r	3/8	← Chrysler
18 1/2	17 1/2	1	1 3/8	2	1/16	9/16	1 1/8	
18 1/2	20	1/16	5/16	7/8	1 7/8	r	r	
CinBel	17 1/2	r	r	r	3/16	r	r	
Cisco	25	14 7/8	s	r	r	s	r	
39 3/4	30	10	11	r	r	7/16	r	
39 3/4	32 1/2	7 1/2	s	r	r	s	r	

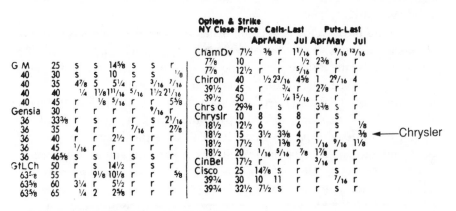

Source: *The Wall Street Journal*, April 16, 1992

EKodak	35	s	r	s	s	1/8	s	
46 3/8	40	r	6 7/8	r	r	7/16	3/4	
46 3/8	45	2 1/8	2 5/8	3 7/8	7/8	1 1/4	2 1/8	←Eastman Kodak
46 3/8	50	1/4	9/16	1 9/16	r	r	r	
46 3/8	55	r	1/8	r	r	r	r	

Source: *The Wall Street Journal*, November 25, 1992

You should know, however, that you need not purchase the stock underlying an option in order to realize your gain. You can sell the option instead. For instance, using the Chrysler example in the previous paragraphs, you will notice that the option was in the money two days before its expiration, and traded at the exact difference ($3.50) between the strike price ($18.50) and the call price ($15.00). In other words, you could have sold it for $3.50 on April 15, 1992 to another investor *and reaped your gain of $300 ($3.50 x 100 less the initial investment of $50) without purchasing the underlying stock.* As a matter of fact, most investors never intend to buy the underlying stock. Instead, they hope to sell their option when it comes into a profit.

Thus, if you buy a call, you're speculating that the stock's price will rise sufficiently to earn you a return (spread) over and above the premium you must pay to buy the option. But suppose it doesn't? Suppose the stock rises only a little, or even falls in value, so that you have the option to buy a stock at a price greater than market value? What then? Would you have to buy the stock from the option writer at the strike price? No, because you have only purchased an *option* to buy. There's no requirement to do so. You can let the option expire without exercising it, and you have only lost your premium.

A *rising* market motivates investors to buy calls. They hope the price of *their* stock will shoot up and they will be able to exercise their option and recover their premium, and then some. This does not necessarily mean that option writers (people who sell the option) are counting on the market to stay flat or even fall. The call writer may have decided to sell a stock if it reaches a certain target level (i.e., take his or her gain after the stock rises a certain number of points). If it does rise, the call writer will receive the increment and the premium; and even if it doesn't, he or she will still receive the premium. Thus, income is the primary motive for writing the option. Instead of waiting for the stock to move up to the target level, the seller writes a call. If it doesn't move up to that price, he or she will still have earned the premium. If it does, he or she will get premium plus capital gain.

Now let's consider the other kind of option and return to the November 25, 1991 issue of the *Journal*, using Kodak as our example. If you had believed on November 22, 1991 that Kodak stock would fall substantially below its current market value of $46.38 (46-3/8), you could have purchased a put contract, and the option writer would have been obliged to buy the put at the strike price, regardless of current market value. Your option to sell at the strike price would give you an opportunity to buy at the lower market value (assuming your forecast was correct) and profit on the difference.

The last three columns in the example on page 185 provide the put contract premiums for December, January, and April. Notice the $2.12 (2 1/8) premium for the April contract. If Kodak fell below 45 before the April 17 expiration date, you could buy Kodak at the market price and sell (put) it to the option writer at the contract price of 45. The difference, less the premium and any brokerage fees, would be your profit.

Let's see what happened. Kodak had fallen to $39.75 (39 3/4) by April 15, 1991 and your put was definitely in the money (see below). You could have purchased Kodak at the market price of $39.75 and sold it to the option write for $45.00, for a gain of $5.25 per share less the $2.12 premium and any brokerage fees.

9 7/8	12 1/2	1/8	3/8	13/16	2	r	2 1/2
IntRec	10	7/8	r	r	r	r	r
IvaxCp	25	r	7 3/8	8 1/2	r	r	r
32 3/8	30	2 5/16	3 1/2	r	1/16	r	r
Ivax o	33 3/8	s	s	2 7/8	s	s	s
IvaxCp	35	r	1	r	2 3/4	3 3/4	r
32 3/8	40	r	r	3/4	r	r	r
K mart	40	s	s	12	s	s	r
51 3/4	45	r	r	r	r	r	1/2
51 3/4	50	2	3 1/8	3 1/2	r	1	r
51 3/4	55	r	1/2	1 1/4	r	r	r
LandsE	35	r	r	2	r	1 7/8	2 3/8
Litton	90	3 1/8	4	r	r	r	r
92 7/8	100	r	r	r	r	8 1/8	r
Loews	100	10	11 3/8	r	r	r	1 3/16
111 3/4	105	r	7	8 3/4	1/8	r	r
111 3/4	110	1 5/8	4	3 3/4	r	r	3
111 3/4	115	r	1 1/8	2 3/8	r	r	r

CyprMn	20	7/8	r	r	r	r	r	
21	22 1/2	r	r	7/8	1 9/16	r	2 1/8	
Delta	55	r	r	7 3/4	r	1/2	1 7/16	
60 5/8	60	1 5/16	2 5/8	4 1/2	3/8	1 3/4	3 1/4	
60 5/8	65	r	3/4	2 3/8	3 3/4	r	6 1/8	
60 5/8	70	r	r	1 1/8	9	r	r	
60 5/8	80	r	s	1/4	r	s	r	
Dryfus	35	r	2 1/4	r	r	r	r	
35 7/8	40	r	r	r	4	r	r	
EKodak	30	s	s	9 5/8	s	s	r	
39 3/4	35	4 3/4	5 1/4	r	r	r	1/2	
39 3/4	40	3/16	1 1/4	1 7/8	3/8	1 1/4	2 1/8	
39 3/4	45	1/16	1/8	3/8	5 3/8	5	r	← Eastman Kodak
39 3/4	50	r	s	1/4	r	s	r	
Eaton	75	r	5 3/4	7 1/2	r	r	r	
Elan	40	7 3/4	7 1/4	9	r	r	3/4	
48	45	2 1/2	3 7/8	4 7/8	1/4	15/16	2	
48	50	1/16	1 1/4	3	2 1/4	r	4 7/8	

Source: *The Wall Street Journal*, April 17, 1992

To be precise, your premium would have been $212 (100 x $2.12). When Kodak fell to $39.75 you could have purchased 100 shares at $3,975 (100 x $39.75) in the market and exercised your option to sell for $4,500 (100 x $45.00) for a gain of $313 ($525 of stock market appreciation less $212 of premium). (Again, you have to subtract the broker's fee from your profit.)

Once again, you should be aware that most options buyers do not exercise their options. They sell them if they show a profit or let them expire if they do not. In this case the premium had risen to 5-3/8 for a net gain of 3-1/4 (5-3/8 less 2-1/8) per share. For 100 shares, that works out to $325.

If you guessed wrong and Kodak rose, so that the market price exceeded the strike price, you wouldn't want to exercise your option to sell at a price below market. Instead, you would permit your option to expire without exercising it. Your loss would be only the premium you paid.

Why would someone write a put? Because he or she is prepared to buy a stock if it should drop to a particular price. The writer earns the premium whether or not the option is exercised. If he or she believes the stock will rise in price, then the writer has little concern that an option holder will put it to him or her at less than the market price. And the writer has collected the premium. But if the market does fall, and falls sufficiently that the contract comes in the money, the writer will have to buy the stock at the contract price, which will be above market. That's not necessarily bad, since the writer had already planned to buy the stock if it fell to the strike price, and he or she has collected a premium, too.

In addition to simply playing the options market for profit, an investor can use options to hedge against price fluctuations of his or her investment in the underlying security. For instance, you can write (sell) call options against a stock you own. If the stock falls in value, you at least get to keep the premium. If it rises above the strike price, you keep the premium and realize a gain on the stock.

Conversely, if you like a stock but think it will fall in value, write (sell) a put instead of buying the stock. If it doesn't fall, you collect the premium anyway. If it does fall, you still collect the premium and purchase the stock at a lower price.

These strategies involve *covered* options, i.e. stock you own or intend to buy. You can write *naked* options on stock you don't own and do not intend to buy. It seems like an easy way to collect a premium. But suppose you've written a call option thinking the stock couldn't possibly rise that far, and it does. You'll have to buy that stock at the market price if the option is exercised and then sell it at the lower strike price. That could hurt.

Conversely, you can write naked put options and collect your premium if you believe a stock could never fall *that* far. But if there's another crash like the one in 1987 and the market collapses, you may find yourself in the embarrassing position of having to buy stock at prices substantially above market. Where are you going to get the money?

That's one of the reasons options are risky business.

And one more comment about leverage. You can minimize risk if you buy options whose strike price is close to the market price, but you also reduce your relative gain. Leverage increases as the strike price increasingly deviates from the market price. That is, not surprisingly, risk and reward move together.

You can spread the risk of options investing by purchasing *index options* (see next page) in the entire market rather than an option on an individual stock. Instead of buying all the stocks in one of the stock market averages (or buying an index mutual fund), you can buy a put or call on an index option (such as the S & P 100), just as you can invest in options on individual stocks.

Take a look at the Thursday April 16, 1992 excerpt from **Index Trading** on next page. You can see that options on both the S&P 100 and 500 permit you to speculate on changes in the broad market without purchasing a large number of stocks.

These index options are more widely traded than options on individual securities, as you can see from the example on page 190 and 191. Notice that the S&P 100 was the most actively traded in Chicago. The S&P 100 was created to represent 100 companies among the S&P 500 stocks for which options are actively traded. This provides the investor with the opportunity to spread the risk over 100 options rather than exposing himself or herself to the risks inherent in a single option.

Finally, as the example on page 192 and 193 illustrates, the investor can purchase longer-term options on some stocks. For instance, IBM traded at $88.50 on April 15, 1992, but you can see that investors willing to gamble on a doubling in IBM's price by the end of the year could have purchased on that day an option for 12-1/2 cents to buy IBM at 165 anytime before the third Friday in January of 1993. That seems like a leap of faith, yet a 100 share contract would have been no more than $12.50. And if IBM did surge and the premium doubled to 25 cents, the investor could have doubled his or her money even if IBM did not

INDEX TRADING

Wednesday, April 15, 1992

Chicago Board

S+P 100

S&P 100 INDEX-$100 times index

Strike	Calls—Last			Puts—Last		
Price	Apr	May	Jun	Apr	May	Jun
340	....	....	....	1/16	....	....
350	....	39¾	....	....	9/16	1⅝
355	35⅛	....	....	1/16	¾	2
360	30⅞	29	....	1/16	15/16	2 7/16
365	25	23¼	27¾	1/16	1 3/16	3
370	20¼	20½	22	1/16	1 11/16	3⅞
375	15⅜	16¼	17½	1/16	2¼	4¾
380	10⅜	12½	15	⅛	3⅛	6
385	5⅜	8⅛	10¾	¼	4⅝	7⅝
390	1⅝	6⅛	8⅞	1 3/16	6⅝	9¾
395	⅛	3½	6¼	5⅛	9½	12¼
400	1/16	2	4¼	9⅞	13½	15½
405	1/16	1½	2¾	....	18⅝	19¾
410	....	½	1¾	....	23	....

Total call volume 202,561 Total call open int. 397,825
Total put volume 201,671 Total put open int. 515,031
The index: High 390.13; Low 386.58; Close 390.12, +3.54

S&P 500 INDEX-$100 times index

Strike	Calls—Last			Puts—Last		
Price	Apr	May	Jun	Apr	May	Jun
325	....	....	....	....	1/16	31/16
350	....	....	67	....	....	9/16
365	....	....	....	....	....	1
370	....	....	46¾	....	7/16	1⅛
375	....	....	....	....	⅝	1½
380	32⅞	....	38½	....	¾	2
385	....	....	....	1/16	....	2⅜
390	....	26⅛	....	....	1¼	2⅞
395	19½	....	....	1/16	1 11/16	3⅞
400	15	17½	20⅝	1/16	2	4½
405	11½	13⅜	16¼	⅛	2⅞	5¾
410	6¾	10¼	13½	3/16	4⅛	7⅛
415	2½	7¼	10	⅞	6	9½
420	¼	4¼	7¼	3¾	8¼	12⅛
425	....	2¾	5	....	11⅜	15¼
430	....	1½	3⅜	15⅜	15¼	18
435	....	⅝	2¼	....	20⅝	....
440	....	....	1¼	....	....	25½
445	....	....	⅜	....	....	....
450	....	....	⅛	35⅝	....	35⅜

Total call volume 37,262 Total call open int. 341,101
Total put volume 32,054 Total put open int. 507,051
The index: High 416.28; Low 412.39; Close 416.28, +3.89

LEAPS-S&P 100 INDEX

Strike	Calls—Last		Puts—Last	
Price	Dec 92	Dec 93	Dec 92	Dec 93
27½	....	....	⅛	⅝
30	....	9⅞	¼	13/16
32½	....	8	½	....
35	....	....	⅞	1⅞
37½	2⅞	....	1 7/16	2¾
40	....	3	2 9/16	3¾

Total call volume 745 Total call open int. 33,194
Total put volume 3,653 Total put open int. 132,448
The index: High 39.01; Low 38.66; Close 39.01, +0.35

LEAPS-S&P 500 INDEX

Strike	Calls—Last		Puts—Last	
Price	Dec 92	Dec 93	Dec 92	Dec 93
32½	....	....	....	⅝
35	....	....	⅜	....
40	....	....	1⅜	2¼
42½	....	....	2¼	....

Total call volume 0 Total call open int. 30,914
Total put volume 1,218 Total put open int. 112,254
The index: High 41.63; Low 41.24; Close 41.63, +0.39

CAPS-S&P 100 INDEX

Strike	Calls—Last		Puts—Last	
Price	Apr 92	Jun 92	Apr 92	Jun 92
380	....	....	....	6¾
400	....	....	13	....

Total call volume 0 Total call open int. 1,496
Total put volume 24 Total put open int. 5,164
The index: High 390.13; Low 386.58; Close 390.12, +3.54

CAPS-S&P 500 INDEX

Strike	Calls—Last		Puts—Last	
Price	Jun 92	Sep 92	Jun 92	Sep 92
410	12	....	....	10

Total call volume 15 Total call open int. 409
Total put volume 400 Total put open int. 2,960
The index: High 416.28; Low 412.39; Close 416.28, +3.89

225	....	....	....	....	....	43

Total call volume 1,475 Total call open int. 24,269
Total put volume 3,502 Total put open int. 30,792
The index: Close 180.72, +5.10

Philadelphia Exchange

GOLD/SILVER INDEX

Strike	Calls—Last			Puts—Last		
Price	Apr	May	Jun	Apr	May	Jun
65	....	5¾	....	....	....	1⅜
70	3/16	2 9/16	....	....	2⅞	....
75	....	13/16	3⅛	....	....	....
80	....	⅜	....	10	....	10½
90	....	....	3/16	....	....	....

Total call volume 116 Total call open int. 2,466
Total put volume 51 Total put open int. 1,142
The index: High 72.40; Low 68.76; Close 69.22, −2.83

VALUE LINE INDEX OPTIONS

Strike	Calls—Last			Puts—Last		
Price	Apr	May	Jun	Apr	May	Jun
350	4	....	....	¼	4	7
355	½	4⅝	....	1¾	5½	8¼
360	....	2⅜	....	....	....	....
375	....	....	1½	....	....	....

Total call volume 303 Total call open int. 6,820
Total put volume 65 Total put open int. 3,175
The index: High 353.80; Low 351.65; Close 353.77, +2.13

UTILITIES INDEX

Strike	Calls—Last			Puts—Last		
Price	Apr	May	Jun	Apr	May	Jun
245	....	....	....	⅛	....	....
250	⅜	2	....	....	....	....
255	....	⅞	....	....	....	....

Total call volume 409 Total call open int. 1,350
Total put volume 10 Total put open int. 907
The index: High 250.66; Low 248.40; Close 250.66, +2.86

Pacific Exchange

FINANCIAL NEWS COMPOSITE INDEX

Strike	Calls—Last			Puts—Last		
Price	Apr	May	Jun	Apr	May	Jun
260	....	....	....	....	....	1 5/16
270	....	....	19½	....	....	....
275	....	13⅛	15½	....	....	3¼
280	5⅞	8⅞	....	....	2⅜	....
285	2⅝	5⅜	....	....	3⅞	....
290	⅜	3⅜	....	4	5¾	....

Total call volume 157 Total call open int. 2,873
Total put volume 295 Total put open int. 1,448
The index: High 288.02; Low 285.47; Close 288.00, +2.53

N.Y. Stock Exchange

NYSE INDEX OPTIONS

Strike	Calls—Last			Puts—Last		
Price	Apr	May	Jun	Apr	May	Jun
220	....	9½	11	....	1 7/16	....
225	3½	6	....	1/16	2 11/16	....
230	1/16	....	....	....	4⅝	6 5/16
235	....	1 1/16	....	....	8¼	....
240	....	....	1 1/16	....	....	....

Total call volume 136 Total call open int. 413
Total put volume 62 Total put open int. 1,156
The index: High 229.15; Low 227.31; Close 229.15, +1.84

Source: *The Wall Street Journal*, April 16, 1992

Chicago Board

LISTED OPTIONS QUOTATIONS

MOST ACTIVE OPTIONS

CHICAGO BOARD

	Sales	Last	Chg	N.Y. Close
CALLS				
SP100 Apr 390	47685	1 5/8	+ 1	390.11
SP100 Apr 385	42426	5 3/8	+ 2 1/2	390.11
SP100 Apr 380	24564	10 3/8	+ 3 1/4	390.11
SP100 May 385	12395	8 7/8	+ 1 7/8	390.11
SP100 Apr 395	10947	1/8	− 1/16	390.11
SP100 Apr 375	10288	15 3/8	+ 3 3/8	390.11
SP100 May 390	9492	6 1/8	+ 1 3/4	390.11
SP500 Apr 415	7278	2 1/2	+ 1 5/8	416.27
SP100 May 395	7159	3 1/2	+ 1 1/16	390.11
SP100 May 400	7112	2	+ 3/4	390.11
PUTS				
SP100 Apr 385	39754	1/4	− 15/16	390.11
SP100 Apr 390	34173	1 3/16	− 2 13/16	390.11
SP100 Apr 380	26763	1/8	− 1/4	390.11
SP100 May 385	17024	4 5/8	− 1 3/8	390.11
SP100 May 380	15237	3 1/4	− 7/8	390.11
SP100 Apr 375	13764	1/16	− 1/8	390.11
SP100 May 390	8307	6 5/8	− 1 7/8	390.11
SP100 May 375	8107	2 1/4	− 5/8	390.11
SP100 May 370	6544	1 11/16	− 5/16	390.11
SP100 Apr 370	5692	1/16	− 1/16	390.11

AMERICAN

	Sales	Last	Chg	N.Y. Close
CALLS				
MMIdx May 300	4000	56 3/8	+ 6 3/8	356.98
MMIdx Apr 355	3418	2 3/4	+ 1 3/8	356.98
Apple Apr 60	2716	2 5/8	+ 1 11/16	60 1/2
MMIdx May 370	2209	1	− 1/16	356.98
U Carb Apr 25	1902	11/16	+ 3/8	25 3/4
A M R Apr 70	1726	1 1/8	+ 1/4	71
Motrla Apr 80	1645	2 1/4	+ 1 3/4	82
USSurg Apr 115	1565	2	− 1/2	115
Centel Jul 45	1554	2 3/8	− 1/4	42
Unisys May 12 1/2	1510	5/16	...	10
PUTS				
MMIdx Apr 355	2289	5/8	− 1 1/16	356.98
MMIdx May 300	2010	1/8	− 1/8	356.98
MMIdx May 370	2010	14	− 6 1/4	356.98
Disney Apr 150	1444	1	− 15/16	150
Merrill Apr 50	1364	1	+ 1/4	49 1/4
MMIdx Apr 350	1294	1/8	− 7/16	356.98
Apple Apr 55	1132	1/8	− 1/4	60 1/2
Dig Eq Jul 45	1100	3 1/4	+ 3/4	44 1/2
Dig Eq Apr 45	1061	3/4	+ 9/16	44 1/2
Dig Eq Jul 40	1043	1 3/8	+ 3/8	44 1/2

PHILADELPHIA

	Sales	Last	Chg	N.Y. Close
CALLS				
Waste May 40	1486	1 3/4	+ 11/16	40 3/4
Abbt L May 70	1236	5/8	− 5/16	66 1/2
F N M Sep 65	1230	6 5/8	+ 1/2	67 5/8
Synrgn Apr 45	1220	1/16	...	38 1/2
Sprint May 22 1/2	1079	1 11/16	+ 1 3/16	23 3/4
Armco Apr 5	1013	3/4	+ 1/4	5 7/8
Waste Apr 40	833	11/16	+ 9/16	40 3/4
USF&G Apr 10	820	1/8	...	10
TimW o Apr 105	741	1/2	+ 1/4	104 1/2
Un Pac May 50	721	1 1/2	+ 9/16	50 1/4
PUTS				
HomeD May 65	860	1 1/8	− 3/8	68 3/8
NBD Bc Oct 35	769	7 3/8	+ 7 3/8	28
Abbt L May 60	719	1/4	+ 1/16	66 1/2
Waste May 40	439	1 3/16	− 7/16	40 3/4
F N M Apr 65	400	1/16	...	67 5/8
FtAmB May 35	386	3 3/4	+ 3 3/4	32 1/2
Strykr Apr 40	330	1/16	− 3/8	40 1/2
Synrgn Apr 40	328	1 7/16	+ 1 1/16	38 1/2
HomeD May 70	320	3 3/8	− 5/8	68 3/8
NBD Bc Apr 30	302	2 1/16	+ 1/4	28

PACIFIC

	Sales	Last	Chg	N.Y. Close
CALLS				
Micsft Apr 120	5228	8 7/8	+ 8 1/4	128 7/8
Micsft Apr 125	3969	4 1/4	+ 4 1/8	128 7/8
Conner Apr 20	3498	11/16	...	20 5/8
Micsft Apr 130	3081	1	+ 15/16	128 7/8
Micsft May 20	1644	11 3/8	+ 6 1/8	128 7/8
Micsft May 130	1464	5	+ 3 1/4	128 7/8
Marion Apr 35	1298	3/8	...	35 1/8
Micsft Apr 115	1188	13 7/8	+ 11	128 7/8
BncOne Apr 40	1150	4 1/4	− 1 1/4	44 3/8
BncOne Nov 40	1030	6 3/8	− 5/8	44 3/8
PUTS				
Micsft Jul 105	5810	2 1/8	− 2 7/8	128 7/8
Micsft Apr 125	2738	5/16	− 7 11/16	128 7/8
Micsft Jul 110	2106	3 1/4	− 3 1/2	128 7/8
Micsft May 125	1539	3 5/8	− 5 5/8	128 7/8
A M D Apr 17 1/2	1043	1/4	− 1/16	17 1/2
Micsft Apr 130	782	2 1/8	− 10 1/2	128 7/8
BncOne May 55	708	10 1/8	+ 1/8	44 3/8
Conner Apr 20	650	1/8	− 7/16	20 5/8
Micsft Apr 110	560	1/16	− 3/16	128 7/8
Compaq Apr 30	537	3 7/8	+ 1/8	26 1/4

NEW YORK

	Sales	Last	Chg	N.Y. Close
CALLS				
TelMex May 60	963	2 1/8	+ 1/2	58 3/4
Maytag Jul 20	768	1 1/16	+ 9/16	19 7/8
Maytag Apr 20	717	1/8	+ 1/16	19 7/8
Maytag Apr 17 1/2	523	2 3/8	+ 1 3/4	19 7/8
TelMex May 65	500	1/2	− 1/16	58 3/4
TritEn Aug 30	395	3 1/2	− 3	28 5/8
Maytag May 20	384	11/16	+ 9/16	19 7/8
Maytag Oct 20	357	1 9/16	+ 9/16	19 7/8
TelMex Apr 55	353	2 15/16	+ 7/16	58 3/4
IngRnd May 65	300	1 3/16	+ 7/16	61 3/8
PUTS				
SumitT Apr 35	265	5/8	− 1 13/16	34 3/4
Q M S May 12 1/2	250	2 3/4	+ 3/4	10
TelMex May 55	205	1 3/8	− 3/16	58 3/4
TelMex Aug 60	200	6	− 3 1/2	58 3/4
Potlch Jun 40	140	1/8	− 3/16	49 7/8
Maytag May 20	130	7/8	− 3/4	19 7/8
BrtStl Oct 12 1/2	111	1 1/4	− 1/4	13 1/4
CumEng Apr 65	110	7	+ 3 7/8	57 1/2
BordCh Apr 20	105	1/16	− 1/8	21 1/2
IMC Frt Jul 50	75	2 9/16	+ 7/16	58 1/2

Source: *The Wall Street Journal*, April 16, 1992

CHICAGO BOARD

CALLS	Sales	Last	Chg	N.Y. Close
SP100 Apr 390	47685	1⅝	+ 1	390.11
SP100 Apr 385	42426	5⅜	+ 2½	390.11
SP100 Apr 380	24564	10⅜	+ 3¼	390.11
SP100 May 385	12395	8⅞	+ 1⅞	390.11
SP100 Apr 395	10947	⅛	− 1/16	390.11
SP100 Apr 375	10288	15⅜	+ 3⅜	390.11
SP100 May 390	9492	6⅛	+ 1¾	390.11
SP500 Apr 415	7278	2½	+ 1⅝	416.27
SP100 May 395	7159	3½	+ 1 11/16	390.11
SP100 May 400	7112	2	+ ¾	390.11

Source: *The Wall Street Journal*, April 16, 1992

double in value. Remember, most options are traded without being exercised (the purchase of the underlying shares).

Many of these possibilities sound intriguing, easy, and potentially profitable. Keep in mind, however, that there are substantial commission costs. Furthermore, as in any leveraged situation, the potential for considerable loss exists. Options are not for novices, and even buying on margin exposes you to up to twice the risk of simply buying a stock with your own money. With leverage you can move a big rock with a small stick—but the stick can also break off in your hands, and the rock can roll back over your feet.

In fact, the whole options game is tricky and multi-faceted. Consequently, before you can invest in options, your broker will evaluate your past investment experience and your current financial position. It will not be easy to qualify.

Short Interest

Instead of speculating on a price increase, some investors borrow stock from their broker in the hope of a price *decrease*. They sell the stock and leave the proceeds of the sale with their broker. If the stock falls, the borrower buys it back at the lower price and returns it to the broker, at which time the broker returns the funds from the original sale to the borrower. The advantage to the borrower is obvious: he or she pockets the difference between the high price when he or she borrowed and sold the stock and the low price when he or she bought and returned the stock.

LONG TERM OPTIONS

CBOE

Option/Exp/Strike	Last
AT&T Jan 93 25	18 1/8
AT&T Jan 93 35	8 3/4
AT&T Jan 93 35 p	13/16
AT&T Jan 93 40	5
AT&T Jan 93 40 p	2 1/4
AT&T Jan 93 50	1 1/16
AT&T Jan 94 30	13 7/8
AT&T Jan 94 30 p	7/8
AT&T Jan 94 40	8
AT&T Jan 94 40 p	3 3/4
AT&T Jan 94 50	3 3/8
BnkAm Jan 93 30	13 7/8
BnkAm Jan 93 40	6 1/2
BnkAm Jan 93 50	2 1/2
BnkAm Jan 94 50	5
Boeing Feb 93 40	9 5/8
Boeing Feb 93 40 p	1 7/8
Boeing Feb 93 50	4
Boeing Feb 93 60	1 3/8
Boeing Feb 93 60 p	13
Boeing Jan 94 40 p	3 3/8
Boeing Jan 94 60	3 3/4
BrMySq Mar 93 60	19 1/4
BrMySq Mar 93 75	9
BrMySq Mar 93 95	2 3/8
BrMySq Jan 94 70	14 3/4
BrMySq Jan 94 70 p	5 1/2
BrMySq Jan 94 85	8 1/4
Centcr Jan 93 20	4 7/8
Centcr Jan 93 20 p	5 1/4
Centcr Jan 93 30	2 3/4
Centcr Jan 93 30 p	12 1/2
Centcr Jan 93 40	1 1/16
Centcr Jan 93 40 p	21 3/8
Centcr Jan 93 55	1/2
Centcr Jan 93 55 p	36 3/8
Centcr Jan 93 70	7/16
Centcr Jan 94 20	7
Centcr Jan 94 20 p	6 1/2
Centcr Jan 94 30	5 1/8
Centcr Jan 94 30 p	13 5/8
Centcr Jan 94 40	3 1/8
Centcr Jan 94 55	1 7/8
Centcr Jan 94 70	1 1/4
Centcr Jan 94 70 p	50 1/2
Citicp Jan 93 12 1/2	5 1/8
Citicp Jan 93 15	3 3/8
Citicp Jan 93 15 p	1 3/8
Citicp Jan 93 17 1/2	2 1/2
Citicp Jan 94 15	4 5/8
CocaCl Feb 93 55	29 1/8
CocaCl Feb 93 80	10 3/8
CocaCl Feb 93 100	2 3/4
CocaCl Jan 94 65	23 7/8
CocaCl Jan 94 80	15
CocaCl Jan 94 95	8 1/2
DeltaA Jan 93 50 p	1 1/2
DowCh Mar 93 40	21 5/8
DowCh Mar 93 55	10 1/2
DowCh Mar 93 70	3 1/8
DowCh Jan 94 40 p	1 1/8
EKodak Jan 93 35	6 1/8
EKodak Jan 93 45	1 1/2
EKodak Jan 94 40	5 1/4
EKodak Jan 94 40 p	5 3/8
EKodak Jan 94 50	2 1/4
Exxon Jan 93 55	5 1/4
Exxon Jan 94 45	14
FordM Jan 93 30	11 3/8
FordM Jan 93 35	7 3/8
FordM Jan 93 40	4 3/8
FordM Jan 93 45	2 1/4
FordM Jan 94 30	13
FordM Jan 94 35	9 3/8
FordM Jan 94 40	7
FordM Jan 94 45	4 5/8
Gap Jan 93 55	2 3/8
Gap Jan 94 30	17 1/4
Gap Jan 94 40	11 1/2
Gap Jan 94 55	6 1/4
GenEl Mar 93 70	11 3/4
GenEl Mar 93 85	3 5/8
GenEl Jan 94 75	12 1/4
GenEl Jan 94 90	5 3/4
GnMotr Mar 93 25	15
GnMotr Mar 93 30	10 1/2
GnMotr Mar 93 30 p	3/4
GnMotr Mar 93 40	4 1/4
GnMotr Mar 93 40 p	4 1/8
GnMotr Mar 93 45	2 3/8
GnMotr Mar 93 45 p	7 1/4
GnMotr Jan 94 30	12
GnMotr Jan 94 30 p	2
GnMotr Jan 94 40	6 3/8
GnMotr Jan 94 40 p	5 3/4
IBM Jan 93 70	19 1/4
IBM → IBM Jan 93 70 p	1 1/2
IBM Jan 93 85	9 1/4
IBM Jan 93 85 p	6
IBM Jan 93 105	2 7/8
IBM Jan 93 135	5/8
IBM Jan 93 165	1/8
IBM Jan 94 70	21 1/2
IBM Jan 94 85	13 3/8
IBM Jan 94 85 p	9
IBM Jan 94 105	7 1/4
JohnJn Jan 93 65	37 1/2
JohnJn Jan 93 80	23 1/2
JohnJn Jan 93 100	9 1/2
JohnJn Jan 93 100 p	7 1/4
JohnJn Jan 93 120	3
JohnJn Jan 93 120 p	20
JohnJn Jan 94 90	21 1/2
JohnJn Jan 94 90 p	6 3/8
K mart Jan 94 40	15 3/4
K mart Jan 94 60	5 3/4
LizCla Jan 93 40	5 1/4
LizCla Jan 94 35	10 1/8
LizCla Jan 94 50	5 1/8
McDonl Mar 93 40	6 3/8
Merck Jan 93 80	75
Merck Jan 93 100	53 5/8
Merck Jan 93 125	32 1/8
Merck Jan 93 125 p	3
Merck Jan 93 150	16 1/2
Merck Jan 93 150 p	10 5/8
Merck Jan 93 175	6
Merck Jan 94 125	39
Merck Jan 94 150	24
Merck Jan 94 150 p	16
Merck Jan 94 175	15 3/4
Mobil Jan 93 70	1 7/8
Mobil Jan 94 65	5 1/2
Pepsi Jan 93 30	6 3/4
Pepsi Jan 93 35	3 5/8
Pepsi Jan 93 35 p	2 3/8
Pepsi Jan 93 40	1 3/8
PepsiC Jan 94 30	9 1/4
PepsiC Jan 94 35	6 5/8
PepsiC Jan 94 40	4 1/8
RJR Nb Jan 93 7 1/2	2 3/4
RJR Nb Jan 93 10	1 1/4
RJR Nb Jan 94 10 p	1 1/2
Sears Jan 93 35	13
Sears Jan 93 35 p	5/8
Sears Jan 93 45	6
Sears Jan 93 45 p	3 1/8
Sears Jan 93 55	1 3/4
Sears Jan 94 55	4 3/8
Syntex Jan 93 35	12 1/2
Syntex Jan 93 40	9
Syntex Jan 93 50	4
Syntex Jan 94 40	12 1/2
Syntex Jan 94 50 p	8 1/4
TexIns Jan 94 30 p	3 5/8
TexIns Jan 94 40	4 7/8
TexInst Jan 93 25	11
TexInst Jan 93 30	7 1/4
TexInst Jan 93 40	3 3/8
UAL Jan 93 50	9
UAL Jan 94 20	33
Upjohn Jan 93 35	4 3/4
Upjohn Jan 93 35 p	3 1/4
Upjohn Jan 93 45	1 1/4
Upjohn Jan 93 45 p	9 3/4
Upjohn Jan 94 35	6 3/4
Upjohn Jan 94 35 p	4 3/8
Upjohn Jan 94 45	3 1/4
Upjohn Jan 94 55	1 3/8
WalMt Jan 93 40	16 5/8
WalMt Jan 93 40 p	9/16
WalMt Jan 93 50	9 1/4
WalMt Jan 93 50 p	2 3/4
WalMt Jan 93 60	3 1/2
WalMt Jan 93 70	1 1/4
WalMt Jan 94 45	15 3/4
WalMt Jan 94 60	7 5/8
Xerox Jan 93 55	21 1/8
Xerox Jan 93 55 p	5/8
Xerox Jan 93 70	8 5/8
Call vol 10,436 **Opint**	272,236
Put vol 879 **Opint**	81,613

AMEX

Option/Exp/Strike	Last
AHome Dec 93 45	34 3/4
AHome Dec 93 75	12
AHome Dec 93 75 p	5 1/2
AHome Dec 93 90	5 1/4
AMR Dec 92 100	1 1/8
AMR Dec 93 80	9
ASA Dec 92 60	1/2
ASA Dec 93 35	9 1/8
ASA Dec 93 60	1 5/8
AmExp Dec 93 15	8 5/8
AmExp Dec 93 20	5 3/4
AmExp Dec 93 30	1 7/8
Amgen Jan 93 50	15
Amgen Jan 93 50 p	3 5/8
Amgen Jan 93 75	3 7/8
Amgen Jan 93 100 p	39 1/4
Amgen Jan 94 75	9 1/2
Amgen Jan 94 75 p	19 3/4
Amgen Jan 94 100	3 1/2
AppleC Dec 92 50	13 1/2
AppleC Dec 92 80	2 3/8
AppleC Dec 93 50	18
AppleC Dec 93 80	6 3/4
BellSo Jan 94 35 p	15/16
BellSo Jan 94 45	3 3/4
BellSo Jan 94 45 p	5
BellSo Jan 94 55 p	12
Chase Dec 92 20	5 1/4
Chase Dec 92 20 p	1 1/8
Chase Dec 92 25	2 1/2
Chase Dec 93 20	6 1/2
Chevrn Dec 93 50	16 1/8
Chevrn Dec 93 50 p	1 1/2
Chevrn Dec 93 75	3 1/2
Digital Dec 93 40	12 1/2
Digital Dec 93 40 p	4 7/8
Digital Dec 93 60	5
Digital Dec 93 60 p	16
Disney Dec 93 100	58 3/8
Disney Dec 93 100 p	3
Disney Dec 93 150	26 1/4
Disney Dec 93 150 p	18 1/4
Disney Dec 93 200	10
DuPont Dec 93 30	19 1/2
DuPont Dec 93 50	5 3/4
GTE Dec 93 25	7 1/2
GTE Dec 93 35	1 7/8
GTE Dec 93 35 p	5 1/2
Glaxo Jan 93 25	6
Glaxo Jan 93 25 p	2 1/8
Glaxo Jan 93 35	1 3/4
Glaxo Jan 93 35 p	7
Glaxo Jan 94 25	8 1/4
Glaxo Jan 94 25 p	3 1/8
Glaxo Jan 94 35	4 5/8
Glaxo Jan 94 45	1 7/8
Intel Dec 92 40	15
Intel Dec 92 40 p	1
Intel Dec 93 40 p	2 3/4
Intel Dec 93 65	7 1/2
Motorla Dec 93 40	44
Motorla Dec 93 40 p	3/8
Motorla Dec 93 100	6 7/8
Pfizer Dec 92 45	29 1/2
Pfizer Dec 92 70	9
Pfizer Dec 92 85	2 15/16
Pfizer Dec 92 85 p	13 3/4
Pfizer Dec 93 45	30 1/4
Pfizer Dec 93 70	13 1/4
Pfizer Dec 93 85	7 1/2
PhilMr Dec 93 60	21 3/4
PhilMr Dec 93 80	9 7/8
PhilMr Dec 93 80 p	9 1/2
PhilMr Dec 93 100	3 3/4
ProctG Dec 93 70	36 3/4
ProctG Dec 93 70 p	1 1/8
ProctG Dec 93 90	22 3/4
ProctG Dec 93 110	11 1/2
ProctG Dec 93 110 p	12 1/4
RJR Nb Jan 93 10	13/16
RJR Nb Jan 93 10 p	1 1/8
RJR Nb Jan 94 12 1/2	1 3/8
RJR Nb Jan 94 12 1/2 p	3
Reebok Dec 93 30	8 7/8
Reebok Dec 93 40	5
Tennco Jan 93 45	1 5/8
Texaco Dec 93 50	11
UCarb Dec 93 15	10 1/2
UCarb Dec 93 25	3 3/4
UCarb Dec 93 25 p	3 1/4
US Sur Jan 93 100	26 1/2
US Sur Jan 93 100 p	7 3/4
US Sur Jan 93 130	13 1/4
US Sur Jan 94 130	24 1/4
USWst Jan 94 35	3 1/8
USWst Jan 94 40	1 1/2
USXMar Jan 94 20	4 1/4
USXMar Jan 94 25	2 1/2
USXMar Jan 94 35	1
USXUSS Jan 94 25	4 3/4
USXUSS Jan 94 25 p	3 7/8
WellsF Jan 94 85	8
vjColGs Jan 94 15 p	2
Call vol 2,587 **Opint**	257,746
Put vol 2,680 **Opint**	254,707

PACIFIC

Option/Exp/Strike	Last
BakrHu Jan 94 20	3 5/8
Compq Jan 93 17 1/2	10
Compq Jan 93 25	5
Compq Jan 93 25 p	3
Compq Jan 93 35	1 11/16
Compq Jan 93 45	9/16
Compq Jan 94 25	8
Compq Jan 94 25 p	4 1/2
Compq Jan 94 35	4 1/2
Compq Jan 94 45	2 7/16
ConrPr Jan 93 12 1/2	8 1/2
ConrPr Jan 93 25	1 3/4
ConrPr Jan 94 15 p	1 1/2
GnMill Jan 93 80	1 3/4
Hilton Jan 93 40	11 3/4
Hilton Jan 93 55	4
Hilton Jan 94 40 p	3
Hilton Jan 94 50	9 1/4
Micsft Jan 93 55	76
Micsft Jan 93 83 3/8 p	2
Micsft Jan 93 85 p	1 1/2
Micsft Jan 93 105	32 1/2
Micsft Jan 93 105 p	5 1/2
Micsft Jan 93 125	20
Micsft Jan 93 125 p	14
Micsft Jan 93 150	10
Micsft Jan 93 150 p	25
Micsft Jan 94 85 p	5 1/4
Micsft Jan 94 105	41
Micsft Jan 94 105 p	9
Micsft Jan 94 125	33
Micsft Jan 94 150	22
Nike B Jan 93 75	8 3/8
Nike B Jan 93 90	2 3/4
Nike B Jan 94 55	21 1/2
Nike B Jan 94 70	14 3/4
PacTel Jan 93 40	2 1/4
SchrPl Feb 93 40	17 3/4
SchrPl Feb 93 60	4
SchrPl Feb 93 70	1 1/2
SchrPl Jan 94 40	18 1/2
SunMic Jan 94 17 1/2 p	1 3/8
Unocal Jan 93 20	3 3/4
Unocal Jan 93 25	1 1/2
Unocal Jan 94 20 p	2 1/8
Call vol 342 **Opint**	36,801
Put vol 176 **Opint**	9,691

PHILADELPHIA

Option/Exp/Strike	Last
AbtLab Jan 93 50	18
AbtLab Jan 93 60	9 1/2
AbtLab Jan 93 75	3 1/8
AbtLab Jan 94 50	20 1/4
AbtLab Jan 94 75	6 3/4
AldSgnl Jan 93 45	11 3/4
AldSgnl Jan 93 55	5 7/8
AldSgnl Jan 94 35	22
AldSgnl Jan 94 45	14 3/8
Anheus Jan 93 50	9 3/4
DomRsc Apr 92 35	13/16
DomRsc Jul 92 36 5/8	1/2
DomRsc Oct 92 35	1 1/2
FedNM Jan 93 70	6 1/2
GaPac Jan 94 75	9 3/8
HomeD Jan 93 55	16 1/8
HomeD Jan 93 55 p	2 1/8
HomeD Jan 93 65	9 5/8
HomeD Jan 93 65 p	5 1/4
HomeD Jan 93 75	5
HomeD Jan 94 35	35
HomeD Jan 94 45	27 3/4
HomeD Jan 94 55	20 1/2
HomeD Jan 94 55 p	4 1/8
HomeD Jan 94 75	10 1/8
Marriot Jan 93 15 p	1 1/2
Marriot Jan 94 15	5 1/8
Marriot Jan 94 25	1 1/2
Morgan Jan 94 50 p	5 1/4
NCNB Jan 94 50 p	9 1/8
Primca Jan 93 40	4
Primca Jan 94 25	16 3/4
QuakrO Jan 93 60	2 5/16
RJR Nb Jan 94 10	2 5/16
TimeW Jan 93 85	23 1/8
TimeW Jan 93 100	13 1/8
TimeW Jan 93 115	7
TimeW Jan 94 100 p	11
TimeW Jan 94 115 p	18 1/2
Waste Jan 93 50	1 1/16
Waste Jan 94 40 p	4 1/8
Waste Jan 94 50	3 3/4
Wolwth Jan 93 30	1 15/16
Call vol 436 **Opint**	52,318
Put vol 83 **Opint**	13,815

NEW YORK

Option/Exp/Strike	Last
CampSp Jan 93 50	1/2
CampSp Jan 94 30 p	2 3/8
FruitL Jan 93 20	18 3/4
FruitL Jan 93 30	9 7/8
Maytag Jan 93 15	5 3/8
Maytag Jan 93 20	2 1/4
Maytag Jan 94 15	6
Maytag Jan 94 20	3 1/8
Nynex Jan 94 65 p	4 1/4
Call vol 61 **Opint**	3,982
Put vol 70 **Opint**	2,760

p-Put.

Source: *The Wall Street Journal*, April 16, 1992

Option/Exp/Strike	Last	
IBM Jan 93 135	5/8	
IBM Jan 93 165	1/8	←IBM
IBM Jan 94 70	21½	
IBM Jan 94 85	13⅜	
IBM Jan 94 85 p	9	
IBM Jan 94 105	7¼	

Source: *The Wall Street Journal*, April 16, 1992

For example, if you borrow a $2 stock from your broker and sell it, you have $2. If it falls to $1, you can buy it on the market and return the stock to the broker and you keep the other dollar. This is called *selling short*. But what advantage does the broker gain? Brokers lend stocks because you have to leave the cash from your sale of the stock with them as collateral for the borrowed stock, and they can then lend (or invest) the cash at interest.

If you borrow a $2 stock from your broker in the hope the it falls to $1, you can easily return the stock to your broker if the market heads south. But what happens if you guess wrong and the stock rises to $3? You have only $2 and therefore cannot repurchase the stock for $3 in order to return it to your broker. How can the broker protect him or herself?

Your broker will insist that you maintain a substantial deposit (margin) at the brokerage firm in order to cover that risk, and if the stock does appreciate you will be required to deposit additional margin. This risk can be substantially reduced if you have a buy-stop order with your broker that instructs the broker to repurchase the stock for your account as soon as it rises to a level slightly higher than the price at which you borrowed it. Your loss will be held to a minimum.

Around the twentieth of each month *The Wall Street Journal* reports **Short Interest Highlights** for each of the Exchanges: NYSE, AMEX, and NASDAQ (OTC) (check the front-page index of the first section). The Friday, March 20, 1992 *Journal* article on page 194 serves as an example. It reports that short interest on the NYSE and AMEX fell for the month ending March 13, 1992, indicating reduced sentiment on the part of the short-sellers that the market would fall.

Short Interest On Big Board Declined 4.2%

Amex Positions Were Down By Under 1% in Period; BankAmerica Had Gain

By Robert J. Brennan
Staff Reporter of The Wall Street Journal

NEW YORK—Short interest fell 4.2% on the New York Stock Exchange and less than 1% on the American Stock Exchange, as short sellers generally cut their losses or ran up the white flag.

"A lot of short-sale funds are out of business, and a lot of clients are reducing their investments or pulling out," said Michael Murphy, a short-sale advocate and director of the Overpriced Stock Service in Half Moon Bay, Calif. "There's just less money committed to short-selling, and a sense of 'give up.' Short sellers are tired of getting beaten up."

While the stock market has generally moved up over the longer term, short sale funds have been sliding in value. Harry Strunk, an investment adviser in West Palm Beach, Fla., who tracks several short-sale funds, said they are down as a group by nearly 10% for the year to date. He said the "pure shorts," those who have no hedging purchases of stocks, are off even more.

BankAmerica again led the list, as its short interest rose to 17.8 million shares from 12.3 million at the mid-February month. Arbitragers continue to short BankAmerica and buy up **Security Pacific** Corp. ahead of the banks' pending merger, which is expected by the end of April. Arbs buy one company's shares and sell short the other's, betting on small market price discrepancies from the valuation of the merger.

SHORT INTEREST HIGHLIGHTS

Largest Short Positions

Rank	Mar. 13	Feb. 14	Change
NYSE			
1 BankAmerica	17,797,725	12,330,722	5,467,003
2 Chrysler	10,787,104	6,311,926	4,475,178
3 Blockbuster Ent	9,109,226	11,722,305	−2,613,079
4 Marriott	7,327,376	8,663,832	−1,336,456
5 Citicorp	7,317,672	10,562,285	−3,244,613
6 Saatchi adr	5,934,569	9,737,802	−3,803,233
7 Fst Intst Bcp	5,636,117	1,209,685	4,426,432
8 Unisys	5,593,594	10,245,383	−4,651,789
9 Bell Atlantic	5,506,672	4,819,249	687,423
10 Wal-Mart Stores	5,065,887	5,047,533	18,354
11 Home Depot	4,766,076	4,913,166	−147,090
12 CUC Intl	4,617,536	4,413,608	203,928
13 AT&T	4,591,958	9,002,341	−4,410,383
14 Chem Waste Mgt	4,533,683	4,701,895	−168,212
15 Ford Motor	4,422,313	3,720,709	701,604
16 Shoney's	4,257,876	4,262,653	−4,777
17 Eastman Kodak	4,231,248	4,253,838	−22,590
18 LTV	4,196,391	1,869,592	2,326,799
19 PacifiCorp	4,138,736	2,663,442	1,475,294
20 Black & Decker	4,006,828	3,927,533	79,295
AMEX			
1 Continental Air	4,134,947	4,515,780	−380,833
2 Alza	3,957,117	3,728,605	228,512
3 Energy Svc	3,639,735	3,726,619	−86,884
4 Turner Bdcst B	2,691,039	2,240,800	450,239
5 Ivax	2,391,964	2,164,706	227,258

Largest Changes

Rank	Mar. 13	Feb. 14	Change
NYSE			
1 BankAmerica	17,797,725	12,330,722	5,467,003
2 Chrysler	10,787,104	6,311,926	4,475,178
3 Fst Intst Bcp	5,636,117	1,209,685	4,426,432
4 GM E	3,708,981	978,838	2,730,143
5 Foodmaker	2,388,070	0	2,388,070
6 LTV	4,196,391	1,869,592	2,326,799
7 Conner Periph	2,438,184	587,234	1,850,950
8 PacifiCorp	4,138,736	2,663,442	1,475,294
1 Tel Espana adr	407,752	9,423,574	−9,015,822
2 Unisys	5,593,594	10,245,383	−4,651,789
3 AT&T	4,591,958	9,002,341	−4,410,383
4 Newell	484,559	4,303,986	−3,819,427
5 Saatchi adr	5,934,569	9,737,802	−3,803,233
6 Citicorp	7,317,672	10,562,285	−3,244,613
7 Blockbuster Ent	9,109,226	11,722,305	−2,613,079
AMEX			
1 Wang Lab B	1,057,724	49,029	1,008,695
2 Turner Bdcst B	2,691,039	2,240,800	450,239
3 US Bioscience	1,411,352	1,024,006	387,346
4 Specialty Chem	360,000	0	360,000
1 Continental Air	4,134,947	4,515,780	−380,833
2 Natl Envr	16,256	370,844	−354,588
3 Fruit Loom	695,177	1,038,731	−343,554
4 Enzo Biochem	233,531	576,105	−342,574

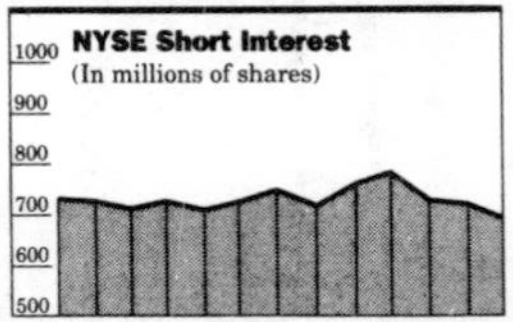

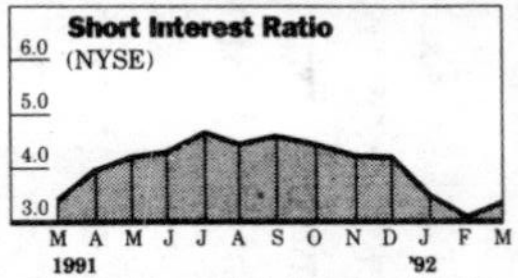

The short interest ratio is the number of days it would take to cover the short interest if trading continued at the average daily volume for the month.

Largest Short Interest Ratios

	Mar. 13 Short Int	Avg Dly Vol-a	Days to Cover
NYSE			
1 A.L. Labs A	2,382,095	25,173	95
2 Cineplex Odeon	2,460,856	27,542	89
3 Nthn Sts Pwr	2,562,633	35,526	72
4 Chock Full O'Nuts	1,321,396	22,410	59
5 CUC Intl	4,617,536	82,900	56
6 Kansas P&L	3,320,404	61,794	54
7 Blackstn N.A. Gvt	1,735,049	36,194	48
8 Midwest Resources	914,994	23,078	40
9 Columbia Gas Sys	3,970,674	105,100	38
10 Orion Pictures	1,273,236	34,215	37
11 Omnicom Group	1,879,912	54,110	35
12 Shoney's	4,257,876	122,931	35
13 Puget Sound P&L	1,373,175	41,047	33
14 Longs Drug Strs	976,914	29,589	33
15 Marriott	7,327,376	229,073	32
16 Nevada Pwr	697,207	22,126	32
17 Freeport-Mc C&G	2,081,050	68,815	30
AMEX			
1 Energy Svc	3,639,735	70,584	52
2 Turner Bdcst B	2,691,039	99,921	27
3 Jan Bell Mktg	1,747,087	65,710	27
4 New Line Cinema	624,250	24,284	26
5 Citizens Fst Bcp	976,839	38,857	25

a-Includes securities with average daily volume of 20,000 shares or more.

r-Revised. The largest percentage increase and decrease sections are limited to issues with previously established short positions in both months.

Largest % Increases

Rank	Mar. 13	Feb. 14	%
NYSE			
1 Blkstn Mun Targ	60,580	220	27,436.4
2 Ntl Westmn adr	341,785	4,733	7,121.3
3 Rhone-Poul un	98,510	1,496	6,484.9
4 General Host	221,006	8,342	2,549.3
5 Bco Santndr adr	94,800	3,749	2,428.7
6 Philips N.V.	1,042,011	41,496	2,411.1
7 Unifi.	80,350	4,300	1,768.6
8 Imperial Chm adr	648,855	39,709	1,534.0
9 Shell TT new adr	675,549	56,719	1,091.0
10 Barclays adr	170,500	18,499	821.7
11 Lomas Fincl new	310,740	39,816	680.4
12 Putnam HY Mun	244,105	32,100	660.5
13 Putnam Prm Inco	109,216	15,757	593.1
14 Savin new	100,485	16,087	524.6
15 MFS Inter Inco	140,008	23,547	494.6
16 Contl Medical Sys	310,213	65,087	376.6
17 Am President Co	105,084	22,364	369.9
18 KN Energy	92,720	19,815	367.9
19 Fst Intst Bcp	5,636,117	1,209,685	365.9
20 Brit Petr adr	1,029,864	222,086	363.7
AMEX			
1 Wang Lab B	1,057,724	49,029	2,057.3
2 DWG	81,175	9,700	736.9
3 Merr Lynch pt wt	102,193	14,393	610.0
4 Turner Bdcst A	250,660	91,010	175.4
5 Parker Parsley	206,187	83,546	146.8

Largest % Decreases

Rank	Mar. 13	Feb. 14	%
NYSE			
1 Brit Gas fin adr	40	1,437,162	−100.0
2 IRT Property	1,899	700,000	−99.7
3 Cyclops Indus	800	72,900	−98.9
4 Beld Heminway	2,347	137,799	−98.3
5 Utd Water Res	9,055	434,103	−97.9
6 Bco Bilbao adr	3,477	143,826	−97.6
7 UGI	7,450	284,450	−97.4
8 Integon	8,250	313,440	−97.4
9 Amphenol A	2,802	74,776	−96.3
10 Tel Espana adr	407,752	9,423,574	−95.7
11 Total adr B	166,020	2,704,435	−93.9
12 Equimark new	119,528	1,935,443	−93.8
13 Bancorp Hawaii	71,508	951,050	−92.5
14 Helene Curtis	7,004	87,334	−92.0
15 Freeport-Mc Res	15,351	179,302	−91.4
16 Van Dorn	7,660	75,438	−89.8
17 Texas Inst $2.26	16,882	155,600	−89.2
18 Newell Co.	484,559	4,303,986	−88.7
19 Nacco Ind A	12,274	102,425	−88.0
20 DPL	94,939	699,233	−86.4
AMEX			
1 CVB Fincl	1,000	66,940	−98.5
2 Halsey Drug	6,000	164,130	−96.3
3 Natl Envr	16,256	370,844	−95.6
4 Hanson wt B	8,284	87,874	−90.6
5 Pn Webber put wt	25,400	97,100	−73.8

Source: *The Wall Street Journal*, March 20, 1992

Short interest is the number of borrowed shares that have not been returned to the lender. A great deal of short interest in a stock indicates widespread speculation that a stock will fall. Remember, however, that these shares must be repaid, and that those who owe stock must buy it in order to repay it. Their stock purchases could bid the stock up.

This ambivalence illustrates the difficulty in using short-interest data. For instance, the charts under **Short Interest Highlights** indicates about 700 million shares had not yet been returned to brokers (NYSE Short Interest) and that this was more than three times recent trading volume (Short Interest Ratio). Despite the fact that this indicates considerable sentiment that stocks will fall, a short-interest ratio of over two has been a rule of thumb that stocks will rise because these borrowed stocks must be repurchased to be repaid. Therefore, it is difficult to find meaning in the ratio.

Nonetheless, this does not mean that you should remain unconcerned if there is a substantial short interest increase in an individual stock in your portfolio. The forces that move the entire market may not be the same as those that move an individual stock. What does the smart money know about your stock that you don't? It's an important question, and one that you should ask. So follow this report each month in the *Journal*.

Foreign Markets

Finally, you can buy shares of stock on **Canadian Markets** and on **Foreign Markets**. The *Journal* provides daily listings, and you can find them in the front page indexes of the first and last sections. Representative samples are included on page 198 from the Friday, June 5, 1992 edition. Remember that when you invest in foreign markets you must be concerned with the fluctuation of foreign currency values as well as the value of the shares you purchase. A rise in the dollar's value against the currency in which your shares are denominated can wipe out your gain, while a fall in the dollar's value could accentuate that gain. In addition, information on foreign stocks is often not as complete and accurate as on U.S. stocks. Let the buyer beware.

In any event, the disparities among the performances of the overseas markets have been huge. Each day the *Journal's* **World Markets** feature (see the front page indexes) carries a report on foreign stock markets that provides detail on recent developments as well as historical trends. (See page 197.)

If these disparities alarm you, there is a way you can invest in foreign firms while keeping your money in dollars and in the U.S. American Depository Receipts (ADRs) are negotiable instruments representing foreign securities that trade like stocks in the U.S. They are listed each day in the *Journal* at the end of the **Nasdaq Bid and Asked Quotations.** For instance, see the page 199 listing under **ADRS** from the June 25, 1992 edition.

EARNINGS AND DIVIDENDS

Many investors focus so heavily upon the potential capital gain (increase in price) of their stock that they ignore the dividends it pays. These dividends can be an important part of a stock's total return, so take a moment to consider corporate earnings and dividends.

Corporations issue stock to raise capital; investors buy shares of it to participate in the growth of the business, to earn dividends, and to enjoy possible capital gains. The ability of a corporation to pay dividends and the potential for increase in the value of a share of stock depend directly on the profits earned by the corporation: the greater the flow of profit (and anticipated profit), the higher the price investors will pay for that share of stock.

The ownership value of assets depends on the income they generate, just as the value of farmland reflects profits that can be reaped by raising crops on it and the value of an apartment building reflects rent that can be collected. Similarly, the value of a share in the ownership of a corporation ultimately depends on the ability of that corporation to create profits. Note that the value of an asset depends not only on the income it currently earns but also on its potential for greater earnings and on investors' willingness to pay for these actual and potential earnings.

A corporation's profit is one of the most important measures of its success. Profit indicates the effectiveness and efficiency with which its assets are managed and employed. Profits calibrate the ability of a firm to make and sell its product or service for more than the cost of production. Profit means that the firm has efficiently combined the labor, material, and capital necessary to produce and market its product at a price that people will pay and that will provide the owners with the financial incentive to expand the operation. When costs exceeds revenues and the

WORLD MARKETS

Stocks Slump in Tokyo and Rebound in London; European Bourses Unsettled by Treaty Outlook

A WALL STREET JOURNAL *News Roundup*

Tokyo stocks slumped in thin trading Thursday, with rumors that President Bush was ill helping to push the Nikkei index below the 18000 level. London shares bounced back from a sell-off to close slightly higher. Frankfurt prices also overcame initial weakness to end with gains.

In Tokyo, the Nikkei 225-stock index, which rose 63.13 points Wednesday, dropped 224.61, or 1.23%, to 17964.07.

On Friday, the Nikkei index fell 103.67 points to close the morning session at 17860.40.

Thursday's first-section volume was estimated at 220 million shares, down from 251.5 million Wednesday. Losers overwhelmed gainers, 659-246.

The Tokyo Stock Price Index of all first section issues, which added 1.8 points Wednesday, fell 12.28 to 1354.10.

Investors continued to stay on the sidelines before the June 12 special quotation on June Nikkei futures, allowing the market to be buffeted by index-related arbitrage activity. The bourse remained lackluster because of a lack of convincing signs that Japan's economy is recovering.

Reports in Tokyo's afternoon session that President Bush had left a theater late Wednesday in the middle of a performance, with the White House providing no explanation, sparked rumors that he was ill. That helped to push down futures prices and then stock prices.

In London, the Financial Times-Stock Exchange 100-share index edged up 1 point to 2681.9, near the intraday high of 2683.6, after recovering from the session low of 2665.2 as sell-offs on the both the futures and bond markets spread to equities. The FT 30-stock averaged added 1.9 points to 2092.6. Volume was 503 million shares, compared with 473.6 million shares a day earlier. Turnover was flat for much of the session because of the loss of part of the stock exchange's electronic information service; the system resumed in the early afternoon, too late for institutional investors to return to the market.

London investors' attention focused on individual stocks affected by corporate news. Investors overall remain unsettled following Denmark's rejection of the European Community's treaty on economic and political integration.

In Frankfurt, the DAX 30-stock index rose 3.73 points to 1792.31. Trading was lively, with volatility attributed to simulated program trading and an unexpected rebound. June futures trading strongly influenced the DAX stocks; though real index trading doesn't exist in Germany, speculators can buy packages of the 10 or so most important DAX stocks and thereby nudge the index.

The reaction to the Danish referendum was mixed on other big European bourses. Paris stocks recovered a bit, after falling in a panic reaction to the Danish rejection of the EC accord. Amsterdam shares closed broadly higher after confidence in European political and economic union was restored, once the Continent's leaders decided to proceed without Denmark. But Madrid stocks had heavy losses on investors' concern about the effect on the Spanish market from a possible collapse of the EC accord. And in Milan, worries that European union may be growing more distant pushed share prices lower. This anxiety also troubled the Stockholm market, where prices fell.

In Seoul, despite action by the Stock Stabilization Fund to support the market, share prices ended lower, weighed down by negative sentiment that a significant market recovery isn't likely soon.

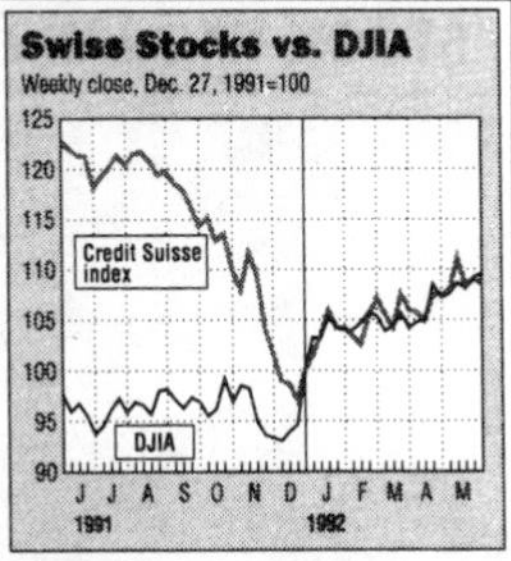

Stock Market Indexes

EXCHANGE	6/4/92 CLOSE	NET CHG	PCT CHG
Tokyo Nikkei Average	17964.07	– 224.61	– 1.23
Tokyo Topix Index	1354.10	– 12.28	– 0.90
London FT 30-share	2092.6	+ 1.9	+ 0.09
London 100-share	2681.9	+ 1.0	+ 0.04
London Gold Mines	107.3	+ 1.0	+ 0.94
Frankfurt DAX	1792.31	+ 3.73	+ 0.21
Zurich Swiss Market	1916.9	+ 1.7	+ 0.09
Paris CAC 40	1994.87	+ 2.26	+ 0.11
Milan Stock Index	972	– 9	– 0.92
Amsterdam ANP-CBS General	215.3	+ 0.6	+ 0.28
Stockholm Affarsvariden	979.7	– 4.2	– 0.43
Brussels Bel-20 Index	1224.1	– 7.13	– 0.58
Australia All Ordinaries	1676.7	– 1.4	– 0.08
Hong Kong Hang Seng	6035.80	– 1.57	– 0.03
Singapore Straits Times	1507.44	– 6.28	– 0.41
Johannesburg J'burg Gold	1086	– 15	– 1.36
Madrid General Index	258.06	– 2.36	– 0.91
Mexico I.P.C.	1895.90	+ 8.97	+ 0.48
Toronto 300 Composite	3403.42	– 3.92	– 0.12
Euro, Aust, Far East MSCI-p	803.9	– 3.5	– 0.43

p-Preliminary
na-Not available

Source: *The Wall Street Journal*, June 5, 1992

FOREIGN MARKETS

Thursday, June 4, 1992

TOKYO
(in yen)

	Close	Prev. Close
ANA	1010	1020
Ajinomoto	1340	1310
Alps Elec	999	999
Amada Co	1050	1070
Ando Elec	1030	1010
Anritsu	935	935
Asahi Chem	670	682
Asahi Glass	1070	1060
Bank of Tokyo	1050	1100
Bk of Yokohama	972	970
Banyu Pharm	1090	1090
Bridgestone	1180	1170
Brother Ind	451	474
C. Itoh	423	424
CSK	2830	2910
Canon Inc	1400	1420
Canon Sales	2450	2450
Casio Computer	1240	1260
Chubu Pwr	2490	2470
Chugai Pharm	1090	1110
Citizen Watch	836	845
Dai Nippon Print	1370	1400
Dai-ichi Kangyo	1370	1420
Daiei	925	910
Daiichi Seiyaku	1470	1510
Dainippon Pharm	1260	1280
Daiwa House	1840	1860
Daiwa Securities	862	885
Eisai	1360	1350
Ezaki Glico	1320	1310
Fanuc	4260	4310
Fuji Bank	1430	1450
Fuji HI	354	357
Fuji Photo Film	2840	2860
Fujisawa Pharm	1100	1100
Fujitsu	656	665
Furukawa Elec	453	465
Green Cross	949	951
Haseko	590	598
Hirose Elec	3400	3490
Hitachi Cable	650	653
Hitachi Credit	1190	1180
Hitachi Ltd	790	800
Hitachi Maxell	1370	1380
Hitachi Metals	790	799
Hitachi Sales	560	575
Honda Motor	1460	1490
Hosiden Elec	1640	1650
Hoya	1780	1830
IHI	446	456
Ind Bank Japan	1790	1830
Intec	1730	1760
Isetan	2290	2260
Isuzu	293	296
Ito-yokado	4400	4470
Iwatsu Elec	405	410
JAL	740	740
JEOL	858	865
JUSCO	1570	1580
Japan Aviat El	610	608
Japan Radio	1980	1970
Jujo Paper	541	553
KDD	9260	9270
Kajima	992	992
Kandenko	2450	2410
Kansai Elec	2400	2430
Kao Corp	1080	1090
Kawasaki HI	421	428
Kawasaki Steel	300	300
Kinki Elec Con	2100	2110
Kirin	1190	1210
Kobe Steel	328	328
Kokusai Elec	2130	2130
Kokuyo	2400	2430
Komatsu Ltd	629	631
Konica	599	600
Kubota	512	525
Kumagai Gumi	547	550
Kuraray	1160	1170
Kureha Chem	465	470
Kyocera	4400	4430
Kyowa Hakko	1000	1040
Kyushu Matsushit	2530	2510
Lion	604	618
Makino Milling	690	693
Makita Elec	1890	1920
Marudai Food	880	880
Marui	1270	1290
Matsushita Com	2120	2110
Mats' Elec Ind	1340	1350
Mats' Elec Wrks	1100	1110
Mazda	487	495
Meiji Seika	690	676
Minolta	392	393
Misawa Homes	1390	1390
Mitsubishi Bank	1780	1790
Mitsubishi Corp	1000	1010
Mitsubishi Elec	482	484
Mitsubishi Real	879	891
Mitsubishi HI	577	587
Mitsubishi Kasei	434	447
Mitsubishi Matl	433	441
Mitsubishi Trust	950	1000
Mitsubishi Whse	1090	1120
Mitsui Fudosan	990	1000
Mitsui Mar&Fire	690	690
Mitsui Trust	813	840
Mitsui & Co	584	586
Mitsukoshi	802	834
Mochida Pharm	3770	3730
NCR Japan	906	907
NEC	928	943
NGK Spark	809	809
NIFCO	1280	1290
NKK	275	277
NSK	594	590
NTN	507	495
NTT	611000	625000
Nihon Unisys Ltd	1370	1390
Nikko Securities	639	637
Nikon Corp	645	660
Nintendo	10600	10600
Nippon Chemi-con	733	748
Nippon Columbia	543	545
Nippon El Glass	1550	1580
Nippon Express	697	705
Nippon Hodo	2410	2430
Nippon Meat	1820	1820
Nippon Mining	471	485
Nippon Oil	707	697
Nippon Sanso	495	496
Nippon Shinpan	686	692
Nippon Steel	293	298
Nissan Motor	603	605
Nissin Food	2200	2220
Nitsuko	650	651
Nomura Securities	1430	1440
OKK	607	601
Obayashi Corp	600	607
Odakyu Railway	725	734
Oji Paper	840	850
Oki Elec Ind	412	421
Okuma Corp	921	937
Olympus Optical	1160	1180
Ono Pharm	6530	6600
Onoda Cement	486	488
Onward	1250	1250
Orient Corp	700	709
Pioneer Electron	3630	3660
Renown	516	510
Ricoh Co	525	529
Royal Co	1250	1250
Ryobi	513	513
SMK	535	525
Sakura Bank	1090	1110
Sankyo Co	2490	2520
Sanrio	1450	1470
Sanwa Bank	1340	1350
Sanyo Elec	460	462
Sapporo Brewery	947	977
Secom	6160	6200
Sekisui House	1290	1300
Seven-eleven	7120	7210
Sharp	1170	1210
Shimizu Corp	1020	1040
Shin-etsu Chem	1500	1510
Shionogi	770	776
Shiseido	1390	1400
Showa Denko	310	310
Skylark	1610	1630
Sony	4390	4390
Sumitomo Bank	1500	1480
Sumitomo Chem	450	461
Sumitomo Corp	874	868
Sumitomo Elec	1010	1050
Sumitomo Marine	728	727
Sumitomo Metal	287	290
Sumitomo Realty	709	719
Sumitomo Trust	950	979
Suzuki Motor	745	753
TDK	4310	4300
Taisei Corp	710	720
Taisho Pharm	1900	1900
Taiyo Yuden	690	701
Takeda Chem	1100	1090
Tanabe Seiyaku	917	930
Teijin	440	452
Toho Co	14400	15000
Tokio Mar&Fire	1010	1010
Tokyo Elec Power	2730	2780
Tokyo Electron	1830	1880
Tokyo Gas	441	448
Tokyo Style	1340	1330
Tokyu Corp	592	604
Tonen Corp	1210	1210
Toppan Print	1090	1100
Toray	635	647
Toshiba	646	645
Toto	1710	1680
Toyo Seikan	3210	3200
Toyobo	405	402
Toyoda Mach	683	692
Toyota Motor	1510	1500
Tsugami	636	636
Uny	1130	1140
Ushio	655	664
Wacoal	890	872
Yamaha	921	986
Yamaichi Sec	572	590
Yamanouchi Phm	2560	2580
Yamatake-Hnywl	1150	1180
Yamato Transport	1020	1020
Yamazaki Baking	1900	1900
Yasuda Fire	633	631
Yokogawa Elec	791	791

LONDON
(in pence)

	Close	Prev. Close
Albert Fisher	74	73.5
Allied-Lyons	657	649
Argyll Group	353	348
Arjo Wiggins	268	266
Assoc Brit Fds	442	443
BAA PLC	659	655
Barclays	369	373
Bass	613	611
BAT Indus	795	810
Blue Circle	247	244
BOC Group	682	681
Body Shop	305	303
Boots	467	490
Borland	2663	2763
Bowater Indus	828	831
BPB Indus	189	181
British Aero	344	343
British Airwys	287	288
British Gas	259	255.5
British Pete	271	268
British Steel	79	80
British Telcom	359	355
BTR	474	476
Burmah Castrol	637	636
Cable&Wireless	555	555
Cadbury Schwp	468	464
Charter Cons	544	545
Coats Viyella	213	212
Commercial Un	500	500
Courtaulds	565	552
Dixons	268	268
Dowty Group	182	176
Eng Ch Clay	569	552
Fisons	362	362
Forte	232	222
GEC	221	220.5
Genrl Accidnt	483	483
GKN	423	427
Glaxo Hldgs	752	756
Granada	283.5	283
Grand Metrop	493	493
Guardian Royal	154	151
Guinness	599	598
Hanson PLC	231	229.25
Hillsdown	175	172
Imp Chem Ind	1331	1328
Jefferson Smurf	545	538
Johnson Mathy	425	425
Kingfisher	535	545
Ladbroke Grp	234	229
Land Securs	412	415
LASMO	197	191
Legal & Genl	390	394
Lloyds Bank	435	438
Lonrho	90	90
Lucas	137	143
Marks&Spencer	325	326
MEPC	315	330
Midland Bank	467	457
Nat Power PLC	242.5	239
Nat Wstmn Bk	361	365
NFC	272	271
P & O	501	502
Pearson	854	865
Pilkgtn Bros	142	145
Prudential	246	249
Racal Elect	63.25	63.75
Rank Org	757	755
Recklt&Colman	649	651
Redland	515	508
Reed Intl	570	580
Reuters	1179	1185
RMC	595	609
Rolls Royce	165	164
Royal Insur	249.5	244
RTZ Corp	619	615
Stchi&Stchi	20.25	20.75
J Sainsbury	471	473
Sears	93	93
Sedgwick Grp	217	215
Shell Trnspt	512	507
Siebe PLC	732	739
Smithkln Bchm	893	904
Smith&Nephew	149.5	150
Std Chartrd	480	483
Storehouse	145	144
Sun Alliance	317	315
Tarmac	129	128
Tate & Lyle	386	389
Tesco	278	278
Thorn EMI	856	850
Trafalgar Hse	136	136
TSB Group	147	147
Utd Biscuits	397	399
Unilever	924	918
Vodafone	378	378
Warburg	553	555
Wellcome	958	963
WPP Group	58	58

South African Mines
(in U.S. dollars)

	Close	Prev. Close
Bracken	0.28	0.28
Deelkraal	1.60	1.60
Doornfontein	0.30	0.30
Durban Deep	4.50	4.50
E. Rand Gold	1.43	1.43
E. Rand Prop	2.50	2.50
Elandsrand	5.25	5.25
Elsburg	0.50	0.45
Grootvlei	1.00	1.00
Harmony	4.85	4.80
Hartebstftn	4.18	4.13
Impala Pltm	14.87	14.81
Kinross	10.38	10.38
Leslie	0.53	0.53
Libanon	0.60	0.55
Loraine	0.48	0.48
Randfontein	4.56	4.37
Rustenburg	23.56	23.16
Southvaal	17.25	17.25
Stilfontein	0.65	0.65
Unisel	2.25	2.25
West Areas	0.78	0.73
Winkelhaak	9.25	9.25

FRANKFURT
(in Marks)

	Close	Prev. Close
AEG	205.5	206.7
Allianz	2270	2255
Asko	809	810
BASF	245.7	246
Bayer	289.3	290
Byr Vereinsbk	410	413
BMW	610	611
Commerzbank	253	254
Continental	271.9	271
Daimler Benz	809.5	808.5
Degussa	366.5	363
Deutsche Bank	692.5	692.5
Dresdner Bank	343.5	341.7
Henkel	618	619
Hochtief	1283	1275
Hoechst	260.5	262
Karstadt	631.5	627.5
Kaufhof	497	496
Linde	861	869
Lufthansa	138.3	137
Mannesmann	306.3	306
MAN	405	404
Metallges	447.5	445
Munchen Ruck	2425	2380
Porsche	n.a.	509
RWE	414.5	415
Schering	747.5	755
Siemens	683.2	680
Thyssen	248	245.5
Veba	408.9	407.5
VEW	214.1	214.1
Volkswagen	409	407.6

BRUSSELS
(in Belgian francs)

	Close	Prev. Close
Arbed	4130	4100
BBL	3505	3505
Bekaert	13050	13075
Delhaize	c1800	9030
Electrabel	4595	4645
GIB	1454	1458
Gevaert	6900	7000
Gen de Bnque	6220	6220
Petrofina	10650	10675
Soc Gen Belg	2240	2255
Solvay	13425	13575

c–five for one stock split.

MILAN
(in lire)

	Close	Prev. Close
Banca Com	3100	3162
Benetton	13875	13990
Ciga	1696	1732
CIR	1745	1775
FIAT Com	5400	5370
FIAT Pref	3528	3615
Generali	29240	29495
Mediobanca	13600	13810
Montedison	1475	1496
Olivetti Com	3065	3100
Olivetti NC	1865	1890
Pirelli Co	4540	4530
Pirelli SpA	1413	1430
Rinascente	6350	6389
RAS	18040	18525
Saipem	1659	1656
SIP	1386	1400
Snia	1161	1174

PARIS
(in French francs)

	Close	Prev. Close
Accor	768	767
Air Liquide	785	780
Alcatel Alstm	648	650
BSN-Gervais	1095	1101
Carrefour	2646	2640
Club Med	523	526
Dassault Avitn	391	380
Elf Aquitaine	391.8	392.4
Elf Sanofi	1074	1079
Euro Disneyld	115.3	115
Generale Eaux	2349	2339
Hachette	142	139.1
Havas	537	538
Imetal	356	352
Lafarge Coppe	369.4	367.5
LVMH	4085	4030
Machines Bull	34	34
Matra	189	188.2
Michelin	216.4	218.8
L'Oreal	897	889
Paribas	408	401.6
Pernod Ricard	1543	1540
Peugeot	769	770
Saint Gobain	588	586
Schneider	771	775
Soc Generale	532	520
Suez	322.2	328
Thomson CSF	161.3	160.9
Total Francais	260	258.4

STOCKHOLM
(in krona)

	Close	Prev. Close
AGA	292	292
Asea	387	390
Astra	545	546
Atlas Copco	325	328
Electrolux	267	268
Ericsson	145	145
SE Bank	37.5	37
Skanska	118	116
SKF	121	121
Volvo	417	421

SWITZERLAND
(in Swiss francs)

	Close	Prev. Close
Alusuisse	517	505
Brown Boveri	4330	4300
Ciba-Geigy br	3510	3510
Ciba-Geigy reg	3560	3560
Ciba-G ptc cff	3460	3450
CS Holding	2030	2020
Hof LaRoch br	4700	4690
Roche div rt	3360	3370
Nestle bearer	9810	9790
Nestle reg	9790	9770
Nestle ptc cff	1920	1920
Sandoz	2870	2840
Sulzer	558	540
Swiss Bnk Cp	273	270
Swiss Reinsur	2590	2580
Swissair	765	765
UBS	3830	3830
Winterthur	3340	3340
Zurich Ins	4180	4220

AMSTERDAM
(in guilders)

	Close	Prev. Close
ABN Amro	44.70	44.70
Aegon	123.70	123.40
Ahold	87.20	86.20
Akzo	158.60	158.60
AMEV	55	55
Buhrmn-Tett	51.40	50.77
DSM	115.30	115.10
Elsevier	114.40	114
Fokker	33.70	34.30
Gist-Brocades	39.90	39.80
Heineken	167.20	166.50
Hoogovens	58.70	57.70
Intl Ndrlndn Gr	48.30	48.10
KLM	40.30	39.50
KNP	49.60	49.20
Nedlloyd	60.40	59.70
Oce-van Grntn	77.30	72.20
Pakhoed Hldg	45.40	45
Philips	38	37.90
Robeco	98.30	98.50
Rodamco	48.60	48.70
Rolinco	96.90	97.20
Rorento	73.50	73.50
Royal Dutch	158.80	158.10
Unilever	184.70	184.70
VOC	42.60	42.40
VNU	87.50	88
VRG-Group	45.70	46.30
Wessanen	92.80	93.40
Wolters Kluwer	74.30	73.80

HONG KONG
(in Hong Kong dollars)

	Close	Prev. Close
Bank E Asia	32.50	32.50
Cathay Pacific	12.80	12.60
Cheung Kong	26.50	26.80
China L & P	35.25	34.75
Dairy Farm	12.30	12.40
Hang Seng Bk	45.75	45.50
HK Electric	19.40	19.10
HK Land	13	12.80
HK Telecom	9.15	9.40
HSBC Hldgs	48.25	47.75
Hutchsn Whmp	19.40	19.50
Jardine Mathsn	62.50	62
Sun Hung Kai	33.25	33.25
Swire Pacific	35	35.50
Wharf Holdings	18	18

SYDNEY
(in Australian dollars)

	Close	Prev. Close
Amcor	7.57	7.59
ANZ Group	4.16	4.18
Ashton	1.51	1.51
Boral	3.22	3.24
Bougainville	0.40	0.40
Brambles Inds	17.62	17.50
Brokn Hill Prp	14.44	14.40
Burns Philp	3.64	3.65
Coles Myer	12.48	12.50
Comalco	4.13	4.08
Centrl Norsemn	0.46	0.47
CRA	14.78	14.86
CSR	4.65	4.65
Foster's	2.10	2.08
Gld Mns Kalgo	0.77	0.79
Goodman	1.55	1.55
Leighton	1.55	1.55
Mayne Nickless	7.68	7.63
MIM Holdings	2.82	2.82
Nat Aust Bnk	7.94	7.97
News Corp	22.22	22.44
Normdy Poseidn	1.05	1.05
Nrth Brk Hill	2.22	2.26
Orbital Engine	3.36	3.38
Pacific Dunlop	5.50	5.48
Pancontinental	0.83	0.80
Renison Gldflds	5.12	5.08
Santos	2.73	2.72
S Pac Pete	0.41	0.40
TNT Ltd	1.83	1.84
Western Mining	5.35	5.33
Westpac	3.55	3.52
Woodside	3.90	3.91

MEXICO
(in pesos)

	Close	Prev. Close
Alfa A	25600	25700
Apasco A	11500	11500
Bimbo 1	12000	12000
Bimbo 2	12850	12900
Banacci C	21700	21000
Cemex B	56000	56000
Cifra B	6050	6050
Cifra C	5125	5200
Femsa B	13450	12800
Gcarso A1	18950	18800
Kimber A	28400	28600
Maseca B2	2500	2500
Tamsa	18800	18700
Tfolmex B2	26300	26000
Vitro	24000	24000

CANADIAN MARKETS

Quotations in Canadian Funds
Quotations in cents unless marked $
Thursday, June 4, 1992

TORONTO

Sales	Stock	High	Low	Close	Chg.
7854	Abti Prce	$16⅛	16	16	− ⅛
13550	Agnico E	$5⅛	5	5	
41700	Air Canada	$5	495	5	
17100	Alt Energy	$12⅝	12½	12⅝	
15000	Alta Nat	$13⅞	13¾	13¾	− ⅛
93650	A Barick	$31¼	30⅝	30⅞	
12800	Atco I f	$11½	11¼	11¼	− ⅜
36234	Aur Res o	275	265	270	+ 2
147640	BCE Inc	$44	43¾	43⅞	− ⅛
12374	BC Gas	$16⅛	16	16⅛	+ ⅛
6041	BF Realty	7½	7	7½	+ ½
3620	BP Canada	$12⅛	12	12	
10300	BtBk Nk ii	$10½	10⅜	10⅜	+ ⅜
3600	BtBk nk iv	$13⅞	13½	13⅞	+ ⅜
2500	BtBk TB w	275	275	275	
136730	Bank N S	$20⅞	20¾	20⅞	
1100	Baton	$7	7	7	
400	BCE Mobl	$25¼	25¼	25¼	+ ⅛
90813	Bramalea	178	165	165	−13
42580	BC Tele	$19¾	19½	19⅝	− ¼
68300	CAE	$6⅛	6	6	− ⅛
3900	CCL B f	$9⅝	9½	9½	
2670	Cambridg	$18¼	18⅛	18¼	
606	Camdev	$7⅝	7⅜	7⅜	− ⅜
87950	Cameco	$17⅝	17½	17½	− ¼
284565	CI Bk Com	$26⅛	25⅝	25¾	− ½
1050	CP Forest	$27½	27½	27½	+ ⅛
744844	CP Ltd	$18¾	18½	18¾	+ ⅛
49421	CTire A f	$18¼	18⅛	18¼	
3663	C Util B	$19¼	19⅛	19¼	+ ⅛
800	Canfor	$28	28	28	− ⅛
2000	Cara	440	435	435	−15
100	Celanese	$43	43	43	− ¼
584	Cntrl Cap	20	16	20	+ 5
131050	Cineplex	380	345	375	+15
875	CocaCBev	$6⅞	6⅝	6⅞	+ ⅛
7800	C Enfield	60	60	60	
32600	Crownx A f	145	141	145	+ 5
6280	Corel Svs	$23	22⅝	22¾	− ⅛
17450	Denison A p	37	34	34	
43500	Derlan	$5¾	5½	5¾	− ⅛
200	Dicknsn A f	405	405	405	+ 5
470668	Dofasco	$12¾	12½	12⅝	− ¼
33400	Du Pont A	$45	45	45	
108400	Dylex A f	395	385	390	
268588	Encor Inc	33½	31	32	−1½
26550	Euro Nev	$16½	16½	16½	
1000	FCA Intl	$7⅜	7⅜	7⅜	
1300	FPI Ltd	405	400	405	+10
10100	Fahnstk A f	$8¾	8⅝	8¾	
5850	Fed Ind A	$6⅝	6½	6½	+ ¼
1120	Finning L	$13⅞	13⅞	13⅞	+ ⅛
2175	Flet CCan A	$14⅝	14⅝	14⅝	− ¼
2550	Flet CInv 2	$24⅛	24	24⅛	+ ⅛
10450	FSesn HI f	$21¼	20⅞	21	
12630	Franco	$26⅛	25¾	26	
7100	Goldcorp f	270	265	265	− 5
52100	Hees Intl	$13⅜	13	13	− ⅜
33920	Hemlo Gld	$9⅛	9	9⅛	
1000	Hollingr I	$10⅝	10⅝	10⅝	
590	Harrows A	23	18	18	− 4
116110	Horsham f	$9⅝	9½	9½	
10102	H Bay Co	$30¼	30	30⅛	− ⅛
106095	Imasco L	$36½	35⅞	35⅞	− ½
20823	Intrprov P	$24⅝	24½	24⅝	+ ⅛
8800	I SemiT Af	$16⅞	16½	16⅝	− ⅛
6517	Ipsco	$18	17⅞	17⅞	− ⅜
8449	ISG Tech	$12	11½	11¾	− ½
6163	Ivaco A f	465	450	450	−25
2200	Jannock	$15⅛	15	15	− ⅛
87788	Labatt	$26¼	26	26⅛	+ ⅛
7050	Loblaw Co	$17	16¾	16¾	
333830	Mackenzie	$6¼	5⅞	6	− ¼
3900	Madelin o	298	290	293	− 7
40540	Magna A f	$34¼	33⅝	33⅝	− ⅝
13413	M L Foods	$16⅝	16⅜	16½	
1500	MDS H A	$17	16¾	16¾	
567192	Maclean H	$12	11¾	11⅞	
3910	Maritime f	$19⅝	19¼	19¼	− ⅜
5109	Mark Res	$5⅛	5	5	− ⅛
31825	Minnova	$16¼	16⅛	16¼	− ⅛
30852	Molson A f	$34	33⅞	34	+ ⅛
221900	Noma A f	$7	6¾	6⅞	
2579	Noranda F	$8¼	8⅛	8⅛	
128559	Noranda I	$18½	18¼	18⅜	
35637	Norcen	$20⅜	20	20⅜	+ ⅜
183406	Nova Cor f	$8⅝	8½	8⅝	+ ⅛
29050	Onex C f	$7⅜	7⅛	7⅜	
5100	Oshawa A f	$17¾	17½	17½	− ⅛
32692	PWA Corp	$5⅝	5⅜	5½	+ ¼
15800	Pgurin A f	450	440	440	− 10
500	PanCan P	$26⅜	26⅛	26⅜	+ ⅜
87642	Petro Cdn	$9⅛	9	9⅛	− ⅛
206214	Placer Dm	$12¼	12	12⅛	+ ⅛
88832	Poco Pete	475	470	470	
8602	Que Sturg o	23	22	22	− 1
700	Rayrock f	$7	7	7	
130415	Renisanc	$15¼	15	15⅛	− ⅛
308400	Rogrs Cn bf	$22⅛	21¾	22	
1100	Rogers A	$15⅜	15⅛	15⅛	− ¼
327131	Rogers B f	$14⅛	13⅞	14	− ⅛
1326	Rothman	$88	86½	86½	−3¾
133815	Royal Bnk	$23⅛	22¾	23⅛	− ¼
116899	Ry Trco	$6⅞	6⅝	6⅝	− ⅛
39875	Saskoil	485	475	480	
152245	Sceptre R	40	36	36	+ 2
3100	Scotts f	$14⅜	14⅜	14⅜	+ ⅛
4593	Sears Can	$8⅝	8⅜	8⅜	− ⅛
39202	SHL Systm	$16⅛	15⅞	16	
33300	Shell Can	$41⅝	41½	41½	− ⅛
92644	Sherritt	$9¼	9	9¼	+ ⅜
19900	Southam	$17	16⅝	16⅞	+ ⅛
5089	Spar Aero f	$17⅜	17¼	17¼	− ⅜
104910	Stelco A	405	365	395	− 15
220820	Teck B f	$20	19¾	20	+ ⅛
34618	Telus Cor	$14	13⅞	13⅞	
78405	ThomCor	$14⅞	14⅝	14¾	− [illegible]
157792	Tor Dm Bk	$16⅞	16½	16¾	− [illegible]
157475	TIPS	1890	1885	1885	− 5
1060	Torstar B f	$21⅞	21½	21⅞	− [illegible]
82804	TrnAlta U	$12¾	12⅝	12¾	
65482	TrCan PL	$17¼	17	17⅛	
45915	Trilon A	$7⅝	7⅜	7⅛	− [illegible]
27000	TrlonF p w	265	255	255	− 5
900	Trimac	$8¼	8¼	8¼	− [illegible]
53741	Trizec A f	465	450	460	− 5
5033	Unicorp A f	170	170	170	
3900	U Energy	$14¼	14¼	14¼	− [illegible]
11064	Westmin	475	455	470	
8090	Weston	$38 [illegible]	38	38	
8057	Woodwd	97	95	95	− 2

Total sales 30,240,667 shares

MONTREAL

Sales	Stock	High	Low	Close	Chg
111747	Bank Mont	$44⅝	44¼	44[illegible]	− [illegible]
67251	Bio Pha	$20¼	19¾	20	
6750	BombrdrA	$14	13⅝	13⅞	[illegible]
696208	BombrdrB	$14¼	13½	13[illegible]	− [illegible]
1350	Cambior	$07¾	07¾	07¾	[illegible]
14731	Cascades	$07⅞	07¾	07¾	[illegible]
2092	DomTxtA	$06¾	06¾	06¾	
800	Donohue	$14¾	14¾	14¾	
176268	NatBk Cda	$09	08¾	08⅞	
238800	Power Corp	$14⅜	14⅛	14⅜	− [illegible]
21110	Provigo	$08¼	08	08¼	− [illegible]
200	Quebecr A	$14⅛	14⅛	14⅛	
11100	Quebecr B	$14¼	14⅛	14¼	
7080	Teleglobe	$13½	13¼	13⅜	
20446	Videotron	$15⅞	15⅝	15⅝	− ⅛

Total Sales 7,451,850 shares; as of 4:00 pm.

F No voting rights or restricted voting rights

Source: *The Wall Street Journal*, June 5, 1992

ADRS

Thursday, June 4, 1992

AngSA	1.15e	12	35 7/8	36 3/8	− 1/8
AngAG	.33e	146	5 3/4	5 15/16	− 1/16
ASEA	1.20e	7	66 5/8	67 3/8	− 3/8
Blyvoor	.10e	11	1 3/8	1 1/2	...
Bwater	1.19e	1	15	15 3/8	− 1/8
Buffels	.41e	6	6 5/8	7	...
BurmhC	1.15e	1	22 3/4	23 1/8	...
DBeer	1.11e	65	25 5/8	25 7/8	− 1/4
DresBk s	.75r	18	21 1/4	21 1/2	+ 1/8
DriefC	.56e	130	10 7/8	11 1/8	− 1/4
Fisons	.81e	398	26 1/2	26 3/4	+ 1/2
FreSCn	.81e	108	8 1/2	8 9/16	− 1/16
FujiPh	.24r	12	44	44 3/4	− 1/2
Gambro	.58e	2	44	45	+ 3/8
Highvld	.23e	49	3 3/4	3 15/16	− 1/16
KloofG	.32e	27	7 5/8	7 7/8	− 3/16
Minorc	.52e	465	13 1/2	13 5/8	...
Nissan	.21e	4	9 3/8	9 5/8	...
OrangF	2.10e	19	18 1/4	18 7/8	− 3/8
Ramtrn		38	3 5/16	3 1/2	...
RankO	.72e	3	13 1/2	13 7/8	...
StHlGd	.69e	2	5 5/8	5 7/8	...
Santos	.58e	1	8 1/8	8 3/8	...
Senetek h		10	7/8	1 1/16	...
SoPcPt		500	19/32	5/8	...
TelMex	.02e	4423	2 25/32	2 13/16	...
Toyota	.29r	101	23 3/8	23 5/8	...
VaalRf	.36e	37	5 3/16	5 1/4	...
WelkG	.54e	1	4 5/8	4 7/8	...
WDeep	1.36e	66	28	29	− 1/2

Source: *The Wall Street Journal*, June 25 ,1992

Waterhouse

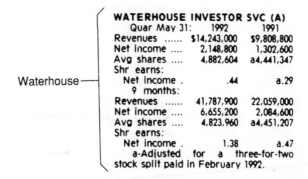

WATERHOUSE INVESTOR SVC (A)

Quar May 31:	1992	1991
Revenues	$14,243,000	$9,808,800
Net income	2,148,800	1,302,600
Avg shares	4,882,604	a4,441,347
Shr earns:		
Net income .	.44	a.29
9 months:		
Revenues	41,787,900	22,059,000
Net income	6,655,200	2,084,600
Avg shares	4,823,960	a4,451,207
Shr earns:		
Net income .	1.38	a.47

a-Adjusted for a three-for-two stock split paid in February 1992.

Source: *The Wall Street Journal*, June 23, 1992

	REGULAR				
Amax →	Amax Inc	Q	.20	9- 1-92	8-10
	Amax Inc pfB	Q	.75	12- 1-92	11-10
	Brady (WH) Co clA	Q	.14	7-31-92	7-13
	Canadian Imper Bk	Q	b.33	7-28-92	6-29
	Canadian Tire Ltd	Q	b.10	9- 1-92	7-31
	Duplex Products	Q	.12	7- 8-92	6-19
	Flexsteel Indus	Q	.12	7- 6-92	6-24
	General Host Corp	Q	.09	7- 3-92	6-19
	Genl Pub Util	Q	.40	8-26-92	7-31
	STOCK				
Intermagnetics →	Intermagnetics Gen		3%	9- 2-92	8- 3
	Momentum Distrib		nn	7- 6-92	6-22
	nn-Three-for-one stock split.				
	Pacificare Health		pp	6-19-92	6- 5
	pp-Distribution of one share of Pacificare Health cl B for each common share held.				

Source: *The Wall Street Journal*, June 5, 1992

firm takes a loss, the amount that the public is willing to pay for the firm's product no longer justifies the cost of producing it.

If you are a stock owner, then, in addition to following the market indexes, you will need to monitor the earnings of particular stocks. You can do so by using *The Wall Street Journal's* **Digest of Earnings Report,** listed as **Earnings Digest** in the front-page index of the first and last sections. The **Digest of Earnings Report** occasionally appears in the second section of the *Journal.*

Find Waterhouse in the June 23, 1992 reprint on pages 199 and 201. The statement reports earnings for the quarter ending May 31, 1992 and compares them with figures for the same period one year earlier. Look for revenues, net income, and net income per share (i.e., total earnings divided by total shares of stock outstanding). As you can see, Waterhouse sales revenue and profits improved.

Improved earnings are important because (among other things) they permit corporations to pay dividends, an important source of income for many stockholders. The stock pages list current annual dividends, and you can also use the *Journal's* daily **Corporate Dividend News** (see the Friday, June 5, 1992 excerpt above and on the next page), listed in the front-page indexes of the first and last sections, to be informed of future dividend payments.

The June 5, 1992 report provides dividend news for June 4. The companies listed under the heading **Regular** will pay regular cash dividends on the payable date to all those who were stockholders on the record date.

DIGEST OF EARNINGS REPORTS

AG SERVICES OF AMERICA (O)

Quar May 31:	1992	1991
Revenues	$25,238,000	$16,002,000
Net income	855,000	490,000
Avg shares	1,744,000	1,000,000
Shr earns:		
Net income	.49	.49

BEST BUY CO. (N)

13 wk May 30:	1992	1991
Revenues	$246,481,000	$165,579,000
Net income	1,244,000	405,000
Avg shares	11,631,000	8,289,000
Shr earns:		
Net income	.11	.05

CABLETRON SYSTEMS INC. (N)

Quar May 31:	1992	1991
Sales	$88,045,000	$60,626,000
Net income	17,589,000	12,187,000
Avg shares	28,079,000	27,861,000
Shr earns:		
Net income	.63	.44

CARNIVAL CRUISE LINES (N)

Quar May 31:	1992	a1991
Revenues	$346,000,000	$307,000,000
Inco cnt op	57,100,000	47,200,000
Inco dis op	....	(3,800,000)
Net income	57,100,000	43,400,000
Avg shares	140,650,000	134,900,000
Shr earns:		
Inco cnt op	.41	.35
Net income	.41	.32
6 months:		
Revenues	674,800,000	599,900,000
Inco cnt op	103,800,000	84,600,000
Inco dis op	....	(10,700,000)
Net income	103,800,000	73,900,000
Avg shares	140,643,000	134,819,000
Shr earns:		
Inco cnt op	.74	.63
Net income	.74	.55

a-Restated to reflect discontinued operations.

Figures in parentheses are losses.

CORNING INC. (N)

12 wk Jun 14:	1992	1991
Sales	$926,700,000	$778,200,000
Income	a71,800,000	73,900,000
bExtrd cred	300,000	2,000,000
Net income	72,100,000	75,900,000
Avg shares	187,834,000	c185,510,000
Shr earns:		
Income	.38	c.40
Net income	.38	c.41
24 weeks:		
Sales	1,719,900,000	1,469,400,000
aIncome	149,600,000	121,100,000
bExtrd cred	600,000	3,200,000
Net income	150,200,000	124,300,000
Avg shares	188,337,000	c184,524,000
Shr earns:		
Income	.79	c.66
Net income	.79	c.67

a-Includes a non-recurring net charge of $16,300,000 in the twelve weeks and a non-recurring net gain of $5,400,000 in the twenty-four weeks of 1992, compared with a non-recurring net gain of $2,600,000 in the twenty-four weeks only of 1991. b-Tax benefit from tax-loss carry-forwards. c-Adjusted for a two-for-one stock split paid in February 1992.

CULBRO CORP (N)

13 wk May 30:	1992	1991
Revenues	$299,198,000	$287,087,000
Net income	2,321,000	(231,000)
Avg shares	4,308,000	4,307,000
Shr earns:		
Net income	.54	(.05)
26 weeks:		
Revenues	561,311,000	522,908,000
Net income	1,475,000	388,000
Avg shares	4,308,000	4,307,000
Shr earns:		
Net income	.34	.09

Figures in parentheses are losses.

EVERGREEN RESOURCES (O)

Year Mar 31:	1992	1991
Revenues	$3,000,000	$3,800,000
Net income	(272,352)	281,276
Shr earns:		
Net income	(.08)	.13

Figures in parentheses are losses.

FDP CORP. (O)

Quar May 31:	1992	1991
Revenues	$5,015,625	$4,441,351
Net income	313,053	161,447
Avg shares	3,485,935	3,372,189
Shr earns:		
Net income	.09	.05
6 months:		
Revenues	9,458,228	8,197,774
Net income	605,532	(70,988)
Avg shares	3,458,543	3,381,956
Shr earns:		
Net income	.18	(.02)

Figures in parentheses are losses.

FSI INTERNATIONAL INC. (O)

13 wk May 30:	1992	1991
Sales	$13,528,000	$11,154,000
Net income	(100,000)	(967,000)
Avg shares	4,203,000	4,048,000
Shr earns:		
Net income	(.02)	(.24)
39 weeks:		
Sales	31,307,000	33,632,000
Net income	(3,394,000)	(3,052,000)
Avg shares	4,119,000	4,031,000
Shr earns:		
Net income	(.82)	(.76)

Figures in parentheses are losses.

FULLER (H.B.) CO. (O)

Quar May 31:	1992	1991
Sales	$234,575,000	$216,347,000
Net income	10,144,000	7,123,000
Shr earns (com & com equiv):		
Net income	.73	a.51
6 months:		
Sales	453,382,000	418,428,000
Net income	16,165,000	10,776,000
Shr earns (com & com equiv):		
Net income	1.16	a.78

a-Adjusted to reflect a three-for-two stock split paid in June 1992.

GENESEE CORP. (O)

Year Apr 30:	1992	1991
Sales	$145,148,000	$134,785,000
aNet income	7,427,000	5,938,000
Shr earns:		
Net income	4.64	3.71

a-Includes non-recurring gains of $1,200,000 in 1992 from litigation settlement and $868,000 in 1991 related to real estate investment.

INTEGRATED SYSTEMS INC. (O)

Quar May 31:	a1992	b1991
Revenues	$7,245,000	$4,487,000
Net income	935,000	712,000
Avg shares	9,518,000	8,400,000
Shr earns:		
Net income	.10	.08

a-Includes the results of Software Components Group Inc., acquired in August 1991. b-Restated.

INTERSTATE BAKERIES (N)

Year May 30:	1992	1991
Sales	$1,145,875,000	$1,106,723,000
Income	25,780,000	(8,035,000)
Extrd chg	a(10,176,000)	....
Net income	15,604,000	(8,035,000)
Avg shares	18,735,000	4,822,000
Shr earns:		
Income	1.49	(1.70)
Net income	.94	(1.70)
12 weeks:		
Sales	276,829,000	262,940,000
Net income	7,881,000	(4,512,000)
Avg shares	21,040,000	4,827,000
Shr earns:		
Net income	.37	(.87)

a-Loss on retirement of debt.

Figures in parentheses are losses.

KLEINERT'S INC. (O)

13 wk May 30:	1992	1991
Sales	$10,786,000	$9,421,000
Net income	251,000	87,000
Avg shares	3,483,000	a3,245,000
Shr earns:		
Net income	.07	a.03
26 weeks:		
Sales	20,257,000	17,046,000
Net income	442,000	157,000
Avg shares	3,431,000	a3,250,000
Shr earns:		
Net income	.13	a.05

a-Adjusted for a five-for-two stock split paid in March 1992.

PARLUX FRAGRANCES INC. (O)

Year Mar 31:	1992	1991
Sales	$28,119,931	$27,154,228
Net income	309,616	161,232
Avg shares	2,421,102	2,397,110
Shr earns (primary):		
Net income	.13	.07
Shr earns (fully diluted):		
Net income	.11	.07
Quarter:		
Sales	7,355,885	7,159,702
Net income	764,617	412,128
Shr earns (primary):		
Net income	.32	.17
Shr earns (fully diluted):		
Net income	.27	.17

(N) New York Stock Exchange (A) American Exchange (O) Over-the-Counter (Pa) Pacific (M) Midwest (P) Philadelphia (B) Boston (T) Toronto (Mo) Montreal (F) Foreign.

ABBREVIATIONS

A partial list of frequently used abbreviations: Acctg adj (Accounting adjustment); Extrd chg (Extraordinary charge); Extrd cred (Extraordinary credit); Inco cnt op (Income from continuing operations); Inco dis op (Income from discontinued operations).

RITE AID CORP. (N)

13 wk May 30:	1992	1991
Sales	$984,046,000	$907,398,000
Net income	33,013,000	28,908,000
Avg shares	87,843,000	84,340,000
Shr earns:		
Net income	.38	.34

ROYAL INTERNATL OPTICAL (O)

Year Mar 31:	1992	1991
Sales	$136,800,000	$145,500,000
Net income	(6,456,000)	(2,822,000)
Avg shares	5,754,020	5,754,010
Shr earns:		
Net income	(1.23)	(.50)
Quarter:		
Sales	35,500,000	38,800,000
Net income	1,100,000	2,501,000
Shr earns:		
Net income	.11	.43

Figures in parentheses are losses.

STANDARD MICROSYSTEMS (O)

Quar May 31:	1992	1991
Revenues	$59,252,000	$18,103,000
Net income	3,361,000	(1,793,000)
Avg shares	12,104,000	11,526,000
Shr earns (com & com equiv):		
Net income	.28	(.16)

Figures in parentheses are losses.

T CELL SCIENCES INC. (O)

Year Apr 30:	1992	1991
Revenues	$10,477,000	$11,149,000
Net income	(4,649,000)	(3,441,000)
Avg shares	13,109,000	10,166,000
Shr earns:		
Net income	(.35)	(.34)
Quarter:		
Revenues	2,713,000	2,783,000
Net income	(1,497,000)	(941,000)
Avg shares	13,285,000	10,333,000
Shr earns:		
Net income	(.11)	(.09)

Figures in parentheses are losses.

TECNOL MEDICAL PRODS (O)

13 wk May 29:	1992	1991
Sales	$17,064,000	$14,279,000
Net income	2,964,000	2,463,000
Avg shares	13,131,000	11,786,000
Shr earns:		
Net income	.23	.21
26 weeks:		
Sales	30,643,000	26,536,000
Net income	5,017,000	4,152,000
Avg shares	13,076,000	11,777,000
Shr earns:		
Net income	.38	.35

UNION CAMP CORP. (N)

Quar Mar 31:	1992	1991
Sales	$760,950,000	$722,129,000
Income	a(15,372,000)	41,239,000
Acctg adj	b40,806,000	
Net income	25,434,000	41,239,000
Avg shares	69,544,799	68,958,071
Shr earns:		
Income	(.22)	.60
Net income	.37	.60

a-Includes a non-recurring net charge of $36,000,000. b-Cumulative effect of accounting changes.

Figures in parentheses are losses.

UNIVAR CORP. (N)

Quar May 31:	1992	1991
Sales	$468,432,000	$377,030,000
Net income	2,455,000	1,073,000
Avg shares	19,700,000	17,834,692
Shr earns:		
Net income	.13	.06

WATERHOUSE INVESTOR SVC (A)

Quar May 31:	1992	1991
Revenues	$14,243,000	$9,808,800
Net income	2,148,800	1,302,600
Avg shares	4,882,604	a4,441,347
Shr earns:		
Net income	.44	a.29
9 months:		
Revenues	41,787,900	22,059,000
Net income	6,655,200	2,084,600
Avg shares	4,823,960	a4,451,207
Shr earns:		
Net income	1.38	a.47

a-Adjusted for a three-for-two stock split paid in February 1992.

Waterhouse

Source: *The Wall Street Journal*, June 23, 1992

CORPORATE DIVIDEND NEWS

Dividends Reported June 4

	Company	Period	Amt.	Payable date	Record date
	REGULAR				
Amax →	Amax Inc	Q	.20	9– 1–92	8–10
	Amax Inc pfB	Q	.75	12– 1–92	11–10
	Brady (WH) Co clA	Q	.14	7–31–92	7–13
	Canadian Imper Bk	Q	b.33	7–28–92	6–29
	Canadian Tire Ltd	Q	b.10	9– 1–92	7–31
	Duplex Products	Q	.12	7– 8–92	6–19
	Flexsteel Indus	Q	.12	7– 6–92	6–24
	General Host Corp	Q	.09	7– 3–92	6–19
	Genl Pub Util	Q	.40	8–26–92	7–31
	Genesee Corp clB	Q	.30	7– 1–92	6–15
	Harnischfeger Ind	Q	.10	7– 9–92	6–25
	Marriott Corp	Q	.07	7–20–92	7– 3
	McDermott Inc pfA	Q	.55	7– 1–92	6–15
	McDermott Inc pfB	Q	.65	7– 1–92	6–15
	McDermott Intl	Q	.25	7– 1–92	6–15
	Midland Co	Q	.12½	7– 9–92	6–20
	ONBANCorp	Q	.10	7– 1–92	6–17
	Pratt & Lambert	Q	.14	7– 1–92	6–15
	Salomon Inc	Q	.16	7– 1–92	6–15
	Salomon Inc depshs	Q	.59⅜	6–30–92	6–15
	Skyline Corp	Q	.12	7– 1–92	6–19
	Tescorp 10%pf	Q	.12½	7–10–92	6–19
	Times Mirror Co	Q	.27	9–10–92	8–21
	Uni-Marts Inc clA	Q	.02½	7–20–92	6–29
	Van Dorn Co	Q	.15	8– 3–92	7–17
	Wal-Mart Stores	Q	.05¼	7– 3–92	6–15
	IRREGULAR				
	Enhance Finl Svcs	–	.06	6–18–92	6–15
	Farrel Corp	–	.04	6–30–92	6–16
	Marriott depshs	–	1.03⅛	7–15–92	7– 3
	FUNDS - REITS - INVESTMENT COS - LPS				
	Amer Capital Bd Fd	Q	h.42	6–30–92	6–12
	Dover Regional Fin	–	.04½	6–30–92	6–15
	Inefficient Mkt Fd	S	.04	6–23–92	6–16
	MLSS Govt Inco Fd	M	h.07½	6– 8–92	6– 8
	MLSS Govt Secs Fd	M	h.039	6– 8–92	6– 8
	MLSS Hi Inco Fd	M	h.05¾	6– 8–92	6– 8
	MLSS NY TaxFree	M	h.036	6– 8–92	6– 8
	MLSS Tax Exempt	M	h.036½	6– 8–92	6– 8
	New Amer Hi Inco	M	.04	6–30–92	6–16
	Oppen Multi-Sector	M	.097	6–26–92	6–12
	Price REIT new	–	.56¼	6–30–92	6–12
	Sabine Royalty Tr	M	.10289	6–29–92	6–15
	S Barney Int Muni	M	.049	7–28–92	7–21
	S Barney Int Muni	M	.049	8–25–92	8–18
	S Barney Int Muni	M	.049	9–22–92	9–15
	Summit TxExmpt Bd	Q	.21	8–15–92	6–30
	TempletonGloblInco	M	h.07	6–30–92	6–16
	Templeton Glb Util	M	h.05	6–30–92	6–16
	TIS Mortgage Inv	Q	.23	7–15–92	6–30
	STOCK				
Intermagnetics →	Intermagnetics Gen		3%	9– 2–92	8– 3
	Momentum Distrib		nn	7– 6–92	6–22
	nn-Three-for-one stock split.				
	Pacificare Health		pp	6–19–92	6– 5
	pp-Distribution of one share of Pacificare Health cl B for each common share held.				
	FOREIGN				
	RoylBk Scotland A	–	t.703⅛	6–30–92	6–15
	RoylBk Scotland B	–	t.70	6–30–92	6–15
	INITIAL				
	Carolina 1st Cp pf	–	.3178	7– 1–92	6–15
	ONBANCorp pfB	–	.30	7–15–92	6–30
	Sadlier (William)	–	.20	7–15–92	6–25
	TNT Freightways	–	.14	7– 1–92	6–19
	ThomasMills A new	Q	.06	6–27–92	6–15
	ThomasMills B new	Q	.06	6–27–92	6–15
	OMITTED				
	ACCEL Intl				

A-Annual; b-Payable in Canadian funds; h-From income k-From capital gains; M-Monthly; Q-Quarterly; S-Semi-annual; t-Approximate U.S. dollar amount per American Depositary Receipt/Share.

* * *

Source: *The Wall Street Journal*, June 5, 1992

Energy	276.86	+	0.67	+	0.24	+	4.2	
Coal	222.07	+	1.40	+	0.63	–	5.9	
Oil drilling	75.64	+	0.58	+	0.77	+	13.2	←Oil drilling
Oil-majors	345.43	+	1.64	+	0.48	+	3.1	
Technology	303.45	–	1.52	–	0.50	+	0.5	
Aerospace/Defense	373.74	+	3.14	+	0.85	–	7.5	
Commu-w/AT&T	403.73	+	1.57	+	0.39	+	9.2	
Commu-wo/AT&T	294.99	+	2.26	+	0.77	+	21.3	
Comptrs-w/IBM	183.71	–	2.48	–	1.33	+	3.1	
Comptrs-wo/IBM	257.79	–	5.04	–	1.92	+	7.2	
Diversified tech	282.34	–	2.30	–	0.81	–	0.1	
Industrial tech	302.10	+	4.84	+	1.63	–	1.6	
Medical/Bio tech	773.69	–	6.30	–	0.81	–	22.7	
Advcd Med Devices	726.53	–	7.54	–	1.03	–	22.0	
Biotechnology	818.05	–	5.31	–	0.64	–	23.2	
Office equipment	304.61	–	2.18	–	0.71	+	5.6	
Semiconductor	310.30	–	6.02	–	1.90	+	4.8	
Software	2420.47	–	5.24	–	0.22	+	1.5	←Software

Source: *The Wall Street Journal*, June 5, 1992

For instance, the June 5 excerpt on page 200 reported that Amax announced a quarterly dividend of 20 cents per share payable on September 1, 1992 to all stockholders of record on August 10, 1992.

Some companies prefer to pay dividends in extra stock rather than cash. Returning to the report, you can see that Intermagnetics announced a three percent stock dividend effective September 2, 1992 for all holders of record on August 3, 1992. That is, each stockholder received an additional amount of stock equal to three percent of his or her holdings.

DOW JONES INDUSTRY GROUPS

June 4, 1992, 4:30 p.m. Eastern Time

GROUPS LEADING (and strongest stocks in group)

GROUP	CLOSE	CHG	%CHG
Auto manufacturers	342.02	+ 12.44	+ 3.77
Gen Motors	43[illegible]	+ 1[illegible]	+ 1.49
Chrysler Corp	20[illegible]	+ [illegible]	+ 3.77
Ford Motor Co	48[illegible]	+ 1[illegible]	+ 2.94
Steel	140.58	+ 4.55	+ 3.34
Armco Inc	6[illegible]	+ [illegible]	+ 5.77
Bethlehem Stl	14[illegible]	+ [illegible]	+ 4.46
Inland Steel	24	+ 1	+ 4.35
Other non-ferrous	281.44	+ 7.63	+ 2.79
Cyprus Minrl	26[illegible]	+ 1[illegible]	+ 7.69
Magma Copper	13[illegible]	+ [illegible]	+ 3.74
Brush Wellman	17[illegible]	+ [illegible]	+ 2.90
Heavy construction	282.30	+ 6.33	+ 2.29
Fluor Corp	43[illegible]	+ 1[illegible]	+ 3.29
Foster Wheeler	25[illegible]	+ [illegible]	+ 0.99
MorrisonKndsn	21[illegible]	+ [illegible]	+ 0.59
Industrial tech	302.10	+ 4.84	+ 1.63
Pall Corp	23[illegible]	+ [illegible]	+ 3.26
Ametek Inc	18	+ [illegible]	+ 2.13
Millipore Corp	34[illegible]	+ [illegible]	+ 1.11

GROUPS LAGGING (and weakest stocks in group)

GROUP	CLOSE	CHG	%CHG
House-Durable	767.87	– 30.14	– 3.78
Rubbermaid	28¾	– 1½	– 4.96
Premark Intl	44	– 1½	– 3.30
Newell Inc	36⅝	– ¾	– 2.01
Other Rec Prod	298.98	– 8.37	– 2.72
Disney (Walt)	37¼	– 1⅞	– 4.79
Polaroid Corp	26	– ½	– 1.89
Eastman Kod	40¼	unch	unch
Cosmetics	640.29	– 16.50	– 2.51
Gillette Co	46¾	– 1½	– 3.11
Avon Products	51½	– 1¼	– 2.37
Tambrands	62⅝	– 1⅜	– 2.15
Beverages	934.95	– 18.43	– 1.93
Coca-Cola Botlg	19½	– ¾	– 3.70
Coca Cola Co	42¾	– 1¼	– 2.84
Whitman Cp	13⅛	– ⅜	– 2.78
Comptrs-wo/IBM	257.79	– 5.04	– 1.92
Hewlett-Pkrd	71⅞	– 3	– 4.01
Wang Labs B	3½	– ⅛	– 3.45
Data General	8	– ¼	– 3.03

INDUSTRY GROUP PERFORMANCE

GROUP	CLOSE	CHG	% CHG	YR TO DATE % CHG
Basic Materials	411.05	– 0.93	– 0.23	+ 10.4
Aluminum	345.35	+ 1.56	+ 0.45	+ 19.5
Other non-ferrous	281.44	+ 7.63	+ 2.79	+ 39.7
Chemicals	495.03	– 4.55	– 0.91	+ 9.6
Chem-Commodity	482.03	– 4.52	– 0.93	+ 11.6
Chem-Specialty	536.60	– 4.69	– 0.87	+ 5.2
Forest products	329.55	+ 1.00	+ 0.30	+ 25.0
Mining,diversified	314.83	– 4.53	– 1.42	– 0.6
Paper products	461.65	+ 0.50	+ 0.11	+ 0.1
Precious metals	224.09	– 1.19	– 0.53	– 3.9
Steel	140.58	+ 4.55	+ 3.34	+ 9.7
Conglomerate	473.61	+ 1.05	+ 0.22	+ 0.4
Consumer,Cyclical	479.79	+ 1.45	+ 0.30	+ 7.4
Advertising	589.53	– 2.00	– 0.34	+ 3.3
Airlines	317.70	+ 1.18	+ 0.37	– 6.9
Apparel	764.78	– 4.76	– 0.62	– 9.4
Clothing/Fabrics	688.59	– 1.51	– 0.22	– 0.9
Footwear	866.24	– 9.10	– 1.04	– 16.9
Auto manufacturers	342.02	+ 12.44	+ 3.77	+ 61.3
Auto parts & equip	343.52	– 0.18	– 0.05	+ 19.3
Casinos	633.76	– 2.02	– 0.32	+ 7.9
Home construction	438.49	– 4.18	– 0.94	+ 0.7
Home furnishings	299.71	+ 1.28	+ 0.43	+ 20.2
Lodging	307.61	– 1.73	– 0.56	+ 13.9
Media	523.36	– 1.06	– 0.20	+ 12.5
Broadcasting	540.98	+ 0.25	+ 0.05	+ 12.7
Publishing	516.04	– 1.71	– 0.33	+ 12.9
Recreation products	306.74	– 4.56	– 1.46	+ 10.2
Entertainment	295.24	+ 2.73	+ 0.93	+ 21.3
Other Rec Prod	298.98	– 8.37	– 2.72	+ 6.2
Toys	410.42	– 0.79	– 0.19	+ 6.8
Restaurants	640.77	– 5.31	– 0.82	+ 16.0
Retailers,apparel	849.78	– 5.11	0.60	23.3
Retailers,broadline	696.23	+ 4.83	+ 0.70	– 0.6
Retailers,drug-base	488.39	– 1.52	– 0.31	– 8.2
Retailers,specialty	575.17	– 1.09	– 0.19	+ 0.4
Consumer,Non-Cycl	705.38	– 7.24	– 1.02	– 10.1
Beverages	934.95	– 18.43	– 1.93	+ 1.9
Consumer services	438.59	– 6.21	– 1.40	– 11.6
Cosmetics	640.29	– 16.50	– 2.51	– 7.7
Food	812.04	– 5.35	0.65	– 14.7
Food retailers	633.82	– 10.01	– 1.55	– 10.0
Health care	315.09	– 3.60	– 1.13	– 7.1
Household products	828.96	– 7.02	– 0.84	+ 5.6
House-Durable	767.87	– 30.14	– 3.78	– 20.0
House-Non-Durable	808.45	3.19	0.39	+ 10.2
Medical supplies	549.03	– 2.85	0.52	– 9.2
Pharmaceuticals	616.10	– 3.03	– 0.49	18.6
Tobacco	1002.34	– 15.61	– 1.53	– 4.9
Energy	276.86	+ 0.67	+ 0.24	+ 4.2
Coal	222.07	+ 1.40	+ 0.63	– 5.9
Oil drilling	75.64	+ 0.58	+ 0.77	+ 13.2
Oil-majors	345.43	+ 1.64	+ 0.48	+ 3.1
Oil-secondary	187.24	– 2.64	– 1.39	+ 1.9
Oilfield equip/svcs	155.60	+ 0.17	+ 0.11	+ 11.1
Pipelines	197.05	+ 0.39	+ 0.20	+ 11.3
Financial	353.10	– 2.13	– 0.60	+ 4.3
Banks,money center	240.44	– 1.80	– 0.74	+ 19.6
Banks,regional	406.99	– 2.19	– 0.54	+ 14.7
Banks-Central	631.72	– 4.17	– 0.66	+ 5.9
Banks-East	331.51	– 0.80	– 0.24	+ 21.1
Banks-South	346.63	– 2.51	– 0.72	+ 13.3
Banks-West	400.92	– 2.02	– 0.50	+ 28.9
Financial services	343.22	– 3.54	– 1.02	– 3.6
Insurance,all	361.80	– 1.21	– 0.33	– 4.9
Ins-Full line	209.13	– 2.18	– 1.03	– 6.1
Ins-Life	564.21	+ 0.52	+ 0.09	+ 0.6
Property/Casualty	460.50	– 1.00	– 0.22	– 6.3
Real estate	357.31	– 1.81	– 0.50	– 8.0
Savings & loans	428.70	– 7.26	– 1.67	– 3.6
Securities brokers	426.36	– 2.59	– 0.60	– 11.1
Industrial	378.77	+ 0.58	+ 0.15	+ 3.9
Air freight	195.29	– 1.33	– 0.68	– 0.1
Building materials	480.49	– 2.31	– 0.48	+ 18.7
Containers/pkging	703.50	+ 1.75	+ 0.25	+ 0.8
Elec comp/equip	351.09	+ 0.65	+ 0.19	– 2.7
Factory equipment	368.53	+ 4.08	+ 1.12	+ 17.0
Heavy construction	282.30	+ 6.33	+ 2.29	– 4.2
Heavy machinery	171.13	– 1.50	– 0.87	+ 17.9
Industrial services	372.42	– 1.41	– 0.38	+ 2.7
Industrial,divers	350.05	+ 0.75	+ 0.21	+ 11.1
Marine transport	425.52	+ 1.74	+ 0.41	– 10.5
Pollution control	756.11	+ 7.81	+ 1.04	– 16.0
Railroads	506.69	– 0.42	– 0.08	+ 7.1
Transport equip	304.55	+ 2.26	+ 0.75	+ 26.6
Trucking	321.07	+ 2.03	+ 0.64	+ 13.7
Technology	303.45	– 1.52	– 0.50	+ 0.5
Aerospace/Defense	373.74	+ 3.14	+ 0.85	– 7.5
Commu-w/AT&T	403.73	+ 1.57	+ 0.39	+ 9.2
Commu-wo/AT&T	294.99	+ 2.26	+ 0.77	+ 21.3
Comptrs-w/IBM	183.71	– 2.48	– 1.33	+ 3.1
Comptrs-wo/IBM	257.79	– 5.04	– 1.92	+ 7.2
Diversified tech	282.34	– 2.30	– 0.81	– 0.1
Industrial tech	302.10	+ 4.84	+ 1.63	– 1.6
Medical/Bio tech	773.69	– 6.30	– 0.81	– 22.7
Advcd Med Devices	726.53	– 7.54	– 1.03	– 22.0
Biotechnology	818.05	– 5.31	– 0.64	– 23.2
Office equipment	304.61	– 2.18	– 0.71	+ 5.6
Semiconductor	310.30	– 6.02	– 1.90	+ 4.8
Software	2420.47	– 5.24	– 0.22	+ 1.5
Utilities	260.41	– 1.13	– 0.43	– 6.6
Telephone	327.75	– 1.35	– 0.41	– 7.3
Electric	228.61	– 1.09	– 0.47	– 5.7
Gas	139.63	– 0.06	– 0.04	– 8.9
Water	411.80	+ 1.34	+ 0.33	– 11.4
DJ Equity Market	389.02	– 1.35	– 0.35	– 0.7

← Software

Oil drilling →

Source: *The Wall Street Journal*, June 5, 1992

INSIDER TRADING SPOTLIGHT

Biggest Individual Trades

(Based on reports filed with regulators last week)

COMPANY NAME	EXCH.	INSIDER'S NAME	TITLE	$ VALUE (000)	NO. OF SHRS. IN TRANS. (000)	% OF HLDNG.	TRANSACTION DATES
BUYERS							
MGM Grand	N	R. R. Maxey	P	**115**	10.0	83.00	5/20/92
Key Tronic	O	K. F. Holtby	D	**103**	14.0	n	5/8/92
Joslyn	O	D. B. Hamister	CB	**91**	3.0	150.00	5/4/92
Mellon Bank	N	B. C. Borgelt	D	**79**	2.0	w	5/1/92
Sysco	N	F. A. Godchaux III x	D	**73**	1.5	38.00	5/18-19/92
KCS Energy	O	J. W. Christmas	P	**73**	7.0	22.00	5/19/92
Fleming Cos	N	J. A. McMillan	D	**60**	2.0	200.00	5/4/92
Sportstown	O	C. B. Cornelius Jr	O	**56**	4.0	1.00	5/1/92
Am Hlthcr Mgmt	A	R. W. Fleming Jr x	VP	**54**	10.3	18.00	4/20/92-5/12/92 †
Mobile Gas Service	O	W. J. Hearin Jr x	D	**53**	3.0	1.00	5/7/92
SELLERS							
Mattel	N	D. M. Mauer	O	**1,138**	31.3	100.00	4/16/92 †r
Fleetwood Enterprises	N	J. A. Nord	O	**861**	20.0	100.00	4/1/92 †r
ITT	N	J. C. Cappello s	VP	**629**	9.3	48.00	5/8/92 r
Concord EFS	O	V. M. Tyler	O	**549**	25.0	13.00	5/1-6/92
Jamesway	N	F. Hall	D	**362**	57.5	15.00	3/23/92-4/1/92 †
Ferro	N	A. Posnick	D	**226**	5.0	4.00	5/4/92
Dynatech	O	T. F. Kelly	O	**193**	10.0	30.00	5/11-12/92
McGraw-Hill	N	R. R. Schulz	O	**177**	2.8	49.00	5/1/92 r
Armco	N	R. E. Boni	D	**167**	29.6	97.00	5/7-8/92
Brown-Forman	N	W. M. Street s	O	**133**	1.8	1.00	5/5/92

Companies With Biggest Net Changes

(Based on actual transaction dates in reports filed through last Friday)

		NET % CHG. IN HOLDINGS OF ACTIVE INSIDERS[1]		LATEST 12 WKS.		LATEST 24 WKS.	
COMPANY NAME	EXCH./SYMBOL	LATEST 12 WEEKS	LATEST 24 WEEKS	NO. OF BUYERS-SELLERS	MULTIPLE OF HIST. NORM[2]	NO. OF BUYERS-SELLERS	MULTIPLE OF HIST. NORM[2]
BUYING							
Morgan Stanley Emr Mkt	N/MSF	**2400**	2800	4-0	4.0*	5-0	2.5
Western Resources	N/WR	**52**	– 5	3-0	6.0	3-1	3.0
Andover Bancorp (Del)	O/ANDB	**43**	43	7-1	3.0	7-1	1.5
Am Hlthcr Mgmt	A/AHI	**42**	370	3-0	3.6	7-0	4.2
Baltimore Bancorp	N/BBB	**28**	28	11-2	2.2	13-4	1.3
First Inter-Bancorp	O/FIBI	**17**	17	6-0	4.3*	6-0	2.2
Kimco Realty	N/KIM	**2**	4	3-1	1.5*	3-1	0.8
SELLING							
Sun Microsystems	O/SUNW	– **44**	– 44	0-11	2.0	0-11	1.0
Cognitronics	A/CGN	– **26**	– 26	0-4	6.9	0-4	3.4
Genlyte Group	O/GLYT	– **25**	– 28	1-5	12.0	2-5	6.0

NOTE: Shows purchases and sales by most officers and directors, which must be reported to the SEC and other regulators by the 10th of the month following the month of the trade. Includes both open-market and private transactions involving direct and indirect holdings. Excludes stocks valued at less than $2 a share, acquisitions through options and companies being acquired. w-1000% or more.

n-No prior holdings. r-sale within two weeks of option exercise equal to 90% or more of shares sold. s-Holds other class of stock. x-Reflects shares held indirectly. †-Late filing. *-Base period is less than 3 years.

CB-chairman. P-president. D-director. VP-vice president. O-officer. Z-other.

[1]Ranked by the net change in shares held by those insiders who bought or sold during the last 12 weeks, expressed as a percentage change of only their holdings at the start of the period. Reflects companies for which filings made last week showed some insider activity during the latest 12 weeks. Excluded: companies with total trades valued under $75,000; option-related sales, companies with fewer than three buyers or sellers, or fewer buyers or sellers than the historical average for the period.

[2]Based on the previous three years.

Source: Invest/Net, Fort Lauderdale, Fla.

Source: *The Wall Street Journal*, June 3, 1992

INDUSTRY GROUPS

This chapter began with a look at the **Markets Diary**, which appears on the first page (C1) of the *Journal's* third section (see page 152). That discussion mentioned the Dow Jones Equity Index (June 30, 1982 = 100) and the 700-odd companies that the index comprises.

Each day the *Journal* breaks out the performance of these stocks in the **Dow Jones Industry Groups** (you can find the index on pages A1 or Cl). In addition, the five industries that enjoyed the greatest relative gain in value the previous trading day and the five that suffered the biggest loss are presented together with the three most important contributing firms in each case. You can use this information to compare the performance of your stock with the average for the entire industry or to compare the performance of a variety of industries. For instance, under **Technology** in the Friday, June 5, 1992 report, note that Software had increased twenty-fold since June 30, 1982, while under **Energy**, Oil-drilling had fallen. (See pages 203 and 204.)

Test yourself, but be honest. Do you think you could have forecast these industry performances back in 1982?

INSIDER TRADING

Finally, if you want to see what the officers and directors of the company in which you own stock are doing, you can follow the **Insider Trading Spotlight** in Wednesday's *Wall Street Journal*. An example from the June 3, 1992 issue is provided on page 205.

If you have an interest in a particular company, it may be worth your while to know whether its key executives and members of its board of directors have purchased its stock recently. Sales are not as important because they can occur for a variety of reasons. Sellers may wish to diversify their portfolios or need cash. Yet you should be alert for massive sell-offs by a number of insiders. Insider purchases of a company's stock are a better indicator of long-term company prospects (why else buy the stock?) because insiders must keep their purchases for six months. The law forbids insiders from selling stock they have purchased until half a year has elapsed from the time of purchase. Nor may insiders sell stock short. This protects the public from insiders profiting from their knowledge at the publics' expense.

Whereas insider trading may be a good clue to the fortunes of a particular company, that does not mean that insider trading can be used to successfully forecast stock market trends and turning points. They may know more than you do about their company, but that doesn't necessarily mean they know more than you do about the entire market. You're better off using the guidelines in this book.

GREED VS. FEAR

Perhaps this chapter has made clear to you how complex the stock market can be, and how many ways there are to invest in stocks. No wonder that even major investors feel they need an expert's advice before they venture their capital.

There is a saying, "Greed and fear drive the stock market." For example, greedy investors fueled the blaze of speculative gains before the crash of 1987, while fear held the market back after the crash.

So far there has been no discussion of investors' psychological dynamics, the herd instinct created by greed and fear. Instead, these chapters treated the fundamentals of investing in terms of the analysis of the outlook for stocks vs. gold and then applied that analysis to a variety of stock market indicators. Here is a brief summary of these approaches.

Fundamental analysis tries to determine the intrinsic value of stocks by discovering their future earnings potential within the context of the business environment, and then concludes whether or not their present market value accurately reflects that intrinsic value.

This book's version of fundamental analysis began with a review of business cycle conditions and inflation's outlook, and the impact of monetary and fiscal policy on them. From there, the analysis proceeded to a discussion of profits under a variety of cyclical and inflationary settings, and delved into the importance of these settings for stocks and gold. At the same time it dealt with the importance of the price-earnings ratio and the importance of current stock market valuation as a determinant of potential appreciation.

This chapter provided some additional assistance in the fundamental analysis of a particular stock. You learned how to compare that stock's performance to its industry's performance, and then compare the industry to the overall market. A company's earnings and its price-earnings ratio are also ingredients in fundamental analysis. Final steps include an appraisal of a company's management as well as a forecast of future prospects founded upon its marketing and technological outlook and the ability to control costs.

If that makes sense, you must nonetheless keep in mind that *technical analysis,* a school with a number of passionate advocates, takes a different approach. It studies the historical price trend of the stock market, a group of stocks, or a single stock to forecast future trends. Technical analysis makes extensive use of charts to comprehend historical developments and thereby predict price movements. This reduces an understanding of the psychology of the market and the forces of greed and fear to an analysis of charts of past price movements. For instance, if stock prices (or the price of a stock) rise and then fall back, only to rise again above the previous high, one school of technical analysis views this as a sign of market strength. On the other hand, failure of the stock to surpass its earlier peak is viewed as a sign of weakness.

Investor's Tip

- To avoid greed and fear, take the long-run view developed in these chapters.

CONCLUSION

You can make money in the stock market if you have the time and expertise required to study it closely. But as you know from Chapters 1 and 8, timing is crucial. You have to know when to get in and when to get out, because it's very difficult to find a stock that will buck the market's trend for long. Just remember that you can invest in that trend, without investing in an individual stock, by investing in an index fund.

CHAPTER 10

COMMODITIES & PRECIOUS METALS

INTRODUCTION

Chapters 1 and 8 observed that stocks and gold move in opposite directions, each reacting differently to the rate of inflation. Chapter 9 reviewed investment opportunities in the stock market. It's now time to turn to gold as an investment opportunity. But before you do let's take a historical step backward to gain a little perspective on commodity and commodity futures markets, where gold (among other things) is traded for delivery and payment at a later date.

Drastic price fluctuations plagued the farmers and producers of commodities throughout our nineteenth-century westward expansion. After a period of rapid western settlement, new farms and ranches flooded the market with their output. Prices plummeted, devastating farmers and ranchers who had hoped for higher prices to cover their debts. Only after the market absorbed the excess capacity did prices firm and rise again, instigating a new round of price increases and cyclical expansion.

Wildly fluctuating prices for cotton, grain, and meat hurt the farmer and rancher as well as the textile manufacturer, flour miller, and meat packer. In order to protect themselves from unpredictable swings in market prices, these "producers" and "consumers" began contracting to buy and sell output *(commodities)* at predetermined prices for future delivery *(forward contracts)*. That way both parties could more accurately forecast revenues and costs and remove some of the uncertainty and risk from their operations.

The contracting parties custom tailored the quantity, quality, delivery date and other conditions of the forward contracts. Soon buyers and sellers felt the need for greater flexibility. Suppose either party wanted to get out of the deal, for whatever reason? Who would take the cotton, hogs, or cattle? As a result commodity producers and users established exchanges to trade these commodities, just as stock exchanges had been established to trade ownership in corporations. And just as a share of stock became a standardized unit of corporate ownership to be exchanged on the open market, commodity contracts were standardized with respect to quantity, quality (grade), delivery date, and price so that they could be traded, too. That established the modern *futures* contract that can be bought and sold anonymously without any special reference to initial producer or ultimate user.

The futures contract is settled at the price initially agreed to when the contract is entered into, regardless of the commodity's market price (cash or spot price) at the time of future delivery and payment, and regardless of any subsequent change in the value of the contract due to changes in the market price. In this way producers, such as farmers and ranchers, who contract to sell their output for future delivery, protect themselves from potentially lower spot (cash) prices, while foregoing the possibility that the actual cash prices might be higher at the time of delivery. Conversely, manufacturers, millers, meat packers, and other commodity processors, who contract to buy goods for future delivery, forego potentially low spot prices at time of delivery to avoid the possible risk of higher prices later. Futures contracts limit both the potential risk and the potential reward of the cash market for producers and consumers, i.e., the price risk is hedged.

For instance, if you are a wheat farmer and wheat's spot and future price is $4 a bushel, you can contract to sell it for the $4 futures price. If the spot price falls to $3, you have protected yourself by hedging (hemming in) your risk. You will have sold your wheat for $1 more than the spot price. Should the price rise to $5, you will not be able to take advantage of that opportunity, although you will have protected yourself (hedged) against the downside risk. In other words, hedging permits you to guarantee a good price while foregoing the risk and reward of extreme prices.

The miller may have the same motivation to lock in $4 with a futures contract and forego either high or low prices.

The futures market protects buyers and sellers of commodities, but it also provides a market for speculative trading. Speculators do not produce or consume the commodities they trade; they hope to profit from fluctuations in commodity prices. The possibility for speculative profits arises as futures prices fluctuate with spot prices.

If wheat sells for $4 a bushel in spot and futures markets, farmers and millers will contract for future delivery of the crop at that price. But if you are smart enough to correctly forecast that wheat will rise to $6 a bushel by the time of future delivery, you may wish to also contract to buy wheat for future delivery at $4 a bushel. Why? Because if you are right, the wheat you bought for delivery at $4 can be resold for $6 on the spot market at a gain of $2 when the day of future delivery arrives.

Moreover, you won't have to take delivery of the wheat, because as the spot price starts to rise, the price of futures contracts will rise, too. After all, other speculators will begin to buy futures contracts as they see the spot price rise, bidding its price up. Therefore, when the price of the futures contract for which you paid $4 reaches $5, you can offset it by contracting for a futures sale at $5. You earn $1 by selling a bushel of wheat for $5 for which you paid only $4.

Conversely, if wheat is $6 a bushel and you correctly forecast that it will fall to $4, you can enter into a contract to sell wheat for future delivery at $6 and then fulfill your obligation on that date by purchasing wheat in the spot market for $4 and reselling it for $6 at a gain of $2. And as the futures price falls to $5 with the spot price, you can make $1 with a $5 purchase of a contract for future delivery by using it to discharge your obligation to sell a contract for $6.

Speculation is important to the futures market because it provides liquidity by increasing sales and purchases of futures contracts. Speculative buying and selling broadens and deepens the market for producers and processors. As a result, fewer than 5 percent of futures contracts are held for actual delivery. The business of the exchange is conducted by traders who make a market for others and buy and sell on their own account.

LONG POSITION

Miller and manufacturer enter into futures contracts to buy commodities for future delivery at a set price. This is called a *long* position.

Investors also take long positions (i.e., purchase futures contracts that enable them to buy commodities at a stipulated price for future delivery) when they expect market prices at the time of delivery to be higher than the present futures price. If the investors' forecast of future cash prices is accurate, they will profit by selling at a high spot price the commodity they purchased for a low futures price. For instance, if you expect gold prices to be higher in October than the current October gold futures contract, you will buy that contract. If you are correct, and in October the spot prices *are* higher than the October futures contract price, your gain will be the difference between the low futures price at which you purchased the gold and the high spot price at which you sell it.

In practice, however, fewer than 5 percent of all futures contracts are actually held to delivery; investors rarely trade the actual commodity. An investor who has taken a long position (i.e., bought a contract for future delivery) can sell the contract before the delivery date. Again, as above, if you are correct and gold prices are rising, the October contract will have risen as well because market forces push future prices toward spot prices as the date of delivery approaches. You will be able to sell your contract to buy gold to someone else at a higher price than you paid for it.

SHORT POSITION

Farmers, ranchers, and miners enter into futures contracts to sell commodities for future delivery at an agreed upon price. This is known as a *short* position.

Investors take short positions when they anticipate that spot prices will be lower than present futures prices. If, for example, you anticipate falling gold prices and feel that spot prices will be lower than present futures contract prices, you can take a short position in gold and thereby contract to sell gold at favorable futures prices. If you wait until the time of delivery, you can buy gold in the cash market at the low spot price and then complete or perform the contract to sell the gold at the higher contracted futures price.

But as you learned earlier, futures contracts are rarely performed; they are generally offset with an opposing trade. As gold prices fall, and therefore futures prices with them, you can buy a contract at the new low price and discharge your obligation to sell a contract at the old high price. Your gain is the difference between the two prices.

FUTURES PRICES

Friday, June 5, 1992

Open Interest Reflects Previous Trading Day.

	Open	High	Low	Settle	Change	Lifetime High	Lifetime Low	Open Interest
Sept	....	....	....	78.00	+ .35	84.00	76.25	116

Est vol 4,103; vol Thur 4,541; open int 59,191, −722.

SUGAR – WORLD (CSCE) – 112,000 lbs.; cents per lb.

	Open	High	Low	Settle	Change	Lifetime High	Lifetime Low	Open Interest
July	10.26	10.44	10.21	10.23	− .11	10.44	7.80	42,649
Oct	9.58	9.65	9.50	9.50	− .11	9.65	7.93	39,636
Mr93	9.44	9.48	9.37	9.37	− .07	9.48	8.20	20,349
May	9.34	9.36	9.30	9.30	− .06	9.37	8.30	2,079
July	9.25	9.25	9.25	9.21	− .06	9.28	8.40	666
Oct	....	....	....	9.05	− .09	9.13	8.69	420

Est vol 13,586; vol Thur 26,634; open int 105,799, +3,003.

SUGAR – DOMESTIC (CSCE) – 112,000 lbs.; cents per lb.

	Open	High	Low	Settle	Change	Lifetime High	Lifetime Low	Open Interest
July	20.91	20.91	20.85	20.86	+ .01	22.39	20.78	768
Sept	21.00	21.00	20.98	20.98	− .02	22.30	20.91	1,812
Nov	21.34	21.35	21.34	21.35	− .02	22.10	21.27	2,048
Ja93	....	....	....	21.44	....	22.00	21.40	345
Mar	21.45	21.45	21.45	21.44	− .01	22.05	21.39	823
May	21.62	21.62	21.62	21.62	− .01	21.86	21.45	702
July	....	....	....	21.74	+ .01	21.85	21.65	463
Sept	....	....	....	21.74	+ .01	21.85	21.65	126

Est vol 267; vol Thur 460; open int 7,087, +75.

COTTON (CTN) – 50,000 lbs.; cents per lb.

	Open	High	Low	Settle	Change	Lifetime High	Lifetime Low	Open Interest
July	58.30	58.99	58.30	58.57	− .01	77.70	54.80	11,756
Oct	59.60	60.15	59.60	59.90	+ .31	70.60	57.65	6,007
Dec	59.42	60.00	59.42	59.60	− .01	69.00	58.45	16,182
Mr93	60.90	61.05	60.65	60.71	− .09	67.30	59.90	3,641
May	61.30	61.40	61.30	61.40	+ .03	66.25	60.40	1,170
Jl93	....	....	....	61.75	+ .03	65.20	61.00	187

Est vol 6,500; vol Thur 6,873; open int 38,943, +604.

ORANGE JUICE (CTN) – 15,000 lbs.; cents per lb.

	Open	High	Low	Settle	Change	Lifetime High	Lifetime Low	Open Interest
July	132.80	134.10	132.60	133.70	+ .90	175.50	115.25	4,622
Sept	125.50	125.75	124.40	125.00	− .25	175.00	117.20	1,639
Nov	118.50	119.00	117.00	117.50	− .75	165.50	112.00	1,457
Ja93	116.50	116.90	115.50	115.60	− .90	178.00	111.75	1,476
Mar	116.75	117.00	115.25	115.15	− 1.10	164.00	112.80	430

Est vol 1,500; vol Thur 841; open int 9,697, −11.

METALS AND PETROLEUM

COPPER-HIGH (CMX) – 25,000 lbs.; cents per lb.

	Open	High	Low	Settle	Change	Lifetime High	Lifetime Low	Open Interest
June	104.00	104.40	103.65	104.35	− .25	104.60	94.80	843
July	104.25	104.40	103.60	104.20	− .20	104.50	92.80	23,028
Aug	....	....	....	104.05	− .20	103.55	95.70	593
Sept	103.90	104.00	103.50	103.90	− .10	104.00	92.80	8,726
Oct	....	....	....	103.75	+ .05	103.70	95.90	455
Nov	103.30	103.50	103.30	103.75	+ .05	103.50	96.00	347
Dec	103.80	103.80	103.35	103.75	− .10	103.85	91.60	6,493
Ja93	....	....	....	103.50	− .10	103.00	93.30	125
Mar	102.80	102.95	102.60	102.90	− .25	103.00	92.80	2,072
May	102.30	102.30	102.25	102.25	− .40	102.30	93.70	995
July	101.70	101.70	101.65	101.80	− .40	101.70	95.80	586
Sept	....	....	....	101.35	− .40	101.25	95.80	549
Dec	100.70	100.75	100.70	100.85	− .40	101.05	97.00	407

Est vol 8,000; vol Thur 15,631; open int 45,251, +3,006.

Gold →

GOLD (CMX) – 100 troy oz.; $ per troy oz.

	Open	High	Low	Settle	Change	Lifetime High	Lifetime Low	Open Interest
June	338.80	339.10	338.50	338.70	+ .10	467.00	334.90	2,016
Aug	340.90	341.40	340.40	340.70	+ .10	426.50	336.60	53,065
Oct	342.60	343.00	342.40	342.60	+ .10	410.80	338.50	4,015
Dec	345.10	345.30	344.40	344.70	+ .10	431.00	340.40	12,018
Fb93	....	....	....	347.00	+ .10	404.20	343.00	9,168
Apr	....	....	....	349.30	+ .10	410.00	346.00	7,961
June	....	....	....	351.70	....	418.50	347.70	5,727
Aug	....	....	....	354.40	....	395.50	354.50	1,870
Oct	....	....	....	357.10	....	395.00	365.60	727
Dec	....	....	....	359.80	....	402.80	356.40	3,583
Fb94	....	....	....	362.70	....	364.50	364.50	339
June	....	....	....	368.90	− .10	379.00	367.00	171
Ju95	....	....	....	389.80	− .10	....	....	100
Dec	....	....	....	400.10	− .10	....	....	100

Est vol 13,000; vol Thur 14,196; open int 100,891, −1,083.

PLATINUM (NYM) – 50 troy oz.; $ per troy oz.

	Open	High	Low	Settle	Change	Lifetime High	Lifetime Low	Open Interest
July	373.50	373.50	368.50	368.30	− 4.70	427.50	331.00	13,443
Oct	378.50	378.50	373.50	374.10	− 3.50	404.00	336.00	4,017
Ja93	377.00	377.00	372.90	372.90	− 4.00	378.50	339.00	2,806
Apr	379.00	379.00	372.70	372.70	− 4.00	384.00	339.00	669

Est vol 5,725; vol Thur 3,285; open int 20,935, +187.

PALLADIUM (NYM) 100 troy oz.; $ per troy oz.

	Open	High	Low	Settle	Change	Lifetime High	Lifetime Low	Open Interest
June	....	....	....	76.80	− .35	101.75	74.50	61
Sept	80.75	81.00	80.50	80.80	− .35	89.30	79.50	2,645
Dec	80.50	80.80	80.50	80.80	− .35	90.65	79.75	1,060

Est vol 42; vol Thur 132; open int 3,802, −115.

SILVER (CMX) – 5,000 troy oz.; cents per troy oz.

	Open	High	Low	Settle	Change	Lifetime High	Lifetime Low	Open Interest
June	405.5	406.0	405.5	405.1	− 2.4	412.0	400.0	4
July	408.5	409.0	405.5	405.8	− 2.5	557.0	388.5	43,023
Sept	411.5	412.0	408.5	408.8	− 2.6	483.0	395.0	7,225
Dec	417.0	417.0	413.0	413.5	− 2.7	507.0	398.0	17,410
Mr93	417.0	420.0	420.0	418.7	− 2.8	513.0	407.0	5,457
May	....	....	....	422.3	− 2.9	473.0	411.0	3,107
July	426.5	426.5	426.5	426.0	− 2.9	470.5	412.5	4,826
Sept	....	....	....	430.3	− 2.9	469.0	418.0	770
Dec	....	....	....	437.0	− 2.9	462.0	431.0	2,014

Est vol 6,000; vol Thur 4,534; open int 83,842, −472.

SILVER (CBT) – 1,000 troy oz.; cents per troy oz.

	Open	High	Low	Settle	Change	Lifetime High	Lifetime Low	Open Interest
June	406.5	406.5	404.0	405.0	− 1.5	494.0	387.0	42
Aug	....	....	....	407.0	− 2.0	495.0	394.0	232
Dec	414.0	415.0	413.0	413.0	− 2.5	460.0	399.0	2,706
Fb93	....	....	....	416.0	− 3.0	448.0	407.0	674
Apr	422.0	422.0	419.0	419.0	− 3.5	454.0	413.0	379
June	427.0	427.0	423.0	423.0	− 3.5	435.0	415.6	679

Est vol 25; vol Thur 17; open int 4,780, −2.

CRUDE OIL, Light Sweet (NYM) 1,000 bbls.; $ per bbl.

	Open	High	Low	Settle	Change	Lifetime High	Lifetime Low	Open Interest
July	22.65	22.70	22.45	22.62	+ .14	22.70	17.90	83,132
Aug	22.62	22.64	22.40	22.55	+ .11	22.64	17.75	66,617
Sept	22.45	22.47	22.24	22.39	+ .10	24.00	17.78	43,390
Oct	22.30	22.32	22.14	22.26	+ .09	22.32	18.42	25,733
Nov	22.15	22.20	22.01	22.13	+ .08	22.18	18.50	18,352
Dec	22.00	22.09	21.90	22.00	+ .07	24.00	18.25	25,813
Ja93	21.85	21.90	21.75	21.85	+ .05	21.90	18.62	19,154
Feb	21.67	21.73	21.62	21.70	+ .03	21.75	18.67	11,021
Mar	21.48	21.55	21.48	21.56	+ .02	21.59	18.51	6,048
Apr	21.35	21.40	21.35	21.42	+ .01	21.52	18.75	2,945
May	21.21	21.26	21.21	21.30	....	21.40	18.93	312
June	21.12	21.13	21.09	21.20	− .01	23.00	18.63	11,400
July	21.07	21.10	21.04	21.11	− .01	22.31	18.97	7,085
Aug	20.95	20.95	20.95	21.03	− .02	21.18	18.99	3,327
Sept	....	....	....	20.98	− .03	21.18	18.90	8,447
Oct	....	....	....	20.96	− .03	21.15	19.05	1,099
Nov	....	....	....	20.95	− .03	21.15	20.24	548
Dec	20.87	20.87	20.87	20.95	− .03	23.00	18.70	9,044
Mr94	....	....	....	20.94	− .03	21.10	19.14	930
June	....	....	....	20.94	− .03	21.35	19.25	11,720
Dec	21.05	21.10	20.95	20.99	− .05	21.26	19.40	5,888
Ju85	....	....	....	21.10	− .05	21.21	20.65	995

Est vol 108,112; vol Thur 76,990; open int 365,700, +2,575

HEATING OIL NO. 2 (NYM) 42,000 gal.; $ per gal.

	Open	High	Low	Settle	Change	Lifetime High	Lifetime Low	Open Interest
July	.6145	.6200	.6110	.6185	+ .0098	.6200	.4950	35,412
Aug	.6200	.6235	.6160	.6220	+ .0084	.6235	.4950	18,898
Sept	.6305	.6325	.6265	.6320	+ .0073	.6325	.5220	9,505
Oct	.6400	.6410	.6360	.6410	+ .0073	.6410	.5315	9,514
Nov	.6485	.6500	.6450	.6495	+ .0068	.6500	.5430	5,536
Dec	.6570	.6585	.6530	.6571	+ .0059	.6585	.5525	8,799
Apr	....	....	....	.5971	+ .0034	.6015	.5525	742
May	....	....	....	.5791	+ .0024	.5740	.4950	126
June	....	....	....	.5701	+ .0014	.5620	.5525	314
July	....	....	....	.5676	+ .0009	.5620	.5095	820
Aug	....	....	....	.5726	+ .0009	....	....	268
Oct	....	....	....	.5936	+ .0009	....	....	200

Est vol 31,674; vol Thur 26,239; open int 100,142, +1,753.

EXCHANGE ABBREVIATIONS
(for commodity futures and futures options)

CBT-Chicago Board of Trade; CME-Chicago Mercantile Exchange; CMX-Commodity Exchange, New York; CRCE-Chicago Rice & Cotton Exchange; CTN-New York Cotton Exchange; CSCE-Coffee, Sugar & Cocoa Exchange, New York; FOX-London Futures and Options Exchange; IPE-International Petroleum Exchange; KC-Kansas City Board of Trade; MCE-MidAmerica Commodity Exchange; MPLS-Minneapolis Grain Exchange; NYM-New York Mercantile Exchange; PBOT-Philadelphia Board of Trade; WPG-Winnipeg Commodity Exchange.

GASOLINE, Unleaded (NYM) 42,000 gal.; $ per gal.

	Open	High	Low	Settle	Change	Lifetime High	Lifetime Low	Open Interest
July	.6760	.6775	.6700	.6724	+ .0007	.6775	.5270	39,678
Aug	.6730	.6735	.6675	.6699	+ .0012	.6735	.5070	15,928
Sept	.6560	.6570	.6520	.6536	+ .0006	.6570	.5465	7,886
Oct	.6280	.6295	.6250	.6256	+ .0006	.6295	.5310	9,632
Nov	.6110	.6110	.6110	.6106	− .0004	.6130	.5300	2,843
Dec	.6020	.6020	.5980	.5991	− .0014	.6050	.5350	2,515
Ja93	.5980	.5980	.5980	.5946	− .0019	.6000	.5465	1,770
Feb	....	....	....	.5970	− .0020	.5970	.5700	247
Mar	....	....	....	.6050	− .0020	.6070	.6070	100

Est vol 22,282; vol Thur 24,785; open int 80,601, +1,051.

NATURAL GAS, (NYM) 10,000 MMBtu.; $ per MMBtu's

	Open	High	Low	Settle	Change	Lifetime High	Lifetime Low	Open Interest
July	1.620	1.655	1.620	1.653	+ .044	1.670	1.156	6,622
Aug	1.595	1.615	1.585	1.600	+ .020	1.625	1.180	7,568
Sept	1.592	1.622	1.592	1.610	+ .028	1.660	1.230	5,555
Oct	1.669	1.690	1.669	1.680	+ .020	1.780	1.360	4,088
Nov	1.875	1.900	1.875	1.890	+ .021	1.985	1.560	4,210
Dec	2.090	2.105	2.085	2.086	+ .007	2.185	1.745	5,498
Ja93	2.140	2.155	2.135	2.140	+ .010	2.230	1.825	6,392
Feb	1.805	1.810	1.795	1.801	+ .011	1.865	1.520	2,853
Mar	1.550	1.565	1.550	1.561	+ .021	1.620	1.150	2,317
Apr	1.525	1.525	1.515	1.516	+ .016	1.550	1.200	1,473
May	1.529	1.529	1.520	1.521	+ .013	1.555	1.200	845
June	1.535	1.540	1.525	1.530	+ .015	1.570	1.215	758
July	1.535	1.550	1.535	1.540	+ .010	1.590	1.180	694
Aug	1.550	1.555	1.550	1.555	+ .016	1.605	1.250	636
Sept	....	....	....	1.580	+ .010	1.660	1.470	300
Oct	1.695	1.695	1.695	1.695	+ .010	1.745	1.655	197
Nov	1.920	1.920	1.920	1.920	+ .009	1.960	1.765	220
Dec	....	....	....	2.144	+ .009	2.180	2.000	203

Est vol 4,455; vol Thur 5,415; open int 50,429, −504.

BRENT CRUDE (IPE) 1,000 net bbls.; $ per bbl.

NOT AVAILABLE

GAS OIL (IPE) 100 metric tons; $ per ton

	Open	High	Low	Settle	Change	Lifetime High	Lifetime Low	Open Interest
June	188.50	189.25	186.75	188.50	+ 2.50	189.25	154.00	17,696
July	188.25	190.25	188.00	189.75	+ 2.75	190.25	155.00	24,258
Aug	190.25	192.25	189.75	191.25	+ 2.25	192.25	158.00	9,829
Sept	191.75	194.25	191.75	193.25	+ 2.25	194.25	159.00	5,166
Oct	194.00	195.75	194.00	195.50	+ 2.25	195.75	166.00	9,943
Nov	196.25	197.50	196.00	197.25	+ 2.25	197.50	169.00	3,827
Dec	197.75	199.00	197.75	198.25	+ 2.25	199.00	174.00	3,844
Ja93	196.25	197.25	196.25	197.25	+ 3.25	197.25	179.25	1,231
Feb	194.25	194.50	194.25	194.25	+ 3.25	194.50	177.00	114

Est vol 15,515; vol Thur 13,762; open int 85,883, −1,034.

INTEREST RATE

TREASURY BONDS (CBT) – $100,000; pts. 32nds of 100%

	Open	High	Low	Settle	Chg	Yield Settle	Yield Chg	Open Interest
June	100-12	101-01	100-05	100-25	+ 11	7.922	− .034	80,608
Sept	99-09	99-31	99-01	99-22	+ 11	8.032	− .035	238,352
Dec	98-00	98-27	97-31	98-18	+ 10	8.147	− .032	13,341
Mr93	97-18	97-24	97-17	97-18	+ 9	8.251	− .029	4,048
June	96-23	96-26	96-19	96-20	+ 8	8.350	− .027	1,419
Sp93	95-23	95-27	95-23	95-25	+ 8	8.440	− .027	288
Dec	95-04	95-04	95-00	95-00	+ 8	8.525	− .028	116
Sp94	....	....	....	93-01	+ 8	8.744	− .028	100

Est vol 380,000; vol Thur 179,584; op int 338,352, −6,563.

TREASURY BONDS (MCE) – $50,000; pts. 32nds of 100%

	Open	High	Low	Settle	Chg	Yield Settle	Yield Chg	Open Interest
June	100-09	101-01	100-09	100-26	+ 12	7.918	− .038	2,011
Sept	99-05	99-31	99-04	99-24	+ 13	8.025	− .042	5,149

Est vol 6,700; vol Thur 4,316; open int 7,180, +405.

T – BONDS (LIFFE) U.S. $100,000; pts of 100%

	Open	High	Low	Settle	Chg	High	Low	Open Interest
June	100-13	100-26	100-13	100-31	+ 0-22	101-15	96-30	716
Sept	9-06	99-28	99-03	99-27	+ 0-22	99-28	98-20	1,184

Est vol 801; vol Thur 992; open int 1,900, −2,444.

GERMAN GOV'T. BOND (LIFFE)
250,000 marks; $ per mark (.01)

	Open	High	Low	Settle	Chg	High	Low	Open Interest
Sept	88.00	88.09	87.86	88.06	+ .16	89.46	86.99	95,183

Est vol n.a; vol Thur n.a.; open int n.a., n.a..

TREASURY NOTES (CBT) – $100,000; pts. 32nds of 100%

	Open	High	Low	Settle	Chg	Yield Settle	Yield Chg	Open Interest
June	103-25	104-10	103-23	104-05	+ 10	7.404	− .044	44,221
Sept	102-22	103-07	102-18	103-00	+ 9	7.567	− .040	77,991

Est vol 35,000; vol Thur 29,708; open int 122,311, −1,980.

5 YR TREAS NOTES (CBT) – $100,000; pts. 32nds of 100%

	Open	High	Low	Settle	Chg	Yield Settle	Yield Chg	Open Interest
June	05-185	05-315	05-155	105-27	+ 7.0	6.609	− .050	39,054
Sept	04-145	104-26	04-095	04-215	+ 7.5	6.880	− .055	94,267

Est vol 36,950; vol Thur 40,739; open int 133,322, +2,518.

2 YR TREAS NOTES (CBT) – $200,000, pts. 32nds of 100%

	Open	High	Low	Settle	Chg	Yield Settle	Yield Chg	Open Interest
June	104-28	04-292	04-272	104-28	+ 4½	5.396	− .073	7,767
Sept	03-265	04-022	03-265	04-007	+ 4½	5.839	− .074	13,294

Est vol 3,000; vol Thur 2,053; open int 21,061, +55.

30-DAY INTEREST RATE (CBT)-$5 million; pts. of 100%

	Open	High	Low	Settle	Chg	Yield Settle	Yield Chg	Open Interest
June	96.24	96.26	96.23	96.24	+ .02	3.76	− .02	2,316
July	96.24	96.29	96.24	96.26	+ .02	3.74	− .02	2,316
Aug	96.22	96.27	96.21	96.24	+ .02	3.76	− .02	1,391
Sept	96.12	96.18	96.11	96.16	+ .05	3.84	− .05	933
Oct	96.10	96.10	96.09	96.10	+ .07	3.90	− .07	528
Nov	96.00	96.00	95.99	96.00	+ .07	4.00	− .07	870
Dec	95.71	95.73	95.71	95.71	+ .04	4.29	− .04	352

Est vol 1,605; vol Thur 441; open int 8,720, +161.

TREASURY BILLS (IMM) – $1 mil.; pts. of 100%

	Open	High	Low	Settle	Chg	Discount Settle	Discount Chg	Open Interest
June	96.27	96.36	96.26	96.31	+ .04	3.69	− .04	16,196
Sept	96.07	96.19	96.05	96.14	+ .07	3.86	− .07	19,901
Dec	95.65	95.75	95.60	95.70	+ .07	4.30	− .07	6,203
Mr93	95.55	95.58	95.46	95.56	+ .09	4.44	− .09	1,686

Est vol 7,939; vol Thur 4,123; open int 43,986, −606.

LIBOR-1 MO. (IMM) – $3,000,000; points of 100%

	Open	High	Low	Settle	Chg	Settle	Chg	Open Interest
June	96.02	96.09	96.02	96.07	+ .05	3.93	− .05	9,569
July	96.00	96.07	96.00	96.05	+ .05	3.95	− .05	8,081
Aug	96.03	96.03	95.99	96.00	+ .05	4.00	− .05	2,553
Sep	95.88	95.90	95.87	95.88	+ .06	4.12	− .06	1,086
Oct	95.78	95.81	95.78	95.79	+ .06	4.21	− .06	1,078
Nov	95.68	95.71	95.67	95.69	+ .06	4.31	− .06	461

Est vol 2,214; vol Thur 3,294; open int 22,828, +1,163.

MUNI BOND INDEX (CBT)-$1,000; times Bond Buyer MBI

	Open	High	Low	Settle	Chg	High	Low	Open Interest
June	95-19	95-26	95-17	95-22	+ 3	97-02	92-14	5,331
Sept	94-14	94-28	94-12	94-22	+ 4	95-10	92-08	4,054

Est vol 2,400; vol Thur 2,320; open int 9,408, +100.
The index: Close 96-01; Yield 6.67.

EURODOLLAR (IMM) – $1 million; pts of 100%

	Open	High	Low	Settle	Chg	Yield Settle	Yield Chg	Open Interest
June	95.95	96.04	95.93	96.01	+ .05	3.99	− .05	206,454
Sept	95.67	95.78	95.65	95.72	+ .05	4.28	− .05	301,143
Dec	95.02	95.15	94.92	95.10	+ .08	4.90	− .08	267,127
Mr93	94.86	95.03	94.83	94.96	+ .09	5.04	− .09	176,254
June	94.42	94.55	94.38	94.51	+ .09	5.49	− .09	111,006
Sept	93.98	94.12	93.96	94.07	+ .09	5.93	− .09	83,513
Dec	93.43	93.58	93.42	93.52	+ .09	6.48	− .09	62,538
Mr94	93.30	93.45	93.29	93.38	+ .08	6.62	− .08	56,620
June	93.03	93.14	93.01	93.10	+ .07	6.90	− .07	36,376
Sept	92.80	92.90	92.78	92.86	+ .06	7.14	− .06	30,346
Dec	92.45	92.55	92.43	92.51	+ .06	7.49	− .06	29,577
Mr95	92.43	92.53	92.41	92.48	+ .05	7.52	− .05	24,429
June	92.22	92.33	92.22	92.29	+ .05	7.71	− .05	17,728
Sept	92.11	92.20	92.10	92.16	+ .05	7.84	− .05	15,438
Dec	91.87	91.95	91.86	91.91	+ .04	8.09	− .04	20,365
Mr96	91.90	91.98	91.89	91.94	+ .04	8.06	− .04	12,747

Est vol 346,252; vol Thur 141,517; open int 1,455,661, +692.

EURODOLLAR (LIFFE) – $1 million; pts of 100%

	Open	High	Low	Settle	Change	Lifetime High	Lifetime Low	Open Interest
June	95.96	96.03	95.95	96.03	+ .07	96.14	90.97	17,510
Sept	95.67	95.78	95.65	95.76	+ .09	95.88	90.97	12,654
Dec	95.02	95.14	94.97	95.14	+ .12	95.37	91.52	5,754
Mr93	94.87	94.98	94.86	95.02	+ .15	95.08	91.45	2,312
June	....	....	....	94.54	+ .13	94.61	92.50	1,433
Sept	....	....	....	94.11	+ .13	94.17	92.50	539
Dec	....	....	....	93.56	+ .12	93.52	92.24	449
Mr94	....	....	....	93.41	+ .11	93.22	93.22	14[illegible]

Est vol 3,489; vol Thur 1,697; open int 40,783, −203.

STERLING (LIFFE) – £500,000; pts of 100%

	Open	High	Low	Settle	Change	Lifetime High	Lifetime Low	Open Interest
June	89.98	89.99	89.93	89.95	− .03	90.46	87.45	52,007
Sept	90.28	90.28	90.18	90.20	.07	90.51	87.46	46,892
Dec	90.50	90.50	90.41	90.44	− .06	90.66	67.55	26,241
Mr93	90.73	90.73	90.67	90.70	− .04	90.91	87.50	19,704
June	90.92	90.92	90.87	90.90	− .03	91.09	87.58	18,086
Sept	91.02	91.02	90.99	91.00	− .30	91.40	87.20	21,784
Dec	91.01	91.02	91.00	91.01	− .02	91.20	88.95	17,204
Mr94	91.00	91.01	90.97	91.00	− .01	91.17	89.87	9,749
June	90.97	90.97	90.94	90.96	− .01	91.16	89.78	5,546

Est vol 39,820; vol Thur 43,495; open int 217,210, −2,444.

LONG GILT (LIFFE) – £50,000; 32nds of 100%

	Open	High	Low	Settle	Change	Lifetime High	Lifetime Low	Open Interest
June	98-14	98-14	97-20	97-30	− 0-09	100-01	93-02	11,367
Sept	98-20	98-21	97-25	98-06	− 0-08	100-24	93-12	57,559

Est vol 58,927; vol Thur 77,111; open int 69,034, −3,732.

CURRENCY

JAPAN YEN (IMM) – 12.5 million yen; $ per yen (.00)

	Open	High	Low	Settle	Change	Lifetime High	Lifetime Low	Open Interest
June	.7863	.7899	.7853	.7885	+ .0043	.8125	.7015	50,036
Sept	.7851	.7886	.7842	.7873	+ .0042	.8080	.7265	17,393
Dec	.7852	.7885	.7845	.7871	+ .0041	.8045	.7410	1,873
Mr93	....	....	....	.7879	+ .0040	.8005	.7445	2,413

Est vol 31,620; vol Thur 25,060; open int 71,715, +1,283.

DEUTSCHEMARK (IMM) – 125,000 marks; $ per mark

	Open	High	Low	Settle	Change	Lifetime High	Lifetime Low	Open Interest
June	.6268	.6308	.6255	.6281	+ .0040	.6490	.5322	64,877
Sept	.6184	.6220	.6165	.6192	+ .0038	.6400	.5685	17,028
Dec	.6105	.6135	.6104	.6114	+ .0036	.6106	.5645	5,270
Mr93	.6033	.6033	.6033	.6048	+ .0834	.6100	.5724	618

Est vol 51,678; vol Thur 54,493; open int 87,792, +162.

CANADIAN DOLLAR (IMM) – 100,000 dlrs.; $ per Can $

	Open	High	Low	Settle	Change	Lifetime High	Lifetime Low	Open Interest
June	.8351	.8385	.8349	.8377	+ .0023	.8820	.8253	19,021
Sept	.8311	.8346	.8308	.8336	+ .0022	.8774	.8191	6,273
Dec	.8290	.8317	.8290	.8305	+ .0025	.8740	.8130	727
Mr93	.8280	.8285	.8275	.8280	+ .0027	.8712	.8115	252

Est vol 8,057; vol Thur 5,500; open int 26,283, −635.

BRITISH POUND (IMM) – 62,500 pds.; $ per pound

	Open	High	Low	Settle	Change	Lifetime High	Lifetime Low	Open Interest
June	1.8266	1.8370	1.8240	1.8310	+ .0092	1.8370	1.6410	28,094
Sept	1.8008	1.8120	1.7980	1.8046	+ .0088	1.8120	1.6490	7,656
Dec	1.7820	1.7840	1.7816	1.7806	+ .0078	1.7840	1.6280	620

Est vol 22,207; vol Thur 16,020; open int 36,370, +477.

SWISS FRANC (IMM) – 125,000 francs; $ per franc

	Open	High	Low	Settle	Change	Lifetime High	Lifetime Low	Open Interest
June	.6865	.6920	.6848	.6878	+ .0059	.7328	.6405	34,429
Sept	.6775	.6830	.6765	.6790	+ .0056	.7265	.6335	8,271

Est vol 24,884; vol 21,398; open int 42,785, +1,682.

AUSTRALIAN DOLLAR (IMM) – 100,000 dlrs.; $ per A.$

	Open	High	Low	Settle	Change	Lifetime High	Lifetime Low	Open Interest
June	.7630	.7637	.7628	.7629	+ .0009	.7670	.7274	2,370
Sept	.7592	.7593	.7592	.7587	+ .0009	.7610	.7430	301

Est vol 144; vol Thur 159; open int 2,716, −6.

U.S. DOLLAR INDEX (FINEX) – 500 times USDX

	Open	High	Low	Settle	Change	Lifetime High	Lifetime Low	Open Interest
June	86.90	87.08	86.46	86.69	− .56	100.15	85.45	5,863
Sept	88.13	88.25	87.70	87.95	− .57	94.20	86.75	76

Est vol 3,120; vol Thur 2,088 open int 6,673, −265.
The index: High 86.92; Low 86.34; Close 86.58 −.50

INDEX

← S+P 500

S&P 500 INDEX (CME) 500 times index

	Open	High	Low	Settle	Chg	High	Low	Open Interest
June	413.25	414.55	411.40	414.30	+ .80	424.40	374.50	108,114
Sept	414.25	415.60	412.50	415.30	+ .75	425.50	376.25	39,952
Dec	415.50	416.75	413.85	416.50	+ .60	427.25	391.40	2,081
Mr93	....	....	....	418.50	+ .60	423.80	397.50	351

Est vol 53,793; vol Thur 42,167; open int 150,503, −4,678.
Indx prelim High 413.85; Low 410.97; Close 413.48 −.22

NIKKEI 225 Stock Average (CME) – $5 times NSA

	Open	High	Low	Settle	Chg	High	Low	Open Interest
June	17750.	17900.	17750.	17850.	− 90.0	26600.	16850.	12,320
Sept	17950.	18060.	17950.	18045.	− 95.0	25300.	17150.	13,297

Est vol 2,662; vol Thur 2,510; open int 25,637, +959.
The index: High 17900.04; Low 17724.31; Close 17790.04
174.03

NYSE COMPOSITE INDEX (NYFE) 500 times index

	Open	High	Low	Settle	Chg	High	Low	Open Interest
June	227.85	228.55	226.85	228.35	+ .40	233.50	206.50	5,278
Sept	228.10	228.85	227.30	228.75	+ .40	233.65	212.55	970
Dec	228.25	229.05	228.20	229.30	+ .40	234.00	218.25	111

Est vol 5,175; vol Thur 4,619; open int 6,367, −182.
The index: High 228.08; Low 226.66; Close 227.88 −.02

MAJOR MKT INDEX (CBT) $500 times index

	Open	High	Low	Settle	Chg	High	Low	Open Interest
June	356.20	356.60	353.95	356.30	+ .30	362.40	340.00	4,764
July	356.00	357.00	354.50	356.75	+ .25	362.60	351.50	1,038
Dec	....	....	....	358.10	+ .30	358.90	346.80	87.

Est vol 1,500; vol Thur 1,216; open int 5,963, +54.
The index: High 356.45; Low 353.18; Close 356.00 +.15

OTHER FUTURES

Settlement prices of selected contracts. Actual volume (from previous session) and open interest of all contract months.

	Vol.	High	Low	Close	Net Change	Lifetime High	Lifetime Low	Open Interest
BRITISH POUND (MCE) 12,500 pounds; $ per pound								
Sep	113	1.8120	1.7980	1.8046	+ .0088	1.8120	1.6490	953
BROILERS (CME) 40,000 lb.; ¢ per lb.								
Jly	20	....	....	54.75	− 1.65	57.00	52.25	433
CATTLE-LIVE (MCE) 20,000 lb.; ¢ per lb.								
Aug	70	71.20	70.67	70.72	− .17	72.60	65.90	192
CORN (MCE) 1,000 bu.; cents per bu.								
Jly	2,148	260¼	257½	258¾	− 4	285	239½	14,509
CRB INDEX (NYFE) – 500 times index								
Jly	142	210.70	209.65	209.80	− 1.20	220.30	205.50	1,044
The index: High 212.15; Low 210.44; Close 210.47 −1.49								
DEUTSCHEMARK (MCE) 62,500 marks; $ per mark								
Sep	425	.6220	.6165	.6192	+ .0038	.6400	.5685	630
DIAMMONIUM PHOSPHATE (CBT 100 tons; $ per ton								
Sep	51	129.60	129.50	129.50	− .30	146.50	129.50	844
5-YR. INT. SWAP (CBT) – $25 per ½ b.p.; pts of 100%								
Sep	0	92.940	92.920	92.920	+ .080	92.95	92.40	957
GOLD-KILO (CBT) 32.15 troy oz.; $ per troy oz.								
Aug	7	341.00	340.70	340.70	+ .10	378.00	336.50	306
HOGS (MCE) 20,000 lb.; ¢ per lb.								
Jly	78	45.55	44.50	44.55	− .95	48.20	43.05	527
JAPANESE YEN (MCE) 6.25 million yen; $ per yen (.00)								
Sep	110	.7886	.7842	.7873	+ .0042	.8080	.7265	280
KC MINI VALUE LINE (KC) – 100 times index								
Sep	77	359.00	356.70	357.95	− .95	363.50	316.25	571
KC VALUE LINE INDEX (KC) – 500 times index								
Sep	72	358.50	356.40	357.95	− .95	364.80	323.25	1,109
The index: High 356.34; Low 354.50; Close 355.48 −.62								
LUMBER (CME) 160,000 bd .ft., $ per 1,000 bd.ft.								
Jly	557	229.60	227.60	228.30	− 1.60	257.00	202.20	1,820
MARK/YEN Cross Rate (CME) DM 125,000; JY per DM								
Sep	18	78.85	78.66	78.66	+ .06	79.80	77.00	982
PROPANE (NYM) 42,000 gal.; ¢ per gal.								
Jly	75	34.25	34.10	34.25	− .20	34.50	25.00	1,643
RICE-ROUGH (CRCE) 2000 cwt; $ per cwt								
Jly	88	6.600	6.555	6.555	− .055	9.080	6.555	1,620
SILVER (MCE) 1,000 troy oz.; cents per troy oz.								
Jly	5	409.0	405.5	405.8	− 2.5	572.5	388.5	1,667
SOYBEANS (MCE) 1,000 bu.; cents per bu.								
Jly	5,007	612	603	606¼	− 13½	668	554	23,203
SOYBEAN MEAL (MCE) 20 tons; $ per ton								
Jly	8	183.00	180.00	180.10	− 3.80	196.00	166.00	267
S&P MIDCAP 400 (CME) – $500 x S&P 400 Stock Index								
Sep	230	145.75	144.75	145.25	.70	156.70	138.70	4,301
The index: High 145.04; Low 143.81; Close 144.29 −.56								
SWISS FRANC (MCE) 62,500 francs; $ per franc								
Sep	237	.6830	.6765	.6790	+ .0056	.7265	.6335	291
WHEAT (MCE) 1,000 bu.; cents per bu.								
Jly	1,271	367	364¼	366½	− 1	429½	279	7,105
WHITE WHEAT (MPLS) 5,000 bu.; cents per bu.								
Sept	1	424	423	425	+ 2	442	352½	133

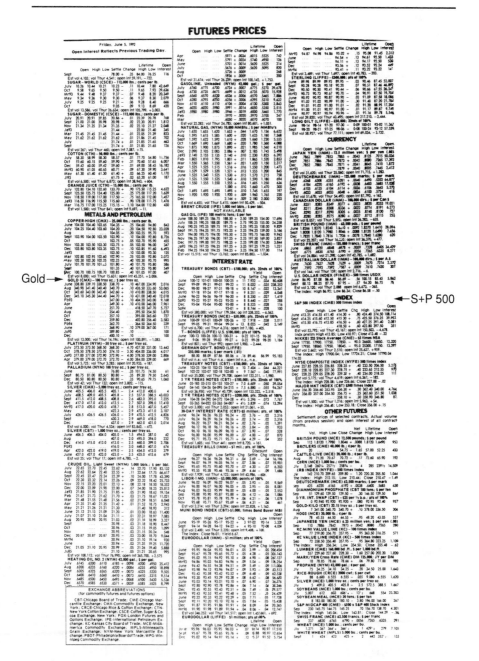

Source: *The Wall Street Journal*, June 8, 1992

MARGIN

Finally, be aware that whether you buy (long position) or sell (short position) a futures contract, your broker will ask you for only a small portion (say, 10 percent) of the contract's value. This margin deposit will protect the broker in the event that prices fall, should you have gone long, or rise if you have sold short. The broker can liquidate your position quickly, as soon as prices move the wrong way, and cover the loss from your deposit. Obviously, your margin can disappear in a hurry.

If wheat's spot price is $4, and you go long because you think it will go to $6, but it falls to $3, will you be able to buy it at $3 in order to sell it at $4? That's why your broker will demand more margin.

But if wheat prices move the right way, your potential profits will accrue to your account.

INVESTING SHORT

The Wall Street Journal reports commodity prices on a daily basis (see the first or last section's index). **Futures Prices** provides quotes for future delivery of specified amounts of each commodity (see pages 213 and 215 for excerpts from the Monday, June 8, 1992 *Wall Street Journal*). The line in boldface across the top tells you the name of the commodity, the exchange where it is traded, the size of a contract, and the unit in which the price is quoted. Take **Gold** as an example. This commodity trades on the Commodity Exchange in New York City (CMX) in contracts of 100 troy ounces at prices quoted in dollars per troy ounce. The quotations are for delivery in June, August, October, and December of 1992.

Using June 1992 for an example in the bottom excerpt on page 215, note how the following information is provided by column:

Open—opening price: $338.80 for June 1992 delivery.

High—highest price for trading day: $339.10.

Low—lowest price for trading day: $338.50.

Settle—settlement price or closing price for the trading day: $338.70.

Change—difference between the latest settlement price and that of previous trading day: increase of $0.10 (10 cents) for June 1992 delivery.

Lifetime High—highest price ever for the June 1992 contract: $467.00.

Lifetime Low—lowest price ever for the June 1992 contract: $334.90.

Open Interest—number of contracts outstanding for June delivery (for the previous trading day): 2,016 contracts have not been offset by an opposing trade or fulfilled by delivery.

The bottom line provides the estimated volume (number of contracts) for the day (13,000) as well as the actual volume for the previous trading day (14,196). Finally, the total open interest is given for all gold contracts (100,891), along with the change in the open interest from the previous trading day (-1,083). Since the previous day, 1,077 contracts were cancelled by a reversing trade.

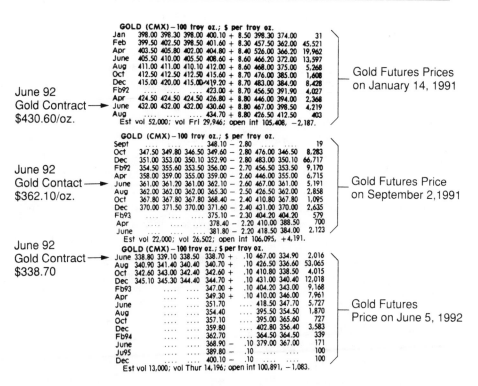

June 92 Gold Contract → $430.60/oz.

Gold Futures Prices on January 14, 1991

GOLD (CMX)–100 troy oz.; $ per troy oz.

Jan	398.00	398.30	398.00	400.10	+ 8.50	398.30	374.00	31
Feb	399.50	402.50	398.50	401.60	+ 8.30	457.50	362.00	45,521
Apr	403.50	405.80	402.00	404.80	+ 8.40	526.00	366.20	19,962
June	405.50	410.00	405.50	408.60	+ 8.60	466.20	372.00	13,597
Aug	411.00	411.00	410.10	412.00	+ 8.60	468.00	375.00	5,268
Oct	412.50	412.50	412.50	415.60	+ 8.70	476.00	385.00	1,608
Dec	415.00	420.00	415.00	419.20	+ 8.70	483.00	384.00	8,428
Fb92	....	....	....	423.00	+ 8.70	456.50	391.90	4,027
Apr	424.50	424.50	424.50	426.80	+ 8.80	446.00	394.00	2,368
June	432.00	432.00	432.00	430.60	+ 8.80	467.00	398.50	4,219
Aug	....	....	....	434.70	+ 8.80	426.50	412.50	403

Est vol 52,000; vol Fri 29,946; open int 105,408, –2,187.

June 92 Gold Contact → $362.10/oz.

Gold Futures Price on September 2,1991

GOLD (CMX)–100 troy oz.; $ per troy oz.

Sept	....	....	....	348.10	– 2.80	....	....	19
Oct	347.50	349.80	346.50	349.60	– 2.80	476.00	346.50	8,283
Dec	351.00	353.00	350.10	352.90	– 2.80	483.00	350.10	66,717
Fb92	354.50	355.60	353.50	356.00	– 2.70	456.50	353.50	9,170
Apr	358.00	359.00	355.00	359.00	– 2.60	446.00	355.00	6,715
June	361.00	361.20	361.00	362.10	– 2.60	467.00	361.00	5,191
Aug	362.00	362.00	362.00	365.30	– 2.50	426.50	362.00	2,858
Oct	367.80	367.80	367.80	368.40	– 2.40	410.80	367.80	1,095
Dec	370.00	371.50	370.00	371.60	– 2.40	431.00	370.00	2,635
Fb93	....	....	....	375.10	– 2.30	404.20	404.20	579
Apr	....	....	....	378.40	– 2.20	410.00	388.50	700
June	....	....	....	381.80	– 2.20	418.50	384.00	2,123

Est vol 22,000; vol 26,502; open int 106,095, +4,191.

June 92 Gold Contract → $338.70

Gold Futures Price on June 5, 1992

GOLD (CMX)–100 troy oz.; $ per troy oz.

June	338.80	339.10	338.50	338.70	+ .10	467.00	334.90	2,016
Aug	340.90	341.40	340.40	340.70	+ .10	426.50	336.60	53,065
Oct	342.60	343.00	342.40	342.60	+ .10	410.80	338.50	4,015
Dec	345.10	345.30	344.40	344.70	+ .10	431.00	340.40	12,018
Fb93		....	....	347.00	+ .10	404.20	343.00	9,168
Apr		....	....	349.30	+ .10	410.00	346.00	7,961
June		....	....	351.70	....	418.50	347.70	5,727
Aug		....	....	354.40	....	395.50	354.50	1,870
Oct		....	....	357.10	....	395.00	365.60	727
Dec		....	....	359.80	....	402.80	356.40	3,583
Fb94		....	....	362.70	....	364.50	364.50	339
June		....	....	368.90	– .10	379.00	367.00	171
Ju95		....	....	389.80	– .10	....	....	100
Dec		....	....	400.10	– .10	....	....	100

Est vol 13,000; vol Thur 14,196; open int 100,891, –1,083.

Source: *The Wall Street Journal*, January 15 & September 3, 1991, June 6, 1992

Suppose that on the eve of Operation Desert Storm you expected gold prices to fall. Apprehension had driven gold prices north, but you anticipated a quick war and expected that gold prices would fall thereafter. How could you have profited from your forecast? Recall that you sell (short) futures contracts when you expect commodity prices to fall. You want to be able to satisfy your commitment to sell at a high price in the future with an offsetting purchase at a lower price in the spot market. Follow the step-by-step example below in order to sharpen your understanding.

1. Turn to page 215 (top excerpt), and note from the excerpt of the Tuesday, January 15, 1991 *Wall Street Journal*, the $430.60 price on Monday, January 14, 1991 of the June 1992 gold contract. Suppose at that time you sold short a June 92 gold futures contract because you believed gold prices would fall. Your broker would adjust your account by $43,060 ($430.60 × 100 troy ounces) to reflect the sale and ask for a good faith deposit (margin) of, say, 10 percent ($4,306) in the event prices rose.
2. By Monday, September 2, 1991 (see the Tuesday, September 3, 1991 *Journal* excerpt on page 215) your forecast proved accurate with the drop in the June 92 gold contract price to $362.10 per ounce.
3. On Friday, June 5, 1992 (see the Monday, June 8, 1992 excerpt on page 215) the June 92 gold contract traded for $338.70 and you realized your gain by instructing your broker to purchase a long position to buy gold for June 92 delivery at that price in order to offset your obligation to sell. In other words, you bought a contract in order to meet your need to sell a contract.
4. In that way you realized the difference between the original high futures price at which you sold and the present low price at which you bought. Your net gain on June 5, 1992, after about a year-and-a-half, is $9,100, reflecting the difference between the contract's original value of $43,060 and its current value of $33,870 ($338.70 per ounce × 100 ounces).

Notice that you did not need to purchase gold. Your desire to liquidate your sell (short) position was offset by someone else's desire to offset their buy (long) position. These obligations cancelled each other.

Return for a moment to your margin deposit of $4,306. This is a performance bond or good faith money, not a down payment. It says you are prepared to meet your contractual obligation to sell gold at the contract price. But remember that you must first buy gold in order to sell it. Since you agreed to deliver gold at $430.60 an ounce, a higher spot price would have placed you in the embarrassing position of buying high in order to sell low. Had gold increased rather than fallen in value, your broker would have asked you to deposit additional margin to cover the difference in price.

For instance, if the spot price rises to $450.60, how does your broker know that you will be able to meet the $2,000 difference ($20 per ounce × 100 ounces) between the $450.60 price you will pay for gold and the $430.60 price at which you must deliver it? And if the spot price rises, the futures price will rise too, as the market adjusts all prices to the rising trend. Therefore, your broker will demand a bigger margin as the price of gold increases. Should the price surge suddenly and unexpectedly before you can respond to your broker's call for more margin, your broker will liquidate your position to cover the difference and protect his or her own position. After all, your broker is liable for the orders he or she exercises on your behalf. You will lose your margin before your broker takes a loss on your behalf.

Commodities trading is risky.

On the other hand, as noted above, your broker will add your potential profits to your margin account if gold prices fall.

Finally, note the higher contract prices in the examples above as settlement dates extend further into the future. Does that mean that traders always anticipated a price increase despite continuously falling prices? No. The increases reflect the time value of money. A dollar tomorrow is worth less than a dollar today at any positive rate of interest. Therefore, the price of an ounce of gold for delivery a year from now must be greater than the price of an ounce of gold today in order to compensate the owner for the interest foregone by holding gold instead of an interest earning asset.

INVESTING LONG

Commodities prices do not always march in lock step. Wheat prices rose at the same time that gold prices fell in the examples above. Use the excerpts below from the *Journal* to track wheat futures on the same dates.

Test your understanding of these concepts by asking yourself (and answering) these questions:

1. What were the prices for the December 91 (January 15 and September 3 excerpts) and July 92 (September 3 and June 8 excerpts) contracts, and by how much did they change?
2. How could an investor have profited from these price movements by purchasing long contracts? By how much would the investor have profited in each case? Note that prices are quoted in cents per bushel and that a contract is 5,000 bushels.

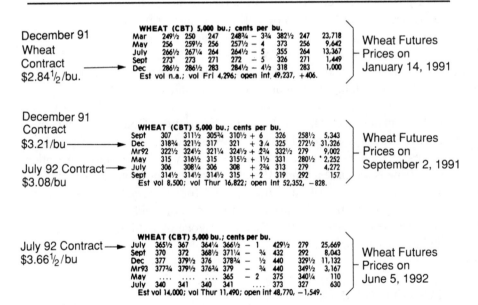

December 91 Wheat Contract $2.84½/bu. →

WHEAT (CBT) 5,000 bu.; cents per bu.

Mar	249½	250	247	248¾	– 3¾	382½	247	23,718
May	256	259½	256	257½	– 4	373	256	9,642
July	266½	267¼	264	264½	– 5	355	264	13,367
Sept	273"	273	271	272	– 5	326	271	1,449
Dec	286½	286½	283	284½	– 4½	318	283	1,000

Est vol n.a.; vol Fri 4,296; open int 49,237, +406.

Wheat Futures Prices on January 14, 1991

December 91 Contract $3.21/bu → (Dec)

July 92 Contract → (July) $3.08/bu

WHEAT (CBT) 5,000 bu.; cents per bu.

Sept	307	311½	305¾	310½	+ 6	326	258½	5,343
Dec	318¾	321½	317	321	+ 3¼	325	272½	31,326
Mr92	322½	324½	321¼	324½	+ 2¾	332½	279	9,002
May	315	316½	315	315½	+ 1½	331	280½	• 2,252
July	306	308¼	306	308	+ 2¾	313	279	4,272
Sept	314½	314½	314½	315	+ 2	319	292	157

Est vol 8,500; vol Thur 16,822; open int 52,352, –828.

Wheat Futures Prices on September 2, 1991

July 92 Contract → $3.66½/bu

WHEAT (CBT) 5,000 bu.; cents per bu.

July	365½	367	364¼	366½	– 1	429½	279	25,669
Sept	370	372	368½	371¼	– ¾	432	292	8,043
Dec	377	379½	376	378¾	– ½	440	329½	11,132
Mr93	377¾	379½	376¾	379	– ¾	440	349½	3,167
May	....	....	....	365	– 2	375	340¼	110
July	340	341	340	341	....	373	327	630

Est vol 14,000; vol Thur 11,490; open int 48,770, –1,549.

Wheat Futures Prices on June 5, 1992

Source: *The Wall Street Journal*, January 15 & September 3, June 8, 1992

OTHER FUTURES AND OPTIONS ON FUTURES CONTRACTS

Turn once again to the excerpts from the Monday, June 8, 1992 *Journal* on page 213 and notice you can purchase futures contracts on investments other than commodities. For instance, futures contracts are available on Treasury bonds, Eurodollars, the S&P 500, the NYSE composite index, and the Major Market Index (which closely tracks the Dow). Whereas futures began with commodities like wheat, trading activity is now far heavier for instruments like Treasury bonds. *Futures options* let you buy options on futures contracts.

Examine the excerpts from the June 8, 1992 *Journal* that portray trading on Friday, June 5, 1992 for Futures and Futures Options on the S&P 500 Index, which closed at 413.48 that day. (See below.)

1. If you had forecast sharply rising stocks prices, you could have purchased a *long* contract on S&P 500 futures, or a *short* contract if you had anticipated the index's decline. The same principles apply as discussed above in the sections on commodity trading. (See below.)

2. As an alternative, you could have purchased either call or put options on the S&P 500 futures index–calls to take advantage of rising prices and puts to take advantage of falling prices. (See pages 220 and 221.)

INDEX

S&P 500 INDEX (CME) 500 times index

	Open	High	Low	Settle	Chg	High	Low	Open Interest
June	413.25	414.55	411.40	414.30	+ .80	424.40	374.50	108,114
Sept	414.25	415.60	412.50	415.30	+ .75	425.50	376.25	39,957
Dec	415.50	416.75	413.85	416.50	+ .60	427.25	391.40	2,081
Mr93	....	....		418.50	+ .60	423.80	397.50	351

Est vol 53,793; vol Thur 42,167; open int 150,503, −4,678.

Indx prelim High 413.85; Low 410.97; Close 413.48 −.22 ← Closing Price

Source: *The Wall Street Journal*, June 8, 1992

FUTURES OPTIONS PRICES

Friday, June 5, 1992.

AGRICULTURAL

CORN (CBT)
5,000 bu.; cents per bu.

Strike Price	Calls–Settle Jly	Sep	Dec	Puts–Settle Jly	Sep	Dec
240	18¾	27	30½	⅛	6	7¾
250	10½	20½	24	1½	9⅝	12
260	5	15¾	20	6	15	17
270	2¼	12½	16½	13½	22½	22½
280	1	10	13¾	22½	29	29½
[illegible]	½	8	10¾	31¾	37	36½

WHEAT (KC)
5,000 bu.; cents per bu.

Strike Price	Calls–Settle Jly	Sep	Dec	Puts–Settle Jly	Sep	Dec
350	17½	26½	35	1	8½	11
360	10¼	21½	29	3½	12¼	14½
370	5	15¾	24½	8¼	17¾	....
380	2	12½	20½	15¾	23½	....
390	1	9	16	23½	30¼	....
400	½	6¾	14½	33½	37¾	

Est. vol. 155;
Thur vol. 137 calls; 45 p[illegible]
Op. int. Thur 4,[illegible]
COTTON [illegible]

						Dec
				.01	1.50	2.05
			....	.01	1.90	2.45
		3.15	3.50	.40	2.40	2.90
	.01	2.75	3.05	1.44	2.84	3.45
61	.01	2.20	2.70	2.44	3.30	3.95
62	.01	1.85	2.25	3.44	3.95	4.60

Est. vol. 1,050;
Thur vol. 584 calls; 682 puts
Op. int. Thur 21,818 calls; 20,074 puts

ORANGE JUICE (CTN)
15,000 lbs.; cents per lb.

Strike Price	Calls–Settle Jly	Sep	Nov	Puts–Settle Jly	Sep	Nov
125	....	4.45	3.50	.05	4.55	....
130	3.70	2.75	2.65	.05	7.55	....
135	.05	1.70	1.80	1.30	11.30	....
140	.05	1.30	1.30	6.30	....	....
145	.05	.85	....	11.30	....	....
150	.05	....	....	16.30	....	....

Est. vol. 60;
Thur vol. 45 calls; 45 puts
Op. int. Thur 2,712 calls; 2,191 puts

COFFEE (CSCE)
37,500 lbs.; cents per lb.

Strike Price	Calls–Settle Jly	Sep	Dec	Puts–Settle Jly	Sep	Dec
57.50	4.05	7.55	11.15	0.00	1.30	1.90
60.00	1.55	5.90	9.53	0.00	2.15	2.78
62.50	0.00	4.50	8.00	0.95	3.25	3.75
65.00	0.00	3.50	6.50	3.45	4.80	4.75
67.50	0.00	2.70	5.65	5.95	6.45	6.40
70.00	0.00	2.10	4.70	8.45	8.35	7.95

Est. vol. 1,817;
Thur vol. 952 calls; 680 puts
Op. int. Thur 41,496 calls; 18,354 [illegible]

SUGAR–WORLD (CSCE)
112,000 lbs.; cent[illegible]
Strike Ca[illegible]
Pric[illegible]

						.0072
					.0125	.0137
				....	....	.0240
		....	.0095	....	....	....
	....	....	.0056	....	....	....

Est. vol. 3,827;
Thur vol. 1,083 calls; 1,544 puts
Op. int. Thur 25,998 calls; 25,517 puts

GASOLINE–Unlead (NYM)
42,000 gal.; $ per gal.

Strike Price	Calls–Settle Jly	Aug	Sep	Puts–Settle Jly	Aug	Sep
64	.0328	.0338	.0275	.0004	.0040	.0140
66	.0143	.0199	.0175	.0019	.0100	....
68	.0037	.0105	.0109	.0113	.0205	....
70	.0007	.0050	.0065	....	....	....
72	.0002	.0025	....	....	....	....
74	....	....	....	....	....	....

Est. vol. 3,689;
Thur vol. 2,213 calls; 2,216 puts
Op. int. Thur 26,996 calls; 23,932 puts

LIVESTOCK

CATTLE-FEEDER (CME)
44,000 lbs.; cents per lb.

Strike Price	Calls–Settle Aug	Sep	Oct	Puts–Settle Aug	Sep	Oct
72	5.05	....	....	0.30	0.50	0.80
74	3.30	....	....	0.55	0.85	1.35
76	1.80	1.60	1.45	1.15	1.50	....
78	0.75	0.65	0.70	2.00		
80	0.15	0.20	0.20			

82	0.05	0.02	0.07	5.30	....	....

Est. vol. 150;
Thur vol. 180 calls; 138 puts
Op. int. Thur 2,339 calls; 4,301 puts

CATTLE-LIVE (CME)
40,000 lbs.; cents per lb.

Strike Price	Calls–Settle Jun	Aug	Oct	Puts–Settle Jun	Aug	Oct
70	3.05	1.67	1.67	0.00	0.95	1.70
72	1.05	0.72	0.82	0.00	1.95	2.80
74	0.00	0.25	0.32	0.95	3.47	....
76	0.00	0.07	0.15	2.95	....	....
78	0.00	0.02	0.02	4.95	....	....
80	0.00	0.02	....	....	....	....

Est. vol. 1,645;
Thur vol. 689 calls; 613 puts

CURRENCY

JAPANESE YEN (IMM)
12,500,000 yen; [illegible]
Strike C[illegible]
Pric[illegible]

						1.10
				.16	0.96	....
			0.89	....	1.28	....
		0.36	0.71	1.15	1.63	....
	....	0.25	....	....	....	....

Est. vol. 9,504;
Thur vol. 4,463 calls; 2,450 puts
Op. int. Thur 45,175 calls; 55,631 puts

DEUTSCHEMARK (IMM)
125,000 marks; cents per mark

Strike Price	Calls–Settle Jun	Jly	Aug	Puts–Settle Jun	Jly	Aug
6200	0.81	0.67	1.03	.00008	0.75	1.11
6250	0.31	0.46	0.82	.00008	1.04	....
6300	0.01	0.31	0.64	0.20	1.39	1.71
6350	.00008	0.20	0.50	0.69	....	....
6400	.00008	0.13	0.37	1.19	....	....
6450	.00008	....	....	1.69	....	....

Est. vol. 23,536;
Thur vol. 20,915 calls; 13,894 puts
Op. int. Thur 93,670 calls; 144,674 puts

CANADIAN DOLLAR (IMM)
100,000 Can.$, cents per Can.$

Strike Price	Calls–Settle Jun	Jly	Aug	Puts–Settle Jun	Jly	Aug
8300	0.77	0.64	0.83	.0000	0.28	....
8350	0.27	0.37	0.57	.0000	0.52	....
8400	.0000	0.18	0.37	0.23	0.83	....
8450	.0000	0.08	0.23	0.73	....	....
8500	.0000	0.03	0.13	1.23	....	....
8550	.0000	....	....	1.73	....	....

Est. vol. 1,624;
Thur vol. 1,065 calls; 1,344 puts
Op. int. Thur 14,466 calls; 16,298 puts

BRITISH POUND (IMM)
62,500 pounds; cents per pound

Strike Price	Calls–Settle Jun	Jly	A[illegible]	P[illegible]		
1775	5.60					
1800						
						....
					.22	....
				6.90	....	....

INTEREST RATE

T-BONDS (CBT)
$100,000; points and 64ths of 100%

Strike Price	Calls–Settle Jly	Sep	Dec	Puts–Settle Jly	Sep	Dec
96	3-45	4-06	3-54	0-01	0-26	1-20
98	1-52	2-34	2-42	0-08	0-56	2-05
100	0-29	1-25	1-45	0-49	1-45	3-07
102	0-03	0-42	1-01	2-23	2-60	4-26
104	0-01	0-16	0-38	....	4-34	5-60
106	0-01	0-06	0-22	....	6-23	7-42

Est. vol. 115,000;
Thur vol. 36,223 calls; 36,175 puts
Op. int. Thur 259,070 calls; 174,517 puts

T-NOTES (CBT)
$100,000; points and 64ths of 100%

Strike Price	Calls–Settle Jly	Sep	Dec	Puts–Settle Jly	Sep	Dec
101	2-02	2-30	....	0-02	0-31	1-27
102	1-10	1-50	....	0-10	0-50	....
103	0-31	1-13	1-17	0-31	1-13	....
104	0-09	0-48	0-59	....	1-48	....
105	0-02	0-29	....	....	2-28	....
106	0-01	0-16	0-29	....	3-15	....

Est. vol. 6,000;
Thur vol. 1,338 calls; 2,545 puts
Op. int. Thur 37,098 calls; 29,627 puts

MUNICIPAL BOND INDEX (CBT)
$100,000; pts. & 64ths of 100%

Strike Price	Calls–Settle Jun	Sep	Dec	Puts–Settle Jun	Sep	Dec
93	2-44		1-62	0-05		0-53
94			1-27	0-06		1-14
95	0-50		0-57	0-07		1-43
96	0-13	....	0-40	0-33	....	2-24
97	0-04	....	....	....	....	....
98	0-03	....	....	2-02	....	....

Est. vol. 0;
Thur vol. 0 calls; 0 puts
Op. int. Thur 5,961 calls; 6,862 puts

5 YR TREAS NOTES (CBT)
$100,000; points and 64ths of 100%

Strike Price	Calls–Settle Jly	Sep	Dec	Puts–Settle Jly	Sep	[illegible]
10350	1-15	1-38	....	0-04		
10400	0-51	1-16	....			
10450	0-28	0-[illegible]				
10500	0-[illegible]					
105[illegible]						

				Puts–Settle		
			....	Sep	Dec	....
		3-51	....	0-15	0-31	....
	2-37	3-03	....	0-25	0-47	....
97	1-54	2-24	....	0-42	1-04	....
98	0-51	1-22	....	1-39	2-20	....
100	n.a.	n.a.	....	2-18	2-41	....
101	0-17	0-42	....	3-05	3-22	....

Est. vol. Fri, 1,324 calls; 8,664 puts
Op. int. Thur, 30,655 calls; 19,840 puts

INDEX

S&P 500 STOCK INDEX (CME) ← S+P 500
$500 times premium

Strike Price	Calls–Settle Jun	Jly	Aug	Puts–Settle Jun	Jly	Aug
405	10.40	13.85	....	1.15	3.60	6.10
410	6.40	10.20	....	2.10	4.95	7.60
415	3.35	7.10	9.75	4.05	6.80	9.45
420	1.40	4.60	7.15	7.10	9.30	11.80
425	0.45	2.70	4.90	11.15	12.30	14.55
430	0.10	1.45	3.15	15.80	16.10	....

Est. vol. 7,141;
Thur vol. 3,135 calls; 3,587 puts
Op. int. Thur 35,794 calls; 74,791 puts

OTHER OPTIONS

Final or settlement prices of selected confracts. Volume and open interest are totals in all contract months.

AUSTRALIAN DOLLAR (IMM)
$100,000; $ per $
Strike Calls–Settle
Price Jun Jlv
7650 ..
E[illegible]

[illegible] Puts–Settle
[illegible]ice .... DayPrice ....
[illegible]hur 0.70 .... Thur 1.00 ....
Est. vol. 0; Thu 10 calls, 5 puts
Op. int. Thu 35 calls, 5 puts

FIVE DAY SILVER (CMX)
5,000 troy oz.; cents per troy oz.

Strike Price	Calls–Settle Jly	Aug	Oct	Puts–Settle Jly	Aug	Oct
360	9.60	17.10	22.60	1.30	3.00	8.50

Est. vol. 95; Thu 95 calls, 1 puts
Op. int. Thu 2,171 calls, 931 puts

PORK BELLIES (CME)
40,000 lbs.; cents per lb.

Strike Price	Calls–Settle Jly	Aug	Nov	Puts–Settle Jly	Aug	Nov
32	1.15	1.35	....	0.55	2.80	....

Est. vol. 164; Thu 90 calls, 142 puts
Op. int. Thu 5,334 calls, 1,522 puts

RICE-ROUGH (CRCE)
2,000 cwt.; $ per cwt.

Strike Price	Calls–Settle Jly	Sep	Nov	Puts–Settle Jly	Sep	Nov
6600	....	....	....	....	.205	....

Est. vol. 50; Thu 3 calls, 25 puts
Op. int. Thu 742 calls, 1,004 puts

SILVER (CBT)
1,000 troy oz.; cents per troy oz.
NOT AVAILABLE

SOYBEANS (MCE)
1,000 bu.; cents per bu.

Strike Price	Calls–Settle Jly	Aug	Sep	Puts–Settle Jly	Aug	Sep
600	16	30½	41½	8¾	20½	26½

Est. vol. 100; Thu 34 calls, 2 puts
Op. int. Thu 3,630 calls, 220 puts

WHEAT (MPLS)
5,000 bu.; cents per bu.

Strike Price	Calls Settle Jly	Sep	Dec	Puts–Settle Jly	Sep	Dec
380	8	10	21	7	21	

Est. vol. 68; Thu 577 calls, 0 puts
Op. int. Thu 1,061 calls, 639 puts

Source: *The Wall Street Journal*, June 8, 1992

INDEX

S&P 500 STOCK INDEX (CME)
$500 times premium

Strike	Calls–Settle			Puts–Settle		
Price	Jun	Jly	Aug	Jun	Jly	Aug
405	10.40	13.85	....	1.15	3.60	6.10
410	6.40	10.20	....	2.10	4.95	7.60
415	3.35	7.10	9.75	4.05	6.80	9.45
420	1.40	4.60	7.15	7.10	9.30	11.80
425	0.45	2.70	4.90	11.15	12.30	14.55
430	0.10	1.45	3.15	15.80	16.10	....

Est. vol. 7,141;
Thur vol. 3,135 calls; 3,587 puts
Op. int. Thur 35,794 calls; 74,791 puts

Source: *The Wall Street Journal*, June 8, 1992

Investor'sTip

- Take a long position in gold futures when you forecast sharply rising inflation and a short position when you forecast a falling rate of inflation.

TRACKING COMMODITIES

Every day, on the first page (Cl) of the third section, *The Wall Street Journal* summarizes recent Commodities activity under the Markets Diary heading. A sample from the Monday, June 8, 1992 edition appears on page 222. The chart presents the Commodities Research Bureau's (CRB) Futures Index, and spot prices for gold, oil, wheat, and steers are also given.

The Wall Street Journal carries a commodities article daily in the third section; on Mondays it includes the Dow Jones Commodity Indexes. See the example from the Monday, June 8, 1992 issue on page 223. You can also use the daily CRB Commodities chart in the Markets Diary (mentioned in the last paragraph) to follow commodity price movements. These indexes will be your most sensitive barometers of inflation.

The Wall Street Journal reports Cash Prices for immediate delivery on a wide variety of commodities on a daily basis. Thus, on Monday, June 8,

1992 the *Journal* published cash prices for Friday, June 5, 1992 (see page 224).

All of these series can be located using the indexes on the front pages of the first and last sections.

CONCLUSION

Commodities investing is far riskier than stock market investing because positions are highly leveraged. You can lose your entire investment if prices move the wrong way. Moreover, individual commodities can be drastically affected by world events—droughts, floods, wars, political upheavals. Yet these markets also present tremendous opportunities for those who can accurately forecast inflation's trend.

COMMODITIES CRB Futures Index (1967=100)

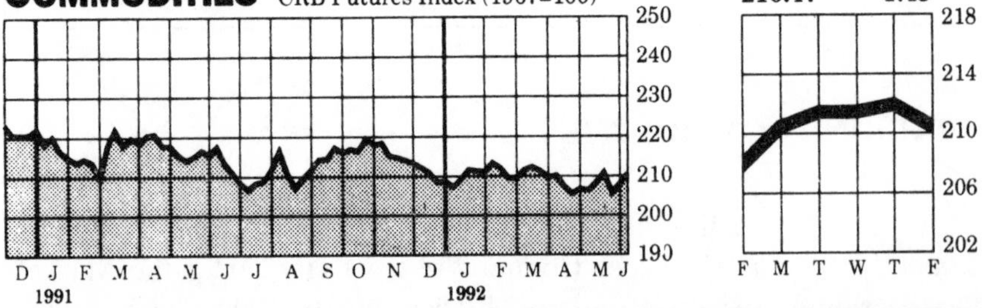

COMMODITY	CLOSE	CHANGE	THU	YR AGO	12-MO HIGH — AT CLOSE —	12-MO LOW
Gold (Comex spot), troy oz.	**$338.70**	$+ 0.10	$338.60	$366.30	$373.70	$335.30
Oil (W. Tex. int. crude), bbl.	**22.60**	+ 0.10	22.50	20.30	24.15	17.85
Wheat (#2 hard KC), bu.	**4.07**	+ 0.05	4.02	2.99	4.77	2.74
Steers (Tex.-Okla. choice), 100 lb.	**73.75**	unch	73.75	75.75	79.75	64.00

NOTE: Monthly charts based on Friday close, except for Federal Funds, which are weekly average rates.

Source: *The Wall Street Journal*, June 8, 1992

Commodity Gains Fit Recovery Scenario

COMMODITIES

By Robert Steiner
And Anita Raghavan
Staff Reporters of The Wall Street Journal

The U.S. economy finally seems to be climbing out of its sickbed and tottering back to health. At this point in the economic cycle, commodity prices typically start moving higher.

Sure enough, in just the past month crude oil has risen 8.7%, copper 4.6% and aluminum 1.5%.

For investors who want to begin playing this development, the bad news is that more adventuresome types already are in the game. They have bid up stocks of big U.S. metals, lumber and energy producers to very pricey levels. The good news is that many investment strategists think money still can be made on shares of smaller commodities producers and, in some cases, in the commodities themselves.

The smaller natural resources stocks will have to be selected very carefully, strategists caution. Many people think the recovery, while definitely under way, mightn't be robust. So, only the most efficient commodity producers – which in many instances also are the largest – may be poised to reap profits soon.

A gutsier approach is advocated by Jim Rogers, now a professor of finance at Columbia University, who made his fame and fortune some years ago as co-manager of Quantum Fund.

"You are always better off investing in the commodity rather than the stock because the moves are much sharper, cleaner, faster and more profitable," he says. He also notes that investors have to put up less money to buy a futures contract than they do to buy a stock, which increases the potential payoff of a prescient pick. Of course, such "leverage" also magnifies the potential losses.

Other strategists suggest that investors anticipating a slow recovery might be safer with a mix of stocks and commodities or simply with stocks alone. Futures don't pay dividends, they note, and they expire regularly, which makes them less suited for long-term strategies.

"Commodities are going to go up if the recovery continues," agrees Victor Sperandeo, president of Rand Management Corp. in Short Hills, N.J. "But I don't think commodities are the way to play the game yet because [they] are only going to move if inflation starts to accelerate."

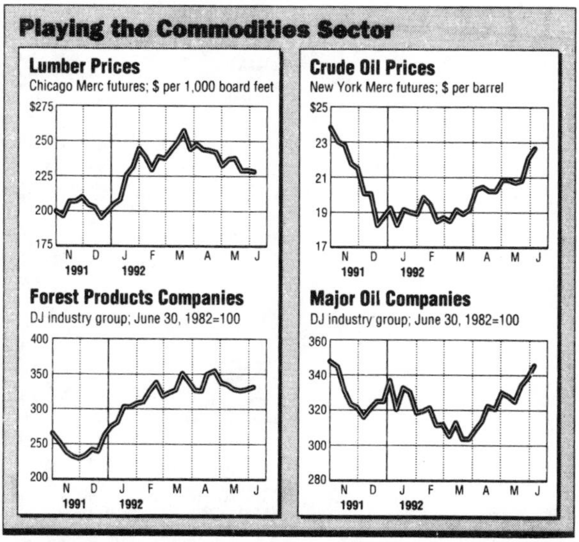

Another caveat to keep in mind is that "not every commodity recovers at the same time," says Abby Cohen, co-chairperson of the investment policy committee at Goldman Sachs. "Each one marches to its own set of demand and supply considerations."

Lumber, for instance, shot up during the first part of the year on speculation that housing construction would take off as interest rates declined. But "if interest rates rise, we could see the gains in lumber evaporate pretty quickly," says Philip Gotthelf, editor of Commodity Futures Forecast, a New Jersey market letter. Lumber for July delivery ended Friday at $228.30 per 1,000 board feet, and Mr. Gotthelf says it could fall to $200 or even as low as $175.

On the other hand, he expects companies making such secondary products as corrugated boxes to do well because the expected drop in lumber prices will improve their profit margins. Investors who

Please Turn to Page C12, Column 3

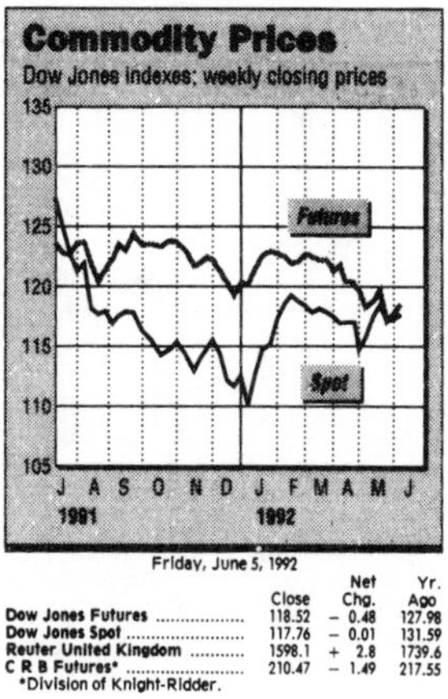

Friday, June 5, 1992

	Close	Net Chg.	Yr. Ago
Dow Jones Futures	118.52	– 0.48	127.98
Dow Jones Spot	117.76	– 0.01	131.59
Reuter United Kingdom	1598.1	+ 2.8	1739.6
C R B Futures*	210.47	– 1.49	217.55

*Division of Knight-Ridder.

Source: *The Wall Street Journal*, June 8, 1992

CASH PRICES

Friday, June 5, 1992.
(Closing Market Quotations)

	Fri	Thur	Yr.Ago
GRAINS AND FEEDS			
Barley, top-quality Mpls., bu	n2.55	2.55	2.30
Bran, wheat middlings, KC ton	63.-65.0	63.-64.0	57.00
Corn, No. 2 yel. Cent-Ill. bu	bp2.52½	2.56½	2.39½
Corn Gluten Feed, Midwest, ton ..	75.-102.	75.-102.	74.00
Cottonseed Meal,			
Clksdle,Miss. ton	130.00	130.00	125.00
Hominy Feed,Cent-Ill. ton	80.00	79.00	70.00
Meat-Bonemeal, 50% pro. Ill. ton.	210.-215.	215.00	200.00
Oats, No. 2 milling, Mpls., bu	n1.55½	1.56½	1.31
Sorghum, (Milo) No. 2 Gulf cwt ...	4.78	4.87	4.46
Soybean Meal,			
Decatur, Illinois ton..................	178.-179.	182.-184.	175.00
Soybeans, No. 1 yel Cent.-Ill. bu ..	bp5.96½	6.10	5.80
Wheat,			
Spring 14%-pro Mpls. bu	4.39½-56½	4.52¼-57¼	3.06
Wheat, No. 2 sft red, St.Lou. bu ...	bp3.62½	3.63½	3.01½
Wheat, No. 2 hard KC, bu	4.06½	4.01⅞	2.99
Wheat, No. 1 sft wht, del Port Ore	4.51	4.51	3.46
FOODS			
Beef, Carcass, Equiv.Index Value,			
choice 1-3,550-700lbs.	113.13	112.98	115.45
Beef, Carcass, Equiv.Index Value,			
select 1-3,550-700lbs.	103.41	103.27	108.25
Broilers, Dressed "A" NY lb	x.5558	.5686	.5251
Broilers, 12-Cty Comp Wtd Av	.5588	.5588	.5096
*Comparable, but not exact.			
Butter, AA, Chgo., lb.	.81¼	.81¼	.99½
Cocoa, Ivory Coast, $metric ton ...	g1,057	1,053	1,150
Coffee, Brazilian, NY lb.	n.48	.48	.72
Coffee, Colombian, NY lb.	n.65	.65	.92
Eggs, Lge white, Chgo doz.	.47-.53	.47-.53	.63
Flour, hard winter KC cwt	10.60	10.55	8.10
Hams, 17-20 lbs, Mid-US lb fob	.60	.60	.76
Hogs, Iowa-S.Minn. avg. cwt	47.50	46.75	55.00
Hogs, Omaha avg cwt	45.50	46.50	53.50
Pork Bellies, 12-14 lbs Mid-US lb ..	.35-.36	.34-.35	.57½
Pork Loins, 14-18 lbs. Mid-US lb ...	1.10-.14	1.08-.12	1.19
Steers, Tex.-Okla. ch avg cwt	73.75	73.75	75.75
Steers, Feeder, Okl Cty, av cwt ...	87.50	87.50	104.25
Sugar, cane, raw, world, lb. fob ...	.1034	.1039	.0885
FATS AND OILS			
Coconut Oil, crd, N. Orleans lb. ...	xxn.28¾	.28¾	.17¼
Corn Oil, crd wet mill, Chgo. lb. ..	n.25	.25	.29½
Corn Oil, crd dry mill, Chgo. lb. ...	n.27½	.27½	.29
Grease, choice white, Chgo lb.	n.11⅞	.11⅛	.11
Lard, Chgo lb.	.13¾	.13	.12½
Palm Oil, ref. bl. deod. N.Orl. lb. .	n.22	.22	.19
Soybean Oil, crd, Decatur, lb.	.2093	.2126	.2010
Tallow, bleachable, Chgo lb.	b.13½	.13½	.12¼
Tallow, edible, Chgo lb.	.15	.15	.13¼
FIBERS AND TEXTILES			
Burlap, 10 oz 40-in NY yd	n.2675	.2675	.2885
Cotton 1 1/16 str lw-md Mphs lb ...	.5607	.5508	.8531
Wool, 64s, Staple, Terr. del. lb.	2.20	2.20	1.80
METALS			
Aluminum			
ingot lb. del. Midwest	q60¼-60¾	.60-.61	.56½
Copper			
cathodes lb.	p1.07⅜-.08	1.07⅜-.09	1.03⅝
Copper Scrap, No 2 wire NY lb	k.88	.88	.81
Lead, lb.	p.35	.35	.31
Mercury 76 lb. flask NY	q195-200	195.-200.	120.00
Steel Scrap 1 hvy mlt Chgo ton	86.-91.0	85.-91.0	89.00
Tin composite lb.	q4.2130	4.2161	3.7157
Zinc Special High grade lb	p.66175	.65240	.48200
MISCELLANEOUS			
Rubber, smoked sheets, NY lb. ...	n.46¼	.46¼	.45
Hides, hvy native steers lb., fob ...	.81	.81	.88
PRECIOUS METALS			
Gold, troy oz			
Engelhard indust bullion	340.03	339.63	368.27
Engelhard fabric prods	357.03	356.61	386.88
Handy & Harman base price	338.80	338.40	367.00
London fixing AM 338.85 PM ...	338.80	338.40	367.00
Krugerrand, whol	a340.00	340.00	367.00
Maple Leaf, troy oz.	a350.00	350.00	378.00
American Eagle, troy oz.	a350.00	350.00	378.00
Platinum, (Free Mkt.)	369.50	373.50	382.00
Platinum, indust (Engelhard)	373.00	374.00	386.00
Platinum, fabric prd (Engelhard)	473.00	474.00	486.00
Palladium, indust (Engelhard) ...	81.50	81.00	98.00
Palladium, fabrc prd (Englhard)	96.50	96.00	113.00
Silver, troy ounce			
Engelhard indust bullion	4.060	4.080	4.525
Engelhard fabric prods	4.385	4.406	4.842
Handy & Harman base price	4.050	4.070	4.510
London Fixing (in pounds)			
Spot (U.S. equiv. $4.0825)	2.2340	2.2340	2.6685
3 months	2.2885	2.2885	2.7425
6 months	2.3425	2.3425	2.8110
1 year	2.4540	2.4545	2.9505
Coins, whol $1,000 face val	a2,975	2,982	3,150

a-Asked. b-Bid. bp-Country elevator bids to producers. c-Corrected. d-Dealer market. e-Estimated. f-Dow Jones International Petroleum Report. g-Main crop, ex-dock, warehouses, Eastern Seaboard, north of Hatteras. j.-f.o.b. warehouse. k-Dealer selling prices in lots of 40,000 pounds or more, f.o.b. buyer's works. n-Nominal. p-Producer price. q-Metals Week. r-Rail bids. s-Thread count 78x54. x-Less than truckloads. z-Not quoted. xx-f.o.b. tankcars.

Spot Lumber and Plywood Prices

Compiled by two trade publications, Crow's and Random Lengths. Prices are a guide only for carload or larger sales to wholesalers; specific sales may be at slightly higher or lower prices.

	Wk Ended 6/05/92	Week Earlier	Year Earlier
SPRUCE-PINE-FIR 2x4s—a			
Crow's	222	233	242
Random Lengths	259	273	228
SHEATHING PLYWOOD, ½-inch—b			
Crow's	254	254	292
Random Lengths	254	248	295

a-Per 1,000 board feet for standard-and-better grade, kiln-dried, random lengths, net f.o.b. British Columbia mills.

b-Per 1,000 square feet, 4-or-5-ply Western exterior, C-D grade,.net f.o.b. mill.

Source: *The Wall Street Journal*, June 8, 1992

CHAPTER 11

LONG-TERM INTEREST RATES

INTRODUCTION

"Gold vs. stocks" is shorthand for the concept that paper assets do well in times of low inflation while tangible assets do not, and vice versa.

Chapter 9 investigated the stock market; this chapter will examine long-term debt instruments. You will discover why they, like stocks, appreciate when prices are stable but become poor investments when inflation turns severe. Begin your investigation with a general discussion of the origin of these investments.

Governments and businesses turn to the credit markets and issue long-term debt instruments to raise large sums whenever their internally generated funds, such as tax revenues or profits, fall short of their current or capital expenditures. The federal government, for instance, began the 1990s by annually borrowing hundreds of billions of dollars in the capital markets because recession suppressed revenue growth while expenditures continued to climb.

Corporations, on the other hand, issue debt (i.e., sell bonds that are redeemed after a long period throughout which they pay interest) in order to finance the purchase of new plant and equipment. Take public utilities for example. Profits cannot cover the cost of new generating and switching stations, satellites, and transmission lines, so the difference has to be made up by borrowing. Since the projects of public utility companies are long-term and generate income for these companies over several decades of useful life, it's appropriate that the financing be long-term too. The stretch-out in earnings on these assets will provide for the regular payment of interest and principal.

You already know that corporations can raise funds by selling shares via the stock market (see Chapter 9). In that process, the ownership of a corporation is subdivided by the issue of new stock. The situation is very different when corporations borrow funds in the credit markets. Ownership does not change hands although, of course, the debt burden is increased.

New credit market debt, whether sold by government or business, is subdivided into discrete units called notes or bonds and issued for a specified length of time. At the conclusion of that period, the issuer redeems the note or bond and repays the initial purchase price. Notes are medium-term debt instruments that are redeemed in one to ten years, whereas bonds are issued with maturities of more than ten years. (Chapter 12 discusses debt instruments with maturities of less than a year.)

Notes and bonds are sold or auctioned in the *primary* (initial issue) market and then traded on the *secondary* market until they mature (redeemed by the issuer). They have a specific face or *par value* (such as $1,000) and pay a specified annual, semiannual, or quarterly amount, known as *coupon interest*. When you purchase a bond, expect to receive an interest return (called the *current* or *true* yield) determined by the relationship between the fluctuating market price of the bond (more, less, or equal to its fixed $1,000 par value) and the fixed periodic payment of coupon interest. If you hold the bond to maturity (i.e., until it is redeemed by the issuer), you will also receive back its par value.

But you need not hold the note or bond to maturity because there is a secondary market for notes and bonds that is separate from the initial-issue market. The existence of this secondary or resale market makes it much easier for government and business to sell bonds in the initial primary market. If note and bond buyers could not sell and resell these instruments over and over again, it would be very difficult for government and business to issue them in the first place. Now you know why these instruments are issued in discrete units (such as $1,000) for convenient trading.

Trading on the secondary market determines all notes' and bonds' market prices and thereby determines their current yields. The secondary market dog wags the primary market tail. Not only are primary market auction or issue prices determined by secondary market trading, but primary market coupon rates will quickly reflect true yields established in the secondary market.

There are three principal issuers of bonds: the United States government and its agencies; corporations; and state and local governments. Examine each of their issues in turn.

TREASURY AND AGENCY ISSUES

Both the U.S. Treasury and a variety of federal agencies issue long-term debt instruments. Treasury debt is classified as bonds, notes, and bills. The Treasury bill will be discussed in Chapter 12. Treasury notes (maturities of 1 to 10 years) and bonds (over 10 years) are issued in $1,000 denominations and pay a stated coupon interest payment semiannually.

Treasury bills, bonds, and notes are referred to collectively as Treasury Securities. These securities are the safest of all debt instruments because they are backed by the full taxing power of the U.S. Government.

The government sells Treasury securities when it needs funds. These primary market sales are made at auction to securities dealers. Dealers then resell them on the secondary market to investors, where they are traded freely until maturity. By the early 1990s, the secondary market, an over-the-counter market in New York, traded $150 billion of Treasury securities daily, about 15 times daily New York Stock Exchange volume. *The Wall Street Journal* reports activity in the primary and secondary markets for long-term Treasury securities in its daily **Credit Markets** article in the third (C) section (see front page index).

The Treasury announces its auction of 2-year notes four times a year on Wednesdays in the middle of February, May, August, and November. The auction takes place about one week after the announcement and the notes are issued on the last day of the month. Five-year, two-month (62 month) notes are auctioned and issued with the two-year notes.

The Treasury generally auctions 3-year notes, l0-year notes, and 30-year bonds during the second week of February, May, August, and November and issues them shortly afterward, on the 15th of the same month. Four-year notes are auctioned in the third week of March, June, September, and December and issued the last day of the month. Finally, 7-year notes are usually auctioned in the middle of January, April, July and October and issued on the 15th of the month.

Bonds and notes are almost always issued in denominations of $1,000, which is referred to as the par value of the bond. Each bond has a coupon rate indicating the dollar amount the security will pay annually until maturity. Interestingly, bonds are seldom auctioned at precisely their par value because market conditions will influence buyers' bids at the auction.

On April 8, 1992 the 7 year note auctioned by the Treasury in the primary market yielded 7.11% → Average price (Rate)

Rates are determined by the difference between the purchase price and face value. Thus, higher bidding narrows the investor's return while lower bidding widens it.

Seven-Year Notes

Applications	$18,794,398,000
Accepted bids	$9,754,610,000
Accepted at low price	62%
Accepted noncompetitively	$474,000,000
Average price (Rate)	99.402 (7.11%)
High price (Rate)	99.510 (7.09%)
Low price (Rate)	99.239 (7.14%)
Interest rate	7%
CUSIP number	912827E81

The notes are dated April 15, 1992, and mature April 15, 1999.

Source: *The Wall Street Journal*, April 9, 1992

The Treasury entertains bids at the primary auction and arrays them from highest to lowest. The Treasury accepts bids starting at the highest price and works down until it has accepted a sufficient number of bids to realize its target funding. The par value and coupon interest rate are established before the auction begins, but the true yield is determined by the price established at the auction. It can be higher or lower than the $1,000 par value. If higher, the true yield will be less than the coupon rate. If lower, the true yield will be more than the coupon rate.

Look at the Thursday, April 9, 1992 *Journal* excerpt from the **Credit Markets** article (see front page index) above that reports on the previous day's 7 percent 7-year note issue. Almost half of $18,794,398,000 in bids was accepted, and $474 million was accepted noncompetitively. These small bidders took the market (average) price established at the auction. Notice that on the average successful bidders paid 99.402 percent of par, so that a $1,000 7-year note cost $994.02 (on the average), which is $5.98 less than par. The coupon rate was 7 percent or $70.00 annually per $1,000 note, but since successful bidders paid on the average only $994.02, the true yield was a higher 7.11 percent. Therefore, the 7.11% yield on these 7-year notes was slightly higher than the coupon rate of 7.0%.

Notice also that some successful bidders were astute or fortunate enough to bid only $992.39 and received a yield of 7.14%. Other bidders paid as much as $995.10 and received only 7.09%.

TREASURY BONDS, NOTES & BILLS

Wednesday, April 8, 1992

Representative Over the Counter quotations based on transactions of $1 million or more.

Treasury bond, note and bill quotes are as of mid-afternoon. Colons in bid-and-asked quotes represent 32nds; 101:01 means 101 1/32. Net changes in 32nds. n-Treasury note. Treasury bill quotes in hundredths, quoted on terms of a rate of discount. Days to maturity calculated from settlement date. All yields are to maturity and based on the asked quote. Latest 13-week and 26-week bills are boldfaced. For bonds callable prior to maturity, yields are computed to the earliest call date for issues quoted above par and to the maturity date for issues below par. -When issued.

Source: Federal Reserve Bank of New York.

U.S. Treasury strips as of 3 p.m. Eastern time, also based on transactions of $1 million or more. Colons in bid-and-asked quotes represent 32nds; 101:01 means 101 1/32. Net changes in 32nds. Yields calculated on the asked quotation. ci-stripped coupon interest. bp-Treasury bond, stripped principal. np-Treasury note, stripped principal. For bonds callable prior to maturity, yields are computed to the earliest call date for issues quoted above par and to the maturity date for issues below par.

Source: Bear, Stearns & Co. via Street Software Technology Inc.

GOVT. BONDS & NOTES

Rate	Maturity Mo/Yr	Bid	Asked	Chg.	Ask Yld.
8 3/8	Nov 92n	102:13	102:15	....	4.15
10 1/2	Nov 92n	103:21	103:23	....	4.13
7 3/8	Nov 92n	101:31	102:01	....	4.13
7 1/4	Dec 92n	102:03	102:05	....	4.19
9 1/8	Dec 92n	103:13	103:15	....	4.21
8 3/4	Jan 93n	103:10	103:12	....	4.22
7	Jan 93n	102:03	102:05	+ 1	4.26
4	Feb 88-93	99:03	99:19	....	4.49
6 3/4	Feb 93	101:31	102:03	+ 1	4.22
7 7/8	Feb 93	102:28	103:00	+ 1	4.24
8 1/4	Feb 93n	103:05	103:07	....	4.35
8 3/8	Feb 93n	103:08	103:10	....	4.36
10 7/8	Feb 93n	105:11	105:13	+ 1	4.33
6 3/4	Feb 93n	102:00	102:02	....	4.36
7 1/8	Mar 93n	102:16	102:18	− 1	4.41
9 5/8	Mar 93n	104:28	104:30	....	4.39
7 3/8	Apr 93n	102:27	102:29	....	4.41
7	Apr 93n	102:17	102:19	+ 1	4.46
7 5/8	May 93n	103:06	103:08	....	4.55
8 5/8	May 93n	104:08	104:10	+ 1	4.55
10 1/8	May 93n	105:26	105:28	....	4.57
6 3/4	May 93n	102:11	102:13	+ 1	4.56
7	Jun 93n	102:23	102:25	....	4.64
8 1/8	Jun 93n	104:01	104:03	....	4.65
7 1/4	Jul 93n	103:00	103:02	....	4.73
6 7/8	Jul 93n	102:18	102:20	....	4.78
8	Aug 93n	104:01	104:03	....	4.83
8 5/8	Aug 93	104:27	104:29	+ 1	4.83
8 3/4	Aug 93n	105:00	105:02	....	4.83
11 7/8	Aug 93n	109:01	109:03	....	4.84
6 3/8	Aug 93n	101:31	102:01	....	4.85
6 1/8	Sep 93n	101:21	101:23	....	4.90
8 1/4	Sep 93n	104:21	104:23	....	4.89
7 1/8	Oct 93n	103:03	103:05	+ 1	4.94
6	Oct 93n	101:13	101:15	+ 1	5.01
7 3/4	Nov 93n	104:02	104:04	....	5.03
8 5/8	Nov 93	105:12	105:14	+ 1	5.04
9	Nov 93n	105:29	105:31	....	5.06
11 3/4	Nov 93n	110:03	110:05	....	5.05
5 1/2	Nov 93n	100:19	100:21	....	5.08
5	Dec 93n	99:25	99:27	....	5.10
7 5/8	Dec 93n	104:00	104:02	....	5.13
7	Jan 94n	102:31	103:01	....	5.18
4 7/8	Jan 94n	99:13	99:15	....	5.19
6 7/8	Feb 94n	102:25	102:27	+ 1	5.24
8 7/8	Feb 94n	106:06	106:08	....	5.28
9	Feb 94	106:15	106:19	+ 1	5.22
5 3/8	Feb 94n	100:05	100:07	....	5.25
5 3/4	Mar 94n	100:26	100:28	+ 1	5.28
8 1/2	Mar 94n	105:26	105:28	+ 2	5.32
7	Apr 94n	103:05	103:07	+ 1	5.29
4 1/8	May 89-94	94:26	95:10	− 1	6.55
7	May 94n	103:02	103:04	+ 1	5.40
9 1/2	May 94n	107:28	107:30	+ 1	5.44
13 1/8	May 94n	115:05	115:07	+ 2	5.36
8 1/2	Jun 94n	106:05	106:07	+ 1	5.49
8	Jul 94n	105:05	105:07	+ 1	5.52
6 7/8	Aug 94n	102:25	102:27	+ 1	5.57
8 5/8	Aug 94n	106:17	106:19	+ 1	5.59
8 3/4	Aug 94	106:28	107:00	+ 1	5.53
12 5/8	Aug 94n	115:09	115:11	....	5.57
8 1/2	Sep 94n	106:15	106:17	+ 1	5.63
9 1/2	Oct 94n	108:24	108:26	+ 1	5.69
6	Nov 94n	100:23	100:25	+ 1	5.67
8 1/4	Nov 94n	105:30	106:00	+ 1	5.73
10 1/8	Nov 94	110:09	110:11	+ 2	5.78
11 5/8	Nov 94n	113:30	114:00	+ 1	5.75
7 5/8	Dec 94n	104:19	104:21	+ 1	5.75
8 5/8	Jan 95n	106:30	107:00	+ 1	5.85
3	Feb 95	94:10	95:10	....	4.78
5 1/2	Feb 95n	99:07	99:09	+ 2	5.78
7 3/4	Feb 95n	104:29	104:31	+ 1	5.83
10 1/2	Feb 95	111:26	111:28	+ 2	5.91
11 1/4	Feb 95n	113:25	113:27	+ 1	5.90
8 3/8	Apr 95n	106:17	106:19	+ 1	5.95
8 1/2	May 95n	106:30	107:00	+ 1	5.99
10 3/8	May 95	111:31	112:01	+ 1	6.06
11 1/4	May 95n	114:15	114:17	+ 2	6.04
12 5/8	May 95	118:14	118:18	− 1	5.97
8 7/8	Jul 95n	107:31	108:01	+ 1	6.12
8 1/2	Aug 95n	106:31	107:01	+ 2	6.15
10 1/2	Aug 95n	112:26	112:28	+ 1	6.19
8 5/8	Oct 95n	107:08	107:10	+ 1	6.27
6 3/4	Feb 97n	99:31	100:01	− 4	6.74
6 7/8	Mar 97n	100:16	100:18	− 4	6.74
8 1/2	Apr 97n	106:31	107:01	− 3	6.82
8 1/2	May 97n	106:30	107:00	− 4	6.85
8 1/2	Jul 97n	106:30	107:00	− 4	6.89
8 5/8	Aug 97n	107:16	107:18	− 4	6.91
8 3/4	Oct 97n	108:01	108:03	− 5	6.96
8 3/8	Aug 95-00	104:06	104:10	− 6	6.91
8 3/4	Aug 00n	108:02	108:04	− 8	7.43
8 1/2	Nov 00n	106:18	106:20	− 7	7.44
7 3/4	Feb 01n	101:30	102:00	− 8	7.44
11 3/4	Feb 01	127:23	127:27	− 7	7.41
8	May 01n	103:15	103:17	− 7	7.46
13 1/8	May 01	137:10	137:14	− 4	7.40
7 7/8	Aug 01n	102:20	102:22	− 9	7.47
8	Aug 96-01	102:29	103:01	− 4	7.18
13 3/8	Aug 01	139:17	139:21	− 7	7.42
7 1/2	Nov 01n	100:16	100:18	− 6	7.42
15 3/4	Nov 01	156:11	156:15	− 14	7.42
14 1/4	Feb 02	146:23	146:27	− 12	7.45
11 5/8	Nov 02	129:13	129:17	− 9	7.53
10 3/4	Feb 03	123:03	123:07	− 10	7.57
10 3/4	May 03	123:10	123:14	− 10	7.59
11 1/8	Aug 03	126:09	126:13	− 10	7.61
11 7/8	Nov 03	132:07	132:11	− 11	7.62
12 3/8	May 04	136:27	136:31	− 12	7.64
13 3/4	Aug 04	148:07	148:11	− 11	7.64
11 5/8	Nov 04	131:06	131:10	− 10	7.70
8 1/4	May 00-05	104:01	104:05	− 6	7.55
12	May 05	134:25	134:29	− 11	7.72
10 3/4	Aug 05	124:25	124:29	− 10	7.73
9 3/8	Feb 06	114:05	114:09	− 9	7.68
7 5/8	Feb 02-07	100:03	100:07	− 9	7.59
7 7/8	Nov 02-07	101:08	101:12	− 8	7.68
8 3/8	Aug 03-08	104:18	104:22	− 11	7.75
8 3/4	Nov 03-08	107:03	107:07	− 9	7.79
9 1/8	May 04-09	110:03	110:07	− 10	7.80
10 3/8	Nov 04-09	120:04	120:08	− 11	7.82
11 3/4	Feb 05-10	131:09	131:13	− 14	7.83
10	May 05-10	117:17	117:21	− 11	7.82
12 3/4	Nov 05-10	140:19	140:23	− 14	7.83
13 7/8	May 06-11	150:29	151:01	− 15	7.83
14	Nov 06-11	152:30	153:02	− 15	7.83
10 3/8	Nov 07-12	121:26	121:30	− 13	7.90
12	Aug 08-13	136:28	137:00	− 14	7.92
13 1/4	May 09-14	149:05	149:09	− 16	7.93
12 1/2	Aug 09-14	142:16	142:20	− 16	7.93
11 3/4	Nov 09-14	135:27	135:31	− 15	7.93
11 1/4	Feb 15	134:10	134:12	− 18	7.96
10 5/8	Aug 15	127:28	127:30	− 18	7.97
9 7/8	Nov 15	120:01	120:03	− 16	7.97
9 1/4	Feb 16	113:16	113:18	− 15	7.97
7 1/4	May 16	92:10	92:12	− 13	7.97
7 1/2	Nov 16	94:28	94:30	− 13	7.97
8 3/4	May 17	108:11	108:13	− 15	7.97
8 7/8	Aug 17	109:29	109:31	− 8	7.95
9 1/8	May 18	112:19	112:21	− 16	7.97
9	Nov 18	111:09	111:11	− 16	7.97
8 7/8	Feb 19	109:29	109:31	− 15	7.97
8 1/8	Aug 19	101:20	101:22	− 15	7.97
8 1/2	Feb 20	105:29	105:31	− 15	7.96
8 3/4	May 20	108:24	108:26	− 15	7.96
8 3/4	Aug 20	108:24	108:26	− 15	7.96
7 7/8	Feb 21	99:01	99:03	− 14	7.96
8 1/8	May 21	101:28	101:30	− 15	7.95
8 1/8	Aug 21	101:28	101:30	− 16	7.95
8	Nov 21	100:23	100:25	− 15	7.93

U.S. TREASURY STRIPS

Mat.	Type	Bid	Asked	Chg.	Ask Yld.
May 92	ci	99:20	99:20	...	3.79
Aug 92	ci	98:20	98:20	+ 1	3.99
Nov 92	ci	97:20	97:20	+ 1	4.07
Feb 93	ci	96:14	96:15	+ 6	4.29
May 93	ci	95:05	95:06	+ 3	4.56
Aug 93	ci	93:20	93:21	+ 1	4.92
Nov 93	ci	92:05	92:06	+ 2	5.16
Feb 94	ci	90:23	90:25	+ 1	5.30
May 94	ci	89:12	89:14	+ 2	5.40
Aug 94	ci	87:22	87:24	+ 4	5.64
Nov 94	ci	86:04	86:06	+ 4	5.81
Nov 94	np	86:01	86:03	+ 1	5.85
Feb 95	ci	84:15	84:17	+ 2	5.99
Feb 95	np	84:12	84:14	+ 2	6.03
May 95	ci	82:28	82:30	+ 1	6.13
May 95	np	82:26	82:28	+ 2	6.16
Aug 95	ci	81:10	81:13	+ 2	6.24
Aug 95	np	81:06	81:09	+ 2	6.29
Nov 95	ci	79:29	79:31	+ 5	6.31
Nov 95	np	79:22	79:24	+ 3	6.39
May 99	np	59:06	59:10	− 4	7.50
Aug 99	ci	57:27	57:31	− 3	7.56
Aug 99	np	57:27	57:31	− 4	7.56
Nov 99	ci	56:24	56:28	− 2	7.57
Nov 99	np	56:24	56:28	− 4	7.57
Feb 00	ci	55:11	55:15	− 4	7.65
Feb 00	np	55:17	55:21	4	7.61
May 00	ci	54:08	54:12	4	7.67
May 00	np	54:12	54:16	4	7.64
Aug 00	ci	53:04	53:08	4	7.69
Aug 00	np	53:10	53:14	4	7.65
Nov 00	ci	52:02	52:06	− 4	7.71
Nov 00	np	52:09	52:13	− 4	7.66
Feb 01	ci	50:26	50:30	− 5	7.77
Feb 01	np	51:05	51:09	4	7.69
May 01	ci	49:25	49:29	7	7.79
May 01	np	50:01	50:05	− 4	7.73
Aug 01	ci	48:25	48:29	7	7.80
Aug 01	np	49:00	49:04	4	7.75
Nov 01	ci	47:27	48:00	− 7	7.80
Nov 01	np	48:01	48:05	4	7.76
Feb 02	ci	46:16	46:20	− 8	7.90
May 02	ci	45:17	45:21	− 8	7.92
Aug 02	ci	44:19	44:23	− 7	7.93
Nov 02	ci	43:21	43:25	− 7	7.95
Feb 03	ci	42:22	42:27	− 9	7.97
May 03	ci	41:25	41:30	− 9	7.99
Aug 03	ci	40:30	41:02	− 8	8.00
Nov 03	ci	40:03	40:07	− 8	8.01
Feb 08	ci	27:21	27:25	− 5	8.25
May 08	ci	27:02	27:06	− 5	8.26
Aug 08	ci	26:16	26:20	− 5	8.26
[illegible] 08	ci	25:30	26:02	− 5	8.27
[illegible]	[illegible]	[illegible]	[illegible]	[illegible]	[illegible]
May 09	ci	24:29	25:01	− 5	8.27
Aug 09	ci	24:13	24:16	− 5	8.27
Nov 09	ci	23:29	24:01	− 5	8.27
Nov 09	bp	23:16	23:20	− 5	8.37
Feb 10	ci	23:12	23:16	− 5	8.28
May 10	ci	22:29	23:01	− 5	8.28
[illegible]	[illegible]	[illegible]	[illegible]	[illegible]	[illegible]
Nov 10	ci	22:00	22:04	− 5	8.28
Feb 11	ci	21:18	21:21	− 5	8.28
May 11	ci	21:04	21:08	− 5	8.28
Aug 11	ci	20:22	20:26	− 5	8.28
Nov 11	ci	20:09	20:13	− 5	8.28
Feb 12	ci	19:28	19:31	− 6	8.28
May 12	ci	19:15	19:19	− 6	8.28
Aug 12	ci	19:02	19:06	− 6	8.28
Nov 12	ci	18:22	18:26	− 6	8.28
Feb 13	ci	18:10	18:14	− 6	8.28
May 13	ci	17:30	18:02	− 6	8.28
Aug 13	ci	17:19	17:22	− 5	8.28
Nov 13	ci	17:07	17:11	− 6	8.28
Feb 14	ci	16:28	17:00	− 6	8.28
May 14	ci	16:17	16:21	− 7	8.28
Aug 14	ci	16:06	16:09	− 6	8.29
Nov 14	ci	15:27	15:31	− 7	8.29
Feb 15	ci	15:17	15:20	− 6	8.29
Feb 15	bp	15:19	15:22	− 4	8.27
May 15	ci	15:07	15:10	− 6	8.29
Aug 15	ci	14:29	15:00	− 6	8.29
Aug 15	bp	14:31	15:02	− 4	8.27
Nov 15	ci	14:20	14:23	− 6	8.29
Nov 15	bp	14:22	14:25	− 4	8.27
Feb 16	ci	14:11	14:14	− 6	8.28
Feb 16	bp	14:17	14:21	− 5	8.22
May 16	ci	14:02	14:05	− 6	8.28
May 16	bp	14:10	14:13	− 5	8.20
Aug 16	ci	13:26	13:29	− 6	8.27
Nov 16	ci	13:18	13:21	− 6	8.26
Nov 16	bp	13:25	13:28	− 4	8.19
Feb 17	ci	13:11	13:14	− 6	8.24
[illegible] 17	ci	13:03	13:06	− 6	8.24
[illegible]	[illegible]	[illegible]	[illegible]	[illegible]	[illegible]
Aug 17	ci	12:26	12:29	− 6	8.24
Aug 17	bp	12:29	13:00	− 8	8.21
Nov 17	ci	12:18	12:21	− 6	8.24
Feb 18	ci	12:11	12:14	− 6	8.23
May 18	ci	12:03	12:06	− 6	8.23
May 18	bp	12:06	12:09	− 7	8.20
Aug 18	ci	11:27	11:30	− 6	8.23
Nov 18	ci	11:21	11:24	− 5	8.22
Nov 18	bp	11:24	11:26	− 7	8.19
Feb 19	ci	11:13	11:16	− 6	8.22
Feb 19	bp	11:17	11:20	− 7	8.18
May 19	ci	11:06	11:09	− 6	8.22
[illegible] 19	ci	[illegible]	[illegible]	− 5	8.21
[illegible]	[illegible]	[illegible]	[illegible]	[illegible]	[illegible]
Nov 19	ci	10:26	10:28	− 5	8.20
Feb 20	ci	10:21	10:24	− 6	8.17
Feb 20	bp	10:23	10:26	− 9	8.15
May 20	ci	10:16	10:18	− 5	8.16
May 20	bp	10:18	10:21	− 7	8.13
Aug 20	ci	10:10	10:12	− 5	8.15
Aug 20	bp	10:13	10:16	− 8	8.11
Nov 20	ci	10:04	10:07	− 5	8.14
Feb 21	ci	9:30	10:01	− 6	8.13
Feb 21	bp	10:02	10:05	− 7	8.09
May 21	ci	9:26	9:29	− 5	8.11
May 21	bp	9:29	9:31	− 8	8.08
Aug 21	ci	9:22	9:25	− 6	8.08
Aug 21	bp	9:23	9:26	− 7	8.07
Nov 21	ci	9:19	9:22	− 3	8.05
Nov 21	bp	9:23	9:26	− 2	8.00

TREASURY BILLS

Maturity	Days to Mat.	Bid	Asked	Chg.	Ask Yld.
Apr 16 '92	6	3.99	3.89	− 0.02	3.96
Oct 22 '92	195	3.97	3.95	− 0.03	4.10
Nov 19 '92	223	3.98	3.96	− 0.04	4.11
Dec 17 '92	251	4.00	3.98	− 0.02	4.14
Jan 14 '93	279	4.04	4.02	− 0.03	4.19
Feb 11 '93	307	4.07	4.05	− 0.03	4.23
Mar 11 '93	335	4.09	4.07	− 0.03	4.25
Apr 08 '93	363	4.13	4.11	− 0.03	4.36

Feb 2001 T-Bond

Nov 2001 T-Bond

May 2016 T-Bond

Bellwether 30 yr T-Bond Nov 2021

Bellwether U.S. Treasury Strip Nov 2021

Source: *The Wall Street Journal*, April 9, 1992

Major financial institutions, not individuals, bid in the primary market for Treasury securities, but your bank or broker can act as your agent if you wish to purchase a Treasury note or bond in the secondary (resale) market. This market is very liquid, which means that you should have no trouble buying or selling securities on any business day. The third section of *The Wall Street Journal* reports trading on the secondary market for Treasury notes and bonds on a daily basis under **Treasury Bonds, Notes & Bills**. (See the report on page 229 for Wednesday, April 8, 1992 in the Thursday, April 9, 1992, *Wall Street Journal.* You can locate it using the front-page index of the first or last section.)

In the first section labeled **Govt. Bonds & Notes**, turn to the *bellwether* (named after the lead sheep in the flock that wears a bell) 30-year Treasury bond in the blowup on page 233. It is listed last because it has the most recent date of issue and therefore has the longest span of time until maturity. The first two columns describe the bond or note in question. Begin with the coupon rate in column one *(Rate)*. Since it is 8, a $1,000 note or bond will pay $80 annually (8% of $1,000). The second column, titled *Maturity-Mo/Yr* (maturation date), provide the year and month of maturity: November, 2021. If the security has two maturity dates, such as 05-10, the bond matures in 2010 but can be called (redeemed) by the Treasury as early as 2005. Thus, if market interest rates drop below the 2005-10 bond's rate, the Treasury may redeem the security in 2005 and reissue the debt at the lower interest rate. For instance, the 12-3/4 2005-10 pays $127.50 per $1,000 bond. If in 2005 the current interest rate is less than 10 percent, the Treasury can redeem the 12-3/4 2005-10 bonds and reissue new securities with lower coupon payments, thus reducing the Treasury's annual coupon obligation.

The letter *n* following the date indicates that the security is a note. All other issues are bonds. You will notice that in the example on page 229 there are no *n's* after November, 2001 because there are no notes with maturities greater than 10 years. The bond issues that mature in less than 10 years (those with no letter following the month) are seasoned issues, sold sometime in the past.

The third *(Bid)* and fourth *(Asked)* columns represent the prices buyers bid or offered and sellers asked. The price quoted is a percentage of par ($1,000) value, with the number after the colon representing 32nds. Thus, a price of 100:23 for the November, 2021 (bellwether) bond means that on April 8, 1992 buyers were willing to pay 100-23/32 percent of the par value, or $1,007.19 (100 + 0.71875 percent of par, or $1,000 x 1.0071875). Whenever the price exceeds par value, the security trades at a *premium;* securities priced below par trade at a *discount*. Thus, the bellwether bond on page 233 traded at a slight premium on April 8, 1992.

The second to last column is the change in bid price, expressed in 32nds, from the previous trading day. The bellwether bond on page 233 fell \$4.69 on April 8 (15/32 of 1% of \$1,000 = \$4.6875).

The last column is the yield to maturity of 7.93%, which is slightly less than the coupon rate of 8% because the bond trades at \$1,007.19, somewhat above its \$1,000 par.

Here's a rough and ready way to approximate the yield.

$$\text{Approximate yield} = \frac{\text{coupon}}{\text{market price}}$$

$$= \frac{\$80}{\$1,007.19}$$

$$= 7.94\%$$

In this particular example the approximate yield to maturity almost exactly equals the actual yield to maturity. That will not always be true, but it nonetheless offers a good approximation.

Why do securities sell at premiums (prices above the \$1,000 par value) and discounts (prices below par)? Once again, market forces provide the answer. If the economy is awash in cash and therefore demand for Treasury securities (the next best thing to cash) is strong on the part of those who desire an interest return, securities buyers will bid

---

8 1/2	Nov 00n	106:18	106:20	– 7	7.44	
7 3/4	Feb 01n	101:30	102:00	– 8	7.44	
11 3/4	Feb 01	127:23	127:27	– 7	7.41	← Feb 2001 T-Bond \$117.50 annual coupon payment, \$1,277.19 price, 7.41% yield
8	May 01n	103:15	103:17	– 7	7.46	
13 1/8	May 01	137:10	137:14	– 4	7.40	
7 7/8	Aug 01n	102:20	102:22	– 9	7.47	
8	Aug 96-01	102:29	103:01	– 4	7.18	
13 3/8	Aug 01	139:17	139:21	– 7	7.42	
7 1/2	Nov 01n	100:16	100:18	– 6	7.42	
15 3/4	Nov 01	156:11	156:15	– 14	7.42	← Nov 2001 T-Bond \$157.50 annual coupon payment, \$1,563.44 price, 7.42% yield
14 1/4	Feb 02	146:23	146:27	– 12	7.45	
11 5/8	Nov 02	129:13	129:17	– 9	7.53	
10 3/4	Feb 03	123:03	123:07	– 10	7.57	
10 3/4	May 03	123:10	123:14	– 10	7.59	
11 1/8	Aug 03	126:09	126:13	– 10	7.61	
11 7/8	Nov 03	132:07	132:11	– 11	7.62	

Source: *The Wall Street Journal*, April 9, 1992

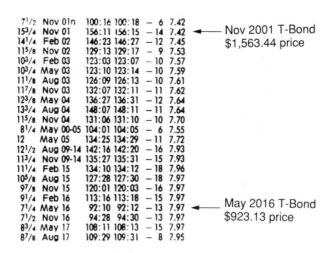

7 1/2	Nov 01n	100:16	100:18	– 6	7.42	
15 3/4	Nov 01	156:11	156:15	– 14	7.42	← Nov 2001 T-Bond $1,563.44 price
14 1/4	Feb 02	146:23	146:27	– 12	7.45	
11 5/8	Nov 02	129:13	129:17	– 9	7.53	
10 3/4	Feb 03	123:03	123:07	– 10	7.57	
10 3/4	May 03	123:10	123:14	– 10	7.59	
11 1/8	Aug 03	126:09	126:13	– 10	7.61	
11 7/8	Nov 03	132:07	132:11	– 11	7.62	
12 3/8	May 04	136:27	136:31	– 12	7.64	
13 3/4	Aug 04	148:07	148:11	– 11	7.64	
11 5/8	Nov 04	131:06	131:10	– 10	7.70	
8 1/4	May 00-05	104:01	104:05	– 6	7.55	
12	May 05	134:25	134:29	– 11	7.72	
12 1/2	Aug 09-14	142:16	142:20	– 16	7.93	
11 3/4	Nov 09-14	135:27	135:31	– 15	7.93	
11 1/4	Feb 15	134:10	134:12	– 18	7.96	
10 5/8	Aug 15	127:28	127:30	– 18	7.97	
9 7/8	Nov 15	120:01	120:03	– 16	7.97	
9 1/4	Feb 16	113:16	113:18	– 15	7.97	
7 1/4	May 16	92:10	92:12	– 13	7.97	← May 2016 T-Bond $923.13 price
7 1/2	Nov 16	94:28	94:30	– 13	7.97	
8 3/4	May 17	108:11	108:13	– 15	7.97	
8 7/8	Aug 17	109:29	109:31	– 8	7.95	

Source: *The Wall Street Journal*, April 9, 1992

their price up. Since the coupon rate is fixed, a higher market price will reduce the yield (see the approximate yield example above). Conversely, a cash shortage will prompt sales of securities on the part of those who need cash, reducing their price and increasing yields.

To illustrate this, note on page 231, that two Treasury bonds with similar maturities can have markedly different coupon rates, although they have similar yields. For example, the 11-3/4 February 2001 bond yields 7.41 percent whereas the 15-3/4 November 2001 bond yields 7.42 percent. Why is there so little difference in the yields when there is a large ($40 a year) difference in the coupon payments? Because these securities have different prices. The February bond's bid price is 127-23/32 or $1,277.19 while the November bond's price is 156-11/32 or $1,563.44. In other words, the $40 coupon difference is offset by an almost $300 difference in market price. Thus, differing prices will ensure that Treasury bonds and notes with similar maturity dates and features will have similar yields whether or not the coupon is markedly different.

Treasury bonds are almost risk-free when held to maturity. Yet their value will fall when interest rates rise, and you will suffer a loss if you must sell your bonds before they mature. For instance, the 7-1/4 May, 2016 bond traded at $923.13 on April 8, 1992 (see above), or $76.87 below par because interest rates had increased somewhat since its issue in

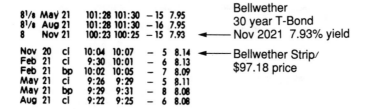

8 1/8	May 21	101:28	101:30	−15	7.95
8 1/8	Aug 21	101:28	101:30	−16	7.95
8	Nov 21	100:23	100:25	−15	7.93

Bellwether
30 year T-Bond
Nov 2021 7.93% yield

Nov	20	ci	10:04	10:07	− 5	8.14
Feb	21	ci	9:30	10:01	− 6	8.13
Feb	21	bp	10:02	10:05	− 7	8.09
May	21	ci	9:26	9:29	− 5	8.11
May	21	bp	9:29	9:31	− 8	8.08
Aug	21	ci	9:22	9:25	− 6	8.08

Bellwether Strip/
$97.18 price

Source: *The Wall Street Journal*, April 9, 1992

1986. If you had purchased it then, and had been obliged to sell it six years later, you would have suffered a loss.

On the other hand, returning to the 15-3/4 November, 2001 bond, its price had risen to $1,563.44, a handsome gain since its 1981 issue at peak interest rates. Substantial capital gains can be earned in low-risk Treasuries while enjoying a comfortable yield (15-3/4 percent at issue in this case).

Bond prices converge on par and fluctuate very little as the maturity date approaches. Thus, bonds with the longest time to maturity offer the greatest opportunities for speculation, the greatest risk of loss, and (usually) the highest yields.

And finally, examine the data on page 229 under **U.S. Treasury Strips**. You can purchase Treasuries in the secondary market that pay no annual interest but are offered at a deep discount so that you receive the equivalent of interest as the price appreciates. For instance, turning to the April 9, 1992 data for April 8, you can see that the most recently issued (bellwether) bond traded at less than $100. If you had purchased it that day, you could count on it appreciating more than ten-fold by maturity. Many investors purchase these securities in order to accumulate a nest egg for a special purpose such as a child's college education.

Investor's Tip

- Bonds are a good investment in low inflation times because falling interest rates send bond prices upward.
- Unload your bonds when inflation threatens because rising interest rates will depress bond prices.

Key Interest Rates

Annualized interest rates on certain investments as reported by the Federal Reserve Board on a weekly-average basis:

	Week Ended: June 19, 1992	June 12, 1992
Treasury bills (90 day)-a	3.63	3.67
Commrcl paper (Dealer, 90 day)-a	3.91	3.93
Certfs of Deposit (Resale, 90 day)	3.83	3.86
Federal funds (Overnight)-b	3.73	3.69
Eurodollars (90 day)-b	3.84	3.86
Treasury bills (one year)-c	4.12	4.18
Treasury notes (three year)-c	5.55	5.67
Treasury notes (five year)-c	6.44	6.56
Treasury notes (ten year)-c	7.24	7.32
Treasury bonds (30 year)-c	7.83	7.87

a-Discounted rates. b-Week ended Wednesday, June 17, 1992 and Wednesday June 10, 1992. c-Yields, adjusted for constant maturity.

Source: *The Wall Street Journal*, June 23, 1992

Since fluctuations in market interest rates are crucial in determining the value of your investment, make a habit of tracking **Key Interest Rates** in Tuesday's *Wall Street Journal* (check the last section's index). See Tuesday, June 23, 1992's report above for the week ending Friday, June 19, 1992.

The Treasury is not the only government agency that issues long-term debt. The *Journal* publishes a **Government Agency & Similar Issues** report daily which you can find using the front-page index of the first or last sections (under Treasury/Agency Issues). The Tuesday, June 23, 1992 edition (see page 235) covered Monday, June 22, 1992 trading activity for these agencies: FNMA, Federal Home Loan Bank, Federal Farm Credit Bank, Student Loan Marketing, World Bank Bonds, Financing Corporation, InterAmerican Development Bank, GNMA Mortgage Issues, Tennessee Valley Authority, Farm Credit Financial Assistance Corporation, Resolution Funding Corporation, and Federal Land Bank. The columns read **Rate, Mat., Bid, Asked,** and **Yld,** and provide the same information as Treasury securities. The discussion below deals with some of these issues.

GOVERNMENT AGENCY & SIMILAR ISSUES

Monday, June 22, 1992

Over-the-Counter mid-afternoon quotations based on large transactions, usually $1 million or more. Colons in bid-and-asked quotes represent 32nds; 101:01 means 101 1/32.

All yields are calculated to maturity, and based on the asked quote. * – Callable issue, maturity date shown. For issues callable prior to maturity, yields are computed to the earliest call date for issues quoted above par, or 100, and to the maturity date for issues below par.

Source: Bear, Stearns & Co. via Street Software Technology Inc.

"Fannie Mae" →

FNMA Issues

Rate	Mat.	Bid	Asked	Yld.
8.45	7-92	100:06	100:10	1.36
7.75	8-92	100:14	100:18	3.24
9.15	9-92	101:02	101:06	3.39
10.60	10-92	101:31	102:03	3.47
8.20	11-92	101:17	101:21	3.72
9.88	12-92	102:19	102:23	3.86
10.90	1-93	103:21	103:25	3.80
7.95	2-93	102:09	102:17	3.80
7.90	3-93	102:18	102:26	3.83
10.95	3-93	104:22	104:30	3.81
7.55	4-93	102:20	102:28	3.85
10.88	4-93	105:07	105:15	3.84
10.75	5-93	105:14	105:22	4.06
8.80	6-93	104:02	104:10	4.16
8.45	7-93	104:01	104:09	4.23
7.75	11-93	104:03	104:11	4.46
7.38	12-93	103:20	103:28	4.60
7.55	1-94	104:05	104:09	4.64
9.45	1-94	106:30	107:06	4.57
7.65	4-94	104:19	104:27	4.80
9.60	4-94	107:29	108:05	4.80
9.30	5-94	107:20	107:24	4.92
8.60	6-94	106:15	106:23	4.96
7.45	7-94*	104:13	104:17	5.09
8.65	7-94*	100:00	100:08	8.51
8.55	8-94*	100:21	100:29	1.40
8.90	8-94	107:11	107:19	5.08
10.10	10-94	109:29	110:05	5.34
9.25	11-94	108:00	108:08	5.49
8.30	12-94*	102:01	102:09	3.33
5.50	12-94	100:06	100:10	5.36
9.00	1-95	108:04	108:12	5.43
11.95	1-95	115:02	115:14	5.37
8.90	2-95*	102:16	102:24	4.38

FHL Bank →

Federal Home Loan Bank

Rate	Mat.	Bid	Asked	Yld.
8.40	6-92	100:00	100:04	0.00
8.45	6-92	100:01	100:05	0.00
8.25	7-92	100:13	100:17	2.36
8.38	7-92	100:13	100:17	2.48
5.63	8-92	100:09	100:11	3.52
8.60	8-92	100:24	100:28	3.31
10.35	8-92	101:02	101:08	2.84
5.68	9-92	100:14	100:16	3.63
8.25	9-92	101:02	101:08	3.20
5.55	10-92	100:16	100:18	3.83
8.00	10-92	101:10	101:14	3.66
8.15	10-92	101:12	101:16	3.62
10.85	10-92	102:09	102:13	3.60
7.65	11-92	101:15	101:19	3.77
8.00	11-92	101:20	101:24	3.74
8.80	11-92	101:31	102:03	3.70
11.10	11-92	102:29	103:03	3.58
7.38	12-92	101:21	101:25	3.81
7.95	12-92	102:00	102:06	3.58
9.05	12-92	102:16	102:22	3.68
9.40	12-92	102:22	102:28	3.65
8.30	1-93	102:13	102:19	3.77
9.35	1-93	103:00	103:06	3.79
9.50	1-93	103:03	103:09	3.77
10.70	1-93	103:25	103:31	3.77
4.38	2-93	100:03	100:05	4.13
8.05	2-93	102:17	102:23	3.88
4.83	3-93	100:17	100:21	3.93
8.10	3-93	102:28	103:02	3.92
10.80	3-93	104:28	105:02	3.89

Federal Farm Credit Bank →

Federal Farm Credit Bank

Rate	Mat.	Bid	Asked	Yld.
4.23	7-92	100:00	100:02	1.00
4.38	7-92	100:00	100:02	1.14
6.55	7-92	100:02	100:04	0.12
13.75	7-92	100:23	100:27	1.94
8.40	7-92	100:12	100:16	2.11
3.85	8-92	100:00	100:02	3.25
4.05	8-92	100:00	100:02	3.42
6.40	8-92	100:08	100:10	3.42
3.85	9-92	100:00	100:04	3.17
4.27	9-92	100:01	100:05	3.38
5.80	9-92	100:10	100:12	3.70
8.25	9-92	100:25	100:27	3.59

Rate	Mat.	Bid	Asked	Yld.
8.60	9-92	100:27	101:01	2.95
4.40	10-92	100:04	100:06	3.66
5.63	10-92	100:14	100:16	3.70
4.03	11-92	100:00	100:02	3.83
5.50	11-92	100:16	100:18	3.87
4.00	12-92	100:00	100:02	3.84
4.90	12-92	100:11	100:13	3.94
7.63	12-92	101:16	101:20	3.82
4.48	1-93	100:07	100:09	3.93
8.13	1-93	102:08	102:14	3.76
10.65	1-93	103:21	103:27	3.77
4.15	2-93	100:00	100:02	4.04
4.53	3-93	100:09	100:13	3.91
4.70	4-93	100:12	100:16	4.03
4.35	5-93	100:04	100:08	4.05
4.32	6-93	100:02	100:06	4.11
6.77	6-93	102:09	102:11	4.18
6.88	8-93	102:14	102:16	4.52
6.48	9-93	102:06	102:10	4.45

Student Loan Marketing ← "Sallie Mae"

Rate	Mat.	Bid	Asked	Yld.
8.25	6-92	100:02	100:06	0.00
8.15	9-92	100:31	101:03	3.35
8.80	12-92	102:01	102:05	3.82
10.50	4-93	105:03	105:09	3.93
7.35	5-93	102:16	102:22	4.13
8.20	5-93	103:09	103:17	4.15
6.87	6-93	102:12	102:16	4.29
8.50	7-93	104:01	104:05	4.34
12.00	12-93	110:06	110:10	4.68
11.88	12-93	110:06	110:10	4.61
7.38	1-94	103:28	104:04	4.58
16.00	2-94	117:18	117:30	4.51
7.43	4-94	104:07	104:15	4.80
7.35	5-94	104:07	104:11	4.93
7.30	5-94	104:05	104:09	4.93
8.50	7-94	106:12	106:16	5.09
7.50	7-94	104:16	104:20	5.09
8.10	7-94	105:23	105:27	5.09
8.25	8-94*	100:17	100:21	1.79
8.30	9-94	105:13	105:17	5.63

World Bank Bonds ← World Bank Bonds

Rate	Mat.	Bid	Asked	Yld.
13.63	9-92	101:24	101:28	3.35
10.90	3-93	104:22	104:26	4.06
10.38	5-93	105:02	105:06	4.36
11.63	12-94	113:30	114:02	5.47
8.63	10-95	108:16	108:20	5.69
7.25	10-96	102:19	102:27	6.47
8.75	3-97	108:24	109:00	6.49
9.88	10-97	113:27	114:03	6.66
8.38	10-99	107:04	107:12	7.06
8.13	3-01	105:02	105:04	7.32
8.85	7-01	102:21	102:29	8.38
6.75	1-02	96:14	96:18	7.25
8.25	5-02*	102:16	102:24	4.94
12.38	10-02	132:07	132:15	7.74
8.25	9-16	100:15	100:23	8.18
8.63	10-16	104:13	104:21	8.18
9.25	7-17	111:02	111:10	8.18
8.88	3-26	107:05	107:13	8.22

GNMA Mtge. Issues ← "Ginnie Mae"

Rate	Mat.	Bid	Asked	a-Bond Yld.
7.00	30Yr	95:14	95:22	7.82
7.50	30Yr	98:08	98:16	7.86
8.00	30Yr	100:31	101:07	7.91
8.50	30Yr	103:29	104:05	7.86
9.00	30Yr	106:07	106:15	7.84
9.50	30Yr	107:24	108:00	7.78
10.00	30Yr	109:05	109:13	7.47
10.50	30Yr	110:01	110:09	7.29
11.00	30Yr	111:23	111:31	6.86
11.50	30Yr	114:10	114:18	7.07
12.00	30Yr	116:01	116:09	7.20
12.50	30Yr	116:23	116:31	6.32

Federal Land Bank ← Federal Land Bank

Rate	Mat.	Bid	Asked	Yld.
7.95	10-96	105:22	105:30	6.36
7.35	1-97	103:07	103:15	6.46

Source: *The Wall Street Journal*, June 23, 1992

FNMA (called "Fannie Mae") stands for the Federal National Mortgage Association, a publicly owned corporation sponsored by the federal government and established to provide a liquid market for mortgage investors. Fannie Mae buys mortgages from mortgage bankers and other mortgage writers, earns the interest payments made by homeowners, and pays for these mortgages with the sale of bonds (debentures) to investors in $10,000 and $5,000 denominations. Pension funds, insurance companies, mutual funds, and other large institutional investors are the principal purchasers of these bonds, which are called Fannie Maes.

The **Federal Home Loan Bank** (FHLB) is a federally chartered, privately owned company charged with regulating the S & L industry. The FHLB borrows by issuing bonds in $10,000 denominations to provide funds to weaker S & Ls with temporary liquidity problems.

The **Federal Farm Credit Bank** assists farmers by helping financial institutions, such as small commercial banks and savings and loan associations (S&Ls), provide credit to farmers for the purchase and sale of commodities and the financing of buildings and new equipment. It is an independent agency of the U.S. Government primarily funded by short-term debt, although it also issues longer-term notes that trade in the secondary market and are listed in the report.

Student Loan Marketing ("Sallie Mae") is a privately owned, government-sponsored corporation that provides a secondary market for government-guaranteed student loans. Sallie Mae sells bonds to investors to raise funds for the purchase of these student loans from financial institutions. The yields on these issues tend to be higher than other government agency issues because of the higher risk of default on student loans.

World Bank Bonds are debt instruments issued by the International Bank for Reconstruction and Development (World Bank) to finance its lending activities to less-developed countries.

GNMA ("Ginnie Mae"), the Government National Mortgage Association, is a government-owned corporation that purchases, packages, and resells mortgages and mortgage purchase commitments in the form of mortgage-backed securities called Ginnie Maes. Each Ginnie Mae bond is backed by a package of residential mortgages, and the holder of a GNMA bond thereby owns a portion of these underlying mortgages. New GNMA bonds cost $25,000, but older, partially repaid GNMAs can cost as little as $5,000.

Mortgage payments of interest and principal are "passed through" to the Ginnie Mae holders. Thus, unlike holders of Treasuries, who receive their principal at maturity, investors in Ginnie Maes are paid interest and principal each month.

Ginnie Maes don't have stated maturity dates because the bond's flow of income depends on the repayment of the underlying mortgages. If all homeowners pay their mortgages regularly for the mortgage's life, with no prepayments, the Ginnie Mae holder receives regular monthly checks for 30 years. However, a homeowner may choose to pay off his or her mortgage prior to maturity, or may pay additional principal in some months. The prepayment or excess principal payments are passed through to the Ginnie Mae holder, who receives a larger monthly check. This prepayment reduces the subsequent monthly payments and the Ginnie Mae's par value.

Ginnie Maes offer higher rates than Treasury bonds because of the unpredictable nature of interest and principal payments. The U.S. Treasury backs these government bonds to remove the risk of homeowner default.

Finally, you can see the mortgage interest rates associated with the various Ginnie Mae pools, as well as the range of prices that determine these bonds' yields.

Federal Land Banks are privately owned organizations, backed by the federal government and organized to finance agricultural activities. They primarily provide first mortgage loans on farm properties with original maturities of around 20 years and fund these mortgages by issuing Consolidated Federal Farm Loan Bonds. The Federal Farm Credit Agency examines the activities of the Federal Land Bank.

CORPORATE BONDS

Corporations are the second principal issuer of long-term debt and, like the government and government agencies, issue credit instruments in order to finance long-term needs.

Most bonds are exchanged over-the-counter, like Treasury securities, by large investment banking firms on behalf of institutional investors. A limited amount of small-lot trading is conducted on the New York Stock Exchange by brokerage firms for individual investors. If you wish to track a corporate bond that is listed on the New York Stock Exchange, you will find it in *The Wall Street Journal* under **New York Exchange Bonds**. Consult the front page of the first or last section for the daily listing. An example from the Tuesday, June 23, 1992 issue appears below and on the next page. (American Stock Exchange Bonds appear under **Amex Bonds** on page 241.)

ATT 5⅝95	5.7	32	99⅜	– ⅛
ATT 5½97	5.7	25	96	+ ⅛
ATT 6s00	6.5	35	92	+ ¼
ATT 5⅛01	6.0	78	85¼	+ ¼
ATT 7s01	7.2	273	97⅜	...
ATT 7⅛03	7.3	83	97¾	– ¼
ATT 8⅝26	8.5	369	101⅜	...
ATT 8⅝31	8.5	17	101½	...
ATT 7⅛02	7.3	433	98	+ ¼
ATT 8⅛22	8.2	397	98½	...

← On 6/22/92 the AT&T bond that will mature in 1995 was worth $993.75 and paid a $56.25 annual coupon interest rate for a yield of 5.7%

Unisys 13⅞92	13.7	3	101⅝	– ⅛
Unisys 10¾95	10.7	80	100½	...
Unisys 8.2s96	8.6	18	95	– 1
Unisy na15s97	...	394	109	– ¼
Unisys 8¼00	cv	436	102¼	– ½

← On 6/22/92 the Unisys bond that will mature in 1995 was worth $1,005 and paid a $107.50 annual coupon interest rate for a yield of 10.7%

Source: *The Wall Street Journal*, June 23, 1992

NEW YORK EXCHANGE BONDS

Quotations as of 4 p.m. Eastern Time
Monday, June 22, 1992

Volume $37,420,000

	Domestic Mon.	Domestic Fri.	All issues Mon.	All issues Fri.
Issues traded	531	511	535	512
Advances	188	173	191	173
Declines	203	190	204	191
Unchanged	140	148	140	148
New highs	30	22	31	22
New lows	8	4	8	4

SALES SINCE JANUARY 1
(000 omitted)

1992	1991	1990
$6,050,038	$6,786,128	$5,208,186

Dow Jones Bond Averages

1991 High	1991 Low	1992 High	1992 Low		1992 Close	1992 Chg.	%Yld	1991 Close	1991 Chg.
98.93	91.30	100.17	98.41	20 Bonds	99.88	−0.27	7.98	94.23	−0.08
100.81	93.44	101.17	98.45	10 Utilities	99.85	−0.11	7.96	95.19	−0.14
97.15	89.06	100.55	97.26	10 Industrials	99.91	−0.43	8.00	93.28	−0.01

CORPORATION BONDS
Volume, $37,250,000

AT&T →

Bonds	Cur Yld	Vol	Close	Net Chg
AForP 5s30	8.9	10	56¼	
AMR 9s16	9.1	438	98⅝	
AMR zr06		52	44	+1
Advst 9s08	cv	27	91	…
AetnLf 8⅛s07	8.1	30	100½	+½
AirbF 6⅞s01	cv	155	81½	−¼
AlaP 9s2000	8.7	29	103⅛	…
AlaP 8⅞s03	8.6	10	103½	+½
AlaP 8¼s03	8.1	1	102	+1¼
AlaP 9⅝s08	9.0	3	106	+1
AlskAr zr06		7	34	+½
AlldC zr92	…	48	98⅝	−1/32
AlldC zr96	…	5	78	−⅛
AlldC zr95	…	10	81⅛	+⅛
AlldC zr03	…	15	40⅜	−1⅜
AlldC zr09	…	15	23	+½
Allwst 7¾14	cv	10	85½	−½
AAirl 4¼92	4.3	1	99½	…
AmBrnd 7⅜99	7.5	10	100⅜	+⅛
ACyan 8⅜06	8.2	40	102	+¾
AmStor 01	cv	58	100	−1⅞
ATT 5⅝95	5.7	32	99⅝	−⅛
ATT 5½97	5.7	25	96	+⅛
ATT 6s00	6.5	35	92	+¼
ATT 5⅛01	6.0	78	85¼	+¼
ATT 7s01	7.2	273	97⅜	…
ATT 7⅛03	7.3	83	97¾	−¼
ATT 8⅝26	8.5	369	101⅜	…
ATT 8⅝31	8.5	[illegible]	101½	…
ATT 7⅛02	7.3	433	98	+¼
ATT 8⅛22	8.2	397	98½	…
vjAmes 7½14f	cv	204	3¼	+½
Amoco 6s98	6.2	395	97	+⅛
Amoco 7⅞07	7.8	25	100¾	+½
Amoco 8⅝16	8.3	20	104¼	…
AmocoCda 7⅜13	6.6	21	112	…
Andarko 6¼14	6.4	5	97½	−1½
Anhr 8s96	7.8	50	102¼	−¼
Anhr 8⅝16	8.5	40	101¾	…
Arml 9.2s00	9.9	16	92½	+1⅝
Arml 8½01	9.8	56	86¾	+3¼
Arml 13½94	12.7	24	106⅛	−¼
AshO 6¾14	cv	4	84¼	+¼
Atchsn 4s95	4.4	1	91⅝	−⅝
ARich 7.7s00	7.6	7	101¼	…
ARch 10½95	10.2	49	102½	+¼
ARch 9⅝96	9.2	12	103¼	…
ARch 9¼93	9.0	30	103	+¼
AubrnHl 16⅞20f	…	58	125	−¼
AutDt zr12	…	1	35½	−¼
Avnet 6s12	cv	35	88¾	−2¼
BRE 9½08	cv	10	105½	−½
Bally 10s06f	cv	37	95⅛	−1⅜
BalGE 8⅜06	8.3	2	101	…
BncFla 9s03	cv	27	81	…
Banka 8⅞05	8.7	100	102	+⅜
Banka 8¾01	8.5	25	102¾	−⅛
Bkam 8.35s07	8.3	6	100¼	−⅛
Bkam zr92	…	23	98 1/16	…
Bkam zr93	…	83	94¾	…
BnkTr 8⅛99	8.1	5	100½	…
Barnt 8½99	8.2	47	103½	…
BellPa 8⅝06	8.4	35	102⅝	−½
BellPa 7⅛12	7.7	10	92⅝	−½
BellPa 7½13	7.9	20	95½	+¼
BellPa 9⅝14	9.1	76	105¼	−¼
BellPa 8¾15	8.5	3	102⅞	+⅛
BellPa 9¼19	8.8	5	105	…
BrkHa zr04	…	90	51¼	…
BethSt 6⅞99	8.1	20	84½	−⅛
BethSt 9s00	9.3	6	96¾	+⅛
BethSt 8.45s05	9.4	116	90	+⅛
BethSt 8⅜01	9.3	10	89¾	…
Bevrly 7⅝03	cv	20	84¾	…
BlkD 8⅜97	8.3	5	101	−⅛
Boeing 8⅜96	7.9	10	106½	+⅛
BoisC 7s16	cv	40	85	…
BwnSh 9¼05	cv	15	93¼	−¼
BwnFer 6¼12	cv	74	85¾	−1
BurNo 8½96	8.4	1	101½	−½
BurNo 9⅝96	9.2	5	104¼	…
CBS 10⅞95	10.7	36	101¼	…
CIGNA 8.2s10	cv	101	102	…
CIT 8¾08	8.5	20	103	+2⅛
CSX 9½16	9.0	62	105½	+1
CaroT 9s08	8.6	10	104⅛	…
Caroico 14s93	18.9	83	74	+3⅞
CaroFrt 6¼11	cv	3	73	−3
Ceridn 8½11	cv	16	85	…
CPoV 8⅝09	8.4	35	102⅛	+⅛
Champ 6½11	cv	14	99	−1
CPoM 8⅞09	8.6	7	103½	+1½
ChmWst zr10	…	1	34⅝	…
Chvrn 8¾96	8.5	29	102½	−¾
Chiquta 9⅛98	9.1	30	100¼	−½
Chiquta 11⅞03	11.2	132	105⅞	−⅛
Chiquta 10½04	10.5	116	100	−⅜
Chiquta 10¼05	10.3	37	100	+⅜
ChckFul 7s12	cv	10	85¾	+¼
ChryF 9.30s94	9.3	177	100½	−⅛
ChryF 12¾99	11.4	160	111⅜	−¼
ChryF 8⅜97	8.9	116	94⅛	−¼
ChryF 8⅛94	8.1	117	99⅞	…
Chryslr 8s98	8.5	13	94⅛	…
Chryslr 13s97	12.2	398	106⅜	−⅛
Chryslr 12s15	11.7	657	102½	−⅜
Chryslr 9.6s94	9.4	254	102⅜	+½
Chryslr 10.95s17	11.1	339	98⅝	+⅛
Chryslr 10.4s99	10.4	201	100⅛	…
vjCircK 12¾97f	…	25	15½	−½
Citicp 8.45s07	8.6	113	98	…
Citicp 8⅛07	8.5	70	95¼	−¼
Clmt zrD00	…	35	46½	…
ClevEl 4⅜94	4.5	14	97	+2⅝
ClevEl 9¼09	9.0	5	103	…

Bonds	Cur Yld	Vol	Close	Net Chg
GreyF zr94	…	64	87	…
Grumn 9¼09	cv	5	99¼	+1¼
Grumn 10½11	10.1	20	103¾	+½
Gulfrd 6s12	cv	6	96	…
GulfMo 5s56f	9.4	10	53	+1
Hallb 7.95s95	7.8	10	102	…
HalwdGp 13½09	…	16	74½	−⅛
Hartfd 8½96	8.5	24	100	…
Hawn 7⅝02	7.7	6	98¾	+¾
HeclMn zr04	…	4	35⅛	−⅞
Hellr 7¾93	7.8	5	100	…
HmGrp 14⅞99	14.5	10	102⅜	…
HomeDp 4½97	cv	52	108¼	+¼
HrzHlt 6¾02	cv	5	84	…
HudFd 14s08	cv	5	107¾	+¾
Huffy 7¼14	cv	1	104	+1
ICN 12⅞98	12.8	148	100⅞	+¼
IllBel 8s04	7.9	60	101½	+⅛
IndBel 8⅛11	8.1	52	100¾	…
IndBel 8s14	8.1	80	99⅛	…
InldStl 8⅞99	9.4	21	94	−1
InldStl 9½00	9.7	10	97½	…
Intlgc 11.99s96	19.3	5	62	−1
IBM 7⅞04	cv	198	102⅜	−⅝
IBM 10¼95	10.1	244	101⅞	…
IBM 9s98	8.4	2	107½	+¼
IntGm dc5½01	cv	4	175	…
Jckpt 8¾14	cv	1	107½	−½
Jamswy 8s05	cv	53	67	−½
vjJonsLl 6¾94f	…	3	4½	−1¼
vjJonsLl 6½88f	…	66	4⅝	−1⅜
vjJoneL 6¾94f	…	2	5⅞	…
K mart 8⅜17	8.5	311	98⅝	…
KerrMc 7¼12	cv	3	104¼	−2¼
Keycrp 7¾02	8.1	10	96	+1
Kolmrg 8¾09	cv	30	78	…
Kraft 8⅜04	8.2	7	102⅜	+1⅛
vjLTV 5s88mf	…	98	5	−¾
vjLTV 9¼97f	…	25	12¼	…
vjLTV 13⅞02f	…	1	11¼	…
vjLTV 14s04f	…	75	11¾	−¼
vjLTV 11½97f	…	44	5¼	−⅛
vjLTV 8¾98f	…	72	4¾	−¾
vjLTV 15s00f	…	25	12½	+½
vjLTV int 5s88f	cv	6	9¼	−1¾
LaQuin 10s02	cv	10	104	…
LaFrg 7s13	cv	7	93¼	−1
Leucadia 10¾02	10.3	192	100⅞	−⅛
LoewCp zr04	…	86	47¼	…
LomNM 10½93f	…	20	58½	−1½
LglsLt 11.7s93	11.3	4	104	−3¼
LglsLt 11¾94	10.6	2	110¾	…
LglsLt 11⅝19	9.5	10	116¾	+½
LouN 2 03r	4.6	1	63	+½
LouLE 8½00	cv	30	99½	+⅛
vjLykes 7½94N f	…	51	2¾	−1⅛
MACOM 9¼06	cv	55	91¾	−¼
MGM Grd 11¾99	11.5	218	102	…
MGM Grd 12s02	11.7	297	102¾	−¾
MGMUA 13s96f	…	220	74⅝	−⅜
MfrH 8⅛04	8.4	77	97⅛	−1⅜
MfrH 8⅛07	8.4	1	97	−⅜
Manvl zr03	…	90	81⅞	−⅛
MarO 8.5s06	8.5	17	100⅛	+⅛
MarO 9½94	9.1	157	104⅞	+⅛
Marriott zr06	…	15	32⅜	−⅜
Masco 5¼12	cv	17	84½	−2
vjMcCro 7½s94f	…	12	15⅝	+½

EXPLANATORY NOTES
(For New York and American Bonds)

Yield is current yield.

cv-Convertible bond. cf-Certificates. cld-Called. dc-Deep discount. ec-European currency units. f-Dealt in flat. il-Italian lire. kd-Danish kroner. m-Matured bonds, negotiability impaired by maturity. na-No accrual. r-Registered. rp-Reduced principal. st-Stamped. t-Floating rate. wd-When distributed. ww-With warrants. x-Ex interest. xw-Without warrants. zr-Zero coupon.

vj-In bankruptcy or receivership or being reorganized under the Bankruptcy Act, or securities assumed by such companies.

Bonds	Cur Yld	Vol	Close	Net Chg.
McDnl zr94	…	25	91⅞	…
McDnl 8⅞19	8.7	1	102½	−⅛
McDnl 8 11	8.3	30	106½	…
McDnlDg 7⅞97	8.2	104	96⅜	−⅛
MeYk 7⅝02	7.9	10	96	…
Mead 6¾12	cv	125	93½	−½
Melln 7¼99	7.3	15	100	…
MesaCap na96	…	15	81	−⅝
MesaCap 13½99	15.9	88	84⅞	−⅜
MichB 7¾11	8.0	30	96⅞	…
MichB 8⅛15	8.0	10	101⅛	…
Mickl dc11½98	11.5	5	100	…
MidlBk 11.35s93	11.1	30	101 13/16	+9/32
MPac 4¼05	6.1	2	70	−2½
MPac 4¾20f	…	6	54⅝	−1⅜
MPac 4¾30f	…	1	52⅝	−1⅛
MobO 7⅜01	7.4	85	99	+⅛
Monog 11s04	11.6	35	95	+5
MorKnd zr05	…	198	39½	+¼
Motrla zr09	…	13	37¼	−¼
MtSTl 7¾13	8.0	13	97	+½
MtSTl 7⅞16	8.1	13	96⅞	+⅛
MtSTl 8s17	8.2	20	97	…
NBD 7¼06	cv	3	110	…
NCNB 8⅜99	8.3	5	101⅜	+⅜
NCNB 11⅛97	10.9	5	101⅞	…
NJBTl 7¾13	8.0	80	96½	+⅜
NJBTl 8s16	8.1	20	98¼	…
vjNtGyp zr04	…	12	3	+⅜
NInd 10s99	11.1	3	90	−2
NStl 8⅜06	9.6	6	87¼	+⅛
NConv 9s08f	cv	14	25½	+1½
NtEdu 6½11	cv	20	67¼	−¾
NavFin 7⅝93	7.7	35	99¼	+⅛
NavFin 7½94	7.7	110	97⅝	+¼
NavFin 11.95s95	11.6	10	102⅝	+1⅝
Navstr 9s04	10.0	10	90¼	+⅛
NwnBl 7½05	7.7	1	98	−⅛
NwnBl 8⅝12	8.3	25	103⅜	+⅜
NwnBl 8⅛17	8.2	15	98¾	…
OcciP 10⅞96	10.5	60	104	…
OcciP 9⅝99	8.9	180	107¾	…
OcciP 10⅛01	9.0	16	112⅜	+¼
OhBIT 7⅞13	8.1	55	97½	−1
OhEd 8½06	8.4	6	100¾	+½
vjOrion 11s98f	…	25	14	…
vjOrion 15¾98f	…	127	22¼	+¾
Oryx 7½14	cv	168	88½	+½
OutbM 7¾96	8.0	35	96¾	−¼
Owill 10¼99	10.2	546	100¼	+⅛
Owill 11s03	10.4	275	105½	−¼
Owill 10½02	10.5	17	100¼	…
OwCor 12s10	11.4	25	105	−½
OxyOG 6⅝99	7.0	25	94¼	…
PcLumb 12s96	11.8	10	102	+¼
PcLumb 12½98	12.4	10	101	+⅛
PNwT 8⅝10	8.4	5	102⅜	…
PNwT 8¾08	8.5	10	102⅝	−⅞
PNwT 9s12	8.7	165	104	+½
PacTT 8.65s05	8.5	5	102¼	−⅛
PacTT 8¾06	8.5	27	102½	−¼
PacTT 7.8s07	7.9	7	98¾	−⅞
PacTT 7¼08	7.7	6	94⅝	+¼
PacTT 9½11	9.1	27	104⅛	−⅛
PacTT 8⅞15	8.6	65	102⅝	−⅛
PacTT 8⅜17	8.4	352	99⅞	…
PacTT 9s18	8.7	50	103¾	…
PacTT 9⅝18	9.0	12	106½	+⅛
PacTT 9⅞16	9.3	15	106¼	−⅜
PacTT 9¾19	9.2	20	105½	−¼
PGE 8⅞s02	8.6	29	103	+⅛
PGE 7½s03	7.7	20	97¼	−1¼
PGE 7½s04	7.7	5	97	−⅞
PGE 9⅛s06	8.8	5	103⅜	−⅛
PGE 8½09	8.3	5	102½	+⅛
ParCm 7s03A	7.6	37	92	+⅜
ParCm 7s03B	7.6	46	92¼	+⅞
PennC 11s97	10.9	124	101⅜	−⅛
Pennzl 8⅜96	8.3	5	100½	−1
Pennzl 8⅝96	8.5	12	102	+¼
Pepsic 7⅝98	7.5	20	102⅛	−⅜
Petrie 8s10	cv	76	108	−1
PhilEl 7¾00	7.8	10	99¾	−⅛
PhilEl 7½98	7.5	5	100¼	−½
PhilEl 9⅛06	8.5	38	104	…
PhilEl 8⅝03	8.5	29	102	+¾
PhilEl 9⅜17	8.9	58	105	−1
PhilP 12¼12	11.3	10	108¾	+¾

Bonds	Cur Yld	Vol	Close	Net Chg
RJR Nb 8.3s99	8.2	60	101½	…
RJR Nb 13½01	11.8	100	114⅝	…
RJR Nb na15s01	…	818	119⅝	−⅛
RJR Nb zr01	…	3492	91⅞	−⅛
RJR Nb 8¾04	8.6	35	101½	…
RJR NbH 17⅜09	9.6	393	181¾	+⅛
RalsP 9½16	9.1	40	104¼	+⅛
RalsP 9s96	8.4	25	107	…
RalsP 9⅜16	9.0	10	104	+⅛
RapA72 7s94f	…	10	1¼	+¼
vjRapA 10¾03f	…	5	1	−⅛
RelFncl 11⅜08	12.0	30	94⅝	+1⅛
RelGp 9⅞98	10.2	100	96¾	−1¾
RelGp 14s96	13.7	448	102	…
RelGp 11s96	12.2	232	90½	−¼
RelGp 11½01	13.1	100	87⅝	+⅝
RelGp 14¼98f	14.1	2	101¼	−¾
vjRepStl 12⅛03f	…	10	4½	−⅜
Revco 11½99	11.4	7	100⅝	+⅛
Revl 10⅞10	10.5	10	103⅛	+⅛
Revln 11¾95	11.7	326	100¼	−¼
RiteA zr06	cv	142	38¾	−¼
RochG 9¼06	9.0	8	103	−2
RocInt 8⅜01	8.3	1	101⅛	−1⅛
Rohr 7s12	cv	53	70½	−½
Rotorx 5s96	cv	35	70	−½
Ryder 9s16	8.9	12	101½	…
Salmnln 8s96	7.9	470	101	+¼
SanD 8¾07	8.7	1	100¾	−1
Scot 8⅞2000	8.8	5	100⅝	…
Scot 8¾2000	8.6	10	101¾	+⅝
Sears 12s94	10.9	2	109¾	+¼
Sears 9½99	8.6	30	109⅞	+⅜
Seltel 9s02	cv	3	99½	…
SensorE 01	cv	14	130	…
Sequa 10½98	10.3	4	101⅝	+⅛
SvceCp 6½11	cv	15	108	…
ShellO 8½00	8.3	11	103	+⅞
ShellO 7¼02	7.3	39	99½	+1
Signl 8s09	cv	16	95	+1½
Solect zr12	…	10	29½	+1
Sonat zr05	…	3	38	−⅜
SoCG 8.85s95	8.7	5	102	−⅜
SoCG 8½97	8.3	41	102	+¼
StBrn 9½04	9.3	12	102¼	+¾
StdOil 7.6s99	7.6	4	99¾	+⅛
StdPac 12¾99	12.6	15	101½	…
StdPac 13⅞04	13.8	58	100½	…
StoneCn 13⅝95	13.5	275	101	−¼
StoneCn 11½99	11.2	221	102½	−½
StoneCn 11⅞98	11.3	185	105½	−⅜
StoneCn 10¾02	10.9	1099	98¼	−½
StrTch 8s15	cv	43	110	−8
SunCo 7⅛02	7.5	10	95	…
vjSunsh 9½94f	…	5	31	−1
vjSunsS 8½95f	…	1	28¾	−½
TCFox 13¼00	12.7	11	104	−½
Tandy 10s94	9.6	5	104¼	+1¾
Teledy 7s99	7.4	9	94½	−½
Teledy 10s04A	9.8	27	101¾	…
Teledy 10s04C	9.8	7	101⅝	−⅛
TencCr 8⅜97	8.3	10	100½	−1½
TencCr 9¾94	9.4	2	103½	−¾
TencoCr 9s95	8.5	10	105⅞	+1¾
TennGas dc6s11	8.3	23	72	−⅜
TennGas 11⅛13	10.5	51	105¾	…
TennGas 9⅝17	9.3	30	100¾	−½
TennGas 13.7s92	13.6	10	100 23/32	−17/32
Terra 8½12	cv	7	93½	−½
Tesor dc12¾01	15.0	70	85¼	+⅛
Texco 9s96	8.4	10	107⅝	−¼
Texco 8.65s98	8.2	20	105⅝	−⅞
Texco 8½03	8.1	10	105⅛	…
Texco 8⅞05	8.6	9	103	…
TxInd 9s08	cv	5	96⅝	+⅛
Tidwtr 7s10	cv	10	90	+1
Time 9⅞09	9.7	25	102	…
Time 8¾17	8.8	83	100	+3⅞
Trvlr 8.7s95	8.6	30	100¾	+¼
Trvlr 7⅝97	7.6	201	100⅝	+⅜
Trvlr 8.32s15	cv	168	92¼	…
TucEP 8⅛01	8.8	30	92⅜	+1⅜
UCCEL 7¼95	cv	25	95⅝	+1¼
UNC 7½06	cv	14	80	…
US West zr11	…	33	26⅜	−⅛
USAir 12⅞00	13.1	604	98	+⅛
USG na16s08	…	1530	14¾	−¼
USLICO 8s11	cv	1	89	…
USX 4⅝96	4.9	73	93½	−⅛
USX 7s17	cv	55	92⅜	+⅛
UnAL 4¼92	4.3	1	99⅝	…
UTelO 7.6s02	7.7	15	98⅛	+1⅜
UCarb 15s06	13.7	13	109¼	−¾
UCarb 7½12	cv	135	91½	−1¾
UnEl 8⅝07	8.4	15	103⅛	+1⅞
UPac 11⅞10	11.1	15	106⅞	+1⅞
Unisys 13⅞92	13.7	3	101⅝	−⅛
Unisys 10¾95	10.7	80	100½	…
Unisys 8.2s96	8.6	18	95	−1
Unisy na15s97	…	394	109	−¼
Unisys 8¼00	cv	436	102¼	−½
Utilicp 6⅝11	cv	3	100	…
VerY 10⅛07	9.5	1	106¾	+2¾
WarC 9⅛96	9.1	101	100¼	+⅛
WarC 11½13	10.7	15	107¾	+1¾
WasteM 01s	…	12	127¼	+1¼
WasteM zr12	…	25	34	−¼
Weingrt 8s09	cv	5	104	…
Wendys 7¼10	cv	25	99½	…
Wendys 7s06	cv	5	109¼	−1¾
WstCNA 7¼15	cv	41	58½	+1
WstDig 9s14	cv	94	66½	−1¼
WstC 7.6s97	7.6	10	99⅝	−⅛
WstgE 9s09	cv	40	125	…
Weyh 7.65s94	7.6	3	101⅛	…
Weyh 5¼17	cv	50	87½	−1
Whirl zr11	…	26	29⅝	+⅛
WilcxGb 7s14	cv	15	70½	−½

← Unisys

Source: *The Wall Street Journal*, June 23, 1992

The top portion of the New York Exchange Bonds quotations provides important information about the previous trading day. **Volume** is the par value of bonds traded on Monday, June 22, 1992: $37,420,000. **Issues traded** lists the number of different bonds sold on that day. **Advances** is the number of bonds that traded at a price higher than the previous day; **Declines** is the number that traded at a price below the previous trading day's, and **Unchanged** is the number of those whose price did not change. New highs lists the number trading at all-time highs. **Dow Jones Bond Averages** is a straight arithmetic summary and average of 20 selected utility and industrial bonds.

If you wish to follow the performance of a particular bond, consider the following illustration from the Tuesday, June 23, 1992 edition.

Bonds	*Cur Yld*	*Vol.*	*Close*	*Net Chg.*
AT&T 5-5/8 95	5.7	32	99 3/8	-1/8
Unisys 10-3/4 95	10.7	80	100 1/2	. . .

You will find a key to all footnotes under **Explanatory Notes** at the bottom of the listing.

In the case of the AT&T bond shown above, the coupon rate at issue per $1,000 bond (5-5/8 or 5.625 percent) and the year of maturity (1995, the year the bond is due for redemption) follow the company's name. (You'll find an "s" after the interest rate when a fraction is absent.)

Corporate bonds are issued in denominations of $1,000, and this particular AT&T bond originally paid an annual fixed-dollar interest return of $56.25 (5.625 percent of $1,000 = $56.25). Thus, AT&T promised to pay the bearer $56.25 a year until it redeemed the bond at maturity.

You can see from the next column that the current yield is 5.7 percent. Volume is reported in thousands of dollars: 32 bonds with a face value of $1,000 were traded on June 22, 1992. You can see the closing price for the day. Since bonds are issued in denominations of $1,000, the reported prices are a percentage of the face value of $1,000. Thus, 99-3/8 means this bond traded at a price of $993.75 (99.375 percent of $1,000 = $993.75) at the day's close. The last column informs you that the June 22 closing price was 1/8 ($1.25=1/8% of $1,000) lower than the previous close.

AMEX BONDS

Volume $2,850,000

SALES SINCE JANUARY 1

1992	1991	1990
$453,010,000	$471,410,000	$343,260,000

	Mon.	Fri.	Thu.	Wed
Issues traded	65	61	71	71
Advances	18	23	23	17
Declines	33	26	33	33
Unchanged	14	12	15	21
New highs	4	2	3	0
New lows	1	0	1	1

AdvMd 7¼02	cv	5	72	...
Alza zr10	...	419	35¾	– 1
Angles 12½95	13.0	60	96½	– ½
Atari 5¼02	cv	35	47	– 1
BSN 7¾01	cv	15	69½	...
BSN 9¼96B	10.6	8	87	+ ½
Benton 8s02	cv	10	103	+ 4½
BrnhP 8½12	cv	3	92½	– 2
ChckFul 8s06	cv	54	91½	– 1½
ChtMd 15.85s08f	...	336	14½	– ⅜
vjCntArHd 15¾92f	...	70	9	– 1½
vjCntArHd 15¾92Bf	...	5	9	– ½
vjCntArHd 14¼93f	...	10	9	...
vjCntArHd 14.9s95f	...	17	8¾	– ¼
Ducom 7¾11	9.9	36	78½	– 2½
Eckerd 11⅛01	11.1	38	100½	...
Eckerd 13s06	12.9	35	100⅝	...
Fthill 9½03	cv	83	107½	– 1½
FruitL 12⅜03	11.7	10	105¾	...
FruitL 7s11	8.8	10	79½	+ ½
Greyhnd 10s01	10.7	5	93½	– ½
Greyhnd 8½07	cv	40	89	– ½
Hadsn 7¾06f	...	5	28	...
vjHlthCr 14⅜95f	...	39	7	+ 2
HomShp 11¾96	11.3	65	104¼	+ ½
HudGn 7s11	cv	35	67	– 1
KellyOG 8½00	cv	58	89¼	– ¼
Koor 8½02rp	8.6	11	98½	+ 1
Lynch 8s06	cv	5	89½	+ 2
Maxam 12½99	12.0	8	101	...
Maxam 14s00	13.6	37	103	– 1
Moog 9⅞06	cv	10	89	– 1½
OBrien 11s11	cv	46	104½	+ ½
Oakwd 7½01	cv	1	104	– 2½
Olsten 7s13	cv	3	113	– 1
Openh 12¾02	12.4	16	103	+ 1
OriolH 12⅞00	12.7	15	101	+ ¼
PlyGm 10s08	cv	32	98⅞	– ⅝
RsrtInt 15s94f	...	250	66	...
RyanM 14s12B	13.1	1	106½	– 1½
Sage 8½05	cv	10	69½	+ 1½
SvcMer 11¾96	11.4	46	103¼	– ⅛
SCE8s96 AA	7.9	10	101¼	– ⅛
StrlEl 10¾09	11.4	22	94	– 2⅛
SwBell 8¾07	8.5	45	102¾	– ½
SwBell 6⅞11	7.8	1	88	+ ¼
SwBell 7¾09	7.9	10	98	...
SwBell 7⅝13	8.0	40	95	+ ¾
SwBell 8¼14	8.3	10	99⅝	...
SwBell 9¼15	8.9	7	103¾	– ⅜
SwBell 8½16	8.4	39	100⅝	+ ⅜
SwBell 8¼17	8.3	10	99⅝	– ⅛
SwBell 8¾18	8.6	31	102¼	+ ¾
SwBell 9⅝19	9.1	7	105½	...
TrnLux 9s05	cv	10	92	– 1
Trump un9½f	...	19	64	– 1
TurnBd zr04	...	30	37⅝	– ½
TurnBd 12s01	11.0	5	109¼	+ ¼
Viacm 9⅛99	9.2	15	99⅜	...
Wang 7¾08	cv	31	55	...
Wang 9s09	cv	51	64	– ½
Westbr 11.7s96	14.7	15	79½	– ¼
Wickes 12s94	11.9	235	100½	+ ⅛
Wickes 7½-10s05	9.0	5	83½	– ⅛
Wickes 11⅞01	11.7	201	101½	+ ½

Source: *The Wall Street Journal*, June 23, 1992

Now, if you bought this bond on June 22, 1992, your yield would be 5.7 percent, slightly *more* than the coupon rate of 5-5/8 (5.625) percent, because on June 22 the bond had a value of $993.75, slightly *less* than its par value of $1,000. An annual yield of $56.25 on an investment of $993.75 is the equivalent of 5.7 percent, not 5-5/8 percent.

If the current yield on securities of similar risk and maturity as the AT&T bond rises above the coupon rate of 5 5/8 percent (as they have here), an investor will pay less than the par value for the bond. When commentators speak of the bond market rising and falling, they mean the *price* of the bond, not the *interest rate*. Bondholders want interest rates to fall so that the value of their bonds will rise. You can see that the AT&T bond went from $1,000 to $993.75 as its yield rose from 5-5/8 percent to 5.7 percent.

Investor's Tip

- Rising inflation, or fear of inflation, which drives interest rates up, hurts corporate bonds as well as Treasuries. Bond prices fall as interest rates rise.

You may have noticed from that some of these bonds carry a 'cv" notation in the *current yield* column. These bonds can be converted to a designated amount of common stock at the discretion of the bond holder, who will ordinarily make the conversion when the stock rises above a certain level. Because of this added feature, convertible bonds trade at a higher price and lower yield than bonds of comparable maturity and credit-worthiness. They are attractive to investors who are drawn to a company's stock but wish to earn interest while waiting to see whether the stock will appreciate.

Not only interest rates, but also the relative strength of the issuing company will affect the price of its bonds. AT&T is an investment of high quality because of its healthy financial condition and secure earnings potential. On the other hand, the Unisys 10-3/4 95 bond on pages 238 and 240, carries a higher coupon payment *and* yield than AT&T because Unisys, a much weaker company, had to pay a higher yield to attract investors' funds.

"Junk" bonds (like Unisys) offer higher rates of interest because of their inherently risky nature. They are issued by companies that have high debt-to-equity ratios and high debt-to-cash flow ratios, and must therefore pay high interest rates to attract investors' money. Any fluctuation in the business of the issuing corporation could affect the timely payment of interest and the repayment of principal on the bonds.

Junk, or high-yield bonds, have been around for a long time and should be distinguished from their well-heeled cousins, the investment-grade bonds issued by financially secure corporations. Interest in junk bonds, especially on the part of institutions such as insurance companies and savings and loan companies, grew in the early 1980s when falling interest rates boosted the prices of all bonds. Investors used the proceeds from the sale of junk bonds to purchase the stock of corporations, particularly conglomerates, that had fallen on hard times. These new owners often hoped to service their junk-bond debt by selling off divisions of the company they had purchased. Sometimes the company was worth more dead than alive and was dismembered. Sometimes top management bought a company from stockholders (called "going private") and then shrank it down to a profitable base. Often, however, the highly-leveraged surviving company was burdened with a huge, high-yield debt. Many companies failed and defaulted on their bonds, so that by the end of the 1980s, and especially during the 1990-91 recession, junk bonds fell out of favor and their prices sank and their yields soared. But the 1992 recovery and falling interest rates resuscitated many of these bonds, so that some investors realized strong capital gains as their prices soared. The example below serves as a case in point.

Bonds	Cur Yld	Vol	Close	Net Chg.
UCarb 9¾94	9.8	170	100	– ¼
UnEl 8⅞06	9.1	3	97¼	– ⅝
Unisys 13⅞92	24.6	353	56½	...
Unisys 10¾95	29.3	367	36¾	+ 1
UnAL 5s91	5.2	10	96 9/16	+ 1/16
UnAL 4¼92	4.5	10	93⅝	+ ⅛
UJer 7¾97	10.8	15	71½	...
VerP 9⅝98	9.7	20	99⅜	+ 2⅝
Vul 10¼2000	10.3	20	99⅞	– ⅝
WarC 10⅞95	11.6	60	93½	...
WarC 11½13	13.2	37	87⅛	– 1⅛
WasteM zr12	...	15	35½	– ¾
WellF 8.6s02	9.6	32	90	– 1
Wendys 7¼10	cv	16	78	...
WUTI 5s92	14.7	20	34	– 1½
WUTI 13¼08	51.0	20	26	+ 1⅛

← On January 14,1991, Unisys 10 3/4 95 bond traded at $367.50 for a yield of 29.3%

Source: *The Wall Street Journal*, January 15, 1991

HIGH YIELD BONDS

Monday June 22, 1992

	Total Daily Return	Index Value	Average Price Change	Vol.
Flash Index	− 0.03%	133.73	− 0.05	L
Cash Pay	− 0.02	130.45	− 0.05	L
Deferred Int	− 0.06	143.94	− 0.06	L
Distressed	− 0.26	141.67	− 0.17	L
Bankrupt	− 0.06	120.51	− 0.03	L

Volume Key: H = Heavy, M = Moderate, L = Light

Index value = 100 on July 1, 1990

Key Gainers	Type/ Coup.	Mat.	3:00P.M. Bid Price	Price Change	Principal Return	Yld to Mat.
EasternAir	c/12.750	11/96	59 3/4	+ 1/2	+ 0.84	z
MascoInd	a/10.000	3/95	101	+ 1/4	+ 0.24	9.56
Key Losers						
CharterMed	h/15.850	8/08	14 1/2	− 1/2	− 3.33	z
Petrolane	a/13.250	10/01	35	− 1/2	− 1.41	z
UnisysCrSns	c/15.000	7/97	108 1/2	− 1 1/4	− 1.07	12.66
EPIC Hldgs	d/12.000	3/02	55	− 1/2	− 0.90	12.58
ColtecInd	c/ 9.750	4/00	99 1/2	− 1/2	− 0.49	9.84
TimeWarner	c/ 0.000	8/02	75 3/4	− 1/4	− 0.33	2.76

Name	Type/Rating	Coup.	Mat.	Close	Net Chg.	% Yld. to Mat.
AdelComm	a /B-	13.000	8/96	101	− 1/4	12.67
AmerStandard	a /B-	12.875	6/00	104 1/2	+ 1/8	11.98
CaesarsWorld	b /BB+	13.500	10/97	103 3/4	unch	12.49
ChryslrAubH	c /B+	16.875	5/20	122 1/8	unch	z
CokeBotSW	b /B	12.000	5/97	100 1/2	+ 1/8	11.85
EPIC Hldgs	d /CCC+	12.000	3/02	55	− 1/2	12.58
FedDeptSerD	e /NR	9.000	8/97	100	+ 3/8	z
GeorgiaGulf	a /B	15.000	4/00	115 1/2	unch	11.89
Kroger	a /B-	12.875	1/99	109	unch	10.91
MagmaCopper	a /BB-	11.500	1/02	104 5/8	+ 1/8	10.71
Magnetek	a /B	10.750	11/98	102 1/2	unch	10.20
McCawCell	a /CCC+	12.950	8/99	105 3/8	unch	11.81
News Corp	c /BB-	12.000	12/01	107	+ 1/2	10.80
QuantumChem	a /B-	12.500	3/99	100	− 1/2	12.50
RH Macy	a /D	14.500	10/98	43 1/2	− 1/4	z
RJR Nabisco	f /BB+	15.000	5/01	119 5/8	unch	12.32
Safeway	g /B+	9.650	1/04	100 1/2	unch	9.58
Southland	c /B+	12.000	12/96	99	unch	12.29
StoneCont	a /B+	10.750	4/02	98 1/4	unch	11.04
Stop & Shop	a /B	9.750	2/02	99 1/4	− 1/2	9.87
SupermktGenl	b /B-	11.625	6/02	100 1/4	unch	11.58
UnisysCrSns	c /B	15.000	7/97	108 1/2	− 1 1/4	12.66
ViacomIntl	a /B+	9.125	8/99	98 3/4	− 1/4	9.36
VonsCompany	a /BB-	9.625	4/02	100 1/2	− 1/2	9.54

Volume indicators are based solely on the traders' subjective judgment given the relative level of inquiry and trading activity on any given day.

a-Senior Sub. b-Subordinated. c-Senior. d-Senior, Split Cpn. e-Secured, VarRt. f-Subordinated, PIK. g-Secured. h-Junior Sub, PIK. z-omitted for reset or bankrupt bonds, or yields above 35%.

Source: Salomon Brothers

Source: *The Wall Street Journal*, June 23, 1992

CREDIT RATINGS

DELTA AIR LINES (Atlanta) – Moody's Investors Service Inc. lowered Delta's long-term debt ratings on $4.6 billion of debt. The ratings concern cited what it considers the continuing poor outlook for Delta's earnings, exacerbated by the latest fare wars. In addition, Moody's expects Delta's leverage will continue to increase because its ability to improve cash flow is eroded by poor profit outlook and continuing heavy capital requirements. Moody's lowered the ratings on secured equipment trust certificates to Baa-1 from A-3; senior unsecured debt issues and industrial revenue bonds to Baa-2 from Baa-1 and industrial revenue bonds to Baa-3 from Baa-2. The Moody's decision follows Standard & Poors Corp.'s recent move to lower its ratings on Delta, affecting about $4.1 billion of debt.

* * *

LOCKHEED Corp. (Calabasas, Calif.) – Standard & Poor's Corp. said it raised its rating on Lockheed commercial paper to A-1 from A-2 and said that it affirmed the single-A rating on senior debt, revising the rating outlook to "stable" from "negative." Lockheed currently has about $100 million of commercial paper outstanding. The company has about $1.1 billion in long-term debt rated by Standard & Poor's. S&P said its upgrading of the commercial paper rating "reflects improved liquidity and reduced financial risk." The rating concern said Lockheed's total debt to capital is expected to average 35% to 40% over time, even with possible share repurchases and acquisitions. "Although weak defense industry fundamentals and higher competition could cause earnings pressures, management is expected to take steps to maintain credit quality," S&P said. S&P's step Friday reversed moves made more than two years ago. The rating concern assigned the "negative" outlook to Lockheed's commercial paper in November 1989 and downgraded the company's commercial paper to A-2 from A-1 at that time.

* * *

NEW YORK STATE – Standard & Poor's Corp. affirmed its single-A-minus rating on the state's $4.8 billion of general obligation bonds, but said it was still concerned about the "fragile" outlook for New York's budget. The ratings concern also assigned the same rating to about $250 million in state serial bonds. S&P said it remains concerned about New York's continuing economic weakness, four years of operating deficits and a growing accumulated deficit. The rating firm said the outlook remains negative "as long as the budget balance is fragile, the economic environment remains weak, and evidence of ongoing prudent fiscal manage-

Source: *The Wall Street Journal*, June 8, 1992

Junk bonds can bring substantial speculative rewards if a troubled company works its way out of difficulty and survives. Compare the Unisys bond listing in the January 15, 1991 *Journal* (see the excerpt on page 243) with the June 23, 1992 listing on page 238. On January 14, 1991 the Unisys 10-3/4 95 traded at $367.50 (36-3/4). By June 22, 1992 it had almost tripled in value to $1,005. Some of this gain can be attributed to falling interest rates, some to greater credibility for all junk bonds, and some to the continued survival of Unisys.

Every day the *Journal* publishes **High Yield Bonds** (see page 244) that summarizes activity in key junk bonds. You should note from the index values that in mid-1992 all junk bonds had appreciated over the past two years.

The *Journal* can help you sort bonds according to credit-worthiness. Each day it publishes **Credit Ratings** (check the last section's index), summarizing the actions of Standard & Poor's and Moody's, the nation's major bond-rating services. (See the example from the June 8, 1992 *Journal* on page 245.) These services rate bonds according to the likelihood of payment of principal and interest. The rating services arrive at their decision by investigating the profitability and strength of the companies issuing the bonds. You will notice that different companies pay varying rates of interest on their debt according to the ratings they have received.

The table below summarizes the format used by the two major-rating services.

Bond Ratings

Moody's	Standard & Poor's	Rating
Aaa	AAA	
Aa	AA	Investment Grade
A	A	
Baa	BBB	
Ba	BB	
B	B	
Caa	CCC	Junk
Ca	CC	
C	C	

NEW SECURITIES ISSUES

The following were among yesterday's offerings and pricings in U.S. and non-U.S. capital markets, with terms and syndicate manager, as compiled by Dow Jones Capital Markets Report:

CORPORATE

AMR Corp. – $200 million of notes, due July 1, 1995, priced as 6¼% at 99.839 to yield 6.31%. The noncallable notes were priced to yield 83 basis points above the Treasury's three-year note. Rated Baa-1 by Moody's Investors Service Inc. and triple-B by Standard & Poor's Corp., the issue will be sold through underwriters led by Lehman Brothers.

Broad Inc. – $125 million of cumulative preferred stock priced through underwriters led by Merrill Lynch & Co. The five million shares of $25-a-share preferred were priced with a dividend yield of 9.25%. The deal is rated Baa-3 by Moody's and single-A-minus by S&P. The preferred shares are noncallable for five years.

Society Corp. – $200 million of subordinated notes, due June 15, 2002, priced at par to yield 8.125%. The noncallable issue was priced at a spread of 89.5 basis points above the Treasury's 10-year note. Rated Baa-1 by Moody's and triple-B-plus by S&P, the issue will be sold through underwriters led by Goldman, Sachs & Co.

MUNICIPALS

Houston – $448.4 million of public improvement general obligation bonds, due March 1, 1997-2005, 2008, and 2012, priced by a Goldman Sachs group to yield from 5.10% in 1997 to 6.45% in 2012. Current interest serial bonds are priced to yield from 5.10% in 1997 to 6.15% in 2005. There are $114 million term bonds priced as 7% at 106.88 to yield 6.30% in 2008, and $76.7 million term bonds priced as 6.40% at 99.44 to yield 6.45% in 2012. The bonds are rated double-A by Moody's and double-A-minus by S&P.

Port of Oakland, Calif. – $153 million of revenue bonds, 1992 Series E, due Nov. 1, 1996-2007, and 2022, priced by a Smith Barney, Harris Upham & Co. group to yield from 5.00% in 1996 to 6.58% in 2022. Current interest serial bonds are priced to yield from 5.00% in 1996 to 6.50% in 2007. There are $112.9 of million term bonds priced as 6.50% at 99 to yield 6.58% in 2022. The bonds are insured by MBIA Corp. and rated triple-A by Moody's and S&P.

Santa Cruz County, Calif. – $50 million of tax and revenue anticipation notes won by a group led by Morgan Stanley & Co. with a bid setting the net interest cost at 3.085%. The notes, due Aug. 1, 1993, carry a coupon rate of 3.75% and are reoffered to yield 3.00%. The notes are rated MIG-1 by Moody's.

EQUITIES

Silicon Graphics Inc. – An offering of 2,150,000 common shares priced at $17.125 each through underwriters led by Morgan Stanley & Co.

Washington Real Estate Investment Trust – An offering of 2.4 million common shares priced at $17 each through underwriters led by Alex Brown & Sons Inc.

EUROBONDS

European Investment Bank (agency) – 350 million European currency units of 9% Eurobonds due July 15, 2002 via Paribas Capital Markets Ltd. Offered to investors intially at a fixed price of 99.17 to yield 9.13%, margin 0.12 above French government's 8½% due 2002. Fees 0.325.

Cie. Bancaire (France) – 1.5 billion French francs of 15% Eurobonds due Jan. 20, 1994, at issue price 100.731 via Paribas Capital Markets. Offered initially at fixed price of 99.86. Fees 1.

State Electricity Commission of Victoria (Australia) – 100 million Australian dollars of 9¼% Eurobonds due July 27, 1999 at issue price 101.65 via Hambros Bank Ltd. Yield 9.32% (annual) after deducting full fees. Guaranteed by State of Victoria. Fees 2.

Mori Seiki Co. (Japan) – 15 billion yen of 5.65% bonds due Oct. 16, 1996 via Yamaichi International Europe Ltd. Fees 1⅝.

Source: *The Wall Street Journal*, June 23, 1992

SECURITIES OFFERING CALENDAR

The following U.S. Treasury, corporate and municipal offerings are tentatively scheduled for sale this week, according to Dow Jones Capital Markets Report:

TREASURY

Monday

$23.2 billion in three- and six-month bills.

CORPORATE

One Day In The Week

Alco Health Distribution Corp. – initial 6.3 million Class A common shares, via Smith Barney, Harris Upham & Co.

Alden Press Co. – initial 3.2 million common shares, via William Blair & Co.

Bradlees Inc. – initial 11,018,625 common shares, via Merrill Lynch & Co.

BroadBand Technologies Inc. – initial 1.8 million common shares, via Bear, Stearns & Co.

Broadway & Seymour Inc. – initial 1.3 million common shares, via Robertson, Stephens & Co.

Cantab Pharmaceuticals PLC – initial two million ordinary shares, represented by American depository shares, via PaineWebber Inc.

Central Point Software – initial three million common shares, via Morgan Stanley & Co.

Coding Sciences Inc. – initial two million common shares, via PaineWebber.

Comcast Cellular Corp. – $1 billion of senior participating zero coupon notes, via Donaldson, Lufkin & Jenrette Securities Corp.

Commerce Bancorp Inc. – 1.5 million common shares, via Legg Mason Wood Walker Inc.

Cone Mills Corp. – initial six million common shares, via Prudential Securities Inc.

Continental Cablevision Inc. – $250 million two-part offering, including $150 million of senior subordinated notes and $100 million of senior subordinated debentures, via Morgan Stanley.

Continuum Co. – 2.5 million common shares, via Lehman Brothers Inc.

CrossComm Corp. – initial 2.7 million common shares, via Donaldson Lufkin.

Eastman Corp. – initial 10.3 million common shares, via Dean Witter Reynolds Inc.

EduCare Community Living Corp. – initial two million common shares, via Kemper Securities.

Fieldcrest Cannon Inc. – $85 million of senior subordinated debentures, via Kidder, Peabody & Co.

Heritage Media Services Inc. – $150 million of senior secured notes, via Goldman, Sachs & Co.

Riverwood International Corp. – $250 million two-part offering, including $125 million of senior notes and $125 million of senior subordinated notes, via J.P. Morgan Securities Inc.

Southwest Gas Corp. – $100 million of debentures, via Salomon Brothers Inc.

Specialty Coatings International Inc. – initial five million common shares, via First Boston Corp.

Trident NGL Inc. – initial 15.5 million common shares, via Donaldson Lufkin.

Ultramar Corp. – initial 33 million common shares, via Goldman Sachs.

Video Lottery Technologies Inc. – two million common shares, via Montgomery Securities.

West One Bancorp – 1.5 million common shares, via Merrill Lynch.

Wisconsin Public Service Corp. – 800,000 common shares, via Smith Barney.

MUNICIPAL

Tuesday

East Bay Regional Park District, Calif. – $60 million of improvement unlimited tax bonds, 1992 Series B, via competitive bid.

Los Angeles – $200 million of wastewater system revenue bonds, 1992 Series B, via competitive bid.

Minnesota – $140 million of various purpose general obligation bonds, via competitive bid.

Virginia Public Building Authority – $91,856,000 of various state building revenue refunding bonds, including $52,130,000 of revenue refunding bonds and $39,726,000 of capital appreciation bonds, via competitive bid.

Wednesday

Fairfax County, Va. – $115,125,000 of public improvement refunding general obligation bonds, 1992 Series B, via competitive bid.

Florida Dept. of Transportation – $193.3 million of turnpike revenue bonds, 1992 Series A, via competitive bid.

Santa Cruz County, Calif. – $50 million of 1992 tax and revenue anticipation notes, via competitive bid.

One Day In The Week

Cape Coral, Fla. – $80 million of waste water and improvement district assessment bonds (FSA-insured), via a PaineWebber group.

Clark County, Nev. – $144 million of industiral development revenue bonds (Nevada Power Co. project), 1992 Series A and B (Alternative Minimum Tax), (FGIC-insured), via a Goldman Sachs group.

Connecticut Housing Finance Authority – $122,530,000 of housing mortgage finance program bonds (AMT and non-AMT), via a PaineWebber group.

Intermountain Power Authority, Utah – $235 million of power supply system refunding revenue bonds, via a Goldman Sachs group.

Los Angeles County, Calif. – $1.5 billion of 1992-93 tax and revenue anticipation notes, including $1 billion of fixed-rate notes and $500 million of notes with a mandatory put option, via a Morgan Stanley group.

Missouri Health and Higher Education Facilities Authority – $82 million of revenue bonds (St. Louis Children's Hospital project), Series 1992, via an A.G. Edwards & Sons Inc. group.

New Hampshire Housing Finance Agency – $90 million of single-family mortgage mandatory revenue bonds (AMT and non-AMT), via a John Nuveen & Co. group.

New York City Municipal Water Finance Authority – $200 million of water and sewer system revenue bonds, Fiscal 1992 Series C, via a Smith Barney group.

New York State Medical Care Facilities Finance Agency – $112 million of mental health revenue bonds, Series B and C, via a Lehman Brothers group.

Oklahoma Municipal Power Authority – $70 million of revenue bonds, via a Lehman Brothers group.

Osceola County, Fla. – $150 million of transportation improvement revenue bonds (Osceola Parkway project), (MBIA Inc.-insured), via a Merrill Lynch group.

South Carolina Public Authority – $170 million of refunding revenue bonds, Series A (Santee Cooper), via Goldman Sachs group.

Tennessee Housing Development Agency – $58 million of home ownership program revenue bonds (AMT and non-AMT), via a Goldman Sachs group.

Vermont Student Assistance Corp. – $100 million of student loan revenue bonds (AMT), (FSA-insured), via a Lehman Brothers group.

Washington Health Care Facilities Authority – $76,520,000 of revenue bonds (Childrens Hospital & Medical Center project), Series 1992, via a John Nuveen group.

Wisconsin Housing and Economic Development Authority – $100 million of single-family mortgage revenue bonds (AMT and non-AMT), via a Lehman Brothers group.

Indefinite

Florida State Board of Education – $311,580,000 of public education capital outlay general obligation bonds, 1992 Series A, via competitive bid.

Source: *The Wall Street Journal*, June 15, 1992

Municipal Bond Index

Merrill Lynch 500

Week ended Tuesday, June 23, 1992

The following index is based on yields that about 500 major issuers, mainly of investment grade, would pay on new long-term tax-exempt securities. The securities are presumed to be issued at par; general obligation bonds have a 20-year maturity and revenue bonds a 30-year maturity. The index, prepared by Merrill Lynch, Pierce, Fenner & Smith Inc., is calculated using yields on major outstanding bonds in the market. Yields are obtained from an internal source.

–500 MUNICIPAL BOND INDEX–

6.52 –0.04

–REVENUE BONDS–

Sub-Index 6.61 –0.05

	6-23	Change In Week
–25-YEAR REVENUE BONDS–		
AAA-Guaranteed ...	6.51	– 0.04
Airport	6.94	– 0.06
Power	6.38	– 0.07
Hospital	6.65	– 0.03
Housing-Single Family	6.87	– 0.02
Housing-Multi Family	6.70	– 0.02
Miscellaneous	6.71	– 0.04
Pollution Control/Ind. Dev.	6.63	– 0.06
Transportation	6.52	+ 0.00
Water	6.57	– 0.06
Advance Refunded .	5.60	– 0.07
–20-YEAR GENERAL OBLIGATIONS–		
Sub-Index	**6.52**	**–0.02**
Cities	6.82	+ 0.00
Counties	6.58	– 0.04
States	6.47	– 0.02
Other Districts	6.57	+ 0.00

The transportation category excludes airports; other districts include school and special districts.

Source: *The Wall Street Journal*, June 26, 1992

You can also follow **New Securities Issues** daily in the *Journal* (check the index in the first or last section). It lists all new corporate, municipal, government agency, and foreign bonds issued on the previous day, and provides pertinent information regarding these securities, including their ratings. (See the excerpt from the June 23, 1992 *Journal* on page 247.)

Finally, Monday's **Securities Offering Calendar** (see the excerpt from the June 15, 1992 edition on page 248) provides information on the week's new issues (check the third section's index under New Offerings).

MUNICIPAL BONDS

Finally, you may wish to purchase municipal (state and local government) or tax-exempt bonds, as they are sometimes called, because earnings from these bonds are not subject to federal income tax and may not be subject to income tax in your state. These bonds were granted tax exemption in order to reduce the borrowing cost of the states, cities, and local districts that issue them. Investors purchase them knowing their return is not taxable and will therefore be satisfied with a yield below that of comparable federal or corporate bonds. State and local governments save billions in interest costs as a result of this indirect subsidy.

Each Friday the *Journal* publishes a **Municipal Bond Index** prepared by Merrill Lynch (see the last section's index). The excerpt from the June 26, 1992 *Journal* on page 249 serves as an example. In addition to an overall index, this report presents the latest yield on a variety of municipal bond categories.

Also, the *Journal* publishes a weekly listing of actively traded municipal bonds on Mondays under the heading **Weekly Tax-Exempts.** (See the excerpt from the June 8, 1992 *Journal.)*

Before deciding on the purchase of a tax-exempt municipal bond, an investor must weigh four considerations: the yield available on the municipal bond, the yield on a taxable bond with the same maturity, the investor's tax bracket, and whether the bond is callable.

If, for example, you are in a 28 percent tax bracket, use the "equivalent tax-exempt yield formula" to calculate your after-tax yield on a security whose income is taxable. This will be the minimum yield a municipal bond must pay you to be of equivalent value to the taxable bond. Here's

WEEKLY TAX-EXEMPTS

Market quotations for some actively traded municipal issues. Yield is to maturity.

Issue	Coupon	Mat.	Bid	Ask	Yld.
California St Dept Wtr	6.000	12-01-21	93¼	93½	6.52
California St G O 12	6.250	09-01-12	97½	97⅝	6.47
Denver Colo Arpt 12	7.250	11-15-12	97¾	98⅛	7.47
Denver Colo Arpt 23	7.250	11-15-23	97⅞	98⅛	7.49
Denver Colo Arpt-25	7.500	11-15-25	98¼	97⅜	7.65
Denver colo Arpt 21	7.750	11-15-21	101⅜	101¾	7.63
Detr Mich Wtr Sys	6.250	07-01-12	97⅛	97½	6.51
Fla St Mun Pwr Agy Rev-12	6.000	10-01-12	94¾	95⅛	6.47
Fla St Mun Pwr Agy Rev-27	6.000	10-01-27	93	93⅛	6.51
Florida St Div Bd	6.250	07-01-13	97⅝	97¾	6.46
Louisiana Pub Facs Auth	6.625	11-15-21	99¼	99⅜	6.68
Mass Muni Whlsl Elec Co	6.625	07-01-18	97½	97¾	6.83
Mass St Wtr Auth Ser A-19	6.500	07-15-19	98⅛	98¼	6.50
Mass St Wtr Auth Ser A-21	6.500	07-15-21	97⅛	97¼	6.72
Metro Atl Rapid Trans 11	6.250	07-01-11	98½	98¾	6.39
Metro Atl Rapid Trans 20	6.250	07-01-20	97½	97¾	6.44
NJ St Tpk Auth Ser A-18	6.200	01-01-18	96⅜	96¾	6.49
NJ St Tpk Auth Ser C-16	6.500	01-01-16	100⅜	100⅝	6.47
NYC G O 09-12	7.100	02-01-09	99⅛	99¼	7.19
NYC G O 16-22	7.000	02-01-16	97¼	97¾	7.25
NYS Engy Resh&Dev 19-22	7.150	09-01-19	101	101¼	7.07
NYS Pwr Auth Rev & Gen	6.250	01-01-23	97¼	97⅝	6.46
Okla St Tpk Auth 1st Ser	6.125	01-01-20	95	95½	6.50
P R Cmwlth Hwy & Trans	6.500	07-01-22	97⅛	97¼	6.72
P R Cmwlth Hwy & Trans	6.625	07-01-18	98¾	98⅞	6.73
P R Cmwlth Hwy & Trans	6.625	07-01-12	99¼	99⅜	6.69
Pa Intrgovrnmntl Coop Auth	6.800	06-15-22	99¾	99⅞	6.82
R I Depositors Econ	6.625	08-01-19	99	99¼	6.69
SC Pub Svc Auth Santee	6.625	07-01-31	98⅞	99	6.70
Sacremento Ca Elec Ser B22	6.375	08-15-22	98½	L	6.49
Sikeston Mo Elec Rev	6.250	06-01-22	97¾	98	6.42
Sikeston Mo Elec Rev	6.250	06-01-12	98	98¼	6.43
Univ of Tex Bd of Regents	6.250	07-01-13	97	97⅛	6.51

L=Locked

Source: J.J. Kenny Drake Inc./McGraw-Hill Municipal Screen Service

Source: *The Wall Street Journal*, June 8, 1992

an instance using a 10 percent yield on the security whose interest is taxable.

$$
\begin{aligned}
\text{Equivalent tax-exempt yield} &= (1 - \text{tax bracket}) \times \text{taxable yield} \\
&= (1 - .28) \times .10 \\
&= .072 \\
&= 7.2 \text{ percent}
\end{aligned}
$$

Thus, in your 28 percent tax bracket, a 7.2 percent tax-exempt yield is the equivalent of a 10 percent taxable yield.

Therefore, if you had the opportunity, you would purchase an 8 percent tax-exempt bond rather than a 10 percent taxable bond with similar maturity and credit-worthiness.

Municipal bond buyers should always determine if the issuing agency can call (redeem) the bond before maturity. It may wish to do so when interest rates are low in order to issue new debt at lower rates. Meanwhile, the purchaser is forced to find another investment at a disadvantageous time. Therefore, an investor that plans to hold a bond until maturity should not purchase a bond that is callable before that date.

TRACKING THE BOND MARKET

It's now time to wrap up this discussion by detailing how you can use the *Journal* every day to follow the bond market. You should begin your daily analysis of bond market activity with a glance at the **Bonds** reports on the first page of the third section under **Markets Diary** (see the excerpt from the Monday June 15, 1992 edition on page 254), which lists five important indexes that track bond market performance and provide current yields. The graph portrays the Shearson Lehman Hutton Treasury Bond Index, a composite index of Treasury securities' yield and price performance. The DJ 20 Bond Index provides the average price and yield of 10 public utility bonds and 10 industrial bonds. You became acquainted with it in the discussion of NYSE bonds. The Salomon mortgage-backed index covers mortgage-backed securities such as Ginnie Maes, Fannie Maes, and Freddie Macs. The Bond Buyer municipal index is compiled by *The Bond Buyer,* a publication that specializes in fixed-income securities, and covers AA-rated and A-rated municipal bonds. The Merrill Lynch corporate bond index, like the Dow index, is a corporate bond composite.

The **Bond Yields** chart appears in Monday's *Wall Street Journal* with the Credit Markets article, as shown in the sample on page 254 from the June 15, 1992 issue. It depicts three series: the top line portrays the yield paid by financially healthy public utilities on debt instruments maturing in 10 years or more, the second series depicts the yield on 15-year and longer Treasury bonds, and the bottom line shows municipal bond yields.

BOND MARKET DATA BANK 6/12/92

MAJOR INDEXES

HIGH	LOW (12 MOS)		CLOSE	NET CHG	% CHG	12-MO CHG	% CHG	FROM 12/31	% CHG
U.S. TREASURY SECURITIES (Lehman Brothers indexes)									
3620.23	3216.88	Intermediate	3620.23	+ 6.35	+ 0.18	+ 402.44	+ 12.51	+ 65.26	+ 1.84
4366.76	3715.27	Long-term	4312.36	+ 10.28	+ 0.24	+ 581.07	+ 15.57	− 39.52	− 0.91
1444.83	1285.27	Long-term(price)	1378.30	+ 2.98	+ 0.22	+ 84.43	+ 6.53	− 64.06	− 4.44
3776.80	3329.11	Composite	3776.80	+ 7.27	+ 0.19	+ 444.58	+ 13.34	+ 39.83	+ 1.07
U.S. CORPORATE DEBT ISSUES (Merrill Lynch)									
583.59	505.59	Corporate Master	583.59	+ 1.56	+ 0.27	+ 78.00	+ 15.43	+ 14.86	+ 2.61
436.88	383.53	1-10 Yr Maturities	436.88	+ 0.99	+ 0.23	+ 53.35	+ 13.91	+ 12.36	+ 2.91
436.32	371.49	10+ Yr Maturities	436.32	+ 1.29	+ 0.30	+ 64.59	+ 17.38	+ 10.83	+ 2.55
259.70	208.10	High Yield	259.70	+ 0.09	+ 0.03	+ 51.60	+ 24.80	+ 25.02	+ 10.66
420.76	363.78	Yankee Bonds	420.76	+ 1.43	+ 0.34	+ 56.80	+ 15.61	+ 6.79	+ 1.64
TAX-EXEMPT SECURITIES (Bond Buyer; Merrill Lynch: Dec. 31, 1986 = 100)									
97-6	91-12	Bond Buyer Municipal	96-10	+ -4	+ 0.13	+ 4-30	+ 5.40	− -6	− 0.19
141.84	127.61	New 10-yr G.O.(AA)	141.70	+ 0.03	+ 0.02	+ 14.09	+ 11.04	+ 2.20	+ 1.58
149.01	130.22	New 20-yr G.O.(AA)	148.50	+ 0.02	+ 0.01	+ 18.28	+ 14.04	+ 4.06	+ 2.81
169.98	143.50	New 30-yr revenue(A)	169.66	+ 0.03	+ 0.02	+ 26.16	+ 18.23	+ 4.73	+ 2.87
MORTGAGE-BACKED SECURITIES (current coupon; Merrill Lynch: Dec. 31, 1986 = 100)									
172.60	149.19	Ginnie Mae(GNMA)	171.86	+ 0.54	+ 0.32	+ 22.67	+ 15.20	− 0.74	− 0.43
173.16	149.37	Fannie Mae(FNMA)	173.16	+ 0.36	+ 0.21	+ 23.79	+ 15.93	+ 1.87	+ 1.09
172.90	149.13	Freddie Mac(FHLMC)	172.90	+ 0.36	+ 0.21	+ 23.77	+ 15.94	+ 2.89	+ 1.70
CONVERTIBLE BONDS (Merrill Lynch: Dec. 31, 1986 = 100)									
154.30	136.67	Investment Grade	153.44	− 0.10	− 0.07	+ 14.05	+ 10.08	+ 4.31	+ 2.89
153.20	122.07	High Yield	151.92	unch		+ 26.86	+ 21.48	+ 13.12	+ 9.45

CORPORATE BONDS

Quotes of representative taxable issues at mid-afternoon New York time, provided by First Boston/CSFB Ltd.

ISSUE (RATING: MOODY'S/S&P)	COUPON	MATURITY	PRICE	CHANGE	YIELD	CHANGE
FINANCIAL						
Chase Manhattan Corp (Ba2/BBB)	9.750	11/01/01	107.121	0.164	8.625	− 0.025
Citicorp (Baa3/BBB+)	9.500	02/01/02	105.128	0.166	8.700	− 0.025
Ford Credit Co (A2/A)	8.875	06/15/99	106.272	0.137	7.700	− 0.025
GMAC (A2/A−)	8.250	08/01/96	104.046	0.450	7.100	− 0.125
Household Fin (A3/A)	7.750	10/01/99	99.702	0.137	7.801	− 0.025
UTILITY						
Commonwlth Ed (A3/A−)	9.625	07/01/19	106.603	0.267	8.971	− 0.025
Pacific G&E (A1/A)	8.125	01/01/97	104.440	1.641	6.971	− 0.420
Sou Bell Tel (Aaa/AAA)	8.500	08/01/29	100.536	0.284	8.451	− 0.025
Sou Cal Ed (Aa3/AA)	9.375	02/15/17	105.469	0.260	8.825	− 0.025
US West Commun (Aa3/AA−)	8.875	06/01/31	102.785	0.284	8.625	− 0.025
INDUSTRIAL						
Amoco (Aaa/AAA)	8.625	12/15/16	102.321	0.265	8.400	− 0.025
Capital Cities (A1/A+)	8.750	03/15/16	101.231	0.252	8.625	− 0.025
Du Pont & Co (Aa2/AA)	6.000	12/01/01	88.101	0.154	7.800	− 0.025
Exxon Shipping (Aaa/AAA)	Zero	09/01/12	19.006	0.097	8.383	− 0.025
East Kodak (A3/A−)	9.125	03/01/98	106.596	0.235	7.674	− 0.050
Mobil (Aa2/AA)	8.625	07/01/94	106.182	0.241	5.400	− 0.125
FOREIGN						
Hydro-Quebec (Aa3/AA−)	8.500	12/01/29	99.771	0.279	8.520	− 0.025
Int Bk Recon Dev (Aaa/AAA)	9.875	10/01/97	112.202	0.112	7.071	− 0.025
Sweden (Aa1/AAA)	8.125	11/01/96	103.456	0.093	7.189	− 0.025
Victoria Finance (Aa2/AA)	8.450	10/01/01	103.224	0.164	7.950	− 0.025

TAX-EXEMPT BONDS

Representative prices for several active tax-exempt revenue and refunding bonds, based on institutional trades. Changes rounded to the nearest one-eighth. Yield is to maturity. n-New. Source: The Bond Buyer.

ISSUE	COUPON	MAT	PRICE	CHG	BID YLD
Brazos Rvr Auth Ser92A	6.750	04-01-22	99½	+ ⅛	6.79
Calif Dept of Wtr Res	6.125	12-01-13	96¼	+ ¼	6.45
Calif St Pub Wrks	6.700	10-01-17	100¼	+ ⅛	6.68
Chgo Ill GO Ser88A,B,C	6.850	01-01-17	101½	+ ⅛	6.72
Contra Costa Calif	6.625	11-01-22	98⅞	+ ⅜	6.71
Cook Co Ill Ser 92A	6.600	11-15-22	99¾	+ ¼	6.65
Dade Co Fla Ser 92	6.250	10-01-21	97⅛	+ ⅛	6.47
Fla State Bd of Ed 91C	6.625	06-01-22	100⅜	...	6.60
Forsyth Montana Ser92	6.800	03-01-22	101⅜	+ ¼	6.69
Gallup N M PCR Ser 92	6.650	08-15-17	100⅛	...	6.64
Harris Co Toll Rd Tx 92	6.500	08-15-17	99⅞	+ ⅛	6.57
Hudson Co NJ Corr Fac	6.600	12-01-21	100⅜	...	6.55
Kans Dept Trans Ser92	6.500	03-01-12	99⅛	...	6.58
L A Calif Wastewater	6.000	12-01-18	94⅜	+ ¼	6.44
L.A. Dept Wtr & Pwr	6.375	02-01-20	98⅛	+ ⅛	6.52
La Pub Fac Auth Ser 92	6.500	05-15-22	98⅛	+ ⅛	6.64
Mass Hlth & Ed	6.550	10-01-22	99¾	+ ⅛	6.57
Mass Hlth & ED Auth	6.875	04-01-22	99⅛	...	6.95
Mass Wtr Res Auth	6.750	07-15-12	99¾	...	6.77
Met Seattle WA SewRev	6.600	01-01-32	99¼	+ ⅛	6.65
Metro Washn Air Auth	6.625	10-01-19	99⅛	+ ⅛	6.69
N.J. Turnpike Au Ser 91	6.200	01-01-18	97⅛	+ ¼	6.43
NJ Sprts & Expo Auth	6.500	03-01-19	100	+ ⅛	6.50
NY Lcl Gvt Asst Corp	6.875	04-01-19	100⅜	+ ⅛	6.82
NY MTA Ser J	6.500	07-01-18	100½	+ ¼	6.46
NYS Engy Res & Dev	6.500	05-15-32	99½	+ ⅛	6.54
NYS Pwr Auth	6.250	01-01-23	97¾	+ ⅛	6.42
NYS Pwr Auth	6.375	01-01-12	99⅞	+ ¼	6.39
Okla Tpke Auth Ser 92A	6.125	01-01-20	95¼	+ ⅛	6.50
Okla Tpke Auth Ser92C&E	6.250	01-01-22	97¾	+ ⅛	6.42
Orange Co Fla	6.500	10-01-19	99⅜	+ ⅛	6.53
Orindo Aviation Auth	6.375	10-01-21	97½	+ ¼	6.56
P.R. El Pwr Ser P	7.000	07-01-21	102½	+ ¼	6.81
P.R. G.O. Pub Imprvmt	6.800	07-01-21	101⅜	...	6.70
P.R. Pub Bldg Auth	6.875	07-01-21	101⅝	...	6.75
S.C. Pub Serv Rev	6.500	07-01-24	99	...	6.57
S.C. Pub Serv Rev	6.625	07-01-31	99	+ ⅛	6.7
Sacramento Ca Ser 92B	6.375	08-15-22	98½	+ ⅛	6.49
Sikeston Mo Elec Sys	6.250	06-01-22	97⅜	+ ⅛	6.43
Univ of Pittsburgh	6.125	06-01-21	95½	+ ⅛	6.47

MORTGAGE-BACKED SECURITIES

Representative issues, quoted by Salomon Brothers Inc.

	REMAINING TERM (Years)	WTD-AVG LIFE (Years)	PRICE (JUNE) (Pts.-32ds)	PRICE CHANGE (32ds)	CASH FLOW YIELD*	YIELD CHANGE (Basis pts.)
30-YEAR						
GNMA 8.0%	29.6	10.7	100-09	unch	8.03%	unch
FHLMC Gold 8.0%	29.4	7.5	100-08	− 7	8.01	+ 4
FNMA 8.0%	29.5	8.1	100-00	− 5	8.07	+ 7
GNMA 9.0%	29.3	9.7	105-18	+ 2	8.11	− 1
FHLMC Gold 9.0%	29.2	6.9	105-06	− 5	7.92	+ 3
FNMA 9.0%	28.5	6.9	105-02	+ 6	7.90	+ 3
GNMA 10.0%	29.0	4.1	108-26	unch	7.22	− 3
FHLMC Gold 10.0%	27.7	2.6	107-22	− 3	6.42	+ 4
FNMA 10.0%	28.0	2.6	107-22	− 3	6.35	+ 7
15-YEAR						
GNMA 8.0%	14.5	6.4	103-00	+ 6	7.41%	− 4
FHLMC Gold 8.0%	14.7	5.3	102-24	+ 6	7.40	unch
FNMA 8.0%	14.7	5.7	102-18	+ 6	7.43	− 1

*Based on projections from Salomon's prepayment model, assuming interest rates remain unchanged from current levels

COLLATERALIZED MORTGAGE OBLIGATIONS

Spread of CMO yields above U.S. Treasury securities of comparable maturity, in basis points (100 basis points = 1 percentage point of interest)

MAT	SPREAD	CHG FROM PREV DAY
NEW ISSUES		
2-year	115	unch
5-year	110	unch
10-year	[illegible]	unch
20-year	95	unch
SEASONED ISSUES		
2-year	105	unch
5-year	100	unch
10-year	105	unch
20-year	90	unch

GUARANTEED INVESTMENT CONTRACTS

Source: T. Rowe Price GIC Index

	1 YEAR RATE	1 YEAR CHG	2 YEARS RATE	2 YEARS CHG	3 YEARS RATE	3 YEARS CHG	4 YEARS RATE	4 YEARS CHG	5 YEARS RATE	5 YEARS CHG
High	4.56%	unch	5.80%	−0.05	6.46%	−0.02	7.00%	unch	7.37%	−0.08
Low	3.50	unch	4.55	−0.06	5.46	+0.78	5.97	−0.06	6.35	−0.09
INDEX	4.14	+0.01	5.34	−0.03	6.07	+0.01	6.62	−0.03	7.09	−0.03
TOP QUARTILE RANGE	4.56%	- 4.49%	5.80%	- 5.56%	6.46%	- 6.29%	7.00%	- 6.83%	7.37%	- 7.25%
SPREAD vs. TREASURYS	+0.03		+0.28		+0.48		+0.56		+0.60	

GIC rates quoted prior to 3 pm (Eastern) net of all expenses, no broker commissions. Rates represent best quote for a $2-$5 million immediate lump sum deposit with annual interest payments. Yield spreads based on U.S. Treasury yields, as of 3 pm (Eastern), versus the index rate unadjusted for semi vs. annual interest payments. CHG reflects change in rate from previous day. INDEX is average of all rates quoted. Universe is investment grade.

INTERNATIONAL GOVERNMENT BONDS

Prices in local currencies, provided by Salomon Brothers Inc.

	COUPON	MATURITY (Mo./yr.)	PRICE	CHANGE	YIELD*
JAPAN (3 p.m. Tokyo)					
#89	5.10%	6/96	99.752	+ 0.033	5.17%
#108	4.80	6/98	96.109	+ 0.022	5.57
#129	6.40	3/00	104.940	unch	5.60
#15	6.70	3/11	105.292	unch	6.21
#73	6.80	6/95	105.596	+ 0.014	4.78
UNITED KINGDOM (5 p.m. London)					
	10.00%	4/93	100.406	+ 0.026	9.45%
	9.00	10/08	99.844	+ 0.062	9.01
	10.00	11/96	102.906	+ 0.186	9.17
	9.75	8/02	104.125	+ 0.125	9.11
	10.00	6/94	101.250	+ 0.031	9.29
GERMANY (5 p.m. London)					
	8.00%	1/02	100.288	− 0.195	7.79%
	8.50	9/96	100.460	− 0.020	8.18
	8.88	7/95	100.460	− 0.060	8.51
	8.38	1/97	100.270	− 0.020	8.12
	6.75	1/99	92.747	− 0.136	8.04
CANADA (3 p.m. EDT)					
	9.50%	6/10	105.700	+ 0.600	8.86%
	8.50	4/02	102.150	+ 0.700	8.17
	9.25	6/22	104.200	+ 0.650	8.85
	8.25	3/97	102.550	+ 0.450	7.59
	7.00	9/94	100.950	+ 0.200	6.55

*Equivalent to semi-annual compounded yields to maturity

Total Rates of Return on International Bonds

In percent, based on Salomon Brothers' world government benchma. k bond indexes

	— LOCAL CURRENCY TERMS —					— U.S. DOLLAR TERMS —				
	1 DAY	1 MO	3 MOS	12 MOS	SINCE 12/31	1 DAY	1 MO	3 MOS	12 MOS	SINCE 12/31
Japan	+ 0.03	+ 0.74	+ 1.14	+ 12.24	+ 2.01	− 0.14	+ 3.80	+ 7.17	+ 25.27	+ 0.52
Britain	+ 0.11	+ 0.92	+ 4.47	+ 14.02	+ 6.28	+ 0.22	+ 2.98	+ 12.83	+ 28.23	+ 5.17
Germany	− 0.06	+ 0.89	+ 0.98	+ 2.50	+ 3.02	− 0.05	+ 3.80	+ 6.84	+ 16.31	− 1.03
France	− 0.07	+ 0.67	+ 1.09	+ 8.81	+ 2.69	− 0.02	+ 3.26	+ 7.91	+ 24.31	+ 0.13
Canada	+ 0.52	+ 2.62	+ 6.86	+ 16.70	+ 3.11	+ 0.64	+ 3.88	+ 7.49	+ 12.07	+ 0.06
Netherlands	+ 0.02	+ 0.94	+ 1.55	+ 8.72	+ 4.38	+ 0.05	+ 3.83	+ 7.37	+ 23.38	+ 0.35
Non-U.S.	NA	NA	NA	NA	NA	+ 0.12	+ 3.59	+ 8.27	+ 21.59	+ 0.87
World*	+ 0.12	+ 1.11	+ 2.45	+ 9.16	+ 3.21	+ 0.14	+ 3.23	+ 7.24	+ 18.67	+ 0.88

*Includes U.S. Treasury benchmark index NA=not applicable

EURODOLLAR BONDS

Provided by First Boston/CSFB Ltd.

ISSUE (RATING: MOODY'S/S&P)	COUPON	MATURITY	PRICE	CHANGE	YIELD	CHANGE
Canada (Aaa/AAA)	9.000	02/27/96	107.020	0.080	6.666	− 0.024
Quebec (Aa3/AA−)	9.125	08/22/01	105.363	0.162	8.112	− 0.024
Belgium (Aa1/NR)	9.625	07/10/98	109.222	0.125	7.524	− 0.024
Italy (Aaa/NR)	9.000	07/28/93	103.986	0.019	5.177	− 0.024
Int Bk Recon Dev (Aaa/AAA)	9.000	07/07/93	103.857	0.017	5.119	− 0.024
Int Bk Recon Dev (Aaa/AAA)	9.000	08/12/97	108.493	0.109	6.858	− 0.024
Lincoln Natl (A1/AA)	9.750	10/20/95	107.741	0.072	6.933	− 0.024

Source: *The Wall Street Journal*, June 15, 1992

BONDS Lehman Brothers T-Bond Index

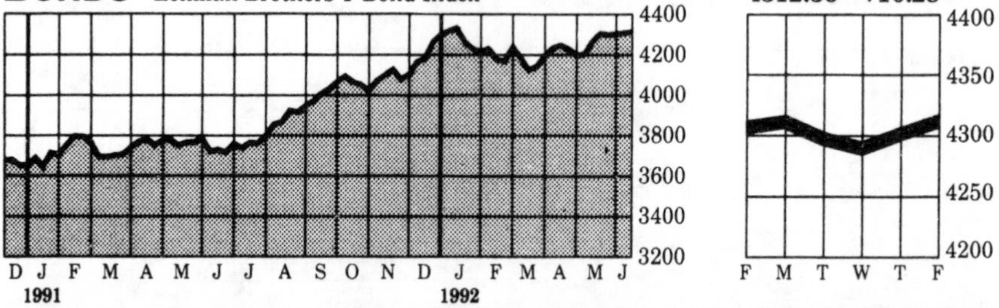

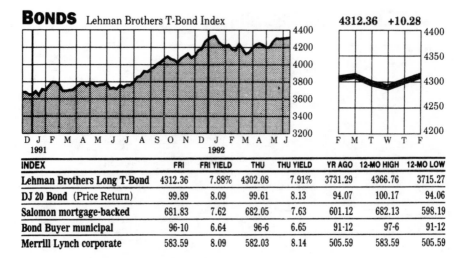

INDEX	FRI	FRI YIELD	THU	THU YIELD	YR AGO	12-MO HIGH	12-MO LOW
Lehman Brothers Long T-Bond	4312.36	7.88%	4302.08	7.91%	3731.29	4366.76	3715.27
DJ 20 Bond (Price Return)	99.89	8.09	99.61	8.13	94.07	100.17	94.06
Salomon mortgage-backed	681.83	7.62	682.05	7.63	601.12	682.13	598.19
Bond Buyer municipal	96-10	6.64	96-6	6.65	91-12	97-6	91-12
Merrill Lynch corporate	583.59	8.09	582.03	8.14	505.59	583.59	505.59

Source: *The Wall Street Journal*, June 15, 1992

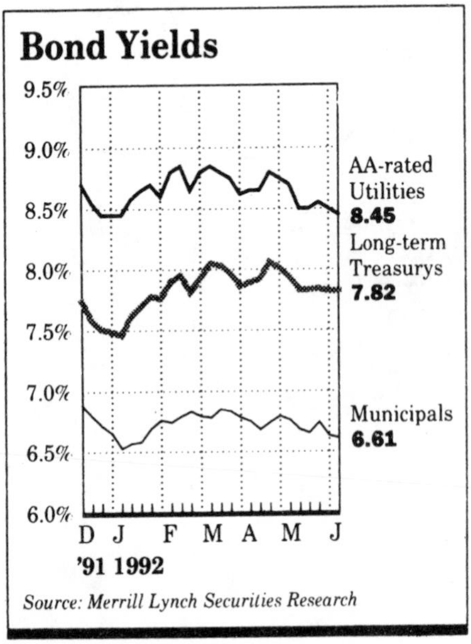

Source: *The Wall Street Journal*, June 15, 1992

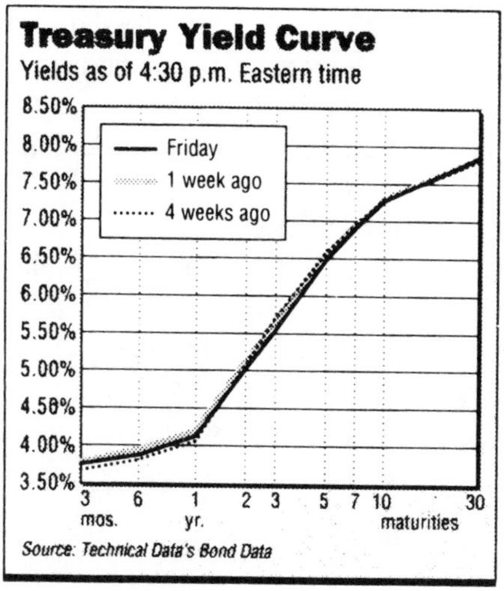

Source: *The Wall Street Journal*, June 15, 1992

YIELD COMPARISONS

Based on Merrill Lynch Bond Indexes, priced as of midafternoon Eastern time.

	6/12	6/11	–52 Week– High	Low
Corp.-Govt. Master	6.81%	6.86%	8.27%	6.53%
Treasury 1-10yr	5.83	5.87	7.61	5.44
10+ yr	7.89	7.92	8.69	7.43
Agencies 1-10yr	6.42	6.45	7.92	6.12
10+ yr	8.31	8.33	8.92	7.80
Corporate				
1-10 yr High Qlty	7.27	7.32	8.67	7.10
Med Qlty	7.69	7.75	9.28	7.69
10+yr High Qlty	8.45	8.48	9.44	8.30
Med Qlty	8.85	8.88	9.84	8.79
Yankee bonds(1)	8.10	8.16	9.24	7.79
Current-coupon mortgages (2)				
GNMA 7.50%	7.98	8.09	9.36	7.40
FNMA 8.00%	8.03	8.07	9.38	7.51
FHLMC8.00%	7.87	7.91	9.33	7.38
High-yield corporates	11.40	11.40	14.40	11.40
New tax-exempts				
10-yr G.O. (AA)	5.85	5.85	6.50	5.60
20-yr G.O. (AA)	6.42	6.42	7.05	6.25
30-yr revenue (A)	6.70	6.70	7.55	6.52

Note: High quality rated AAA-AA; medium quality A-BBB/Baa; high yield, BB/Ba-C.

(1) Dollar-denominated, SEC-registered bonds of foreign issuers sold in the U.S. (2) Reflects the 52-week high and low of mortgage-backed securities indexes rather than the individual securities shown.

Source: *The Wall Street Journal*, June 15, 1992

The Journal publishes its **Bond Market Data Bank** (find it in the front page index of the first and last sections) daily toward the center of Section C, as in the example from the Monday, June 15, 1992 issue on page 253. The Data Bank thoroughly covers the bond market for the preceding trading day and contains more information than you may ever want to know.

Finally, you can compare the yield on a variety of long-term instruments by using the **Yield Comparisons** table that appears daily with the **Credit Markets** article and also check the yield on the entire range of Treasury securities in the **Treasury Yield Curve** (see the excerpts from the June 15, 1992 issue on page 255). Notice the normal shape of the yield curve: yields increase with length of maturity.

MUTUAL FUNDS

If you recall the discussion of mutual funds in Chapter 9, you will remember that mutual funds often specialize in particular types of investments. Bond funds are mutual funds that invest primarily in debt instruments, permitting you to diversify your bond investments without venturing a large sum of capital. For example, new Ginnie Mae issues require a $25,000 minimum investment, which would be out of the reach of the small investor. Mutual funds pool large sums of money in order to invest in instruments like Ginnie Maes from which small individual investors can then benefit.

Recall as well Chapter 9's description of two types of mutual funds. Open-end funds issue shares as needed, while closed-end fund's shares are limited and fixed. Once all the shares are sold, no more shares will be issued. On Mondays, the *Journal* reports on Closed-End Bond Funds and Publicly Traded Funds (find them in the last section's index), as in the examples from the June 8, 1992 edition on pages 257 and 258.

CONCLUSION

If all this detail has set your head swimming, regain your perspective by recalling that stocks' and bonds' values should move together in the long haul and that both are paper investments that thrive in low inflation.

CLOSED-END BOND FUNDS

Friday, June 5, 1992

Unaudited net asset values of closed-end bond fund shares, reported by the companies as of Friday's close. Also shown is the closing listed market price or a dealer-to-dealer asked price of each fund's shares, with percentage of difference.

Fund Name	Stock Exch.	N.A. Value	Stock Price		% Diff.
Bond Funds					
ACM Govt Inco Fund	NYSE	10.31	10 7/8	+	5.48
ACM Govt Oppor Fd	NYSE	9.32	9 5/8	+	3.27
ACM Govt Securities	NYSE	10.25	10 3/4	+	4.88
ACM Govt Spectrum	NYSE	a8.70	9 1/8	+	4.89
ACM Mgd Inco	NYSE	8.84	9 5/8	+	8.88
AIM Strategic Inco	AMEX	9.26	8 5/8	–	6.86
American Adj Rate '95	NYSE	ac9.86	10 3/8	+	5.22
American Adj Rate '96	NYSE	ac9.61	10 1/8	+	5.36
American Adj Rate '97	NYSE	ac9.55	10 1/8	+	6.02
American Adj Rate '98	NYSE	ac9.52	9 3/4	+	2.42
American Capital Bond	NYSE	b19.92	19 7/8	–	0.23
American Govt Income	NYSE	ac7.84	8 5/8	+	10.01
American Gov't Portf	NYSE	ac 10.18	10 3/4	+	5.60
American Govt Term	NYSE	ac9.77	11	+	12.59
American Opp Inco Fund	NYSE	ac 10.30	11	+	6.80
American Strat Inc	NYSE	ac 13.67	15 1/4	+	11.56
AMEV Securities	NYSE	10.12	11 1/4	+	11.17
Blackstone Advtg Trm	NYSE	10.50	11	+	4.76
Blackstone Income Tr	NYSE	9.52	10 5/8	+	11.61
Blackstone Inv Qual Term	NYSE	9.61	9 7/8	+	2.76
Blackstone 1998 Term	NYSE	10.26	10 1/4	–	0.10
Blackstone Strat Trm	NYSE	9.96	10 3/4	+	7.93
Blackstone Target Trm	NYSE	10.19	10 5/8	+	4.27
Bunker Hill Income Sec	NYSE	15.81	16 1/2	+	4.37
CIGNA High Income	NYSE	7.13	7 7/8	+	10.45
Colonial Int High Inco	NYSE	6.51	6 1/2	–	0.15
Colonial Intrmkt Inco I	NYSE	11.49	11 1/4	–	2.09
Current Income Shares	NYSE	12.89	13 1/8	+	1.82
Dean Witter Govt Inco	NYSE	a9.63	9 3/8	–	2.65
Dreyfus Strt Gov Inco	NYSE	11.02	11 3/8	+	3.22
1838 Bond-Deb Trad	NYSE	21.55	23 3/4	+	10.21
Excelsior Inco Shares	NYSE	c18.38	18	–	2.07
First Boston Inco Fd	NYSE	8.70	8 3/4	+	0.57
First Boston Strategic	NYSE	9.91	11 1/2	+	16.04
Ft Dearborn Income	NYSE	15.93	15 1/2	–	2.70
John Hancock Income	NYSE	16.27	16 3/4	+	2.95
John Hancock Invest	NYSE	21.65	23	+	6.24
Hatteras Income Secs	NYSE	16.08	17 5/8	+	9.61
High Yield Income Fd	NYSE	7.39	8 3/8	+	13.33
High Yield Plus Fund	NYSE	7.98	8	+	0.25
Hyperion Total Ret	NYSE	a10.97	11 7/8	+	8.25
INA Investments	NYSE	18.34	17 3/4	–	3.22
Independence Sq	OTC	17.61	17 1/2	–	0.62
Kemper High Inco Tr	NYSE	8.84	9 3/8	+	6.05
Kemper Inter Govt Tr	NYSE	8.98	9 1/2	+	5.79
Kemper Multi Inco Tr	NYSE	11.10	11	–	0.90
Liberty Tm Tr 1999	NYSE	9.55	9 7/8	+	3.40
Lincoln Natl Inco	NYSE	cd 29.85	28 3/4	–	3.69
MFS Charter Inco	NYSE	10.67	11	+	3.09
MFS Govt Mkts Inco	NYSE	7.97	8 1/4	+	3.51
MFS Intermed Inco Tr	NYSE	8.21	8 1/4	+	0.49
MFS Multimkt Inco Tr	NYSE	7.93	8 3/8	+	5.61
MFS Special Value Tr	NYSE	15.06	16	+	6.24
Montgomery Street	NYSE	19.14	19 3/4	+	3.19
Mutual Omaha Int Shs	NYSE	13.85	14 3/4	+	6.50
New America Hi Inco	NYSE	c 4.17	4 1/8	–	1.08
Oppenhmr Multi-Govt	NYSE	8.81	9 3/8	+	6.41
Oppenhmr Multi-Sectr	NYSE	10.76	10 3/4	–	0.09
Pacific Amer Inco Shs	NYSE	bc 15.95	15 7/8	–	0.47
Prospect St Hi Inco Fd	NYSE	4.18	3 7/8	–	7.30
RAC Income Fund	NYSE	c11.41	12 7/8	+	12.84
State Mutual Securities	NYSE	11.10	11	–	0.90
Transamerica Income	NYSE	24.28	24 5/8	+	1.42
Tyler Cabot Mort Sec Fd	NYSE	11.20	12 3/8	+	10.49
USF&G Pacholder Fd	NYSE	19.38	19 3/8	–	0.03
USLife Income Fund	NYSE	9.66	9 5/8	–	0.36
VanKamp Intmdt Hi Inc	NYSE	6.39	7 1/2	+	17.37
VanKamp Ltd Hi Inc	NYSE	8.38	8 1/2	+	1.43
Vestaur Securities	NYSE	c14.93	14 5/8	–	2.04
Zenix Income Fund	NYSE	6.28	6 7/8	+	9.47
Convertible Bond Funds					
Lincoln Natl Convert	NYSE	c18.81	16 5/8	–	11.62
International Bond Funds					
ACM Mgd Multi-Market	NYSE	10.96	11 5/8	+	6.07
First Australia Prime	NYSE	11.03	11 1/2	+	4.26
First Commonwealth	NYSE	14.46	14 5/8	+	1.14
Global Govt Plus Fd	NYSE	8.16	7 7/8	–	3.49
Global Income Plus	NYSE	9.84	9 7/8	+	0.36
Global Yield Fund	NYSE	8.91	8 5/8	–	3.20
Kleinwort Benson Aust	NYSE	11.57	10 3/4	–	7.09
Strat Global Income	NYSE	14.24	14 1/8	–	0.81
Templeton Glbl Gov Inco	NYSE	8.91	9 3/4	+	9.43
Templeton Global Inco	NYSE	8.74	9 3/8	+	7.27
Municipal Bond Funds					
Allstate Mun Inc Op	NYSE	a8.90	9 1/2	+	6.74
Allstate Mun Inc Op II	NYSE	a9.09	9 3/4	+	7.26
Allstate Mun Inc Op III	NYSE	a9.46	9 3/4	+	3.07
Allstate Mun Inc	NYSE	a10.50	10 5/8	+	1.19
Allstate Mun Inc II	NYSE	a10.26	10 1/8	–	1.32
Allstate Mun Inc III	NYSE	a9.57	9 3/4	+	1.88
Allstate Muni Pr Inco	NYSE	a9.97	10 3/8	+	4.06
Amer Muni Term Tr	NYSE	ac 10.00	10 1/4	+	2.50
Amer Muni Term Tr II	NYSE	ac9.72	10	+	2.88
Apex Muni Fund	NYSE	10.36	11 1/8	+	7.38
Blackstone Insured Muni	NYSE	9.52	9 7/8	+	3.73
Blackstone Muni Tar Trm	NYSE	9.59	9 3/4	+	1.67
Colonial Hi Inco Muni	NYSE	8.77	8 3/4	–	0.23
Colonial Inv Gr Muni	NYSE	10.87	11 3/4	+	8.10
Colonial Muni Inco Tr	NYSE	7.90	8 1/8	+	2.85
Dreyfus Cal Muni Inco	AMEX	9.28	9 3/8	+	1.02
Dreyfus Muni Inco	AMEX	9.85	10 3/8	+	5.33
Dreyfus NY Muni Inco	AMEX	9.80	9 3/4	–	0.51
Dreyfus Strategic Muni	NYSE	9.68	9 3/4	+	0.72
Dreyfus Strategic Munis	NYSE	9.98	10 3/4	+	7.72
Duff & Phelps Util Tx-Fr	NYSE	14.24	15	+	5.34
Intercap Insured Muni	NYSE	a14.74	15 7/8	+	7.70
Intercap Ins Muni Tr	NYSE	a14.21	15	+	5.56
Intercap Qual Muni	NYSE	a14.41	15	+	4.09
Kemper Muni Inco Tr	NYSE	12.18	12 5/8	+	3.65
Kemper Strategic Inco	NYSE	11.77	12 3/8	+	5.14
MFS Muni Inco Tr	NYSE	8.88	9 1/2	+	6.98
Minnesota Muni Term Tr	NYSE	ac9.68	10	+	3.31
Minnesota Muni Trm Tr II	AMEX	c 9.53	10 1/8	+	6.24
Municipal High Income	NYSE	9.47	9 5/8	+	1.64
MuniEnhanced Fund	NYSE	12.02	12 3/4	+	6.07
MuniInsured Fd Inc	NYSE	10.02	10	–	0.20
MuniVest Fund Inc	NYSE	9.89	10 7/8	+	9.96
MuniYield CA	NYSE	14.30	14 5/8	+	2.27
MuniYield FL	NYSE	14.25	15	+	5.26
MuniYield Fund	NYSE	14.75	14 7/8	+	0.85
MuniYield Insured	NYSE	14.41	14 3/4	+	2.36
MuniYield MI	NYSE	14.30	14 3/4	+	3.15
MuniYield New Jersey	NYSE	14.31	15 1/4	+	6.57
MuniYield NY Ins	NYSE	14.42	15	+	4.02
New York Tax-Exempt	AMEX	10.33	10 5/8	+	2.86
Nuveen CA Inv Qual Muni	NYSE	14.98	15 1/4	+	1.80
Nuveen CA Muni Inco	NYSE	12.03	12 1/2	+	3.91
Nuveen CA Muni Mkt Opp	NYSE	15.17	15 1/2	+	2.18
Nuveen CA Muni Val	NYSE	10.38	10 7/8	+	4.77
Nuveen CA Perf Plus	NYSE	15.18	15 1/8	–	0.36
Nuveen CA Qual Inc Muni	NYSE	14.15	14	–	1.06
Nuveen CA Sel Qual Muni	NYSE	14.69	14 3/4	+	0.41
Nuveen FL Inv Qual Muni	NYSE	14.76	15 1/2	+	5.01
Nuveen FL Qual Inc Muni	NYSE	14.28	14 3/4	+	3.29
Nuveen Ins Muni Opp	NYSE	14.40	14 5/8	+	1.56
Nuveen Ins Quality Muni	NYSE	15.11	15 7/8	+	5.06
Nuveen Inv Quality Muni	NYSE	15.37	16 1/8	+	4.91
Nuveen MI Qual Inc Muni	NYSE	14.31	15 1/4	+	6.57
Nuveen Muni Adv	NYSE	15.16	15 1/2	+	2.24
Nuveen Muni Inco	NYSE	12.09	12 7/8	+	6.49
Nuveen Muni Mkt Opp	NYSE	15.42	16	+	3.76
Nuveen Muni Value	NYSE	10.51	11 1/8	+	5.85
Nuveen NJ Inv Qual Muni	NYSE	14.56	15 3/8	+	5.60
Nuveen NJ Qual Inc Muni	NYSE	14.31	14 3/4	+	3.07
Nuveen NY Inv Qual Muni	NYSE	15.35	15 3/4	+	2.61
Nuveen NY Muni Inco	AMEX	11.98	12 3/8	+	3.30
Nuveen NY Muni Mkt Opp	NYSE	15.48	16	+	3.36
Nuveen NY Muni Val	NYSE	10.53	11 1/8	+	5.65
Nuveen NY Perf Plus	NYSE	15.18	15 7/8	+	4.58
Nuveen NY Qual Inc Muni	NYSE	14.20	14 1/4	+	0.35
Nuveen NY Sel Qual Muni	NYSE	14.82	15	+	1.21
Nuveen OH Qual Inc Muni	NYSE	14.11	14 7/8	+	5.42
Nuveen PA Inv Qual Muni	NYSE	14.85	15 5/8	+	5.22
Nuveen PA Qual Inc Muni	NYSE	14.38	14 7/8	+	3.44
Nuveen Perf Plus	NYSE	14.98	15 1/8	+	0.97
Nuveen Prem Inco	NYSE	15.81	16 3/8	+	3.57
Nuveen Prem Ins Muni	NYSE	14.07	14 3/8	+	2.17
Nuveen Prem Muni Inc	NYSE	14.04	14 1/4	+	[illegible]
Nuveen Qual Inco Muni	NYSE	14.67	14 7/8	+	1.40
Nuveen Sel Qual Muni	NYSE	14.94	14 7/8	–	0.44
Nuveen Sel Tx-Fr Inc	NYSE	14.26	14 3/4	+	3.44
Nuveen Sel Tx-Fr Inc 2	NYSE	13.98	15	+	7.30
Nuveen TX Qual Inc Muni	NYSE	14.23	14 3/4	+	3.65
Seligman Quality Muni	NYSE	14.08	14 1/8	+	0.32
Seligman Select Muni	NYSE	12.04	12 1/8	+	0.71
Smith Barney Int Mun	AMEX	10.14	10	–	1.38
Taurus Muni CA Hldgs	NYSE	11.66	12 7/8	+	10.42
Taurus Muni NY Hldgs	NYSE	11.85	13	+	9.70
VanKamp CA Muni Tr	NYSE	9.94	10	+	0.60
VanKamp CA Qual Muni	NYSE	15.19	14 5/8	–	3.72
VanKamp FL Qual Muni	NYSE	15.43	15 1/4	–	1.17
VanKamp Inv Gr CA	NYSE	15.08	14 5/8	–	3.02
VanKamp Inv Gr FL	NYSE	15.17	14 7/8	–	1.94
VanKamp Inv Gr Muni	NYSE	11.33	12 3/8	+	9.22
VanKamp Inv Gr NJ	NYSE	15.15	15	–	0.99
VanKamp Inv Gr NY	NYSE	15.08	15	–	0.53
VanKamp Inv Gr PA	NYSE	15.24	15	–	1.57
VanKamp Muni Inc Tr	NYSE	10.46	11	+	5.16
VanKamp Muni Trust	NYSE	15.63	15 1/2	–	0.83
VanKamp NY Qual Muni	NYSE	15.42	15	–	2.72
VanKamp OH Qual Muni	NYSE	15.27	15 7/8	+	3.96
VanKamp PA Qual Muni	NYSE	15.63	15 5/8	–	0.03
VanKamp Tr For Ins Muni	NYSE	15.32	14 3/4	–	3.72
VanKamp Tr Inv Gr Muni	NYSE	15.45	14 7/8	–	3.72
Voyageur Minn Muni Inc	AMEX	13.98	15 1/4	+	9.08

a-Ex-dividend. b-Fully diluted. c-As of Thursday's close.
d-NAV 5/29/92 was 29.69.
Source: Lipper Analytical Services, Denver Colorado.

Source: *The Wall Street Journal*, June 8, 1992

PUBLICLY TRADED FUNDS

Friday, June 5, 1992

Following is a weekly listing of unaudited net asset values of publicly traded investment fund shares, reported by the companies as of Friday's close. Also shown is the closing listed market price or a dealer-to-dealer asked price of each fund's shares, with the percentage of difference.

Fund Name	Stock Exch.	N.A. Value	Stock Price		% Diff.
Diversified Common Stock Funds					
Adams Express	NYSE	19.84	18 3/4	–	5.49
Allmon Trust	NYSE	10.41	9 3/4	–	6.34
Baker Fentress	NYSE	21.69	18 7/8	–	12.98
Blue Chip Value	NYSE	7.77	7 7/8	+	1.35
Clemente Global Gro	NYSE	b10.91	9 1/4	–	15.22
Gemini II Capital	NYSE	17.96	13 7/8	–	22.74
Gemini II Income	NYSE	9.56	13 1/8	+	37.29
General Amer Invest	NYSE	26.99	27 1/4	+	0.96
Jundt Growth Fd	NYSE	14.24	13 1/4	–	6.95
Liberty All-Star Eqty	NYSE	10.70	10 3/4	+	0.47
Niagara Share Corp.	NYSE	15.28	14 5/8	–	4.29
Quest For Value Cap	NYSE	25.25	20 1/4	–	19.80
Quest For Value Inco	NYSE	11.69	13 3/8	+	14.41
Royce Value Trust	NYSE	12.14	11 1/2	–	5.27
Salomon Fd	NYSE	15.27	13 3/4	–	9.95
Source Capital	NYSE	41.50	46 3/4	+	12.65
Tri-Continental Corp.	NYSE	28.21	27 3/4	–	1.63
Worldwide Value	NYSE	16.70	14 1/4	–	14.67
Zweig Fund	NYSE	11.45	12 1/2	+	9.17
Closed End Bond Funds					
CIM High Yield Secs	AMEX	7.70	7 5/8	–	0.97
Franklin Multi Inc Tr	NYSE	b10.38	10	–	3.66
Franklin Prin Mat Tr	NYSE	b8.44	7 3/4	–	8.18
Franklin Universal Tr	NYSE	b8.74	8	–	8.47
Flexible Portfolio Funds					
America's All Seasn	OTC	5.77	5	–	13.34
European Warrant Fd	NYSE	8.21	6 3/4	–	17.78
Zweig Total Return Fd	NYSE	a9.14	9 3/4	+	6.67
Loan Participation Funds					
Pilgrim Prime Rate	NYSE	9.98	8 5/8	–	13.58
Specialized Equity and Convertible Funds					
Alliance Global Env Fd	NYSE	12.39	10 3/8	–	16.26
American Capital Conv	NYSE	22.23	19 3/8	–	12.84
Argentina Fd	NYSE	13.34	15	+	12.44
ASA Ltd	NYSE	bc40.72	43 1/2	+	6.83
Asia Pacific	NYSE	14.86	16 1/4	+	9.35
Austria Fund	NYSE	9.69	8 1/2	–	12.28
Bancroft Convertible	AMEX	22.56	19 3/8	–	14.12
Bergstrom Capital	AMEX	95.03	107	+	12.60
BGR Precious Metals	TOR	be7.98	5 7/8	–	26.38
Brazil	NYSE	b19.58	21 3/8	+	9.17
Brazilian Equity Fd	NYSE	b13.16	14 3/4	+	12.08
CNV Holdings Capital	NYSE	11.71	7 5/8	–	34.88
CNV Holdings Income	NYSE	9.56	12 1/4	+	28.14
Castle Convertible	AMEX	24.74	21 1/4	–	14.11
Central Fund Canada	AMEX	b4.21	3 13/16	–	9.44
Central Securities	AMEX	a12.19	9 7/8	–	18.99
Chile Fund	NYSE	39.69	37 1/8	–	6.46
Couns Tandem Secs	NYSE	15.28	13 3/8	–	12.47
Duff&Phelps Utils Inc.	NYSE	9.22	10	+	8.46
Ellsw Conv Gr&Inc	AMEX	9.10	7 7/8	–	13.46
Emerging Ger Fd	NYSE	9.43	8	–	15.16
Emerging Mexico Fd	NYSE	b23.44	20 1/4	–	13.61
Engex	AMEX	11.37	8 7/16	–	25.79
Europe Fund	NYSE	13.48	12 3/8	–	8.20
1stAustralia	AMEX	10.99	9 3/8	–	14.70
First Financial Fund	NYSE	10.63	10 3/8	–	2.40
First Iberian	AMEX	9.52	8 1/8	–	14.65
First Philippine Fund	NYSE	14.11	12 1/2	–	11.41
France Growth Fund	NYSE	11.88	9 7/8	–	16.88
Future Germany Fund	NYSE	15.60	13 1/4	–	15.06
Gabelli Equity Trust	NYSE	10.84	11	+	1.48
Germany Fund	NYSE	11.79	11 1/8	–	5.64
Global Health Sciences Fd	NYSE	12.80	12 1/4	–	4.30
Growth Fund Spain	NYSE	11.72	9 7/8	–	15.74
GT Greater Europe Fd	NYSE	11.46	9 7/8	–	13.83
H&Q Healthcare Inv	NYSE	w18.95	20	+	5.54
H&Q Life Sciences Inv Fd	NYSE	13.89	15 1/8	+	8.89
Hampton Utils Tr Cap	AMEX	b14.43	13 1/4	–	8.18
Hampton Utils Tr Pref	AMEX	b50.13	50 5/8	+	0.99
India Growth Fund	NYSE	f19.60	19 3/8	–	1.15
Indonesia Fund	NYSE	9.36	10 1/4	+	9.51
Inefficient Market Fund	AMEX	11.42	9 7/8	–	13.53
Irish Investment Fd	NYSE	9.59	7 3/4	–	19.19
Italy Fund	NYSE	10.03	9	–	10.27
Jakarta Growth Fd	NYSE	7.08	8 1/8	+	14.76
Japan OTC Equity Fund	NYSE	8.82	10 1/8	+	14.80
Korea Fund	NYSE	11.24	11 1/4	+	0.09
Korean Investment Fd	NYSE	10.26	9 5/8	–	6.19
Latin America Equity Fd	NYSE	19.85	18	–	9.32
Latin America Inv Fd	NYSE	33.28	30 5/8	–	7.98
Malaysia Fund	NYSE	15.08	13 7/8	–	7.99
Mexico Equity Inc Fd	NYSE	b17.91	15 5/8	–	12.76
Mexico Fund	NYSE	b29.41	24 7/8	–	15.42
Morgan Grenf SmCap	NYSE	11.62	11 1/8		4.26
Morgan Stan Em Mks Fd	NYSE	17.84	17 7/8	+	0.20
New Germany Fund	NYSE	13.64	11 5/8	–	14.77
Pacific Eur Growth Fd	NYSE	b10.77	10 1/4	–	4.83
Patriot Prem Div Fd	NYSE	9.81	9 3/4	–	0.61
Patriot Prem Div Fd II	NYSE	11.70	11 3/8	–	2.78
Patriot Select Div Trust	NYSE	15.49	16 7/8	+	8.94
Petrol & Resources	NYSE	28.96	27 1/4	–	5.90
Pilgrim Regional	NYSE	11.68	11 3/8	–	2.61
Portugal Fund	NYSE	11.66	12 1/8	+	3.99
Preferred Income Fd	NYSE	18.20	18 5/8	+	2.34
Preferred Inc Opport Fd	NYSE	12.40	12 3/4	+	2.82
Rl Estate Sec Inco Fd	AMEX	7.56	7 7/8	+	4.17
ROC Taiwan Fund	NYSE	b9.70	9 5/8	–	0.77
Scudder New Asia	NYSE	15.86	16 1/4	+	2.46
Scudder New Europe	NYSE	10.48	9 1/4	–	11.74
SE Thrift & Bank Fd	OTC	b12.04	11	–	8.64
Singapore Fd	NYSE	b12.09	11 5/8	–	3.85
Spain Fund	NYSE	11.85	10 3/4	–	9.28
Swiss Helvetia Fd	NYSE	14.77	14 1/4	–	3.52
Taiwan Fund	NYSE	b21.94	22 1/8	+	0.84
TCW Convertible Secs	NYSE	8.22	9 1/8	+	11.01
Templeton Em Mkts	NYSE	b20.12	25 1/4	+	25.50
Templeton Global Util	AMEX	b13.22	13 3/8	+	1.17
Thai Capital Fund	NYSE	9.05	8 1/4	–	8.84
Thai Fund	NYSE	15.43	16 3/8	+	6.12
Turkish Inv Fund	NYSE	4.85	6 1/2	+	34.02
United Kingdom Fund	NYSE	11.68	10 1/8	–	13.31
Z-Seven	OTC	17.13	19	+	10.92

a-Ex-dividend. b-As of Thursday's close. c-Translated at Commercial Rand exchange rate. e-In Canadian Dollars. f-As of Wednesday's close, using the Free – Market Spot Rate. w–As of 5/29, NAV was 13.92.

Source: *The Wall Street Journal*, June 8, 1992

CHAPTER 12

MONEY MARKET INVESTMENTS

INTRODUCTION

Maybe the risk and bother of investing in stocks, bonds, and commodities inhibit you. If that's so, you may be satisfied with an investment whose yield just covers the rate of inflation, provided that you can readily convert it to cash. In other words, you want your money's purchasing power to be unchanged a year or two from now and you want the assurance that you can get your hands on your money at will.

Many circumstances might justify this point of view. Everyone's future involves some degree of uncertainty. If you are retired, your nest egg may have to meet unexpected medical bills. You don't want to be penalized for cashing out in a hurry. And investors of every age may wish to park their money for brief periods in anticipation of other planned uses of their funds. Whatever the situation, you might have a number of good reasons not to tie up your funds in riskier investments even if they offer higher returns.

If you wish to make a short-term investment that is relatively risk-free and can be quickly converted to cash, the money market offers a variety of selections that range from one day to one year and may be obtained for large or small amounts. Most of these are probably familiar to you: bank savings accounts, interest-bearing checking accounts (money market checking accounts), certificates of deposit, money market mutual funds, and Treasury bills (T-bills). Market forces determine their yields, and the markets for all are interrelated.

As a general rule, the greater the liquidity (ease with which it is converted into cash) and safety of an investment, the lower the yield. A smaller investment commitment and a shorter maturity also reduce the yield.

This chapter describes the money market investments available to individual investors and shows you how to track those investments in *The Wall Street Journal*.

CONSUMER SAVINGS AND INTEREST-EARNING CHECKING ACCOUNTS

Your interest-earning checking account, NOW (negotiable order of withdrawal), or savings account at the bank or savings and loan company (S&L) is a short-term liquid investment because you can withdraw your funds quickly and easily with relatively few restrictions. Moreover, these accounts are insured up to $100,000 by the Federal Deposit Insurance Corporation (FDIC). In the hierarchy of short-term interest rate yields, consumer checking and savings rates tend to be on the bottom because of their liquidity and safety, and because of the inertia that prevents many savers from shopping for the higher yields available on alternative investments.

Consumer Savings Rates

Money Market Deposits-a	3.31%
Super-NOW Accounts-a	2.71%
Six-month Certificates-a	3.65%
One-year Certificates-a	3.98%
Thirty-month Accounts-a	4.83%
Five-Year Certificates-a	5.98%
U.S. Savings Bonds-b	5.58%

a-Average rate paid yesterday by 100 large banks and thrifts in the 10 largest metropolitan areas as compiled by Bank Rate Monitor.
b-Current annual yield. Guaranteed minimum 6% for bonds held five years or longer.

Source: *The Wall Street Journal*, June 25, 1992

BANK MONEY MARKET ACCOUNTS

You can open a money market account with a minimum daily balance ranging from $500 to $5,000, depending on the bank. This is a highly liquid investment because you can withdraw from the account at any time simply by writing a check, although most banks have restrictions regarding the number and frequency of checks written. These accounts offer relatively low yields because of their check-writing privileges, although the yields do tend to be a little higher than on savings accounts due to higher required minimum balances. They are also insured up to $100,000 by the FDIC.

Every Thursday *The Wall Street Journal* publishes **Consumer Savings Rates** (check the third section's index), a listing prepared by the *Bank Rate Monitor* that reports on the average rate paid by 100 banks on the previous day for a variety of money market and certificate of deposit (CD) accounts. See the page 260 excerpt from the June 25,1992 *Journal.* According to this report, money market deposits paid 3.31 percent on June 24, 1992, Super-NOWs paid less, and a variety of certificates of deposit as well as U.S. Savings Bonds earned more.

On Friday of each week, on the next to the last page of the last section, the *Journal* publishes **Banxquote Money Markets** together with **High Yield Savings** and **High Yield Jumbos** (see the excerpt from the June 26, 1992 *Journal* on the next page). The Banxquote Money Market report lets you compare your yield on a variety of money market accounts and certificate of deposit accounts at different maturities with the average earned nationally (Bank Average) and in six key states: New York, California, Pennsylvania, Illinois, Texas, and Florida. You can also find the weekly change in the national average. In the week ended June 25, 1992, for instance, the average short-term account earned 3.27 percent and had fallen 0.01 percent over the previous week. The **High Yield Savings** figures represent the rates available at individual institutions for accounts requiring a small minimum balance (some as low as $500), and the **High Yield Jumbos** are rates offered with minimum balances of $95,000 to $100,000.

Banks and S&Ls created the money market accounts to stem withdrawals of funds lost to competing money market mutual funds offering higher rates than savings accounts. Although interest paid by the money market accounts fluctuates with short-term market rates, these accounts do not enjoy yields as high as those paid by money market

BANXQUOTE MONEY MARKETS

Survey ended Thursday, June 25, 1992

AVERAGE YIELDS OF MAJOR BANKS

	MMI*	One Month	Two Months	Three Months	Six Months	One Year	Two Years	Five Years
NEW YORK								
Savings	3.08%	z	z	3.15%	3.21%	3.66%	4.57%	6.13%
Jumbos	3.72%	3.28%	3.40%	3.45%	3.60%	3.93%	4.40%	5.36%
CALIFORNIA								
Savings	3.35%	z	z	3.23%	3.33%	3.72%	4.65%	6.30%
Jumbos	3.49%	3.25%	3.28%	3.37%	3.48%	3.90%	4.78%	6.60%
PENNSYLVANIA								
Savings	3.41%	z	z	3.38%	3.64%	4.00%	4.18%	5.84%
Jumbos	3.77%	3.32%	3.34%	3.42%	3.53%	3.82%	4.48%	5.58%
ILLINOIS								
Savings	3.33%	z	z	3.47%	3.56%	3.98%	4.63%	6.13%
Jumbos	3.51%	3.49%	3.54%	3.61%	3.71%	4.17%	4.87%	6.31%
TEXAS								
Savings	3.26%	z	z	3.38%	3.57%	3.92%	4.77%	6.09%
Jumbos	3.26%	3.45%	3.48%	3.53%	3.70%	4.10%	4.74%	6.11%
FLORIDA								
Savings	3.15%	z	z	2.99%	3.41%	3.67%	4.75%	5.75%
Jumbos	3.26%	3.01%	3.01%	3.17%	3.37%	3.70%	4.73%	5.97%
BANK AVERAGE								
Savings	3.26%	z	z	3.27%	3.45%	3.83%	4.59%	6.04%
Jumbos	3.50%	3.30%	3.34%	3.42%	3.56%	3.94%	4.68%	6.05%
WEEKLY CHANGE (in percentage point)								
Savings	....	z	z	−0.01	+0.01	−0.02	−0.02	−0.04
Jumbos	−0.02	....	+0.01	....	....	−0.02	−0.04	−0.06

The average short-term account earned 3.27% in the week ending June 25, 1992 →

SAVINGS CD YIELDS OFFERED THROUGH LEADING BROKERS

	Three Months	Six Months	One Year	Two Years	Five Years
BROKER AVERAGE	3.30%	3.45%	3.80%	4.35%	6.15%
WEEKLY CHANGE	....	....	−0.15	−0.10	−0.05

Broker average, 3.3% →

*Money Market Investments include MMDA, NOW, savings deposits, passbook and other liquid accounts.

Each depositor is insured by the Federal Deposit Insurance Corp. (FDIC) up to $100,000 per issuing institution.

COMPOUND METHODS: c-Continuously. d-Daily. w-Weekly. m-Monthly. q-Quarterly. s-Semi-annually. a-Annually. si-Simple interest.

F-Floating rate. P-Prime CD. T-T-Bill CD.

YIELD BASIS: A-365/365. B-360/360. C-365/360.

The information included in this table has been obtained directly from broker-dealers, banks and savings institutions, but the accuracy and validity cannot be guaranteed. Rates are subject to change. Yields, terms and capital adequacy should be verified before investing. Only well capitalized or adequately capitalized depository institutions are quoted.

z-Unavailable.

HIGH YIELD SAVINGS

Small minimum balance, generally $500 to $25,000

Money Market Investments*	Rate		Yield
JC Penney NB, Harrington De	4.41%	dA	4.51%
Columbia First, Arlington Va	4.25%	dC	4.40%
Metropolitan Bank, Arlington Va	4.30%	mA	4.39%
Key Bank USA, Albany NY	4.15%	mA	4.23%
New South FSB, Birmingham Al	4.15%	qA	4.22%
One Month CDs	**Rate**		**Yield**
Valley View State, Ovrlnd Prk Ks	4.00%	siA	4.00%
Pioneer Svgs, Newport Beach Ca	3.90%	dA	3.98%
Loyola Federal, Baltimore Md	3.75%	dA	3.82%
Topa Savings, Los Angeles Ca	3.80%	siA	3.80%
Colonial Bank, Santa Ana Ca	3.75%	siA	3.75%
Two Months CDs	**Rate**		**Yield**
Pioneer Svgs, Newport Beach Ca	4.00%	dA	4.08%
Valley View State, Ovrlnd Prk Ks	4.00%	siA	4.00%
Colonial Bank, Santa Ana Ca	4.00%	siA	4.00%
New South FSB, Birmingham Al	3.75%	siA	3.75%
Standard Pac, Newport Beach Ca	3.55%	dC	3.66%
Three Months CDs	**Rate**		**Yield**
Pioneer Svgs, Newport Beach Ca	4.10%	dA	4.18%
Eastern Savings, Baltimore Md	3.92%	dA	4.00%
Valley View State, Ovrlnd Prk Ks	4.00%	siA	4.00%
Colonial Bank, Santa Ana Ca	4.00%	siA	4.00%
New South FSB, Birmingham Al	3.95%	siA	3.95%

Pioneer Savings, 4.08% →

Six Months CDs	Rate		Yield
JC Penney NB, Harrington De	4.41%	dA	4.51%
Colonial National, Wilmington De	4.31%	dA	4.40%
AFBA Industrial, Colordo Sps Co	4.31%	dA	4.40%
Pioneer Svgs, Newport Beach Ca	4.30%	dA	4.39%
Fidelity Federal, Richmond Va	4.25%	qA	4.32%
One Year CDs	**Rate**		**Yield**
AFBA Industrial, Colordo Sps Co	4.78%	dA	4.90%
JC Penney NB, Harrington De	4.65%	dA	4.76%
Colonial National, Wilmington De	4.55%	dA	4.65%
First Deposit, Tilton NH	4.53%	dA	4.63%
Valley View State, Ovrlnd Prk Ks	4.50%	dA	4.60%
Two Years CDs	**Rate**		**Yield**
JC Penney NB, Harrington De	5.41%	dA	5.56%
Key Bank USA, Albany NY	5.30%	mA	5.43%
Fidelity Federal, Richmond Va	5.25%	qA	5.35%
Washington Savings, Waldorf Md	5.25%	qA	5.35%
Home Federal, Washington DC	5.15%	dA	5.28%
Five Years CDs	**Rate**		**Yield**
Astoria Federal, Lake Success NY	6.55%	dC	6.87%
Metropolitan Bank, Arlington Va	6.65%	qA	6.82%
New South FSB, Birmingham Al	6.60%	qA	6.77%
Domestic Bank, Cranston RI	6.56%	mA	6.76%
MBNA America, Newark De	6.50%	dA	6.72%

HIGH YIELD JUMBOS

Large minimum balance, generally $95,000 to $100,000

Money Market Investments*	Rate		Yield
JC Penney NB, Harrington De	4.41%	dA	4.51%
Columbia First, Arlington Va	4.25%	dC	4.40%
Metropolitan Bank, Arlington Va	4.30%	mA	4.39%
First Signature, Portsmouth NH	4.22%	dA	4.31%
Eastern Savings, Baltimore Md	4.21%	dA	4.30%
One Month Jumbo CDs	**Rate**		**Yield**
Astoria Federal, Lake Success NY	4.05%	siC	4.11%
Colonial Bank, Santa Ana Ca	4.00%	siA	4.00%
Valley View State, Ovrlnd Prk Ks	3.90%	siC	3.95%
Colonial National, Wilmington De	3.90%	siA	3.90%
Fidelity Federal, Glendale Ca	3.85%	siA	3.85%
Two Months Jumbo CDs	**Rate**		**Yield**
Astoria Federal, Lake Success NY	4.05%	siC	4.11%
Colonial Bank, Santa Ana Ca	4.00%	siA	4.00%
Colonial National, Wilmington De	3.95%	siA	3.95%
Valley View State, Ovrlnd Prk Ks	3.90%	siC	3.95%
Fidelity Federal, Glendale Ca	3.90%	siA	3.90%
Three Months Jumbo CDs	**Rate**		**Yield**
Comerce Securty, Sacramento Ca	4.25%	siA	4.25%
Astoria Federal, Lake Success NY	4.10%	siC	4.16%
Valley View State, Ovrlnd Prk Ks	4.00%	siC	4.06%
Fidelity Federal, Glendale Ca	4.05%	siA	4.05%
Colonial National, Wilmington De	4.00%	siA	4.00%

Six Months Jumbo CDs	Rate		Yield
Comerce Securty, Sacramento Ca	4.50%	siA	4.50%
AFBA Industrial, Colordo Sps Co	4.31%	dA	4.40%
Valley View State, Ovrlnd Prk Ks	4.25%	siC	4.31%
JC Penney NB, Harrington De	4.30%	siA	4.30%
Pioneer Svgs, Newport Beach Ca	4.30%	siA	4.30%
One Year Jumbo CDs	**Rate**		**Yield**
AFBA Industrial, Colordo Sps Co	4.78%	dA	4.90%
First Deposit, Tilton NH	4.55%	dA	4.65%
Comerce Securty, Sacramento Ca	4.63%	siA	4.63%
Valley View State, Ovrlnd Prk Ks	4.50%	siC	4.56%
Commercial Center, Santa Ana Ca	4.55%	siA	4.55%
Two Years Jumbo CDs	**Rate**		**Yield**
Key Bank USA, Albany NY	5.30%	mA	5.43%
First Deposit NCCB, Concord NH	5.18%	dA	5.32%
Ventura County, Oxnard Ca	5.25%	siA	5.25%
Commercial Center, Santa Ana Ca	5.25%	siA	5.25%
AFBA Industrial, Colordo Sps Co	5.12%	dA	5.25%
Five Years Jumbo CDs	**Rate**		**Yield**
MBNA America, Newark De	6.60%	dA	6.82%
Metropolitan Bank, Arlington Va	6.61%	mA	6.81%
Prudential Bank, Atlanta Ga	6.55%	dA	6.77%
Domestic Bank, Cranston RI	6.56%	mA	6.76%
New South FSB, Birmingham Al	6.75%	siA	6.75%

For more information call MASTERFUND at (800) 325-3242. MASTERFUND is registered with the FDIC as a deposit broker.

Source: BANXQUOTE, Wilmington, De. BANXQUOTE is a registered trademark and service mark of MASTERFUND INC.

Source: *The Wall Street Journal*, June 26, 1992

mutual funds. Your account will, however, be insured by the FDIC, which is not the case with money market mutual funds. Remember: the smaller the risk, the smaller the reward.

MONEY MARKET MUTUAL FUNDS

Investment companies establish mutual funds to pool the capital of many investors and thus create a large shared portfolio of investments. (Recall the earlier discussions of mutual funds in Chapter 9.) Individuals invest in mutual funds by purchasing shares in the fund, and the return on the portfolio is passed through to the investor according to the number of shares held. An enormous variety of mutual funds is available, designed for different types of investors and bearing a wide variety of yields.

Money market mutual funds invest principally in short-term investment instruments such as Treasury bills, commercial paper, bank certificates of deposit, bankers acceptances, and other liquid assets denominated in large amounts and therefore unavailable to the small

The Highest Yielders

Top performing money-market mutual funds.

NAME OF FUND	YIELD*	ASSETS (MILLIONS)	MIN. INITIAL INVESTMENT	CHECK WRITING
US Govt. Securities	4.69%	$103.7	$1,000	$500 min.
Dreyfus Basic MM	4.30	63.3	25,000	$1,000 min./fee
Olde Premium Plus	4.30	62.5	25,000	$500 min.
Aetna Money Market	4.20	27.1	1,000	$250 min.
Dreyfus Basic Govt.	4.17	33.1	25,000	$1,000 min./fee
Harbor Money Market	4.15	53.8	2,000	$500 min.
Riverside Capital	4.11	167.8	1,000	Not Available
Standby Reserve	4.07	637.5	2,000	$100 min.
Alger MM Portfolio	4.02	145.5	1,000	$500 min.
Value Line Cash	4.01	484.7	1,000	$500 min.

* *Seven-day compound yield, which assumes reinvestment of dividends, for week ended June 23, 1992.*
Source: IBC/Donoghue's Money Fund Report

Source: *The Wall Street Journal*, June 25, 1992

Money-Fund Assets Fall by $5.14 Billion

By a WALL STREET JOURNAL *Staff Reporter*

WASHINGTON – Assets of the nation's 595 money-market mutual funds fell by $5.14 billion to a total of $491.97 billion for the week ended Wednesday, the Investment Company Institute reported.

Assets of 283 general-purpose funds fell by $313.7 million to $172.43 billion. Assets of 219 institutional funds fell by $3.8 billion to $180.53 billion, and assets of the 93 broker-dealer funds fell by $1.03 billion to $139.02 billion.

There were no revisions of the figures of the prior week ended June 17.

Money Market Funds

Assets, in billions of dollars

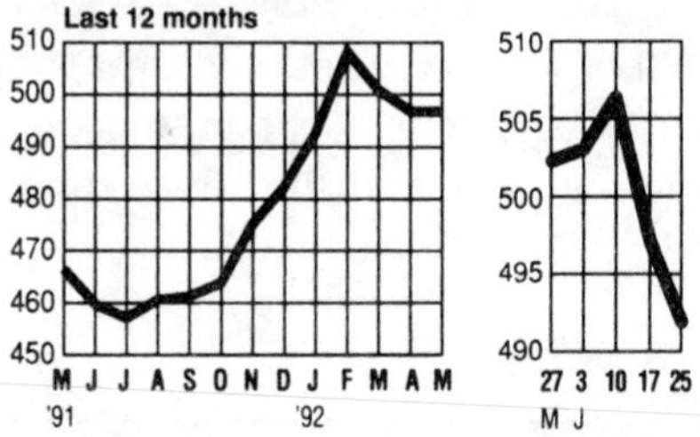

Source: Investment Company Institute

Source: *The Wall Street Journal*, June 26, 1992

investor. A money market mutual fund permits you to participate in the return on a variety of short-term investments and enjoy the benefits of diversification without employing large sums of your own capital. You also take advantage of the professional management skills of the investment company.

Most money market mutual funds are *no-load funds*. They do not charge a sales commission fee because they are directly marketed by the investment company. However, "management" fees are subtracted from the yield you receive. Money market mutual funds are issued and trade at a par value of one dollar. The dividends you receive are expressed as percentage yield.

Although money market funds sell their shares for a dollar each, most have minimum investment requirements ranging from $1,000 to $25,000. As an incentive, many money market funds also have check-writing privileges. Although these funds are not insured by the federal government, they are safe and liquid investments whose yields tend to be higher than the yields on bank money market accounts. Page 263 has an excerpt from the June 25, 1992 *Journal* that lists some of the top yielding funds at that time.

In the early 1980s, when the Federal Reserve applied a chokehold on the economy and interest rates climbed to the sky, money market mutual funds became popular among investors and savers. Since banks and S&Ls at the time were prohibited from offering above-passbook rates to small depositors, huge sums poured into the money market funds as their yields climbed above the legal passbook minimums. When the interest rate ceilings were removed from small denomination accounts at banks and S&Ls, and these accounts began to offer rates that moved with market conditions (and thus competed with the money market mutual funds), some investors deserted the money market funds. Once again, however, money market fund (not insured) rates generally outdo those at the banks (insured) and consequently remain very popular.

You can use a variety of reports in *The Wall Street Journal* to compare the performance of your money fund with others.

Every Thursday the *Journal* publishes a report and a chart called **Yields for Consumers** that compares money market fund yields with yields on bank certificates of deposit and money market accounts as well as a report on the size of money market funds' assets. As you can see from the June 25, 1992 excerpt on page 266, both yields and assets fell in the latest week. Notice that the average maturity of the investments in

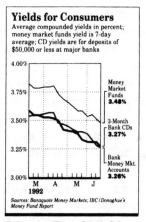

Yields for Consumers

Average compounded yields in percent; money market funds yield is 7-day average; CD yields are for deposits of $50,000 or less at major banks

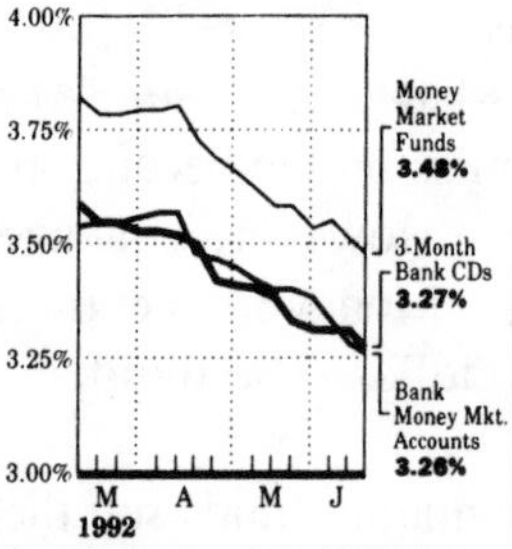

Sources: Banxquote Money Markets; IBC/Donoghue's Money Fund Report

Money-Fund Yields Slipped to New Lows In the Latest Week

By a WALL STREET JOURNAL *Staff Reporter*

Yields on money-market mutual funds slid to new lows in the latest week, as fund assets also declined.

The average seven-day compound yield on taxable funds eased to 3.48% from 3.50%, according to IBC/Donoghue's Money Fund Report. Compound yields assume reinvestment of dividends.

Assets of 548 taxable funds tracked by the Ashland, Mass., newsletter fell by $1.3 billion, to $486.3 billion. Institutional investors pulled $1.6 billion out of the 123 funds open only to them, while individual investors added $321 million to the remaining 425 funds.

Average Maturity

Average maturity of the funds' investments, which include commercial paper (short-term corporate IOUs) and Treasury bills, remained at 61 days, a sign that portfolio managers don't expect a drastic change in short-term interest rates any time soon.

Yield

The average seven-day simple yield on taxable funds slipped to 3.42% from 3.44%, while the average 30-day simple yield eased to 3.45% from 3.46% and the average 30-day compound yield slipped to 3.51% from 3.52%.

Yields on tax-exempt money funds dropped more sharply. The average seven-day compound yield fell to 2.44% from 2.53%, Donoghue's said. The latest yield is equivalent to a taxable 3.39% for an investor in the 28% tax bracket and to 3.54% for an investor paying 31% in taxes.

Assets of 301 tax-free funds tracked by Donoghue's fell by $873.7 million, to $95.1 billion. Average maturity lengthened by two days to 55 days.

Source: *The Wall Street Journal*, June 25, 1992

Average Maturity–Fourth Paragraph

Average maturity of the funds' investments, which include commercial paper (short-term corporate IOUs) and Treasury bills, remained at 61 days, a sign that portfolio managers don't expect a drastic change in short-term interest rates any time soon.

Source: The *Wall Street Journal*, June 25, 1992

Yield–Fifth and Sixth Paragraph

The average seven-day simple yield on taxable funds slipped to 3.42% from 3.44%, while the average 30-day simple yield eased to 3.45% from 3.46% and the average 30-day compound yield slipped to 3.51% from 3.52%.

Yields on tax-exempt money funds dropped more sharply. The average seven-day compound yield fell to 2.44% from 2.53%, Donoghue's said. The latest yield is equivalent to a taxable 3.39% for an investor in the 28% tax bracket and to 3.54% for an investor paying 31% in taxes.

Source: The *Wall Street Journal*, June 25, 1992

these funds (T-bills, CDs, commercial paper, etc.) "remained at 61 days." Many fund managers lock in longer yields on longer maturities in order to enjoy those higher yields for as long as possible if they think interest rates will fall, and shorter maturities when they believe rates will rise. Since the length of maturity had remained unchanged, the author of the article felt that money fund managers had taken a wait-and-see attitude.

MONEY MARKET MUTUAL FUNDS

The following quotations, collected by the National Association of Securities Dealers Inc., represent the average of annualized yields and dollar-weighted portfolio maturities ending Wednesday, June 24, 1992. Yields don't include capital gains or losses.

Fund	Avg. Mat.	7Day Yld.	e7Day Yld.	Assets
Money Market:				
FrkIFTGS	46	3.62	3.69	195
FrkFdl b	18	2.93	2.97	151
FrnkGvt	30	3.63	3.70	45
FreeCsh	52	3.18	3.23	1083
FreeGv	62	3.19	3.24	321
FremntMM	67	3.36	3.42	30
FrkMny	35	3.00	3.05	1199
FdTrMny	65	3.49	3.52	44
GT Mny	51	2.90	2.94	93
GW Glob	68	3.80	3.87	72
GW Gv	72	3.34	3.40	44
Gab OC DP	39	3.52	3.58	164
Gab OC Mgr	46	3.44	3.50	17
Gab OC UST	71	3.43	3.49	322
GalaxyGv	22	3.60	3.67	460
GalxyMM	56	3.53	3.59	708
GalaxTr	61	3.49	3.55	427
GnGvSec	87	3.62	3.69	648
GnMMkt	87	3.47	3.53	698
GSILGv f	60	3.52	3.58	2680
GSILMM f	63	3.76	3.83	1241
GSILTrsOblg f	51	3.48	3.54	1836
GSILPO f	62	3.64	3.71	4659
GSILTrsInst	57	3.53	3.60	329
GvInvTr	52	2.76	2.80	108
GradCshR	56	3.43	3.48	602
GradUS	66	3.18	3.23	32
GrtHallGv	58	3.19	3.24	61
GrtHallPr	63	3.33	3.38	842
GrdCsFd	22	3.35	3.41	347
GrdCsMg	23	3.13	3.18	39
HTInsgtCs	64	3.45	3.51	248
HTInsgtGv	77	3.36	3.42	159
HanvCsh	60	3.31	3.36	252
HanvGov	69	3.36	3.42	402
HanvTreas	83	3.37	3.43	217
HelmsPr	67	3.48	3.54	954
HelmsUS	48	3.30	3.35	398
HrtgCsh	37	3.16	3.20	949
InfCCR	88	3.04	3.08	231
InflnPeg	65	4.11	4.19	201
InstCsh	84	3.83	3.90	439
InstFd	36	3.30	3.35	8
InstGov	30	3.63	3.70	202
InvCshGv	19	3.46	3.52	108
Invesco	16	3.65	3.72	133
InvCshRsv	49	2.98	3.02	16
IvyMny	15	3.06	3.01	18
JanMS Gov	55	3.19	3.24	262
JanMS MM	62	3.27	3.32	282
JHanCshM	62	3.27	3.32	216
KemperGvt	16	3.64	3.70	992
KemperM	45	3.53	3.59	5767
KeyLqd	55	2.97	3.01	233
KldPeCsh	41	3.17	3.21	1890
KldPeGv	38	3.15	3.20	415
KldPePr	40	3.21	3.26	859
LandUSTr	65	3.19	3.24	454
LdmkCs	48	3.29	3.34	489
LdmkPrmLq	48	3.59	3.65	582
LaurlUSO	22	3.39	3.45	37
LaurGII	45	3.68	3.75	436
LaurPrI	57	3.57	3.64	105
LaurPrII	59	3.73	3.80	791
LaurlUSI	59	3.47	3.53	73
LauUSTr	44	3.63	3.69	494
LegMUS	80	3.41	3.47	175
LegMCR f	84	3.45	3.51	774
LehPFd	56	3.73	3.80	2869
LehPFdT	43	3.73	3.80	381
LehPTCs	39	3.82	3.89	3008
LehPTFd	44	3.73	3.80	1406
LehPTmp	29	3.72	3.79	25109
LehPTrs	54	3.55	3.61	1596
LexGvSc a	55	2.88	2.92	19
Lexingt a	55	3.02	3.06	121
LibtyUS	41	3.18	3.23	1110
Liq Ins Gv	43	3.46	3.52	129
LiqInt	36	3.60	3.66	300
LiqCshTr f	2	3.70	3.77	853
LqdGrTr	50	2.87	2.92	136
LrdAbCR	35	2.74	2.78	148
LosanvPr	58	3.34	3.40	105
LosnTr	47	3.31	3.37	362
LuthrnBr	47	2.88	2.92	370
MIMLIC a	32	3.06	3.11	27
MainSty	57	3.42	3.47	191
MngdCsh	77	3.59	3.66	343
MngdGv	26	3.30	3.36	99
Map Gvt	79	3.65	3.72	37
MarinCsh	67	3.81	3.88	266
MarineGv	79	3.89	3.96	215
MarinerUS	49	3.30	3.35	192
MassCash	58	3.01	3.06	456
MassCsGv	66	2.95	2.99	44
McDonald	87	3.17	3.22	276
McDnldUS	83	3.50	3.56	148
ML CBAMon	80	3.54	3.60	1259
ML CMAGv	72	3.36	3.42	4188
ML CMAMn	86	3.47	3.53	27440
MerLyGv	55	3.54	3.60	1332
MerLITr	56	3.23	3.28	294
MerLyIn	69	3.68	3.75	2009
MerLyRdy	87	3.43	3.49	8158
MerLyRet	88	3.47	3.53	6568
ML CMATr	80	3.15	3.20	1172
MerLyUSA	79	3.21	3.26	587
ML US Tr	79	3.10	3.15	61
MetLfStMM	47	3.21	3.26	167
MdIncTrGv	58	3.02	3.07	96
MdIninst	57	3.44	3.50	51
NationsFdTr	43	3.39	3.45	94
Natns FGvt	57	3.50	3.56	391
Natns FMM	53	3.59	3.65	548
NatwMM	46	3.25	3.30	516
NeubCsh	72	3.31	3.36	292
NeubGvt	82	3.32	3.37	318
Newton	47	3.59	3.67	264
Nicholas	24	3.42	3.48	153
OldeMM	84	3.23	3.27	149
OldePrPl	89	4.22	4.30	62
OldePrem	86	3.69	3.76	197
OppMoney	57	3.52	3.58	798
OvldExMM	70	3.23	3.29	230
PFAMCo MM	38	3.52	3.58	10
PNC Gvt	46	3.46	3.52	183
PNC Prm	55	3.46	3.52	592
PcHrzPr	69	3.71	3.77	7639
PcHrzTr	50	3.42	3.47	2730
PacificGv	82	3.56	3.62	188
Pacifica	77	3.78	3.85	135
PW Cash	56	3.49	3.55	3915
PW MstrM b	67	1.75	1.77	28
PW RMA	61	3.58	3.64	4123
PW RM US	69	3.44	3.50	868
PW Retr	60	3.37	3.43	2182
ParagTr	52	3.60	....	312
ParkPr	65	3.53	3.59	700
ParkUS	87	3.56	3.62	390
Phonix	64	3.27	3.32	178
PillarPrObA	41	3.00	3.04	32
PillarUST A	46	2.96	3.00	233
PionrCs	47	3.18	3.23	67
PionUS	48	3.26	3.31	25
PiprMM	62	3.08	3.12	1196
PiprUS	65	3.13	3.18	198
PortgeGv	43	3.18	3.23	49
PortInstMn	38	3.62	3.68	698
PortMM	50	3.48	3.54	151
PortUS	41	3.41	3.47	191
PortUSFed	31	3.32	3.38	42
Prem US	65	3.44	3.50	169
PrimeCsh	34	3.22	3.27	205
PrVlCsh	74	3.85	3.92	1328
PrVlRdy	65	3.65	3.72	174
PrVlUS	41	3.56	3.62	592
PrVlTr	82	3.46	3.52	352
PrincorCash	61	3.42	3.48	233
PrvMut	25	2.39	2.41	34
PruCdGvt	66	3.42	3.48	377
PruCdMny	58	3.46	3.52	2175
RimcoTrs	45	3.40	3.46	60
RIMCOPrm	68	3.89	3.96	169
RiversdeCap	21	4.02	4.10	165
RdSqMM	64	3.59	3.65	742
RdSqUS	39	3.40	3.46	414
RshFGI	38	3.08	3.13	752
Rshmre	17	3.06	3.11	96
SBK MMFT	52	3.18	3.23	46
SBK TMMFT	50	3.11	3.16	154
SBSF MM	62	3.48	3.54	15
SEI CsPrB	59	3.57	3.63	12
SEI CsPrC	59	3.37	3.42	81
SEI CsFd	50	3.45	3.51	242
SEI CsGv	60	3.77	3.84	528
SEI CsMM	48	3.75	3.82	247
SEI CsPr	59	3.87	3.94	1582
SEI LqCl	30	3.40	3.46	20
SEI LqGv	60	3.73	3.80	406
SEI LqPr	59	3.66	3.72	1538
SEI LqTr	49	3.66	3.73	2311
SEI LqTII	48	3.46	3.52	42
SEICsTrA	54	3.69	3.75	296
SEICsTrB	54	3.39	3.45	23
Safeco f	47	3.32	3.37	172
StClair	52	3.32	3.38	216
SalTMMI	43	3.45	3.51	187
SalmMMI	76	3.31	3.36	67
SalTMMT	43	3.75	3.82	297
SalomonUST	70	3.50	3.56	43
SchbValAdv	73	3.84	3.91	52
SchwbGv	77	3.48	3.54	1624
SchbMM	74	3.46	3.52	5594
Schb UST	79	3.28	3.33	78
ScudCshIn	55	3.35	3.41	1385
Scud UST	69	3.36	3.42	316
SecurityCsh	41	2.87	2.91	63
SelectGv	39	3.00	3.04	23
SelectIn	33	3.22	3.27	124
SeligCsh Gvt	50	3.09	3.13	25
SeligCsh pr	33	3.13	3.18	219
SentinelCsh	59	2.87	2.91	49
SevnSea f	76	3.86	3.93	3429
SvnSeaGv r	89	3.68	3.75	115
SLB MMP	79	3.03	3.08	249
ShrtTrA	36	3.34	3.40	20
ShrtTmMM a	60	3.56	3.62	697
ShTrInUS a	48	3.33	3.38	581
SmBarCash	54	3.40	3.46	1789
SmBarGvt	54	3.40	3.46	408
SmBarRetir	57	3.35	3.40	1010
Standby	80	3.99	4.07	641
StarbGovT	63	3.40	3.46	166
StarbMMT	65	3.73	3.80	178
SteinroeCRs	62	3.48	3.54	726
SteinroeGvt	63	3.33	3.39	133
Strong	74	3.75	3.82	441
StrongUST	84	3.67	3.74	25
SumtCsh	51	3.19	3.24	229
SunamCs	32	2.66	2.74	30
SunamMM	53	2.70	2.78	233
TCW MM	69	3.88	3.95	184
TNE MN	68	3.48	3.54	927
TNE USGv	73	3.26	3.31	80
TRAK GovMon	86	3.40	3.46	21
TRowPRF f	68	3.28	3.33	3879
TRowUST f	68	3.25	3.30	610
TempltnM	59	2.83	2.87	132
ThomMB	19	2.91	2.94	54
ThmNtGv	41	3.08	3.13	99
ThmNtl	44	3.24	3.29	2359
ThoroPO	32	3.36	3.41	189
ThoroUS	58	3.27	3.32	250
USAA Mutl	71	3.81	3.88	941
USAA Treas	77	3.63	3.70	22
USFG Cs	37	3.17	3.22	30
UST Gvt	29	3.51	3.57	1109
UST Mny	40	3.58	3.64	747
UST Treas	76	3.29	3.34	201
USTrCshIns	46	3.56	3.62	94
US TreCs	44	3.22	3.27	51
UnionInst	77	3.73	3.79	257
UnionInv	77	3.48	3.54	142
UtdCshM	68	2.87	2.91	451
UtdGvt	72	4.60	4.70	104
VIMMP	60	3.88	3.96	230
ValLin	57	3.92	4.00	484
VnEckUS a	29	2.10	2.12	27
VanKmpMM	60	2.77	2.80	25
VangFdl f	60	3.70	3.77	1925
VangPr f	59	3.72	3.79	12836
VangUST	59	3.59	3.66	2239
VantgCsh	55	3.38	3.44	1108
VantgGvt	51	3.33	3.38	307
VlsnMM	48	3.74	3.81	143
VlsnTr	40	3.50	3.56	106
VistaUS	47	3.18	3.23	331
Voyager	48	3.38	3.44	76
WPG GovMM	49	2.97	3.01	104
WestcrCs	30	3.51	3.50	200
WestcrGv	40	3.34	3.35	88
WestcrPr	34	3.51	3.51	86
WestcrTr	49	3.28	3.32	128
WoodGv	71	3.71	3.71	287
WoodMM	65	3.65	3.72	992
WorkAsets	60	3.11	3.16	227
WrightMgd	39	3.24	3.29	21
ZweigGvt	64	3.63	3.70	98
Tax Exempt:				
AARPHTe	46	1.95	1.97	129
ASO TxEx	53	2.45	2.48	35
AT OhioTx	46	2.44	2.47	259
ActAsCal	52	1.79	1.80	176
ActAstTx	43	2.24	2.26	1323
AlxB TF	40	2.11	2.13	268
AllMuNY	76	2.72	2.76	101
AllIaMun	69	2.61	2.64	951
AllTxCal	58	2.62	2.65	125
AmExCal	30	2.33	2.36	638
AmExTxDD	66	2.34	2.37	3434
AmExNY	71	2.15	2.17	561
AmbTxFr	68	2.66	2.70	96
ArchFd	44	2.10	2.12	134
CalvTxFr	14	2.96	3.00	1692
CapTFB	39	2.40	2.43	11
CardTx	17	1.93	1.95	85
CashEq	45	2.45	2.48	1315
CsTrIIMun	49	2.61	2.65	85
CshTrMuni	55	2.31	2.34	543
Centn CA	23	2.31	2.34	49
CentenTx	38	2.35	2.38	947
ColTEx	48	2.13	2.15	28
CmpPATx	13	2.27	2.29	24
Comp NJ Tx	72	2.10	2.12	33
CompCap	23	2.42	2.45	64
CmpCshTx	60	2.36	2.39	36
CnstgTF	25	2.54	2.58	56
ConnDly	39	1.98	2.00	164
Core TF	58	2.47	2.50	76
CortldTx	49	2.33	2.35	204
DallTx c	11	2.79	2.83	648
DWSears	56	2.16	2.19	744
DWSrCal	56	2.32	2.34	304
DWSrNY	40	1.58	1.59	51
DelaTax	78	2.32	2.35	55
DryInvMuni	87	3.08	3.13	179
DryCTMu	70	2.49	2.52	213
DreyCalTx	45	2.60	2.63	312
DrMI Mun	34	2.53	2.56	95
DrNJMun	36	2.45	2.48	811
DrNYTE	74	2.11	2.13	407
DRPA Mun	60	2.81	2.85	121
DreyTxEx c	70	2.27	2.30	1493
DyrMAMun	53	2.61	2.64	65
DryOHMu	62	2.81	2.85	49
EatnVn	10	2.17	2.20	36
Emblem	56	2.21	2.24	158
EvgrnCal	51	2.80	2.84	38
EvgrnTE	65	2.99	3.03	436
FFB PA TF	45	2.64	2.67	20
FFB TF	53	2.47	2.50	95
FMMNCsh	49	2.34	2.36	77
FMOHIns	53	2.80	2.84	82
FMPACsh	63	2.24	2.27	19
FN Netwk	56	2.13	2.15	49
FMMASv	51	2.37	2.40	89
FMPASvc	63	2.64	2.68	305
FMMNIn	49	2.74	2.77	149
FMCTSvc	65	2.21	2.24	115
FdOHMuII	53	2.50	2.53	81
FedTxF c	51	2.50	2.53	1715
FldTxEx	50	2.70	2.74	2563
FldCA	51	2.28	2.30	547
FldCT	48	2.28	2.30	379
FldDlyTE	60	2.45	2.48	415
FldMA	45	1.87	1.88	642
FldMI	42	2.39	2.42	179
FldNJ	75	2.36	2.38	358
FldNY	62	2.15	2.17	528
FldOH	55	2.62	2.66	261
FldSpCA	49	2.77	2.81	938
FldSpCT	51	2.75	2.79	48
FldSpNJ	78	2.78	2.82	343
FldSpNY	62	2.31	2.34	468
FldSpPA	42	2.58	2.61	253
FldTxEx	55	2.53	2.56	2718
FldSpMu	65	3.02	3.07	1228
FldSpMA	68	2.54	2.57	282
FinclTxFr	37	2.36	2.39	62
FtInvTax	40	2.34	2.37	26
FtPraTE	33	2.46	2.49	221
FrkCal	21	2.20	2.22	765
FrkNYTE	36	1.77	1.78	63
FrkTx c	41	2.26	2.29	213
Free CA	19	2.33	2.36	62

← Tax-exempt funds

Merrill Lynch Cash Management Account → (ML CMAMn)

Source: The *Wall Street Journal*, June 25, 1992

Merrill Lynch Cash Management Account → ML CMAMn

McDonald	87	3.17	3.22	276
McDnldUS	83	3.50	3.56	148
ML CBAMon	80	3.54	3.60	1259
ML CMAGv	72	3.36	3.42	4188
ML CMAMn	86	3.47	3.53	27440
MerLyGv	55	3.54	3.60	1332
MerLITr	56	3.23	3.28	294
MerLyIn	69	3.68	3.75	2009
MerLyRdy	87	3.43	3.49	8158
MerLyRet	88	3.47	3.53	6568
ML CMATr	80	3.15	3.20	1172
MerLyUSA	79	3.21	3.26	587
ML US Tr	79	3.10	3.15	61
MetLfStMM	47	3.21	3.26	167
MdIncTrGv	58	3.02	3.07	96

Source: The *Wall Street Journal*, June 25, 1992

Money Market Mutual Funds, published every Thursday in the *Journal,* lists the most popular money market mutual funds (see the index on page C1). Several statistics are given for each: the average maturity of the investments in the fund, the 7-day yield for the week (average yield), the effective 7-day yield (after reinvesting and compounding interest earned), and the total assets in millions of dollars as of the previous day. (See the above examples from the June 25, 1992 *Journal.*)

You can track the performance of your money market mutual fund and most others with this report. For instance, Merrill Lynch's Cash Management fund had an average maturity of 86 days, yields of 3.47 percent and 3.53 percent, and assets of $27.44 billion. Finally, note that tax-exempt funds are listed separately and have lower yields.

CERTIFICATES OF DEPOSIT

Certificates of deposit (CDs) are like savings accounts for which you receive a "certificate of deposit" from the bank or savings and loan company. Banks and S&Ls issue certificates of deposit to compete with Treasury bills and commercial paper for the investor's dollar. CDs that have maturities of one year or less are part of the money market.

CDs offer higher rates than bank money market accounts, but you pay a price in penalties for early withdrawal of funds. Jumbo ($90,000-$100,000) certificates purchased through a broker are the only exception and then only if the broker can sell the CD to another investor. When you

Yields on CDs Show Little Change in Week

By a WALL STREET JOURNAL *Staff Reporter*

NEW YORK – Yields on certificates of deposit at major banks and brokerage firms were little changed in the week ended Tuesday.

The average yields on small-denomination consumer CDs sold directly by banks were mixed. The average yield on six-month consumer CDs rose to 3.46% from 3.44%, according to an 18-bank survey by Banxquote Money Markets, a Wilmington, Del., information service. The average yield on five-year consumer CDs slipped to 6.07% from 6.08%.

BANXQUOTE® INDEX

Tuesday, June 23, 1992

AVERAGE YIELDS OF 18 LEADING BANKS

	Savings Yield	Wkly Chg.	Jumbo Yield	Wkly Chg.
Money Market	3.26	....	3.50	−0.02
1 Month CD	....	....	3.31	+0.01
2 Month CD	....	....	3.34	+0.01
3 Month CD	3.27	−0.01	3.43	+0.01
6 Month CD	3.46	+0.02	3.57	+0.01
1 Year CD	3.84	−0.01	3.95	−0.01
2 Year CD	4.62	+0.01	4.70	−0.02
5 Year CD	6.07	−0.01	6.08	−0.03

AVERAGE YIELDS OF LEADING BROKERS

	3 Mo.	6 Mo.	1 Yr.	2 Yr.	5 Yr.
Savings CD	3.30	3.45	3.80	4.35	6.15
Weekly Change	....	....	−0.15	−0.10	−0.05

Source: BANXQUOTE, WILMINGTON De.

At leading brokerage firms, the average yield on six-month CDs remained at 3.45%, while the five-year average yield dropped to 6.15% from 6.20%.

On jumbo CDs at major banks, which typically require deposits of $90,000 or more, the average yield on six-month CDs inched up to 3.57% from 3.56%. The average yield for five-year jumbo CDs eased to 6.08% from 6.11%.

Source: The *Wall Street Journal*, June 24, 1992

tie up your funds until maturity, the CD becomes a non-liquid asset. This disadvantage is offset to some extent by FDIC deposit insurance.

You can often get a higher CD rate from your broker than your local bank or S&L because your broker can shop nationally for the highest CD rate. You won't pay a fee for this service because the bank pays the broker.

Every Wednesday *The Wall Street Journal* publishes an article on current certificates of deposit yields which accompanies the **Banxquote Index.** Page 270 provides an example from the June 24, 1992 issue. The **Banxquote Index** presents the average yields paid by 18 leading banks for money market accounts and for one, two, three, and six months and for one, two, and five year CDs (minimum balance of $500 to $10,000) and jumbos (minimum balance of $90,000 to $100,000) along with weekly interest rate changes and rates paid on accounts offered by brokers.

HIGH YIELD SAVINGS

Small minimum balance, generally $500 to $25,000

Pioneer Savings, 4.0% rate, 4.08% yield →

Valley View State Bank, 4.0% rate, 4.0% yield →

Money Market Investments*	Rate		Yield
JC Penney NB, Harrington De	4.41%	dA	4.51%
Columbia First, Arlington Va	4.25%	dC	4.40%
Metropolitan Bank, Arlington Va ...	4.30%	mA	4.39%
Key Bank USA, Albany NY	4.15%	mA	4.23%
New South FSB, Birmingham Al	4.15%	qA	4.22%
One Month CDs	**Rate**		**Yield**
Valley View State, Ovrlnd Prk Ks ..	4.00%	slA	4.00%
Pioneer Svgs, Newport Beach Ca ...	3.90%	dA	3.98%
Loyola Federal, Baltimore Md	3.75%	dA	3.82%
Topa Savings, Los Angeles Ca	3.80%	slA	3.80%
Colonial Bank, Santa Ana Ca	3.75%	slA	3.75%
Two Months CDs	**Rate**		**Yield**
→ Pioneer Svgs, Newport Beach Ca ...	4.00%	dA	4.08%
→ Valley View State, Ovrlnd Prk Ks ..	4.00%	slA	4.00%
Colonial Bank, Santa Ana Ca	4.00%	slA	4.00%
New South FSB, Birmingham Al	3.75%	slA	3.75%
Standard Pac, Newport Beach Ca ..	3.55%	dC	3.66%
Three Months CDs	**Rate**		**Yield**
Pioneer Svgs, Newport Beach Ca ...	4.10%	dA	4.18%
Eastern Savings, Baltimore Md	3.92%	dA	4.00%
Valley View State, Ovrlnd Prk Ks ..	4.00%	slA	4.00%
Colonial Bank, Santa Ana Ca	4.00%	slA	4.00%
New South FSB, Birmingham Al	3.95%	slA	3.95%

Six Months CDs	Rate		Yield
JC Penney NB, Harrington De	4.41%	dA	4.51%
Colonial National, Wilmington De ..	4.31%	dA	4.40%
AFBA Industrial, Colordo Sps Co ...	4.31%	dA	4.40%
Pioneer Svgs, Newport Beach Ca ...	4.30%	dA	4.39%
Fidelity Federal, Richmond Va	4.25%	qA	4.32%
One Year CDs	**Rate**		**Yield**
AFBA Industrial, Colordo Sps Co ...	4.78%	dA	4.90%
JC Penney NB, Harrington De	4.65%	dA	4.76%
Colonial National, Wilmington De ..	4.55%	dA	4.65%
First Deposit, Tilton NH	4.53%	dA	4.63%
Valley View State, Ovrlnd Prk Ks ..	4.50%	dA	4.60%
Two Years CDs	**Rate**		**Yield**
JC Penney NB, Harrington De	5.41%	dA	5.56%
Key Bank USA, Albany NY	5.30%	mA	5.43%
Fidelity Federal, Richmond Va	5.25%	qA	5.35%
Washington Savings, Waldorf Md ...	5.25%	qA	5.35%
Home Federal, Washington DC	5.15%	dA	5.28%
Five Years CDs	**Rate**		**Yield**
Astoria Federal, Lake Success NY .	6.55%	dC	6.87%
Metropolitan Bank, Arlington Va ...	6.65%	qA	6.82%
New South FSB, Birmingham Al	6.60%	qA	6.77%
Domestic Bank, Cranston RI	6.56%	mA	6.76%
MBNA America, Newark De	6.50%	dA	6.72%

Source: The *Wall Street Journal*, June 1992

Two days later, on Fridays, the *Journal* publishes the more comprehensive **Banxquote Money Markets, High Yield Savings**, and **High Yield Jumbos**. Return to the June 26, 1992 example on page 262 (and blown-up on page 271). It reports CD interest rates by locale, maturity, and size. Note that CDs are quoted by rate and yield in the "high yield" portions of the table. The more frequently interest is compounded, the higher the yield for each rate. Look under **High Yield Savings**, two-month CDs and you'll notice that both Pioneer Savings in Newport Beach, California and Valley View State Bank in Overland Park, Kansas quote rates of 4.00 percent. However, because Pioneer compounds daily (denoted by *dA*) and Valley View pays simple interest (*siA*), the yield is higher at Pioneer (4.08 percent) than at Valley View (4.00 percent).

It pays to shop, too. You can see on page 262 that while the average 3-month CD paid 3.27 percent, the broker average was 3.3 percent, and Pioneer's yield was 4.08 percent.

TREASURY BILLS

Our national debt made the news when it passed $4 trillion, and it continues to grow. Treasury bills (T-bills) constitute about a quarter of the total national debt, and this huge dollar volume makes Treasury bills one of the most important short-term investment instruments.

The U.S. Treasury borrows by selling bills at auction (primary market) every Monday in New York, and in the following day's *Journal* you will find a summary at the end of the **Credit Markets** article of the U.S. Treasury's Monday auction of 13- and 26-week bills (see the indexes at the front of the first and last sections). An example drawn from the Tuesday, June 23, 1992 edition of the *Journal* appears on pages 273 and 274.

Treasury bills are sold on a discount basis. Buyers pay less than the $10,000 face value (par value), the amount they will receive when the bill matures and is redeemed by the U.S. Treasury. If bidding is strong and the price is high, the effective rate of interest will be low and vice versa.

To understand how this works, place yourself in the role of a buyer. If you pay $9,750 for a bill maturing in 91 days (about a quarter of a year), your effective annual yield is approximately 10 percent. Remember, $250 in a quarter-year is the equivalent of $1,000 in a year, or 10 percent of a $10,000 base. (Use $10,000 as the base for calculating the discount rate,

CREDIT MARKETS

Treasury Securities

Bond prices ended modestly lower in quiet trading.

The Treasury's 30-year bond was quoted late at 101 24/32 to yield 7.84% down from 101 27/32 to yield 7.83%.

The Treasury auctioned $23.37 billion in three-month and six-month bills at its regular weekly auction. Three-month bills were sold at an average discount rate of 3.67% for a coupon-equivalent yield of 3.76%. Six-month bills were sold at an average discount rate of 3.77% to yield 3.90%.

The average discount rates for both the three-month and six-month issues were up from last week's auction when they were 3.66% and 3.75%, respectively.

Here are the details of yesterday's auction by the Treasury of 13-week and 26-week bills:

Rates are determined by the difference between the purchase price and face value. Thus, higher bidding narrows the investor's return while lower bidding widens it. The percentage rates are calculated on a 360-day year, while the coupon-equivalent yield is based on a 365-day year.

	13-Week	26-Week
Applications	$46,743,360,000	$36,345,760,000
Accepted bids	$11,732,380,000	$11,641,680,000
Accepted at low price	38%	58%
Accepted noncompet'ly ...	$1,294,085,000	$858,540,000
Average price (Rate)	99.072 (3.67%)	98.094 (3.77%)
High price (Rate)	99.077 (3.65%)	98.104 (3.75%)
Low price (Rate)	99.072 (3.67%)	98.094 (3.77%)
Coupon equivalent	3.76%	3.90%
CUSIP number	912794YY4	912794ZW7

Both issues are dated June 25. The 13-week bills mature Sept. 24, 1992, and the 26-week bills mature Dec. 24, 1992.

Source: The *Wall Street Journal*, June 23, 1992

On Monday, June 22, 1992 the U.S. Treasury auctioned 13-week bills in the primary market at an average price of $9,907.20 and a discount of $92.80, for a discount rate of 3.67% and a coupon equivalent of 3.76%.

Here are the details of yesterday's auction by the Treasury of 13-week and 26-week bills:

Rates are determined by the difference between the purchase price and face value. Thus, higher bidding narrows the investor's return while lower bidding widens it. The percentage rates are calculated on a 360-day year, while the coupon-equivalent yield is based on a 365-day year.

	13-Week	26-Week
Applications	$46,743,360,000	$36,345,760,000
Accepted bids	$11,732,380,000	$11,641,680,000
Accepted at low price	38%	58%
Accepted noncompet'ly ...	$1,294,085,000	$858,540,000
Average price (Rate)	99.072 (3.67%)	98.094 (3.77%)
High price (Rate)	99.077 (3.65%)	98.104 (3.75%)
Low price (Rate)	99.072 (3.67%)	98.094 (3.77%)
Coupon equivalent	3.76%	3.90%
CUSIP number	912794YY4	912794ZW7

Both issues are dated June 25. The 13-week bills mature Sept. 24, 1992, and the 26-week bills mature Dec. 24, 1992.

Source: The *Wall Street Journal*, June 23, 1992

rather than $9,750, because Treasury bills' yields are usually quoted on a discount basis; that is, the discount—$250—is measured against face value—$10,000.) If strong bidding drives the price to $9,875, your yield falls to 5 percent. If weak bidding or selling pressure permits the price to fall to $9,500, the effective yield rises to 20 percent. The more you pay for the Treasury bill, the lower your yield and vice versa. These examples are summarized here. You can easily approximate the following discount rates using this simple table.

Face (redemption) Value	$10,000	$10,000	$10,000
Selling Price	$9,875	$9,750	$9,500
(note: prices falling)			
Discount (difference)	$125	$250	$500
Approximate Yield (Discount Rate)	5%	10%	20%
(note: yield rising)			

Take a moment to review the method used to compute the discount rate in the bottom row of the above table. The following calculations show how the 10 percent rate was obtained. Discount rate (Yield) = Discount expressed as a percentage of par (yield) × Time factor multiplier (which is needed to generate the annual rate).

$$\text{Approximate discount rate (yield)} = \frac{\text{Discount}}{\text{Face or par value}} \times 4 \quad \text{(because 91 days are about a quarter of a 365-day year)}$$

$$= \frac{\$250}{\$10{,}000} \times 4$$

$$= 2.5\% \times 4$$

$$= 10\%$$

The true discount-rate formula is very close to this approximation. The "time factor multiplier" is somewhat different because the "year" is 360 days. Again returning to the example, the discount rate would be calculated as follows:

$$\text{Discount rate} = \frac{\text{Discount}}{\text{Par value}} \times \text{Time multiplier}$$

$$= \frac{\$250}{\$10{,}000} \times \frac{360}{91}$$

$$= 0.0989$$

$$= 9.89\%$$

You can see that the true discount rate of 9.89 is less than the 10 percent approximation calculated above because the time multiplier (360/91) is less than 4.

The discount rate is only an approximation of the true yield to maturity or coupon equivalent. In the first place, the purchase price of the T-bill was $9,750, not $10,000. So in the fraction below, $9,750 replaces $10,000. And secondly, a year is 365 days, not 360. Thus, the correct time multiplier is 365/91.

Now calculate the actual yield, called the investment yield to maturity, for the same example.

$$\text{Yield to maturity} = \frac{\text{Discount}}{\text{Purchase price}} \times \text{Time Factor}$$

$$= \frac{\$250}{\$9,750} \times \frac{365}{91}$$

$$= 0.1029$$

$$= 10.29\%$$

You can see that the discount rate of 9.89% is less than the true yield of 10.29 percent because the discount is expressed as a percentage of the purchase price rather than par, and the year is calculated at 365 rather than 360 days.

Why are T-bills quoted on a discount- rather than true-yield basis? Because the arithmetic is much easier to deal with, and that was important years ago before the advent of data processing equipment.

Now that you understand the relationship between the discount rate and the yield to maturity (coupon equivalent), look at the illustration on page 274 from the Tuesday, June 23, 1992 *Journal*. Potential buyers submitted $46,743,360,000 in bids of which the Treasury accepted $11,732,380,000. The Treasury took the highest bid of $9,907.70 (99.077 percent of par) and then accepted progressively lower bids until it generated the required funds, stopping at the low bid of $9,907.20 (9907.20 percent of $10,000). On the average, the U.S. Treasury received $9,907.20 (99.072 percent of face value) for each $10,000 bill auctioned (same as the low price) on Monday, June 22, 1992 for a discount rate of 3.67 percent and a coupon equivalent yield of 3.76 percent. Note that in over $11 billion of successful bids, only 50 cents separated the high and low bids. It's a tough business.

Here is how you calculate the discount rate using the Treasury auction figures on page 274.

$$\text{Discount Rate} = \frac{\text{Discount}}{\text{Par value}} \times \text{Time multiplier}$$

$$= \frac{\$92.80 \text{ (i.e., } \$10,000 - \$9,907.20)}{\$10,000} \times \frac{360}{91}$$

$$= 0.0367$$

$$= 3.67\%$$

You can also compute the true (coupon equivalent) yield as follows.

$$\text{Yield to maturity} = \frac{\text{Discount}}{\text{Purchase price}} \times \text{Time multiplier}$$

$$= \frac{\$92.80}{\$9{,}907.20} \times \frac{365}{91}$$

$$= 0.0376$$

$$= 3.76\%$$

Your motivation for buying Treasury bills is probably quite simple: you have idle cash on which you wish to earn an interest return. If you and all other bidders for Treasury bills have ample funds and are eager to buy, you will drive the price close to $10,000 and earn a low rate of return. If you and all other bidders do not have ample funds, you can be enticed only by a very low price for the right to receive $10,000 in 91 days, and you will earn a high rate of return.

Now, this discussion has been presented as if you could participate in the bidding for Treasury bills. Well, you can't. The auction is conducted in New York by the Fed, acting as the Treasury's agent, and bidding is conducted by large firms that deal in, and make a market for, Treasury bills. They bid for the bills at the weekly Monday auction (primary market) so they can resell them at a markup on any business day (secondary market).

You *can* go to your local regional Federal Reserve Bank and buy Treasury bills, but you'll have to do so noncompetitively at the average rate (discount) established at the New York auction. (For instance, the 3.67 percent discount rate and 3.76 percent yield in the example on page 274). Note that the Treasury accepted $1,294,085,000 of bids noncompetitively on June 22, 1992. These were bids made directly to the Fed by individuals and small institutions who could not participate in the auction.

There are two ways to buy T-bills from the Fed: immediately or by opening an account that permits purchases at a later date.

TREASURY BONDS, NOTES & BILLS

Wednesday, April 8, 1992

Representative Over-the-Counter quotations based on transactions of $1 million or more.

Treasury bond, note and bill quotes are as of mid-afternoon. Colons in bid-and-asked quotes represent 32nds; 101:01 means 101 1/32. Net changes in 32nds. n-Treasury note. Treasury bill quotes in hundredths, quoted on terms of a rate of discount. Days to maturity calculated from settlement date. All yields are to maturity and based on the asked quote. Latest 13-week and 26-week bills are boldfaced. For bonds callable prior to maturity, yields are computed to the earliest call date for issues quoted above par and to the maturity date for issues below par. -When issued.

Source: Federal Reserve Bank of New York.

U.S. Treasury strips as of 3 p.m. Eastern time, also based on transactions of $1 million or more. Colons in bid-and-asked quotes represent 32nds; 101:01 means 101 1/32. Net changes in 32nds. Yields calculated on the asked quotation. ci-stripped coupon interest. bp-Treasury bond, stripped principal. np-Treasury note, stripped principal. For bonds callable prior to maturity, yields are computed to the earliest call date for issues quoted above par and to the maturity date for issues below par.

Source: Bear, Stearns & Co. via Street Software Technology Inc.

GOVT. BONDS & NOTES

Rate	Maturity Mo/Yr	Bid	Asked	Chg.	Ask Yld.
11¾	Apr 92n	100:04	100:06	– 1	0.00
8⅞	Apr 92n	100:08	100:10	– 1	3.06
6⅝	May 92n	100:08	100:10	....	3.28
9	May 92n	100:15	100:17	....	3.34
13¾	May 92n	100:30	101:00	....	3.14
8½	May 92n	100:19	100:21	....	3.65
8¼	Jun 92n	100:31	101:01	....	3.50
8⅜	Jun 92n	100:30	101:00	– 1	3.76
10⅜	Jul 92n	101:20	101:22	– 1	3.82
8	Jul 92n	101:06	101:08	....	3.83
4¼	Aug 87-92	99:19	100:03	+ 3	3.95
7¼	Aug 92	101:02	101:04	+ 1	3.94
7⅞	Aug 92n	101:08	101:10	....	4.01
8¼	Aug 92n	101:13	101:15	....	3.93
8⅛	Aug 92n	101:17	101:19	....	3.93
8⅛	Sep 92n	101:27	101:29	....	4.01
8¾	Sep 92n	102:05	102:07	....	3.96
4⅞	Jan 94n	99:13	99:15	....	5.19
6⅞	Feb 94n	102:25	102:27	+ 1	5.24
8⅞	Feb 94n	106:06	106:08	....	5.28
9	Feb 94	106:15	106:19	+ 1	5.22
5⅜	Feb 94n	100:05	100:07	....	5.25
5¾	Mar 94n	100:26	100:28	+ 1	5.28
8½	Mar 94n	105:26	105:28	+ 2	5.32
7	Apr 94n	103:05	103:07	+ 1	5.29
4⅛	May 89-94	94:26	95:10	– 1	6.55
7	May 94n	103:02	103:04	+ 1	5.40
9½	May 94n	107:28	107:30	+ 1	5.44
13⅛	May 94n	115:05	115:07	+ 2	5.36
8½	Jun 94n	106:05	106:07	+ 1	5.49
8	Jul 94n	105:05	105:07	+ 1	5.52
6⅞	Aug 94n	102:25	102:27	+ 1	5.57
8⅝	Aug 94n	106:17	106:19	+ 1	5.59
8¾	Aug 94	106:28	107:00	+ 1	5.53
12⅝	Aug 94n	115:09	115:11	....	5.57
8½	Sep 94n	106:15	106:17	+ 1	5.63
9½	Oct 94n	108:24	108:26	+ 1	5.69
6	Nov 94n	100:23	100:25	+ 1	5.67
8¼	Nov 94n	105:30	106:00	+ 1	5.73
10⅛	Nov 94	110:09	110:11	+ 2	5.78
11⅝	Nov 94n	113:30	114:00	+ 1	5.75
7⅝	Dec 94n	104:19	104:21	+ 1	5.75
8⅝	Jan 95n	106:30	107:00	+ 1	5.85
3	Feb 95	94:10	95:10	....	4.78
5½	Feb 95n	99:07	99:09	+ 2	5.78
7¾	Feb 95n	104:29	104:31	+ 1	5.83
10½	Feb 95	111:26	111:28	+ 2	5.91
11¼	Feb 95n	113:25	113:27	+ 1	5.90
8⅜	Apr 95n	106:17	106:19	+ 1	5.95
8½	May 95n	106:30	107:00	+ 1	5.99
10⅜	May 95	111:31	112:01	+ 1	6.06
11¼	May 95n	114:15	114:17	+ 2	6.04
12⅝	May 95	118:14	118:18	– 1	5.97
8⅞	Jul 95n	107:31	108:01	+ 1	6.12
8½	Aug 95n	106:31	107:01	+ 2	6.15
10½	Aug 95n	112:26	112:28	+ 1	6.19
8⅝	Oct 95n	107:08	107:10	+ 1	6.27
8½	Nov 95n	106:29	106:31	+ 1	6.30
9½	Nov 95n	110:03	110:05	+ 1	6.30
11½	Nov 95	116:13	116:17	+ 1	6.29
9¼	Jan 96n	109:08	109:10	....	6.43
7½	Jan 96n	103:18	103:20	....	6.41
7⅞	Feb 96n	104:23	104:25	....	6.45
8⅞	Feb 96n	108:02	108:04	– 1	6.46
7½	Feb 96n	103:16	103:18	– 1	6.45
7¾	Mar 96n	104:10	104:12	– 1	6.48
9⅜	Apr 96n	109:26	109:28	– 3	6.54
7⅝	Apr 96n	103:24	103:26	– 2	6.54
7⅜	May 96n	102:25	102:27	– 3	6.57
7⅝	May 96n	103:21	103:23	– 3	6.58
7⅞	Jun 96n	104:17	104:19	– 2	6.61
7⅞	Jul 96n	104:15	104:17	– 3	6.64
7⅞	Jul 96n	104:16	104:18	– 3	6.64
7¼	Aug 96n	102:05	102:07	– 3	6.66
7	Sep 96n	101:08	101:10	– 2	6.66
8	Oct 96n	104:30	105:00	– 3	6.70
6⅞	Oct 96n	100:22	100:24	– 3	6.68
7¼	Nov 96n	102:02	102:04	– 3	6.71
6½	Nov 96n	99:08	99:10	– 4	6.67
6⅛	Dec 96n	97:30	98:00	– 4	6.62
8	Jan 97n	104:31	105:01	– 3	6.75
6¼	Jan 97n	98:05	98:07	– 4	6.69
6¾	Feb 97n	99:31	100:01	– 4	6.74
6⅞	Mar 97n	100:16	100:18	– 4	6.74
8½	Apr 97n	106:31	107:01	– 3	6.82
8½	May 97n	106:30	107:00	– 4	6.85
8½	Jul 97n	106:30	107:00	– 4	6.89
8⅝	Aug 97n	107:16	107:18	– 4	6.91
8¾	Oct 97n	108:01	108:03	– 5	6.96
8⅞	Nov 97n	108:19	108:21	– 5	6.98
7⅞	Jan 98n	103:28	103:30	– 4	7.03
8⅛	Feb 98n	105:01	105:03	– 2	7.05
7⅞	Apr 98n	103:25	103:27	– 4	7.08
7	May 93-98	100:09	100:17	– 1	6.49
9	May 98n	109:04	109:06	– 4	7.12
8¼	Jul 98n	105:13	105:15	– 5	7.15
9¼	Aug 98n	110:14	110:16	– 3	7.16
7⅛	Oct 98n	100:00	100:02	– 4	7.11
3½	Nov 98	94:27	95:27	+ 1	4.23
8⅞	Nov 98n	108:20	108:22	– 4	7.20
6⅜	Jan 99n	96:03	96:05	– 3	7.10
8⅞	Feb 99n	108:21	108:23	– 4	7.24
8½	May 94-99	104:19	104:27	– 2	6.01
9⅛	May 99n	110:02	110:04	– 4	7.27
8	Aug 99n	103:29	103:31	– 5	7.29
7⅞	Nov 99n	103:05	103:07	– 5	7.32
7⅞	Feb 95-00	102:04	102:30	– 3	6.97
9¼	Feb 16	113:16	113:18	– 15	7.97
7¼	May 16	92:10	92:12	– 13	7.97
7½	Nov 16	94:28	94:30	– 13	7.97
8¾	May 17	108:11	108:13	– 15	7.97
8⅞	Aug 17	109:29	109:31	– 8	7.95
9⅛	May 18	112:19	112:21	– 16	7.97
9	Nov 18	111:09	111:11	– 16	7.97
8⅞	Feb 19	109:29	109:31	– 15	7.97
8⅛	Aug 19	101:20	101:22	– 15	7.97
8½	Feb 20	105:29	105:31	– 15	7.96
8¾	May 20	108:24	108:26	– 15	7.96
8¾	Aug 20	108:24	108:26	– 15	7.96
7⅞	Feb 21	99:01	99:03	– 14	7.96
8⅛	May 21	101:28	101:30	– 15	7.95
8⅛	Aug 21	101:28	101:30	– 16	7.95
8	Nov 21	100:23	100:25	– 15	7.93

U.S. TREASURY STRIPS

Mat.	Type	Bid	Asked	Chg.	Ask Yld.
May 92	ci	99:20	99:20	....	3.79
Aug 92	ci	98:20	98:20	+ 1	3.99
Nov 92	ci	97:20	97:20	+ 1	4.07
Feb 93	ci	96:14	96:15	+ 6	4.29
May 93	ci	95:05	95:06	+ 3	4.56
Aug 93	ci	93:20	93:21	+ 1	4.92
Nov 93	ci	92:05	92:06	+ 2	5.16
Feb 94	ci	90:23	90:25	+ 1	5.30
May 94	ci	89:12	89:14	+ 2	5.40
Aug 94	ci	87:22	87:24	+ 4	5.64
Nov 94	ci	86:04	86:06	+ 4	5.81
Nov 94	np	86:01	86:03	+ 1	5.85
Feb 95	ci	84:15	84:17	+ 2	5.99
Feb 95	np	84:12	84:14	+ 2	6.03
May 95	ci	82:28	82:30	+ 1	6.13
May 95	np	82:26	82:28	+ 2	6.16
Aug 95	ci	81:10	81:13	+ 2	6.24
Aug 95	np	81:06	81:09	+ 2	6.29
Nov 95	ci	79:29	79:31	+ 5	6.31
Nov 95	np	79:22	79:24	+ 2	6.39
Feb 96	ci	77:24	77:26	+ 1	6.62
Feb 96	np	77:21	77:24	– 2	6.65
May 96	ci	76:08	76:11	+ 1	6.70
May 96	np	75:31	76:02	– 2	6.79
Aug 96	ci	74:25	74:28	+ 4	6.77
Nov 96	ci	73:14	73:17	+ 3	6.80
Nov 96	np	73:09	73:12	– 2	6.85
Feb 97	ci	71:22	71:26	– 3	6.95
May 97	ci	70:09	70:12	+ 5	7.01
May 97	np	69:22	69:26	– 4	7.18
Aug 97	ci	68:25	68:28	+ 4	7.09
Aug 97	np	68:15	68:18	– 3	7.18
Nov 97	ci	67:16	67:19	+ 5	7.12
Nov 97	np	66:30	67:02	– 4	7.27
Feb 98	ci	65:26	65:30	– 1	7.25
Feb 98	np	65:17	65:20	– 3	7.33
May 98	ci	64:15	64:19	– 1	7.30
May 98	np	64:10	64:14	– 4	7.34
Aug 98	ci	63:05	63:09	– 1	7.34
Aug 98	np	63:03	63:06	– 3	7.36
Nov 98	ci	61:31	62:03	– 1	7.36
Nov 98	np	61:12	61:16	– 4	7.51
Feb 99	ci	60:13	60:16	– 1	7.47
Feb 99	np	60:10	60:14	– 4	7.49
May 99	ci	59:02	59:06	– 3	7.53
May 99	np	59:06	59:10	– 4	7.50
Aug 99	ci	57:27	57:31	– 3	7.56
Aug 99	np	57:27	57:31	– 4	7.56
Nov 99	ci	56:24	56:28	– 2	7.57
Nov 99	np	56:24	56:28	– 4	7.57
Feb 00	ci	55:11	55:15	– 4	7.65

Mat.	Type	Bid	Asked	Chg.	Bid Yld.
Feb 00	np	55:17	55:21	– 4	7.61
May 00	ci	54:08	54:12	– 4	7.67
May 00	np	54:12	54:16	– 4	7.64
Aug 00	ci	53:04	53:08	– 4	7.69
Aug 00	np	53:10	53:14	– 4	7.65
Nov 00	ci	52:02	52:06	– 4	7.71
Nov 00	np	52:09	52:13	– 4	7.66
Feb 01	ci	50:26	50:30	– 5	7.77
Feb 01	np	51:05	51:09	– 4	7.69
May 01	ci	49:25	49:29	– 7	7.79
May 01	np	50:01	50:05	– 4	7.73
Aug 01	ci	48:25	48:29	– 7	7.80
Aug 01	np	49:00	49:04	– 4	7.75
Nov 01	ci	47:27	48:00	– 7	7.80
Nov 01	np	48:01	48:05	– 4	7.76
Feb 02	ci	46:16	46:20	– 8	7.90
May 02	ci	45:17	45:21	– 8	7.92
Aug 02	ci	44:19	44:23	– 7	7.93
Nov 02	ci	43:21	43:25	– 7	7.95
Feb 03	ci	42:22	42:27	– 9	7.97
May 03	ci	41:25	41:30	– 9	7.99
Aug 03	ci	40:30	41:02	– 8	8.00
Nov 03	ci	40:03	40:07	– 8	8.01
Feb 04	ci	39:07	39:11	– 4	8.03
May 04	ci	38:12	38:16	– 4	8.05
Aug 04	ci	37:16	37:21	– 5	8.07
Nov 04	ci	36:25	36:29	– 4	8.07
Nov 04	bp	36:24	36:28	– 5	8.08
Feb 05	ci	35:29	36:02	– 6	8.10
May 05	ci	35:06	35:10	– 5	8.11
May 05	bp	35:07	35:11	– 6	8.10
Aug 05	ci	34:15	34:19	– 6	8.11
Aug 05	bp	34:12	34:16	– 6	8.13
Nov 05	ci	33:26	33:30	– 5	8.11
Feb 06	ci	32:27	33:00	– 12	8.17
Feb 06	bp	33:03	33:07	– 5	8.12
May 06	ci	32:05	32:10	– 12	8.18
Aug 06	ci	31:15	31:19	– 13	8.19
Nov 06	ci	30:26	30:30	– 14	8.20
Feb 07	ci	30:06	30:10	– 8	8.20
Feb 17	ci	13:11	13:14	– 6	8.24
May 17	ci	13:03	13:06	– 6	8.24
May 17	bp	13:06	13:09	– 7	8.21
Aug 17	ci	12:26	12:29	– 6	8.24
Aug 17	bp	12:29	13:00	– 8	8.21
Nov 17	ci	12:18	12:21	– 6	8.24
Feb 18	ci	12:11	12:14	– 6	8.23
May 18	ci	12:03	12:06	– 6	8.23
May 18	bp	12:06	12:09	– 7	8.20
Aug 18	ci	11:27	11:30	– 6	8.23
Nov 18	ci	11:21	11:24	– 5	8.22
Nov 18	bp	11:24	11:26	– 7	8.19
Feb 19	ci	11:13	11:16	– 6	8.22
Feb 19	bp	11:17	11:20	– 7	8.18
May 19	ci	11:06	11:09	– 6	8.22
Aug 19	ci	11:00	11:02	– 5	8.21
Aug 19	bp	11:04	11:07	– 7	8.16
Nov 19	ci	10:26	10:28	– 5	8.20
Feb 20	ci	10:21	10:24	– 6	8.17
Feb 20	bp	10:23	10:26	– 9	8.15
May 20	ci	10:16	10:18	– 5	8.16
May 20	bp	10:18	10:21	– 7	8.13
Aug 20	ci	10:10	10:12	– 5	8.15
Aug 20	bp	10:13	10:16	– 8	8.11
Nov 20	ci	10:04	10:07	– 5	8.14
Feb 21	ci	9:30	10:01	– 6	8.13
Feb 21	bp	10:02	10:05	– 7	8.09
May 21	ci	9:26	9:29	– 5	8.11
May 21	bp	9:29	9:31	– 8	8.08
Aug 21	ci	9:22	9:25	– 6	8.08
Aug 21	bp	9:23	9:26	– 7	8.07
Nov 21	ci	9:19	9:22	– 3	8.06
Nov 21	bp	9:23	9:26	– 2	8.00

TREASURY BILLS

Treasury Bills

Maturity	Days to Mat.	Bid	Asked	Chg.	Ask Yld.
Apr 16 '92	6	3.99	3.89	– 0.02	3.96
Apr 23 '92	13	4.00	3.90	....	3.97
Apr 30 '92	20	3.94	3.84	– 0.04	3.91
May 07 '92	27	3.80	3.70	– 0.06	3.77
May 14 '92	34	3.80	3.76	– 0.04	3.84
May 21 '92	41	3.83	3.79	– 0.03	3.87
May 28 '92	48	3.83	3.79	– 0.02	3.87
Jun 04 '92	55	3.84	3.80	– 0.04	3.89
Jun 11 '92	62	3.83	3.81	– 0.03	3.90
Jun 18 '92	69	3.84	3.82	– 0.02	3.91
Jun 25 '92	76	3.84	3.82	....	3.92
Jul 02 '92	83	3.88	3.86	– 0.02	3.96
Jul 09 '92	**90**	**3.87**	**3.85**	....	**3.95**
Jul 16 '92	97	3.85	3.83	– 0.03	3.93
Jul 23 '92	104	3.87	3.85	– 0.04	3.96
Jul 30 '92	111	3.87	3.85	– 0.04	3.96
Aug 06 '92	118	3.90	3.88	– 0.02	4.00
Aug 13 '92	125	3.91	3.89	– 0.02	4.01
Aug 20 '92	132	3.92	3.90	– 0.01	4.02
Aug 27 '92	139	3.93	3.91	– 0.02	4.04
Sep 03 '92	146	3.94	3.92	– 0.02	4.04
Sep 10 '92	153	3.94	3.92	– 0.02	4.04
Sep 17 '92	160	3.94	3.92	– 0.02	4.04
Sep 24 '92	167	3.93	3.91	– 0.02	4.05
Oct 01 '92	174	3.96	3.94	– 0.01	4.07
Oct 08 '92	**181**	**3.96**	**3.94**	**– 0.02**	**4.08**
Oct 22 '92	195	3.97	3.95	– 0.03	4.10
Nov 19 '92	223	3.98	3.96	– 0.04	4.11
Dec 17 '92	251	4.00	3.98	– 0.02	4.14
Jan 14 '93	279	4.04	4.02	– 0.03	4.19
Feb 11 '93	307	4.07	4.05	– 0.03	4.23
Mar 11 '93	335	4.09	4.07	– 0.03	4.25
Apr 08 '93	363	4.13	4.11	– 0.03	4.30

Source: *The Wall Street Journal*, June 23, 1992

TREASURY BILLS

Maturity	Days to Mat.	Bid	Asked	Chg.	Ask Yld.
Jun 25 '92	1	2.85	2.75	−0.22	2.80
Jul 02 '92	8	3.57	3.47	+0.10	3.53
Jul 09 '92	15	3.45	3.35	+0.02	3.41
Jul 16 '92	22	3.50	3.40	+0.02	3.46
Jul 23 '92	29	3.51	3.47	+0.05	3.54
Jul 30 '92	36	3.52	3.48	+0.02	3.55
Aug 06 '92	43	3.55	3.51	+0.02	3.58
Aug 13 '92	50	3.54	3.50	+0.02	3.58
Aug 20 '92	57	3.55	3.51	−0.01	3.59
Aug 27 '92	64	3.57	3.55	−0.01	3.63
Sep 03 '92	71	3.59	3.57	−0.02	3.65
Sep 10 '92	78	3.61	3.59	−0.01	3.67
Sep 17 '92	**85**	**3.64**	**3.62**	**−0.01**	**3.70**
Sep 24 '92	92	3.66	3.64	−0.01	3.74
Oct 01 '92	99	3.67	3.65	....	3.74
Oct 08 '92	106	3.68	3.66	+0.01	3.75
Oct 15 '92	113	3.69	3.67	....	3.76
Oct 22 '92	120	3.69	3.67	−0.01	3.78
Oct 29 '92	127	3.70	3.68	−0.01	3.78
Nov 05 '92	134	3.72	3.70	−0.01	3.80
Nov 12 '92	141	3.73	3.71	−0.01	3.82
Nov 19 '92	148	3.74	3.72	....	3.84
Nov 27 '92	156	3.75	3.73	....	3.84
Dec 03 '92	162	3.75	3.73	−0.01	3.85
Dec 10 '92	169	3.75	3.73	....	3.85
Dec 17 '92	**176**	**3.75**	**3.73**	**−0.01**	**3.86**
Jan 14 '93	204	3.77	3.75	−0.01	3.89
Feb 11 '93	232	3.83	3.81	−0.02	3.95
Mar 11 '93	260	3.85	3.83	−0.03	3.97
Apr 08 '93	288	3.90	3.88	−0.02	4.03
May 06 '93	316	3.94	3.92	−0.02	4.08
Jun 03 '93	344	3.95	3.93	−0.02	4.10

On Monday, June 22,1992, → the 91-day T-bill rate on the open (secondary) market was 3.64% for bills auctioned on Monday June 15, issued on Thursday, June 18 and maturing 13 weeks later on Thursday, September 17.

Source: *The Wall Street Journal*, June 23, 1992

INTEREST Fed Funds (NY Fed, Babcock Fulton Prebon)

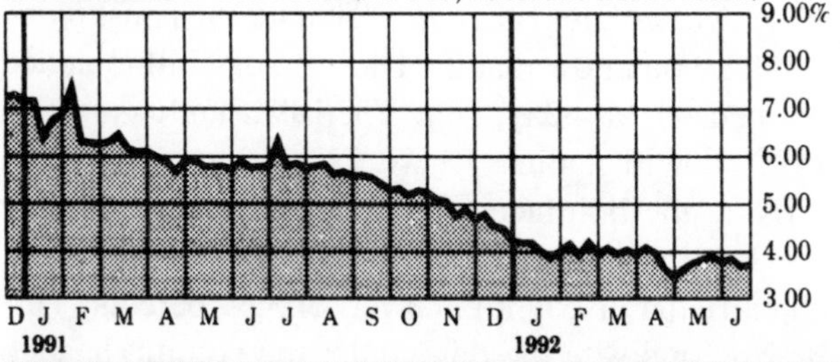

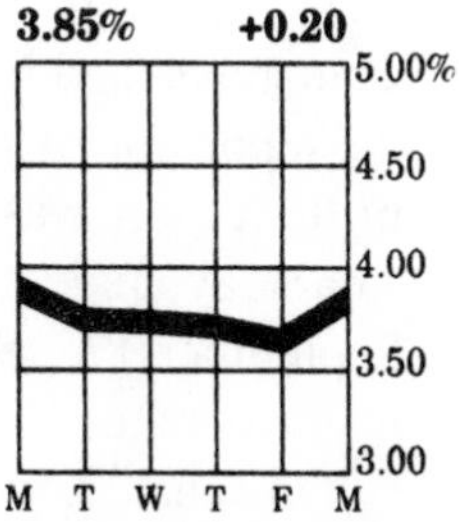

ISSUE	CLOSE	FRI	YEAR AGO	12-MO HIGH	12-MO LOW
3-month T-bill	**3.64%**	3.65%	5.56%	5.61%	3.54%
3-month CD (new)	**3.41**	3.41	5.80	5.80	3.41
Dealer Comm. Paper (90 days)	**3.90**	3.88	6.08	6.15	3.78
3-month Eurodollar deposit	**4.00**	3.94	6.19	6.19	3.81

Source: *The Wall Street Journal*, June 23, 1992

If you want to purchase Treasuries right away, obtain what is called a "Tender" form from the Fed or your bank, fill out the "Direct Deposit" section and include a money order or certified check for $10,000. The Fed will mail you your change (the discount) and return the $10,000 at maturity (91 days).

If you wish to open an account to purchase Treasuries in the near future, complete and return the "New Account Application." Once the application is received and you are given an account number, you can then contact the Fed by phone and purchase Treasuries with a tender offer and certified check for the exact amount.

If you purchase a Treasury bill from the Fed, you must hold it to maturity, which is not the case if you have purchased it from your bank or broker in the secondary market. Your bank or broker can sell it on the open or secondary market for you at any time, but be prepared to pay a flat fee of $25 to $50 per transaction. In order to gain clients with large assets, however, some brokerage houses do not charge a fee if an investor purchases more than $100,000 of Treasury bills.

The Wall Street Journal reports on activity in the secondary market each day, under the heading **Treasury Bonds, Notes & Bills**. Find this table by using the index on the front page or the index on the first page of Section C.

Look at the excerpt from the Tuesday, June 23, 1992 *Journal* on pages 278 and 279. The data represent quotations for Monday, June 22, 1992. Keep in mind that these bills are auctioned on Mondays, issued on Thursdays, and mature 13 weeks later (also on a Thursday). Thus, using the report for June 22, 1992, you know that the latest 91-day bill included in the report was auctioned on Monday, June 15, 1992, and issued on Thursday, June 18, 1992. It will mature 13 weeks later, on Thursday, September 17, 1992. (Note the boldface type for the 13- and 26-week maturity dates.)

On June 22, that bill carried a discount rate (bid) of 3.64 percent. This figure is located in the row opposite the date under the column headed "Bid." Buyers (bidders) paid a price (less than $10,000) that would yield 3.64 percent if the Treasury bill were held to maturity and cashed in for $10,000. Sellers on September 18 were asking a higher price (lower interest rate) equivalent to 3.62 percent. The last column gives the true yield of 3.70 percent. (The other maturity dates are for older bills and for bills with maturities of more than 91 days.)

It is now time to complete this discussion of short-term interest rates with a description of how you can track the yield on your own interest-earning investments and compare them with market rates.

TRACKING SHORT-TERM INTEREST RATES

Every day you can use the **Markets Diary** report on the left side of the first page (Cl) of the *Journal's* last section to follow some of the most important short-term interest rates. Consult the excerpt from the Tuesday, June 23, 1992 edition on page 279, starting with the chart labeled **Interest**, which displays the *federal funds* rate for the preceding 18 months. This is the rate banks charge one another for overnight loans of reserves in amounts of $1 million or more. The federal funds rate was 3.85 percent on June 22, 1992. Four more interest rates follow. Except for Treasury bills, which were discussed above, these quotes are for instruments purchased by financial institutions in very large amounts. Nonetheless, they provide a good daily snapshot of current short-term rates. Note that the yields increase with increased risk and reduced liquidity. The June 22, 1992 rates were 3-month T-bills, 3.64 percent (as noted above), new 3-month certificates of deposit, 3.41 percent, 90-day commercial paper (short-term corporate debt), 3.90 percent; and 3-month Eurodollar deposits ("dollar" denominated deposits held at European banks), 4.00 percent.

You can follow an even larger array of interest rates each day in **Money Rates**, a report that lists the current yields on most of the major money market interest-rate instruments. Look for it in the front-page index of the first and last sections. The example from the Tuesday, June 23, 1992 *Journal* on page 282 reports the rates for Monday, June 22, 1992. **Money Rates** tracks the following domestic rates: *Prime Rate* (rate banks charge their corporate customers), *Federal Funds, Discount Rate* (rate the Federal Reserve charges its member banks), *Call Money* (rate banks charge brokers), *Commercial Paper, Certificates of Deposit, Bankers Acceptances* (rates on corporate or business credit used in international trade, backed by a bank), *Treasury Bills, Federal Home Loan Mortgage Corp.* (rates on a variety of mortgages), *Federal National Mortgage Association* (also rates on a variety of mortgages), and *Merrill*

MONEY RATES

Monday, June 22, 1992

The key U.S. and foreign annual interest rates below are a guide to general levels but don't always represent actual transactions.

PRIME RATE: 6½%. The base rate on corporate loans posted by at least 75% of the nation's 30 largest banks.

FEDERAL FUNDS: 3⅞% high, 3¾% low, 3 13/16% near closing bid, 3⅞% offered. Reserves traded among commercial banks for overnight use in amounts of $1 million or more. Source: Babcock Fulton Prebon (U.S.A.) Inc.

DISCOUNT RATE: 3½%. The charge on loans to depository institutions by the Federal Reserve Banks.

CALL MONEY: 5¾% to 6%. The charge on loans to brokers on stock exchange collateral.

COMMERCIAL PAPER placed directly by General Electric Capital Corp.: 3.80% 30 to 119 days; 3.82% 120 to 149 days; 3.85% 150 to 179 days; 3.87% 180 to 199 days; 3.97% 200 to 270 days. Commercial Paper placed directly by General Motors Acceptance Corp.: 3.80% 30 to 149 days; 3.85% 150 to 179 days; 3.90% 180 to 270 days.

COMMERCIAL PAPER: High-grade unsecured notes sold through dealers by major corporations in multiples of $1,000: 3.88% 30 days; 3.88% 60 days; 3.90% 90 days.

CERTIFICATES OF DEPOSIT: 3.32% one month; 3.36% two months; 3.41% three months; 3.51% six months; 3.73% one year. Average of top rates paid by major New York banks on primary new issues of negotiable C.D.s, usually on amounts of $1 million and more. The minimum unit is $100,000. Typical rates in the secondary market: 3.80% one month; 3.85% three months; 3.90% six months.

BANKERS ACCEPTANCES: 3.75% 30 days; 3.75% 60 days; 3.76% 90 days; 3.78% 120 days; 3.83% 150 days; 3.84% 180 days. Negotiable, bank-backed business credit instruments typically financing an import order.

LONDON LATE EURODOLLARS: 3 15/16% - 3 13/16% one month; 3 15/16% - 3 13/16% two months; 4% - 3⅞% three months; 4 1/16% - 3 15/16% four months; 4 1/16% - 3 15/16% five months; 4⅛% -4% six months.

LONDON INTERBANK OFFERED RATES (LIBOR): 3 15/16% one month; 4% three months; 4⅛% six months; 4½% one year. The average of interbank offered rates for dollar deposits in the London market based on quotations at five major banks. Effective rate for contracts entered into two days from date appearing at top of this column.

FOREIGN PRIME RATES: Canada 7%; Germany 11%; Japan 5.25%; Switzerland 11.38%; Britain 10%. These rate indications aren't directly comparable; lending practices vary widely by location.

TREASURY BILLS: Results of the Monday, June 22, 1992, auction of short-term U.S. government bills, sold at a discount from face value in units of $10,000 to $1 million: 3.67%, 13 weeks; 3.77%, 26 weeks.

FEDERAL HOME LOAN MORTGAGE CORP. (Freddie Mac): Posted yields on 30-year mortgage commitments. Delivery within 30 days 8.27%, 60 days 8.34%, standard conventional fixed-rate mortgages; 5.75%, 2% rate capped one-year adjustable rate mortgages. Source: Telerate Systems Inc.

FEDERAL NATIONAL MORTGAGE ASSOCIATION (Fannie Mae): Posted yields on 30 year mortgage commitments (priced at par) for delivery within 30 days 8.25%, 60 days 8.33%, standard conventional fixed rate-mortgages; 5.85%, 6/2 rate capped one-year adjustable rate mortgages. Source: Telerate Systems Inc.

MERRILL LYNCH READY ASSETS TRUST: 3.44%. Annualized average rate of return after expenses for the past 30 days; not a forecast of future returns.

Source: The *Wall Street Journal*, June 23, 1992

Lynch Ready Assets Trust (a money market mutual fund). **Money Rates** also tracks foreign money market rates including: *London Late Eurodollars, London Interbank Offered Rates* (similar to federal funds), and *Foreign Prime Rates* of different countries. These interest rates are discussed more thoroughly below.

Federal Funds Rate

Banks lend reserves to one another overnight at the federal funds rate. This practice is profitable for lender banks because they earn interest on funds ($1 million or more) that would otherwise be idle, and it is profitable for the borrower banks because they acquire reserves that enable them to make additional loans and still meet their reserve requirement.

Notice that under *Federal Funds* in the *Money Rates* column on page 282, four different percentages are listed: 3-7/8 percent high, 3-3/4 percent low, 3-13/16 percent near closing bid, and 3-7/8 percent offered. These numbers show that during trading on Monday, June 22, 1992, 3-7/8 percent was the highest interest rate proposed by a potential lender bank, and 3-3/4 percent was the lowest interest rate proposed by a prospective borrower. The last two percentages describe the state of trading near the end of the day: lender banks were offering 3-7/8 percent, and borrower banks were bidding 3-13/16 percent. Use the closing bid (3-13/16 percent) when following this interest rate.

This rate is closely watched as an indicator of Federal Reserve monetary policy. A rising federal funds rate is a sign that the Fed is draining reserves from the banks via its open market operations, forcing some banks to borrow excess reserves from other banks and thereby driving up the federal funds rate. A falling rate would indicate an easy money policy. But beware: sharp fluctuations occur from day to day. This is such a short-term market that the rate changes on an "as needed" basis.

Investor's Tip

- Follow the federal funds chart under Interest in the Markets Diary on page Cl, because it presents a weekly average that smooths out sharp daily movements.

Commercial Paper

The excerpt on page 282 (second set of quotes) lists 3.9 percent as the going rate for 90-day commercial paper on June 22, 1992. Commercial paper is short-term, unsecured debt issued by the very largest corporations. It is the equivalent of the Treasury bill, so in order to attract investors, its rate of interest has to be higher.

Corporations issue commercial paper to avoid the higher interest rate (prime rate) levied by banks on business borrowers and is issued for maturities up to 270 days. There are very large minimums set on commercial paper purchases (often in excess of $1 million), and this instrument is very popular with money market funds.

Prime Rate

This is the rate that large commercial banks charge their best corporate customers. Although it does not change as frequently as other market rates, it is an important indicator of supply and demand in the capital markets. Banks raise the prime rate whenever they have difficulty meeting the current demand for funds, or when the Federal Reserve drains away their reserves through its open market operations.

Bankers Acceptances

Bankers Acceptances are used to finance international trade. Large institutions, investment companies, and money market mutual funds purchase bankers acceptances because they offer high yields for relatively short periods of time. Individual investors benefit from the higher yields when they invest in funds that include these instruments.

Call Rates

The call rate is the rate that banks charge brokers, who generally add 1 percent on loans to their clients.

Key Interest Rates

Annualized interest rates on certain investments as reported by the Federal Reserve Board on a weekly-average basis:

	Week Ended: June 19, 1992	June 12, 1992
Treasury bills (90 day)-a	3.63	3.67
Commrcl paper (Dealer, 90 day)-a	3.91	3.93
Certfs of Deposit (Resale, 90 day)	3.83	3.86
Federal funds (Overnight)-b	3.73	3.69
Eurodollars (90 day)-b	3.84	3.86
Treasury bills (one year)-c	4.12	4.18
Treasury notes (three year)-c	5.55	5.67
Treasury notes (five year)-c	6.44	6.56
Treasury notes (ten year)-c	7.24	7.32
Treasury bonds (30 year)-c	7.83	7.87

a-Discounted rates. b-Week ended Wednesday, June 17, 1992 and Wednesday June 10, 1992. c-Yields, adjusted for constant maturity.

Source: The *Wall Street Journal*, June 23, 1992

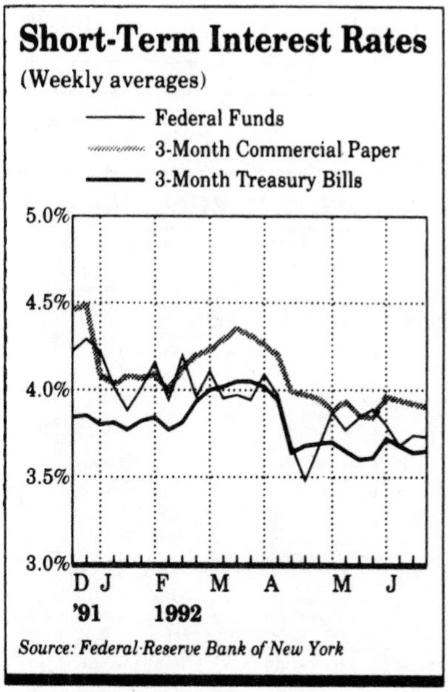

Source: The *Wall Street Journal*, June 25, 1992

Key Interest Rates

Every Tuesday, under the heading **Key Interest Rates,** the *Journal* reports the weekly average of most important interest rates, including long-term rates. See the example from the June 23, 1992 edition of the *Journal* on page 285. In the week ended June 19, 1992, Treasury bills averaged 3.63 percent; commercial paper, 3.91 percent; CDs, 3.83 percent; and federal funds, 3.73 percent. Once again, notice the interest rate hierarchy.

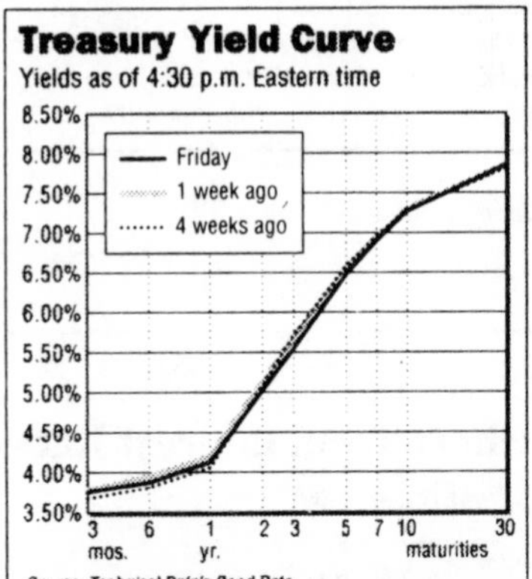

Source: Technical Data's Bond Data

YIELD COMPARISONS

Based on Merrill Lynch Bond Indexes, priced as of midafternoon Eastern time.

			–52 Week–	
	6/12	**6/11**	**High**	**Low**
Corp.-Govt. Master	6.81%	6.86%	8.27%	6.53%
Treasury 1-10yr	5.83	5.87	7.61	5.44
10+ yr	7.89	7.92	8.69	7.43
Agencies 1-10yr	6.42	6.45	7.92	6.12
10+ yr	8.31	8.33	8.92	7.80
Corporate				
1-10 yr High Qlty	7.27	7.32	8.67	7.10
Med Qlty	7.69	7.75	9.28	7.69
10+yr High Qlty	8.45	8.48	9.44	8.30
Med Qlty	8.85	8.88	9.84	8.79
Yankee bonds(1)	8.10	8.16	9.24	7.79
Current-coupon mortgages (2)				
GNMA 7.50%	7.98	8.09	9.36	7.40
FNMA 8.00%	8.03	8.07	9.38	7.51
FHLMC8.00%	7.87	7.91	9.33	7.38
High-yield corporates	11.40	11.40	14.40	11.40
New tax-exempts				
10-yr G.O. (AA)	5.85	5.85	6.50	5.60
20-yr G.O. (AA)	6.42	6.42	7.05	6.25
30-yr revenue (A)	6.70	6.70	7.55	6.52

Note: High quality rated AAA-AA; medium quality A-BBB/Baa; high yield, BB/Ba-C.

(1) Dollar-denominated, SEC-registered bonds of foreign issuers sold in the U.S. (2) Reflects the 52-week high and low of mortgage-backed securities indexes rather than the individual securities shown.

Source: The *Wall Street Journal*, June 25, 1992

Short-Term Interest Rates Chart

Also, the *Journal* provides a **Short-Term Interest Rates** chart each Thursday in the daily **Credit Markets** report (consult the front-page index of the first and last sections for location of the *Credit Markets* article), as in the example from the June 25, 1992 edition of the *Journal* on page 285. The **Short-Term Interest Rate** chart portrays Federal Funds, 3-Month Commercial Paper, and 3-Month T-Bill rates over the past six months.

Treasury Yield Curve

The yield curve charts the relationship between interest rates and length of maturity for all debt instruments at a particular time. A normal yield curve slopes upward, so that longer-term investments have higher yields. Thus, short-term Treasury bill rates are usually lower than long-term Treasury bond rates. Abnormal yield curves can be flat, inverted, or peaked in the middle (higher short-term rates than long-term rates).

The Wall Street Journal publishes a **Treasury Yield Curve** chart daily with the **Credit Markets** article. See the excerpt from the Thursday, June 25, 1992 edition on page 286. You can see the normal pattern of rising rates associated with longer maturities.

Buying and Borrowing

Each Monday, the *Journal* reports a variety of figures that investors follow, under the heading ***Buying & Borrowing***, including bank money market deposit account rates. See the June 22, 1992 example on page 288.

CONCLUSION

If the risk and bother of investing in stocks, bonds, and commodities seems excessive to you, a wide variety of relatively risk-free and highly liquid money market instruments is available to you. Use *The Wall Street Journal*'s data services to check the hierarchy of rates and then choose the instrument that's right for you.

Buying & Borrowing

Here are some recent figures on financial trends affecting consumers and individual investors.

—DOW JONES INDUSTRIALS—

Close: 3285.35. Year earlier: 2965.56.

—MOODY'S CORPORATE YIELDS—

Average for double-A-rated bonds:

8.53%. Year earlier: 9.30%.

—FEDERAL HOUSING FINANCE BOARD—

Average effective rate for conventional fixed-rate mortgage on new homes:

8.96%. Year earlier: 9.84%.

Average price on new homes:

$162,500. Year earlier: $151,400.

—BANK MONEY MARKET DEPOSITS—

Rates for accounts with minimum balance of $1,000:

At one major commercial bank: 2.95%.

At one major savings & loan association: 3.60%.

Source: *The Wall Street Journal*, June 22, 1992

PART III

FINE TUNING: REFINING YOUR SENSE OF THE ECONOMY AND THE RIGHT INVESTMENT DECISION

CHAPTER 13

LEADING ECONOMIC INDICATORS

Now that you have examined the business cycle in detail and learned to use *The Wall Street Journal*'s statistical series, you may be looking for a device to make analysis somewhat easier. Perhaps, while wading through the stream of data, you felt the need for a single indicator that could predict changes in the business cycle. You wanted something akin to the meteorologist's barometer, to inform you of rain or shine without a detailed examination of cloud formations.

Unfortunately, economists have never agreed on a single economic indicator to predict the future. Some indicators are better than others, but none is consistently accurate; all give a false signal on occasion. To deal with this, economists have devised a composite or combination of statistical series drawn from a broad spectrum of economic activity, each of which tends to move up or down ahead of the general trend of the business cycle. These series are referred to as leading indicators because of their predictive quality, and 11 have been combined into the composite index of leading economic indicators.

The components of the index are as follows:

1. Average weekly hours of production or non-supervisory workers, manufacturing.
2. Average weekly initial claims for unemployment insurance, state programs.
3. Manufacturers' new orders in 1982 dollars, consumer goods and materials industries.
4. Vendor performance—slower deliveries diffusion index.
5. Contracts and orders for plant and equipment in 1982 dollars.
6. New private housing units authorized by local building permits.

7. Change in manufacturers' unfilled orders in 1982 dollars, durable goods industries.
8. Change in sensitive materials prices.
9. Stock prices, 500 common stocks.
10. Money supply—M2—in 1982 dollars.
11. Index of consumer expectations.

There are three general criteria for inclusion in the index. First, each series must accurately lead the business cycle. Second, the various series should provide comprehensive coverage of the economy by representing a wide and diverse range of economic activity. And, third, each series must be available monthly, with only a brief lag until publication, and must be free from large subsequent revisions.

The leading indicators meet these criteria, and weaving these series into a composite provides a statistic that is more reliable and less erratic than any individual component by itself.

Finally, some of the indicators measure activity in physical units, others in current dollars, still others in constant dollars, and some with an index form. This variety of measurements is reduced to an index with 1982 assigned a base value of 100. All other months and years are expressed as a percentage of the base year.

The May index, published in the Wednesday, July 1, 1992 issue of *The Wall Street Journal*, is representative. The series usually appears around the first of the month. The chart accompanying the article and the second paragraph inform you that the index rose 0.6 percent to 149.9 (1982 = 100) in May.

Chart 13-1 on page 295 complements the chart on page 293 that accompanied the article. Both show the 1990-91 recession's dip as well as the recovery's stall in late 1991.

You can see that the index did a good job of forecasting recession except in 1981-1982 and 1990-91. For all other instances the index the downturn by at least five months. In 1981-82 you should observe that the two-month lead is a difficult call because the index double-clutched just prior to the recession's start. The first pump on the clutch is at least a half-year before the downturn begins. For 1990-91 there was no advance warning, although the index had been lethargic in the late 80s. This lends credence to the observation made earlier there would have been no recession in 1990-91 had it not been for the Persian Gulf crisis.

Economic Index Advanced Again During May

Leading Indicators Continue String of Small Increases, Commerce Agency Says

ECONOMY

By CHRYSTAL CARUTHERS
Staff Reporter of THE WALL STREET JOURNAL

WASHINGTON – The government's main economic forecasting gauge, the index of leading indicators, continued its string of small increases in May.

The index, which tends to move in advance of the general economy, rose 0.6% in May after increasing 0.3% in April and 0.4% in March, the Commerce Department said.

Index of Leading Indicators

Leading Indicators

In percent (1982 = 100).

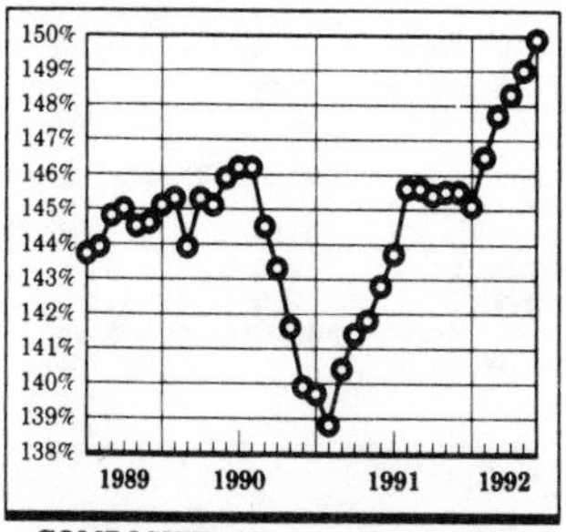

COMPOSITE of key indicators of future economic activity rose in May to 149.9% of the 1982 average, from a revised 149.0% in April, the Commerce Department reports.

The figures indicate the U.S. economy is growing, but not fast enough to bring the unemployment rate down. "Unemployment rates increase in the early stages of a recovery," noted John Silvia, chief economist at Kemper Financial Services Inc. The statistics indicate a recovery, he said, but many people are saying, 'I'm sure not feeling it.' "

In what he termed a "creepy-crawly" recovery, Robert Dederick, chief economist at Northern Trust Co. in Chicago, said, "We need a dose of hiring and spending to give consumers more income to increase their confidence levels so that they can increase spending."

In the index of leading indicators, five of the 11 measures rose in May: commodity prices, the length of the average workweek, delays in the delivery of goods by vendors, stock prices, and an index of consumer expectations as measured by the University of Michigan. The components that fell were new orders for consumer goods and materials, money supply, contracts and orders for plant and equipment, manufacturers' backlogs of orders, building permits and new claims for state unemployment insurance.

The index of coincident indicators, which is designed to measure the current status of the economy, was unchanged in May, and the index of lagging indicators, which trails economic changes, decreased 1.2%.

Here are the net contributions of the components of the Commerce Department's index of leading indicators. After various adjustments, they produced a 0.6% increase in the index for May and a 0.3% increase for April.

	May 1992	April 1991
Workweek	.15	.00
Unemployment claims	−.01	.11
Orders for consumer goods	−.03	.09
Slower deliveries	.11	−.09
Plant and equipment orders	−.03	−.03
Building permits	−.01	−.09
Durable order backlog	−.03	.00
Materials prices	.23	.34
Stock prices	.10	.00
Money supply	−.03	−.13
Consumer expectations	.03	.01

The seasonally adjusted index numbers (1982=100) for May, and the change from April, are:

Index of leading indicators	149.9	0.6%
Index of coincident indicators	124.8	0.0%
Index of lagging indicators	106.0	−1.2%

The ratio of coincident to lagging indicators was 1.18, up from 1.16 in the previous month.

Source: *The Wall Street Journal*, July 1, 1992

Index of Leading Indicators– Second Paragraph

The index, which tends to move in advance of the general economy, rose 0.6% in May after increasing 0.3% in April and 0.4% in March, the Commerce Department said.

Source: *The Wall Street Journal*, July 1, 1992

Statistical Summary–End of Article

Here are the net contributions of the components of the Commerce Department's index of leading indicators. After various adjustments, they produced a 0.6% increase in the index for May and a 0.3% increase for April.

	May 1992	April 1991
Workweek	.15	.00
Unemployment claims	−.01	.11
Orders for consumer goods	−.03	.09
Slower deliveries	.11	−.09
Plant and equipment orders	−.03	−.03
Building permits	−.01	−.09
Durable order backlog	−.03	.00
Materials prices	.23	.34
Stock prices	.10	.00
Money supply	−.03	−.13
Consumer expectations	.03	.01

The seasonally adjusted index numbers (1982=100) for May, and the change from April, are:

Index of leading indicators	149.9	0.6%
Index of coincident indicators	124.8	0.0%
Index of lagging indicators	106.0	−1.2%

The ratio of coincident to lagging indicators was 1.18, up from 1.16 in the previous month.

Source: *The Wall Street Journal*, July 1, 1992

But you can also see the false alarms of 1962, 1966, 1984, and 1987. In each case the index fell for at least three consecutive months although no recession followed. The 1962 decline followed on the heels of President Kennedy's forced rollback of Big Steel's price increase.

The stock market went into shock and business activity slowed, but you can see that the setback was brief. This decline was clearly a random event and of no cyclical significance.

The indicators' 1966 setback was more like developments in the 1980s. The Vietnam War had begun and inflation was climbing. The Fed

CHART 13-1
Composite Index of 11 Leading Indicators

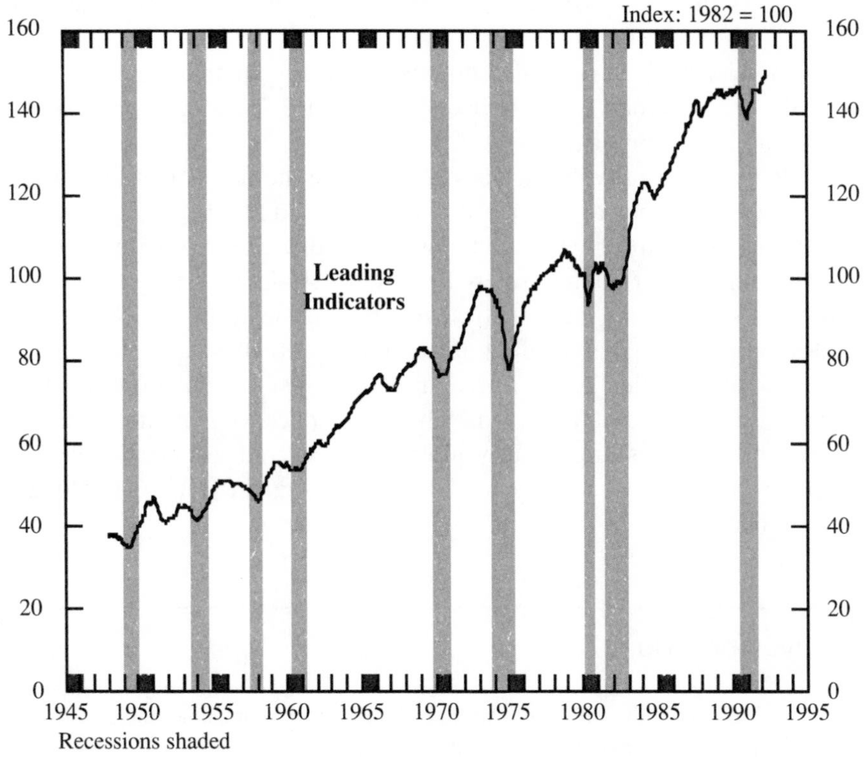

Source: U.S. Department of Commerce, *Business Cycle Indicators*, Series 910.

tightened in response, in order to raise interest rates and curb consumer and business demand. Housing starts crashed and it was "nip-and-tuck" for a while, but the Fed quickly eased when alarm spread so that recession never took hold.

The Fed faced similar conditions and tightened in 1984 as the cycle came roaring back from the 1981-1982 recession. The economy went into the doldrums temporarily and the leading indicators fell, but once again the Fed eased as soon as inflation subsided and the economy emerged with only a scratch.

The October 1987 stock market crash was as severe as 1962's decline, but this time the market's own dynamic created the problem, rather than the actions of the president. Nonetheless, fears of recession swirled about for several months and the composite index headed south. Soon, however, everyone realized the crash had nothing to do with the economy's fundamentals, and concern evaporated as the index snapped back.

Moreover, keep in mind that this statistic is not an analytical tool that permits you to probe beneath the cycle's surface in order to analyze its dynamic. The composite does not provide a step-by-step diagnosis that reveals the cycle's rhythm. It does not disclose the forces that lead from one set of conditions to another. It only averages a number of convenient series that are themselves leading indicators, but are otherwise unrelated.

This series is of interest solely because it provides an omen of future events. You need all the statistical reports appearing in the *Journal* in order to build an understanding of the timing, direction, and strength of the business cycle. After all, a meteorologist needs more than a barometer, and most Americans who make decisions in the business community, or wish to be fully informed of current economic events, need far more than a crude, general directional signal to guide their long-range planning.

Investor's Tip

- The composite index of leading economic indicators is not the square root of the universe. There is no single index or formula that provides all the answers to the problem of business forecasting.

CHAPTER 14

INVENTORIES

A DESTABILIZING FORCE

Inventories are stocks of goods on hand: raw materials, goods in process, or finished products. Individual businesses use them to bring stability to their operations, and yet you'll see that they actually have a destabilizing effect on the business cycle.

Businesses view inventories as a necessary evil. A manufacturer, wholesaler, or retailer can't live from hand to mouth, continually filling sales orders from current production. Stocks of goods "on the shelf" are a cushion against unexpected orders and slowdowns in production. On the other hand, inventories are an investment in working capital and incur an interest cost. If the firm borrows capital to maintain inventories, the direct interest cost is obvious. Even if the firm has not borrowed, however, working capital tied up in inventories represents an interest cost. Any funds invested in inventories could have earned the going interest rate in the money market, and this loss can substantially crimp profits.

Therefore, business attempts to keep inventories at an absolute minimum consistent with smooth operations. For a very large business, literally millions of dollars are at stake. This is why you see modern automated cash registers (i.e., the ones that automatically "read" the black and white bar code on packages) in large chain supermarkets and retail establishments. These cash registers came into use not chiefly because they record your purchases more quickly (which of course they do), but because they also tie into a computer network that keeps track of inventories of thousands of items on a daily basis.

But why do inventories, so necessary to the smooth functioning of an individual business, exacerbate the business cycle?

Consider the upswing of the cycle first. As demand increases rapidly, businesses must boost production to meet the growing volume of orders. If they are not quick enough, and sales grow more rapidly than output, an unplanned drawdown of inventories will occur as orders are filled. This is known as involuntary inventory depletion. If inventories are severely depleted, shortages can result and sales may be jeopardized. To protect itself against such developments once it is confident of the unfolding expansion, business will boost output and defensively accumulate inventories more rapidly than its sales are growing. Since all firms are stockpiling to prevent shortages, industrial production increases more vigorously than it otherwise would, accentuating the cyclical expansion and the swift rise in capacity utilization. For the entire economy, production grows more rapidly than sales. This, of course, hastens the inevitable decrease in labor productivity and increase in unit labor costs associated with this phase of the cycle. Hence, inventory accumulation adds to inflationary pressures.

Now consider the downswing of the cycle. No firm willingly maintains production in a sales slump because unsold goods would pile up on the shelf. As sales weaken and fall, business curtails production in order to prevent involuntary inventory accumulation. Indeed, once business recognizes the severity of the slump, it will begin to liquidate the large volume of (now unnecessary) inventories built up during the previous expansion. These stockpiles of goods are no longer needed and can be disposed of. But as goods are sold from inventories, output and employment are reduced more than sales, since orders can be filled from inventories rather than from current production. This aggravates the cycle's downturn.

Thus, inventories play an important destabilizing role in the cycle through their influence on industrial production, boosting output during expansion and depressing it during slump. This destabilizing influence is compounded by inventory's impact on inflation. When rapid expansion is heightened by inventory accumulation, contributing to inflationary pressures, business firms increase their inventory buildup. They want to stockpile goods at current prices and sell them later at inflated prices. And when inventory liquidation in a recession contributes to deflationary pressures, falling prices can trigger a panic sell-off, which drives prices down even more steeply.

Here's how it works. Business stockpiles goods during the expansionary phase of the cycle to prevent involuntary inventory depletion and shortages, and prices start to rise. Firms quickly discover that goods held in inventory increase in value along with the general rise in prices. They have an incentive to buy now while prices are low, hold the goods in inventory, and sell them later at higher prices and profits. If prices are rising rapidly enough, widespread speculation can set in, which adds to the general increase in production and reinforces the inflation.

Recall, for example, the rapid increase in sugar prices in 1973-1974. Sugar manufacturers and industrial users of sugar (canners, soft drink bottlers, confectioners, and bakers) produced sugar and sweetened products and held them in inventory while their prices were low, hoping to make large profits from sales when their prices increased. This speculative stockpiling contributed to the price increase by bidding up production (and costs) out of proportion to sales.

Of course, when the inevitable contraction comes, liquidation of the inventory overhang helps halt the inflationary spiral. Businesses panic when faced with the prospect of selling at a price that will not recoup interest costs. If sufficiently severe, the sell-off can force prices down. More important, output plummets and layoffs mount as orders are filled from the shelf. Liquidation continues until inventories are in proper relation to sales.

Thus, speculative inventory accumulation and liquidation become a self-fulfilling prophecy. Firms pile up inventories in anticipation of a price increase, and the large volume of orders bids prices upward. When the recession begins, firms sell inventories in haste, afraid of a drop in prices, and the sell-off forces prices downward.

Now you understand why inventories and their relationship to sales are such important economic indicators. They not only confirm the stage of the cycle, they also provide advance warning of turning points and of the strength or severity of impending boom and bust.

And you also understand the irony that inventories exacerbate the business cycle even though individual businesses use inventories to smooth operations. Production will rise more rapidly than sales during cyclical expansion, the difference accumulating as inventories, thereby forcing capacity utilization and costs up more rapidly, intensifying the expansion and thus hastening inflation and recession. And after recession begins, firms will reduce output more rapidly than the drop in sales, drawing upon inventories to make up the difference. Therefore, the cycle's downswing will be more severe.

RECENT EXPERIENCE

Inventory accumulation and liquidation reinforce the business cycle. The consumer sets the cycle's pace; inventories exacerbate it. The cyclical experience of the early 1970s will serve as an illustration, followed by an examination of more recent developments.

To begin with, *The Wall Street Journal* publishes the Commerce Department's inventory, sales, and inventory/sales ratio data around the middle of each month.

In the excerpt on page 301 from the *Journal*'s Friday, May 15, 1992 edition, the statistical summary at the end of the article informs you that inventories were \$816.26 billion, sales were \$547.90 billion, and inventories were 1.49 times sales.

Inventories and sales are straightforward concepts. The inventory-sales ratio tells you how many months it would take to sell off inventories at the prevailing sales pace. You can calculate the ratio by dividing monthly inventory by monthly sales. Typically, inventories have been roughly 1.5 times sales over the cycle. A rise in the ratio indicates that inventories are growing out of proportion to sales and that inventory liquidation and recession are imminent. A fall in the ratio informs you that sales are outpacing inventory growth and that economic expansion is under way. This is a key indicator; you should follow it closely.

Return to the *Journal* article after examining the inventory cycle of the early 1970s (see Chart 14-1 on page 303). This cycle concluded with a good example of inventory accumulation and speculation followed by inventory liquidation. To trace these events, follow the steep rise in inventories from 1972 through 1974 and the 1975 liquidation; note the decline in the inventory-sales ratio in 1971-72 and the increase in 1973 and 1974; and note that the inventory and sales curves are nearly congruent, with inventories lagging behind sales by a year or so.

You can observe the decline of the inventory-sales ratio as the business cycle moved from recovery to expansion in 1971-1972. Sales were expanding, but it was still too early for business to rebuild inventories.

As increasing demand boosted sales, 1973 displayed all the symptoms of the expansion-to-peak phase of the cycle: strong and rapidly growing sales, strained capacity utilization and slower deliveries, and a rising rate of inflation. Under these circumstances, business sought to defend itself against possible shortages by adding to inventories more rapidly than sales grew. The long decline in the inventory- sales ratio was reversed,

Business Inventories Rose 0.4% in March; All Categories Gained

ECONOMY

By a WALL STREET JOURNAL *Staff Reporter*

WASHINGTON – Business stockpiles increased 0.4% in March, the Commerce Department said, with inventory growth rippling across all categories.

Retail stockpiles rose the most, climbing 0.8%. Within the retail category, automotive dealers and general merchandise stores posted the largest increases, while stockpiles of food and furniture stores fell.

Manufacturers' and wholesalers' inventories also showed small increases. The inventory growth was the first in two months. Total business sales in March rose 0.5%.

The ratio of inventories to sales held steady at 1.49 during the month. That means it would take businesses 1.49 months to run through their stockpiles at the current sales rate.

All figures have been adjusted for normal seasonal variations.

Here is a summary of the Commerce Department's report on business inventories and sales in March. The figures are seasonally adjusted:

	(billions of dollars) March 1992	Feb. 1992	March 1991
Total business inventories	816.26	813.18	818.53
Manufacturers	372.85	372.80	385.98
Retailers	245.02	243.06	236.52
Wholesalers	198.39	197.31	196.03
Total business sales	547.90	545.38	523.38
Inventory/sales ratio	1.49	1.49	1.56

Statistical Summary

Business Inventories

In billions of dollars.

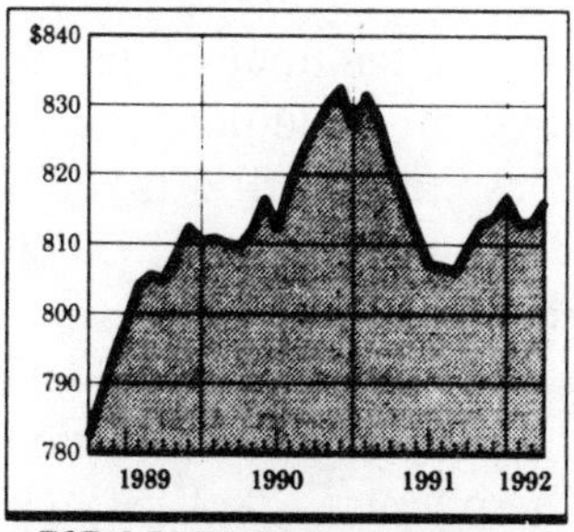

TOTAL BUSINESS INVENTORIES rose in March to $816.26 billion after seasonal adjustments from $813.18 billion in February, the Commerce Department reports.

Source: *The Wall Street Journal*, May 15, 1992

Statistical Summary–End of Article

Here is a summary of the Commerce Department's report on business inventories and sales in March. The figures are seasonally adjusted:

	(billions of dollars)		
	March 1992	Feb. 1992	March 1991
Total business inventories	816.26	813.18	818.53
Manufacturers	372.85	372.80	385.98
Retailers	245.02	243.06	236.52
Wholesalers	198.39	197.31	196.03
Total business sales	547.90	545.38	523.38
Inventory/sales ratio	1.49	1.49	1.56

Source: *The Wall Street Journal*, May 15, 1992

and speculation began. Business boosted inventories in the expectation of rising prices, hoping to make a profit as goods increased in value. This intensified inflationary pressure (recall sugar) as a share of production went on the shelf instead of toward satisfying consumer demand. You can see that the inventory run-up dwarfed all other postwar increases up to that date.

As the cycle's peak approached, in 1974, sales stopped growing. Unplanned inventory accumulation became a problem; the inventory sales ratio rose even more rapidly; and business firms had to deal with ever-larger stockpiles of goods. Sensing that a sell-off was around the corner, they tried to bring inventories under control. Unfortunately, this was more easily said than done. Orders had to be canceled and production curtailed more than once because business underestimated the situation's severity.

But beginning in late 1974 and continuing into 1975, inventory liquidation finally began. Under panic conditions, business desperately dumped goods on the market. Despite the sell-off, you'll notice that the inventory-sales ratio remained high until early 1975. This is evidence of the collapse in sales and the recession's severity—the reason business went to such lengths to unload its stocks of goods. Other postwar recessions had been mild by comparison. Industrial production plunged as business firms cut output sharply and filled the meager volume of orders from overstocked inventories. Two million workers were laid off between the fall of 1974 and the spring of 1975, and the unemployment rate brushed 10 percent. There is no doubt that inventory accumulation and liquidation played a key role in the recession's harshness.

CHART 14-1
Manufacturing and Trade Inventory/Sales Ratio (constant dollars), **and Change in Book Value of Manufacturing and Trade Inventories** (current dollars)

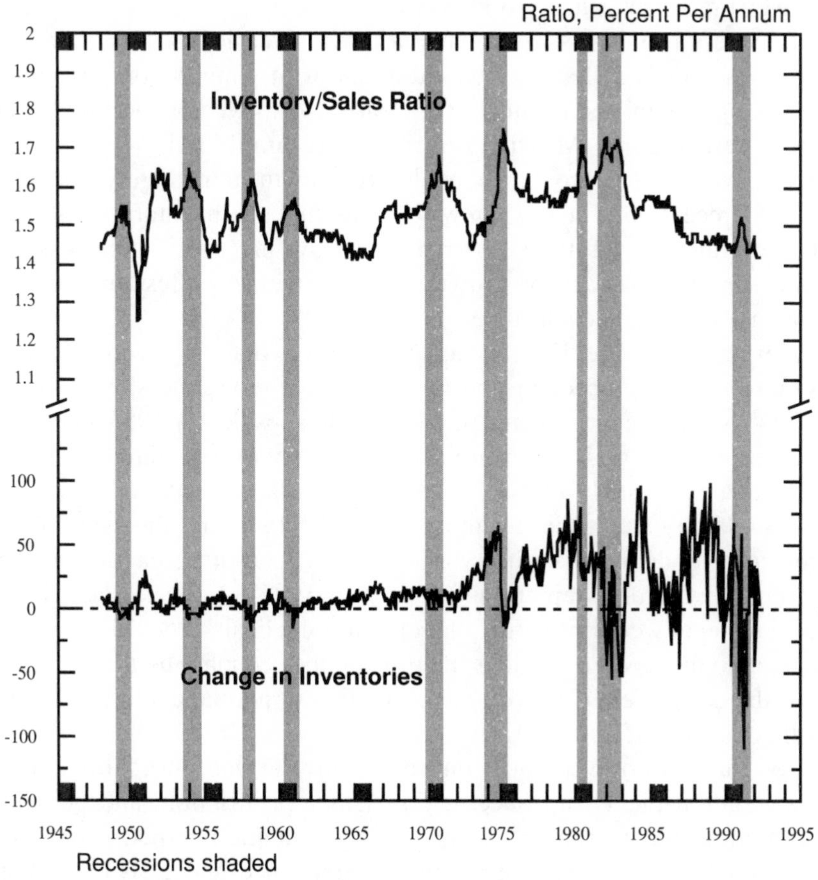

Source: U.S. Department of Commerce, *Business Cycle Indicators*, Series 31, 77

Unlike the cycle of the early 70s, the 1981-82 recession can't be used as a typical example of inventory accumulation and liquidation because of the Fed's role in aborting the 1981 recovery. Sales were doing well and the inventory-sales ratio was low when the Fed's tight money policy clamped a vise on the economy in 1981. Sales shrank and involuntary inventory accumulation drove up both inventories and the inventory-sales ratio. As soon as possible, business began a massive inventory liquidation program that continued through early 1983. As you can tell from Chart 14-1 on page 303, a desperate bout of inventory liquidation accompanied the worst recession since World War II.

Recovery began as soon as the Fed provided easier credit conditions. And you can see that business did not wait long before it began restocking its depleted inventories. By early 1984 inventory accumulation set a new record. Massive inventory accumulation contributed impressively to the economy's explosive growth immediately after the 1981-82 recession. Yet sales grew so strong that the inventory-sales ratio declined throughout 1983 and remained low in 1984. There was no indication that inventory growth had outstripped sales or that the economy was near a cyclical peak.

Nevertheless, the Fed became concerned that the recovery and expansion were proceeding too rapidly. It fine-tuned the slowdown of mid-84, and inventory accumulation began to subside. By 1985 and early 1986 economic conditions were slack and inventory accumulation had fallen to a moderate level.

To a large extent, the inventory run-up of 1984 and the subsequent drop to a moderate pace in 1985-86 were a one-time reaction to the extreme inventory depletion during the 1981-82 recession. These developments were not part of the ordinary cyclical scene; they were a reaction to the credit conditions imposed on the economy by the Fed. In a way, the decks were cleared for a resumption of normal cyclical patterns by the second half of the 80s.

As the economy's pace improved in the late 80s, inventory accumulation picked up once again. Although inflation, and perhaps speculation, were minimal, inventory accumulation turned robust by 1988 and then declined as the Fed tightened up once again. By the end of the decade circumstances were similar to 1985-86: a jump in interest rates had led to slack conditions and the absence of inventory build-up.

Then Iraq invaded Kuwait and the economy plunged into recession. Businesses were caught by surprise and the inventory-sales ratio climbed as unsold goods piled up on shelves. But businesses brought the unintended inventory accumulation under control by sharply reducing inventories in 1991. By early 1992 the inventory-sale ratio was back to normal levels and inventories had begun to expand once again.

Another glance at Chart 14-1 on page 303 will demonstrate the 1990-91 recession's peculiar nature. No signs of serious speculation, such as a rising inventory-sales ratio, can be seen before the recession's start. Even after the slump begins, and despite massive inventory liquidation, the inventory-sales ratio's rise is moderate by the standard of previous recessions. Many observers ventured that the ratio's relatively smooth sailing provided evidence of business's better inventory-control methods and that relatively low inventory levels coming out of recession meant a snappy recovery and expansion. That remained to be seen by late 1992.

THE OUTLOOK

Return to the May 15, 1992 *Journal* article on pages 301 and 302. It informs you of a 1.49 inventory-sales ratio and Chart 14-1 on page 303 confirms that this was fairly low figure. This is partly a consequence of the improved technology that enables business to keep a closer watch over its inventories. But it's also a sign of a lean economy.

How long will the inventory-sales ratio remain low, and how long will it be before inventory accumulation exacerbates the expansion and contributes to the next recession? That depends on the strength of the expansion as determined by the growth in consumer demand. If demand grows too quickly and inflation speeds up, business will begin stockpiling for self-protection and speculation, and the inventory-sales ratio will start to climb. This will be a dead giveaway that inventory accumulation is contributing to boom conditions and that the peak of the cycle cannot be far off. On the other hand, if the expansion is restrained, the inventory-sales ratio should remain flat for a long time. In that case, inventory accumulation will not aggravate the expansion and the business cycle will not be brought to a peak prematurely.

Investor'sTip

- Watch these figures carefully. If boom conditions drive inventories out of moderate proportion to sales and the inventory-sales ratio rises rapidly and exceeds 1.6, you know recession can't be far behind.

CHAPTER 15

BUSINESS CAPITAL EXPENDITURES

WHY BUSINESS INVESTS

John Maynard Keynes could not have known America's modern consumer economy when he wrote his General Theory in 1936 (see Chapters 3 and 5). Keynes assumed the absence of any dynamic in British consumer expenditures and believed consumption behaved passively, expanding and contracting with consumer income. As far as Keynes was concerned, business investment determined the cycle's dynamic. So Keynes built his theory of aggregate economic activity around the forces that determine business investment in plant and equipment.

But business's expenditures on factories, warehouses, offices, machinery, and equipment, like its accumulation of inventories, reinforce the business cycle; they do not lead it. Business waits for its signal from the economy before committing its capital. Similarly, only after the expansion is over does business begin to cut back on capital expenditures in anticipation of reduced sales.

There are six principal factors influencing business decisions to spend on new plant and equipment.

First, old facilities may wear out and need to be replaced.

Second, the rate of capacity utilization may be high. Putting it simply, if sales are strong, business will invest in new machinery and equipment in order to have the capacity necessary to fill the orders. During a recession, however, the rate of capacity utilization is low and business has more than enough plant and equipment on hand to satisfy the low volume of orders. Why add to plant and equipment when the existing level is already more than adequate?

Third, old facilities, whether fully utilized or not, will be scrapped and replaced by new facilities if operating costs can be sufficiently reduced through innovation in the process of production. Competition leaves business no choice: if equipment is no longer cost-effective, it must be replaced even though it could still be used.

Fourth, new plant and equipment may be required to produce a new or redesigned product even if existing facilities are operating at full capacity and have a continued useful life. Model and style changes have forced the automobile industry to spend billions replacing still-functional equipment, for instance.

Fifth, spending on plant and equipment is sensitive to current and anticipated profits. Business will invest in additional facilities if it expects long-range profit growth beyond any short-run cyclical fluctuation. In addition, profits plowed back into the business provide the cash flow necessary to finance capital expenditures. A recession will limit business's ability to finance capital expenditures; an expansion will generate the necessary cash flow.

The final factor is interest rates. Business must borrow to finance plant and equipment expenditures if internally generated funds are not adequate. When interest rates are very high the cost of borrowing may be prohibitive, and so business firms postpone or cancel their capital expenditure plans. Or they may feel that for the time being they can get a better return by investing their own funds at high rates of interest than by making expenditures on new productive facilities.

Keep these factors in mind when evaluating business's capital expansion plans and their role in the current cycle. You can keep abreast of capital expenditures by following a series published monthly in *The Wall Street Journal*: the Commerce Department report on new orders for nondefense capital goods.

NONDEFENSE CAPITAL GOODS

The Wall Street Journal publishes preliminary data for nondefense capital goods, such as the Thursday, June 25, 1992 release (see page 310), on the Thursday or Friday of the next-to-the-last week of the month, and then publishes the final report about a week later. You will have to keep your eyes open for these figures because they are part of an overall report

Factory Orders Rose 1% in April, 4th Gain in a Row

By CHRYSTAL CARUTHERS
Staff Reporter of THE WALL STREET JOURNAL

WASHINGTON – Orders to U.S. factories continued to improve in April, the Commerce Department said, rising 1.0% to $243.85 billion.

The increase was broad-based and continues a string of gains that began in January, although orders for durable goods, big-ticket factory items intended to last more than three years, rose a bit less than the department estimated in a preliminary report last week. Led by electronic components, primary metals and transportation equipment, orders for durables increased 1.3% in April instead of the 1.4% reported originally.

New orders for nondurable goods rose 0.7%, with large increases in food, petroleum and coal products offsetting declines in tobacco and textile mill products.

Also encouraging was a 0.2% increase in shipments in April. Michael Penzer, senior economist for Bank of America in San Francisco, said that since shipments can lag several days to several years behind orders, the increase shows the manufacturing sector is "going forward."

But one dim spot in the Commerce Department's report is that unfilled orders for durable goods declined for the eighth consecutive month in April, this time by 0.2%.

Durable-goods inventories also fell by 0.5% to $235.66 billion, their lowest level since late 1988. "Manufacturers are still reluctant to replenish their inventories after filling their orders," said Evelina M. Tainer, an economic consultant in Chicago. The fact that unfilled orders continue to decline suggests that manufacturing employment will be slow to pick up.

All figures have been adjusted for normal seasonal variations.

FACTORY ORDER

Here are the Commerce Department's latest figures for manufacturers in billions of dollars, seasonally adjusted.

	April 1992	Mar. 1992	%Chg.
All industries	**243.85**	**241.42**	**1.0**
Durable goods	125.27	123.62	1.3
Nondurable goods	118.59	117.80	0.7
Capital goods industries	**40.13**	**41.09**	....
Nondefense	31.73	34.11	– 7.0
Defense	8.40	6.98	20.4
Total shipments	**244.74**	**244.18**	**0.2**
Inventories	**371.55**	**372.76**	**– 0.3**
Backlog of orders	**501.77**	**502.67**	**– 0.2**

Source: *The Wall Street Journal*, June 4, 1992

Orders for Durables Fell 2.4% in May, Raising Doubts on Economic Recovery

By MONICA MILLER
Staff Reporter of THE WALL STREET JOURNAL

WASHINGTON – Orders for big-ticket factory items dropped 2.4% in May, the Commerce Department said, raising doubts about the strength of the economic recovery.

The drop in durable-goods orders, to $119.53 billion, followed increases of 1.9% in April and 2.1% in March. A 27.7% plunge in defense orders accounted for much of the May decline, as orders for aircraft and navigation equipment fell sharply. Orders for electronic equipment and industrial machinery also declined. Durable goods are defined as those that are likely to last at least three years.

Nondefense capital goods

Orders for nondefense capital goods, considered by economists a barometer of business investment, rose 1.4% following a 7.1% decrease in April. Excluding aircraft and parts, however, this measure increased only 0.7%.

Particularly troubling in the Commerce Department report was a 0.6% decline in factories' backlog of orders, the ninth monthly decrease. The drop suggests that manufacturers will be slow to hire new workers, or may even lay some off, because demand isn't keeping pace with current production.

"If the backlog isn't moving, production will have to be scaled back," predicted Doug Handler, an economist with Dun & Bradstreet. He said the latest numbers confirm declining optimism among the nation's manufacturers that things will continue to get better. Said Mr. Handler, "The good numbers that we saw in the past months will not continue."

But other economists saw the report as a reflection of fluctuations in the aircraft industry and not the American economy as a whole. "The overall picture is positive," said Thomas Runiewicz, industrial economist for the WEFA Group in suburban Philadelphia. "This is not an indication that the economy is back in a recession, but rather that it is moving at a sluggish pace."

Shipments of durable goods declined 1% to $122.26 billion in May, the second consecutive monthly drop.

All the figures are adjusted to remove normal seasonal fluctuations.

DURABLE GOODS

Here are the Commerce Department's latest figures on new orders for durable goods (seasonally adjusted, in billions):

	April	May	% Chg.
Total	$122.52	$119.53	– 2.4
Primary Metals	11.05	10.98	– 0.6
Nonelect. machinery	20.14	19.96	– 0.9
Electrical machinery	17.17	16.94	– 1.3
Transportation equip.	33.00	30.94	– 6.2
Capital goods	38.02	36.20	– 4.8
Nondefense	29.89	30.32	1.4
Defense	8.13	5.87	– 27.7

Source: *The Wall Street Journal*, June 25, 1992

on durable goods. The revised data, appearing a week later, is included with a general release on factory orders. The June 4, 1992 article on page 309 covering the previous month, is a good example.

You will notice that the third paragraph (see page 312) of the June 25 durable goods article states that orders for nondefense capital goods rose 1.4 percent in May and that the statistical summary at the end of the article (see below) reports a figure of $30.32 billion.

This series presents new orders received by manufacturers of durable goods other than military equipment. (Durable goods are defined as those having a useful life of more than three years.) Nondefense capital goods represent approximately one fifth to one third of all durable goods production. The series includes engines; construction, mining, and materials handling equipment; office and store machinery; electrical transmission and distribution equipment and other electrical machinery (excluding household appliances and electronic equipment); and railroad, ship and aircraft transportation equipment. Military equipment is excluded because new orders for such items do not respond directly to the business cycle.

Chart 15-1 on page 313 provides a good illustration of the relationship between nondefense capital goods orders and the business cycle. We track orders rather than shipments in order to obtain maximum advance notice of business cycle developments and turning points.

By the late 80s, nondefense orders were hovering around $35 billion and had advanced rapidly over the past half-decade. Yet you should notice, in a development remarked upon earlier in the discussion on inventories, that the 1980s expansion stumbled in the middle and end of the decade. Then nondefense orders dropped into the $30 billion range with the 1990-91 recession.

Statistical Summary–End of Article

Statistical Summary

DURABLE GOODS

Here are the Commerce Department's latest figures on new orders for durable goods (seasonally adjusted, in billions):

	April	May	% Chg.
Total	$122.52	$119.53	– 2.4
Primary Metals	11.05	10.98	– 0.6
Nonelect. machinery	20.14	19.96	– 0.9
Electrical machinery	17.17	16.94	– 1.3
Transportation equip.	33.00	30.94	– 6.2
Capital goods	38.02	36.20	– 4.8
Nondefense	29.89	30.32	1.4
Defense	8.13	5.87	– 27.7

Source: *The Wall Street Journal*, June 25, 1992

Nondefense Capital Goods–Third Paragraph

Orders for nondefense capital goods, considered by economists a barometer of business investment, rose 1.4% following a 7.1% decrease in April. Excluding aircraft and parts, however, this measure increased only 0.7%.

Source: *The Wall Street Journal*, June 25, 1992

SUMMARY

In conclusion, Chart 15-1 illustrates business cycle developments in the 1970s, when expenditures, like inventory accumulation, reinforced the cycle rather than initiated it. Business responded to consumer orders by adding plant and equipment. As the expansion developed into the peak of the cycle and productive capacity became strained, business added facilities and equipment. Their completion swelled the level of demand and contributed to generally inflationary conditions.

After recession begins, some of the investment projects are canceled, but most are completed, and these expenditures ease the downturn. Time elapses before a new cycle's expansionary phase encourages another round of capital expenditures. Until this occurs, the depressed level of plant and equipment expenditures holds demand down and prevents the economy from heating up too quickly. When capital expenditures do recover, the economy is once again approaching the cycle's peak.

Returning one last time to the articles and charts for an overview of the process, it's clear that the cycle developed differently in the 1980s than it had in the 1970s. The economy did not overheat in the 80s because the Fed's fine-tuning cooled it at the middle and end of the decade. Unfortunately, conditions were still chilly when the Persian Gulf crisis began, and then quickly slipped into recession.

Investor's Tip

- Treat these statistics like inventory accumulation: too much of a good thing is dangerous.

CHART 15-1
Nondefense Orders for Capital Goods

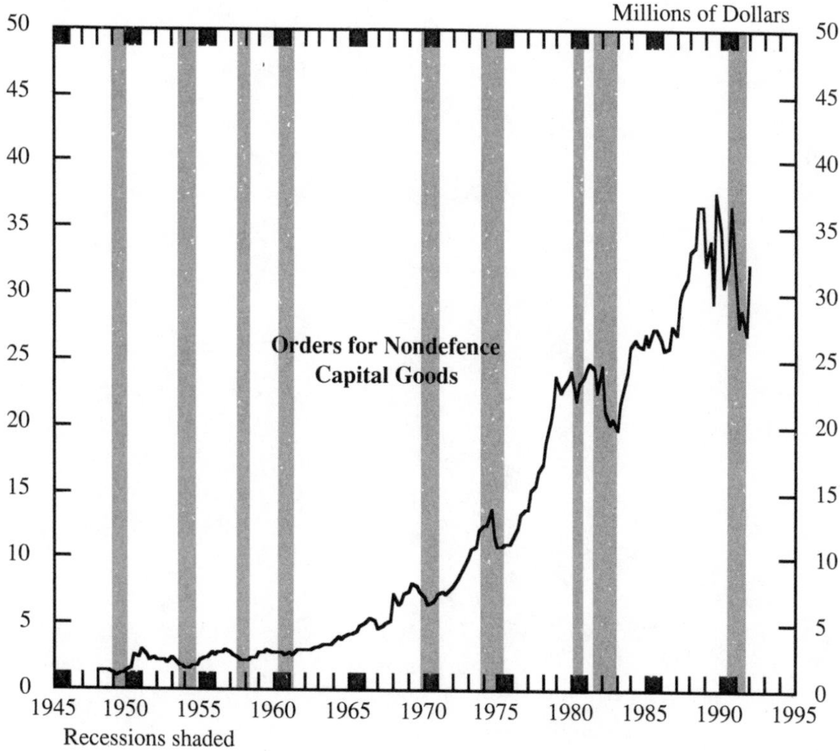

Source: U.S. Department of Commerce, *Business Cycle Indicators*, Series 24

CHAPTER 16

U.S. INTERNATIONAL TRANSACTIONS

POSTWAR PERSPECTIVE

The phrases of international commerce were continuously in the financial news in the early 1990s. Foreign exchange rates, IMF, balance of trade, balance of payments, and the other terms used to discuss America's international economic relations can certainly be defined and described in the context of current events. But to understand them thoroughly, you must think back to World War II. Most of our modern international economic institutions were formed at the end of the war and immediately afterward, when the American dollar assumed the central role in the world's economy that it still plays today. Take the time to review postwar international economic developments before plunging into the current data and terminology.

In the summer of 1944, in the resort town of Bretton Woods, New Hampshire, well before World War II came to a close, the United States hosted a conference to plan international monetary affairs for the postwar years, since the Allies were already certain of victory. The United States knew that the war was taking a drastic toll on the rest of the world's economies, while the U.S. economy was growing stronger. Both victor and vanquished would need food, fuel, raw materials, and equipment, but only the United States could furnish these requirements. How were other nations to pay for these imports? They had very little that Americans wanted. If they sold their money for dollars in order to buy goods from us, the strong selling pressure on their currencies and their strong demand for dollars would drive their currencies down in value and the dollar up. Soon the dollar would be so expensive, in terms of foreign currency, that the rest of the world could not afford to buy the American goods necessary to rebuild.

It would have been very easy to say that this was everyone else's problem, not ours, but America's statesmen knew that it was our problem as well. This lesson had been learned the hard way during the aftermath of World War I. Following that war, the United States had washed its hands of international responsibilities; consequently, the world economy had suffered a severe dollar shortage. Many nations were forced to devalue their currencies. Other nations used gold in desperation to settle their accounts with the United States, so America ended up with most of the world's gold supply. Moreover, each nation sought shelter in shortsighted protectionist devices, shattering the world economy. Economic nationalism spilled into the diplomatic arena where its malevolent force accelerated the world into the second global war.

Determined to avoid these mistakes the second time around, the United States convened the Bretton Woods Conference to anticipate such problems and establish institutions to handle them. The conference's principal task was to prevent runaway depreciation of other currencies after the war. It therefore created the International Monetary Fund (IMF), a pool of currencies to which all nations (but mostly the United States) contributed and from which any nation could borrow in order to shore up the value of its own currency. If a nation's currency was under selling pressure, and weak and falling in value compared to other currencies, buying pressure designed to drive its price upward could be implemented with strong currencies borrowed from the IMF. For instance, Britain could borrow dollars from the IMF to buy pounds, thus supporting the price of the pound.

The dollar was pegged to gold at $35 an ounce, and all other currencies were pegged to the dollar (e.g., a dollar was worth a fixed number of francs or pounds). At the time, the United States had most of the world's gold and other nations had hardly any, so the entire system was tied to gold through the U.S. dollar. This system of fixed exchange rates was constructed to provide stability in international economic relationships. Traders and investors knew exactly what a contract for future delivery of goods or future return on investment was worth in terms of the foreign exchange in which a contract was written. There was no incentive to speculate on shifting exchange rates, which could wipe out profit margins or generate large losses.

To draw an analogy, consider a shipment of oranges from California to New York and investments made by Californians on the New York

Stock Exchange. Californians must be concerned about the price of oranges in New York and the price of a share of stock on the exchange, but they need not be concerned about fluctuations in the value of New York currency versus California currency, since both states use dollars.

Now think how much more difficult selling and investing in New York would be for Californians if the exchange rate between their currencies fluctuated. The diplomats wished to avoid precisely that problem after World War II, and that's why the Bretton Woods Conference established the IMF and a system of fixed exchange rates.

Unfortunately, after the war the U.S. balance-of-trade surplus (the amount by which the revenue of all exports exceeds the cost of all imports) created a greater dollar shortage than the conference had anticipated. Other nations were continually selling their currencies in order to buy American dollars with which to purchase American goods. Selling pressure forced down the price of other currencies despite the IMF, which was not large enough to bail them out, and many of these currencies faced runaway depreciation against the dollar.

The United States responded to this crisis with the Marshall Plan. George C. Marshall, a career soldier, had been chairman of the Joint Chiefs of Staff during the war. At the war's end, President Truman appointed him Secretary of State. Marshall understood that a shortage of essential items such as food, fuel, raw materials, and machinery and equipment hobbled Europe's recovery. Only the United States could supply Europe's needs in sufficient quantities. He further understood that the dollar shortage prevented Europe from importing what it needed from the United States.

He proposed, and President Truman and Congress approved, a plan whereby the European nations drew up a list of their needs and the United States gave (not loaned) them the dollars they required to satisfy those needs. This reduced the strain on Europe's balance of payments and freed their currencies from the pressure of devaluation. American exports, of course, benefited as our dollars bounced right back to us for purchases of American goods.

By the time of the Korean War, everyone was talking about the "economic miracle of Europe." The Marshall Plan had been extended to victor and vanquished alike, probably history's greatest example of benevolence as enlightened self-interest. The United States had learned from its mistakes following World War I. Isolationism was myopic; the United States had to play an active role in world affairs. And our generosity would be repaid many times over as foreign markets for our goods recovered rapidly.

The Marshall Plan became a cornerstone of American foreign policy. The United States provided the rest of the world with desperately needed dollars in this and also a number of other ways, not all of them purposeful. For example, the United States began to maintain a substantial military presence overseas, and our foreign bases salted their host countries with dollars when native civilians were employed at the bases and American personnel spent their paychecks. In addition, American business firms resumed overseas investing, especially in Europe, spending dollars to purchase subsidiaries and to build facilities. Finally, Americans started to travel abroad in great numbers, seeding Europe with funds. All of these activities meant that dollars were sold for foreign exchange (foreign currency) and so they helped offset the constant sale by other nations of their currency in order to buy American goods.

Furthermore, whenever foreign banks, businesses, or individuals received more dollars than were immediately required, they were delighted to deposit those dollars in either American or foreign banks in order to hold them for a rainy day. Since dollars were in vigorous demand because of the continuing need to buy American exports, those dollars could always be sold in the future, and meanwhile they were a handy private reserve.

To summarize, there were four principal outflows of dollars from the United States: foreign aid (such as the Marshall Plan), foreign investment, military presence overseas, and tourism. Two principal influxes of foreign exchange offset these outflows: foreign purchase of American exports, which greatly exceeded our purchases of imports, and foreigners' willingness to hold dollars as a liquid investment. The four outflows of dollars (roughly) equaled the two influxes of foreign exchange.

By the late 50s and early 60s, however, some foreign banks, businesses, and individuals found that they had more dollars than they could use. They did not wish to buy American goods, and they had found making other investments more attractive than holding dollars, so they decided to sell them.

The United States did not have to rely on the IMF to support the dollar and maintain a fixed exchange rate between the dollar and other currencies. Rather, the U.S. Treasury stood ready to redeem dollars with gold whenever selling pressure on the dollar became heavy: the United

States propped up the price of the dollar relative to other currencies by buying the dollar for gold. Since a foreign holder of dollars could buy gold at $35 per ounce and sell that gold for foreign exchange anywhere in the world, there was no need to sell dollars below the fixed rate of exchange. Whenever the dollar fell a little, foreigners would buy gold with their dollars and cash that gold in for other currencies at full value, which kept the dollar up. And the U.S. price of $35 per ounce of gold set the world price for gold, simply because the United States had most of the world's supply. As a result, a stream of gold started to leave the United States as dollars were redeemed for it. American holdings of gold were cut almost in half by the time increasing alarm was voiced in the early 60s.

An alternative solution had to be found, or else the U.S. supply of gold would disappear. The foreign central banks stepped in and agreed to support the price of the dollar as part of their obligation to maintain fixed exchange rates under the Bretton Woods agreement. They had potentially limitless supplies of their own currencies. If a bank, business, or individual in another nation wanted to sell dollars, and this selling pressure tended to force the price of the dollar down in terms of that nation's currency, the foreign central bank would buy the dollars for its currency and thus support the price of the dollar.

Neither the U.S. Treasury or the Federal Reserve System could support the dollar in this way because neither had limitless supplies of foreign currency. As long as the foreign central banks were willing to buy and accumulate dollars, private citizens, banks, and businesses in other countries were satisfied. In this way, the system of fixed exchange rates survived.

However, by the late 60s and early 70s the situation had once again become ominous. The United States no longer had a favorable balance of trade. Other nations were selling more to, and buying less from, the United States. America's favorable balance of trade had been the single big plus in its balance of payments, offsetting the outflows of dollars mentioned earlier: foreign aid (the Marshall Plan), American tourism, foreign investment, and the American military presence overseas. Now the dollar holdings of foreign central banks began to swell ever more rapidly as their citizens liquidated dollar holdings. These central banks realized that they were acquiring an asset that ultimately would be of little value to them. Having been put in a position of continually buying dollars they would never be able to sell, they insisted that the United States do something to remedy the situation.

The French suggested that the dollar be officially devalued as a first step, because it had had a very high value in terms of other currencies ever since World War II. They reasoned that if the dollar were worth less in terms of other currencies, American exports would be cheaper for the rest of the world, imports would be more expensive in the United States, and thus the U.S. balance of trade would shift from negative to positive as the United States exported more and imported less. In addition, if foreign currencies were more expensive, Americans would be less likely to travel and invest overseas. This would partially stem the dollar hemorrhage. Others suggested that the foreign central banks stop supporting (buying) the dollar and that the dollar be allowed to float downward to a more reasonable level as foreigners sold off their holdings.

For many years, the United States resisted both devaluation and flotation, until, in a series of developments between 1971 and 1973, the U.S. ceased redeeming the dollar for gold and permitted it to float. It promptly fell, relative to other currencies, because foreign central banks no longer felt obliged to purchase it in order to support its price.

At the same time, the price of gold increased because the United States would no longer redeem dollars with gold. The willingness of the United States to sell gold virtually without limit at $35 per ounce had kept its value from rising, but now the price of gold could increase according to the forces of private supply and demand. Consequently, it fluctuated with all other commodity prices, rising rapidly during the general inflation at the end of the 1970s and then falling with commodity prices after 1980.

The dollar fell until the summer of 1973, and then it fluctuated in value until the end of the 1970s. Although foreign central banks no longer felt an obligation to buy dollars, they occasionally did so to keep it from plummeting too far or too fast. They took this action in their own interest at the suggestion of exporters, who knew that a low value for the dollar and a high value for their own currencies made it difficult to export to the United States. Nevertheless, by the end of the 70s the dollar's value was at a postwar low.

The history of the dollar in the 1980s through the early 1990s is a roller coaster ride. At first the dollar's value headed steeply up and rose to a new postwar high by mid-decade. After that it fell once again, so that by the late 80s and early 90s it had retreated back down to its late 70s level. What caused these ups and downs, and what does the future hold? You can find an answer in *The Wall Street Journal*'s coverage of the balance of payments, the balance of trade, and foreign exchange rates.

These few statistical series portraying America's international transactions have generated more confusion in public perception than perhaps any others, but you will see that they are really not difficult to grasp and follow on a regular basis.

BALANCE OF PAYMENTS AND BALANCE OF TRADE

In order to comprehend the *balance-of-payments* accounts, think of yourself as representing the United States in all dealings with the rest of the world. If you wish to do business with the rest of the world, you must buy its currencies (called *foreign exchange*). Likewise, in order to do business in the United States, the rest of the world must buy dollars.

Now set up an accounting statement. The left side will include all the uses you had for all the foreign exchange you purchased. The right side of the account will include all the uses for the dollars that the rest of the world purchased. The two sides must balance: *for every dollar's worth of foreign exchange that you buy with a dollar, the rest of the world must use a dollar's worth of foreign exchange to buy that dollar.* There are no leaks. It is impossible for you to buy any amount of foreign currency without the seller of that currency buying an equivalent value of dollars. It doesn't matter what you do with the foreign exchange you bought nor what they do with the dollars they bought (even if both of you do *nothing* with your newly purchased money). The balance of payments statement merely records what both parties do with their funds.

Congratulations. You have just constructed a balance-of-payments statement.

U.S. Balance of Payments

Money going out (–)	Money coming in (+)
Uses by United States for all foreign exchange purchased with U.S. dollars	Uses by rest of world for all U.S. dollars purchased with foreign exchange

Once the accounting statement has been set up, you may add other details. Each side of the statement will have a *current account* and a *capital account*. Subdivide the current account into merchandise trade, services, and foreign aid; subdivide the capital account into private investment and central bank transactions.

U.S. Balance of Payments

U.S. purchase of foreign money (debit) (–)	**Foreign purchase of U.S. money (credit) (+)**
Current account payments by United States to rest of world	Current account payments to United States by rest of world
Goods and services imports by United States	Goods and services exports by United States
Merchandise trade imports	Merchandise trade exports
Services for which United States pays rest of world	Services United States sells rest of world
Foreign aid payments by United States to rest of world	Foreign aid payments by rest of world to United States
Capital account outflows of funds from United States	Capital account inflows of funds to United States
Private investment by United States in rest of world	Private investment by rest of world in United States
Central bank transactions such as Fed buys foreign currencies	Central bank transactions such as foreign central banks buy dollars

To summarize: the left side of this account (*debit*) shows what you, representing the United States, are doing with the foreign exchange you purchased with American dollars. The right side of the account (*credit*) shows what the rest of the world is doing with the dollars it purchased with its money. Remember, *the two sides must be equal*; a transaction can take place only if things of equal worth are exchanged. Although the *total* for each side must be equal, however, the individual categories need not be. Thus, you can balance one category against another in order to arrive at a merchandise trade balance, goods and services balances, and so on. Each category in the balance of payments will be examined in turn.

The Current Accounts

Balance on Goods and Services

Merchandise Trade

You can use the foreign exchange you have purchased to buy foreign goods, and the rest of the world can use dollars to buy American goods. Thus, if you import goods into the United States, you have incurred a debit (-) because you have sold dollars to buy foreign currency in order to make the transaction; in other words, money has left the United States. On the other hand, if the rest of the world buys American goods, you have earned a credit (+). It is customary to talk about the *balance on merchandise trade* by netting imports against exports to determine whether we have an export (+) surplus or an import (-) deficit.

Services

If you use your dollars to buy foreign currency in order to travel in a foreign country, or to use a foreign air carrier, or to pay interest on a foreign debt, all this would be classified as an outflow of funds or a debit (-). On the other hand, if the rest of the world uses the dollars it buys to travel in the United States, or to fly with an American air carrier, or to pay interest on a debt to the United States, that flow of money into the United States would be a credit (+).

If the net credit (+) or debit (-) balance on this account is added to the credit (+) or debit (-) balance of the merchandise trade account, this subtotal is referred to as the *balance on goods and services.*

Foreign Aid

If you use the foreign money you have purchased to make a gift to the rest of the world, that's a debit (-); if the rest of the world uses the dollars it has purchased to make a gift to the United States, that's a credit (+). Until the Persian Gulf war, and our request to our allies that they compensate us for Operation Desert Storm, foreign aid had always been a debit (-) entry for the U.S. But in 1991 it temporarily switched to credit (+) and, as you will see, made a big difference in our balance of payments that year.

When the foreign aid transaction is combined with the balance on goods and services, it completes the *balance on current account*, which will be a debit (-) balance or a credit (+) balance, depending on whether more funds flowed out of or into the United States.

The Capital Accounts

Private Investments

As a private investor, you may wish to sell U.S. dollars and buy foreign exchange in order to make an investment somewhere else in the world. This could be a direct investment in the form of plant and equipment expenditures or the purchase of a foreign company, or it could be a financial asset, either long-term or short-term. (Stocks and bonds, for instance, are long-term investments, while a foreign bank account or a holding in foreign currency is a short-term investment.)

Any of these transactions will be a debit (-) in the American account because dollars have left the United States. Conversely, when a private investor in another country sells foreign exchange in order to have U.S. dollars to make a direct or financial investment in the United States, whether long-term or short-term, this is classified as a credit (+).

Central Bank Transactions

If, as a representative of the Federal Reserve System, you sell dollars in order to buy foreign currency, this too is a debit (-), and when foreign central banks buy dollars, it is a credit (+).

These central bank transactions conclude the discussion of balance-of-payments components.

A further point must be made before you plow into the data. References are constantly being made to deficits or surpluses in the balances on trade, goods and services, and current account. Now and then you may encounter a comment about a deficit or a surplus in the balance of payments despite this chapter's assertion that it always balances. How can you explain this apparent paradox?

Trade, goods and services, and current account are easy. You already know that there can be a surplus (+) or a deficit (-) in these separate accounts. But how could anyone speak of a deficit in the total balance of payments when it *must always balance*? Because that is the shorthand way of saying that the nation's currency is under selling pressure and that the value of the currency will fall unless some remedial action is taken.

Trade Deficit Grew Sharply In 2nd Quarter

By David Wessel
Staff Reporter of The Wall Street Journal

Current Account Deficit

WASHINGTON – The broadest measure of the U.S. trade deficit expanded to $17.8 billion in the second quarter from $5.9 billion in the first, the Commerce Department said.

The second-quarter current-account deficit, which reflects financial flows as well as trade in goods and services, was the largest for a quarter since the $22.7 billion deficit in the fourth quarter of 1990.

The wider deficit reflected a sharp increase in the merchandise trade deficit, mostly from a rise in imports. Surpluses in services and investment income narrowed.

Because of contributions from U.S. allies to pay for the Persian Gulf War, the U.S. ran a current-account surplus in the first half of last year. But with foreign economies weakening and demand for U.S. goods falling, the deficit is growing again.

Merchandise Trade, Services, and Foreign Aid

The merchandise trade deficit widened to $24.4 billion in the second quarter from $17.2 billion in the first. The trade surplus on services contracted to $13 billion from $13.8 billion. The surplus in dividends, interest and other investment income shrank to $1.4 billion from $4.5 billion. And government and private transfers to foreign recipients came to $7.7 billion, up from $7 billion in the first quarter.

The Commerce Department also reported that net capital inflows, the difference between foreign capital flowing into the U.S. and U.S. capital flowing abroad, increased to $37.4 billion in the second quarter from $14.3 billion in the first.

U.S. purchases of foreign securities showed little change in the quarter. But foreign investors, after cutting back on purchases of U.S. securities in the first quarter, increased them in the second. Foreigners bought U.S. Treasury securities valued at $10.3 billion after selling $800 million of the securities in the first quarter.

Purchases of private securities rose to $10.9 billion in the second quarter from $4.6 billion in the first. An additional $6 billion of foreign direct investment in U.S. plants and companies was recorded in the second quarter; in the first, foreign direct investment fell by $3.8 billion.

The breakdown of capital flows is imprecise. The department said its statistical discrepancy, or the sum of all errors and omissions in recorded capital transactions, amounted to an unusually large $19.6 billion in the second quarter.

Source: *The Wall Street Journal*, September 16, 1992

For instance, at the time the foreign central banks supported the value of the dollar, their purchases of dollars constituted a "plus" (+) in the American balance of payments because they sopped up the excess dollars that their own economies didn't need. (Had they not done so, the dollar would have fallen in value.) Obviously, if you remove a plus from an accounting system that is in the balance, what remains has a negative bottom line. Since a remedial action made the account balance, and since without it the account would have been negative, reference was made to a deficit in the balance of payments.

Current Account Deficit – First Paragraph

WASHINGTON – The broadest measure of the U.S. trade deficit expanded to $17.8 billion in the second quarter from $5.9 billion in the first, the Commerce Department said.

Merchandise Trade, Services, and Foreign Aid – Fifth Paragraph

The merchandise trade deficit widened to $24.4 billion in the second quarter from $17.2 billion in the first. The trade surplus on services contracted to $13 billion from $13.8 billion. The surplus in dividends, interest and other investment income shrank to $1.4 billion from $4.5 billion. And government and private transfers to foreign recipients came to $7.7 billion, up from $7 billion in the first quarter.

When the United States still sold gold internationally in order to redeem the dollar, these sales were plus (+) entries in our balance of payments. If you wonder why the loss of gold is a plus, remember that anything sold by the United States is a plus because the rest of the world must pay us for it. When you remove gold sales from the balance of payments, the remaining items must net out to a negative balance. Therefore, people often referred to the size of the U.S. gold loss as the deficit in the U.S. balance of payments.

And now for one final tip before you look at the data: keep your eyes on the money. That's the best way to determine whether something is a plus (+) or minus (-) in the balance of payments. If *we* pay for it, it's a minus because money is going out. If *they* pay for it, it's a plus.

The Wall Street Journal regularly publishes two Commerce Department reports dealing with the balance of payments and the balance of trade that will be useful to you.

1. *Balance-of-payments* figures for the previous *quarter* appear in the third week of the last month of each quarter.
2. *Monthly balance-of-trade* figures for the previous month are also released in the third week of each month.

Look for the following in the September 16, 1992 balance of payments article: *current account balance*, *merchandise trade balance*, *services*, and *foreign aid*. Very few of the items in the capital account are reported, so the article will not present a complete record of the balance of payments.

According to the first paragraph, the current account deficit was $17.8 billion in the second quarter of 1992. This was generated by the merchandise trade deficit of $24.4 billion (fifth paragraph) and foreign aid payments of $7.7 billion (fifth paragraph), and occurred despite net service (including investment) income of $14.4 billion (fifth paragraph).

The outflow due to the trade deficit and foreign aid swamped service income—hence, the current account deficit.

Use Chart 16-1 (below) to focus on these developments.

CHART 16-1
Balance of Payments (quarterly data)**: Current Account Balance, Goods and Services Balance and Merchandise Trade Balance.**

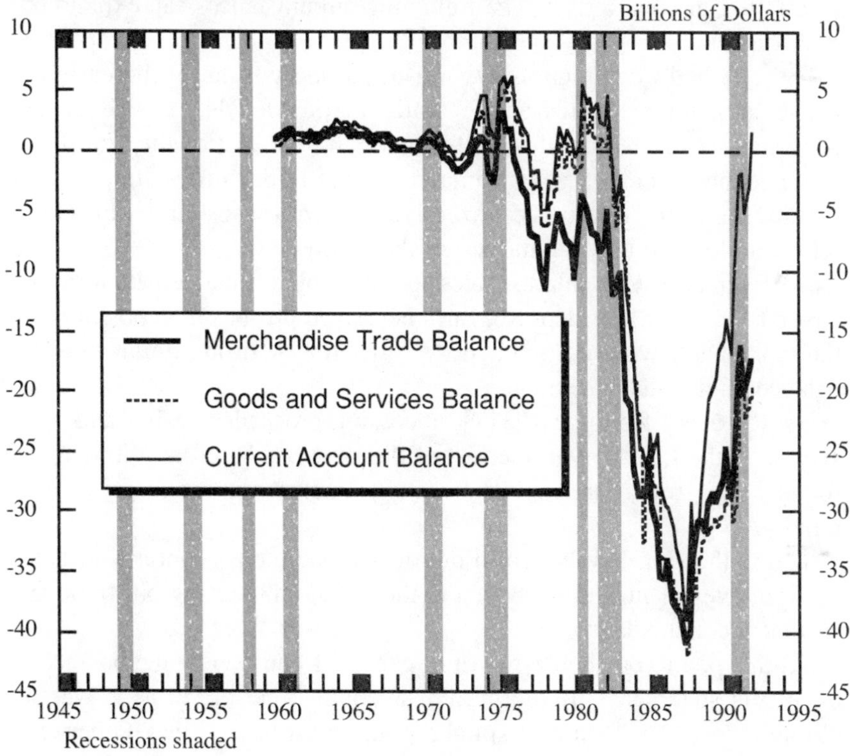

Source: U.S. Department of Commerce, *Business Cycle Indicators*, Series 622, 627; U.S. Department of Commerce *Business Statistics*

First, the merchandise trade balance dropped like a stone in the early 80s, dragging the current account deficit with it.

Second, the merchandise trade deficit stopped falling in the late 80s, halting the deterioration in the current account balance.

Third, the current account balance moved back above zero in 1991, although the merchandise trade balance lagged behind.

Service income, such as the net earnings that the United States receives from foreign investments, the sale of banking, transport, and insurance services, and foreign tourism in the United States, comprises most of the gap between the current account and merchandise trade balance. Notice that until the late 70s and early 80s, U.S. service earnings grew so rapidly that the balance on current account remained positive (+) despite a negative (-) merchandise trade balance.

Then the U.S. merchandise trade balance and the balance on current account dropped off the end of the world so that by the mid-80s both numbers exceeded $150 billion at annual rates. (The numbers in the Chart 16-1 are quarterly.) The following circumstances can explain this development.

1. The Fed's contractionary, anti-inflationary stand in the early 80s drove U.S. interest rates above world market levels. Consequently, Americans were reluctant to sell dollars and the rest of the world was eager to buy them. Strong demand for the dollar drove its price up, making imports relatively attractive to Americans and our goods relatively less attractive in the rest of the world.

2. Even after U.S. interest rates fell, the dollar remained an attractive haven because of President Reagan's perceived pro-business position and the fear of left-wing governments elsewhere. A strong dollar hurt our balance on merchandise trade.

3. Recovery from the 1981-82 recession proceeded earlier and more swiftly in the U.S. than in the rest of the world. Therefore, our demand for imports grew more rapidly because American incomes grew more rapidly.

4. As the U.S. led the world out of recession, our economy attracted foreign investment, further boosting the dollar and hurting our trade and current account balances.

At this point you should return to page 321 and review the balance of payments statement. If the current account is negative, as it was all through the 1980s, then the capital account must be positive. Otherwise, the balance of payments cannot balance. But a positive balance on capital account means that the rest of the world is acquiring American assets. In other words, if we buy Toyotas, they buy Rockefeller Center.

Put it in simple terms. If we export $2 and import $3, the rest of the world has at its disposal an additional dollar. Why? Because of the $3 it earned selling goods to us, it used only $2 to buy our goods. Keeping the extra dollar in its pocket constitutes a foreign investment by the rest of the world in the U.S. But of course the rest of the world won't just keep the dollar in its pocket. Instead it will purchase U.S. Treasury securities or a baseball team, or some other investment.

The U.S. ran a balance of trade and current account surplus for most years in the first three-quarters of the twentieth century and thereby became the world's greatest creditor nation. Reversing the example in the previous paragraph, we had extra money to invest in the rest of the world. But after 1980 we became the world's greatest debtor nation as the flow of capital into the U.S. offset our deficit in the current account.

By the mid-1980s President Reagan and his advisers viewed the situation with alarm. Free traders, they didn't want Congress imposing tariffs in order to reduce imports. So we proposed that our major trading partners dump some of the dollars they had accumulated in the 1970s and thereby force down the dollar's value. As our export prices fell and import prices rose, the problem would take care of itself.

This agreement, negotiated at New York's Plaza Hotel in 1985, became known as the Plaza Accord and began to work in 1987. You can see from Chart 16-1 on page 327 that our trade and current account balances began to improve in 1987 and that by the early 90s these deficits had shrunk considerably.

But they had help. Europe's economies began to break out of their malaise by the end of the 80s. As their incomes grew more rapidly, so did their imports of American goods. This helped stabilize our balance of trade.

In any event, you can see that even though the dollar had fallen all the way back down to its pre-1980 level, our balance of trade deficit persisted in the early 1990s. Obviously, more was involved than the dollar's value and the relative health of the European economy. What about the issues of competitiveness and trade fairness on Japan's part?

We'll examine that soon, but one last point regarding the current account before turning to the trade data in *The Wall Street Journal.* Our balance on current account popped back up above zero briefly in 1991 because of payments made to us by our Desert Storm allies. Those payments offset the continued trade deficit and momentarily pushed the current account into the black.

You can use the *Journal* to follow the Commerce Department's monthly merchandise trade report. The April 17, 1992 article provides data for February 1992. Focus your attention on imports, exports, and the balance between the two. (See pages 332 and 333).

According to the second paragraph, the United States ran a $3.38 billion trade deficit in February 1992 due to exports of $37.81 billion and imports of $41.20 billion. But the text of the article makes clear that this was an unusually small number.

Investor's Tip

- There is no long-run correlation between our balance of trade and the stock market's or gold's performance. If the trade figures improve, less and less attention will be paid to them. And when the balance of trade is no longer a headline-grabber, the stock and gold markets will pay less attention to it.

FOREIGN EXCHANGE RATES

Each day *The Wall Street Journal* publishes several reports on foreign exchange trading activity. Start with the report on the last section's first page (Cl), under the **Markets Diary** heading, labeled **U.S. Dollar**. The excerpt on page 333 from the Monday, June 22, 1992 issue is an example. The Chart provides a record of the dollar's value compared with a trade-weighted average of 15 currencies. Below that is a record of the dollar's value against five major currencies.

The *Journal* also publishes daily a table on **Currency Trading** (check the front page index of the first and last sections under **Foreign Exchange**). The June 22, 1992 table appears on page 336. You can use it to keep abreast of the dollar's value against a wide range of currencies. For instance, on Friday, June 19, 1992, the British pound was worth approximately $1.85, the Canadian dollar about $0.83, the French franc approximately $0.18, the Japanese yen about $0.007, the Swiss franc approximately $0. 70, and the German mark approximately $0.63.

You can see that these quotations portray the value of a single unit of foreign exchange in terms of the American dollar. However, foreign currencies are often quoted in units per American dollar. Thus on June 19 the dollar was worth 127.10 Japanese yen and 1.573 German marks.

Most foreign exchange trading is conducted by banks on behalf of their customers. Banks will also provide future delivery of foreign exchange for customers who want a guaranteed price in order to plan their operations and limit risk due to exchange rate fluctuation. The price for future delivery is known as the forward rate, and you can see forward quotes for the major currencies immediately beneath the current rate.

Finally, the *Journal* also provides exchange rates for major currencies in terms of each other's value and a weekly comparison of the dollar's value against almost every currency in the world on Mondays. See **Key Currency Cross Rates** on page 335 and **World Value of the Dollar** from the June 22, 1992 issue on page 337.

Recall the brief outline of the dollar's postwar history presented earlier.

Chart 16-2 on page 334 provides graphic evidence that the value of foreign currencies in terms of dollars has risen dramatically (i.e., the dollar has fallen in value) since the mid-80s. The French franc has jumped from $0.10 to $0.18; the British pound from a little over $1.00 to $1.85; the Swiss franc from $0.35 to $0.70; the Japanese yen from $0.004 to $0.007; and the German mark from $0.30 to $0.63. The balance-of-payments discussion will aid your understanding of the dollar's fall.

The dollar fell to its post-World War II low against most currencies in the late 70s (see Chart 16-2) because of severe inflation here at home and its impact on our trade balance. (You can observe the increase in value of the key currencies in Chart 16-2.) The merchandise trade balance sank dramatically, as rising prices impeded our ability to sell and whetted our appetite for imports (Chart 16-1 on page 327). Since people in the rest of the world needed fewer dollars (because they weren't buying as many of our goods) and we needed more foreign exchange (because we were buying more of their goods), the dollar's value plunged. The dollar's rally in the early 80s was a two-phase process. The first phase in 1981-82 had two major causes.

First, high interest rates strengthened the dollar. When interest rates in the United States are higher than interest rates elsewhere, foreign exchange is sold for dollars and the capital accounts will show a net flow of private investment into the United States. The Fed's tight money policy pushed interest rates in the United States higher than those in Europe and

U.S. Trade Gap Cut in February To $3.38 Billion

ECONOMY

By JONATHAN WEIL
Staff Reporter of THE WALL STREET JOURNAL

WASHINGTON – The U.S. posted its smallest trade deficit in nine years in February as a surge in aircraft sales helped pull exports out of their three-month slump.

Balance of Trade

The February trade gap shrank to $3.38 billion from $5.95 billion in January, the Commerce Department said. Exports climbed 6.8% in February to $37.81 billion, their first increase since October. More than half the rise was accounted for by a 9.4% increase in exports of non-automotive capital goods, principally civilian aircraft. Auto exports also rose sharply. Imports were down 0.4% to $41.20 billion.

For the first two months of 1992, exports were 8.1% greater than a year earlier. But economists figure the strong performance won't be sustainable until the economies improve among U.S. trading partners, notably Western Europe and Japan.

"We can expect continued strong export performance once our major trading partners emerge from their current economic doldrums," said Barry Rogstad, president of American Business Conference, a group of 100 fast-growing midsized companies.

Import levels are expected to rise, however, as the U.S. recovery progresses.

Civilian aircraft exports grew 30.3% in February, and auto exports climbed 12.8%. Both industries typically are volatile, however, suggesting a shaky base for the export growth.

"No one in their wildest imagination thinks that auto exports will be able to sustain" such an increase, said Lyle Gramley, chief economist for Mortgage Bankers Association. Aircraft and autos "are very large items. They're lumpy and tend to go up one month and down the next."

Food exports shot up 17.8% in February, as seafood shipments more than doubled. Exports of industrial supplies were down 4.3%, however, as fuel oil exports tumbled.

Meanwhile, imports of food, industrial supplies and autos all registered significant declines. Imports of both capital and consumer goods increased. Crude oil imports were slashed 13.7% in February, while auto imports fell 4.1%. But the U.S. continues importing semiconductors and computers, with imports climbing by 6.9% and 8.9%, respectively.

All figures are adjusted for seasonal fluctuations.

U. S. Trade Deficit

In billions of dollars

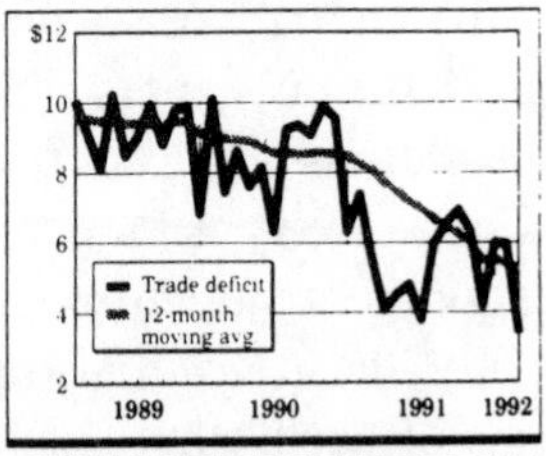

THE U.S. MERCHANDISE TRADE deficit narrowed in February to a seasonally adjusted $3.38 billion from a revised $5.95 billion in January, the Commerce Department reports. The 12-month moving average narrowed to $5.20 billion in February from a revised $5.38 billion in January. (See story on page A2.)

Source: *The Wall Street Journal*, April 17, 1992

Merchandise Trade Balance–Second Paragraph

The February trade gap shrank to $3.38 billion from $5.95 billion in January, the Commerce Department said. Exports climbed 6.8% in February to $37.81 billion, their first increase since October. More than half the rise was accounted for by a 9.4% increase in exports of non-automotive capital goods, principally civilian aircraft. Auto exports also rose sharply. Imports were down 0.4% to $41.20 billion.

Source: *The Wall Street Journal,* April 17, 1992

U.S. DOLLAR J. P. Morgan Index vs. 15 Currencies

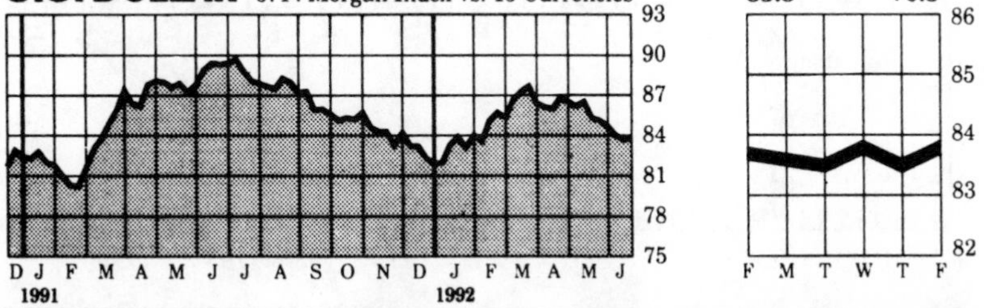

CURRENCY	LATE NY	LATE THU	DAY'S HIGH	DAY'S LOW	12-MO HIGH — LATE NY —	12-MO LOW
British pound (in U.S. dollars)	**1.8595**	1.8635	1.8650	1.8549	1.8855	1.6010
Canadian dollar (in U.S. dollars)	**0.8352**	0.8345	0.8364	0.8340	0.8928	0.8291
Swiss franc (per U.S. dollar)	**1.4195**	1.4140	1.4128	1.4230	1.3405	1.5903
Japanese yen (per U.S. dollar)	**127.06**	126.87	126.73	127.25	123.35	139.60
German mark (per U.S. dollar)	**1.5735**	1.5684	1.5667	1.5760	1.5075	1.8356

Source: *The Wall Street Journal,* June 22, 1992

CHART 16-2
Foreign Exchange Rates

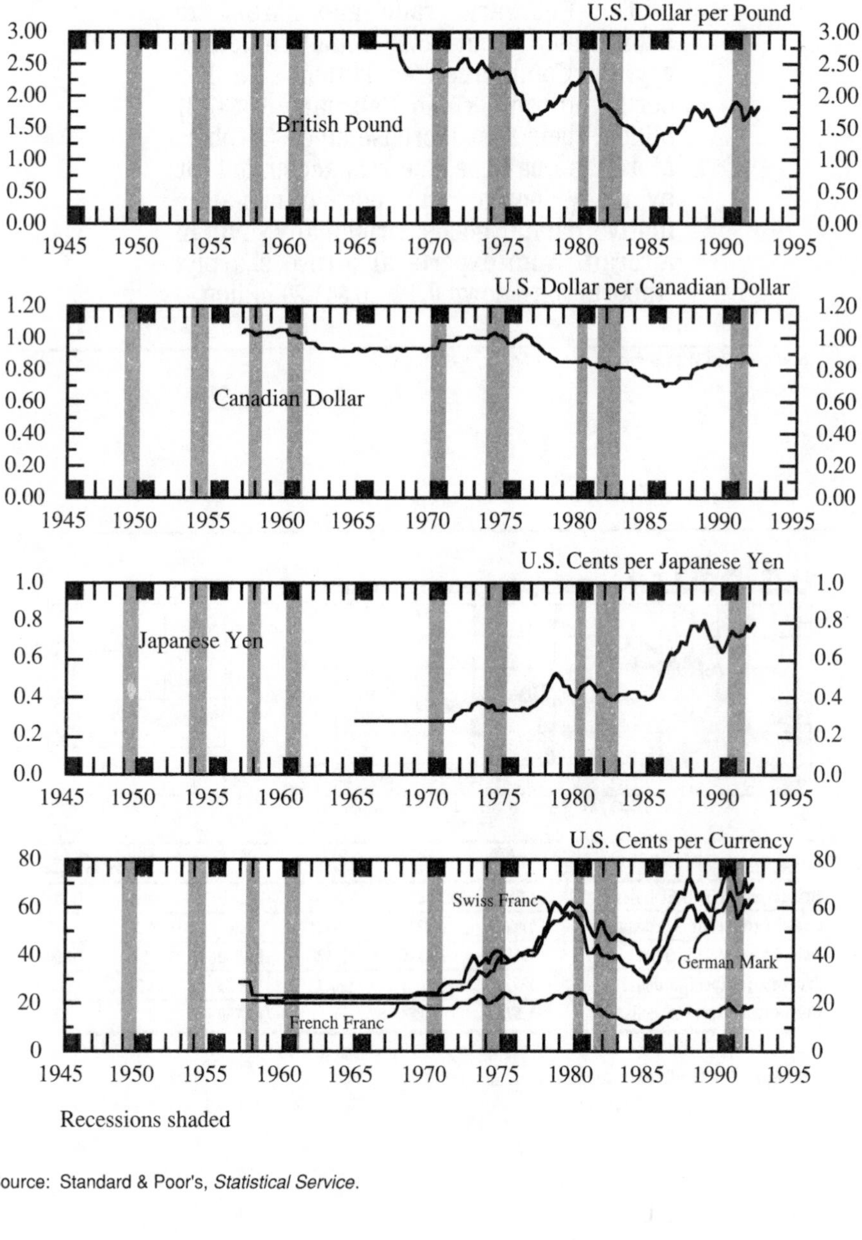

Recessions shaded

Source: Standard & Poor's, *Statistical Service*.

Key Currency Cross Rates Late New York Trading June 19, 1992

	Dollar	Pound	SFranc	Guilder	Yen	Lira	D-Mark	FFranc	CdnDlr
Canada	1.1972	2.2262	.84340	.67543	.00942	.00101	.76085	.22599	....
France	5.2975	9.851	3.7319	2.9887	.04169	.00445	3.3667	....	4.4249
Germany	1.5735	2.9259	1.1085	.88773	.01238	.00132	....	.29703	1.3143
Italy	1190.8	2214.2	838.85	671.79	9.372	....	756.75	224.78	994.6
Japan	127.06	236.27	89.510	71.684	....	.10671	80.750	23.985	106.13
Netherlands ...	1.7725	3.2960	1.2487	....	.01395	.00149	1.1265	.33459	1.4805
Switzerland	1.4195	2.6396	....	.80085	.01117	.00119	.90213	.26796	1.1857
U.K.	.53778	....	.37885	.30340	.00423	.00045	.34177	.10152	.44920
U.S.	....	1.8595	.70447	.56417	.00787	.00084	.63553	.18877	.83528

Source: Telerate

Source: *The Wall Street Journal*, June 22, 1992

Japan, prompting heavy dollar purchases by foreign investors who wished to enjoy the high interest rates available here.

Second, the U.S. balance on current account improved dramatically until late 1982 because of rapidly growing service income and despite a sharply negative balance of trade. This positive element in the American balance of payments not only generated a flow of dollars into the United States but also encouraged private businesses and individuals in the rest of the world to invest in dollars because they believed that the dollar would remain strong in the future.

The second phase in 1983-84 is somewhat more complex. The interest rate differential between the United States and the rest of the world had narrowed since mid 82 (see the first cause listed above), while the balance on current account deteriorated rapidly (see the second cause listed above) due to the plunge in our merchandise trade balance (see Chart 16-1 on page 327). Under these circumstances, the dollar's value should have fallen.

Nevertheless, it improved, because of the continuing flow of investment dollars into the United States and the continuing reduced flow of our investment dollars to the rest of the world. The rest of the world believed America to be the safest, most profitable home for its funds. To foreigners (indeed, to many Americans) President Reagan symbolized America's protection of, and concern for, business interests. Certainly, the United States was a secure haven: investments would not be expropriated nor would their return be subject to confiscatory taxation. And the return was good; even if the interest rate differential between here and abroad had narrowed, U.S. rates were still higher than those in most other countries. Moreover, profits had been strong, and the stock market

CURRENCY TRADING

EXCHANGE RATES

Friday, June 19, 1992

The New York foreign exchange selling rates below apply to trading among banks in amounts of $1 million and more, as quoted at 3 p.m. Eastern time by Bankers Trust Co., Telerate and other sources. Retail transactions provide fewer units of foreign currehcy per dollar.

		U.S. $ equiv.		Currency per U.S. $	
	Country	**Fri.**	**Thurs.**	**Fri.**	**Thurs.**
	Argentina (Peso)	1.01	1.01	.99	.99
	Australia (Dollar)	.7521	.7545	1.3296	1.3254
	Austria (Schilling)	.09038	.09071	11.06	11.02
	Bahrain (Dinar)	2.6522	2.6522	.3771	.3771
	Belgium (Franc)	.03089	.03102	32.38	32.24
	Brazil (Cruzeiro)	.00032	.00032	3106.91	3106.91
British Pound →	**Britain** (Pound)	1.8590	1.8645	.5379	.5363
	30-Day Forward	1.8496	1.8551	.5407	.5391
	90-Day Forward	1.8316	1.8370	.5460	.5444
	180-Day Forward	1.8071	1.8125	.5534	.5517
Canadian Dollar →	**Canada** (Dollar)	.8352	.8360	1.1973	1.1962
	30-Day Forward	.8338	.8345	1.1994	1.1983
	90-Day Forward	.8315	.8322	1.2027	1.2017
	180-Day Forward	.8284	.8292	1.2072	1.2060
	Czechoslovakia (Koruna)				
	Commercial rate	.0361141	.0362188	27.6900	27.6100
	Chile (Peso)	.002898	.002898	345.09	345.09
	China (Renminbi)	.181984	.181984	5.4950	5.4950
	Colombia (Peso)	.001731	.001731	577.78	577.78
	Denmark (Krone)	.1652	.1657	6.0535	6.0355
	Ecuador (Sucre)				
	Floating rate	.000712	.000712	1404.00	1404.00
	Finland (Markka)	.23348	.23411	4.2830	4.2715
French Franc →	**France** (Franc)	.18879	.18956	5.2970	5.2755
	30-Day Forward	.18782	.18857	5.3243	5.3030
	90-Day Forward	.18586	.18660	5.3805	5.3592
	180-Day Forward	.18323	.18391	5.4575	5.4375
German Mark →	**Germany** (Mark)	.6357	.6384	1.5730	1.5663
	30-Day Forward	.6327	.6353	1.5806	1.5740
	90-Day Forward	.6265	.6291	1.5962	1.5895
	180-Day Forward	.6182	.6208	1.6175	1.6108
	Greece (Drachma)	.005211	.005230	191.90	191.20
	Hong Kong (Dollar)	.12928	.12925	7.7350	7.7370
	Hungary (Forint)	.0130412	.0129820	76.6800	77.0300
	India (Rupee)	.03560	.03560	28.09	28.09
	Indonesia (Rupiah)	.0004931	.0004931	2028.03	2028.03
	Ireland (Punt)	1.7001	1.7057	.5882	.5863
	Israel (Shekel)	.4158	.4164	2.4052	2.4013
	Italy (Lira)	.0008389	.0008425	1192.05	1186.99
	Japan (Yen)	.007868	.007886	127.10	126.80
	30-Day Forward	.007863	.007882	127.17	126.87
	90-Day Forward	.007859	.007875	127.25	126.99
	180-Day Forward	.007859	.007873	127.25	127.01
	Jordan (Dinar)	1.5094	1.5094	.6625	.6625
	Kuwait (Dinar)	3.4483	3.4483	.2900	.2900
	Lebanon (Pound)	.000562	.000562	1780.00	1780.00
	Malaysia (Ringgit)	.3975	.3973	2.5160	2.5170
	Malta (Lira)	3.2206	3.2206	.3105	.3105
	Mexico (Peso)				
	Floating rate	.0003206	.0003206	3119.01	3119.01
	Netherland (Guilder)	.5643	.5667	1.7721	1.7647
	New Zealand (Dollar)	.5464	.5436	1.8302	1.8396
	Norway (Krone)	.1626	.1632	6.1490	6.1270
	Pakistan (Rupee)	.0400	.0400	24.97	24.97
	Peru (New Sol)	.8752	.8752	1.14	1.14
	Philippines (Peso)	.03891	.03891	25.70	25.70
	Poland (Zloty)	.00007931	.00007920	12609.00	12626.01
	Portugal (Escudo)	.007662	.007683	130.51	130.16
	Saudi Arabia (Riyal)	.26738	.26738	3.7400	3.7400
	Singapore (Dollar)	.6164	.6166	1.6223	1.6217
	South Africa (Rand)				
	Commercial rate	.3560	.3564	2.8093	2.8058
	Financial rate	.2778	.2778	3.6000	3.6000
	South Korea (Won)	.0012411	.0012411	805.75	805.75
	Spain (Peseta)	.010107	.010134	98.94	98.68
	Sweden (Krona)	.1761	.1767	5.6800	5.6605
Swiss Franc →	**Switzerland** (Franc)	.7047	.7074	1.4191	1.4137
	30-Day Forward	.7016	.7042	1.4254	1.4200
	90-Day Forward	.6953	.6980	1.4382	1.4327
	180-Day Forward	.6877	.6901	1.4541	1.4490
	Taiwan (Dollar)	.040881	.040895	24.46	24.45
	Thailand (Baht)	.03940	.03940	25.38	25.38
	Turkey (Lira)	.0001450	.0001448	6895.00	6908.00
	United Arab (Dirham)	.2723	.2723	3.6725	3.6725
	Uruguay (New Peso)				
	Financial	.000321	.000321	3114.00	3114.00
	Venezuela (Bolivar)				
	Floating rate	.01536	.01538	65.11	65.01
	SDR	1.41202	1.41305	.70821	.70769
	ECU	1.30400	1.30840	....	....

Special Drawing Rights (SDR) are based on exchange rates for the U.S., German, British, French and Japanese currencies. Source: International Monetary Fund.

European Currency Unit (ECU) is based on a basket of community currencies.

Source: *The Wall Street Journal*, June 22, 1992

World Value of the Dollar

The table below, compiled by Bank of America, gives the rates of exchange for the U.S. dollar against various currencies as of Friday June 19, 1992. Unless otherwise noted, all rates listed are middle rates of interbank bid and asked quotes, and are expressed in foreign currency units per one U.S. dollar. The rates are indicative and aren't based on, nor intended to be used as a basis for, particular transactions.

BankAmerica International doesn't trade in all the listed foreign currencies.

Country (Currency)	Value 6/19	Value 6/12
Afghanistan (Afghani -c)	1162.50	1162.50
Albania (Lek)	50.00	50.00
Algeria (Dinar)	21.36	21.50
Andorra (Peseta)	98.87	99.46
Andorra (Franc)	5.2895	5.3075
Angola (New Kwanza -8)	550.00	550.00
Antigua (E Caribbean $)	2.70	2.70
Argentina (Peso)	0.9906	0.9901
Aruba (Florin)	1.79	1.79
Australia (Australia Dollar)	1.3256	1.3141
Austria (Schilling)	11.0538	11.0765
Bahamas (Dollar)	1.00	1.00
Bahrain (Dinar)	0.377	0.377
Bangladesh (Taka)	38.70	38.70
Barbados (Dollar)	2.0113	2.0113
Belgium (Franc)	32.333	32.405
Belize (Dollar)	2.00	2.00
Benin (C.F.A. Franc)	264.475	265.375
Bermuda (Dollar)	1.00	1.00
Bhutan (Ngultrum)	28.28	28.35
Bolivia (Boliviano -f)	3.86	3.85
Bolivia (Boliviano -o)	3.87	3.865
Botswana (Pula)	2.1258	2.1191
Bouvet Island (Norwegian Krone)	6.145	6.166
Brazil (Cruzeiro -c)	3202.45	3086.30
Brunei (Dollar)	1.6225	1.6218
Bulgaria (Lev)	23.104	23.086
Burkina Faso (C.F.A. Franc)	264.475	265.375
Burma (Kyat)	6.0347	6.0437
Burundi (Franc)	193.6777	193.9666
Cambodia (Riel)	850.00	850.00
Cameroon (C.F.A. Franc)	264.475	265.375
Canada (Dollar)	1.1983	1.1933
Cape Verde Isl (Escudo)	66.90	68.52
Cayman Islands (Dollar)	0.85	0.85
Centrl African Rp (C.F.A. Franc)	264.475	265.375
Chad (C.F.A. Franc)	264.475	265.375
Chile (Peso -m)	355.76	353.41
Chile (Peso -o)	386.00	385.11
China (Renminbi Yuan)	5.4747	5.48
Colombia (Peso -o)	755.95	753.57
Commwlth Ind Sts (Rouble -m)	85.00	85.00
Comoros (C.F.A. Franc)	264.475	265.375
Congo, People Rp (C.F.A. Franc)	264.475	265.375
Costa Rica (Colon)	123.50	125.13
Cuba (Peso)	1.3203	1.3203
Cyprus (Pound *)	2.2299	2.2202
Czechoslovakia (Koruna -c)	28.39	28.54
Denmark (Danish Krone)	6.0465	6.0765
Djibouti (Djibouti Franc)	177.72	177.72
Dominica (E Caribbean $)	2.70	2.70
Dominican Rep (Peso -d)	13.00	13.00
Ecuador (Sucre -o-1)	1423.09	1419.55
Ecuador (Sucre -d-1)	1517.50	1475.50
Egypt (Pound)	3.30	3.375
El Salvador (Colon -d)	8.20	8.21
Equatorial Guinea (C.F.A. Franc)	264.475	265.375
Ethiopia (Birr -o)	2.07	2.07
Faeroe Islands (Danish Krone)	6.0465	6.0765
Falkland Islands (Pound *)	1.8604	1.8499
Fiji (Dollar)	1.4782	1.4765
Finland (Markka)	4.2815	4.2945
France (Franc)	5.2895	5.3075
French Guiana (Franc)	5.2895	5.3075
French Pacific Isl (C.F.P. Franc)	96.1726	96.4999
Gabon (C.F.A. Franc)	264.475	265.375
Gambia (Dalasi)	8.79	8.79
Germany (Mark)	1.5705	1.5759
Ghana (Cedi)	412.00	412.00
Gibraltar (Pound *)	1.8604	1.8499
Greece (Drachma)	191.95	191.56
Greenland (Danish Krone)	6.0465	6.0765
Grenada (E Caribbean $)	2.70	2.70
Guadeloupe (Franc)	5.2895	5.3075
Guam (U.S. $)	1.00	1.00
Guatemala (Quetzal)	5.13	5.13
Guinea Bissau (Peso)	5000.00	5000.00
Guinea Rep (Franc)	812.29	812.29
Guyana (Dollar)	124.10	124.10
Haiti (Gourde)	5.00	5.00
Honduras Rep (Lempira -d)	5.54	5.56
Hong Kong (Dollar)	7.7375	7.7345
Hungary (Forint -2)	78.05	78.29
Iceland (Krona)	57.22	57.47
India (Rupee -m-10)	28.28	28.35
Indonesia (Rupiah)	2030.00	2032.25
Iran (Rial -d)	1437.00	1437.00
Iraq (Dinar)	0.3125	0.3125
Ireland (Punt *)	1.7022	1.6948
Israel (New Shekel)	2.468	2.461
Italy (Lira)	1188.25	1193.00
Ivory Coast (C.F.A. Franc)	264.475	265.375
Jamaica (Dollar -o)	22.00	22.70
Japan (Yen)	126.81	126.50
Jordan (Dinar)	0.676	0.677
Kenya (Shilling)	28.7151	28.7579
Kiribati (Australia Dollar)	1.3256	1.3141
Korea, North (Won)	2.18	2.18
Korea, South (Won)	791.40	789.30
Kuwait (Dinar)	0.2904	0.2902
Laos, People DR (Kip)	710.00	710.00
Lebanon (Pound)	1685.00	1780.00
Lesotho (Maloti)	2.8048	2.8061
Liberia (Dollar)	1.00	1.00
Libya (Dinar)	0.2723	0.2727
Liechtenstein (Franc)	1.4203	1.43
Luxembourg (Lux.Franc)	32.333	32.405
Macao (Pataca)	7.9928	7.9897
Madagascar DR (Franc)	1883.99	1883.99
Malawi (Kwacha -9)	4.078	3.9466
Malaysia (Ringgit)	2.52	2.516
Maldive (Rufiyaa)	9.91	9.91
Mali Rep (C.F.A. Franc)	264.475	265.375
Malta (Lira *)	3.2217	3.1862
Martinique (Franc)	5.2895	5.3075
Mauritania (Ouguiya)	84.92	84.92
Mauritius (Rupee)	15.55	15.62
Mexico (Peso -d)	3093.30	3092.30
Monaco (Franc)	5.2895	5.3075
Mongolia (Tugrik -o)	40.00	40.00
Montserrat (E Caribbean $)	2.70	2.70
Morocco (Dirham)	8.2546	8.3128
Mozambique (Metical)	2430.27	2355.29
Namibia (Rand -c)	2.8048	2.8061
Nauru Islands (Australia Dollar)	1.3256	1.3141
Nepal (Rupee -11)	46.63	46.63
Netherlands (Guilder)	1.7698	1.7748
Netherlands Ant'les (Guilder)	1.79	1.79
New Zealand (N.Z.Dollar)	1.8371	1.8387
Nicaragua (Gold Cordoba)	5.00	5.00
Niger Rep (C.F.A. Franc)	264.475	265.375
Nigeria (Naira -d-5)	18.46	18.46
Norway (Norwegian Krone)	6.145	6.166
Oman, Sultanate of (Rial)	0.385	0.385
Pakistan (Rupee)	25.08	25.1049
Panama (Balboa)	1.00	1.00
Papua N.G. (Kina)	0.9555	0.9521
Paraguay (Guarani -d)	1470.00	1465.00
Peru (New Sol -d)	1.185	1.195
Philippines (Peso)	25.739	26.256
Pitcairn Island (N.Z.Dollar)	1.8371	1.8387
Poland (Zloty -o)	13677.00	13755.00
Portugal (Escudo)	130.32	131.20
Puerto Rico (U.S. $)	1.00	1.00
Qatar (Riyal)	3.64	3.64
Republic of Yemen (Dinar)	0.465	0.465
Republic of Yemen (Rial)	12.00	12.00
Republic of Yemen (Rial -o)	18.00	18.00
Reunion, Ile de la (Franc)	5.2895	5.3075
Romania (Leu)	283.00	251.00
Rwanda (Franc -7)	142.8308	143.0439
Saint Christopher (E Caribbean $)	2.70	2.70
Saint Helena (Pound Sterling *)	1.8604	1.8499
Saint Lucia (E Caribbean $)	2.70	2.70
Saint Pierre (Franc)	5.2895	5.3075
Saint Vincent (E Caribbean $)	2.70	2.70
Samoa, American (U.S. $)	1.00	1.00
Samoa, Western (Tala)	2.4248	2.4248
San Marino (Lira)	1188.25	1193.00
Sao Tome & Principe (Dobra)	240.00	240.00
Saudi Arabia (Riyal)	3.7503	3.7503
Senegal (C.F.A. Franc)	264.475	265.375
Seychelles (Rupee)	5.1311	5.1388
Sierra Leone (Leone)	415.00	420.00
Singapore (Dollar)	1.6225	1.6218
Solomon Islands (Solomon Dollar)	2.874	2.874
Somali Rep (Shilling -d)	2620.00	2620.00
South Africa (Rand -f)	3.6166	3.5026
South Africa (Rand -c)	2.8048	2.8061
Spain (Peseta)	98.87	99.46
Sri Lanka (Rupee)	44.05	43.85
Sudan Rep (Dinar -4)	10.00	10.00
Sudan Rep (Pound -c)	90.00	90.00
Surinam (Guilder)	1.785	1.785
Swaziland (Lilangeni)	2.8048	2.8061
Sweden (Krona)	5.677	5.691
Switzerland (Franc)	1.4203	1.43
Syria (Pound -h)	20.25	20.25
Taiwan (Dollar -o)	24.71	24.73
Tanzania (Shilling)	300.76	299.47
Thailand (Baht)	25.39	25.37
Togo, Rep (C.F.A. Franc)	264.475	265.375
Tonga Islands (Pa'anga)	1.3256	1.3141
Trinidad & Tobago (Dollar)	4.25	4.25
Tunisia (Dinar)	0.8663	0.8728
Turkey (Lira)	7086.89	6867.07
Turks & Caicos (U.S. $)	1.00	1.00
Tuvalu (Australia Dollar)	1.3256	1.3141
Uganda (Shilling -l)	1165.49	1161.29
United Arab Emir (Dirham)	3.671	3.671
United Kingdom (Pound Sterling *)	1.8604	1.8499
Uruguay (Peso -m)	3009.00	2990.00
Vanuatu (Vatu)	111.04	111.04
Vatican City (Lira)	1188.25	1193.00
Venezuela (Bolivar -d)	66.16	66.03
Vietnam (Dong -o)	11200.00	11250.00
Virgin Is, Br (U.S. $)	1.00	1.00
Virgin Is, US (U.S. $)	1.00	1.00
Yugoslavia (Dinar -3)	316.62	317.74
Zaire Rep (Zaire -6)	130000.00	130000.00
Zambia (Kwacha)	155.02	151.33
Zimbabwe (Dollar)	5.0501	5.0156

*U.S. dollars per National Currency unit. (a) Free market central bank rate. (b) Floating rate. (c) Commercial rate. (d) Free market rate. (e) Controlled. (f) Financial rate. (g) Preferential rate. (h) Nonessential imports. (i) Floating tourist rate. (j) Public transaction rate. (k) Agricultural products. (l) Priority rate. (m) Market rate. (n) Essential imports. (o) Official rate. (p) Exports. (n.a.) Not available.

(1) Ecuador, 29 May 1992: Sucrê devalued by approx 4% (2) Hungary, 16 March 1992: Forint devalued by approx 1.9% (3) Yugoslavia, 13 April 1992: Dinar devalued by approx 57%, now 200 dinars to DM1. (4) Sudan Rep., 18 May 1992: New currency called the Dinar introduced (5) Nigeria, 5 March 1992: Naira now floating. (6) Zaire Rep., 29 May 1992: Rate as of 15.5.92 (7) Rwanda, 11 June 1992: Franc devalued by approx 14.9% (8) Angola, 15 April 1992: New Kwanza devalued by approx 67.2% (9) Malawi, 11 June 1992: Kwacha devalued by approx 22%. (10) India, 3 March 1992: Rupee now partially convertible (11) Nepal, 4 March 1992: Rupee now partially convertible.

Further information available at BankAmerica International. Source: Bank of America Global Trading, London

Source: *The Wall Street Journal*, June 22, 1992

reflected this. Foreign investors who had a stake in American business were rewarded handsomely.

Thus the dollar remained strong because the huge net capital flow into the United States bid the dollar's price up and forced other currencies down. The rise in the dollar's value, together with the quicker economic expansion here than abroad, depressed our exports and stimulated our imports. Consequently, the deterioration in our merchandise trade balance in 1983 and 1984 was a result of the dollar's appreciation, not a cause of it.

But by 1985 the merchandise trade balance had deteriorated to such an extent, while American interest rates continued to slide, that the dollar began to weaken. Foreign demand for our currency was not strong enough to offset our demand for the rest of the world's currencies. In addition, we began to pressure our major trading partners, requesting their assistance in reducing our trade deficit by driving the dollar's value down. They (i.e., their central banks) complied by agreeing to the Plaza Accord and sold dollars, contributing to the dollar's slide. As a result, by the late 80s, the dollar had lost most of the increase of the early 80s.

The dollar stabilized at the end of the decade because our balance-of-trade deficit stopped growing due to rapid export growth. American interest rates rose, and foreign central banks actively supported the dollar once again. These developments stimulated dollar purchase and helped halt the dollar's decline. The foreign central banks had begun to respond to their own industrial interests and were no longer willing to let the dollar fall in order to protect our markets.

The dollar remained near its all-time low in the early 1990s but our merchandise trade deficit remained substantial and foreign investment dollars continued to flow into the U.S.

Investor's Tip

- This brief history should warn you how hard it is to predict the dollar's value and the course of international economic events. That's why foreign exchange speculation is not for amateurs. Even some pros go broke doing it.

CHAPTER 17

SUMMARY AND PROSPECT

So what will you have for the 1990s? Stocks and other paper securities, or gold and similar tangible assets? The best investment all depends on the course of inflation and the business cycle.

But, you may ask, didn't we tame both inflation and the business cycle in the 1980s? The decade came to an end after seven good years of steady expansion, with both low unemployment and low inflation. Wasn't this evidence that the Fed had done a great job?

Yes, the Fed did perform admirably and effectively in the 1980s, so that by the end of the decade, escalating debt and inflation and the business cycle's roller coaster ride appeared to be mere relics of the past, confined to the years 1965 through 1980. Could it be that those years, with all their problems, were an exception, a kind of rough patch that is now behind us? Once again, we must turn to the historical record for some perspective.

The early 1960s followed the Eisenhower years, which President Kennedy and his advisers criticized severely for sluggish economic performance and too many recessions. They excoriated the fiscal policy of President Eisenhower's administration and the monetary policy of the Federal Reserve for excessive concern with inflation and complacency about slow economic growth and unemployment. These critics charged that because of the attempt to restrain demand in order to combat "creeping inflation," the economy's growth rate had fallen and recovery from frequent recessions in the 1950s had been weak.

Yet the Eisenhower years had been the best of times for stock market investors. The Dow climbed from 200 in 1950 to almost 1,000 in 1965, a fivefold increase in 15 years. Some said that stocks had been a good hedge against the negligible inflation of those years. In truth, they had done well because of inflation's absence.

But as the middle 60s approached, the economy rapidly gained steam. The low level of inflation (inherited from the Eisenhower years) and the

Fed's easy money policy (in response to Kennedy administration requests) were the most important ingredients in the rapid economic expansion that began in the 1960s.

Modest increases in the CPI permitted strong growth in real consumer income. As a result, consumer sentiment steadily improved. This, together with the ready availability of loans at low interest rates, prompted consumers to resort to record levels of mortgage borrowing and consumer credit. Home construction and automobile production set new highs. Business responded by investing heavily in new plant and equipment, so that general boom conditions prevailed by the middle of the decade.

The tax cut proposed by President Kennedy has received most of the credit for this prosperity. Inconveniently, however, it was not enacted until 1964, after his death, and it is difficult to understand how an expansion that began in 1962 can be attributed to a tax cut two years later.

The expansion's relaxed and easy progress was its most important early feature. There was no overheating. Housing starts, auto sales, consumer credit, and retail sales gradually broke through to new highs. By 1965 there had been three solid years of expansion, reflected in a strong improvement in labor productivity and a solid advance in real compensation.

The problems began in the late 60s when the Fed did not exercise enough restraint on the boom. Its half-hearted measures were too little and too late. Most observers blamed the Vietnam War for the inflation, but the federal deficit never exceeded $15 billion in the late 60s. Meanwhile, private borrowing hit $100 billion annually, thereby dwarfing federal fiscal stimuli. Private borrowing and spending on residential construction, autos, and other consumer durables and business capital expenditures—not federal borrowing and spending on the Vietnam War—generated the inflation of the late 60s.

As the inflation progressed, it created a nightmare for stock and bond holders in the 1970s. During the entire decade, their investments did not gain in value; some even fell. Meanwhile, real estate boomed and gold and other precious metals went through the roof.

And as you know from the earlier discussion, the Fed's attempts to deal with inflation remained inadequate throughout the 70s, so that its stop-go policies only exacerbated inflation over the course of the cycle.

It was not until Paul Volcker persuaded the Fed to take a stand in the early 80s with a policy of continued restraint that inflation was brought under control and stability ensured for the rest of the decade. By the end of the 80s, Americans enjoyed better economic conditions than at any time since the early 60s.

And as had happened during the good old days of low inflation, paper assets such as stocks and bonds did well in the low inflation 80s while gold and precious metals collapsed. Real estate appeared to be an an anomaly because it did well in key urban areas which enjoyed strong demographic and job growth. But that obscured real estate's weakness in most markets. Real estate was a bad investment all across rural America, in oil-producing regions, and in many metropolitan areas in the 1980s.

Will the 1990s be like the late 80s and the early 60s? Will the economy expand slowly and gradually, bringing prosperity without severe fluctuation and inflation? And will stocks and bonds do better than real estate and precious metals?

Yes. The rate of inflation remains low, with substantial slack in the economy. The Fed's change in direction in the early 1980s means that the years from 1965 to 1980 were an anomaly, a bad patch that is now behind us. Spiraling debt and inflation should be a thing of the past as we look forward to continued monetary restraint.

But that doesn't mean that the U.S. faces a rosy economic future. Long-run forces are at work that will weaken America's future growth unless they are dealt with soon. The U.S. economy can't compete the way it once did and Americans have noticed that the shares of the pie are shrinking. That's a bad sign that became increasingly clear as we emerged from the 1990-91 recession. The old confidence was lacking.

Capitalism is a moving target, always changing and always evolving—constrained by indigenous institutions and shaped by contemporary events. The description of its dynamic, contained in these chapters, is appropriate for the present time and place. This dynamic would not have explained conditions 50 years earlier, nor will it describe them 50 years hence. The system will evolve in ways that no one can predict. Yet for the time being, the Fed has managed to wrestle the business cycle and inflation to the mat, so that they will be restrained, although not absent, in the 1990s.

APPENDIX A

MISCELLANEOUS STATISTICAL INDICATORS

A number of statistical indicators have not yet been discussed although they appear regularly in *The Wall Street Journal*. These indicators are not directly applicable to the earlier chapters' analyses. They are important, however, and the following commentary should help you put them in perspective.

EMPLOYMENT DATA

The Wall Street Journal usually publishes the Labor Department's *monthly employment report* on Monday of the second week. Perhaps because of the July 4 holiday weekend, June's report appeared early in the Friday, July 3, 1992 *Wall Street Journal* (see page 344). The first and fifth paragraphs inform you that the *unemployment rate* rose to 7.8% and that *non-farm payrolls* fell by 117,000, bad news that took most people by surprise because the consensus forecast had been for continued recovery from the 1990-91 recession. Now more observers would take a wait and see attitude.

You should also track the *average workweek* and *factory overtime* because they, too, portray the economy's strength and are important determinants of consumer sentiment. They appear in the last paragraph. Appendix Charts 1-1 and 1-2 on pages 345 and 346 clearly show that the workweek and overtime had recovered well from the 1990-91 recession despite June's disappointing unemployment report. You should also observe that these indicators generally improve during expansion, flatten with boom conditions, and plummet in recession. Their relationship to consumer sentiment is probably obvious.

Jobless Figures For June Show Recovery Is Thin

Unemployment Rose to 7.8% While Jobs Dwindled; May Factory Orders Fell

By RICK WARTZMAN
Staff Reporter of THE WALL STREET JOURNAL

Unemployment Rate

WASHINGTON – Underscoring the feebleness of the economy's recovery, the unemployment rate in June jumped to 7.8% while the number of payroll jobs dropped sharply, and May factory orders fell.

"There were a few bombshells," said Jeff Thredgold, senior vice president and chief economist at KeyCorp., an Albany, N.Y., bank holding company.

He and others maintained that the avalanche of statistics didn't signal an end to the recovery, but rather showed just how weak it really is.

Growth Estimates May Fall

Analysts who had been encouraged by an earlier string of positive economic reports and had been expecting the recovery to gain some momentum "may now find themselves reassessing" that outlook, Mr. Thredgold said. Specifically, he said, those who forecast overall economic growth in the second half of 3% or more probably will be inclined to scale that prediction back to about 2%.

Non-farm Payrolls

The biggest shocker was the payroll-jobs figure. Many economists had expected it to rise by 90,000 or more. Instead, the Labor Department reported that businesses reduced employee ranks by 117,000 last month, after adding a revised 93,000 jobs in May.

The drop was widespread. Manufacturing jobs slipped by 58,000 after showing little movement the previous four months. At the same time, the service sector showed weakness, losing 21,000 jobs.

John Silvia, chief economist at Kemper Financial Services, said that both the manufacturing and construction industries had failed to add jobs at the rate that they usually do at this time of year, resulting in especially large statistical declines after seasonal adjustments. He also pointed out that the payroll numbers often are revised and said he expects the Labor Department to revise them upward.

Data Breeds Uncertainty

"This number clearly overstates what's going on in the economy," said Mr. Silvia. Still, he acknowledged that the magnitude of the drop surprised him and "introduces a lot of uncertainty into the picture."

The unemployment rate, typically played down by economists and trumpeted by politicians, rose three-tenths of a percentage point in June to its highest level since March 1984. More than half the increase in the latest month was among teen-agers, whose unemployment rate rose 3.6 percentage points to 23.6%, the highest it has been since June 1983.

The increase in the rate reflected in part the continuing expansion of the labor force, which grew in June by 389,000 to 127.5 million. Since November, the labor force has swelled by about 2.2 million. The labor force participation rate, the portion of the population over 16 years of age that's either working or looking for work, returned to its pre-recession high of 66.6%.

The average factory workweek was shortened by two-tenths of an hour in June to 41.1 hours, erasing May's increase but still a high number by historical standards. Average overtime for factory workers fell one-tenth of an hour to 3.9 hours.

Average Workweeks and Overtime

Source: *The Wall Street Journal*, July 3, 1992

APPENDIX CHART 1-1
Average Workweek of Production Workers, Manufacturing

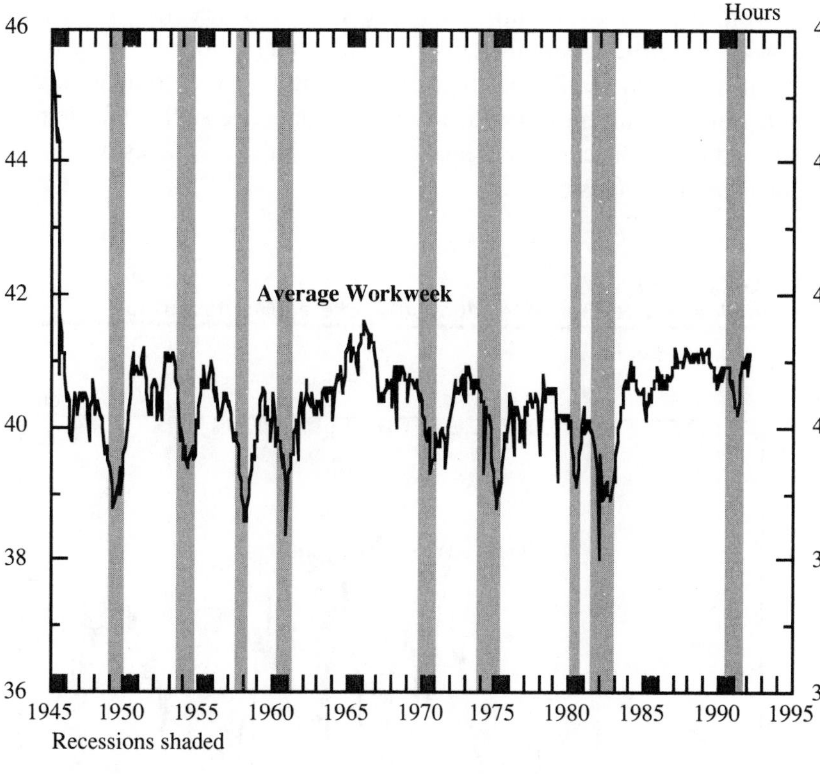

Source: U.S. Department of Commerce, *Business Cycle Indicators*, Series 1

True, manufacturing production workers typically do not control the length of their workweek or whether they will work overtime. Yet the extra income afforded by overtime is welcome and bolsters the consumer sentiment of those earning it. Together with the low rate of inflation, strong overtime helps explain robust consumer sentiment throughout the late 80s. In general, marginal employment adjustments are a reinforcing element of the business cycle through their impact on consumer sentiment.

PERSONAL INCOME

The Commerce Department's monthly personal income report appears in *The Wall Street Journal* during the third week. The second paragraph of the April 30, 1992 article informs you that personal income grew by 1.1 percent in March 1992, and the statistical summary accompanying the article puts the current figure at $4.991 trillion. The statistical summary at the end of the article also breaks out the major components of personal income and its disposition.

APPENDIX CHART 1-2
Average Weekly Overtime of Production Workers, Manufacturing

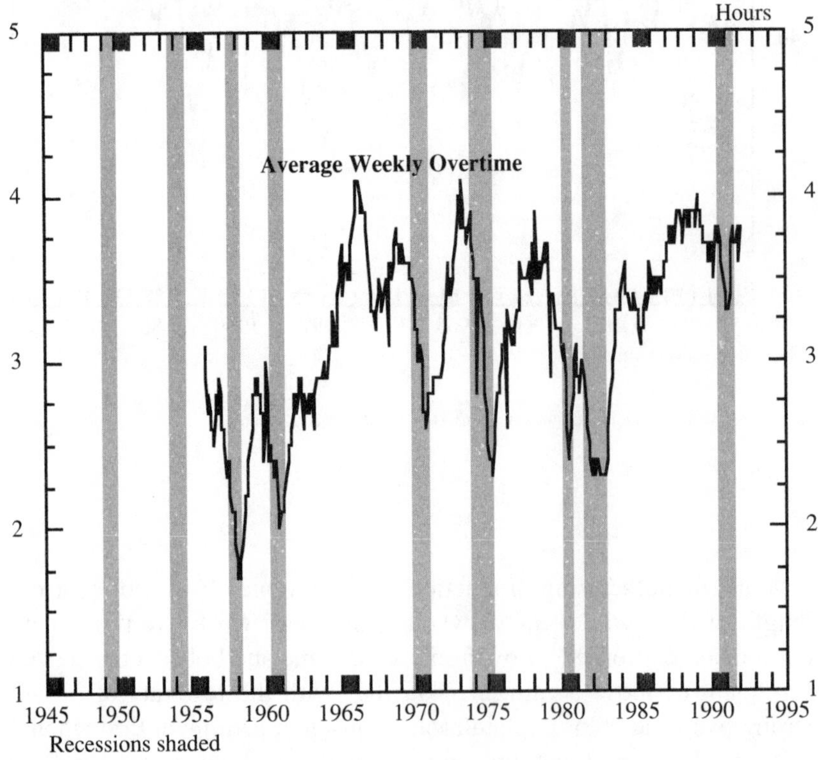

Source: U.S. Department of Commerce, *Business Cycle Indicators*, Series 21

Personal Income Rose in March, Spending Fell

ECONOMY

By Lucinda Harper
Staff Reporter of The Wall Street Journal

WASHINGTON – Americans made more money last month than in February and spent less of it, the Commerce Department said.

Personal Income

After-tax personal income rose 0.6% in March after adjusting for inflation, while personal spending fell 0.2%. In February, real, or inflation-adjusted, personal income rose 0.5% and spending increased 0.3%. Before adjusting for inflation, personal income grew 1.1% last month and spending rose 0.3%.

While spending jumped more than 5% for the entire first quarter, the March income and spending figures illustrate how spending continues to be damped by slow wage growth.

Wages and salaries increased $11.7 billion in March after surging $33.6 billion in February. Most of last month's growth in personal income came from such government payments as farm subsidies and life insurance dividends to veterans. Excluding those benefits, personal income grew slightly less than 0.5% last month before adjustments for inflation.

"Since November, more than half of personal income gains have come from government transfer payments. Real spending growth is driven by increases in wages and salaries," said Sandra Shaber, an economist with the Futures Group Inc. here. "The question is, are we going to start hiring people and pay them enough so they can spend?"

The slow growth in wages and salaries is worrisome because consumer spending accounts for two-thirds of the nation's total economic activity, but economists say the economy is getting stronger.

"This report shouldn't be discouraging. It points to slowing, but not a slump," said John Godfrey, chief economist at Barnett Banks Inc. in Jacksonville, Fla.

The decline in spending in March was met with a strong rise in the savings rate. Americans tucked away a hefty 5.3% of disposable income last month, up from 4.5% in February and 4.3% in January.

Savings Rate

"Consumers are more optimistic about the future, but they don't want to go back to spending the way they did in the '80s," said Andy Borinstein of DYG Inc. in New York.

All figures have been adjusted for normal seasonal variations.

PERSONAL INCOME

Here is the Commerce Department's latest report on personal income. The figures are at seasonally adjusted annual rates in trillions of dollars.

	March 1992	Feb. 1992
Personal income	4.991	4.963
Wages and salaries	2.882	2.870
Factory payrolls	0.562	0.561
Transfer payments	0.833	0.829
Disposable personal income	4.384	4.337
Personal outlays	4.151	4.140
Consumption expenditures	4.041	4.030
Other outlays	0.110	0.110
Personal saving	0.233	0.197

Statistical Summary

Personal Income

Annual rate, in trillions of dollars.

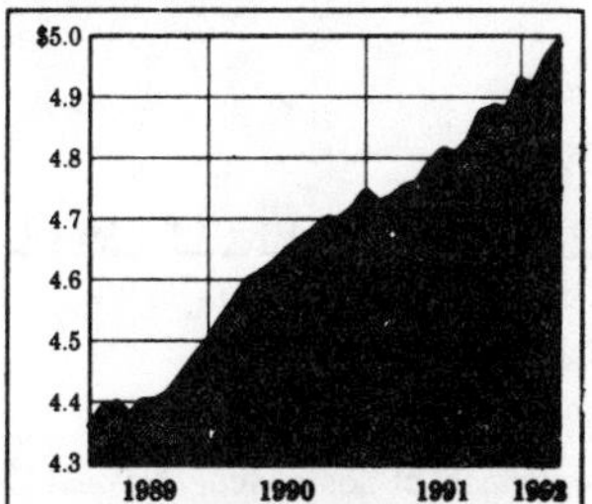

PERSONAL INCOME rose in March to a seasonally adjusted rate of $4.991 trillion from a revised $4.963 trillion a month earlier, the Commerce Department reports. (See story on page A2.)

APPENDIX CHART 1-3
Personal Income (constant dollars)

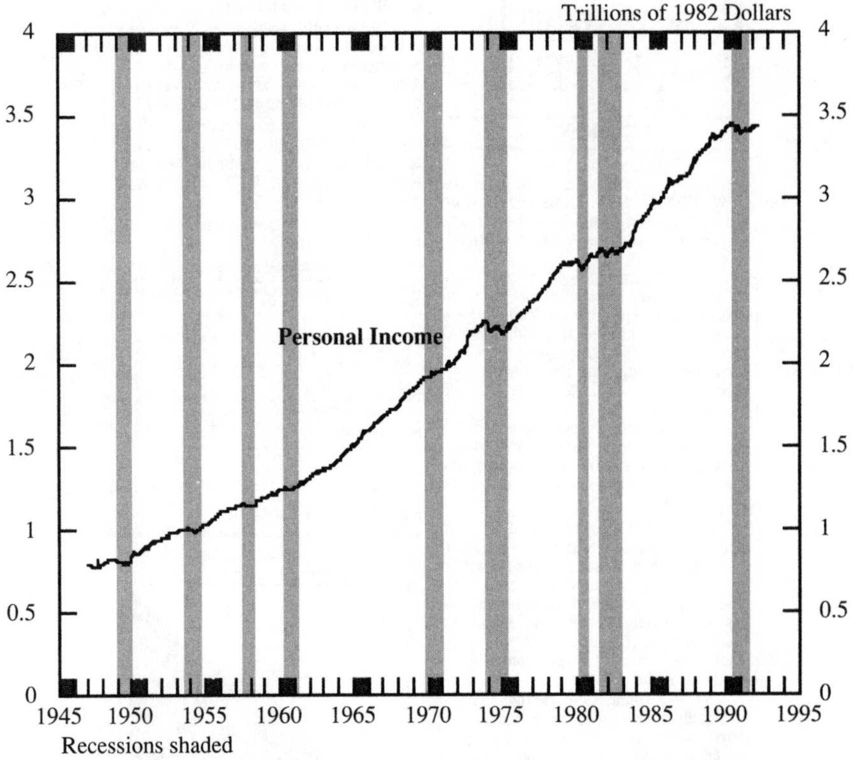

Source: U.S. Department of Commerce, *Business Cycle Indicators*, Series 52

Personal income is all the income we earn (wages, salaries, fringe benefits, profit, rent, interest, and so on) plus the transfer payments we receive (such as veterans' benefits, social security, unemployment compensation, and welfare), minus the social security taxes we pay to the government. Therefore, the federal government's ability to borrow from banks, and use these borrowed funds to pay out to us in transfer payments more than it receives from us in taxes, provides a cushion that keeps personal income growing even in recession, when earned income is down. Paragraphs three, four, and five of the article discuss this relationship in the context of current events.

Producer Prices Post Biggest Increase In 19 Months; Retail Sales Rise 0.2%

By Lucinda Harper
Staff Reporter of The Wall Street Journal

WASHINGTON – Wholesale inflation and retail spending in May were both disappointing, but don't mean the economy is off-track.

Prices at the wholesale level climbed 0.4% last month, the largest jump in the Labor Department's producer price index in 19 months. Excluding the volatile food and energy sectors, producer prices jumped an even more troubling 0.6%.

Retail Sales

In another report, the Commerce Department said retail sales rose a scant 0.2% in May. Also disheartening: April's retail sales figures were reduced to a 0.4% gain, compared with the 0.9% pickup estimated earlier. Previously, February and March's retail sales figures were revised downward.

The retail sales figures, though extremely sluggish, weren't completely surprising. Household incomes have been virtually stagnant, and consumers have shown an unwillingness to take on debt.

Initial Jobless Claims Unchanged

The Labor Department also said that initial claims for state unemployment benefits in the week ended May 30 were unchanged at 407,000, pointing to a stagnant labor market.

"We're not going to get any real exciting pickup in economic activity until wages pick up" and the job market gets better, said David Cross, a retailing analyst with the Futures Group here.

The small increase that did occur in retail sales came from a 0.4% jump in car sales. In the non-durable goods sector, a 0.7% increase in general-merchandise store sales offset declines in food, gasoline and clothing purchases.

The three consecutive downward revisions to retail sales numbers suggest that consumer spending won't be a big contributor to economic growth in the second quarter.

Said Alan Gayle, Crestar Bank chief economist: "The consumer pulled back in the second quarter and is taking a breather."

Retail Sales

In billions of dollars, seasonally adjusted.

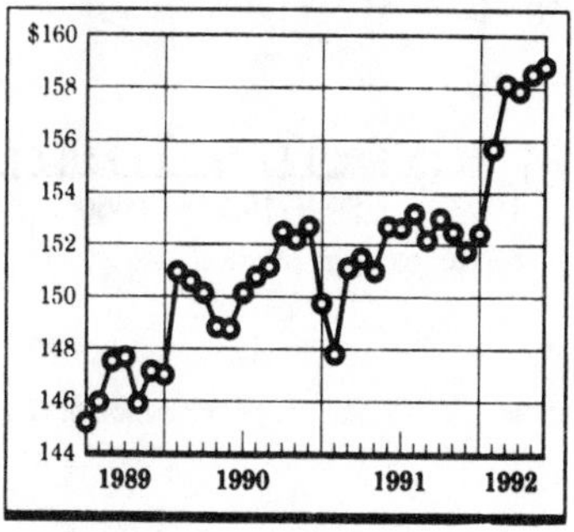

Source: *The Wall Street Journal,* June 12, 1992

APPENDIX CHART 1-4
Retail Sales (constant dollars)

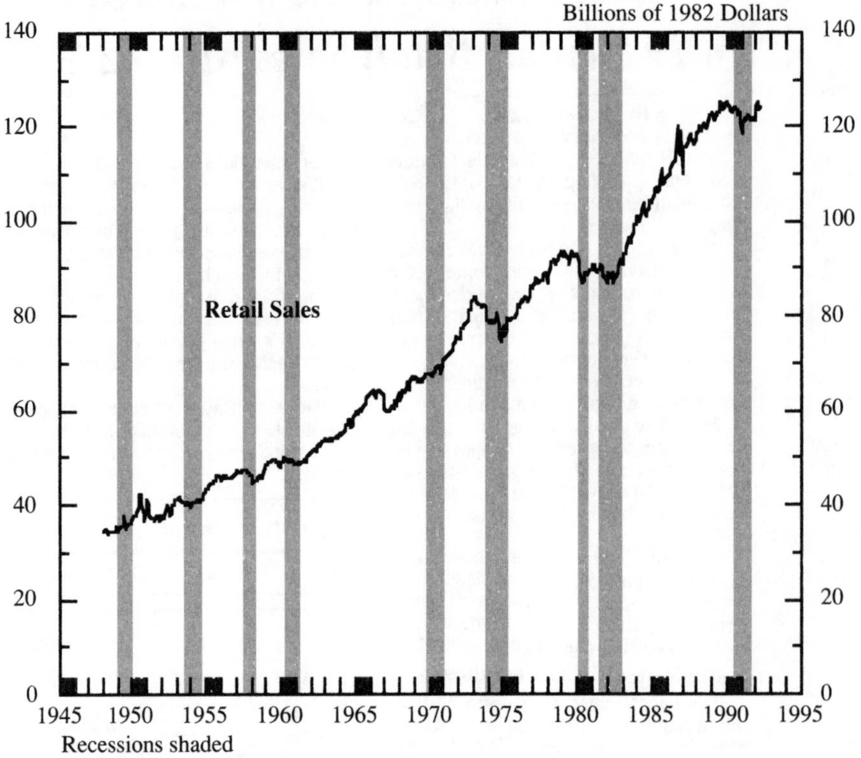

Source: U.S. Department of Commerce, *Business Cycle Indicators*, Series 59

The huge federal deficits generated by the 1990-91 recession helped maintain personal income's growth trend (see chart accompanying article on page 347) despite rising unemployment in those years. This kept a floor under personal consumption expenditures.

For this reason, as you can see from the historical data (Appendix Chart 1-3 on page 348), personal income has grown so steadily that it is difficult to use as a cyclical indicator, even after adjustments for inflation. That's why the article's second paragraph presents personal income in current and constant dollars.

Finally, the second paragraph and the third paragraph from the end of the article discuss the inverse relationship between consumption and saving. Savings rose in March of 92 because of sluggish consumer spending.

RETAIL SALES

The U.S. Department of Commerce's monthly release on *retail sales* appears in *The Wall Street Journal* around the second week. You can see from the headline and third paragraph of the Friday, June 12, 1992 article on page 349 that retail sales stalled in mid 1992. This reinforces the impression created by the article on personal income, discussed above, that consumer expenditures weakened in those months.

As you can see from Appendix Chart 1-4, however, retail sales has not been a volatile series even when measured in constant dollars, so using retail sales to trace the course of the business cycle is not so easy nor satisfactory as using auto sales, housing starts, or consumer credit.

APPENDIX B

ALPHABETICAL LISTING OF STATISTICAL SERIES PUBLISHED IN *THE WALL STREET JOURNAL*

Chapter Introduced	*Series Description*	*Publication Schedule*
9	Advance/decline (stocks)	Daily
9	American Stock Exchange composite transactions	Daily
11	Amex bonds	Daily
6	Auto sales	Monthly
16	Balance of payments	Quarterly
16	Balance of trade	Monthly
12	Banxquote index (deposit & CD interest rates)	Weekly
12	Banxquote money markets (deposit & CD interest rates)	Weekly
11	Bond market data bank	Daily
11	Bond yields (chart)	Weekly
12	Buying and borrowing (interest rates)	Weekly
9	Canadian markets (stocks)	Daily
7	Capacity utilization	Monthly
10	Cash prices (commodities)	Daily
11	Closed-end bond funds	Weekly
10	Commodities (article)	Daily
10	Commodity indexes	Daily
6	Consumer confidence	Monthly
6	Consumer credit	Monthly
6	Consumer price index	Monthly
12	Consumer savings rates	Weekly
9	Corporate dividend news	Daily

Chapter Introduced	Series Description	Publication Schedule
8	Corporate profits (Commerce Department)	Quarterly
8	Corporate profits (*The Wall Street Journal* survey)	Quarterly
11 and 12	Credit markets (article)	Daily
11	Credit ratings	Daily
16	Currency trading	Daily
9	Digest of earnings report	Daily
9	Dow Jones Averages (six-month charts)	Daily
10	Dow Jones commodity indexes (chart)	Weekly
9	Dow Jones industry groups	Daily
15	Durable goods orders	Monthly
Appendix A	Employment	Monthly
16	Foreign exchange rates	Daily
9	Foreign markets (stocks)	Daily
10, 11, 12	Futures options prices	Daily
10, 11, 12	Futures prices	Daily
7	GDP	Quarterly
11	Government agency issues	Daily
11	High yield bonds	Daily
6	Housing starts	Monthly
9	Index trading (options)	Daily
7	Industrial production	Monthly
9	Insider trading spotlight	Weekly
14	Inventories	Monthly
6	Key currency cross rates	Daily
12	Key interest rates	Weekly
13	Leading indicators	Monthly
9	Listed options quotations	Daily
9	Long term options (stocks)	Daily
15	Manufacturers' orders	Monthly
9–12	Markets diary	Daily
12	Money-fund yields	Weekly
12	Money market funds assets	Weekly
12	Money market mutual funds	Weekly
12	Money rates	Daily
11	Municipal bond index	Weekly
9	Mutual fund quotations	Daily
9	Mutual fund scorecard	Daily
9	NASDAQ bid & asked quotations	Daily
9	NASDAQ national market issues	Daily
11	New securities issues	Daily
11	New York exchange bonds	Daily
9	NYSE composite transactions	Daily
9	NYSE highs/lows	Daily
9	Odd-Lot trading	Daily
8	P/E ratios	Weekly

Chapter Introduced	*Series Description*	*Publication Schedule*
Appendix A	Personal income	Monthly
7	Producer price index	Monthly
7	Productivity	Quarterly
9	Publicly traded funds	Weekly
Appendix A	Retail sales	Monthly
11	Securities offering calendar	Weekly
9	Short interest (stocks)	Monthly
12	Short-term interest rates (chart)	Weekly
9	Stock market data bank	Daily
11 and 12	Treasury auction	Weekly
11 and 12	Treasury bonds, notes and bills	Daily
11 and 12	Treasury yield curve	Daily
11	Weekly tax-exempts (bonds)	Weekly
9	World markets (stocks)	Daily
16	World value of the dollar	Daily
11 and 12	Yield comparisons	Daily
12	Yield for consumers	Daily

APPENDIX C

STATISTICAL SERIES PUBLISHED IN *THE WALL STREET JOURNAL* IN CHAPTER ORDER

Chapter Introduced	*Series Description*	*Publication Schedule*
6	Auto sales	Monthly
6	Consumer confidence	Monthly
6	Consumer credit	Monthly
6	Consumer price index	Monthly
6	Housing starts	Monthly
7	Capacity utilization	Monthly
7	GDP	Quarterly
7	Industrial production	Monthly
7	Producer price index	Monthly
7	Productivity	Quarterly
8	Corporate profits (Commerce Department)	Quarterly
8	Corporate profits (*The Wall Street Journal* survey)	Quarterly
8	P/E ratios	Weekly
9–12	Markets Diary	Daily
9	Advance/decline (stocks)	Daily
9	American Stock Exchange composite transactions	Daily
9	Canadian markets (stocks)	Daily
9	Corporate dividend news	Daily
9	Digest of earnings report	Daily

Chapter Introduced	*Series Description*	*Publication Schedule*
9	Dow Jones Averages (six-month charts)	Daily
9	Dow Jones industry groups	Daily
9	Foreign markets (stocks)	Daily
9	Index trading (options)	Daily
9	Insider trading spotlight	Weekly
9	Listed options quotations	Daily
9	Long term options (stocks)	Daily
9	Mutual fund quotations	Daily
9	Mutual fund scorecard	Daily
9	NASDAQ bid & asked quotations	Daily
9	NASDAQ national market issues	Daily
9	NYSE composite transactions	Daily
9	NYSE highs/lows	Daily
9	Odd-Lot trading	Daily
9	Publicly traded funds	Weekly
9	Short interest (stocks)	Monthly
9	Stock market data bank	Daily
9	World markets (stocks)	Daily
10	Cash prices (commodities)	Daily
10	Commodities (article)	Daily
10	Commodity indexes	Daily
10	Dow Jones commodity indexes (chart)	Weekly
10,11,12	Futures options prices	Daily
10,11,12	Futures prices	Daily
11	Amex bonds	Daily
11	Bond market data bank	Daily
11	Closed-end bond funds	Weekly
11 and 12	Credit markets (article)	Daily
11	Credit ratings	Daily
11	Government agency issues	Daily
11	High yield bonds	Daily
11	Municipal bond index	Weekly
11	New securities issues	Daily
11	New York exchange bonds	Daily
11	Securities offering calendar	Weekly
11 and 12	Treasury auction	Weekly
11 and 12	Treasury bonds, notes and bills	Daily
11 and 12	Treasury yield curve	Daily
11	Weekly tax-exempts (bonds)	Weekly
11 and 12	Yield comparisons	Daily

Chapter Introduced	*Series Description*	*Publication Schedule*
12	Key interest rates	Weekly
12	Banxquote index (deposit & CD interest rates)	Weekly
12	Banxquote money markets (deposit & CD interest rates)	Weekly
12	Buying and borrowing (interest rates)	Weekly
12	Consumer savings rates	Weekly
12	Money-fund yields	Weekly
12	Money market funds assets	Weekly
12	Money market mutual funds	Weekly
12	Money rates	Daily
12	Short-term interest rates (chart)	Weekly
12	Yields for consumers	Daily
13	Leading indicators	Monthly
14	Inventories	Monthly
15	Durable goods orders	Monthly
15	Manufacturers' orders	Monthly
16	Balance of payments	Quarterly
16	Balance of trade	Monthly
16	Currency trading	Daily
16	Foreign exchange rates	Daily
16	Key currency cross rates	Daily
16	World value of the dollar	Daily
Appendix A	Employment	Monthly
Appendix A	Personal income	Monthly
Appendix A	Retail sales	Monthly

APPENDIX D

LISTING OF STATISTICAL SERIES ACCORDING TO *THE WALL STREET JOURNAL* PUBLICATION SCHEDULE

Day of Month Usually Published in The Wall Street Journal	*Series Description*	*Chapter Introduced*
	Quarterly	
Two months after end of quarter	Corporate profits (*The Wall Street Journal* survey)	8
Middle of last month of quarter	Balance of payments	16
25th of month	GDP	7
25th of last month of quarter	Corporate profits (Commerce Department)	8
Month after end of quarter	Productivity	7
	Monthly	
1st	Leading indicators	13
1st week	Manufacturers' orders	15
1st week	Consumer confidence	6
5th, 15th, 25th	Auto sales	6
2nd week	Consumer credit	6
Monday of 2nd week	Employment	Appendix A
Middle of 2nd week	Retail sales	Appendix A
Midmonth	Producer price index	7
Midmonth	Industrial production	7

Day of Month Usually Published in The Wall Street Journal	*Series Description*	*Chapter Introduced*
	Monthly	
Midmonth	Inventories	14
Midmonth	Capacity utilization	7
Midmonth	Consumer price index	6
17th to 20th	Housing starts	6
20th	Short Interest (stocks)	9
Thurs or Fri of 3rd week	Durable goods orders	15
3rd week	Personal income	16
4th week	Balance of trade	Appendix A

Day of Week Usually Published in The Wall Street Journal	*Series Description*	*Chapter Introduced*
	Weekly	
Monday	Bond yields (chart)	11
Monday	Buying and borrowing (interest rates)	12
Monday	Closed-end bond funds	11
Monday	Dow Jones commodity indexes (chart)	10
Monday	P/E ratios	8
Monday	Publicly traded funds	9
Monday	Securities offering calendar	11
Monday	Weekly tax-exempts (bonds)	11
Tuesday	Key interest rates	11 and 12
Tuesday	Treasury auction	11 and 12
Wednesday	Banxquote index (deposit & CD interest rates)	12
Wednesday	Insider trading spotlight	9
Thursday	Consumer savings rates	12
Thursday	Money market mutual funds	12
Thursday	Money-fund yields	12
Thursday	Short-term interest rates (chart)	12
Friday	Banxquote money markets (deposit & CD interest rates)	12
Friday	Money market funds assets	12
Friday	Municipal bond index	11

Series Description	*Chapter Introduced*
Daily	
Advance/decline (stocks)	9
American Stock Exchange composite transactions	9
Amex bonds	11
Bond market data bank	11
Canadian markets (stocks)	9
Cash prices (commodities)	10
Commodities (article)	10
Commodity indexes	10
Corporate dividend news	9
Credit markets (article)	11 and 12
Credit ratings	11
Currency trading	16
Digest of earnings report	9
Dow Jones Averages (six-month charts)	9
Dow Jones industry groups	9
Foreign exchange rates	16
Foreign markets (stocks)	9
Futures options prices	10,11,12
Futures prices	10,11,12
Government agency issues	11
High yield bonds	11
Index trading (options)	9
Interest rate instruments (options)	11
Key currency cross rates	6
Listed options quotations	9
Long term options (stocks)	9
Markets diary	9–12
Money rates	12
Mutual fund quotations	9
Mutual fund scorecard	9
NASDAQ bid & asked quotations	9
NASDAQ national market issues	9
New securities issues	11
New York exchange bonds	11
NYSE composite transactions	9
NYSE highs/lows	9
Odd-Lot trading	9
Stock market data bank	9
Treasury bonds, notes and bills	11 and 12
Treasury yield curve	11 and 12
World markets (stocks)	9
World value of the dollar	16
Yield comparisons	11 and 12
Yields for consumers	12

APPENDIX E

FURTHER REFERENCES*

These references were selected to assist you with further research into the many topics covered in this book. The listings include some of the best books and other resources on numerous investment topics. In certain cases, a title may be out-of-print, but copies will be available at most larger public and educational facility libraries.

All Business One Irwin (formerly Dow Jones-Irwin) titles are available in bookstores, or directly from Business One Irwin, 1818 Ridge Road, Homewood, Illinois 60430. Customer Service 1-800-634-3966.

BASICS

American Association of Individual Investors
625 North Michigan Avenue, Suite 1900
Chicago, IL 60611
(312) 280-0170

Member benefits include a subscription to the excellent monthly, *AAII Journal*. The Association also publishes home study courses, audio tapes, and presents seminars. There is a local chapter network. (Annual membership, $49.00.)

*The author gratefully acknowledges the assistance of Bob Meier in compiling these references.

"Classics: An Investor's Anthology" and *"Classics II"*, edited by Charles D. Ellis and James Vertin.

These two volumes are the most comprehensive, yet compact, source of Wall Street wisdom. They present the best practical ideas and commentaries of over 100 gifted economists and investment industry thinkers on financial analysis, investing, and economic history, from the past 200 years. ("Classics" 759 pages, hardbound $37.50; "Classics II", 480 pages, hardbound, $42.50, Business One Irwin.)

Business One Irwin One Hour Guide Series

a. *How To Be a Successful Investor* by Bailard, Biehl & Kaiser (230 pages, $10.95)

b. *How To Pick The Best No-Load Mutual Fund for Solid Growth and Safety* by Sheldon Jacobs (300 pages, $12.95, Business One Irwin.)

c. *How To Set and Achieve Your Financial Goals* by Bailard, Biehl, and Kaiser (229 pages, $10.95)

CONSUMER PROTECTION

What Every Investor Should Know
Consumer Information Center K
P.O. Box 100
Pueblo, CO 81002

Basic information on choosing and safeguarding investments, trading securitites, and protections guaranteed by law. Written by the Securitites & Exchange Commission. When ordering, make checks payable to the "Superintendent of Documents" and include the publication number, #146V. (35 pages, $1.25).

INTERNATIONAL INVESTING

FullerMoney
Chart Analysis Ltd.
7 Swallow Street
London W1R 7HD
United Kingdom

A monthly newsletter featuring long-term charts and commentary for 27 world stock and bond markets, all major currencies, and precious metals. This service is one of the best resources for the serious international investor. (Annual subscription, $340.00.)

PSYCHOLOGY

Investment Psychology Consulting
337 Lochside Drive
Cary, NC 27511

Books and audio cassettes by Dr. Van K. Tharp to help investors and traders overcome the psychological barriers to objective interpretation of economic news and successful investment decisions. (Write for catalog.)

GENERAL REFERENCE

Ellis, Charles. *Investment Policy, 2nd Edition*. Homewood: Business One Irwin, 1992.

Graham, Benjamin. *The Intelligent Investor*. New York: Harper & Row, 1965.

Hirt, Geoffrey, and Block, Stanley B. *The New Complete Investor: Instruments, Markets, and Methods*. Homewood: Business One Irwin, 1990.

Levine, Sumner. *The Business One Irwin Business and Investment Almanac*. Homewood: Business One Irwin, 1993.

Malkiel, Burton G. *A Random Walk Down Wall Street, 4th Ed*. New York: W.W. Norton & Company, 1985.

Nichols, Donald R. *Starting Small, Investing Smart: What to Do With $5 to $5,000*. Homewood: Business One Irwin, 1990.

Pressin, Allan H., and Ross, Joseph A. *The Complete Words of Wall Street* and *More Words of Wall Street*. Homewood: Business One Irwin, 1986.

Skousen, Mark. *Economics on Trial*. Homewood: Business One Irwin, 1992.

Veale, Stuart R., ed. *Stocks, Bonds, Options, Futures: Investments and Their Markets*. New York: New York Institute of Finance; Prentice-Hall, 1987.

FUTURES & OPTIONS

Futures & Options Trading Kit
Fox Investments
Attn: Susan Rutsen, Consumer Affairs
Suite 1800A
141 West Jackson Blvd.
Chicago, IL 60604

Collection of basic "how to" brochures, article reprints, and other information on the potential risks and rewards of futures and options trading, including managed accounts and funds. Indicate any special areas of interest. (Free.)

Options Edge
P.O. Box 268031
Chicago, Illinois 60626

A monthly newsletter with many charts and tables and frequent extra bulletins on stock index, currency, bond and other option contracts. Content includes a monthly "Beginner's Trade", unique option strategies, including ways to hedge stock portfolio risks and increase money market fund "yields". (Semi-annual subscription with all extra bulletins, $100.00.)

Options Institute. *Options: Essential Concepts and Trading Strategies*. Homewood: Business One Irwin, 1990.

Clasing, Henry. *Currency Options*. Homewood: Business One Irwin, 1992.

LONG-TERM INTEREST RATES AND MONEY MARKET INVESTMENTS

Ray, Christina. *The Bond Market: Trading and Risk Management*. Homewood: Business One Irwin, 1992.

Stigum, Marcia, with Mann, John. *Money Market Calculations: Yields, Break Evens and Arbitrage*. Homewood: Business One Irwin, 1987.

Stigum, Marcia and Robinson, Franklin. *Fixed Income Calculations, Volume One: Money Market Paper and Bonds*. Homewood: Business One Irwin, 1992.

COMPUTERS

Technical Analysis of Stocks & Commodities
3517 SW Alaska Street
Seattle, Washington 98126

This monthly magazine has articles and case studies on a wide range of computerized investing topics, plus reviews of the newest hardware, software and databases. Various special product and services directories are issued throughout the year. (12 issues, $64.95.)

FINANCIAL AND ECONOMIC ONLINE DATA RETRIEVAL

A number of computer information subscription services provide up to the minute financial and economic information.

Dow Jones New Retrieval (DJN/R): 1-609-452-1511

Compuserve: 1-800-848-8990

GEnie: 1-800-638-9636

The Source: 1-800-336-3366

These services will give you access to many of the following:

- S & P Online
- Value Line Data Base
- Futures Focus
- Money Market Services
- OTC News
- Bond Prices and Volumes
- Stock Quotes
- Commodities Futures Prices
- Company Information
- *and much more*

CHART SERVICES

Commodity Research Bureau
30 S. Wacker Drive, Suite 1820
Chicago, IL 60601

Weekly and monthly chart services, plus yearbooks, covering all commodity futures and options on futures contracts. (Write for catalog.)

Chartcraft, Inc.
Investors Intelligence
30 Church Street, Box 2046
New Rochelle, NY 10802

Fifteen different chart service combinations, featuring the point and figure charting method. (Write for catalog.)

Securities Research Company
208 Newbury Street
Boston, MA 02116

Monthly and quarterly chart services covering 1,000 stocks each, plus wall charts and books. (Write for catalog.)

Standard & Poor's Corporation
25 Broadway
New York, NY 10004

Comprehensive subscriber package, including the Trendline Chart Service, tracking over 1,400 active stacks, and the Security Owner's Stock Guide, presenting statistics on over 5,300 stocks. (Write for catalog.)

STOCKS

Alger, David. *Raging Bull: How to Invest in the Growth Stocks of the 90s*. Homewood: Business One Irwin, 1991.

Jacobs, Sheldon. *The Handbook for No-Load Fund Investors*. Homewood: Business One Irwin, 1992.

Merriman, Paul. *Investing for a Lifetime: Paul Merriman's Guide to Mutual Fund Strategies*. Homewood: Business One Irwin, 1991.

Pierce, Phyllis, ed. *The Dow Jones Averages, 1885 to 1990*. Homewood: Business One Irwin.

Pierce, Phyllis, ed. *The Dow Jones Investor's Handbook*. Homewood: Business One Irwin, 1992.

Powell, James. *Super Investment Trends: Cashing In On the Dynamic 90s*. Homewood: Business One Irwin, 1991.

TECHNICAL ANALYSIS

"Technical Analysis Explained" by Martin J. Pring
Pring Market Review
P.O. Box 329
Washington, CT 06794

One of the most definitive and comprehensive references on technical ananlysis. The book, now in its third edition, features over 150 charts and illustrations. Danish, Italian, German, and Japanese editions are also availabe. (521 pages, $49.95.)

Stan Weinstein's Secrets for Profiting in Bull and Bear Markets by Stan Weinstein.
Professional Tape Reader
P.O. Box 2407
Hollywood, FL 33022

A popular book with primary emphasis on technical analysis of stocks. (348 pages, $24.95.)

COMMODITIES AND PRECIOUS METALS

Kroll, Stanley and Paulenoff, Michael. *The Business One Irwin Guide to the Futures Markets*. Homewood: Business One Irwin, 1991.

Labuszewski, John W., and Singuefield, Jeanne Cairns. *Inside the Commodity Options Markets*. New York: John Wiley & Sons, 1985.

LeBeau, Charles and Lucas, David. *Technical Traders Guide to Computer Analysis of the Futures Market*. Homewood: Business One Irwin, 1991.

Markham, Jerry W. *The History of Commodity Futures Trading and Its Regualtion*, New York: Praeger, 1987.

Nix, William E., ed. *Futures Markets: Their Ecomonic Role*. Washington D.C.: American Enterprise Institute for Public Policy Research, 1985.

INDEX